Worlds of History

Worlds of History

A Comparative Reader

Volume Two: Since 1400

Kevin Reilly
Raritan Valley College

Bedford/St. Martin's
Boston ◆ New York

To My Teachers: Eugene Meehan, Traian Stoianovich, Donald Weinstein, and the memory of Warren Susman

For Bedford/St. Martin's
History Editor: Katherine E. Kurzman
Developmental Editor: Charisse Kiino
Production Editor: Stasia Zomkowski
Production Supervisor: Catherine Hetmansky
Marketing Manager: Charles Cavaliere
Editorial Assistant: Chip Turner
Production Assistant: Helaine Denenberg
Copyeditor: Marie Salter
Text Design: George McLean
Cover Design: Ann Gallager
Cover Art: Utagawa Yoshitora, *Imported Silk Reeling Machine at Tsukiji in Tokyo*, Oban Triptych (detail). The Metropolitan Museum of Art, Gift of Lincoln Kirstein, 1959. (JP3346) Photograph by Otto E. Nelson, Photograph ©1986 The Metropolitan Museum of Art. BAL2726 William Bell Scott (1811–90), *Industry of the Tyne: Iron and Coal,* 1861 (oil on canvas). Wallington Hall, Northumberland, UK/Bridgeman Art Library, London/NewYork.
Composition: Pine Tree Composition, Inc.
Printing and Binding: Haddon Craftsmen, Inc.

President: Charles H. Christensen
Editorial Director: Joan E. Feinberg
Director of Editing, Design, and Production: Marcia Cohen
Managing Editor: Elizabeth M. Schaaf

Library of Congress Catalog Card Number: 98–87546

Manufactured in the United States of America.

4   3   2   1
f   e   d   c

For information, write: Bedford/St. Martin's, 75 Arlington Street, Boston, MA 02116 (617-399-4000)

ISBN: 0–312–15789–4 (Volume 1)
      0–312–15788–6 (Volume 2)

Acknowledgments

Chinua Achebe, excerpts from *Things Fall Apart.* Copyright © 1958 by Chinua Achebe. Reprinted with the permission of Heinemann Educational Publishers, a division of Reed Educational & Professional Publishing, LTD.

Acknowledgments and copyrights are continued at the back of the book on pages 548–52, which constitute an extension of the copyright page. It is a violation of the law to reproduce these selections by any means whatsoever without the written permission of the copyright holder.

Preface

Worlds of History is designed to meet a need that marks a new stage in the maturation of world history as an introductory course. In 1982 when the World History Association was founded, there were just three college textbooks and one reader devoted to the topic. In those early years, defining the subject matter of world history, creating a canon of sources, and distinguishing world history from other fields of history were our top priorities.

In recent years, as world history has matured in content and importance, becoming *the* introductory course in the college history curriculum, our attentions have turned to how and what students learn. We teach subject matter, but we must also teach certain skills — what the Romans called "habits of mind." This book is meant to address both these needs, conferring knowledge and critical thinking skills. These invaluable skills (for example, how to approach historical evidence, argument, and interpretation) inform how students think about the past, present, and future, and will serve them well throughout their lives.

Meant for the introductory world history course, Volume Two of this two-volume reader contains ninety-four primary and secondary source selections that answer the question "What is essential for students to learn?", in terms of content and thinking skills. Fourteen chapters, organized chronologically, should correspond to general survey texts and to most instructors' syllabi. Understanding that some variation might exist, I have included a correlation chart in the new instructor's manual (*Editor's Notes to Accompany* WORLDS OF HISTORY) that matches each reading in this text with related chapters in sixteen of the most widely used survey texts. By dividing *Worlds of History* into two volumes, I hope to accommodate those instructors whose world history survey courses are divided into two terms, with a break at around 1500. In response to recent arguments that modern history began before 1500, this volume begins around 1400.

TOPICAL ORGANIZATION

After thirty years of teaching, I am convinced that students are generally more interested in topics than eras, and that an appreciation of period and process can be taught by focusing on topics. Some of the topics in this volume have precise chronological parameters (for example, the Opium War and the First World War) and form the basis of a single chapter; other topics, such as slavery and industrialization, provide a basis for comparison across long spans of time. Chapter 2 asks students to compare the impact of Europeans on Africa and the Americas over the course of the centuries. Chapter 6 distinguishes the effects of capitalism and industrialization in Europe and Asia over a century and a half.

Different periodization also calls for different analytical skills; in general, brief periods require more focused analysis, and longer periods, broader synthesis. Thus, Chapter 7, Free Trade and the Opium War, provides students with an opportunity to examine the gradual change in tenor of debates as the war approached. Chapter 9, Independence and Westernization, on the other hand, asks students to understand a process, without regard to its different local chronologies. As a result, students are exposed to a variety of dimensions of human history and gain experience in thinking about history's breadth and depth.

Readings can function as discrete entities and at the same time relate clearly to each other, offering numerous opportunities for analysis, evaluation, and synthesis. As a collection of fourteen topical chapters, this comparative anthology works incrementally — through fascinating, varied, and relevant readings — to direct student learning and to encourage intellectual development.

COMPARATIVE APPROACH

History demands careful comparison. In *Worlds of History*, the connections among readings in a single chapter encourage students to compare one reading with another. On a more basic level, the recognition of similarities and differences helps students make useful connections that are at the root of all critical thinking. Each chapter is constructed around a general, directed comparison. In some, students are asked to compare the same process in two areas (for example, Chinese and European oceanic expansion or slavery in Africa and the Americas); in others, two sides of an encounter or war; in still others, two effects of an event or two historical interpretations. Clearly, understanding world history involves more than comparison, but careful analysis, well-chosen examples, and discerning judgments are vital beginnings.

THINKING HISTORICALLY

In recent years, world historians have begun to show great interest in pedagogical issues. Carnegie Mellon University and Northeastern University, among others, have developed courses and materials that attempt to delineate steps in the learning process, to specify the nature of historical understanding. Such attempts reflect the growing national interest in general education, the academy's attention to "critical thinking skills," and the wide acceptance of world history as valuable basic training in cultural literacy and global awareness. This book continues that effort.

Each chapter in *Worlds of History* teaches a particular historical thinking skill; further, these skills are organized in a sequence from the easiest to the most difficult, so that a student's capacity to manipulate knowledge — to analyze, synthesize, and interpret — builds one step at a time. Volume Two does not assume complete mastery of the skills taught in Volume One. Still, students will build their skills progressively and with regular use come to grasp more complex and sophisticated ways of thinking. Thus, they move from using primary and secondary sources and sifting evidence to causation, changing debates, contradictions, the nature of historical knowledge, constructing theory, and discerning the broadest patterns of the past.

To emphasize both skill building and content, each chapter and every reading have a dual introduction. The first, "Historical Context," concerns subject matter, while the second, "Thinking Historically," focuses on skill acquisition and mastery. The two parts, while related, have been separated to allow instructors maximum flexibility. Each chapter concludes with "Reflections," a section that summarizes or extends the chapters' lessons. Visual images and maps are included. A companion instructor's manual provides the rationale for the selection and organization of the readings; it also highlights some teaching strategies and provides information about ancillary resources, including films and Internet sites.

Not all instructors will agree that these are the most important skills on which to focus. Regardless, my pedagogical choices were guided by the readings and topics of each chapter, as well as by their success in my own classroom. I would be grateful for classroom feedback on these learning exercises and for suggestions for other skills to emphasize in future editions. Please post your remarks and suggestions on the Bedford/St. Martin's Web site at www.bedfordstmartins.com.

ACKNOWLEDGMENTS

A book like this cannot be written without the help and advice, even if sometimes unheeded, of a vast army of colleagues and professionals. I count myself enormously fortunate to have met and known such a large group of gifted and generous scholars and teachers in my years with the World History Association. Among them, I would like to thank those who were reviewers and questionnaire respondents for this book: Helen

E. Anderson, University of Indianapolis; Charlotte Beahan, Murray State University; Norman R. Bennett, Boston University; Robert Berry, Salisbury State University; Fritz Blackwell, Washington State University; Jurgen Buchenau, Wingate University; Nancy Clark, California Polytechnic State University, San Luis Obispo; Ralph Croizier, University of Victoria; Ross E. Dunn, San Diego State University; Martha L. Edwards, Truman State University; Mark Finlay, Armstrong Atlantic State University; Basil D. Georgiadis; Major Bradley T. Gericke, United States Military Academy; Lorraine Gesick, University of Nebraska–Omaha; Samuel Goldberger, Capital Community Technical College; Sumaiya Hamdani, George Mason University; Ed Haynes, Winthrop University; Karen Jolly, University of Hawaii at Manoa; Newton Key, Eastern Illinois University; Sharon McGee, Thomas More College; Marian P. Nelson, University of Nebraska–Omaha; Joseph M. Norton, Dutchess Community College; Donathon Olliff, Auburn University; Patricia O'Neill, Central Oregon Community College; William G. Palmer, Marshall University; Maarten L. Pereboom, Salisbury State University; Vera Blinn Reber, Shippensburg State University; Colonel Carl Reddel, United States Air Force Academy; Sarah E. Sharbach, Salisbury State University; Marc J. Stern, Bentley College; Ronald J. Weber, University of Texas at El Paso; Sally West, Truman State University; and Ken Wolf, Murray State University.

Other friends and colleagues contributed selections, suggestions, and advice for the book in other ways. Among them, I would like to thank the following: Michael Adas, Rutgers University; Jerry Bentley, University of Hawaii; David Berry, Essex County Community College; Catherine Clay, Shippensburg University; Roger Cranse, Norwich University; Philip Curtin, Johns Hopkins University; Steve Gosch, University of Wisconsin at Eau Claire; Gregory Guzman, Bradley University; Brock Haussamen, Raritan Valley College; Sarah Hughes, Shippensburg University; Allen Howard, Rutgers University; Karen Jolly, University of Hawaii; Maghan Keita, Villanova University; Pat Manning, Northeastern University; William H. McNeill, University of Chicago; John Mears, Southern Methodist University; Gyan Prakash, Princeton University; Heidi Roupp, Aspen High School; Richard Rosen, Drexel University; Robert Rosen, University of California at Los Angeles; John Russell-Wood, Johns Hopkins University; Lynda Shaffer, Tufts University; Anthony Snyder, Brookdale Community College; Leften Stavrianos, University of California at San Diego; Peter Stearns, Carnegie Mellon University; Robert Tignor, Princeton University; Mary Evelyn Tucker, Bucknell University; John Voll, Georgetown University; and Judith Zinsser, Miami University.

I also want to thank the people at Bedford/St. Martin's, especially Charles Christensen, President, and Joan Feinberg, Editorial Director, who inherited the third edition of *Readings in World Civilization* almost at the moment it was published, for not being satisfied with only a fourth edition of a proven success but encouraging me to transform the book for a new generation of students. Katherine Kurzman, History Editor, put together a superb team headed by Charisse Kiino, Developmental Editor, whose thoroughness, intelligence, and good humor lightened the load while lighting the way. Editorial Assistant Chip Turner provided invaluable support. The production team, headed by Elizabeth Schaaf, Managing Editor, proved a model of "just-in-time" publishing. Stasia Zomkowski, Production Editor, and Marie Salter, Copyeditor, queried widely and well, and polished my pedestrian prose. Donna Dennison, Art Director, coordinated the cover design. Carole Frohlich, Photo Researcher, and Ann Gallager, Cover Designer, tracked down illustrations and designed the beautiful covers.

While writing this book, memories of my own introduction to history and critical thinking have come flooding back to me. I was blessed at Rutgers in the 1960s with teachers I still aspire to emulate. Eugene Meehan taught me that learning could be both hard work and fun. Traian Stoianovich, who introduced me to the work of his own teacher, Fernand Braudel, demonstrated a vision of history that was boundless, and demanded only originality from this graduate student. Donald Weinstein taught me to listen to students as if they were Stradivarii. And Warren Susman filled a room with more life than I ever knew existed. I dedicate this book to them.

Finally, I want to thank my own institution, Raritan Valley College, for nurturing my career, allowing me to teach whatever I wanted, and entrusting me with some of the best students one could encounter anywhere. I could not ask for anything more. Except, of course, a loving wife like Pearl.

Introduction

You have here fourteen lessons in world history, each of which deals with a particular historical period and topic since the fifteenth century. (A companion volume addresses human history to 1550.) Some of the topics are narrow and specific, covering events such as the Opium War in detail, while others are broad and general, such as colonialism and globalization.

As you learn about historical periods and topics, you also will be coached to think systematically. The "Thinking Historically" passages in each chapter encourage habits of mind that I associate with my own study of history. They are not necessarily intended to turn you into historians but, rather, to give you skills that will help you in all of your college courses and throughout your life. For example, the first chapter distinguishes primary sources (eye-witness accounts) from secondary sources (historical interpretations) — certainly something that historians do. But the true value of this exercise, and of the others that build on it, is in helping you to differentiate between fact and opinion, clearly an ability as necessary at work, on a jury, in the voting booth, and in discussions with friends as it is in the study of history.

World history is nothing less than everything ever done or imagined, so we cannot possibly cover it all. In his famous novel *Ulysses,* James Joyce imagines the thoughts and actions of a few friends on a single day in Dublin, June 16, 1904. The book runs almost a thousand pages. Obviously, there were many more than a few people in Dublin on that particular day, countless other cities in the world, and infinitely more days than that one particular day in world history. So we are forced to choose places and times.

In this volume our choices include some particular days, like the day in 1519 that Cortés and Montezuma met, but our attention will be directed mainly toward much longer periods. And while we will visit particular places like Mexico City in 1519, typically we will study more than one place at a time by using a comparative approach.

Comparisons can be enormously useful in studying world history. When we compare Chinese and European mariners, merchants in Malacca and Persia, science in India and England, growing up in Algeria and Nigeria, we learn about the general and the specific at the same time. My hope is that by comparing some of the various worlds of history, an understanding of world history will emerge.

Contents

3. Asian Continental Empires and Maritime States   *78*

The rich and powerful continental empires of Asia were alike in some respects, but important characteristics differentiated land empires from the dynamic maritime merchant city-states of the new era. In distinguishing the societies, economics, politics, and cultures of these societies, we learn to understand their differences and the implications these differences had for their ultimate survival and success.

HISTORICAL CONTEXT: Malacca, China,
and Muslim Empires, 1500–1700   *78*

THINKING HISTORICALLY: Sifting Evidence: Social,
Economic, Political, and Cultural   *79*

4. The Scientific Revolution   *117*

The seventeenth-century scientific revolution occurred in Europe, but it had important roots in Asia and its consequences reverberated throughout the world. To understand exactly what changed and how, we must study the "before" and "after."

HISTORICAL CONTEXT: Europe, America, India, China,
and Japan, 1600–1800   *117*

THINKING HISTORICALLY: Sifting Evidence:
"Before" and "After"   *117*

5. Enlightenment and Revolution   *157*

The eighteenth-century Enlightenment applied scientific reason to politics, but reason meant different things to different people and societies. What were the goals of the political revolutions produced by the Enlightenment? A close reading of period texts reveals disagreement and shared dreams.

HISTORICAL CONTEXT: Europe and the Americas, 1650–1850   *157*

THINKING HISTORICALLY: Close Reading and Interpretation of Texts   *158*

6. Capitalism and the Industrial Revolution   *187*

Modern society has been shaped dramatically by capitalism and the industrial revolution, but these two forces are not the same. Which one is principally responsible for the creation of our modern world: the economic system of the market or the technology of the industrial revolution? Distinguishing different "causes" allows us to gauge their relative effects and legacies.

HISTORICAL CONTEXT: Europe and the World, 1750–1900   *187*

THINKING HISTORICALLY: Distinguishing Causes of Change   *188*

7. Free Trade and the Opium War   *224*

Conflict is the impetus for war, and so it was in the Opium War between Britain and China. With each step toward war, internal conflicts within Britain and China escalated as well. Was war inevitable, or did it only seem inevitable as each side continued to limit its respective diplomatic options? We examine evidence, in words, graphs, and pictures, as many debates merge into one.

8. Colonized and Colonizers   264

Colonialism resulted in a world divided between the colonized and the colonizers, a world in which people's identities were defined by their power relationships with others who looked and often spoke differently. The meeting of strangers and their forced adjustment to predefined roles inspired a number of great literary works that we look to in this chapter for historical guidance.

9. Independence and Westernization   303

Becoming "independent" of the colonizers often required that the colonized adopt their conquerors' ways. Whether or how much to Westernize was one of the fundamental questions national independence movements sought to answer. We must appreciate contradiction and paradox to understand the high stakes involved for those fighting for their freedom.

10. World War and Its Consequences   *344*

The First World War brutally ended an era — the world would never be the same after such death and destruction. We read historical accounts so we can begin to understand the war's far-reaching chain of causes and consequences.

11. Fascism, World War II, and Genocide   *381*

The rise of fascism in Europe and Asia led to genocide and world war. How could people allow their governments, armies, families, and friends to commit such unspeakable acts? How does the unforgivable happen?

12. New States and New Struggles   *423*

New states were created in the wake of colonialism and in the ashes of war, but all too often they were unable to resolve the conflicts that occasioned their creation. What are the fault lines of modern society and culture? Does the present recapitulate the past?

HISTORICAL CONTEXT: Middle East, South Africa, China, and Vietnam, 1945–1975   *423*

THINKING HISTORICALLY: Diagnosing Rifts and Noting the Uses of History   *424*

13. Women's World   *464*

The lives of women in the modern world are as diverse as those of men. Can you find any patterns in these personal accounts and stories? Can you develop any theories about women's lives in the modern world?

HISTORICAL CONTEXT: The World, 1950–2000   *464*

THINKING HISTORICALLY: Constructing Theory   *465*

14. Globalization   *503*

Globalization *is a word with many meanings and a process with many causes. What are the forces most responsible for the shrinking of the world into one global community? Ultimately, understanding history enables us to understand the process of change.*

Worlds of History

1

Chinese and European Expansion

HISTORICAL CONTEXT:
China and Europe, 1400–1600

Between 1400 and 1500, the balance between Chinese and European sea power changed drastically. Before 1434, Chinese shipbuilding technology was the envy of the world. Chinese ships were larger, more numerous, safer, and better outfitted than European ships. The Chinese navy made frequent trips through the South China Sea to the Spice Islands, through the Indian Ocean, and as far as East Africa and the Persian Gulf. Every island, port, and kingdom along the route was integrated into the Chinese system of tributaries. Goods were exchanged, marriages arranged, and princes taken to visit the Chinese emperor.

In the second half of the fifteenth century, the Chinese navy virtually disappeared. At the same time, the Portuguese began a series of explorations down the coast of Africa and into the Atlantic Ocean. In 1434, Portuguese ships rounded the treacherous Cape Bojador, just south of Morocco. In 1488, Bartholomeu Dias rounded the Cape of Good Hope. Vasco de Gama sailed into the Indian Ocean, arriving in Calicut the following year. And in 1500 a fortuitous landfall in Brazil by Pedro Cabral gave the Portuguese a claim from the western Atlantic to the Indian Ocean. By 1512, Portuguese ships had reached the Bandas and Moluccas — the Spice Islands of what is today eastern Indonesia.

The Spanish, beginning slightly later than the Portuguese but right on the heels of unification and the defeat of the Moors (Muslims) in 1492, claimed most of the Western Hemisphere until challenged by the Dutch, English, and French, who also struggled with the Portuguese in Asia. European control in the Americas penetrated far deeper than in Asia, where it was limited to enclaves on the coast, and where European nations were in an almost perpetual state of war with each

1

other. Taken together, the nations of Western Europe dominated the seas of the world after 1500.

What accounts for the different fortunes of China and Europe in the fifteenth century? Was the decline of China and the rise of Europe inevitable? Probably no objective observer of the time would have thought so. In what ways were the expansions of China and Europe similar? In what ways were they different? Think about these questions as you reflect on the readings in this chapter.

THINKING HISTORICALLY:
Reading Primary and Secondary Sources

This chapter contains both primary and secondary sources. *Primary sources* are actual pieces of the past and include anything — for example, art, letters, essays, and so on — from the historical period being studied. If a future historian were to study and research students in American colleges at the end of the twentieth century, possible primary sources might include diaries, letters, e-mail messages, class notes, school newspapers, transcripts, textbooks, tests, and official and unofficial records. *Secondary sources* are usually books and articles *about* the past — interpretations of the past. That is, these sources are "secondary" because they must be based on primary sources; therefore, a history written after an event occurs is a secondary source.

In your studies, you will be expected to distinguish primary from secondary sources. A quick glance at the introductions to this chapter's four readings tells you that the first article, published in the *New York Times,* is written by a modern journalist, whereas the fourth article, also written by a contemporary author, is taken from a book published in 1991. In contrast, Zhang Han, author of the second selection, recorded his thoughts in the sixteenth century, whereas Christopher Columbus penned the fourth selection more than five hundred years ago. These latter sources are firsthand accounts of long past worlds.

Having determined whether selections are primary or secondary sources, we also explore some of the subtle complexities that are overlooked by such designations.

1

NICHOLAS D. KRISTOF

1492: *The Prequel*

Almost a century before Columbus, Zheng He, a eunich admiral in the court, sailed from China with three hundred ships and twenty-eight thousand men. His fleet stopped at ports in the Indian Ocean and jour-neyed as far as the east coast of Africa. Nicholas Kristof travels to the east African island of Pate to find traces of these fifteenth-century Chi-nese sailors. What types of evidence is he seeking? What does Kristof's brief history suggest about China, India, and Europe, and their roles in the making of the modern world? How would today's world be differ-ent if Chinese ships had reached the Western Hemisphere before Columbus?

Thinking Historically

In his secondary account of Zheng He's voyages, Kristof alludes to certain possible primary sources. What sorts of primary sources are available to historians interested in reconstructing the life and voyages of Zheng He? What primary sources are not available? Why are they not available? Has Kristof's recent voyage led to the discovery of a new primary source?

From the sea, the tiny East African island of Pate, just off the Kenyan coast, looks much as it must have in the 15th century: an impenetrable shore of endless mangrove trees. As my little boat bounced along the waves in the gray dawn, I could see no antennae or buildings or even gaps where trees had been cut down, no sign of human habitation, nothing but a dense and mysterious jungle.

The boatman drew as close as he could to a narrow black-sand beach, and I splashed ashore. My local Swahili interpreter led the way through the forest, along a winding trail scattered with mangoes, coconuts, and oc-casional seashells deposited by high tides. The tropical sun was firmly overhead when we finally came upon a village of stone houses with thatched roofs, its dirt paths sheltered by palm trees. The village's inhabi-tants, much lighter-skinned than people on the Kenyan mainland, emerged barefoot to stare at me with the same curiosity with which I was

---

Nicholas D. Kristof, "1492: The Prequel," *New York Times Magazine*, 6 June 1999, 6, 80:1.

studying them. These were people I had come halfway around the world to see, in the hope of solving an ancient historical puzzle.

"Tell me," I asked the first group I encountered, "where did the people here come from? Long ago, did foreign sailors ever settle here?" The answer was a series of shrugs. "I've never heard about that," one said. "You'll have to ask the elders."

I tried several old men and women without success. Finally the villagers led me to the patriarch of the village, Bwana Mkuu Al-Bauri, the keeper of oral traditions. He was a frail old man with gray stubble on his cheeks, head, and chest. He wore a yellow sarong around his waist; his ribs pressed through the taut skin on his bare torso. Al-Bauri hobbled out of his bed, resting on a cane and the arm of a grandson. He claimed to be 121 years old; a pineapple-size tumor jutted from the left side of his chest.

"I know this from my grandfather, who himself was the keeper of history here," the patriarch told me in an unexpectedly clear voice. "Many, many years ago, there was a ship from China that wrecked on the rocks off the coast near here. The sailors swam ashore near the village of Shanga — my ancestors were there and saw it themselves.

"The Chinese were visitors, so we helped those Chinese men and gave them food and shelter, and then they married our women. Although they do not live in this village, I believe their descendants still can be found somewhere else on this island."

I almost felt like hugging Bwana Al-Bauri. For months I had been poking around obscure documents and research reports, trying to track down a legend of an ancient Chinese shipwreck that had led to a settlement on the African coast. My interest arose from a fascination with what to me is a central enigma of the millennium: Why did the West triumph over the East?

For most of the last several thousand years, it would have seemed far likelier that Chinese or Indians, not Europeans, would dominate the world by the year 2000, and that America and Australia would be settled by Chinese rather than by the inhabitants of a backward island called Britain. The reversal of fortunes of East and West strikes me as the biggest news story of the millennium, and one of its most unexpected as well.

As a resident of Asia for most of the past thirteen years, I've been searching for an explanation. It has always seemed to me that the turning point came in the early 1400s, when Admiral Zheng He sailed from China to conquer the world. Zheng He (prounounced JUNG HUH) was an improbable commander of a great Chinese fleet, in that he was a Muslim from a rebel family and had been seized by the Chinese Army when he was still a boy. Like many other prisoners of the time, he was castrated, his sexual organs completely hacked off, a process that killed many of those who suffered it. But he was a brilliant and tenacious boy who grew up to be physically imposing. A natural leader, he had the good fortune to be assigned, as a houseboy, to the household of a great prince, Zhu Di.

In time, the prince and Zheng He grew close, and they conspired to overthrow the prince's nephew, the Emperor of China. With Zheng He as one of the prince's military commanders, the revolt succeeded and the prince became China's Yongle Emperor. One of the emperor's first acts (after torturing to death those who had opposed him) was to reward Zheng He with the command of a great fleet that was to sail off and assert China's pre-eminence in the world.

Between 1405 and 1433, Zheng He led seven major expeditions, commanding the largest armada the world would see for the next five centuries. Not until World War I did the West mount anything comparable. Zheng He's fleet included twenty-eight thousand sailors on three hundred ships, the longest of which were four hundred feet. By comparison, Columbus in 1492 had ninety sailors on three ships, the biggest of which was eighty-five feet long. Zheng He's ships also had advanced design elements that would not be introduced in Europe for another 350 years, including balanced rudders and watertight bulwark compartments.

The sophistication of Zheng He's fleet underscores just how far ahead of the West the East once was. Indeed, except for the period of the Roman Empire, China had been wealthier, more advanced, and more cosmopolitan than any place in Europe for several thousand years. Hangzhou, for example, had a population in excess of a million during the time it was China's capital (in the twelfth century), and records suggest that as early as the seventh century, the city of Guangzhou had 200,000 foreign residents: Arabs, Persians, Malays, Indians, Africans, and Turks. By contrast, the largest city in Europe in 1400 was probably Paris, with a total population of slightly more than 100,000.

A half-century before Columbus, Zheng He had reached East Africa and learned about Europe from Arab traders. The Chinese could easily have continued around the Cape of Good Hope and established direct trade with Europe. But as they saw it, Europe was a backward region, and China had little interest in the wood, beads, and wine Europe had to trade. Africa had what China wanted — ivory, medicines, spices, exotic woods, even specimens of native wildlife.

In Zheng He's time, China and India together accounted for more than half of the world's gross national product, as they have for most of human history. Even as recently as 1820, China accounted for 29 percent of the global economy and India another 16 percent, according to the calculations of Angus Maddison, a leading British economic historian.

Asia's retreat into relative isolation after the expeditions of Zheng He amounted to a catastrophic missed opportunity, one that laid the groundwork for the rise of Europe and, eventually, America. Westerners often attribute their economic advantage today to the intelligence, democratic habits, or hard work of their forebears, but a more important reason may well have been the folly of fifteenth-century Chinese rulers. That is why I came to be fascinated with Zheng He and set out earlier this year to retrace his journeys. I wanted to see what legacy, if any, remained of his achievement, and to figure out why his travels did not remake the world in the way that Columbus's did.

Zheng He lived in Nanjing, the old capital, where I arrived one day in February. Nanjing is a grimy metropolis on the Yangtze River in the heart of China. It has been five centuries since Zheng He's death, and his marks on the city have grown faint. The shipyards that built his fleet are still busy, and the courtyard of what had been his splendid seventy-two-room mansion is now the Zheng He Memorial Park, where children roller-skate and old couples totter around for exercise. But though the park has a small Zheng He museum, it was closed — for renovation, a caretaker told me, though he knew of no plans to reopen it.

I'd heard that Zheng He's tomb is on a hillside outside the city, and I set out to find it. It wasn't long before the road petered out, from asphalt to gravel to dirt to nothing. No tomb was in sight, so I approached an old man weeding a vegetable garden behind his house. Tang Yiming, seventy-two, was still lithe and strong. His hair was gray and ragged where he had cut it himself, disastrously, in front of a mirror. Evidently lonely, he was delighted to talk, and offered to show me the path to the tomb. As we walked, I mentioned that I had read that there used to be an old Ming Dynasty tablet on Zheng He's grave.

"Oh, yeah, the old tablet," he said nonchalantly. "When I was a boy, there was a Ming Dynasty tablet here. When it disappeared, the Government offered a huge reward to anyone who would return it — a reward big enough to build a new house. Seemed like a lot of money. But the problem was that we couldn't give it back. People around here are poor. We'd smashed it up to use as building materials."

A second mystery concerned what, if anything, is actually buried in Zheng He's tomb, since he is believed to have died on his last voyage and been buried at sea. So I said in passing that I'd heard tell the tomb is empty, and let my voice trail off.

"Oh, there's nothing in there," Tang said, a bit sadly. "No bones, nothing. That's for sure."

"How do you know?"

"In 1962, people dug up the grave, looking for anything to sell. We dug up the ground to one and a half times the height of a man. But there was absolutely nothing in there. It's empty."

The absence of impressive monuments to Zheng He in China today should probably come as no surprise, since his achievement was ultimately renounced. Curiously, it is not in China but in Indonesia where his memory has been most actively kept alive. Zheng He's expeditions led directly to the wave of Chinese immigration to Southeast Asia, and in some countries he is regarded today as a deity. In the Indonesia city of Semarang, for example, there is a large temple honoring Zheng He, located near a cave where he once nursed a sick friend. Indonesians still pray to Zheng He for a cure or good luck.

Not so in his native land. Zheng He was viewed with deep suspicion by China's traditional elite, the Confucian scholars, who made sure to destroy the archives of his journey. Even so, it is possible to learn something about his story from Chinese sources — from imperial archives and even the memoirs of crewmen. The historical record makes clear, for example, that it was not some sudden impulse of extroversion that led to Zheng He's achievement. It grew, rather, out of a long sailing tradition. Chinese accounts suggest that in the fifth century a Chinese monk sailed to a mysterious "far east country" that sounds very much like Mayan Mexico, and Mayan art at that time suddenly began to include Buddhist symbols. By the thirteenth century, Chinese ships regularly traveled to India and occasionally to East Africa.

Zheng He's armada was far grander, of course, than anything that came before. His grandest vessels were the "treasure ships," 400 feet long and 160 feet wide, with nine masts raising red silk sails to the wind, as well as multiple decks and luxury cabins with balconies. His armada included supply ships to carry horses, troop transports, warships, patrol boats, and as many as twenty tankers to carry fresh water. The full contingent of 28,000 crew members included interpreters for Arabic and other languages, astrologers to forecast the weather, astronomers to study the stars, pharmacologists to collect medicinal plants, ship-repair specialists, doctors, and even two protocol officers to help organize official receptions.

In the aftermath of such an incredible undertaking, you somehow expect to find a deeper mark on Chinese history, a greater legacy. But perhaps the faintness of Zheng He's trace in contemporary China is itself a lesson. In the end, an explorer makes history but does not necessarily change it, for his impact depends less on the trail he blazes than on the willingness of others to follow. The daring of a great expedition ultimately is hostage to the national will of those who remain behind.

In February I traveled to Calicut, a port town in southwestern India that was (and still is) the pepper capital of the world. The evening I arrived, I went down to the beach in the center of town to look at the coastline where Zheng He once had berthed his ships. In the fourteenth and fifteenth centuries, Calicut was one of the world's great ports, known to the Chinese as "the great country of the Western ocean." In the early fifteenth century, the sight of Zheng He's fleet riding anchor in Calicut harbor symbolized the strength of the world's two greatest powers, China and India.

On this sultry evening, the beach, framed by long piers jutting out to sea, was crowded with young lovers and ice-cream vendors. Those piers are all that remain of the port of Calicut, and you can see at a glance that they are no longer usable. The following day I visited the port offices, musty with handwritten ledgers of ship visits dating back nearly a century. The administrator of the port, Captain E. G. Mohanan, explained matter-of-factly what had happened. "The piers got old and no proper maintenance was ever carried out," he said, as a ceiling fan whirred tiredly overhead. "By the time we thought of it, it was not economical to fix it up." So in 1989, trade was halted, and one of the great ports of the world became no port at all.

The disappearance of a great Chinese fleet from a great Indian port symbolized one of history's biggest lost opportunities — Asia's failure to dominate the second half of this millennium. So how did this happen?

While Zheng He was crossing the Indian Ocean, the Confucian scholar-officials who dominated the upper echelons of the Chinese Government were at political war with the eunuchs, a group they regarded as corrupt and immoral. The eunuchs' role at court involved looking after the concubines, but they also served as palace administrators, often doling out contracts in exchange for kickbacks. Partly as a result of their legendary greed, they promoted commerce. Unlike the scholars — who owed their position to their mastery of two thousand-year-old texts — the eunuchs, lacking any such roots in a classical past, were sometimes outward-looking and progressive. Indeed, one can argue that it was the virtuous, incorruptible scholars who in the mid-fifteenth century set China on its disastrous course.

After the Yongle Emperor died in 1424, China endured a series of brutal power struggles; a successor emperor died under suspicious circumstances and ultimately the scholars emerged triumphant. They ended the voyages of Zheng He's successors, halted construction of new ships, and imposed curbs on private shipping. To prevent any backsliding, they destroyed Zheng He's sailing records and, with the backing of the new emperor, set about dismantling China's navy.

By 1500 the Government had made it a capital offense to build a boat with more than two masts, and in 1525 the Government ordered the destruction of all oceangoing ships. The greatest navy in history, which a century earlier had 3,500 ships (by comparison, the United States Navy today has 324), had been extinguished, and China set a course for itself that would lead to poverty, defeat, and decline.

Still, it was not the outcome of a single power struggle in the 1440s that cost China its worldly influence. Historians offer a host of reasons for why Asia eventually lost its way economically and was late to industrialize; two and a half reasons seem most convincing.

The first is that Asia was simply not greedy enough. The dominant social ethos in ancient China was Confucianism and in India it was caste, with the result that the elites in both nations looked down their noses at business. Ancient China cared about many things — prestige, honor, culture, arts, education, ancestors, religion, filial piety — but making money came far down the list. Confucius had specifically declared that it was wrong for a man to make a distant voyage while his parents were alive, and he had condemned profit as the concern of "a little man." As it was, Zheng He's ships were built on such a grand scale and carried such lavish gifts to foreign leaders that the voyages were not the huge money spinners they could have been.

In contrast to Asia, Europe was consumed with greed. Portugal led the age of discovery in the fifteenth century largely because it wanted spices, a precious commodity; it was the hope of profits that drove its ships steadily farther down the African coast and eventually around the Horn to Asia. The profits of this trade could be vast: Magellan's crew once sold a cargo of twenty-six tons of cloves for ten thousand times the cost.

A second reason for Asia's economic stagnation is more difficult to articulate but has to do with what might be called a culture of complacency. China and India shared a tendency to look inward, a devotion to past ideals and methods, a respect for authority, and a suspicion of new ideas. David S. Landes, a Harvard economist, has written of ancient China's "intelligent xenophobia"; the former Indian Prime Minister Jawaharlal Nehru referred to the "petrification of classes" and the "static nature" of Indian society. These are all different ways of describing the same economic and intellectual complacency.

Chinese elites regarded their country as the "Middle Kingdom" and believed they had nothing to learn from barbarians abroad. India exhibited much of the same self-satisfaction. "Indians didn't go to Portugal not because they couldn't but because they didn't want to," mused M. P. Sridharan, a historian, as we sat talking on the porch of his home in Calicut.

The fifteenth-century Portuguese were the opposite. Because of its coastline and fishing industry, Portugal always looked to the sea, yet rivalries with Spain and other countries shut it out of the Mediterranean trade. So the only way for Portugal to get at the wealth of the East was by conquering the oceans.

The half reason is simply that China was a single nation while Europe was many. When the Confucian scholars reasserted control in Beijing and banned shipping, their policy mistake condemned all of China. In contrast, European countries committed economic suicide selectively. So when Portugal slipped into a quasi-Chinese mind-set in the sixteenth century, slaughtering Jews and burning heretics, and driving astronomers and scientists abroad, Holland and England were free to take up the slack.

When I first began researching Zheng He, I never thought I'd be traveling all the way to Africa to look for traces of his voyages. Then I came across a few intriguing references to the possibility of an ancient

Chinese shipwreck that might have left some Chinese stranded on the island of Pate (pronounced PAH-tay). One was a skeptical reference in a scholarly journal, another was a casual conversation with a Kenyan I met a few years ago, and the third was the epilogue of Louise Levathes's wonderful 1994 book about China's maritime adventures, "When China Ruled the Seas." Levathes had traveled to Kenya and found people who believed they were descended from survivors of a Chinese shipwreck. So, on a whim and an expense account, I flew to Lamu, an island off northern Kenya, and hired a boat and an interpreter to go to Pate and see for myself.

Pate is off in its own world, without electricity or roads or vehicles. Mostly jungle, it has been shielded from the twentieth century largely because it is accessible from the Kenyan mainland only by taking a boat through a narrow tidal channel that is passable only at high tide. Initially I was disappointed by what I found there. In the first villages I visited, I saw people who were light-skinned and had hair that was not tightly curled, but they could have been part Arab or European rather than part Chinese. The remote villages of Chundwa and Faza were more promising, for there I found people whose eyes, hair, and complexion hinted at Asian ancestry, though their background was ambiguous.

And then on a still and sweltering afternoon I strolled through the coconut palms into the village of Siyu, where I met a fisherman in his forties named Abdullah Mohammed Badui. I stopped and stared at the man in astonishment, for he had light skin and narrow eyes. Fortunately, he was as rude as I was, and we stared at each other in mutual surprise before venturing a word. Eventually I asked him about his background and appearance.

"I am in the Famao clan," he said. "There are fifty or one hundred of us Famao left here. Legend has it that we are descended from Chinese and others.

"A Chinese ship was coming along and it hit rocks and wrecked," Badui continued. "The sailors swam ashore to the village that we now call Shanga, and they married the local women, and that is why we Famao look so different."

Another Famao, with the same light complexion and vaguely Asian features, approached to listen. His name was Athman Mohammed Mzee, and he, too, told of hearing of the Chinese shipwreck from the elders. He volunteered an intriguing detail: The Africans had given giraffes to the Chinese.

Salim Bonaheri, a fifty-five-year-old Famao man I met the next day, proudly declared, "My ancestors were Chinese or Vietnamese or something like that." I asked how they had got to Pate.

"I don't know," Bonaheri said with a shrug. Most of my conversations were like that, intriguing but frustrating dead ends. I was surrounded by people whose appearance seemed tantalizingly Asian, but who had only the vaguest notions of why that might be. I kept at it, though, and eventually found people like Khalifa Mohammed Omar, a fifty-five-year-old Famao fisherman who looked somewhat Chinese and who also clearly remembered the stories passed down by his grandfather. From him and others, a tale emerged.

Countless generations ago, they said, Chinese sailors traded with local African kings. The local kings gave them giraffes to take back to China. One of the Chinese ships struck rocks off the eastern coast of Pate, and the sailors swam ashore, carrying with them porcelain and other goods from the ship. In time they married local women, converted to Islam, and named the village Shanga, after Shanghai. Later, fighting erupted among Pate's clans, Shanga was destroyed, and the Famao fled, some to the mainland, others to the village of Siyu.

Every time I heard the story about the giraffes my pulse began to race. Chinese records indicate that Zheng He had brought the first giraffes to China, a fact that is not widely known. The giraffe caused an enormous stir in China because it was believed to be the mythical qilin, or Chinese unicorn. It is difficult to imagine how African villagers on an island as remote as Pate would know about the giraffes unless the tale had been handed down to them by the Chinese sailors.

Chinese ceramics are found in many places along the east African coast, and their presence on Pate could be the result of purchases from Arab traders. But the porcelain on Pate was overwhelmingly concentrated among the Famao clan, which could mean that it had been inherited rather than purchased. I also visited some ancient Famao graves that looked less like traditional Kenyan graves than what the Chinese call "turtle-shell graves," with rounded tops.

Researchers have turned up other equally tantalizing clues. Craftsmen on Pate and the other islands of Lamu practice a kind of basketweaving that is common in southern China but unknown on the Kenyan mainland. On Pate, drums are more often played in the Chinese than the African style, and the local dialect has a few words that may be Chinese in origin. More startling, in 1569 a Portuguese priest named Monclaro wrote that Pate had a flourishing silk-making industry — Pate, and no other place in the region. Elders in several villages on Pate confirmed to me that their island had produced silk until about half a century ago.

When I asked my boatman, Bakari Muhaji Ali, if he thought it was possible that a ship could have wrecked off the coast near Shanga, he laughed. "There are undersea rocks all over there," he said. "If you don't know exactly where you're going, you'll wreck your ship for sure."

If indeed there was a Chinese shipwreck off Pate, there is reason to think it happened in Zheng He's time. For if the shipwreck had predated him, surviving sailors would not have passed down stories of the giraffes. And if the wreck didn't occur until after Zheng He, its survivors could not have settled in Shanga, since British archeological digs indicate that the village was sacked, burned, and abandoned in about 1440 — very soon after Zheng He's last voyage.

Still, there is no hard proof for the shipwreck theory, and there are plenty of holes in it. No ancient Chinese characters have been found on tombs in Pate, no nautical instruments have ever turned up on the island, and there are no Chinese accounts of an African shipwreck. This last lacuna might be explained by the destruction of the fleet's records. Yet if one of Zheng He's ships did founder on the rocks off Pate, then why didn't some other ships in the fleet come to the sailors' rescue?

As I made my way back through the jungle for the return trip, I pondered the significance of what I'd seen on Pate. In the faces of the Famao, in those bits of pottery and tantalizing hints of Chinese culture, I felt as though I'd glimpsed the shadowy outlines of one of the greatest might-have-beens of the millennium now ending. I thought about the Columbian Exchange, the swap of animals, plants, genes, germs, weapons, and peoples that utterly remade both the New World and the Old, and I couldn't help wondering about another exchange — Zheng He's — that never took place, yet could have.

If ancient China had been greedier and more outward-looking, if other traders had followed in Zheng He's wake and then continued on, Asia might well have dominated Africa and even Europe. Chinese might have settled in not only Malaysia and Singapore, but also in East Africa, the Pacific Islands, even in America. Perhaps the Famao show us what the mestizos of such a world might have looked like, the children of a hybrid culture that was never born. What I'd glimpsed in Pate was the highwater mark of an Asian push that simply stopped — not for want of ships or know-how, but strictly for want of national will.

All this might seem fanciful, and yet in Zheng He's time the prospect of a New World settled by the Spanish or English would have seemed infinitely more remote than a New World made by the Chinese. How different would history have been had Zheng He continued on to America? The mind rebels; the ramifications are almost too overwhelming to contemplate. So consider just one: This magazine would have been published in Chinese.

ZHANG HAN
Essay on Merchants

Zhang Han (1511–1593) was a Chinese official whose family had become wealthy in the textile trade. How would you describe his attitude toward merchants?

The previous selection called our attention to the role of the Chinese government, specifically of the emperor and his staff of eunuchs, in maritime trade. In this selection we are reminded that there were private maritime merchants as well as official treasure ships and that the activity of private mariners could be greatly restricted by imperial policy. What kinds of trade restrictions does Zhang Han find unwise? How would you describe the relationship between merchants and officials in China during this period?

Thinking Historically

Though primary sources are the building blocks of history, they can also challenge the historical interpretations of a secondary source. Consider how this primary source supports or disputes Kristof's interpretation in the previous selection. Keep in mind that this primary source was written in the sixteenth century (1500s), whereas Kristof writes in the twentieth century about the fifteenth. What, according to Kristof, is the crucial event that occurred between 1433 and the 1500s? What signs do you see of this event in Zhang Han's essay? In what ways does Zhang Han's essay support or challenge Kristof's explanation of Chinese withdrawal from ocean trade?

Money and profit are of great importance to men. They seek profit, then suffer by it, yet they cannot forget it. They exhaust their bodies and spirits, run day and night, yet they still regard what they have gained as insufficient. . . .

Those who become merchants eat fine food and wear elegant clothes. They ride on beautifully caparisoned, double-harnessed horses — dust flying as they race through the streets and the horses' precious sweat falling like rain. Opportunistic persons attracted by

Zhang Han, "Songchuang meng yu" (1896 edition), trans. Lily Hwa, in *Chinese Civilization and Society: A Sourcebook*, ed. Patricia Buckley Ebrey, 2nd ed. (New York: The Free Press, 1993), 216–18.

their wealth offer to serve them. Pretty girls in beautiful long-sleeved dresses and delicate slippers play string and wind instruments for them and compete to please them.

Merchants boast that their wisdom and ability are such as to give them a free hand in affairs. They believe that they know all the possible transformations in the universe and therefore can calculate all the changes in the human world, and that the rise and fall of prices are under their command. They are confident that they will not make one mistake in a hundred in their calculations. These merchants do not know how insignificant their wisdom and ability really are. As the *Zhangzi* says: "Great understanding is broad and unhurried; little understanding is cramped and busy."

Because I have traveled to many places during my career as an official, I am familiar with commercial activities and business conditions in various places. The capital is located in an area with mountains at its back and a great plain stretching in front. The region is rich in millet, grain, donkeys, horses, fruit, and vegetables, and has become a center where goods from distant places are brought. Those who engage in commerce, including the foot peddler, the cart peddler, and the shopkeeper, display not only clothing and fresh foods from the fields but also numerous luxury items such as priceless jade from Kunlun, pearls from the island of Hainan, gold from Yunnan, and coral from Vietnam. These precious items, coming from the mountains or the sea, are not found in central China. But people in remote areas and in other countries, unafraid of the dangers and difficulties of travel, transport these items step by step to the capital, making it the most prosperous place in the empire. . . .

South of the capital is the province of Henan, which is the center of the empire. Going from Kaifeng, its capital, northwards to Weizhong, one can reach the Yangzi and Han rivers. Thus, Kaifeng is a great transportation center; one can travel by either boat or carriage from this spot to all other places, which makes it a favorite gathering place for merchants. The area is rich in lacquer, hemp, sackcloth, fine linen, fine gloss silk, wax, and leather. In antiquity, the Zhou dynasty had its capital here. The land is broad and flat, the people are rich and prosperous, and the customs are refined and frugal. . . .

In general, in the Southeast area the greatest profits are to be had from fine gauze, thin silk, cheap silk, and sackcloth. Sanwu in particular is famous for them. My ancestors' fortunes were based solely on such textile businesses. At the present time, a great many people in Sanwu have become wealthy from the textile industry.

In the nations' Northwest, profits are greatest in wool, coarse woolen serge, felt, and fur garments. Guanzhong is especially famous for these items. There is a family named Zhang in that area which has engaged in the animal-breeding business generation after generation.

They claim to have ten thousand sheep. Their animal-breeding enterprise is the largest in the Northwest and has made them the richest family in the area. In the surrounding areas of Yan, Zhou, Qin, and Jin, many other people have also become rich from animal breeding. From there, merchants seeking great profits go west to Sichuan and south to Guangdong. Because of the nature of the special products from the latter area — fine and second-grade pearls, gold, jade, and precious woods — profits can be five- or ten-fold or more.

The profits from the tea and salt trades are especially great but only large-scale merchants can undertake these businesses. Furthermore, there are government regulations on their distribution, which prohibit the sale of tea in the Northwest and salt in the Southeast. Since tea is produced primarily in the Southeast, prohibiting its sale to the non-Chinese on the northern border is wise and can be enforced. Selling privately produced salt where it is manufactured is also prohibited. This law is rigidly applied to all areas where salt was produced during the Ming dynasty. Yet there are so many private salt producers there now that the regulation seems too rigid and is hard to enforce.

Profits from selling tea and the officials' income from the tea tax are usually 10 to 20 percent of the original investment. By contrast, merchants' profits from selling salt and the officials' income from the salt tax can reach 70 to 80 percent of the original invested capital. In either case, the more the invested capital, the greater the profit; the less the invested capital, the less the profit. The profits from selling tea and salt enrich the nation as well as the merchants. Skillful merchants can make great profits for themselves while the inept ones suffer losses. This is the present state of the tea and salt business.

In our Zhejiang province it appears that most of the rich gain their wealth from engaging in salt trade. But the Jia family in Wuling became rich from selling tea and have sustained their prosperity for generations. The "Book of Zhou" says: "If farmers do not work, there will be an insufficiency of food; if craftsmen do not work, there will be an insufficiency of tools; if merchants do not work, circulation of the three necessities will be cut off, which will cause food and materials to be insufficient."[1]

As to the foreign trade on the northwestern frontier and the foreign sea trade in the Southeast, if we compare their advantages and disadvantages with respect to our nation's wealth and the people's well-being, we will discover that they are as different as black and white. But those who are in charge of state economic matters know only the benefits of the Northwest trade, ignoring the benefits of the sea trade. How can they be so blind?

---

[1] The "Book of Zhou" is a section of the *Book of Documents,* one of the oldest of the classics.

In the early years of the frontier trade, China traded sackcloth and copper cash to the foreigners. Now we use silk and gold but the foreigners repay us only with thin horses. When we exchanged sackcloth and copper cash for their thin horses, the advantage of the trade was still with China and our national wealth was not endangered. But now we give away gold and silk, and the gold, at least, will never come back to us once it flows into foreign lands. Moreover, to use the silk that China needs for people's clothing to exchange for useless, inferior horses is clearly unwise.

Foreigners are recalcitrant and their greed knows no bounds. At the present time our nation spends over one million cash yearly from our treasury on these foreigners, still we cannot rid ourselves of their demands. What is more, the greedy heart is unpredictable. If one day they break the treaties and invade our frontiers, who will be able to defend us against them? I do not think our present trade with them will ensure us a century of peace.

As to the foreigners in the Southeast, their goods are useful to us just as ours are to them. To use what one has to exchange for what one does not have is what trade is all about. Moreover, these foreigners trade with China under the name of tributary contributions. That means China's authority is established and the foreigners are submissive. Even if the gifts we grant them are great and the tribute they send us is small, our expense is still less than one ten-thousandth of the benefit we gain from trading with them. Moreover, the Southeast sea foreigners are more concerned with trading with China than with gaining gifts from China. Even if they send a large tribute offering only to receive small gifts in return, they will still be content. In addition, trading with them can enrich our people. So why do we refrain from the trade?

Some people may say that the Southeast sea foreigners have invaded us several times so they are not the kind of people with whom we should trade. But they should realize that the Southeast sea foreigners need Chinese goods and the Chinese need their goods. If we prohibit the natural flow of this merchandise, how can we prevent them from invading us? I believe that if the sea trade were opened, the trouble with foreign pirates would cease. These Southeast sea foreigners are simple people, not to be compared to the unpredictable Northeast sea foreigners. Moreover, China's exports in the Northwest trade come from the national treasury. Whereas the Northwest foreign trade ensures only harm, the sea trade provides us with only gain. How could those in charge of the government fail to realize this? . . .

CHRISTOPHER COLUMBUS

Letter to King Ferdinand and Queen Isabella

Christopher Columbus sent this letter to his royal backers, King Ferdinand and Queen Isabella of Spain, on his return in March 1493 from his first voyage across the Atlantic.

An Italian sailor from Genoa, Columbus tried to make his fortune in Portugal in the 1480s. The Genoese had banking and trading contacts with Portugal, and it is possible that Columbus may have represented one of these contacts. In 1483–84 Columbus tried to convince King John II of Portugal to underwrite his plan to sail across the western ocean to the spice-rich East Indies. Relying on a Florentine map that used Marco Polo's overstated distance from Venice to Japan across Asia and an understated estimate of the circumference of the globe, Columbus believed that Japan lay only 2,500 miles west of the Portuguese Azores. King John II rejected the proposal because he had more accurate estimates that indicated sailing around Africa was shorter. In 1488 the Portuguese navigator Bartholomeu Dias returned with news that he had rounded the Cape of Good Hope, the southernmost point in Africa, which enabled him to sail to the Indies, ending any interest in Columbus's plan.

The new Spanish monarchs, Ferdinand of Aragon and Isabella of Castile, were less knowledgeable about navigation than the Portuguese king. As a result they supported Columbus and financed his plan to sail west to Asia. In four voyages, Columbus touched a number of Caribbean islands and the coast of Central America, settled Spaniards on Hispaniola (Española), and began to create one of the largest empires in world history for Spain — all the while thinking he was near China and Japan, in the realm of the Great Khan whom Marco Polo had met and who had died hundreds of years earlier.

In what ways was the voyage of Columbus similar to that of Zheng He? In what ways was it different? How were the relationships of the explorers with their kings similar and different? Were the motives driving Chinese and European expansion more alike or different?

"First Voyage of Columbus," in *The Four Voyages of Columbus*, ed. Cecil Jane (New York: Dover, 1988), 1–18.

Thinking Historically

Because this document comes from the period we are studying and is written by Columbus himself, it is a primary source. Primary sources have a great sense of immediacy and can often "transport" us to the past intellectually. However, involvement when reading does not always lead to understanding. Think critically about the source and the writer's intended audience as you read. Is the author reliable? Is the information accurate? Might the author represent a particular bias or point of view? We can only determine these things through careful analysis.

First, we must determine the source of the document. Where does it come from? Is it original? If not, is it a copy or a translation? Next, we must determine who wrote it, when it was written, and for what purpose. After answering these questions, we are able to read the document with a critical eye, which leads to greater understanding.

Now, let us analyze this selection. The original letter by Columbus has been lost. This selection is an English translation based on three different printed Spanish versions of the letter. So this text is a reconstruction, not an original, though it is believed to be quite close to the original.

The original letter was probably composed during a relaxed time on the return voyage before its date of February 15, 1493 — possibly as early as the middle of January — and sent to the Spanish monarchs from Lisbon in order to reach them by the time Columbus arrived in Barcelona.

Columbus wanted the readers — let us assume Ferdinand and Isabella — to learn that his voyage from the Canary Islands to the Indies took thirty-three days. Can we believe him? Columbus might have exaggerated his speed or, conversely, the amount of time it took; or a scribe or a printer might have gotten it wrong. As it turns out, we can believe that Columbus's trip took thirty-three days because we have another source that corroborates the information: Columbus's detailed ship's log or diary.

Of course, a close rereading of the opening sentence tells us that the amount of time the voyage took is only part of the message Columbus wanted to impart to Ferdinand and Isabella. First and foremost, he wants them to know that he reached the Indies, that the voyage was a success. And so, the letter's opening sentence tells us something that Columbus certainly did not intend or know. We learn that on his return in 1493, Columbus thought he had been to the Indies when in fact he had not. (It is due to Columbus's confusion that we call the islands he visited the West Indies and Native Americans "Indians.")

We might infer many other things from the first sentence. Did Columbus know that Ferdinand and Isabella were "pleased at the great victory with which Our Lord ha[d] crowned [his] voyage"? No, but we learn that Columbus hoped they would be and that he is writing persuasively. Do we learn that the "Lord ha[d] crowned" the voyage? No, but we learn that Columbus wanted Ferdinand and Isabella to view the voyage as a crowning success and that invoking the name of the Lord was not overreaching in his mind.

Knowing what the author wants a reader to believe is useful information because it serves as a point of reference for other statements the author makes. The success of Columbus's voyage is a case in point. Columbus does not admit to the loss of one of his ships in his letter, nor does he explain fully why he had to build a fort at Navidad and leave some of his crew there, returning home without them. Clearly, Columbus had reason to worry that his voyage would be viewed as a failure. He had not found the gold mines he sought or the Asian cities described by Marco Polo. He thought he had discovered many spices, though only the chili peppers were new. Notice, as you read this letter, how Columbus presents his voyage in the best light.

Every sentence in this letter could be closely analyzed and scrutinized, an exhausting enterprise. As you read the letter, ask yourself the following questions: What does Columbus want the reader to learn? How does he describe his voyage in positive ways? Aside from what Columbus intends, what facts do you learn from the letter about Columbus, his first voyage, and his encounter with the New World? What seems to drive Columbus to do what he does? What is Columbus's attitude toward the "Indians"? What does Columbus's letter tell us about the society and culture of the Taino — the people he met in the Caribbean?

Sir, As I know that you will be pleased at the great victory with which Our Lord has crowned my voyage, I write this to you, from which you will learn how in thirty-three days, I passed from the Canary Islands to the Indies with the fleet which the most illustrious king and queen, our sovereigns, gave to me. And there I found very many islands filled with people innumerable, and of them all I have taken possession for their highnesses, by proclamation made and with the royal standard unfurled, and no opposition was offered to me. To the first island which I found, I gave the name *San Salvador,* in remembrance of the Divine Majesty, Who has marvellously bestowed all this; the Indians call it "Guanahani." To the second, I gave the name *Isla de Santa María de Concepción;* to the third, *Fernandina;* to the fourth, *Isabella;* to the fifth, *Isla Juana,* and so to each one I gave a new name.

When I reached Juana, I followed its coast to the westward, and I found it to be so extensive that I thought that it must be the mainland, the province of Catayo. And since there were neither towns nor villages on the seashore, but only small hamlets, with the people which I could not have speech, because they all fled immediately, I went forward on the same course, thinking that I should not fail to find great cities and towns. And, at the end of many leagues, seeing that there was no change and that the coast was bearing me northwards, which I wished to avoid, since winter was already beginning and I proposed to make from it to the south, and as moreover the wind was carrying me forward, I determined not to wait for a change in the weather and retraced my path as far as a certain harbour known to me. And from that point, I sent two men inland to learn if there were a king or great cities. They travelled three days' journey and found an infinity of small hamlets and people without number, but nothing of importance. For this reason, they returned.

I understood sufficiently from other Indians, whom I had already taken, that this land was nothing but an island. And therefore I followed its coast eastwards for one hundred and seven leagues to the point where it ended. And from that cape, I saw another island, distant eighteen leagues from the former, to the east, to which I at once gave the name "Española." And I went there and followed its northern coast, as I had in the case of Juana, to the eastward for one hundred and eighty-eight great leagues in a straight line. This island and all the others are very fertile to a limitless degree, and this island is extremely so. In it there are many harbours on the coast of the sea, beyond comparison with others which I know in Christendom, and many rivers, good and large, which is marvellous. Its lands are high, and there are in it very many sierras and very lofty mountains, beyond comparison with the island of Teneriffe. All are most beautiful, of a thousand shapes, and all are accessible and filled with trees of a thousand kinds and tall, and they seem to touch the sky. And I am told that they never lose their foliage, as I can understand, for I saw them as green and as lovely as they are in Spain in May, and some of them were flowering, some bearing fruit, and some in another stage, according to their nature. And the nightingale was singing and other birds of a thousand kinds in the month of November there where I went. There are six or eight kinds of palm, which are a wonder to behold on account of their beautiful variety, but so are the other trees and fruits and plants. In it are marvellous pine groves, and there are very large tracts of cultivatable lands, and there is honey, and there are birds of many kinds and fruits in great diversity. In the interior are mines of metals, and the population is without number. Española is a marvel.

The sierras and mountains, the plains and arable lands and pastures, are so lovely and rich for planting and sowing, for breeding cattle of every kind, for building towns and villages. The harbours of the sea here are such as cannot be believed to exist unless they have been seen, and so with the rivers, many and great, and good waters, the majority of which contain gold. In the trees and fruits and plants, there is a great difference from those of Juana. In this island, there are many spices and great mines of gold and of other metals.

The people of this island, and of all the other islands which I have found and of which I have information, all go naked, men and women, as their mothers bore them, although some women cover a single place with the leaf of a plant or with a net of cotton which they make for the purpose. They have no iron or steel or weapons, nor are they fitted to use them, not because they are not well built men and of handsome stature, but because they are very marvellously timorous. They have no other arms than weapons made of canes, cut in seeding time, to the ends of which they fix a small sharpened stick. And they do not dare to make use of these, for many times it has happened that I have sent ashore two or three men to some town to have speech, and countless people have come out to them, and as soon as they have seen my men approaching they have fled, even a father not waiting for his son. And this, not because ill has been done to anyone; on the contrary, at every point where I have been and have been able to have speech, I have given to them of all that I had, such as cloth and many other things, without receiving anything for it; but so they are, incurably timid. It is true that, after they have been reassured and have lost their fear, they are so guileless and so generous with all they possess, that no one would believe it who has not seen it. They never refuse anything which they possess, if it be asked of them; on the contrary, they invite anyone to share it, and display as much love as if they would give their hearts, and whether the thing be of value or whether it be of small price, at once with whatever trifle of whatever kind it may be that is given to them, with that they are content. I forbade that they should be given things so worthless as fragments of broken crockery and scraps of broken glass, and ends of straps, although when they were able to get them, they fancied that they possessed the best jewel in the world. So it was found that a sailor for a strap received gold to the weight of two and a half *castellanos,* and others much more for other things which were worth much less. As for new *blancas,* for them they would give everything which they had, although it might be two or three *castellanos'* weight of gold or an *arroba* or two of spun cotton. . . . They took even the pieces of the broken hoops of the wine barrels and, like savages, gave what they had, so that it seemed to me to be wrong and I forbade it. And I gave a thousand handsome good things, which I had brought, in order that they might conceive affection, and more than that, might become Christians and be inclined to the love and service of their highnesses and of the whole Castilian nation, and strive to aid us and to give us of the things which they have in abundance and which are necessary to us. And they do not know any creed and are not idolaters; only they all believe that power and good are in the heavens, and they are very firmly convinced that I, with these ships and men, came from the heavens, and in this belief they everywhere received me, after they had overcome their fear. And this does not come because they are ignorant; on the contrary, they are of a very acute intelligence and are men who navigate all those seas, so that it is amazing how good an account they give of everything, but it is because they have never seen people clothed or ships of such a kind.

And as soon as I arrived in the Indies, in the first island which I found, I took by force some of them, in order that they might learn and give me information of that which there is in those parts, and so it was that they soon understood us, and we them, either by speech or signs, and they have been very serviceable. I still take them with me, and they are always assured that I come from Heaven, for all the intercourse which they have had with me; and they were the first to announce this wherever I went, and the others went running from house to house and to the neighbouring towns, with loud cries of, "Come! Come to see the people from Heaven!" So all, men and women alike, when their minds were set at rest concerning us, came, so that not one, great or small, remained behind, and all brought something to eat and drink, which they gave with extraordinary affection. In all the island, they have very many canoes, like rowing *fustas,* some larger, some smaller, and some are larger than a *fusta* of eighteen benches. They are not so broad, because they are made of a single log of wood, but a *fusta* would not keep up with them in rowing, since their speed is a thing incredible. And in these they navigate among all those islands, which are innumerable, and carry their goods. One of these canoes I have seen with seventy and eighty men in her, and each one with his oar.

In all these islands, I saw no great diversity in the appearance of the people or in their manners and language. On the contrary, they all understand one another, which is a very curious thing, on account of which I hope that their highnesses will determine upon their conversion to our holy faith, towards which they are very inclined.

I have already said how I have gone one hundred and seven leagues in a straight line from west to east along the seashore of the island Juana, and as a result of that voyage, I can say that this island is larger than England and Scotland together, for, beyond these one hundred and seven leagues, there remain to the westward two provinces to which I have not gone. One of these provinces they call "Avan," and there the people are born with tails; and these provinces cannot have a length of less than fifty or sixty leagues, as I could understand from those Indians whom I have and who know all the islands.

The other, Española, has a circumference greater than all Spain, from Colibre, by the sea-coast, to Fuenterabia in Vizcaya, since I voyaged along one side one hundred and eighty-eight great leagues in a straight line from west to east. It is a land to be desired and, seen, it is never to be left. And in it, although of all I have taken possession for their highnesses and all are more richly endowed than I know how, or am able, to say, and I hold them all for their highnesses, so that they may dispose of them as, and as absolutely as, of the kingdoms of Castile, in this Española, in the situation most convenient and in the best position for the mines of gold and for all intercourse as well with the mainland here as with that there, belonging to the Grand Khan, where will be great trade and gain, I have taken possession of a large town, to which I gave the name *Villa de Navidad,* and in it I have made fortifications and a fort, which now will by this time be entirely finished, and I have left in it sufficient men for such a purpose with arms and artillery and provisions for more than a year, and a *fusta,* and one, a master of all seacraft, to build others, and great friendship with the king of that land, so much so, that he was proud to call me, and to treat me as, a brother. And even if he were to change his attitude to one of hostility towards these men, he and his do not know what arms are and they go naked, as I have already said, and are the most timorous people that there are in the world, so that the men whom I have left there alone would suffice to destroy all that land, and the island is without danger for their persons, if they know how to govern themselves.

In all these islands, it seems to me that all men are content with one woman, and to their chief or king they give as many as twenty. It appears to me that the women work more than the men. And I have not been able to learn if they hold private property; what seemed to me to appear was that, in that which one had, all took a share, especially of eatable things.

In these islands I have so far found no human monstrosities, as many expected, but on the contrary the whole population is very well-formed, nor are they negros as in Guinea, but their hair is flowing, and they are not born where there is intense force in the rays of the sun; it is true that the sun has there great power, although it is distant from the equinoctial line twenty-six degrees. In these islands, where there are high mountains, the cold was severe this winter, but they endure it, being used to it and with the help of meats which they eat with many and extremely hot spices. As I have found no monsters, so I have had no report of any, except in an island "Quaris," the second at the coming into the Indies, which is inhabited by a people who are regarded in all the islands as very fierce and who eat human flesh. They have many canoes with which they range through all the islands of India and pillage and take as many as they can. They are no more malformed than the others, except that they have the custom of wearing their hair long like women, and they use bows and arrows of the same cane stems, with a small piece of wood at the end, owing to lack of iron which they do not possess. They are ferocious among these other people who are cowardly to an excessive degree, but I make no more account of them than of the rest. These are those who have intercourse with the women of "Matinino," which is the first island met on the way from Spain to the Indies, in which there is not a man. These women engage in no feminine occupation, but use bows and arrows of cane, like those already mentioned, and they arm and protect themselves with plates of copper, of which they have much.

In another island, which they assure me is larger than Española, the people have no hair. In it, there is gold incalculable, and from it and from the other islands, I bring with me Indians as evidence.

In conclusion, to speak only of that which has been accomplished on this voyage, which was so hasty, their highnesses can see that I will give them as much gold as they may need, if their highnesses will render me very slight assistance; moreover, spice and cotton, as much as their highnesses shall command; and mastic, as much as they shall order to be shipped and which, up to now, has been found only in Greece, in the island of Chios, and the Seignory sells it for what it pleases; and aloe wood, as much as they shall order to be shipped, and slaves, as many as they shall order to be shipped and who will be from the idolaters. And I believe that I have found rhubarb and cinnamon, and I shall find a thousand other things of value, which the people whom I have left there will have discovered, for I have not delayed at any point, so far as the wind allowed me to sail, except in the town of Navidad, in order to leave it secured and well established, and in truth, I should have done much more, if the ships had served me, as reason demanded.

This is enough . . . and the eternal God, our Lord, Who gives to all those who walk in His way triumph over things which appear to be impossible, and this was notably one; for, although men have talked or have written of these lands, all was conjectural, without suggestion of ocular evidence, but amounted only to this, that those who heard for the most part listened and judged it to be rather a fable than as having any vestige of truth. So that, since Our Redeemer has given this victory to our most illustrious king and queen, and to their renowned kingdoms, in so great a matter, for this all Christendom ought to feel delight and make great feasts and give solemn thanks to the Holy Trinity with many solemn prayers for the great exaltation which they shall have, in the turning of so many peoples to our holy faith, and afterwards for temporal benefits, for not only Spain but all Christians will have hence refreshment and gain.

This, in accordance with that which has been accomplished, thus briefly.

Done in the caravel,[1] off the Canary Islands, on the fifteenth of February, in the year one thousand four hundred and ninety-three.

At your orders.   El Almirante.

---

[1] Sailing ship, in this case the *Santa María*. [Ed.]

After having written this, and being in the sea of Castile, there came on me so great a south-south-west wind, that I was obliged to lighten ship. But I ran here to-day into this port of Lisbon, which was the greatest marvel in the world, whence I decided to write to their highnesses. In all the Indies, I have always found weather like May; where I went in thirty-three days and I had returned in twenty-eight, save for these storms which have detained me for fourteen days, beating about in this sea. Here all the sailors say that never has there been so bad a winter nor so many ships lost.

Done on the fourth day of March.

4

KIRKPATRICK SALE

secondary

From *The Conquest of Paradise*

In this selection from his popular study of Columbus, Sale is concerned with Columbus's attitude toward nature in the New World. Do you think Sale's comments are accurate? Are they insightful? Do they help us understand Columbus?

Sale regards Columbus as a symbol of European expansion. Let us for the moment grant him that. If Columbus is distinctly European, what is Sale saying about European expansion? How and what does Sale add to your understanding of the similarities and differences between Chinese and European expansion?

Was Columbus much different from Zheng He? Or were the areas and peoples they visited causes for different responses?

Thinking Historically

Clearly, this selection is a secondary source; Sale is a modern writer, not a fifteenth-century contemporary of Columbus. Still, you will not have to read very far into the selection to realize that Sale has a distinct point of view. Secondary sources, like primary ones, should be analyzed for bias and perspective and should identify the author's interpretation.

Kirkpatrick Sale, *The Conquest of Paradise* (New York: Penguin, 1991), 92–104.

Sale is an environmentalist and a cultural critic. Do his beliefs and values hinder his understanding of Columbus, or do they inform and illuminate aspects of Columbus that might otherwise be missed? Does Sale help you recognize things you would not have seen on your own, or does he persuade you to see things that might not truly be there?

Notice how Sale uses primary sources in his text. He quotes from Columbus's journal and his letter to Santangel.[1] Do these quotes help you understand Columbus, or do they simply support Sale's argument? What do you think about Sale's use of the Spanish "Colón" for "Columbus"? Does Sale "take possession" of Columbus by, in effect, "renaming" him for modern readers? Is the effect humanizing or debunking?

Notice how Sale sometimes calls attention to what the primary source did *not* say rather than what it did say. Is this a legitimate way to understand someone, or is Sale projecting a twentieth-century perspective on Columbus to make a point?

Toward the end of the selection, Sale extends his criticism beyond Columbus to include others. Who are the others? What is the effect of this larger criticism?

Admiral Colón spent a total of ninety-six days exploring the lands he encountered on the far side of the Ocean Sea — four rather small coralline islands in the Bahamian chain and two substantial coastlines of what he finally acknowledged were larger islands — every one of which he "took possession of" in the name of his Sovereigns.

The first he named San Salvador, no doubt as much in thanksgiving for its welcome presence after more than a month at sea as for the Son of God whom it honored; the second he called Santa María de la Concepcíon, after the Virgin whose name his flagship bore; and the third and fourth he called Fernandina and Isabela, for his patrons, honoring Aragon before Castile for reasons never explained (possibly protocol, possibly in recognition of the chief sources of backing for the voyage). The first of the two large and very fertile islands he called Juana, which Fernando says was done in honor of Prince Juan, heir to the Castilian throne, but just as plausibly might have been done in recognition of Princess Juana, the unstable child who eventually carried on the line; the second he named la Ysla Española, the "Spanish Island," because it resembled (though he felt it surpassed in beauty) the lands of Castile.

It was not that the islands were in need of names, mind you, nor indeed that Colón was ignorant of the names that native peoples had al-

---

[1] Letter to King Ferdinand and Queen Isabella (See selection 3.)

ready given them, for he frequently used those original names before endowing them with his own. Rather, the process of bestowing new names went along with "taking possession of" those parts of the world he deemed suitable for Spanish ownership, showing the royal banners, erecting various crosses, and pronouncing certain oaths and pledges. If this was presumption, it had an honored heritage: It was Adam who was charged by his Creator with the task of naming "every living creature," including the product of his own rib, in the course of establishing "dominion over" them.

Colón went on to assign no fewer than sixty-two other names on the geography of the islands — capes, points, mountains, ports — with a blithe assurance suggesting that in his (and Europe's) perception the act of name-giving was in some sense a talisman of conquest, a rite that changed raw neutral stretches of far-off earth into extensions of Europe. The process began slowly, even haltingly — he forgot to record, for example, until four days afterward that he named the landfall island San Salvador — but by the time he came to Española at the end he went on a naming spree, using more than two-thirds of all the titles he concocted on that one coastline. On certain days it became almost a frenzy: on December 6 he named six places, on the nineteenth six more, and on January 11 no fewer than ten — eight capes, a point, and a mountain. It is almost as if, as he sailed along the last of the islands, he was determined to leave his mark on it the only way he knew how, and thus to establish his authority — and by extension Spain's — even, as with baptism, to make it thus sanctified, and real, and official. . . .

This business of naming and "possessing" foreign islands was by no means casual. The Admiral took it very seriously, pointing out that "it was my wish to bypass no island without taking possession" (October 15) and that "in all regions [I] always left a cross standing" (November 16) as a mark of Christian dominance. There even seem to have been certain prescriptions for it (the instructions from the Sovereigns speak of "the administering of the oath and the performing of the rites prescribed in such cases"), and Rodrigo de Escobedo was sent along as secretary of the fleet explicitly to witness and record these events in detail.

But consider the implications of this act and the questions it raises again about what was in the Sovereigns' minds, what in Colón's. Why would the Admiral assume that these territories were in some way *un*possessed — even by those clearly inhabiting them — and thus available for Spain to claim? Why would he not think twice about the possibility that some considerable potentate — the Grand Khan of China, for example, whom he later acknowledged (November 6) "must be" the ruler of Española — might descend upon him at any moment with a greater military force than his three vessels commanded and punish him for his territorial presumption? Why would he make the ceremony of possession his very first act on shore, even before meeting the inhabitants

or exploring the environs, or finding out if anybody there objected to
being thus possessed — particularly if they actually owned the great
treasures he hoped would be there? No European would have imagined
that anyone — three small boatloads of Indians, say — could come up
to a European shore or island and "take possession" of it, nor would a
European imagine marching up to some part of North Africa or the
Middle East and claiming sovereignty there with impunity. Why were
these lands thought to be different?

Could there be any reason for the Admiral to assume he had
reached "unclaimed" shores, new lands that lay far from the domains
of any of the potentates of the East? Can that really have been in his
mind — or can it all be explained as simple Eurocentrism, or Eurosupe-
riority, mixed with cupidity and naiveté? . . .

Once safely "possessed,"[2] San Salvador was open for inspection.
Now the Admiral turned his attention for the first time to the "naked
people" staring at him on the beach — he did not automatically give
them a name, interestingly enough, and it would be another six days
before he decided what he might call them — and tried to win their
favor with his trinkets.

> They all go around as naked as their mothers bore them; and also the
> women, although I didn't see more than one really young girl. All that
> I saw were young people *[mancebos]*, none of them more than 30
> years old. They are very well built, with very handsome bodies and
> very good faces; their hair [is] coarse, almost like the silk of a horse's
> tail, and short. They wear their hair over their eyebrows, except for a
> little in the back that they wear long and never cut. Some of them paint
> themselves black (and they are the color of the Canary Islanders, nei-
> ther black nor white), and some paint themselves white, and some red,
> and some with what they find. And some paint their faces, and some of
> them the whole body, and some the eyes only, and some of them only
> the nose.

It may fairly be called the birth of American anthropology.

A crude anthropology, of course, as superficial as Colón's descriptions always were when his interest was limited, but simple and
straightforward enough, with none of the fable and fantasy that characterized many earlier (and even some later) accounts of new-found
peoples. There was no pretense to objectivity, or any sense that these
people might be representatives of a culture equal to, or in any way a
model for, Europe's. Colón immediately presumed the inferiority of the
natives, not merely because (a sure enough sign) they were naked, but

---

[2] Given Spanish names. [Ed.]

because (his society could have no surer measure) they seemed so technologically backward. "It appeared to me that these people were very poor in everything," he wrote on that first day, and, worse still, "they have no iron." And they went on to prove their inferiority to the Admiral by being ignorant of even such a basic artifact of European life as a sword: "They bear no arms, nor are they acquainted with them," he wrote, "for I showed them swords and they grasped them by the blade and cut themselves through ignorance." Thus did European arms spill the first drops of native blood on the sands of the New World, accompanied not with a gasp of compassion but with a smirk of superiority.

Then, just six sentences further on, Colón clarified what this inferiority meant in his eyes:

> They ought to be good servants and of good intelligence *[ingenio]*. . . . I believe that they would easily be made Christians, because it seemed to me that they had no religion. Our Lord pleasing, I will carry off six of them at my departure to Your Highnesses, in order that they may learn to speak.

No clothes, no arms, no possessions, no iron, and now no religion — not even speech: hence they were fit to be servants, and captives. It may fairly be called the birth of American slavery.

Whether or not the idea of slavery was in Colón's mind all along is uncertain, although he did suggest he had had experience as a slave trader in Africa (November 12) and he certainly knew of Portuguese plantation slavery in the Madeiras and Spanish slavery of Guanches in the Canaries. But it seems to have taken shape early and grown ever firmer as the weeks went on and as he captured more and more of the helpless natives. At one point he even sent his crew ashore to kidnap "seven head of women, young ones and adults, and three small children"; the expression of such callousness led the Spanish historian Salvador de Madariaga to remark, "It would be difficult to find a starker utterance of utilitarian subjection of man by man than this passage [whose] form is no less devoid of human feeling than its substance."

To be sure, Colón knew nothing about these people he encountered and considered enslaving, and he was hardly trained to find out very much, even if he was moved to care. But they were in fact members of an extensive, populous, and successful people whom Europe, using its own peculiar taxonomy, subsequently called "Taino" (or "Taíno"), their own word for "good" or "noble," and their response when asked who they were. They were related distantly by both language and culture to the Arawak people of the South American mainland, but it is misleading (and needlessly imprecise) to call them Arawaks, as historians are wont to do, when the term "Taino" better establishes their ethnic and historical distinctiveness. They had migrated to the islands from the mainland at about the time of the birth of Christ, occupying the three large islands we now call the Greater Antilles and arriving at Guanahani (Colón's San Salvador) and the end of the Bahamian chain probably sometime around A.D. 900. There they displaced an earlier people, the Guanahacabibes (sometimes called Guanahatabeys), who by the time of the European discovery occupied only the western third of Cuba and possibly remote corners of Española; and there, probably in the early fifteenth century, they eventually confronted another people moving up the islands from the mainland, the Caribs, whose culture eventually occupied a dozen small islands of what are called the Lesser Antilles.

The Tainos were not nearly so backward as Colón assumed from their lack of dress. (It might be said that it was the Europeans, who generally kept clothed head to foot during the day despite temperatures regularly in the eighties, who were the more unsophisticated in garmenture — especially since the Tainos, as Colón later noted, also used their body paint to prevent sunburn.) Indeed, they had achieved a means of living in a balanced and fruitful harmony with their natural surroundings that any society might well have envied. They had, to begin with, a not unsophisticated technology that made exact use of their available resources, two parts of which were so impressive that they were picked up and adopted by the European invaders: *canoa* (canoes) that were carved and fire-burned from large silk-cotton trees, "all in one piece, and wonderfully made" (October 13), some of which were capable of carrying up to 150 passengers; and *hamaca* (hammocks) that were "like nets of cotton" (October 17) and may have been a staple item of trade with Indian tribes as far away as the Florida mainland. Their houses were not only spacious and clean — as the Europeans noted with surprise and appreciation, used as they were to the generally crowded and slovenly hovels and huts of south European peasantry — but more apropos, remarkably resistant to hurricanes; the circular walls were made of strong cane poles set deep and close together ("as close as the fingers of a hand," Colón noted), the conical roofs of branches and vines tightly interwoven on a frame of smaller poles and covered with heavy palm leaves. Their artifacts and jewelry, with the exception of a few gold trinkets and ornaments, were based largely on renewable materials, including bracelets and necklaces of coral, shells, bone, and stone, embroidered cotton belts, woven baskets, carved statues and chairs, wooden and shell utensils, and pottery of variously intricate decoration depending on period and place.

Perhaps the most sophisticated, and most carefully integrated, part of their technology was their agricultural system, extraordinarily productive and perfectly adapted to the conditions of the island environment. It was based primarily on fields of knee-high mounds, called *conucos,* planted with *yuca* (sometimes called manioc), *batata* (sweet potato), and various squashes and beans grown all together in multi-crop harmony: The root crops were excellent in resisting erosion and producing minerals and potash, the leaf crops effective in providing shade and moisture, and the mound configurations largely resistant to erosion and flooding and adaptable to almost all topographic conditions including steep hillsides. Not only was the *conuco* system environmentally appropriate — "conuco agriculture seems to have provided an exceptionally ecologically well-balanced and protective form of land use," according to David Watts's recent and authoritative *West Indies* — but it was also highly productive, surpassing in yields anything known in Europe at the time, with labor that amounted to hardly more than two or three hours a week, and in continuous yearlong harvest. The pioneering American geographical scholar Carl Sauer calls Taino agriculture "productive as few parts of the world," giving the "highest returns of food in continuous supply by the simplest methods and modest labor," and adds, with a touch of regret, "The white man never fully appreciated the excellent combination of plants that were grown in conucos."

In their arts of government the Tainos seem to have achieved a parallel sort of harmony. Most villages were small (ten to fifteen families) and autonomous, although many apparently recognized loose allegiances with neighboring villages, and they were governed by a hereditary official called a *kaseke* (*cacique,* in the Spanish form), something of a cross between an arbiter and a prolocutor, supported by advisers and elders. So little a part did violence play in their system that they seem, remarkably, to have been a society without war (at least we know of no war music or signals or artifacts, and no evidence of intertribal combats) and even without overt conflict (Las Casas reports that no Spaniard ever saw two Tainos fighting). And here we come to what was obviously the Tainos' outstanding cultural achievement, a proficiency in the social arts that led those who first met them to comment unfailingly on their friendliness, their warmth, their openness, and above all — so striking to those of an acquisitive culture — their generosity.

"They are the best people in the world and above all the gentlest," Colón recorded in his *Journal* (December 16), and from first to last he was astonished at their kindness:

> They became so much our friends that it was a marvel. . . . They traded and gave everything they had, with good will [October 12].
>
> I sent the ship's boat ashore for water, and they very willingly showed my people where the water was, and they themselves carried the full barrels to the boat, and took great delight in pleasing us [October 16].

They are very gentle and without knowledge of what is evil; nor do they murder or steal [November 12].

Your Highnesses may believe that in all the world there can be no better or gentler people . . . for neither better people nor land can there be. . . . All the people show the most singular loving behavior and they speak pleasantly [December 24].

I assure Your Highnesses that I believe that in all the world there is no better people nor better country. They love their neighbors as themselves, and they have the sweetest talk in the world, and are gentle and always laughing [December 25].

Even if one allows for some exaggeration — Colón was clearly trying to convince Ferdinand and Isabella that his Indians could be easily conquered and converted, should that be the Sovereigns' wish — it is obvious that the Tainos exhibited a manner of social discourse that quite impressed the rough Europeans. But that was not high among the traits of "civilized" nations, as Colón and Europe understood it, and it counted for little in the Admiral's assessment of these people. However struck he was with such behavior, he would not have thought that it was the mark of a benign and harmonious society, or that from it another culture might learn. For him it was something like the wondrous behavior of children, the naive guilelessness of prelapsarian creatures who knew no better how to bargain and chaffer and cheat than they did to dress themselves: "For a lacepoint they gave good pieces of gold the size of two fingers" (January 6), and "They even took pieces of the broken hoops of the wine casks and, like beasts [*como besti*], gave what they had" (Santangel Letter). Like beasts; such innocence was not human.

It is to be regretted that the Admiral, unable to see past their nakedness, as it were, knew not the real virtues of the people he confronted. For the Tainos' lives were in many ways as idyllic as their surroundings, into which they fit with such skill and comfort. They were well fed and well housed, without poverty or serious disease. They enjoyed considerable leisure, given over to dancing, singing, ballgames, and sex, and expressed themselves artistically in basketry, woodworking, pottery, and jewelry. They lived in general harmony and peace, without greed or covetousness or theft. . . .

It is perhaps only natural that Colón should devote his initial attention to the handsome, naked, naive islanders, but it does seem peculiar that he pays almost no attention, especially in the early days, to the spectacular scenery around them. Here he was, in the middle of an old-growth tropical forest the likes of which he could not have imagined before, its trees reaching sixty or seventy feet into the sky, more varieties than he knew how to count much less name, exhibiting a lushness that stood in sharp contrast to the sparse and denuded lands he had known in the Mediterranean, hearing a melodious multiplicity of bird songs and parrot calls — why was it not an occasion of wonder, excitement, and the sheer joy at nature in its full, arrogant abundance? But there is not a word of that: He actually said nothing about the physical surroundings on the first day, aside from a single phrase about "very green trees" and "many streams," and on the second managed only that short sentence about a big island with a big lake and green trees. Indeed, for the whole two weeks of the first leg of his voyage through the Bahamas to Cuba, he devoted only a third of the lines of description to the phenomena around him. And there are some natural sights he seems not to have noticed at all: He did not mention (except in terms of navigation) the nighttime heavens, the sharp, glorious configurations of stars that he must have seen virtually every night of his journey, many for the first time.

Eventually Colón succumbed to the islands' natural charms as he sailed on — how could he not? — and began to wax warmly about how "these islands are very green and fertile and the air very sweet" (October 15), with "trees which were more beautiful to see than any other thing that has ever been seen" (October 17), and "so good and sweet a smell of flowers or trees from the land" (October 19). But his descriptions are curiously vapid and vague, the language opaque and lifeless:

> The other island, which is very big [October 15] . . . this island is very large [October 16] . . . these islands are very green and fertile [October 15] . . . this land is the best and most fertile [October 17] . . . in it many plants and trees . . . if the others are very beautiful, this is more so [October 19] . . . here are some great lagoons . . . big and little birds of all sorts . . . if the others already seen are very beautiful and green and fertile, this one is much more so [October 21] . . . full of very good harbors and deep rivers [October 28].

You begin to see the Admiral's problem: He cares little about the features of nature, at least the ones he doesn't use for sailing, and even when he admires them he has little experience in assessing them and less acquaintance with a vocabulary to describe them. To convey the lush density and stately grandeur of those tropical forests, for example, he had little more than the modifiers "green" and "very": "very green trees" (October 12), "trees very green" (October 13), "trees . . . so green and with leaves like those of Castile" (October 14), "very green and very big trees" (October 19), "large groves are very green" (October 21), "trees . . . beautiful and green" (October 28). And when he began to be aware of the diversity among those trees, he was still unable to make meaningful distinctions: "All the trees are as different from ours as day from night" (October 17), "trees of a thousand kinds" (October 21), "a thousand sorts of trees" (October 23), "trees . . . different from ours"

(October 28), "trees of a thousand sorts" (November 14), "trees of a thousand kinds" (December 6).

Such was his ignorance — a failing he repeatedly bemoaned ("I don't recognize them, which gives me great grief," October 19) — that when he did stop to examine a species he often had no idea what he was looking at. "I saw many trees very different from ours," he wrote on October 16, "and many of them have branches of many kinds, and all on one trunk, and one twig is of one kind and another of another, and so different that it is the greatest wonder in the world how much diversity there is of one kind from the other. That is to say, one branch has leaves like a cane, and another like mastic, and thus on one tree five or six kinds, and all so different." There is no such tree in existence, much less "many of them," and never was: Why would anyone imagine, or so contrive, such a thing to be?

Colón's attempts to identify species were likewise frequently wrongheaded, usually imputing to them commercial worth that they did not have, as with the worthless "aloes" he loaded such quantities of. The "amaranth" he identified on October 28 and the "oaks" and "arbutus" of November 25 are species that do not grow in the Caribbean; the "mastic" he found on November 5 and loaded on board to sell in Spain was gumbo-limbo, commercially worthless. (On the other hand, one of the species of flora he deemed of no marketable interest — "weeds [tizon] in their hands to drink in the fragrant smoke" [November 6] — was tobacco.) Similarly, the "whales" he spotted on October 16 must have been simply large fish, the "geese" he saw on November 6 and again on December 22 were ducks, the "nightingales" that kept delighting him (November 6; December 7, 13) do not exist in the Americas, and the skulls of "cows" he identified on October 29 were probably not those of land animals but of manatees.

This all seems a little sad, revealing a man rather lost in a world that he cannot come to know, a man with a "geographic and naturalistic knowledge that doesn't turn out to be very deep or nearly complete," and "a limited imagination and a capacity for comparisons conditioned by a not very broad geographic culture," in the words of Gaetano Ferro, a Columbus scholar and professor of geography at the University of Genoa. One could not of course have expected that an adventurer and sailor of this era would also be a naturalist, or necessarily even have some genuine interest in or curiosity about the natural world, but it is a disappointment nonetheless that the Discoverer of the New World turns out to be quite so simple, quite so inexperienced, in the ways of discovering his environment.

Colón's limitations, I hasten to say, were not his alone; they were of his culture, and they would be found in the descriptions of many others — Vespucci, Cortés, Hawkins, Juet, Cartier, Champlain, Ralegh — in the century of discovery to follow. They are the source of what the distinguished English historian J. H. Elliott has called "the problem of description" faced by Europeans confronting the uniqueness of the New World: "So often the physical appearance of the New World is either totally ignored or else described in the flattest and most conventional phraseology. This off-hand treatment of nature contrasts strikingly with the many precise and acute descriptions of the native inhabitants. It is as if the American landscape is seen as no more than a backcloth against which the strange and perennially fascinating peoples of the New World are dutifully grouped." The reason, Elliott thinks, and this is telling, may be "a lack of interest among sixteenth-century Europeans, and especially those of the Mediterranean world, in landscape and in nature." This lack of interest was reflected in the lack of vocabulary, the lack of that facility common to nature-based peoples whose cultures are steeped in natural imagery. Oviedo, for example, setting out to write descriptions for his *Historia general* in the next century, continually threw his hands up in the air: "Of all the things I have seen," he said at one point, "this is the one which has most left me without hope of being able to describe it in words"; or at another, "It needs to be painted by the hand of a Berruguete or some other excellent painter like him, or by Leonardo da Vinci or Andrea Mantegna, famous painters whom I knew in Italy." Like Colón, visitor after visitor to the New World seemed mind-boggled and tongue-tied trying to convey the wonders before them, and about the only color they seem to have eyes for is green — and not very many shades of that, either. . . .

REFLECTIONS

In this chapter, we compared Chinese and European expansion as well as Zheng He and Columbus. We also considered the motivations of the Chinese and Spanish monarchies. Such comparisons help us to think critically and are ways of pinpointing the differences between Chinese and European civilization.

But how did Europe replace China as "ruler of the seas"? There are a number of ways to answer that question. Compare Kristof's "two and a half reasons" with those suggested by Sales. What evidence do you find for any of these interpretations in the primary sources? Could it be that Chinese expansion was more expensive than European expansion because Chinese trading partners in Asia and East Africa were strong enough to strike hard bargains? Might their trading partners be a key to their respective levels of success? For example, perhaps the merchants of India were too wealthy and too strong to pay tribute to the Chinese? On the other hand, the Tainos could easily be overwhelmed by Columbus. We might ask why the Chinese treasure ships were essentially merchant ships and the Spanish caravels were war ships. We might compare the Chinese impact on people in India, the Middle East, and Africa, all of whom shared the same immunities, with the Spanish impact on Native Americans, who did not.

In the New World, Europeans were able to conquer and take virtually all they wanted. At least one modern scholar, James M. Blaut in *The Colonizer's Model of the World,* argues that the European theft of American treasure fueled European expansion and growth for centuries, though causing high inflation in Europe in the sixteenth century. The rise of European power has also been attributed to improved European technology in sailing vessels and the development of powerful cannons. A classic account of this is Carlo Cipolla's *Guns, Sails, and Empires.*

Still, we might ask how Europeans were able to gain a technological advantage that had been enjoyed previously by the Chinese. Similarly, how were Europeans able to create a profitable maritime empire in the Indian Ocean and South China Sea so soon after China's withdrawal?

These questions raise yet a larger question: Were there more pervasive differences between Chinese and European civilization that contributed to Europe's military and maritime advantage after 1450? Since you have begun a comparison of these two civilizations, you might also begin to answer that question.

2

Europeans, Americans, and Africans in the Atlantic World

HISTORICAL CONTEXT
Africa and the Americas, 1500–1750

European expansion in the Atlantic that began with Portuguese voyages along the African coast in the 1440s and Columbus's discovery of the Americas in 1492 had by 1750 created a new Atlantic zone of human contact and communication that embraced four continents and one ocean. Until this point, nothing — neither the Chinese contacts with Africa in the early fifteenth century, nor the expansion of Islam throughout Eurasia in the almost thousand years since the Prophet Muhammad's death in 632 — had so thoroughly and so permanently changed the human and ecological balance of the world.

Sub-Saharan Africa had already been integrated into the world of Eurasia by 1450. African populations became more mixed, as peoples from the Niger River area migrated east and south throughout the continent during the fifteen hundred years before the arrival of the Portuguese. Muslims from North Africa and the Middle East had aided or established Muslim states and trading ports south of the Sahara in East and West Africa after 1000. Cultural and technical innovations of the Middle East, like the literacy that came with Islam, penetrated slowly, and the spread of the many plants and animals of the northern hemisphere was slowed by the Sahara and equator. However, microbes traveled swiftly and easily from Eurasia to Africa, creating a single set of diseases and immunities for the peoples of the Afro-Eurasian Old World.

The peoples of the Americas, having been isolated ecologically for more than a thousand years, were not so fortunate. The arrival of Europeans and Africans in the Americas after 1492 had devastating consequences for Native American populations. Old World diseases like smallpox were responsible for millions of Native American deaths — a tragedy far worse in scope than the casualties caused by wars. To work the mines and plantations of the New World, Europeans used Indian labor, but increasingly, especially for lowland plantations, they used African slaves. By 1750, the combination of Indian "die off" and African and European migration resulted in vastly different populations in the Americas. On some Caribbean islands and in plantation areas like north-eastern Brazil, Indian populations were entirely replaced by Africans. At the same time, European animals (for example, goats, cattle, horses) multiplied in the absence of natural predators, in some cases entirely replacing Native Americans who were wiped out by European disease.

The new Atlantic ecological system was not a uniform zone, however. Coastal regions in Western Europe and towns on the eastern seaboard of the Americas prospered, while American interiors and African populations in Africa stagnated or declined. The Atlantic Ocean became a vast lake that united port cities and plantations with sailing ships that carried African slaves to the Caribbean, Caribbean sugar and rum to North American and European industrial ports, and guns, pots, and liquor to the African "Slave Coast."

Thus, the Atlantic world was integrated with the Old World. Trade routes that began in Boston or Bahia, Brazil, stretched across Eurasia and around southern Africa into the Indian Ocean and the China Sea. Crops that had previously been known only to Native Americans — corn, potatoes, and tomatoes — fueled population explosions from Ireland to China and graced the tables of peasants and princes in between. What began as an effort by European merchants to import Asian spices directly became after 1650 (as European tastes for pepper and Asian spices moderated) a new global pantry of possibilities.

In this chapter, we will read selections that describe some of the first contacts that led to this new global balance. We will read of Europeans in Mexico, North America, and West Africa. We will also explore some of the African and American responses to this European expansion. When reading these accounts, notice how these individuals at the frontier of a new age understand and treat each other. Consider how these initial exchanges, so apparently fortuitous and transitory at the time, changed the face of the world.

THINKING HISTORICALLY
Comparing Primary Sources

By comparing and contrasting one thing with another, we learn more about each, and by examining related works in their proper context, we learn more about the whole of which they are part. In the first chapter we compared China and Europe or Chinese and European (mainly

Spanish) expansion in the fifteenth century. In this chapter we look at
the Atlantic world, specifically at Europeans in Africa and the Americas. We begin with two views of the Spanish conquest of Mexico —
separate accounts by the Spanish conquistadors and by the Mexicans.
The third selection recounts the Dutch conquest of the Algonquin nation in North America (in what is today New York City) and allows us
to compare the methods of the Dutch with those of the Spanish.

The final three readings examine encounters between Europeans and
Africans and the development of the Atlantic slave trade. Do Europeans
treat Native Americans differently than they do Africans? If so, why?

In selection 8 an African ruler responds to the European slave
trade. This account contrasts with the encounter of Europeans with the
Mexican ruler, Montezuma, in selections 5 and 6. The chapter concludes with an account of a European slave trader and the memoir of
an African who was enslaved. Do you notice any discrepancies in these
accounts? Which is more believable and why?

5

BERNAL DÍAZ

From *The Conquest of New Spain*

Bernal Díaz del Castillo was born in Spain in 1492, the year Columbus sailed to America. After participating in two explorations of the
Mexican coast, Díaz joined the expedition of Hernán Cortés to Mexico City in 1519. He wrote this history of the conquest much later,
when he was in his seventies; he died circa 1580, a municipal official
with a small estate in Guatemala.

The conquest of Mexico did not automatically follow from the first
Spanish settlements in Santo Domingo, Hispaniola, and then Cuba in
the West Indies. The Spanish crown had given permission for trade
and exploration, not colonization. But the fortune-seeking peasant-
soldiers whose fathers had fought to rid Spain of Muslims and Jews
were eager to conquer their own lands and develop populations of dependent Indians.

Bernal Díaz, *The Conquest of New Spain*, trans. J. M. Cohen (Baltimore: Penguin Books,
1963), 217–19, 221–25, 228–38, 241–43.

Cortés, of minor noble descent but a failed student at the University of Salamanca, sailed to the Indies at the age of nineteen, where he enjoyed a sizeable estate on the island of Hispaniola. When he heard stories of Montezuma's gold from an Indian woman who was given to him in tribute, he determined to find the fabled capital of the Aztec empire, Tenochtitlán (modern Mexico City). He gathered more than five hundred amateur soldiers, eleven ships, sixteen horses, and several pieces of artillery, then sailed across the Caribbean and Gulf of Mexico to a settlement he christened Veracruz, and there began the long march from the coast up to the high central plateau of Mexico.

The Aztecs were new to central Mexico, arriving from the North American desert only about two hundred years before the Spanish, around 1325. They settled on an island in the middle of the large lake on the central plain, shunned by the peoples of other cities who thought themselves to be more sophisticated and cultured. In less than two hundred years, this band of uncouth newcomers established dominion over almost all other city-states of Mexico, by 1500 ruling an empire that stretched as far south as Guatemala and as far east as the Mayan lands of the Yucatan Peninsula.

Aztec power relied on a combination of old and new religious ideas and a military system that conquered through terror. The older religious traditions that the Aztecs adopted were those of the classical Toltec culture at the center of which stood the god Quetzalcoatl — the feathered serpent, god of creation and brotherhood. The nurturing forces of Quetzalcoatl continued in Aztec society in a system of universal and obligatory education and in festivals dedicated to life, creativity, and procreation. But the Aztecs also celebrated a god they had brought with them from the north, Huitzilopochtli — a warrior god primed for death and sacrifice. Huitzilopochtli (rendered as Huichilobos in this selection) was given dominant status in the Aztec pantheon by Tlacaelel, an adviser behind the Aztec throne of Montezuma's predecessor, Itzcoatl (r. 1428–1440). Tlacaelel envisioned Huitzilopochtli as a force for building a powerful Aztec empire. Drawing on the god's need for human sacrifice — a need not unknown among religions of central Mexico (or Christians) — Tlacaelel built altars to Huitzilopochtli at Tenochtitlán, Cholula, and other sites. According to the tenets of the religion, the war god required a never-ending supply of human hearts, a need that prompted armies to ever-more remote sections of Central America in search of sacrificial victims and creating an endless supply of enemies of the Aztecs. Among these, the Tlaxcalans, whom the Aztecs left independent so they could be conquered at will for war captives, proved to be an eager ally of Cortés and the Spanish. As the Aztec star waned, other Mexican peoples eagerly joined the Spanish-Tlaxcalan alliance.

With the help of his Indian captive and companion Doña Marina —
called La Malinche by some of the Indians (thus, Montezuma sometimes calls Cortés "Lord Malinche" in the selection) — Cortés was
able to communicate with the Tlaxcalans and other Indians who were
tired of Aztec domination. On his march toward Tenochtitlán, Cortés
stopped to join forces with the Tlaxcalans, perhaps cementing the relationship and demonstrating his resolve through a brutal massacre of
the people of Cholula, an Aztec ally and arch enemy of the Tlaxcalans.
By the time Cortés arrived at Tenochtitlán, Montezuma knew of the
defeat of his allies at Cholula.

This selection from Bernal Díaz begins with the Spanish entry into
Tenochtitlán. What impresses Díaz, and presumably other Spanish
conquistadors, about the Mexican capital city? What parts of the city
attract his attention the most? What conclusions does he draw about
Mexican (or Aztec) civilization? Does he think Spanish civilization is
equal, inferior, or superior to that of Mexico?

Thinking Historically

Díaz gives us a dramatic account of the meeting of Cortés and Montezuma. What do you think each is thinking and feeling? Do you see
any signs of tension in their elaborate greetings? Why are both behav-
ing so politely? What do they want from each other?

Notice how the initial hospitality turns tense. What causes this? Is
either side more to blame for what happens next? Was conflict inevitable? Could the encounter have ended in some sort of peaceful resolution?

Remember, we are going to compare Díaz's view with a Mexican
view of these events. From your reading of Díaz, does he seem able to
understand the Mexican point of view? Would you call him a sympathetic observer?

... When Cortes saw, heard, and was told that the great Montezuma
was approaching, he dismounted from his horse, and when he came
near to Montezuma each bowed deeply to the other. Montezuma welcomed our Captain, and Cortes, speaking through Doña Marina, answered by wishing him very good health. Cortes, I think, offered Montezuma his right hand, but Montezuma refused it and extended his
own. Then Cortes brought out a necklace which he had been holding.
It was made of those elaborately worked and coloured glass beads
called *margaritas,* ... and was strung on a gold cord and dipped in
musk to give it a good odour. This he hung round the great Montezuma's neck, and as he did so attempted to embrace him. But the

great princes who stood round Montezuma grasped Cortes' arm to prevent him, for they considered this an indignity.

Then Cortes told Montezuma that it rejoiced his heart to have seen such a great prince, and that he took his coming in person to receive him and the repeated favours he had done him as a high honour. After this Montezuma made him another complimentary speech, and ordered two of his nephews who were supporting him, the lords of Texcoco and Coyoacan, to go with us and show us our quarters. Montezuma returned to the city with the other two kinsmen of his escort, the lords of Cuitlahuac and Tacuba; and all those grand companies of *Caciques*[1] and dignitaries who had come with him returned also in his train. And as they accompanied their lord we observed them marching with their eyes downcast so that they should not see him, and keeping close to the wall as they followed him with great reverence. Thus space was made for us to enter the streets of Mexico without being pressed by the crowd.

Who could now count the multitude of men, women, and boys in the streets, on the roof-tops and in canoes on the waterways, who had come out to see us? It was a wonderful sight and, as I write, it all comes before my eyes as if it had happened only yesterday.

They led us to our quarters, which were in some large houses capable of accommodating us all and had formerly belonged to the great Montezuma's father, who was called Axayacatl. Here Montezuma now kept the great shrines of his gods, and a secret chamber containing gold bars and jewels. This was the treasure he had inherited from his father, which he never touched. Perhaps their reason for lodging us here was that, since they called us *Teules*[2] and considered us as such, they wished to have us near their idols. In any case they took us to this place, where there were many great halls, and a dais hung with the cloth of their country for our Captain, and matting beds with canopies over them for each of us.

On our arrival we entered the large court, where the great Montezuma was awaiting our Captain. Taking him by the hand, the prince led him to his apartment in the hall where he was to lodge, which was very richly furnished in their manner. Montezuma had ready for him a very rich necklace, made of golden crabs, a marvellous piece of work, which he hung round Cortes' neck. His captains were greatly astonished at this sign of honour.

After this ceremony, for which Cortes thanked him through our interpreters, Montezuma said: "Malinche, you and your brothers are in your own house. Rest awhile." He then returned to his palace, which was not far off.

[1] Chiefs. [Ed.]
[2] Gods. [Ed.]

We divided our lodgings by companies, and placed our artillery in a convenient spot. Then the order we were to keep was clearly explained to us, and we were warned to be very much on the alert, both the horsemen and the rest of us soldiers. We then ate a sumptuous dinner which they had prepared for us in their native style.

So, with luck on our side, we boldly entered the city of Tenochtitlán or Mexico on 8 November in the year of our Lord 1519.

The Stay in Mexico

. . . Montezuma had ordered his stewards to provide us with everything we needed for our way of living: maize, grindstones, women to make our bread, fowls, fruit, and plenty of fodder for the horses. He then took leave of us all with the greatest courtesy, and we accompanied him to the street. However, Cortes ordered us not to go far from our quarters for the present until we knew better what conduct to observe.

Next day Cortes decided to go to Montezuma's palace. But first he sent to know whether the prince was busy and to inform him of our coming. He took four captains with him: Pedro de Alvarado, Juan Velazquez de Leon, Diego de Ordaz, and Gonzalo de Sandoval, and five of us soldiers.

When Montezuma was informed of our coming, he advanced into the middle of the hall to receive us, closely surrounded by his nephews, for no other chiefs were allowed to enter his palace or communicate with him except upon important business. Cortes and Montezuma exchanged bows, and clasped hands. Then Montezuma led Cortes to his own dais, and setting him down on his right, called for more seats, on which he ordered us all to sit also.

Cortes began to make a speech through our interpreters, saying that we were all now rested, and that in coming to see and speak with such a great prince we had fulfilled the purpose of our voyage and the orders of our lord the King. The principal things he had come to say on behalf of our Lord God had already been communicated to Montezuma through his three ambassadors, on that occasion in the sandhills when he did us the favour of sending us the golden moon and sun. We had then told him that we were Christians and worshipped one God alone, named Jesus Christ, who had suffered His passion and death to save us; and that what they worshipped as gods were not gods but devils, which were evil things, and if they were ugly to look at, their deeds were uglier. But he had proved to them how evil and ineffectual their gods were, as both the prince and his people would observe in the course of time, since, where we had put up crosses such as their ambassadors had seen, they had been too frightened to appear before them.

The favour he now begged of the great Montezuma was that he should listen to the words he now wished to speak. Then he very carefully expounded the creation of the world, how we are all brothers, the children of one mother and father called Adam and Eve; and how such a brother as our great Emperor, grieving for the perdition of so many souls as their idols were leading to hell, where they burnt in living flame, had sent us to tell him this, so that he might put a stop to it, and so that they might give up the worship of idols and make no more human sacrifices — for all men are brothers — and commit no more robbery or sodomy. He also promised that in the course of time the King would send some men who lead holy lives among us, much better than our own, to explain this more fully, for we had only come to give them warning. Therefore he begged Montezuma to do as he was asked.

As Montezuma seemed about to reply, Cortes broke off his speech, saying to those of us who were with him: "Since this is only the first attempt, we have now done our duty."

"My lord Malinche," Montezuma replied, "these arguments of yours have been familiar to me for some time. I understand what you said to my ambassadors on the sandhills about the three gods and the cross, also what you preached in the various towns through which you passed. We have given you no answer, since we have worshipped our own gods here from the beginning and know them to be good. No doubt yours are good also, but do not trouble to tell us any more about them at present. Regarding the creation of the world, we have held the same belief for many ages, and for this reason are certain that you are those who our ancestors predicted would come from the direction of the sunrise. As for your great King, I am in his debt and will give him of what I possess. For, as I have already said, two years ago I had news of the Captains who came in ships, by the road that you came, and said they were servants of this great king of yours. I should like to know if you are all the same people."

Cortes answered that we were all brothers and servants of the Emperor, and that they had come to discover a route and explore the seas and ports, so that when they knew them well we could follow, as we had done. Montezuma was referring to the expeditions of Francisco Hernandez de Cordoba and of Grijalva, the first voyages of discovery. He said that ever since that time he had wanted to invite some of these men to visit the cities of his kingdom, where he would receive them and do them honour, and that now his gods had fulfilled his desire, for we were in his house, which we might call our own. Here we might rest and enjoy ourselves, for we should receive good treatment. If on other occasions he had sent to forbid our entrance into his city, it was not of his own free will, but because his vassals were afraid. For they told him we shot out flashes of lightning, and killed many Indians with our horses, and that we were angry *Teules,* and other such childish stories. But now that he had seen us, he knew that we were of flesh and blood

and very intelligent, also very brave. Therefore he had a far greater es-
teem for us than these reports had given him, and would share with us
what he had.

We all thanked him heartily for his . . . good will, and Montezuma
replied with a laugh, because in his princely manner he spoke very
gaily: "Malinche, I know that these people of Tlascala with whom you
are so friendly have told you that I am a sort of god or *Teule,* and keep
nothing in any of my houses that is not made of silver and gold and
precious stones. But I know very well that you are too intelligent to believe this and will take it as a joke. See now, Malinche, my body is
made of flesh and blood like yours, and my houses and palaces are of
stone, wood, and plaster. It is true that I am a great king, and have inherited the riches of my ancestors, but the lies and nonsense you have
heard of us are not true. You must take them as a joke, as I take the
story of your thunders and lightnings."

Cortes answered also with a laugh that enemies always speak evil
and tell lies about the people they hate, but he knew he could not hope
to find a more magnificent prince in that land, and there was good reason why his fame should have reached our Emperor.

While this conversation was going on, Montezuma quietly sent one
of his nephews, a great *Cacique,* to order his stewards to bring certain
pieces of gold, which had apparently been set aside as a gift for Cortes,
and ten loads of fine cloaks which he divided: the gold and cloaks between Cortes and the four captains, and for each of us soldiers two
gold necklaces, each worth ten pesos, and two loads of cloaks. The
gold that he then gave us was worth in all more than a thousand pesos,
and he gave it all cheerfully, like a great and valiant prince.

As it was now past midday and he did not wish to be importunate,
Cortes said to Montezuma: "My lord, the favours you do us increase,
load by load, every day, and it is now the hour of your dinner." Montezuma answered that he thanked us for visiting him. We then took our
leave with the greatest courtesy, and returned to our quarters, talking
as we went of the prince's fine breeding and manners and deciding to
show him the greatest respect in every way, and to remove our quilted
caps in his presence, which we always did.

The great Montezuma was about forty years old, of good height,
well proportioned, spare and slight, and not very dark, though of the
usual Indian complexion. He did not wear his hair long but just over
his ears, and he had a short black beard, well-shaped and thin. His face
was rather long and cheerful, he had fine eyes, and in his appearance
and manner could express geniality or, when necessary, a serious com-
posure. He was very neat and clean, and took a bath every afternoon.
He had many women as his mistresses, the daughters of chieftains, but
two legitimate wives who were *Caciques* in their own right, and when
he had intercourse with any of them it was so secret that only some of

his servants knew of it. He was quite free from sodomy. The clothes he wore one day he did not wear again till three or four days later. He had a guard of two hundred chieftains lodged in rooms beside his own, only some of whom were permitted to speak to him. When they entered his presence they were compelled to take off their rich cloaks and put on others of little value. They had to be clean and walk barefoot, with their eyes downcast, for they were not allowed to look him in the face, and as they approached they had to make three obeisances, saying as they did so, "Lord, my lord, my great lord!" Then, when they had said what they had come to say, he would dismiss them with a few words. They did not turn their backs on him as they went out, but kept their faces towards him and their eyes downcast, only turning round when they had left the room. Another thing I noticed was that when other great chiefs came from distant lands about disputes or on business, they too had to take off their shoes and put on poor cloaks before entering Montezuma's apartments; and they were not allowed to enter the palace immediately but had to linger for a while near the door, since to enter hurriedly was considered disrespectful. . . .

Montezuma had two houses stocked with every sort of weapon; many of them were richly adorned with gold and precious stones. There were shields large and small, and a sort of broadsword, and two-handed swords set with flint blades that cut much better than our swords, and lances longer than ours, with five-foot blades consisting of many knives. Even when these are driven at a buckler or a shield they are not deflected. In fact they cut like razors, and the Indians can shave their heads with them. They had very good bows and arrows, and double and single-pointed javelins as well as their throwing-sticks and many slings and round stones shaped by hand, and another sort of shield that can be rolled up when they are not fighting, so that it does not get in the way, but which can be opened when they need it in battle and covers their bodies from head to foot. There was also a great deal of cotton armour richly worked on the outside with different coloured feathers, which they used as devices and distinguishing marks, and they had casques and helmets made of wood and bone which were also highly decorated with feathers on the outside. They had other arms of different kinds which I will not mention through fear of prolixity, and workmen skilled in the manufacture of such things, and stewards who were in charge of these arms. . . .

I have already described the manner of their sacrifices. They strike open the wretched Indian's chest with flint knives and hastily tear out the palpitating heart which, with the blood, they present to the idols in whose name they have performed the sacrifice. Then they cut off the arms, thighs, and head, eating the arms and thighs at their ceremonial banquets. The head they hang up on a beam, and the body of the sacrificed man is not eaten but given to the beasts of prey. They also had many vipers in this accursed house, and poisonous snakes which have something that sounds like a bell in their tails. These, which are the deadliest snakes of all, they kept in jars and great pottery vessels full of feathers, in which they laid their eggs and reared their young. They were fed on the bodies of sacrificed Indians and the flesh of the dogs that they bred. We know for certain, too, that when they drove us out of Mexico and killed over eight hundred and fifty of our soldiers, they fed those beasts and snakes on their bodies for many days, as I shall relate in due course. These snakes and wild beasts were dedicated to their fierce idols, and kept them company. As for the horrible noise when the lions and tigers roared, and the jackals and foxes howled, and the serpents hissed, it was so appalling that one seemed to be in hell.

I must now speak of the skilled workmen whom Montezuma employed in all the crafts they practised, beginning with the jewellers and workers in silver and gold and various kinds of hollowed objects, which excited the admiration of our great silversmiths at home. Many of the best of them lived in a town called Atzcapotzalco, three miles from Mexico. There were other skilled craftsmen who worked with precious stones and *chalchihuites*,[3] and specialists in feather-work, and very fine painters and carvers. We can form some judgement of what they did then from what we can see of their work today. There are three Indians now living in the city of Mexico, named Marcos de Aquino, Juan de la Cruz, and El Crespillo, who are such magnificent painters and carvers that, had they lived in the age of the Apelles of old, or of Michael Angelo, or Berruguete in our own day, they would be counted in the same rank.

Let us go on to the women, the weavers and sempstresses, who made such a huge quantity of fine robes with very elaborate feather designs. These things were generally brought from some towns in the province of Cotaxtla, which is on the north coast, quite near San Juan de Ulua. In Montezuma's own palaces very fine cloths were woven by those chieftains' daughters whom he kept as mistresses; and the daughters of other dignitaries, who lived in a kind of retirement like nuns in some houses close to the great *cue*[4] of Huichilobos, wore robes entirely of feather-work. Out of devotion for that god and a female deity who was said to preside over marriage, their fathers would place them in religious retirement until they found husbands. They would then take them out to be married.

Now to speak of the great number of performers whom Montezuma kept to entertain him. There were dancers and stilt-walkers, and some who seemed to fly as they leapt through the air, and men

---

3 Green stone. [Ed.]
4 Plaza or square. [Ed.]

rather like clowns to make him laugh. There was a whole quarter full of these people who had no other occupation. He had as many work-men as he needed, too, stonecutters, masons, and carpenters, to keep his houses in repair.

We must not forget the gardens with their many varieties of flowers and sweet-scented trees planted in order, and their ponds and tanks of fresh water into which a stream flowed at one end and out of which it flowed at the other, and the baths he had there, and the variety of small birds that nested in the branches, and the medicinal and useful herbs that grew there. His gardens were a wonderful sight, and required many gardeners to take care of them. Everything was built of stone and plastered; baths and walks and closets and rooms like summerhouses where they danced and sang. There was so much to see in these gar-dens, as everywhere else, that we could not tire of contemplating his great riches and the large number of skilled Indians employed in the many crafts they practised. . . .

We carried our weapons, as was our custom, both by night and day. Indeed, Montezuma was so used to our visiting him armed that he did not think it strange. I say this because our Captain and those of us who had horses went to Tlatelolco mounted, and the majority of our men were fully equipped. On reaching the market-place, escorted by the many *Caciques* whom Montezuma had assigned to us, we were as-tounded at the great number of people and the quantities of merchan-dise, and at the orderliness and good arrangements that prevailed, for we had never seen such a thing before. The chieftains who accompa-nied us pointed everything out. Every kind of merchandise was kept separate and had its fixed place marked for it. . . .

When our Captain and the Mercedarian friar realized that Mon-tezuma would not allow us to set up a cross at Huichilobos'[5] *cue* or build a church there, it was decided that we should ask his stewards for masons so that we could put up a church in our own quarters. For every time we had said mass since entering the city of Mexico we had had to erect an altar on tables and dismantle it again.

The stewards promised to tell Montezuma of our wishes, and Cortes also sent our interpreters to ask him in person. Montezuma granted our request and ordered that we should be supplied with all the necessary material. We had our church finished in two days, and a cross erected in front of our lodgings, and mass was said there each day until the wine gave out. For as Cortes and some other captains and a friar had been ill during the Tlascalan campaign, there had been a run on the wine that we kept for mass. Still, though it was finished, we still

---

[5] The temple of the sun god who demanded human sacrifice. [Ed.]

went to church every day and prayed on our knees before the altar and images, firstly because it was our obligation as Christians and a good habit, and secondly so that Montezuma and all his captains should observe us and, seeing us worshipping on our knees before the cross — especially when we intoned the Ave Maria — might be inclined to imitate us.

It being our habit to examine and inquire into everything, when we were all assembled in our lodging and considering which was the best place for an altar, two of our men, one of whom was the carpenter Alonso Yañez, called attention to some marks on one of the walls which showed that there had once been a door, though it had been well plastered up and painted. Now as we had heard that Montezuma kept his father's treasure in this building, we immediately suspected that it must be in this room, which had been closed up only a few days before. Yañez made the suggestion to Juan Velazquez de Leon and Francisco de Lugo, both relatives of mine, to whom he had attached himself as a servant; and they mentioned the matter to Cortes. So the door was secretly opened, and Cortes went in first with certain captains. When they saw the quantity of golden objects — jewels and plates and ingots — which lay in that chamber they were quite transported. They did not know what to think of such riches. The news soon spread to the other captains and soldiers, and very secretly we all went in to see. The sight of all that wealth dumbfounded me. Being only a youth at the time and never having seen such riches before, I felt certain that there could not be a store like it in the whole world. We unanimously decided that we could not think of touching a particle of it, and that the stones should immediately be replaced in the doorway, which should be blocked again and cemented just as we had found it. We resolved also that not a word should be said about this until times changed, for fear Montezuma might hear of our discovery.

Let us leave this subject of the treasure and tell how four of our most valiant captains took Cortes aside in the church, with a dozen soldiers who were in his trust and confidence, myself among them, and asked him to consider the net or trap in which we were caught, to look at the great strength of the city and observe the causeways and bridges, and remember the warnings we had received in every town we had passed through that Huichilobos had counselled Montezuma to let us into the city and kill us there. We reminded him that the hearts of men are very fickle, especially among the Indians, and begged him not to trust the good will and affection that Montezuma was showing us, because from one hour to another it might change. If he should take it into his head to attack us, we said, the stoppage of our supplies of food and water, or the raising of any of the bridges, would render us helpless. Then, considering the vast army of warriors he possessed, we should be incapable of attacking or defending ourselves. And since all the houses stood in the water, how could our Tlascalan allies come in to help us? We asked him to think over all that we had said, for if we wanted to preserve our lives we must seize Montezuma immediately, without even a day's delay. We pointed out that all the gold Montezuma had given us, and all that we had seen in the treasury of his father Axayacatl, and all the food we ate was turning to poison in our bodies, for we could not sleep by night or day or take any rest while these thoughts were in our minds. If any of our soldiers gave him less drastic advice, we concluded, they would be senseless beasts charmed by the gold and incapable of looking death in the eye.

When he had heard our opinion, Cortes answered: "Do not imagine, gentlemen, that I am asleep or that I do not share your anxiety. You must have seen that I do. But what strength have we got for so bold a course as to take this great lord in his own palace, surrounded as he is by warriors and guards? What scheme or trick can we devise to prevent him from summoning his soldiers to attack us at once?"

Our captains (Juan Velazquez de Leon, Diego de Ordaz, Gonzalo de Sandoval, and Pedro de Alvarado) replied that Montezuma must be got out of his palace by smooth words and brought to our quarters. Once there, he must be told that he must remain as a prisoner, and that if he called out or made any disturbance he would pay for it with his life. If Cortes was unwilling to take this course at once, they begged him for permission to do it themselves. With two very dangerous alternatives before us, the better and more profitable thing, they said, would be to seize Montezuma rather than wait for him to attack us. Once he did so, what chance would we have? Some of us soldiers also remarked that Montezuma's stewards who brought us our food seemed to be growing insolent, and did not serve us as politely as they had at first. Two of our Tlascalan allies had, moreover, secretly observed to Jeronimo de Aguilar that for the last two days the Mexicans had appeared less well disposed to us. We spent a good hour discussing whether or not to take Montezuma prisoner, and how it should be done. But our final advice, that at all costs we should take him prisoner, was approved by our Captain, and we then left the matter till next day. All night we prayed God to direct events in the interests of His holy service. . . .

6

From *The Broken Spears:*
The Aztec Account of
the Conquest of Mexico

This Aztec account of the encounter between the Spanish and the Indians of Mexico was written some years after the events described. Spanish Christian monks helped a postconquest generation of Aztec Nahuatl speakers translate the illustrated manuscripts of the conquest period. According to this account, how did Montezuma respond to Cortés? Was Montezuma's attitude toward the Spanish shared by other Aztecs? How reliable is this account, do you think, in describing Montezuma's thoughts, motives, and behavior?

Thinking Historically

How does the Aztec account of the conquest differ from that of the Spanish, written by Díaz? Is this difference merely a matter of perspective, or do the authors disagree about what happened? To the extent to which there are differences, how do you decide which account to believe and accept?

Speeches of Motecuhzoma and Cortes

When Motecuhzoma had given necklaces to each one, Cortes asked him: "Are you Motecuhzoma? Are you the king? Is it true that you are the king Motecuhzoma?"

And the king said: "Yes, I am Motecuhzoma." Then he stood up to welcome Cortes; he came forward, bowed his head low and addressed him in these words: "Our lord, you are weary. The journey has tired you, but now you have arrived on the earth. You have come to your city, Mexico. You have come here to sit on your throne, to sit under its canopy.

"The kings who have gone before, your representatives, guarded it and preserved it for your coming. The kings Itzcoatl, Motecuhzoma the Elder, Axayacatl, Tizoc and Ahuitzol ruled for you in the City of

The Broken Spears: The Aztec Account of the Conquest of Mexico, ed. Miguel Leon-Portilla (Boston: Beacon Press, 1990), 64–76.

Mexico. The people were protected by their swords and sheltered by their shields.

"Do the kings know the destiny of those they left behind, their posterity? If only they are watching! If only they can see what I see!

"No, it is not a dream. I am not walking in my sleep. I am not seeing you in my dreams. . . . I have seen you at last! I have met you face to face! I was in agony for five days, for ten days, with my eyes fixed on the Region of the Mystery. And now you have come out of the clouds and mists to sit on your throne again.

"This was foretold by the kings who governed your city, and now it has taken place. You have come back to us; you have come down from the sky. Rest now, and take possession of your royal houses. Welcome to your land, my lords!"

When Motecuhzoma had finished, La Malinche translated his address into Spanish so that the Captain could understand it. Cortes replied in his strange and savage tongue, speaking first to La Malinche: "Tell Motecuhzoma that we are his friends. There is nothing to fear. We have wanted to see him for a long time, and now we have seen his face and heard his words. Tell him that we love him well and that our hearts are contented."

Then he said to Motecuhzoma: "We have come to your house in Mexico as friends. There is nothing to fear."

La Malinche translated this speech and the Spaniards grasped Motecuhzoma's hands and patted his back to show their affection for him.

Attitudes of the Spaniards and the Native Lords

The Spaniards examined everything they saw. They dismounted from their horses, and mounted them again, and dismounted again, so as not to miss anything of interest.

The chiefs who accompanied Motecuhzoma were: Cacama, king of Tezcoco; Tetlepanquetzaltzin, king of Tlacopan; Itzcuauhtzin the Tlacochcalcatl, lord of Tlatelolco; and Topantemoc, Motecuhzoma's treasurer in Tlatelolco. These four chiefs were standing in a file.

The other princes were: Atlixcatzin [chief who has taken captives][1]; Tepeoatzin, The Tlacochcalcatl; Quetzalaztatzin, the keeper of the chalk; Totomotzin; Hecateupatiltzin; and Cuappiatzin.

When Motecuhzoma was imprisoned, they all went into hiding. They ran away to hide and treacherously abandoned him!

---

[1] Military title given to a warrior who had captured four enemies.

The Spaniards Take Possession of the City

When the Spaniards entered the Royal House, they placed Motecuhzoma under guard and kept him under their vigilance. They also placed a guard over Itzcuauhtzin, but the other lords were permitted to depart.

Then the Spaniards fired one of their cannons, and this caused great confusion in the city. The people scattered in every direction; they fled without rhyme or reason; they ran off as if they were being pursued. It was as if they had eaten the mushrooms that confuse the mind, or had seen some dreadful apparition. They were all overcome by terror, as if their hearts had fainted. And when night fell, the panic spread through the city and their fears would not let them sleep.

In the morning the Spaniards told Motecuhzoma what they needed in the way of supplies: tortillas, fried chickens, hens' eggs, pure water, firewood, and charcoal. Also: large, clean cooking pots, water jars, pitchers, dishes, and other pottery. Motecuhzoma ordered that it be sent to them. The chiefs who received this order were angry with the king and no longer revered or respected him. But they furnished the Spaniards with all the provisions they needed — food, beverages, and water, and fodder for the horses.

The Spaniards Reveal Their Greed

When the Spaniards were installed in the palace, they asked Motecuhzoma about the city's resources and reserves and about the warriors' ensigns and shields. They questioned him closely and then demanded gold.

Motecuhzoma guided them to it. They surrounded him and crowded close with their weapons. He walked in the center, while they formed a circle around him.

When they arrived at the treasure house called Teucalco, the riches of gold and feathers were brought out to them: ornaments made of quetzal feathers, richly worked shields, disks of gold, the necklaces of the idols, gold nose plugs, gold greaves and bracelets and crowns.

The Spaniards immediately stripped the feathers from the gold shields and ensigns. They gathered all the gold into a great mound and set fire to everything else, regardless of its value. Then they melted down the gold into ingots. As for the precious green stones, they took only the best of them; the rest were snatched up by the Tlaxcaltecas. The Spaniards searched through the whole treasure house, questioning and quarreling, and seized every object they thought was beautiful.

The Seizure of
Motecuhzoma's Treasures

Next they went to Motecuhzoma's storehouse, in the place called Toto-calco [Place of the Palace of the Birds],[2] where his personal treasures were kept. The Spaniards grinned like little beasts and patted each other with delight.

When they entered the hall of treasures, it was as if they had arrived in Paradise. They searched everywhere and coveted everything; they were slaves to their own greed. All of Motecuhzoma's possessions were brought out: fine bracelets, necklaces with large stones, ankle rings with little gold bells, the royal crowns and all the royal finery — everything that belonged to the king and was reserved to him only. They seized these treasures as if they were their own, as if this plunder were merely a stroke of good luck. And when they had taken all the gold, they heaped up everything else in the middle of the patio.

La Malinche called the nobles together. She climbed up to the palace roof and cried: "Mexicanos, come forward! The Spaniards need your help! Bring them food and pure water. They are tired and hungry; they are almost fainting from exhaustion! Why do you not come forward? Are you angry with them?"

The Mexicans were too frightened to approach. They were crushed by terror and would not risk coming forward. They shied away as if the Spaniards were wild beasts, as if the hour were midnight on the blackest night of the year. Yet they did not abandon the Spaniards to hunger and thirst. They brought them whatever they needed, but shook with fear as they did so. They delivered the supplies to the Spaniards with trembling hands, then turned and hurried away.

The Preparations for the Fiesta

The Aztecs begged permission of their king to hold the fiesta of Huitzilopochtli. The Spaniards wanted to see this fiesta to learn how it was celebrated. A delegation of the celebrants came to the palace where Motecuhzoma was a prisoner, and when their spokesman asked his permission, he granted it to them.

---

[2] The zoological garden attached to the royal palaces.

As soon as the delegation returned, the women began to grind seeds of the chicalote.[3] These women had fasted for a whole year. They ground the seeds in the patio of the temple.

The Spaniards came out of the palace together, dressed in armor and carrying their weapons with them. They stalked among the women and looked at them one by one; they stared into the faces of the women who were grinding seeds. After this cold inspection, they went back into the palace. It is said that they planned to kill the celebrants if the men entered the patio.

The Statue of Huitzilopochtli

On the evening before the fiesta of Toxcatl, the celebrants began to model a statue of Huitzilopochtli. They gave it such a human appearance that it seemed the body of a living man. Yet they made the statue with nothing but a paste made of the ground seeds of the chicalote, which they shaped over an armature of sticks.

When the statue was finished, they dressed it in rich feathers, and they painted crossbars over and under its eyes. They also clipped on its earrings of turquoise mosaic; these were in the shape of serpents, with gold rings hanging from them. Its nose plug, in the shape of an arrow, was made of gold and was inlaid with fine stones.

They placed the magic headdress of hummingbird feathers on its head. They also adorned it with an *anecuyotl,* which was a belt made of feathers, with a cone at the back. Then they hung around its neck an ornament of yellow parrot feathers, fringed like the locks of a young boy. Over this they put its nettle-leaf cape, which was painted black and decorated with five clusters of eagle feathers.

Next they wrapped it in its cloak, which was painted with skull and bones, and over this they fastened its vest. The vest was painted with dismembered human parts: skulls, ears, hearts, intestines, torsos, breasts, hands, and feet. They also put on its *maxtlatl,* or loincloth, which was decorated with images of dissevered limbs and fringed with amate paper. This *maxtlatl* was painted with vertical stripes of bright blue.

They fastened a red paper flag at its shoulder and placed on its head what looked like a sacrificial flint knife. This too was made of red paper; it seemed to have been steeped in blood.

The statue carried a *tehuehuelli,* a bamboo shield decorated with four clusters of fine eagle feathers. The pendant of this shield was blood-red, like the knife and the shoulder flag. The statue also carried four arrows.

---

3 Edible plants also used in medicines.

Finally, they put the wristbands on its arms. These bands, made of coyote skin, were fringed with paper cut into little strips.

The Beginning of the Fiesta

Early the next morning, the statue's face was uncovered by those who had been chosen for that ceremony. They gathered in front of the idol in single file and offered it gifts of food, such as round seedcakes or perhaps human flesh. But they did not carry it up to its temple on top of the pyramid.

All the young warriors were eager for the fiesta to begin. They had sworn to dance and sing with all their hearts, so that the Spaniards would marvel at the beauty of the rituals.

The procession began, and the celebrants filed into the temple patio to dance the Dance of the Serpent. When they were all together in the patio, the songs and the dance began. Those who had fasted for twenty days and those who had fasted for a year were in command of the others; they kept the dancers in file with their pine wands. (If anyone wished to urinate, he did not stop dancing, but simply opened his clothing at the hips and separated his clusters of heron feathers.)

If anyone disobeyed the leaders or was not in his proper place they struck him on the hips and shoulders. Then they drove him out of the patio, beating him and shoving him from behind. They pushed him so hard that he sprawled to the ground, and they dragged him outside by the ears. No one dared to say a word about this punishment, for those who had fasted during the year were feared and venerated; they had earned the exclusive title "Brothers of Huitzilopochtli."

The great captains, the bravest warriors, danced at the head of the files to guide the others. The youths followed at a slight distance. Some of the youths wore their hair gathered into large locks, a sign that they had never taken any captives. Others carried their headdresses on their shoulders; they had taken captives, but only with help.

Then came the recruits, who were called "the young warriors." They had each captured an enemy or two. The others called to them: "Come, comrades, show us how brave you are! Dance with all your hearts!"

The Spaniards Attack the Celebrants

At this moment in the fiesta, when the dance was loveliest and when song was linked to song, the Spaniards were seized with an urge to kill the celebrants. They all ran forward, armed as if for battle. They closed the entrances and passageways, all the gates of the patio: the Eagle Gate in the lesser palace, the Gate of the Canestalk and the Gate of the

Serpent of Mirrors. They posted guards so that no one could escape, and then rushed into the Sacred Patio to slaughter the celebrants. They came on foot, carrying their swords and their wooden or metal shields.

They ran in among the dancers, forcing their way to the place where the drums were played. They attacked the man who was drumming and cut off his arms. Then they cut off his head, and it rolled across the floor.

They attacked all the celebrants, stabbing them, spearing them, striking them with their swords. They attacked some of them from behind, and these fell instantly to the ground with their entrails hanging out. Others they beheaded: they cut off their heads, or split their heads to pieces.

They struck others in the shoulders, and their arms were torn from their bodies. They wounded some in the thigh and some in the calf. They slashed others in the abdomen, and their entrails all spilled to the ground. Some attempted to run away, but their intestines dragged as they ran; they seemed to tangle their feet in their own entrails. No matter how they tried to save themselves, they could find no escape.

Some attempted to force their way out, but the Spaniards murdered them at the gates. Others climbed the walls, but they could not save themselves. Those who ran into the communal houses were safe there for a while; so were those who lay down among the victims and pretended to be dead. But if they stood up again, the Spaniards saw them and killed them.

The blood of the warriors flowed like water and gathered into pools. The pools widened, and the stench of blood and entrails filled the air. The Spaniards ran into the communal houses to kill those who were hiding. They ran everywhere and searched everywhere; they invaded every room, hunting and killing.

DAVID PIETERZEN DEVRIES

A Dutch Massacre of the Algonquins

David Pieterzen DeVries was a ship's captain who became a landlord or "patroonship" holder in the Dutch colony of New Amsterdam (now New York). After a disastrous venture to establish a farming and whaling colony, Swanendael on the Delaware River (near modern Philadelphia), he was granted the first patroonship on Staten Island. There he had frequent contact with the Algonquin and Raritan Indians. He was a member of the Board of Directors (the Twelve Men), responsible to the Dutch West India Company for the governance of New Amsterdam. When in 1642, a new governor, Dutch merchant Willem Kieft, urged increased settlement and Indian removal, DeVries urged caution. He described what happened in February 1643 in his book, *Voyages from Holland to America*.

Why did DeVries oppose the governor's plan to attack the Algonquins? What does his story suggest about Dutch-Indian relations before 1643? What were the consequences of the massacre?

Thinking Historically

How is the Dutch treatment of the Algonquins different from the Spanish treatment of the Mexicans? What accounts for these differences?

Do you think an Algonquin account of this encounter would be significantly different from that of DeVries? How might it differ?

The 24th of February, sitting at a table with the Governor, he began to state his intentions, that he had a mind to *wipe the mouths* of the savages; that he had been dining at the house of Jan Claesen Damen, where Maryn Adriaensen and Jan Claesen Damen, together with Jacob Planck, had presented a petition to him to begin this work. I answered him that they were not wise to request this; that such work could not be done without the approbation of the Twelve Men; that it could not take place without my assent, who was one of the Twelve Men; that moreover I was the first patroon, and no one else hitherto had risked

David Pieterzen DeVries, *Voyages from Holland to America, A.D. 1632–1644*, trans. H. C. Murphy (New York: Billing Brothers, 1853), 114–17.

there so many thousands, and also his person, as I was the first to come from Holland or Zeeland to plant a colony; and that he should consider what profit he could derive from this business, as he well knew that on account of trifling with the Indians we had lost our colony in the South River at Swanendael, in the Hoere-kil, with thirty-two men, who were murdered in the year 1630; and that in the year 1640, the cause of my people being murdered on Staten Island was a difficulty which he had brought on with the Raritan Indians, where his soldiers had for some trifling thing killed some savages. . . . But it appeared that my speaking was of no avail. He had, with his comurderers, determined to commit the murder, deeming it a Roman deed, and to do it without warning the inhabitants in the open lands that each one might take care of himself against the retaliation of the savages, for he could not kill all the Indians. When I had expressed all these things in full, sitting at the table, and the meal was over, he told me he wished me to go to the large hall, which he had been lately adding to his house. Coming to it, there stood all his soldiers ready to cross the river to Pavonia to commit the murder. Then spoke I again to Governor Willem Kieft: "Let this work alone; you wish to break the mouths of the Indians, but you will also murder our own nation, for there are none of the settlers in the open country who are aware of it. My own dwelling, my people, cattle, corn, and tobacco will be lost." He answered me, assuring me that there would be no danger; that some soldiers should go to my house to protect it. But that was not done. So was this business begun between the 25th and 26th of February in the year 1643. I remained that night at the Governor's, sitting up. I went and sat by the kitchen fire, when about midnight I heard a great shrieking, and I ran to the ramparts of the fort, and looked over to Pavonia. Saw nothing but firing, and heard the shrieks of the savages murdered in their sleep. I returned again to the house by the fire. Having sat there awhile, there came an Indian with his squaw, whom I knew well, and who lived about an hour's walk from my house, and told me that they two had fled in a small skiff, which they had taken from the shore at Pavonia; that the Indians from Fort Orange had surprised them; and that they had come to conceal themselves in the fort. I told them that they must go away immediately; that this was no time for them to come to the fort to conceal themselves; that they who had killed their people at Pavonia were not Indians, but the Swannekens, as they call the Dutch, had done it. They then asked me how they should get out of the fort. I took them to the door, and there was no sentry there, and so they betook themselves to the woods. When it was day the soldiers returned to the fort, having massacred or murdered eighty Indians, and considering they had done a deed of Roman valor, in murdering so many in their sleep; where infants were torn from their mothers' breasts, and hacked to pieces in the presence of the parents, and the pieces thrown into the fire and in the water, and other sucklings, being bound to small boards, were cut, stuck, and pierced, and miserably massacred in a manner to move a heart of stone. Some were thrown into the river, and when the fathers and mothers endeavored to save them, the soldiers would not let them come on land but made both parents and children drown — children from five to six years of age, and also some old and decrepit persons. Those who fled from this onslaught, and concealed themselves in the neighboring sedge, and when it was morning, came out to beg a piece of bread, and to be permitted to warm themselves, were murdered in cold blood and tossed into the fire or the water. Some came to our people in the country with their hands, some with their legs cut off, and some holding their entrails in their arms, and others had such horrible cuts and gashes, that worse than they were could never happen. And these poor simple creatures, as also many of our own people, did not know any better than that they had been attacked by a party of other Indians — the Maquas. After this exploit, the soldiers were rewarded for their services, and Director Kieft thanked them by taking them by the hand and congratulating them. At another place, on the same night, on Corler's Hook near Corler's plantation, forty Indians were in the same manner attacked in their sleep, and massacred there in the same manner. Did the Duke of Alva in the Netherlands ever do anything more cruel? This is indeed a disgrace to our nation, who have so generous a governor in our Fatherland as the Prince of Orange, who has always endeavored in his wars to spill as little blood as possible. As soon as the savages understood that the Swannekens had so treated them, all the men whom they could surprise on the farmlands, they killed; but we have never heard that they have ever permitted women or children to be killed. They burned all the houses, farms, barns, grain, haystacks, and destroyed everything they could get hold of. So there was an open destructive war begun. They also burnt my farm, cattle, corn, barn, tobacco-house, and all the tobacco. My people saved themselves in the house where I alone lived, which was made with embrasures, through which they defended themselves. Whilst my people were in alarm the savage whom I had aided to escape from the fort in the night came there, and told the other Indians that I was a good chief, that I had helped him out of the fort, and that the killing of the Indians took place contrary to my wish. Then they all cried out together to my people that they would not shoot them; that if they had not destroyed my cattle they would not do it, nor burn my house; that they would let my little brewery stand, though they wished to get the copper kettle, in order to make darts for their arrows; but hearing now that it had been done contrary to my wish, they all went away, and left my house unbesieged. When now the Indians had destroyed so many farms and men in revenge for their people, I went to Governor Willem Kieft, and asked him if it was not as I had said it would be, that he would only effect the spilling of Christian blood. Who would now compensate us for our losses? But he gave me no answer. He said he wondered that no Indians came to the fort. I told him that I did not wonder at it; "why should the Indians come here where you have so treated them?"

8

NZINGA MBEMBA

Appeal to the King of Portugal

Europeans were unable to conquer Africa as they did the Americas until the end of the nineteenth century. Rivers that fell steeply to the sea, military defenses, and diseases like malaria proved insurmountable to Europeans before the age of the steamship, the machine gun, and quinine pills. Before the last half of the nineteenth century, Europeans had to be content with alliances with African kings and rulers. The Portuguese had been the first to meet Africans in the towns and villages along the Atlantic coast, and they became the first European missionaries and trading partners.

Nzinga Mbemba, whose Christian name was Affonso, was king of the west African state of Congo (comprising what is today parts of Angola as well as the two Congo states) from about 1506 to 1543. He succeeded his father, King Nzinga a Kuwu who, shortly after their first Portuguese contact in 1483, sent officials to Lisbon to learn European ways. In 1491 father and son were baptized, and Portuguese priests, merchants, artisans, and soldiers were provided with a coastal settlement.

What exactly is the complaint of the King of Congo? What seems to be the impact of Portuguese traders (factors) in the Kongo? What does King Affonso want the King of Portugal to do?

Thinking Historically

This selection offers an opportunity to compare European expansion in the Americas and Africa. Portuguese contact with Nzinga Mbemba

Basil Davidson, *The African Past* (Boston: Little, Brown, and Company, 1964), 191–94.

of the Congo was roughly contemporaneous with the Spanish expedition to Mexico. What differences do you see between these two cases
of early European expansion? Can you think of any reasons that
Congo kings converted to Christianity while Mexican kings did not?

Compare the European treatment of Africans with their treatment
of Native Americans. Why did Europeans enslave Africans and not,
for the most part, American Indians?

Sir, Your Highness [of Portugal] should know how our Kingdom is
being lost in so many ways that it is convenient to provide for the necessary remedy, since this is caused by the excessive freedom given by
your factors and officials to the men and merchants who are allowed
to come to this Kingdom to set up shops with goods and many things
which have been prohibited by us, and which they spread throughout
our Kingdoms and Domains in such an abundance that many of our
vassals, whom we had in obedience, do not comply because they have
the things in greater abundance than we ourselves; and it was with
these things that we had them content and subjected under our vas-
salage and jurisdiction, so it is doing a great harm not only to the service of God, but to the security and peace of our Kingdoms and State
as well.

And we cannot reckon how great the damage is, since the mentioned merchants are taking every day our natives, sons of the land and
the sons of our noblemen and vassals and our relatives, because the
thieves and men of bad conscience grab them wishing to have the
things and wares of this Kingdom which they are ambitious of; they
grab them and get them to be sold; and so great, Sir, is the corruption
and licentiousness that our country is being completely depopulated,
and Your Highness should not agree with this nor accept it as in your
service. And to avoid it we need from those [your] Kingdoms no more
than some priests and a few people to teach in schools, and no other
goods except wine and flour for the holy sacrament. That is why we
beg of Your Highness to help and assist us in this matter, commanding
your factors that they should not send here either merchants or wares,
because it is *our will that in these Kingdoms there should not be any
trade of slaves nor outlet for them.*[1] Concerning what is referred above,
again we beg of Your Highness to agree with it, since otherwise we
cannot remedy such an obvious damage. Pray Our Lord in His mercy
to have Your Highness under His guard and let you do for ever the
things of His service. I kiss your hands many times.

---

[1] Emphasis in the original.

At our town of Congo, written on the sixth day of July.
João Teixeira did it in 1526.
The King. Dom Affonso.
[On the back of this letter the following can be read:
To the most powerful and excellent prince Dom João, King our Brother.]

Moreover, Sir, in our Kingdoms there is another great inconvenience which is of little service to God, and this is that many of our people [*naturaes*], keenly desirous as they are of the wares and things of your Kingdoms, which are brought here by your people, and in order to satisfy their voracious appetite, seize many of our people, freed and exempt men; and very often it happens that they kidnap even noblemen and the sons of noblemen, and our relatives, and take them to be sold to the white men who are in our Kingdoms; and for this purpose they have concealed them; and others are brought during the night so that they might not be recognized.

And as soon as they are taken by the white men they are immediately ironed and branded with fire, and when they are carried to be embarked, if they are caught by our guards' men the whites allege that they have bought them but they cannot say from whom, so that it is our duty to do justice and to restore to the freemen their freedom, but it cannot be done if your subjects feel offended, as they claim to be.

And to avoid such a great evil we passed a law so that any white man living in our Kingdoms and wanting to purchase goods in any way should first inform three of our noblemen and officials of our court whom we rely upon in this matter, and these are Dom Pedro Manipanza and Dom Manuel Manissaba, our chief usher, and Gonçalo Pires our chief freighter, who should investigate if the mentioned goods are captives or free men, and if cleared by them there will be no further doubt nor embargo for them to be taken and embarked. But if the white men do not comply with it they will lose the aforementioned goods. And if we do them this favor and concession it is for the part Your Highness has in it, since we know that it is in your service too that these goods are taken from our Kingdom, otherwise we should not consent to this. . . .

Sir, Your Highness has been kind enough to write to us saying that we should ask in our letters for anything we need, and that we shall be provided with everything, and as the peace and the health of our Kingdom depend on us, and as there are among us old folks and people who have lived for many days, it happens that we have continuously many and different diseases which put us very often in such a weakness that we reach almost the last extreme; and the same happens to our children, relatives, and natives owing to the lack in this country of physicians and surgeons who might know how to cure properly such diseases. And as we have got neither dispensaries nor drugs which might help us in this forlornness, many of those who had been already confirmed and instructed in the holy faith of Our Lord Jesus Christ perish and die; and the rest of the people in their majority cure themselves with herbs and breads and other ancient methods, so that they put all their faith in the mentioned herbs and ceremonies if they live, and believe that they are saved if they die; and this is not much in the service of God.

And to avoid such a great error and inconvenience, since it is from God in the first place and then from your Kingdoms and from Your Highness that all the good and drugs and medicines have come to save us, we beg of you to be agreeable and kind enough to send us two physicians and two apothecaries and one surgeon, so that they may come with their drug-stores and all the necessary things to stay in our kingdoms, because we are in extreme need of them all and each of them. We shall do them all good and shall benefit them by all means, since they are sent by Your Highness, whom we thank for your work in their coming. We beg of Your Highness as a great favor to do this for us, because besides being good in itself it is in the service of God as we have said above.

9

WILLEM BOSMAN

Slave Trader

Willem Bosman was the chief agent of the Dutch West India Company on the African coast. Here, in a letter to a friend in Holland, he explains how slaves were bought to Whydah, an English fort on the coast of Dahomey (between the Gold Coast of Ghana and the slave coast of Nigeria). Bosman discusses various ways in which he received slaves. What were these ways? Which does he seem to prefer?

Willem Bosman, *A New and Accurate Description of the Coast of Guinea, Divided into the Gold, Slave, and the Ivory Coasts*, trans. from Dutch, 2nd ed. (London: 1721), 339–45.

Thinking Historically

Compare Bosman's description of the slave trade with that of Nzinga Mbemba in the preceding selection. How do you account for the differences? Are they due to Dutch and Portuguese practice, to policies of the Congo and Dahomey, or to the passage of time between 1526 and 1700?

The author, a Dutchman, makes certain comparisons between Dutch slave ships and those of other Europeans. Do you see any evidence for his claims?

The first business of one of our factors [agents] when he comes to Fida [Whydah], is to satisfy the customs of the king and the great men, which amounts to about a hundred pounds in Guinea value, as the goods must yield there. After which we have free license to trade, which is published throughout the whole land by the crier.

But yet before we can deal with any person, we are obliged to buy the king's whole stock of slaves at a set price, which is commonly one third or one fourth higher than ordinary; after which, we obtain free leave to deal with all his subjects, of what rank soever. But if there happen to be no stock of slaves, the factor must then resolve to run the risk of trusting the inhabitants with goods to the value of one or two hundred slaves; which commodities they send into the inland country, in order to buy with them slaves at all markets, and that sometimes two hundred miles deep in the country. For you ought to be informed, that markets of men are here kept in the same manner as those of beasts with us.

Not a few in our country fondly imagine that parents here sell their children, men their wives, and one brother the other. But those who think so, do deceive themselves; for this never happens on any other account but that of necessity, or some great crime; but most of the slaves that are offered to us, are prisoners of war, which are sold by the victors as their booty.

When these slaves come to Fida, they are put in prison all together; and when we treat concerning buying them, they are all brought out together in a large plain; where, by our surgeons, whose province it is, they are thoroughly examined, even to the smallest member, and that naked, both men and women, without the least distinction or modesty. Those that are approved as good, are set on one side; and the lame or faulty are set by as invalids, which are here called *mackrons*: these are such as are above five and thirty years old, or are maimed in the arms, legs, or feet; have lost a tooth, are grey-haired, or have films over their eyes; as well as all those which are affected with any venereal distemper, or several other diseases.

The invalids and the maimed being thrown out, as I have told you, the remainder are numbered, and it is entered who delivered them. In the meanwhile, a burning iron, with the arms or name of the companies, lies in the fire, with which ours are marked on the breast. This is done that we may distinguish them from the slaves of the English, French, or others (which are also marked with their mark), and to prevent the Negroes exchanging them for worse, at which they have a good hand. I doubt not but this trade seems very barbarous to you, but since it is followed by mere necessity, it must go on; but we yet take all possible care that they are not burned too hard, especially the women, who are more tender than the men.

We are seldom long detained in the buying of these slaves, because their price is established, the women being one fourth or fifth part cheaper than the men. The disputes which we generally have with the owners of these slaves are, that we will not give them such goods as they ask for them, especially the *boesies* [cowry shells] (as I have told you, the money of this country) of which they are very fond, though we generally make a division on this head, in order to make one part of the goods help off another; because those slaves which are paid for in *boesies,* cost the company one half more than those bought with other goods. . . .

When we have agreed with the owners of the slaves, they are returned to their prison; where, from that time forwards, they are kept at our charge, cost us two pence a day a slave; which serves to subsist them, like our criminals, on bread and water: so that to save charges, we send them on board our ships with the very first opportunity, before which their masters strip them of all they have on their backs; so that they come to us stark-naked, as well women as men: in which condition they are obliged to continue, if the master of the ship is not so charitable (which he commonly is) as to bestow something on them to cover their nakedness.

You would really wonder to see how these slaves live on board; for though their number sometimes amounts to six or seven hundred, yet by the careful management of our masters of ships, they are so [well] regulated, that it seems incredible. And in this particular our nation exceeds all other Europeans; for as the French, Portuguese, and English slave-ships are always foul and stinking; on the contrary, ours are for the most part clean and neat.

The slaves are fed three times a day with indifferent good victuals, and much better than they eat in their own country. Their lodging place is divided into two parts; one of which is appointed for the men, the other for the women, each sex being kept apart. Here they lie as close together as it is possible for them to be crowded.

We are sometimes sufficiently plagued with a parcel of slaves which come from a far inland country, who very innocently persuade one another, that we buy them only to fatten, and afterwards eat them as a delicacy. When we are so unhappy as to be pestered with many of this sort, they resolve and agree together (and bring over the rest of their party) to run away from the ship, kill the Europeans, and set the vessel ashore; by which means they design to free themselves from being our food.

I have twice met with this misfortune; and the first time proved very unlucky to me, I not in the least suspecting it; but the uproar was timely quashed by the master of the ship and myself, by causing the abettor to be shot through the head, after which all was quiet.

But the second time it fell heavier on another ship, and that chiefly by the carelessness of the master, who having fished up the anchor of a departed English ship, had laid it in the hold where the male slaves were lodged, who, unknown to any of the ship's crew, possessed themselves of a hammer, with which, in a short time they broke all their fetters in pieces upon the anchor: After this, they came above deck, and fell upon our men, some of whom they grievously wounded, and would certainly have mastered the ship, if a French and English ship had not very fortunately happened to lie by us; who perceiving by our firing a distressed-gun, that something was in disorder on board, immediately came to our assistance with shallops and men, and drove the slaves under deck: notwithstanding which, before all was appeased, about twenty of them were killed.

The Portuguese have been more unlucky in this particular than we; for in four years time they lost four ships in this manner.

10

OLAUDAH EQUIANO

Enslaved Captive

primary

This selection is part of the autobiography of an enslaved African, Olaudah Equiano. He was born in 1745 in what is today Nigeria, sold to British slavers at the age of eleven, and shipped off to the British West Indies. In 1766 he was able to buy his freedom and became involved in the antislavery movement in England. What was slavery in Africa like, and how did it differ from slavery in the Americas? For

---

"Olaudah Equiano of the Niger Ibo," ed. G. I. Jones, in *Africa Remembered,* ed. Philip D. Curtin (Madison: University of Wisconsin Press, 1967), 60–98.

those, like Equiano, who survived, what were the worst aspects of the Atlantic slave trade? What do you think of Equiano's criticism of "nominal Christians"?

Thinking Historically

Compare Equiano's attitude toward slavery with one of the other authors' in this chapter. Is Equiano opposed to all forms of slavery or only to certain kinds of slavery? How does Equiano's attitude compare with others you have read in this chapter?

I hope the reader will not think I have trespassed on his patience in introducing myself to him with some account of the manners and customs of my country. They had been implanted in me with great care, and made an impression on my mind, which time could not erase, and which all the adversity and variety of fortune I have since experienced served only to rivet and record; for, whether the love of one's country be real or imaginary, or a lesson of reason, or an instinct of nature, I still look back with pleasure on the first scenes of my life, though that pleasure has been for the most part mingled with sorrow.

My father, besides many slaves, had a numerous family, of which seven lived to grow up, including myself and a sister, who was the only daughter. As I was the youngest of the sons, I became, of course, the greatest favourite with my mother, and was always with her; and she used to take particular pains to form my mind. I was trained up from my earliest years in the arts of agriculture and war: My daily exercise was shooting and throwing javelins; and my mother adorned me with emblems, after the manner of our greatest warriors. In this way I grew up till I was turned the age of eleven, when an end was put to my happiness in the following manner: — Generally, when the grown people in the neighbourhood were gone far in the fields to labour, the children assembled together in some of the neighbour's premises to play; and commonly some of us used to get up a tree to look out for any assailant, or kidnapper, that might come upon us; for they sometimes took those opportunities of our parents' absence, to attack and carry off as many as they could seize. One day, as I was watching at the top of a tree in our yard, I saw one of those people come into the yard of our next neighbour but one, to kidnap, there being many stout young people in it. Immediately, on this, I gave the alarm of the rogue, and he was surrounded by the stoutest of them, who entangled him with cords, so that he could not escape till some of the grown people came and secured him. But alas! ere long, it was my fate to be thus attacked, and to be carried off, when none of the grown people were nigh. One day, when all our people were gone out to their works as usual, and only I and my dear sister were left to mind the house, two men and a woman got over our walls, and in a moment seized us both; and, without giving us time to cry out, or make resistance, they stopped our mouths, and ran off with us into the nearest wood. Here they tied our hands, and continued to carry us as far as they could, till night came on, when we reached a small house, where the robbers halted for refreshment, and spent the night. We were then unbound; but were unable to take any food; and, being quite overpowered by fatigue and grief, our only relief was some sleep, which allayed our misfortune for a short time. The next morning we left the house, and continued travelling all the day. For a long time we had kept the woods, but at last we came into a road which I believed I knew. I had now some hopes of being delivered; for we had advanced but a little way before I discovered some people at a distance, on which I began to cry out for their assistance, but my cries had no other effect than to make them tie me faster and stop my mouth, and then they put me into a large sack. They also stopped my sister's mouth, and tied her hands; and in this manner we proceeded till we were out of sight of these people. When we went to rest the following night they offered us some victuals; but we refused them; and the only comfort we had was in being in one another's arms all that night, and bathing each other with our tears. But alas! We were soon deprived of even the smallest comfort of weeping together. The next day proved a day of greater sorrow than I had yet experienced; for my sister and I were then separated, while we lay clasped in each other's arms: it was in vain that we besought them not to part us: she was torn from me, and immediately carried away, while I was left in a state of distraction not to be described. I cried and grieved continually; and for several days did not eat any thing but what they forced into my mouth. At length, after many days travelling, during which I had often changed masters, I got into the hands of a chieftain, in a very pleasant country. This man had two wives and some children, and they all used me extremely well, and did all they could to comfort me; particularly the first wife, who was something like my mother. Although I was a great many days journey from my father's house, yet these people spoke exactly the same language with us. This first master of mine, as I may call him, was a smith; and my principal employment was working his bellows, which were the same kind as I had seen in my vicinity. They were in some respects not unlike the stoves here in gentlemen's kitchens; and were covered over with leather; and in the middle of that leather a stick was fixed, and a person stood up, and worked it, in the same manner as is done to pump water out of a cask with a hand pump. I believe it was gold he worked, for it was of a lovely bright yellow colour, and was worn by the women on their wrists and ankles. . . .

Soon after this my master's only daughter and child by his first wife sickened and died, which affected him so much that for some time he was almost frantic, and really would have killed himself, had he not been watched and prevented. However, in a small time afterwards he recovered; and I was again sold. I was now carried to the left of the sun's rising, through many dreary wastes and dismal woods, amidst the hideous roarings of wild beasts. The people I was sold to used to carry me very often, when I was tired, either on their shoulders or on their backs. I saw many convenient well-built sheds along the roads, at proper distances, to accommodate the merchants and travellers, who lay in those buildings along with their wives, who often accompany them; and they always go well armed.

From the time I left my own nation I always found somebody that understood me till I came to the sea coast. The languages of different nations did not totally differ, nor were they so copious as those of the Europeans, particularly the English. They were therefore easily learned; and, while I was journeying thus through Africa, I acquired two or three different tongues. . . .

I came to a town called Timnah, in the most beautiful country I had yet seen in Africa. It was extremely rich, and there were many rivulets which flowed through it, and supplied a large pond in the centre of the town, where the people washed. Here I first saw and tasted cocoa nuts, which I thought superior to any nuts I had ever tasted before; and the trees, which were loaded, were also interspersed amongst the houses, which had commodious shades adjoining, and were in the same manner as ours, the insides being neatly plastered and white-washed. Here I also saw and tasted for the first time sugar-cane. Their money consisted of little white shells, the size of the fingernail: they were known in this country by the name of core.[1] I was sold here for one hundred and seventy-two of them by a merchant who lived and brought me there. I had been about two or three days at his house, when a wealthy widow, a neighbour of his, came there one evening, and brought with her an only son, a young gentleman about my own age and size. Here they saw me: and, having taken a fancy to me, I was bought of the merchant, and went home with them. Her house and premises were situated close to one of those rivulets I have mentioned, and were the finest I ever saw in Africa: they were very extensive, and she had a number of slaves to attend her. The next day I was washed and perfumed, and when mealtime came, I was led into the presence of my mistress, and ate and drank before her with her son. This filled me

---

[1] Cowrie, a seashell obtained from the Maldive Islands and used as currency in many parts of West Africa. [Ed.]

with astonishment; and I could scarce help expressing my surprise that the young gentleman should suffer me, who was bound, to eat with him who was free; and not only so, but that he would not at any time either eat or drink till I had taken first, because I was the eldest, which was agreeable to our custom. Indeed every thing here, and all their treatment of me, made me forget that I was a slave. The language of these people resembled ours so nearly, that we understood each other perfectly. They had also the very same customs as we. There were likewise slaves daily to attend us, while my young master and I, with other boys, sported with our darts and bows and arrows, as I had been used to do at home. In this resemblance to my former happy state, I passed about two months, and I now began to think I was to be adopted into the family, and was beginning to be reconciled to my situation, and to forget by degrees my misfortunes, when all at once the delusion vanished; for, without the least previous knowledge, one morning early, while my dear master and companion was still asleep, I was awakened out of my reverie to fresh sorrow, and hurried away even amongst the uncircumcised.

Thus, at the very moment I dreamed of the greatest happiness, I found myself most miserable; and it seemed as if fortune wished to give me this taste of joy only to render the reverse more poignant. The change I now experienced was as painful as it was sudden and unexpected. It was a change indeed from a state of bliss to a scene which is inexpressible by me, as it discovered to me an element I had never before beheld, and till then had no idea of, and wherein such instances of hardship and fatigue continually occurred as I can never reflect on but with horror.

The first object which saluted my eyes when I arrived on the coast was the sea, and a slaveship, which was then riding at anchor, and waiting for its cargo. These filled me with astonishment, which was soon converted into terror, which I am yet at a loss to describe, nor the then feelings of my mind. When I was carried on board I was immediately handled, and tossed up, to see if I were sound, by some of the crew; and I was now persuaded that I had got into a world of bad spirits, and that they were going to kill me. Their complexions too differing so much from ours, their long hair, and the language they spoke, which was very different from any I had ever heard, united to confirm me in this belief. Indeed, such were the horrors of my views and fears at the moment, that, if ten thousand worlds had been my own, I would have freely parted with them all to have exchanged my condition with that of the meanest slave in my own country. When I looked round the ship too, and saw a large furnace of copper boiling, and a multitude of black people of every description chained together, every one of their countenances expressing dejection and sorrow, I no longer doubted of my fate; and, quite overpowered with horror and anguish, I fell motionless on the deck and fainted. When I recovered a little, I found some black people about me, who I believed were some of those who brought me on board, and had been receiving their pay; they talked to me in order to cheer me, but all in vain. I asked them if we were not to be eaten by those white men with horrible looks, red faces, and long hair. They told me I was not; and one of the crew brought me a small portion of spirituous liquor in a wine-glass; but, being afraid of him, I would not take it out of his hand. One of the blacks therefore took it from him, and gave it to me, and I took a little down my palate, which, instead of reviving me, as they thought it would, threw me into the greatest consternation at the strange feeling it produced having never tasted any such liquor before. Soon after this, the blacks who brought me on board went off, and left me abandoned to despair. I now saw myself deprived of all chance of returning to my native country, or even the least glimpse of hope of gaining the shore, which I now considered as friendly; and I even wished for my former slavery, in preference to my present situation, which was filled with horrors of every kind, still heightened by my ignorance of what I was to undergo. I was not long suffered to indulge my grief; I was soon put down under the decks, and there I received such a salutation in my nostrils as I had never experienced in my life; so that, with the loathsomeness of the stench, and crying together, I became so sick and low that I was not able to eat, nor had I the least desire to taste any thing. I now wished for the last friend, death, to relieve me; but soon, to my grief, two of the white men offered me eatables; and, on my refusing to eat, one of them held me fast by the hands, and laid me across, I think, the windlass, and tied my feet while the other flogged me severely. I had never experienced any thing of this kind before; and, although not being used to the water, I naturally feared that element the first time I saw it; yet, nevertheless, could I have got over the nettings, I would have jumped over the side; but I could not; and, besides, the crew used to watch us very closely who were not chained down to the decks, lest we should leap into the water: and I have seen some of these poor African prisoners most severely cut for attempting to do so, and hourly whipped for not eating. This indeed was often the case with myself. In a little time after, amongst the poor chained men, I found some of my own nation, which in a small degree gave ease to my mind. I inquired of them what was to be done with us? They gave me to understand we were to be carried to these white people's country to work for them. I then was a little revived, and thought, if it were no worse than working, my situation was not so desperate: but still I feared I should be put to death, the white people looked and acted, as I thought, in so savage a manner; for I had never seen among any people such instances of brutal cruelty; and this not only shown towards us blacks, but also to some of the whites themselves. One white man in particular I saw, when we were permitted to be on deck, flogged[2] so unmercifully with a large rope near the fore-mast, that he died in consequence of it; and they tossed him over the side as they would have done a brute. This made me fear these people the more; and I expected nothing less than to be treated in the same manner. I could not help expressing my fears and apprehensions to some of my countrymen: I asked them if these people had no country, but lived in this hollow place the ship? They told me they did not, but came from a distant one. "Then," said I, "how comes it in all our country we never heard of them?" They told me, because they lived so very far off. I then asked, where were their women? Had they any like themselves? I was told they had. "And why," said I, "do we not see them?" They answered, because they were left behind. I asked how the vessel could go? They told me they could not tell; but that there were cloth put upon the masts by the help of the ropes I saw, and then the vessel went on; and the white men had some spell or magic they put in the water when they liked in order to stop the vessel. I was exceedingly amazed at this account, and really thought they were spirits. I therefore wished much to be from amongst them, for I expected they would sacrifice me: but my wishes were vain; for we were so quartered that it was impossible for any of us to make our escape. While we stayed on the coast I was mostly on deck; and one day, to my great astonishment, I saw one of these vessels coming in with the sails up. As soon as the whites saw it, they gave a great shout, at which we were amazed; and the more so as the vessel appeared larger by approaching nearer. At last she came to an anchor in my sight, and when the anchor was let go, I and my countrymen who saw it were lost in astonishment to observe the vessel stop; and were now convinced it was done by magic. Soon after this the other ship got her boats out, and they came on board of us, and the people of both ships seemed very glad to see each other. Several of the strangers also shook hands with us black people, and made motions with their hands, signifying, I suppose, we were to go to their country; but we did not understand them. At last, when the ship we were in had got in all her cargo, they made ready with many fearful noises, and we were all put under deck, so that we could not see how they managed the vessel. But this disappointment was the least of my sorrow. The stench of the hold while we were on the coast was so intolerably loathsome, that it was dangerous to remain there for any time, and some of us had been permitted to stay on the deck for the fresh air; but now that the whole ship's cargo were confined together, it became absolutely pestilential. The closeness of the place, and the heat of the climate, added to the number in the ship, which was so crowded that

[2] Such brutal floggings were at this time considered essential to the maintenance of discipline in the British navy and on ships engaged in the slave trade. [Ed.]

each had scarcely room to turn himself, almost suffocated us. This produced copious perspirations, so that the air soon became unfit for respiration, from a variety of loathsome smells, and brought on a sickness amongst the slaves, of which many died, thus falling victims to the improvident avarice, as I may call it, of their purchasers. This wretched situation was again aggravated by the galling of the chains, now become insupportable; and the filth of the necessary tubs, into which the children often fell, and were almost suffocated. The shrieks of the women, and the groans of the dying, rendered the whole a scene of horror almost inconceivable. Happily perhaps for myself I was soon reduced so low here that it was thought necessary to keep me almost always on deck; and from my extreme youth I was not put in fetters. In this situation I expected every hour to share the fate of my companions, some of whom were almost daily brought upon deck at the point of death, which I began to hope would soon put an end to my miseries. Often did I think many of the inhabitants of the deep much more happy than myself; I envied them the freedom they enjoyed, and as often wished I could change my condition for theirs. Every circumstance I met with served only to render my state more painful, and heighten my apprehensions and my opinion of the cruelty of the whites. One day they had taken a number of fishes; and when they had killed and satisfied themselves with as many as they thought fit, to our astonishment who were on the deck, rather than give any of them to us to eat, as we expected, they tossed the remaining fish into the sea again, although we begged and prayed for some as well as we could, but in vain; and some of my countrymen, being pressed by hunger, took an opportunity, when they thought no one saw them, of trying to get a little privately; but they were discovered, and the attempt procured them some very severe floggings.

One day, when we had a smooth sea, and moderate wind, two of my wearied countrymen, who were chained together (I was near them at the time), preferring death to such a life of misery, somehow made through the nettings, and jumped into the sea; immediately another quite dejected fellow, who, on account of his illness, was suffered to be out of irons, also followed their example; and I believe many more would very soon have done the same, if they had not been prevented by the ship's crew, who were instantly alarmed. Those of us that were the most active were in a moment put down under the deck; and there was such a noise and confusion amongst the people of the ship as I never heard before, to stop her, and get the boat out to go after the slaves. However, two of the wretches were drowned, but they got the other, and afterwards flogged him unmercifully, for thus attempting to prefer death to slavery. In this manner we continued to undergo more hardships than I can now relate; hardships which are inseparable from this accursed trade. Many a time we were near suffocation, from the want of fresh air, which we were often without for whole days together. This, and the stench of the necessary tubs, carried off many. During our passage I first saw flying fishes, which surprised me very much: They used frequently to fly across the ship, and many of them fell on the deck. I also now first saw the use of the quadrant. I had often with astonishment seen the mariners make observations with it, and I could not think what it meant. They at last took notice of my surprise; and one of them, willing to increase it, as well as to gratify my curiosity, made me one day look through it. The clouds appeared to me to be land, which disappeared as they passed along. This heightened my wonder, and I was now more persuaded than ever that I was in another world, and that every thing about me was magic. At last, we came in sight of the island of Barbadoes, at which the whites on board gave a great shout, and made many signs of joy to us. We did not know what to think of this; but, as the vessel drew nearer, we plainly saw the harbour, and other ships of different kinds and sizes; and we soon anchored amongst them off Bridge Town. Many merchants and planters now come on board, though it was in the evening. They put us in separate parcels, and examined us attentively. They also made us jump, and pointed to the land, signifying we were to go there. We thought by this we should be eaten by these ugly men, as they appeared to us; and when, soon after we were all put down under the deck again, there was much dread and trembling among us, and nothing but bitter cries to be heard all the night from these apprehensions, insomuch that at last the white people got some old slaves from the land to pacify us. They told us we were not to be eaten, but to work, and were soon to go on land where we should see many of our country people. This report eased us much; and sure enough, soon after we landed, there came to us Africans of all languages. We were conducted immediately to the merchant's yard, where we were all pent up together like so many sheep in a fold, without regard to sex or age. As every object was new to me, everything I saw filled me with surprise. What struck me first was, that the houses were built with bricks, in stories, and in every other respect different from those I have seen in Africa; but I was still more astonished on seeing people on horseback. I did not know what this could mean; and indeed I thought these people were full of nothing but magical arts. While I was in this astonishment, one of my fellow prisoners spoke to a countryman of his about the horses, who said they were the same kind they had in their country. I understood them, though they were from a distant part of Africa, and I thought it odd I had not seen any horses there; but afterwards, when I came to converse with different Africans, I found they had many horses amongst them, and much larger than those I then saw. We were not many days in the merchant's custody, before we were sold after their usual manner, which is this: On a signal given (as the beat of a drum), the buyers rush at once into the yard where the slaves are confined, and make choice of that parcel they like best. The noise and clamour with which this is attended, and the eagerness visible in the countenances of the buyers, serve not a little to increase the apprehension of the terrified Africans, who may well be supposed to consider them as the ministers of that destruction to which they think themselves devoted. In this manner, without scruple, are relations and friends separated, most of them never to see each other again. I remember in the vessel in which I was brought over, in the men's apartment, there were several brothers who, in the sale, were sold in different lots; and it was very moving on this occasion to see and hear their cries at parting. O, ye nominal Christians! Might not an African ask you, learned you this from your God? Who says unto you, Do unto all men as you would men should do unto you. Is it not enough that we are torn from our country and friends to toil for your luxury and lust of gain? Must every tender feeling be likewise sacrificed to your avarice? Are the dearest friends and relations, now rendered more dear by their separation from their kindred, still to be parted from each other, and thus preventing from cheering the gloom of slavery with the small comfort of being together, and mingling their sufferings and sorrows? Why are parents to love their children, brothers their sisters, or husbands their wives? Surely this is a new refinement in cruelty, which, while it has no advantage to atone for it, thus aggravates distress, and adds fresh horrors even to the wretchedness of slavery.

REFLECTIONS

This chapter asks you to compare European encounters with Native Americans and Africans. Why did Europeans enslave Africans and not, for the most part, American Indians? Because so many Africans were brought to the Americas to work on plantations, this topic is especially compelling.

Initially, of course, Indians *were* enslaved. Recall the letter of Columbus (selection 3). Part of the reason this enslavement did not continue was the high mortality of Native Americans exposed to smallpox and Old World diseases. In addition, Native Americans who survived the bacterial onslaught had the "local knowledge" and support needed to escape from slavery.

Above and beyond this were the humanitarian objections of Spanish priests like Bartolomeo de Las Casas and the concerns of the Spanish monarchy that slavery would increase the power of the conquistadors at the expense of the crown. In 1542, the enslavement of Indians was outlawed in Spanish dominions of the New World. Clearly, these "New Laws" were not always obeyed by Spaniards in the Americas or by the Portuguese subjects of the unified Spanish-Portuguese crown between 1580 and 1640. Still, the different legal positions of Africans and Indians in the minds of Europeans require further explanation.

Some scholars have suggested that the difference in treatment lies in the differing needs of the main European powers involved in the encounter. The anthropologist Marvin Harris makes the argument this way:

> The most plausible explanation of the New Laws [of 1542] is that they represented the intersection of the interests of three power groups: the Church, the Crown, and the colonists. All three of these interests sought to maximize their respective control over the aboriginal populations. Outright enslavement of the Indians was the method preferred by the colonists. But neither the Crown nor the Church could permit this to happen without surrendering their own vested and potential interests in the greatest resource of the New World — its manpower.

Why then did they permit and even encourage the enslavement of Africans? In this matter all three power groups stood to gain. Africans who remained in Africa were of no use to anybody, since effective military and political domination of that continent by Europeans was not achieved until the middle of the nineteenth century. To make use of African manpower, Africans had to be removed from their homelands. The only way to accomplish this was to buy them as slaves from dealers on the coast. For both the Crown and the Church, it was better to have Africans under the control of the New World colonists than to have to have Africans under the control of nobody but Africans.[1]

What do you think of this argument? Does it work for Portugal as well as for Spain? Does it explain the behavior of the Protestant Dutch or English? Can you offer an alternative explanation?

Finally, let us return to the more global perspective of the first chapter. We have not explored Chinese expansion in the same detail as we did European expansion, but a few comparisons might be possible. First, was slavery unique to European expansion, or was it practiced in the course of Chinese expansion as well? Remember the distinction between China's northern neighbors (Mongols and Manchus) and its trading partners of the Southeast; how did China treat these two regions differently? Was the difference between Chinese treatment of the Mongols and Chinese treatment of the peoples of the Southeast (India, Hormuz, and East Africa) similar to the difference between European treatment of Africans and Native Americans?

---

[1] Marvin Harris, *Patterns of Race in the Americas* (New York: Norton, 1964), 17.

3

Asian Continental Empires
and Maritime States

HISTORICAL CONTEXT
Malacca, China, and
Muslim Empires, 1500–1700

From 1500 to 1700, there were two kinds of states in Asia — large inland empires and maritime states. Most of the Asian landmass was dominated by a few large inland empires: the Chinese, Turkish Ottoman, Persian Safavid, and Indian Mughal. In addition, there were a number of small coastal or island-based maritime states: Hormuz on the Persian Gulf, Calicut on the southwest coast of India, and Malacca on the Malay Peninsula, among others. These maritime states along important trade routes relied on trade more than agriculture for their livelihoods. In Hormuz, saline soil prevented any agriculture at all, but even those states that were self-sufficient agriculturally earned the bulk of their livelihoods from commerce, taxing and reshipping the goods that came through their ports.

In this chapter, we will try to determine how land empires were different from maritime states. Clearly, land empires were much larger in territory, but were there benefits or drawbacks to size?

How did the populations of these two types of states differ? As we might suspect, compared with maritime states, a smaller proportion of the inhabitants of continental empires were fishermen, sailors, shipbuilders, or fish eaters, though all of these could be found to some extent in land-based empires, and many inhabitants of the smallest island states were none of these. Agriculturalists and armies tended to be more influential in landed empires while both were also needed in maritime states, and long-distance merchants, foreigners, and traders were less of a force in inland empires, though they were also much in evidence. Maritime states depended more than continental empires on their merchant fleets and navies, but none were larger

78

than the navy launched by China before 1450 or the Ottoman navy until 1571.

Historians have speculated on some of the consequences of these differences. They have argued, for instance, that because maritime states devoted a greater proportion of their resources to trade and shipping and a lesser proportion to farming, merchants played a greater role there than in landed states; trade goods and money were valued more than land; and such capitalist institutions as banking, joint stock companies, bills of credit, market pricing, and profit planning were developed more fully. Larger territorial states seemed richer than maritime states, but often their wealth came from tribute extracted from an unwilling peasantry and was frequently displayed in extravagant spectacles of power.

How important were such differences in size, occupation, defense, and homogeneity? Were territorial empires more conservative, slower to change? Did their greater size mean greater productivity than that of smaller, more capitalist states? Or were they more centralized, authoritarian, uniform, and inflexible?

In retrospect, we see that the modern world was shaped more by the innovative, capitalist merchant states; the territorial empires were the dinosaurs. But was this "obsolescence" inevitable? How viable, adaptable, and innovative could the territorial empires be?

THINKING HISTORICALLY
Sifting Evidence: Social, Economic, Political, and Cultural

In order to more easily compare entire states and empires, it helps to break them down into their component parts. Historians do this by distinguishing between society, economy, politics, and culture. Of course, none of these "parts" is completely distinct. Rather, they are analytical constructs or divisions that provide us with frames of reference and allow us to categorize a wide range of historical information. (For this chapter, you might find it useful to divide your notebook into sections for social, economic, political, and cultural material.)

For a frame of reference to be helpful, we must understand what the selected categories mean. *Society* would include information on family life, the roles of men and women, and of adults and children. Society also encompasses the community beyond the family: city and country, social class or caste, issues of status and prestige, and social customs regarding such things as marriage, child-rearing, and education. General information about the society is included as well: How many people are there? How dense is the population? Is it increasing or decreasing? What are the standards of health and well-being?

Some social issues are closely related to economics. But when we analyze economics, we think of finances, how people work, make, and spend (receive and distribute) the fruits of their labor; how they save and invest; and whether they are rich or poor, becoming richer or poorer, and to what extent. On a broader scale, we want to know about societal standards of living, the types of jobs people have, local and distant trade, and what products are produced. Though sometimes technology is considered separately, we include it here. What tools do people use? Is it an agrarian or industrial society? Is the society innovative? How does innovation occur?

Politics covers all areas of governance and power. Who makes decisions? With what advice or consultation are decisions made? Is power limited to a particular person, to particular groups of people, or to particular classes of people? Is power tyrannical, democratic, representative, competent, fair, just, efficient? How is power transferred from one leader to another? How knowledgeable are the decision makers? How heavy-handed is the government in its relations with the people?

Culture involves matters of the mind and spirit: art, music, literature, philosophy, religion, ethics, beliefs, goals. It also includes feelings, emotions, dreams, fears, anxieties, and hopes. Culture can be viewed in terms of the individual and in terms of society at large. It includes dance, ritual, custom, law, superstition, methods of learning, and methods of communication.

The overlap between these categories is clear: People can have ideas about anything. Notions of work are both cultural and economic; emotions can be cultural and social; education has cultural and social implications, not to mention its economic and political impact. You get the idea. As you begin recording "data" from each selection, do not concern yourself with overlap. Simply record information in the category that seems most appropriate. Later, you can examine and analyze, compare and contrast, your findings. Note that primary and secondary sources are used in this chapter.

11

SARNIA HAYES HOYT

From *Old Malacca*

We begin this chapter with one of the most important maritime states of the sixteenth century. Malacca was founded in 1402 by a Sumatran prince, Paramesvara, on the Malay Peninsula at one of its closest points to the island of Sumatra. The passage between Sumatra and the Malay Peninsula was the shortest distance between the Spice Islands or southern China and the Indian Ocean routes to Europe, the Middle East, and East Africa. Paramesvara's efforts to establish Malacca as a vital trade port were initially thwarted by Thailand, Chinese pirates, and the kingdom of Majapahit on neighboring Java, all of which enjoyed a percentage of the passing trade. With the help of the great Chinese expeditionary fleet under Admiral Zheng He, which eliminated the pirates and established a special relationship with Paramesvara, Malacca became a preeminent port, fostering trade between the China Sea and the Indian Ocean by 1500. The Portuguese arrived in 1509 and took the port by force.

The secondary source that follows is based in part on the primary account of Ma Huan, an Arabic-speaking Chinese Muslim who sailed with Zheng He. Ma Huan's account of Malacca is preserved in his *Ying-Yai Sheng-Lan,* or *General Account of the Shores of the Ocean.*

In the selection, what signs do you see that the Malacca empire was primarily based on trade? How important were merchants in Malacca?

Thinking Historically

How would you distinguish between political and economic powers in Malacca? Did political or economic leaders have greater social status? How would you describe the culture of Malacca?

... Ma Huan found a city surrounded by a palisade with four gates and watch-towers, and patrolled at night by watchmen ringing bells. Inside the city walls was a second fortress where godowns (warehouses), money, and provisions were kept. A city plan dividing the town into two parts separated by the river had been established, a pat-

Sarnia Hayes Hoyt, *Old Malacca* (Oxford and Kuala Lumpur: Oxford University Press, 1993), 15, 17–19, 21.

tern that endures today. The hill on the south side was maintained as a royal and aristocratic preserve where the sultan, his court, and body-guards lived. Here also was the main mosque.

A bridge spanned the river, connecting the north and south banks with a market-place of twenty pavilions where commodities of all kinds were sold. North of the river lived the merchants, organized into separate ethnic communities — and trading centres — according to country of origin. These heterogeneous communities enjoyed considerable autonomy over their own affairs. Both Kampong Upeh (Tranquerah) and Bandar Hilir began as settlements of the Javanese, who controlled the rice trade. Especially numerous were the Klings (Hindus) and Bengalis from the east coast of India, the Tamils from south India, the Gujaratis (Muslims), the Chinese, and Japanese, but there were also Moors, Arabs, Jews, Filipinos, Burmese, Siamese, and Borneans.

Ma Huan reports that the king and his subjects revered the laws of Islam, observing its fasts and penances. The men got up at dawn and turned their faces toward heaven, invoking the name of Allah. Business deals were sealed with a handshake and a glance at heaven.

The Chinese visitor also took note of local fashions. Most men wore sarongs while the more distinguished wore short silk coats that hid their weapons. "The king wore a white turban of fine local cloth, a long floral robe of fine green calico, and leather shoes. . . ." Ordinary men also covered their heads in a square piece of cloth. Olive-skinned, dark-haired women wore their hair knotted at the back, but the wives of important people were never seen.

Well-to-do merchants were favoured by the trading system which required the stockpiling of a large inventory over several months. Rich traders did not hesitate to show off their wealth — besides offices in town they owned residences staffed with slaves and servants among orchards outside the town wall, and wore "robes of honour" for prestige.

Hwang Chung, author of the *Hai-Yu* ("Words About the Sea"), published in 1537 (quoted in Groeneveldt), commented that people in Malacca were well-mannered: "When people meet each other, they put their hands on each other's heart as a sign of politeness." They enjoyed music, ballads, and poetry. The men cultivated the arts of war, taking pride in their ability with the kris[1]; even a boy of two was allowed to carry a small dagger. People also took offence easily, reacting with fierce tempers, especially when someone put a hand on another's head or shoulder.

Hunting, fishing, and washing tin were important occupations among the lower classes. Malay *orang laut* (sea people) lived along the

---

[1] A dagger used in fighting and ceremony in dance. [Ed.]

sea-shores or river banks. Their houses were built on piles about a metre off the ground, with floors made of split coconut trees fastened with rattan where people spread their mats. They sat, slept, and cooked in the same space.

Tomé Pires, a Portuguese apothecary, accountant, scholar, and diplomat came to Malacca in 1512, just after the Portuguese conquest, stayed for two years, and found 100,000 people speaking eighty-four languages living there. His *Suma Oriental,* intended as a reference for the Portuguese rulers, has been widely quoted even though Pires is biased and his praises sound fulsome. As quoted in Cortesâo, he reported, for example, that Malacca was "a land of such freshness, of such fertility and of such good living . . . for it is certainly one of the outstanding things of the world, with beautiful orchards of trees and shades, many fruits, abundant fresh waters which come from the enchanted hills."

Trade

Malacca was an international market-place, a capital, in Pires' words, "made for merchandise." He wrote that "no trading port as large as Malacca is known, nor any where they deal in such fine and highly prized merchandise. Goods from all over the east are found here; goods from all over the west are sold here." He goes on, "There is no doubt that the affairs of Malacca are of great importance, and of much profit and great honour. It is a land [that] cannot depreciate, on account of its position, but must always grow."

Today, spices are taken for granted, but in medieval Europe curries and peppers were in great demand to preserve and flavour meats, for it was too expensive to feed animals through the long winters. Pepper, for instance, was so scarce and so prized in England in 1607 that a single peppercorn could pay a nominal rent.

Malacca's location made it the most convenient place to receive goods like silk, camphor, and pottery from China, sugar from the Philippines, and cloves, nutmeg, and sandalwood from the Moluccas. April, the busiest trading month, was the time when Chinese traders departed after warehousing their goods in Malacca, leaving behind an agent to sell them to the Indians and Arabs.

These Western traders would soon arrive on the south-west monsoon, bringing with them many kinds of printed cottons, copper weapons, seeds, grains, incense, tapestries, dyes, and opium.

Malacca's trade was complex. Traders had to know where to get the best spices at the best prices, how to get there, and what to barter in exchange for the greatest profits. Wooden ships had to be loaded with a small volume of high-value items, with the bulk of the cargo as ballast, for it would have ruined the richest merchant to lose a ship laden only with luxury goods. Most lucrative was the "blue water trade," collecting and distributing spices, silks, porcelain, and tea destined for Europe through the Middle East and Venice. Thus, Pires was able to write that "whoever is lord of Malacca has his hand on the throat of Venice."

China wanted little from Europe except silver bullion in exchange for its porcelain and silks, but it was still part of the "blue water trade." Certain products from South-East Asia, such as spices, birds' nests, and woods became highly prized.

Malacca also played a key role in the local distributive trade, bringing in goods such as pottery, arrack (liquor), pepper, rice, gold, musk, and tin from regional centres. As the sultanate expanded, Malacca offered goods in both the luxury and bulk trade, goods destined for distant ports as well as for local and regional consumption.

Despite the variety of its goods, Malacca's market-place still had curious anomalies. Gold was so ordinary that children played with it, but garlic and onions were valued, according to Piers, "more than musk, benzoin, and other precious things."

┌─────┐
│ *12* │
└─────┘

JONATHAN SPENCE

The Late Ming Empire

This is a secondary account of the Chinese Empire by a leading modern historian of China. Jonathan Spence provides us with a view of the Ming dynasty (1368–1644) at its height around 1600, but he also helps us understand some of the reasons that it fell to the Manchus from the northeast in 1644.

Remember that Spence is describing the Ming Empire after China's great oceangoing expeditions had ceased in the 1430s. Those expeditions filled Ming treasuries with tribute payments and gifts, and they

Jonathan D. Spence, *The Search for Modern China* (New York: W. W. Norton, 1990), 7–16.

established trading relationships between China and ports as far-flung as East Africa. Do you see any signs here that Chinese trade has declined with the suspension of maritime trade?

How was China different from the rest of the world in 1600? How was it different from Malacca, as described in the previous selection?

Thinking Historically

As you read this selection, take notes under the four categories: social, economic, political, and cultural. This process will help you get a feel for what the different categories mean. Notice how Spence discusses each of these aspects separately, and how he relates one to the other. Specifically, how does Spence use examples of Chinese culture to illustrate aspects of Chinese society, economics, and politics?

Though Spence begins his survey in 1600 — the height of the Ming dynasty — he is most interested in understanding how Ming China changed and how it declined. What changes does he see in society, economics, politics, and culture? Does Spence argue that the causes of Ming decline were more social, economic, political, or cultural?

In the year A.D. 1600, the empire of China was the largest and most sophisticated of all the unified realms on earth. The extent of its territorial domains was unparalleled at a time when Russia was only just beginning to coalesce as a country, India was fragmented between Mughal and Hindu rulers, and a grim combination of infectious disease and Spanish conquerors had laid low the once great empires of Mexico and Peru. And China's population of some 120 million was far larger than that of all the European countries combined.

There was certainly pomp and stately ritual in capitals from Kyoto to Prague, from Delhi to Paris, but none of these cities could boast of a palace complex like that in Peking, where, nestled behind immense walls, the gleaming yellow roofs and spacious marble courts of the Forbidden City symbolized the majesty of the Chinese emperor. Laid out in a meticulous geometrical order, the grand stairways and mighty doors of each successive palace building and throne hall were precisely aligned with the arches leading out of Peking to the south, speaking to all comers of the connectedness of things personified in this man the Chinese termed the Son of Heaven.

Rulers in Europe, India, Japan, Russia, and the Ottoman Empire were all struggling to develop systematic bureaucracies that would expand their tax base and manage their swelling territories effectively, as well as draw to new royal power centers the resources of agriculture and trade. But China's massive bureaucracy was already firmly in place, harmonized by a millennium of tradition and bonded by an immense body of statutory laws and provisions that, in theory at least, could offer pertinent advice on any problem that might arise in the daily life of China's people.

One segment of this bureaucracy lived in Peking, serving the emperor in an elaborate hierarchy that divided the country's business among six ministries dealing respectively with finance and personnel, rituals and laws, military affairs and public works. Also in Peking were the senior scholars and academicians who advised the emperor on ritual matters, wrote the official histories, and supervised the education of the imperial children. This concourse of official functionaries worked in uneasy proximity with the enormous palace staff who attended to the emperor's more personal needs: the court women and their eunuch watchmen, the imperial children and their nurses, the elite bodyguards, the banquet-hall and kitchen staffs, the grooms, the sweepers, and the water carriers.

The other segment of the Chinese bureaucracy consisted of those assigned to posts in the fifteen major provinces into which China was divided during the Ming dynasty. These posts also were arranged in elaborate hierarchies, running from the provincial governor at the top, down through the prefects in major cities to the magistrates in the countries. Below the magistrates were the police, couriers, militiamen, and tax gatherers who extracted a regular flow of revenue from China's farmers. A group of officials known as censors kept watch over the integrity of the bureaucracy both in Peking and in the provinces.

The towns and cities of China did not, in most cases, display the imposing solidity in stone and brick of the larger urban centers in post-Renaissance Europe. Nor, with the exception of a few famous pagodas, were Chinese skylines pierced by towers as soaring as those of the greatest Christian cathedrals or the minarets of Muslim cities. But this low architectural profile did not signify an absence of wealth or religion. There were many prosperous Buddhist temples in China, just as there were Daoist temples dedicated to the natural forces of the cosmos, ancestral meeting halls, and shrines to Confucius, the founding father of China's ethical system who had lived in the fifth century B.C. A scattering of mosques dotted some eastern cities and the far western areas, where most of China's Muslims lived. There were also some synagogues, where descendants of early Jewish travelers still congregated, and dispersed small groups with hazy memories of the teachings of Nestorian Christianity, which had reached China a millenium earlier. The lesser grandeur of China's city architecture and religious centers represented not any absence of civic pride or disesteem of religion, but rather a political fact: The Chinese state was more effectively centralized than those elsewhere in the world; its religions were more effectively controlled; and the growth of powerful, independent cities was prevented by a watchful government that would not tolerate rival centers of authority.

With hindsight we can see that the Ming dynasty, whose emperors had ruled China since 1368, was past its political peak by the early seventeenth century; yet in the years around 1600, China's cultural life was in an ebullient condition that few, if any, other countries could match. If one points to the figures of exceptional brilliance or insight in late sixteenth-century European society, one will easily find their near equivalents in genius and imagination working away in China at just the same time. There was no Chinese dramatist with quite the range of Shakespeare, but in the 1590s Tang Xianzu was writing plays of thwarted, youthful love, of family drama and social dissonance, that were every bit as rich and complex as *A Midsummer Night's Dream* or *Romeo and Juliet.* And if there was no precise equal to Miguel de Cervantes, whose *Don Quixote* was to become a central work of Western culture, it was in the 1590s that China's most beloved novel of religious quest and picaresque adventure, the *Journey to the West,* was published. This novel's central hero, a mischievous monkey with human traits who accompanies the monk-hero on his action-filled travels to India in search of Buddhist scriptures, has remained a central part of Chinese folk culture to this day. Without pushing further for near parallels, within this same period in China, essayists, philosophers, nature poets, landscape painters, religious theorists, historians, and medical scholars all produced a profusion of significant works, many of which are now regarded as classics of the civilization.

Perhaps in all this outpouring, it is the works of the short-story writers and the popular novelists that make the most important commentary about the vitality of Ming society, for they point to a new readership in the towns, to new levels of literacy, and to a new focus on the details of daily life. In a society that was largely male-dominated, they also indicate a growing audience of literate women. The larger implications of expanding female literacy in China were suggested in the writings of late Ming social theorists, who argued that educating women would enhance the general life of society by bringing improvements in morals, child rearing, and household management.

These many themes run together in another of China's greatest novels, *Golden Lotus,* which was published anonymously in the early 1600s. In this socially elaborate and sexually explicit tale, the central character (who draws his income both from commerce and from his official connections) is analyzed through his relationships with his five consorts, each of whom speaks for a different facet of human nature. In many senses, *Golden Lotus* can be read as allegory, as a moral fable of the way greed and selfishness destroy those with the richest opportunities for happiness; yet it also has a deeply realistic side, and illuminates the tensions and cruelties within elite Chinese family life as few other works have ever done.

Novels, paintings, plays, along with the imperial compendia on court life and bureaucratic practice, all suggest the splendors — for the wealthy — of China in the late Ming. Living mainly in the larger commercial towns rather than out in the countryside, the wealthy were bonded together in elaborate clan or lineage organizations based on family descent through the male line. These lineages often held large amounts of land that provided income for support of their own schools, charity to those fallen on hard times, and the maintenance of ancestral halls in which family members offered sacrifices to the dead. The spacious compounds of the rich, protected by massive gates and high walls, were filled with the products of Chinese artisans, who were sometimes employed in state-directed manufactories but more often grouped in small, guild-controlled workshops. Embroidered silks that brought luster to the female form were always in demand by the rich, along with the exquisite blue and white porcelain that graced the elaborate dinner parties so beloved at the time. Glimmering lacquer, ornamental jade, feathery latticework, delicate ivory, cloisonné, and shining rosewood furniture made the homes of the rich places of beauty. And the elaborately carved brush holders of wood or stone, the luxurious paper, even the ink sticks and the stones on which they were rubbed and mixed with water to produce the best and blackest ink, all combined to make of every scholar's desk a ritual and an aesthetic world before he had even written a word.

Complementing the domestic decor, the food and drink of these wealthier Chinese would be a constant delight: pungent shrimp and bean curd, crisp duck and water chestnuts, sweetmeats, clear teas, smooth alcohol of grain or grape, fresh and preserved fruits and juices — all of these followed in stately sequence at parties during which literature, religion, and poetry were discussed over the courses. After the meal, as wine continued to flow, prize scroll paintings might be produced from the family collection, and new works of art, seeking to capture the essence of some old master, would be created by the skimming brushes of the inebriated guests.

At its upper social and economic levels, this was a highly educated society, held together intellectually by a common group of texts that reached back before the time of Confucius to the early days of the unification of a northern Chinese state in the second millennium B.C. While theorists debated its merits for women, education was rigorous and protracted for the boys of wealthy families, introducing them to the rhythms of classical Chinese around the age of six. They then kept at their studies in school or with private tutors every day, memorizing, translating, drilling until, in their late twenties or early thirties, they might be ready to tackle the state examinations. Success in these examinations, which rose in a hierarchy of difficulty from those held locally to those conducted in the capital of Peking, allegedly under the supervision of the emperor himself, brought access to lucrative bureaucratic office and immense social prestige. Women were barred by law from taking the state examinations; but those of good family often learned to write classical poetry from their parents or brothers, and courtesans in the city pleasure quarters were frequently well trained in poetry and song, skills that heightened their charms in the eyes of their educated male patrons. Since book printing with wooden blocks had been developing in China since the tenth century, the maintenance of extensive private libraries was feasible, and the wide distribution of works of philosophy, poetry, history, and moral exhortation was taken for granted.

Though frowned on by some purists, the dissemination of popular works of entertainment was also accelerating in the late sixteenth century, making for a rich and elaborate cultural mix. City dwellers could call on new images of tamed nature to contrast with their own noise and bustle, and find a sense of order in works of art that interpreted the world for them. The possibilities for this sense of contentment were caught to perfection by the dramatist Tang Xianzu in his play *The Peony Pavilion* of 1598. Tang puts his words into the mouth of a scholar and provincial bureaucrat named Du Bao. One side of Du Bao's happiness comes from the fact that administrative business is running smoothly:

> The mountains are at their loveliest
> and court cases dwindle,
> "The birds I saw off at dawn,
> at dusk I watch return,"
> petals from the vase cover my seal box,
> the curtains hang undisturbed.

This sense of peace and order, in turn, prompts a more direct response to nature, when official duties can be put aside altogether, the literary overlays forgotten, and nature and the simple pleasures enjoyed on their own terms:

> Pink of almond fully open,
> iris blades unsheathed,
> fields of spring warming to season's life.
> Over thatched hut by bamboo fence juts a tavern flag,
> rain clears, and the smoke spirals from kitchen stoves.

It was a fine vision, and for many these were indeed glorious days. As long as the country's borders remained quiet, as long as the bureaucracy worked smoothly, as long as the peasants who did the hard work in the fields and the artisans who made all the beautiful objects remained content with their lot — then perhaps the splendors of the Ming would endure.

Town and Farm

The towns and cities of Ming China, especially in the more heavily populated eastern part of the country, had a bustling and thriving air. Some were busy bureaucratic centers, where the local provincial officials had their offices and carried out their tax gathering and administrative tasks. Others were purely commercial centers, where trade and local markets dictated the patterns of daily life. Most were walled, closed their gates at night, and imposed some form of curfew.

As with towns and cities elsewhere in the world, those in China could be distinguished by their services and their levels of specialization. Local market towns, for instance, were the bases for coffin makers, ironworkers, tailors, and noodle makers. Their retail shops offered for sale such semispecial goods as tools, wine, headgear, and religious supplies, including incense, candles, and special paper money to burn at sacrifices. Such market towns also offered winehouses for customers to relax in. Larger market towns, which drew on a flow of traders and wealthy purchasers from a wider region, could support cloth-dyeing establishments, shoemakers, iron foundries, firecracker makers, and sellers of bamboo, fine cloth, and teas. Travelers here found bathhouses and inns, and could buy the services of local prostitutes. Rising up the hierarchy to the local cities that coordinated the trade of several regional market towns, there were shops selling expensive stationery, leather goods, ornamental lanterns, altar carvings, flour, and the services of tinsmiths, seal cutters, and lacquer-ware sellers. Here, too, visitors could find pawnshops and local "banks" to handle money exchanges, rent a sedan chair, and visit a comfortably appointed brothel. As the cities grew larger and their clientele richer, one found ever more specialized luxury goods and services, along with the kinds of ambience in which wealth edged — sometimes dramatically, sometimes unobtrusively — into the realms of decadence, snobbery, and exploitation.

At the base of the urban hierarchy, below the market towns, there were the small local townships where the population was too poor and scattered to support many shops and artisans, and where most goods were sold only by traveling peddlers at periodic markets. Such townships housed neither the wealthy nor any government officials; as a result, the simplest of teahouses, or perhaps a roadside stall, or an occasional temple fair would be the sole focus for relaxation. Nevertheless, such smaller townships performed a vast array of important functions, for they served as the bases for news and gossip, matchmaking, simple schooling, local religious festivals, traveling theater groups, tax collection, and the distribution of famine relief in times of emergency.

Just as the towns and cities of Ming China represented a whole spectrum of goods and services, architecture, levels of sophistication, and administrative staffing, making any simple generalization about them risky, so, too, was the countryside apparently endless in its variety. Indeed the distinction between town and country was blurred in China, for suburban areas of intensive farming lay just outside and sometimes even within the city walls, and artisans might work on farms in peak periods, or farmers work temporarily in towns during times of dearth.

It was south of the Huai River, which cuts across China between the Yellow River and the Yangzi, that the country was most prosperous, for here climate and soil combined to make intensive rice cultivation possible. The region was crisscrossed by myriad rivers, canals, and irrigation streams that fed lush market gardens and paddies in which the young rice shoots grew, or flowed into lakes and ponds where fish and ducks were raised. Here the seasonal flooding of the paddy fields returned needed nutrients to the soil. In the regions just south of the Yangzi River, farmers cultivated mulberry trees for the leaves on which silk worms fed, as well as tea bushes and a host of other products that created extra resources and allowed for a richly diversified rural economy. Farther to the south, sugarcane and citrus were added to the basic crops; and in the mountainous southwest, forests of bamboo and valuable hardwood lumber brought in extra revenue. Water transport was fast, easy, and cheap in south China. Its villages boasted strong lineage organizations that helped to bond communities together.

Although there were many prosperous farming villages north of the Huai River, life there was harsher. The cold in winter was extreme, as icy winds blew in from Mongolia, eroding the land, filling the rivers with silt, and swirling fine dust into the eyes and noses of those who could not afford to shelter behind closed doors. The main crops were wheat and millet, grown with much toil on overworked land, which the scattered farming communities painstakingly fertilized with every scrap of human and animal waste they could recycle. Fruit trees such as apple and pear grew well, as did soybeans and cotton; but by the end of the sixteenth century, much of the land was deforested, and the Yellow River was an unpredictable force as its silt-laden waters meandered across the wide plains to the sea. Unhindered by the dikes, paddies, and canals of the South, bandit armies could move men and equipment easily across the northern countryside, while cavalry forces could race ahead and to the flanks, returning to warn the slower foot soldiers of any danger from opposing forces or sorties from garrison towns. Lineage organizations were weaker here, villages more isolated, social life often more fragmented, and the tough-minded owner-cultivator, living not far above subsistence level, more common than either the prosperous landlord or the tenant farmer.

China's rural diversity meant that "landlords" could not be entirely distinguished from "peasants." For every wealthy absentee landlord living in one of the larger towns, for example, there might be scores of smaller-scale local landlords living in the countryside, perhaps renting out some of their land or hiring part-time labor to till it. Similarly, there were millions of peasant proprietors who owned a little more land than they needed for subsistence, and they might farm their own land with the help of some seasonal laborers. Others, owning a little *less* land than they needed for subsistence, might rent an extra fraction of an acre or hire themselves out as casual labor in the busy seasons. And in most peasant homes, there was some form of handicraft industry that connected the rural family to a commercial network.

The social structure was further complicated by the bewildering variety of land-sale agreements and rental contracts used in China. While the state sought extra revenue by levying a tax on each land deal, in return for which it granted an official contract with a red seal, many farmers — not surprisingly — tried to avoid these surcharges by drawing up their own unofficial contracts. The definition of a land sale, furthermore, was profoundly ambiguous. Most land sales were conducted on the general understanding that the seller might at some later date reclaim the land from the buyer at the original purchase price, or that the seller retained "subsurface" rights to the soil while the purchaser could till the land for a specified period. If land rose in price, went out of cultivation, became waterlogged, or was built upon, a maze of legal and financial problems resulted, leading often to family feuds and even to murder.

For centuries, whether in the north or the south, the peasantry of China had shown their ability to work hard and to survive even when sudden natural calamities brought extreme deprivation. In times of drought or flood, there were various forms of mutual aid, loans, or relief grain supplies that could help to tide them and their families over. Perhaps some sort of part-time labor could be secured, as a porter, an irrigation worker, or barge puller. Children could be indentured, on short- or long-term contracts, for domestic service with the rich. Female children could be sold in the cities; and even if they ended up in brothels, at least they were alive and the family freed of an extra mouth to feed. But if, on top of all the other hardships, the whole fabric of law and order within the society began to unravel, then the situation became hopeless indeed. If the market towns closed their gates, if bands of desperate men began to roam the countryside, seizing the few stores that the rural families had laid in against the coming winter's cold, or stealing the last seed grain carefully hoarded for the next spring's planting, then the poor farmers had no choice but to abandon their fields —

whether the land was rented or privately owned — and to swell the armies of the homeless marchers.

In the early 1600s, despite the apparent prosperity of the wealthier elite, there were signs that this dangerous unraveling might be at hand. Without state-sponsored work or relief for their own needy inhabitants, then the very towns that barred their gates to the rural poor might erupt from within. Driven to desperation by high taxes and uncertain labor prospects, thousands of silk weavers in the Yangzi-delta city of Suzhou went on strike in 1601, burnt down houses, and lynched hated local tyrants. That same year, southwest of Suzhou, in the Jiangxi province porcelain-manufacturing city of Jingdezhen, thousands of workers rioted over low wages and the Ming court's demand that they meet heightened production quotas of the exquisite "dragon bowls" made for palace use. One potter threw himself into a blazing kiln and perished to underline his fellows' plight. A score of other cities and towns saw some kind of social and economic protest in the same period.

Instability in the urban world was matched by that in the countryside. There were incidents of rural protest in the late Ming, as in earlier periods, that can be seen as having elements of class struggle inherent in them. These incidents, often accompanied by violence, were of two main kinds: protests by indentured laborers or "bondservants" against their masters in attempts to regain their free status as farmers, and strikes by tenants who refused to pay their landlords what they regarded as unjust rents.

Even if they were not common, there were enough such incidents to offer a serious warning to the wealthier Chinese. In that same play, *The Peony Pavilion*, in which he speaks glowingly of the joys of the official's life, Tan Xianzu gently mocks the rustic yokels of China, putting into deliberately inelegant verse the rough-and-ready labor of their days:

> Slippery mud,
> sloppery thud,
> short rake, long plough, clutch 'em as they slide.
> After rainy night sow rice and hemp,
> when sky clears fetch out the muck,
> then a stink like long-pickled fish
> floats on the breeze.

The verses sounded amusing. But Tang's audience had not yet begun to think through the implications of what might happen when those who labored under such conditions sought to overthrow their masters.

13

GHISLAIN DE BUSBECQ
The Ottoman Empire under Suleiman

Not all territorial states were the same. China's empire was vast and possessed such a long history that it must be viewed as unique. But how unique was China when compared with, say, the Ottoman Empire, the oldest of the three great Muslim territorial empires of the sixteenth and seventeenth centuries?

Far from China in Western Asia, the Ottoman Empire consisted of what is today Turkey, Greece, the Balkans, Syria, Iraq, Georgia, Ukraine, Palestine, Israel, Jordan, and parts of Saudi Arabia and Egypt. Turkish-speaking people from Central Asia invaded what is present-day Turkey in the 1300s, and between 1500 and 1700 the Ottoman Empire spanned from the Middle East to India. In 1453 the Ottoman Turks captured the city of Constantinople, which they renamed Istanbul, the successor to the thousand-year-old Byzantine Empire.

In this selection we use a primary source instead of a secondary one to enter the world of the Ottomans. Ghislain de Busbecq (1522–1590), a European diplomat, traveled to Istanbul in 1555. A Flemish nobleman, he had been sent on a diplomatic mission by the Hapsburg ruler Ferdinand I, Archduke of Austria and King of Hungary and Bohemia (later to become Holy Roman Emperor from 1556 to 1564). At the time, all of Europe — especially the Hapsburg Empire — was threatened by Ottoman expansion. In 1543 most of Ferdinand's Hungary had come under Ottoman domination, and the continual border wars between the Ottoman and Hapsburg Empires were to favor the Turks until as late as 1683. It is not surprising, then, that Busbecq finds much to admire and fear in Ottoman society. As well, he arrived in Istanbul in its heyday, during the reign of Suleiman I (r. 1520–1566), known as "Suleiman the Magnificent" and "Suleiman the Law Giver," one of the great Ottoman sultans.

What similarities do you see between the Ottoman sultan and his court and that of the emperor of China in the previous selection? What, according to Busbecq, are the main differences between the Ottoman system of government and that of European states like his own

The Turkish Letters of Ogier Ghislain de Busbecq, Imperial Ambassador at Constantinople, 1534–1562, trans. Edward S. Foster (Oxford: Clarendon Press, 1927), 58–62, 65–66, 109–14.

Hapsburg Empire? Do you think he exaggerates any of these differences? What advantages does Busbecq see in the Ottoman army? Do you see any disadvantages in the Ottoman army?

This chapter asks you to make comparisons on a number of different levels: continental empires versus maritime states; Ming China versus the Muslim empires; one Muslim empire with another. As you read this and the following two selections, consider how these large Muslim territorial empires are similar and different. Then compare the three Muslim empires with the Chinese empire.

Writing specifically of the great Muslim empires — Ottoman, Persian, and Indian — the historian Marshall Hodgson has classified them as "gunpowder empires" because gunpowder enabled their rulers to level the walls of rebellious cities and to control legions of nomadic cavalry and vast agricultural regions. If cannon and heavy artillery tipped the traditional balance from nomads and tribal federations to imperial industries and trained armies, older states like China and new non-Muslim ones like Russia might also be called gunpowder states. Indeed, the success of the maritime empires of Europe owed much to their ability to mount heavy cannons on wide-beamed ocean-going vessels as well as to employ field cannon in land wars.

The great Muslim empires also have been called "bureaucratic army states" due to the centralized bureaucracy that acted as a military arm and facilitated military rule. The founders of the great Muslim dynasties (that is, Ottoman, Safavid, and Mughal) owed their power to armed tribal leaders who, they feared, might always change allegiances. Thus, they had to find ways to undercut the power of these potentially dangerous rivals. Muslim leaders used the power of the state to confiscate and reward lands to a new military nobility. They also created armies of captured slaves, who, because they were foreign, had no loyalties to other clans or chieftains and provided a protective buffer against well-connected rivals.

The Ottoman Janissaries were such a Muslim "slave army," which explains, at least partially, Busbecq's remark that family, rank, and inheritance had no meaning for them. They were taken from their Christian families and raised as wards of the sultan, to whom they owed their lives and loyalties. Unable to marry or raise their own families (until 1572 when this practice changed), Janissaries were unlikely to develop their own dynastic ties or ambitions, so they were used by the sultan to counter the ambitions of other princes and other Turkish clan and tribal leaders. What evidence do you see here of the Ottoman's reliance on these slave soldiers? On what other soldiers did the empire rely? How effective was each of these armies? What social groups in Ottoman society had more status or prestige than soldiers? What social groups in China had more status or prestige than soldiers?

Thinking Historically

Organize Busbecq's description under the categories of economics, society, politics, and culture. Notice again how these categories overlap. What aspect of social organization does Busbecq think is the strength of Ottoman political power?

When Busbecq discusses the Ottoman army campaigns against Persia, he praises certain aspects of the Turkish force. What are these aspects, and would you term them social, economic, political, or cultural? What, according to Busbecq, is the source of Ottoman political strength? Is it social, economic, or cultural?

On reaching Amasya we were taken to pay our respects to Achmet, the Chief Vizier, and the other Pashas (for the Sultan himself was away), and we opened negotiations with them in accordance with the [King Ferdinand's] injunctions. The Pashas, anxious not to appear at this early stage prejudiced against our cause, displayed no opposition but postponed the matter until their master could express his wishes. On his return we were introduced into his presence; but neither in his attitude nor in his manner did he appear very well disposed to our address, or the arguments, which we used, or the instructions which we brought.

The Sultan was seated on a rather low sofa, not more than a foot from the ground and spread with many costly coverlets and cushions embroidered with exquisite work. Near him were his bow and arrows. His expression, as I have said, is anything but smiling, and has a sternness which, though sad, is full of majesty. On our arrival we were introduced into his presence by his chamberlains, who held our arms — a practice which has always been observed since a Croatian sought an interview and murdered the Sultan Amurath [Murad II] in revenge for the slaughter of his master, Marcus the Despot of Serbia. After going through the pretence of kissing his hand, we were led to the wall facing him backwards, so as not to turn our backs or any part of them towards him. He then listened to the recital of my message, but, as it did not correspond with his expectations (for the demands of my imperial master were full of dignity and independence, and, therefore, far from acceptable to one who thought that his slightest wishes ought to be obeyed), he assumed an expression of disdain, and merely answered "Giusel, Giusel," that is, "Well, Well." We were then dismissed to our lodging.

The Sultan's head-quarters were crowded by numerous attendants, including many high officials. All the cavalry of the guard were there . . . , and a large number of Janissaries. In all that great assembly no single man owed his dignity to anything but his personal merits and bravery; no one is distinguished from the rest by his birth, and honour is paid to each man according to the nature of the duty and offices which he discharges. Thus there is no struggle for precedence, every man having his place assigned to him in virtue of the function which he performs. The Sultan himself assigns to all their duties and offices, and in doing so pays no attention to wealth or the empty claims of rank, and takes no account of any influence or popularity which a candidate may possess; he only considers merit and scrutinizes the character, natural ability, and disposition of each. Thus each man is rewarded according to his deserts, and offices are filled by men capable of performing them. In Turkey every man has it in his power to make what he will of the position into which he is born and of his fortune in life. Those who hold the highest posts under the Sultan are very often the sons of shepherds and herdsmen, and, so far from being ashamed of their birth, they make it a subject of boasting, and the less they owe to their forefathers and to the accident of birth, the greater is the pride which they feel. They do not consider that good qualities can be conferred by birth or handed down by inheritance, but regard them partly as the gift of heaven and partly as the product of good training and constant toil and zeal. Just as they consider that an aptitude for the arts, such as music or mathematics or geometry, is not transmitted to a son and heir, so they hold that character is not hereditary, and that a son does not necessarily resemble his father, but his qualities are divinely infused into his bodily frame. Thus, among the Turks, dignities, offices, and administrative posts are the rewards of ability and merit; those who were dishonest, lazy, and slothful never attain to distinction, but remain in obscurity and contempt. This is why the Turks succeed in all that they attempt and are a dominating race and daily extend the bounds of their rule. Our method is very different; there is no room for merit, but everything depends on birth; considerations of which alone open the way to high official position. On this subject I shall perhaps say more in another place, and you must regard these remarks as intended for your ears only.

Now come with me and cast your eye over the immense crowd of turbaned heads, wrapped in countless folds of the whitest silk, and bright raiment of every kind and hue, and everywhere the brilliance of gold, silver, purple, silk, and satin. A detailed description would be a lengthy task, and no mere words could give an adequate idea of the novelty of the sight. A more beautiful spectacle was never presented to my gaze. Yet amid all this luxury there was a great simplicity and economy. The dress of all has the same form whatever the wearer's rank; and no edgings or useless trimmings are sewn on, as is the custom with us, costing a large sum of money and worn out in three days. Their most beautiful garments of silk or satin, even if they are embroidered, as they usually are, cost only a ducat to make. . . .

The Sultan, when he sets out on a campaign, takes as many as 40,000 camels with him, and almost as many baggage-mules, most of whom, if his destination is Persia, are loaded with cereals of every kind, especially rice. Mules and camels are also employed to carry tents and arms and warlike machines and implements of every kind. The territories called Persia which are ruled by the Sophi,[1] as we call him (the Turkish name being Kizilbash), are much less fertile than our country; and, further, it is the custom of the inhabitants, when their land is invaded, to lay waste and burn everything, and so force the enemy to retire through lack of food. The latter, therefore, are faced with serious peril, unless they bring an abundance of food with them. They are careful, however, to avoid touching the supplies which they carry with them as long as they are marching against their foes, but reserve them, as far as possible, for their return journey, when the moment for retirement comes and they are forced to retrace their steps through regions which the enemy has laid waste, or which the immense multitude of men and baggage animals has, as it were, scraped bare, like a swarm of locusts. It is only then that the Sultan's store of provisions is opened, and just enough food to sustain life is weighed out each day to the Janissaries and the other troops in attendance upon him. The other soldiers are badly off, if they have not provided food for their own use; most of them, having often experienced such difficulties during their campaigns — and this is particularly true of the cavalry — take a horse on a leading-rein loaded with many of the necessities of life.[2] These include a small piece of canvas to use as a tent, which may protect them from the sun or a shower of rain, also some clothing and bedding and a private store of provisions, consisting of a leather sack or two of the finest flour, a small jar of butter, and some spices and salt; on these they support life when they are reduced to the extremes of hunger. They take a few spoonfuls of flour and place them in water, adding a little butter, and then flavour the mixture with salt and spices. This, when it is put on the fire, boils and swells up so as to fill a large bowl. They eat of it once or twice a day, according to the quantity, without any bread, unless they have with them some toasted bread or biscuit. They thus contrive to live on short rations for a month or even longer, if necessary. Some soldiers take with them a little sack full of beef dried and reduced to a powder, which they employ in the same manner as the

---

[1] That is, Sûfî, Ismâ'îl II, Safavid Shâh. The Turks called the Safavids Kizilbash (red-headed or hatted) because of their distinctive red headgear. [Ed.]

[2] This refers to those irregular "feudal" troops called up during a general mobilization and responsible for their own supplies. [Ed.]

flour, and which is of great benefit as a more solid form of nourishment. Sometimes, too, they have recourse to horseflesh; for in a great army a large number of horses necessarily dies, and any that die in good condition furnish a welcome meal to men who are starving. I may add that men whose horses have died, when the Sultan moves his camp, stand in a long row on the road by which he is to pass with their harness or saddles on their heads, as a sign that they have lost their horses, and implore his help to purchase others. The Sultan then assists them with whatever gift he thinks fit.

All this will show you with what patience, sobriety, and economy the Turks struggle against the difficulties which beset them, and wait for better times. How different are our soldiers, who on campaign despise ordinary food and expect dainty dishes (such as thrushes and beccaficoes) and elaborate meals. If these are not supplied, they mutiny and cause their own ruin; and even if they are supplied, they ruin themselves just the same. For each man is his own worst enemy and has no more deadly foe than his own intemperance, which kills him if the enemy is slow to do so. I tremble when I think of what the future must bring when I compare the Turkish system with our own; one army must prevail and the other be destroyed, for certainly both cannot remain unscathed. On their side are the resources of a mighty empire, strength unimpaired, experience and practice in fighting, a veteran soldiery, habituation to victory, endurance of toil, unity, order, discipline, frugality, and watchfulness. On our side is public poverty, private luxury, impaired strength, broken spirit, lack of endurance and training; the soldiers are insubordinate, the officers avaricious; there is contempt for discipline; licence, recklessness, drunkenness, and debauchery are rife; and, worst of all, the enemy is accustomed to victory, and we to defeat. Can we doubt what the result will be? Persia alone interposes in our favour; for the enemy, as he hastens to attack, must keep an eye on this menace in his rear. But Persia is only delaying our fate; it cannot save us. When the Turks have settled with Persia, they will fly at our throats supported by the might of the whole East; how unprepared we are I dare not say!

But to return to the point from which I digressed. I mentioned that baggage animals are employed on campaign to carry the arms and tents, which mainly belong to the Janissaires. The Turks take the utmost care to keep their soldiers in good health and protected from the inclemency of the weather; against the foe they must protect themselves, but their health is a matter for which the State must provide. Hence one sees the Turk better clothed than armed. He is particularly afraid of the cold, against which, even in the summer, he guards himself by wearing three garments, of which the innermost — call it shirt or what you will — is woven of coarse thread and provides much warmth. As a further protection against cold and rain tents are always carried, in which each man is given just enough space to lie down, so that one tent holds twenty-five or thirty Janissaries. The material for the garments to which I have referred is provided at the public expense. To prevent any disputes or suspicion of favour, it is distributed in the following manner. The soldiers are summoned by companies in the darkness to a place chosen for the purpose — the balloting station or whatever name you like to give it — where are laid out ready as many portions of cloth as there are soldiers in the company; they enter and take whatever chance offers them in the darkness, and they can only ascribe it to chance whether they get a good or a bad piece of cloth. For the same reason their pay is not counted out to them but weighed, so that no one can complain that he has received light or chipped coins. Also their pay is given them not on the day on which it falls due but on the day previous.

The armour which is carried is chiefly for the use of the household cavalry, for the Janissaries are lightly armed and do not usually fight at close quarters, but use muskets. When the enemy is at hand and a battle is expected, the armour is brought out, but it consists mostly of old pieces picked up in various battlefields, the spoil of former victories. These are distributed to the household cavalry, who are otherwise protected by only a light shield. You can imagine how badly the armour, thus hurriedly given out, fits its wearers. One man's breastplate is too small, another's helmet is too large, another's coat of mail is too heavy for him to bear. There is something wrong everywhere; but they bear it with equanimity and think that only a coward finds fault with his arms, and vow to distinguish themselves in the fight, whatever their equipment may be; such is the confidence inspired by repeated victories and constant experience of warfare. Hence also they do not hesitate to re-enlist a veteran infantryman in the cavalry, though he has never fought on horseback, since they are convinced that one who has warlike experience and long service will acquit himself well in any kind of fighting. . . .

14

JOHN CHARDIN

From *Travels in Persia, 1673–1677*

John Chardin (1643–1713) was born into a wealthy Protestant family in Paris and was a jeweler like his father, but unlike his father he used his business to travel and learn about the world. In 1666 he traveled through the Ottoman Empire from Istanbul through the Black Sea to Persia, where he remained for eighteen months. After securing an order for jewelry from the ruler Shah Abbas II, who died in the fall of 1666, Chardin observed the succession and coronation of the Shah's son Sulayman (r. 1666–1694) and began his studies of Turkish and Persian language and culture. On his return to Paris, he wrote *The Coronation of Soleiman II*[1] and traveled throughout Europe to secure stones for the commissioned jewelry, now presumably destined for the new shah.

In 1672 Chardin returned to Persia with the finished jewelry and spent the next four years studying Persian culture and literature, "frequenting the most eminent and most Knowing Men of the Nation, the better to inform myself in all things that were Curious and New to us in Europe" and becoming — as he also put it — as fluent in Persian as in French and as knowledgeable of Isfahan, the Persian capital, as he was of Paris, where he was born and bred. After his return to Europe, characteristically by way of southern Africa to extend his travels, Chardin decided to settle in England, as Protestants were increasingly threatened in France. In addition to continuing his studies of Persia and writing an account of his travels from which this selection is taken, Chardin served as court jeweler to King Charles II of England and agent of the East India Company of Holland.

The seventeenth-century English edition of Chardin's *Travels,* excerpted here, was published in two volumes: The first describes Chardin's activities in Persia; the second introduces the reader to various aspects of Persian life: its climate, food, customs, crafts, manufactures, and trade, among others. This selection includes parts from each volume.

The Persian Safavid Empire was somewhat smaller than the Ottoman Empire to the west and the Indian Mughal Empire to the east.

---

[1] Note the variety of spellings. Busbecq used Suleiman; modern scholars use Sulayman or Suleyman. [Ed.]

N. M. Penzer, *Sir John Chardin: Travels in Persia, 1673–1677* (1927; reprint, New York: Dover Publications, 1988), 6–9, 188–89, 192–95, 279–81, 282–83.

It was founded later than the Ottoman, around 1500, about the same time as the Mughal. Its founder and namesake, Ismail Safavi, was a leader of a radical Shia sect of Turkish tribesmen; he was crowned shah by his own decree in 1502. In 1508 he conquered Baghdad and defeated the Uzbeks at Bokhara in Central Asia. The Ottoman army stopped Safavi's efforts at western expansion in 1514, but the two empires remained in an almost perpetual state of war for more than a hundred years. The conflict between Shia and Sunni Muslims was then and remains one of the great rifts in Islam, much like the rift between Protestants and Catholics in the Christian wars of the sixteenth century.

The power of the Safavi state reached its peak under Shah Abbas the Great (r. 1587–1629), who made Isfahan a great garden city and capital. In 1666, when Chardin was first at Isfahan, Persia was prosperous and at peace. Yet with peace may have come the decline of Persian military forces. The story is told that late in the reign of Abbas II, a parade of the dwindling Persian military forces had to be marched past the Shah several times. Abbas II died at the age of thirty-three, possibly of syphilis. Despite his distinctly un-Muslim life of dissipation, he was an effective ruler. His son inherited more of his vices than his leadership skills, however. He took the name Safi II in 1666, but rededicated his reign two years later, after a series of natural disasters, as Sulayman, his title when Chardin returned in 1672. The last years of his rule were more fortunate, owing to an absence of natural disasters and costly military campaigns, but Sulayman lessened the vitality of a dynasty that came to an abrupt end when his son and successor was defeated by an Afghan army in 1722.

Chardin writes in the beginning of this selection of the shah's drunkenness and rage. Persian kings thought themselves above such Muslim laws as the prohibition of alcohol, and they sometimes governed their subjects as if they were the captive slaves of armed conquest. Further, the fear of rivals to the throne lurking in their midst led to cruel punishments of those close to them. Often crown princes were blinded or murdered when the shah suspected they were being groomed by rival tribal chieftains, with the connivance of harem eunuchs. The absolute power of the king could be a source of great accomplishment, but in a weak king it also could herald instability and decline. Who are Chardin's closest associates in Isfahan? Why is he concerned about who will be prime minister?

The second section on the manners and customs of the Persians is Chardin's attempt to describe Persian behavior in general. What aspects of Persian behavior strike him? What do you make of his comparisons of Persian and European customs?

On the subject of the third section, trade, Chardin is more of an expert. After all, he is a merchant himself. What does Chardin think of the similarities and differences in trade practices between Persia and Europe? From these observations, would you judge Persia as more or less mercantile than Europe at the time? How would you compare the importance of trade in Persia with its importance in the Ottoman Empire and in China?

Thinking Historically

Take notes on the reading under four categories: politics, economy, society, and culture. As described by Chardin, what are the leading three or four characteristics of Persian society in each of these categories? Which of these characteristics are also found in Busbecq's description of the Ottoman Empire? Which do you find in Spence's history of Ming China?

I spent the first Day of my coming to *Ispahan,* and all the next, in receiving Visits from the *Europeans* of the Place, from several *Persians* and *Armenians,* with whom I had contracted a Friendship after my first Journey thither, and with whom I consulted about the Conduct and Management of my Affairs. The Court was very much alter'd from what it was the first Time I saw it, and in the greatest Confusion; almost all the Noblemen belonging to the late King were dead, or in Disgrace. Interest, and Favour, were in the Hands of certain young Lords, who had neither Generosity nor Merit. The Prime Minister, nam'd *Cheic Ali can,* had for fourteen Months past been under Disgrace; three of the chief Officers of the Crown discharg'd his Duty: But the worst thing of all for me, was, that they talk'd of restoring his Place to him, and reinstating him in the Royal Favour; for he being on one Hand a great Enemy to the *Christians* and *Europeans,* and on the other, inaccessible, by Recommendations and Presents, and having always made it apparent during the time he was in Office, that he had nothing more at Heart than to inlarge the Treasure of his Master; I had Reason to fear, that he would hinder the King from Purchasing the Jewels, which I brought by the express Command of the late King his Father, and made according to the Patterns which I had receiv'd from his own Hands: This Consideration made me come to a Resolution immediately of notifying my return to the King; my difficulty lay in the Choice of an Introductor to the *Nazir,* who is the great and supreme Intendant over the King's Household, his Wealth, his Affairs, and over all those who are employ'd in them; I mean, who I should pitch upon to give the first Admittance; I was advis'd by some to *Zerguer bachi,* or chief of the Jewellers, and Goldsmiths in *Persia;* others propos'd *Mirza Thaer* to me, the Comptroller General of the King's Household. I had done better to have trusted to the Conduct of the first, as I found afterwards, but because I had known the Comptroller General a long time, I re-solv'd to put my Trust in him.

On the 26th, the Superior of the *Capuchins* took the Trouble of going to visit him in my Behalf. I beg'd of him to tell him, that an Indisposition hinder'd me from coming to pay him my Respects, but that the Goodness he had shewn me six Years before, make me take the Liberty of Addressing my self to him, to be presented to the *Nazir,* or Superintendant, for that I was sure I could not be introduced by a better Hand; that I most humbly intreated him, to represent to that Minister, the Order which I had receiv'd from the late King, to go into my own Country, and get him some rich Works of Jewels made there, and bring them to him my self, which I had accordingly perform'd in such a Manner, that I durst perswade my self it was not possible to do better. To this I added great Promises of Recompence, which I knew was necessary to be done in such Cases. The Answer I had from this Lord was, That I was welcome, that I might depend upon him, and that he would, to the best of his Power, answer the Expectations I had of his good Offices towards me; but that I might assure my self, the King had but little Inclination for Jewels, that the Court was very bare of Money, and that to my great Misfortune, the Prime Minister, who was a Man so averse to those sort of Expences, and so disingag'd from all Interest, was again coming into Favour; that he order'd this to be told me not to discourage me, but to dispose me to sell them cheap, to make a great many Presents, to take a deal of Pains, and have a World of Patience; that as for the rest, he would notify my Arrival to the *Nazir,* in the best Manner he could, and that I should place my Hopes in the Clemency of God. The *Persians* always conclude their Deliberations with these Words, being as much as to say, that God will give Overtures to those Affairs, which Men are in Pain to bring about with Success.

I at the same time receiv'd a Piece of News, which confirm'd those Advices. This was, that the Day before, the King getting Drunk, as it had been his daily Custom almost for some Years, fell into a Rage against a Player on the Lute, who did not play well to his Taste, and commanded *Nesralibec,* his Favourite, Son to the Governour of *Irivan,* to cut his Hands off. The Prince in pronouncing that Sentence, threw himself on a Pile of Cushions to Sleep. The Favourite, who was not so Drunk, and knowing no Crime in the condemn'd Person, thought that the King had found none neither, and that this cruel Order was only a transport of Drunkenness, he therefore contented himself with Reprimanding the Player very severely, in that he did not study to please his Master better; the King wak'd in an Hours time, and seeing the Musician touch the Lute as before, he call'd to Mind the Orders he had given to his Favourite against the Musician, and flying into a great Passion with the young Lord, he commanded the Lord high Steward to cut off the Hands and Feet of them both; the Lord Steward threw himself at the King's Feet, to implore Mercy for the Favourite; the King, in the extream Violence of his Indignation and Fury, cry'd out to his Eunucks and his Guards, to execute his Sentence upon all three; *Cheic-ali-can,* that Grand Vizier who was out of his Post, happen'd to be there, as good Luck would have it, he flung himself at the King's Feet, and embracing them, he beseech'd him to show them Mercy; the King making a little Pause upon it, say'd to him, *thou art very bold to hope, that I should grant what thou desirest of me, I who can't obtain of thee to resume the Charge of Prime Minister. Sir,* reply'd the Suppliant, *I am your Slave, I will ever do what your Majesty shall command me.* The King being hereupon appeas'd, Pardon'd all the condemn'd Persons, and next Morning sent a *Calaat* to *Cheic-ali-can:* By that Name they call the Garments which the King presents great Men to do them Honour; he sent him besides the Garment, a Horse, with a Saddle, and Trappings of Gold, set with Diamonds, A Sword and Ponyard of the same kind, with the Inkhorn, Letters Patents, and other Marks, with denote the Post of the Prime Minister. . . .

Manners and Customs

. . . They walk gravely, make their Prayers and Purgations at set Times, and with the greatest Shew of Devotion; they hold the Wisest and Godliest Conversation possible, discoursing constantly of God's Glory, and of his Greatness, in the Nobelest Terms, and with all the outward Shew of the most fervent Faith. Altho' they be naturally dispos'd to good Nature, Hospitality, Pitty, Contempt of the World, and of its Riches, they affect them nevertheless, that they may appear to be possest of a larger Share of them than they really are. Whoever sees them only passing by, or in a Visit, will always give them the best Character in the World; but he that deals with them; and pries into their Affairs, will find that there is little Honesty in them; and that most of them are *Whited Sepulcres,* according to our Saviours Expression, which I think the more proper here, because the *Persians* study particularly a strict Observation of the Law. That is the Character of the Generality of the *Persians:* But there is without doubt, an Exception to that general Depravation; for among some of the *Persians,* there is as much Justice, Sincerity, Virtue and Piety to be found, as among those who profess the best Religions. But the more one Converses with that Nation, the fewer one finds included in the Exception, the Number of Truly, Honest and Courteous *Persians* being very small. . . .

The *Persians* neither love walking Abroad, nor Travelling. As to that of walking Abroad, they look upon that Custom of ours to be very Absurd; and they look upon the walking in the Alley, as Actions only proper for a Madman. They ask very gravely for what one goes to the End of the Alley, and why one does not stand still, if one has Business to go there. This proceeds no doubt from their living in a Climate that is more even than ours. They are not so Sanguine as we are *Northward,* nor so Fiery. The most Spirituous part of their Blood perspiring more than it does with us, which is the Reason that they are not so subject to the Motions of the Body, which look so like Lightness and Disquietude, and which go often to Extravagence, and even to Madness. They don't know such a Remedy in *Persia,* as that which we call *Exercise;* they are much better sitting or leaning, than walking. The *Women* and the *Eunuchs* generally Speaking, use no Exercise, and are always sitting or lying, without prejudicing the Health: For the Men, they ride on Horseback, but never walk, and their Exercises are only for Pleasure, and not for Health. The climate of each People is always, as I believe, the principal Effect of the Inclinations and Customs of the Men, which are no more different among them, than that of the Temper of the Air is different from one Place to another. As for what relates to travelling, those Journeys that are made out of pure Curiosity, are still more inconceivable to the *Persians,* than walking Abroad. They have no Taste of the Pleasure we enjoy in seeing different Manners from ours, and hearing of a Language which we do not Understand. . . . They ask'd me if it was possible that there should be such People amongst us, who would travel two or three thousand Leagues with so much Danger, and Inconveniency, only to see *how they were made, and what they did in Persia, and upon no other Design.* These people are of Opinion, as I have observ'd, that one cannot better attain to Virtue, nor have a fuller Taste of Pleasure than by resting and dwelling at Home, and that it is not good to Travel, but to acquire Riches. They believe likewise, that every Stranger is a Spy if he be not a Merchant, or a Handicrafts-Man, and the People of Quality look upon it to be a Crime against the State to receive 'em among them, or to Visit them. It is from this Spirit of theirs no doubt, that the *Persians* are so grosly Ignorant of the present State of other Nations of the World, and that they do not so much as understand *Geography,* and have no Maps; which comes from this, that having no Curiosity to see other Countries, they never mind the Distance, nor Roads, by which they might go thither. They have no such thing among 'em as Accounts of Foreign Countries, neither *Gazetts, News A-la-main,* nor *Offices* of *Intelligence.* This would seem very strange to People who pass their time in asking after News, and whose Health and Rest in a Manner, are Interested in it, as well as to those who apply themselves with so much care to the Study of the Maps and other Accounts; but this is however very true; and as I have represented the *Persians,* it is plain, that all that Knowledge is not requisite for the Pleasure and Tranquility of the Mind. The Ministers of

State generally Speaking, know no more what passes in *Europe,* than in the World of the Moon. The greatest Part, even have but a confus'd Idea of *Europe,* which they look upon to be some little Island in the *North* Seas, where there is nothing to be found that is either Good or Handsome; *from whence it comes,* say they, *that the Europeans go all over the World, in search of fine Things, and of those which are Necessary, as being destitute of them.*

Yet notwithstanding what I have been saying, it is certainly true, that there is not that Country in the World, which is less dangerous to travel in from the Security of the Roads, for which they provide with a great deal of Care; neither is it less Expensive any where, by Reason of the great Number of publick Buildings, which they keep for Travellers, in all Parts of the Empire, as well in the Cities, as in the Country. They lodge in those Houses without being put to any Charge; besides which, there are Bridges and Causways, in all the Places where the Roads are too bad, which are made for the Sake of the Caravans, and of all those who travel from a motive of Gain. . . .

Commerce or Trade

Trading is a very honourable Profession in the *East,* as being the best of those that have any Stability, and are not so liable to change. 'Tis not to be wonder'd at, for it cannot be otherwise in Kingdoms, where on the one hand there is no Title of Nobility, and therefore little Authority annexed to the Birth; and where on the other Hand, the form of Government being altogether Despotick and Arbitrary, the Authority annexed to Places and Employments cannot last longer than the Employments themselves, which are likewise precarious; for which Reason Trading is much set by in that part of the World, as a lasting and independent Station. Another Reason why it is valu'd is, because the Noblemen profess it, and the Kings also; they have their Deputies as the Merchants have, and under the same Denomination: They have most of them their Trading Ships, and their Store-Houses. The King of *Persia,* for Instance, sells and sends to the Neighbouring Kingdoms, Silk, Brocades, and other rich Goods, Carpets and Precious Stones. The Name of Merchant, is a Name much respected in the *East,* and is not allowed to Shop-keepers or Dealers in trifling Goods; nor to those who Trade not in foreign Countries: 'Tis allow'd only to such as employ Deputies or Factors in the remotest Countries: And those Men are sometimes rais'd to the highest Ranks, and are usually employed in Embassies. There are Merchants in *Persia* who have Deputies in all parts of the world: And when those Deputies are returned Home, they wait on their Master, under no better Denomination than that of a Servant, standing up always before them, and waiting at Table, tho' some of those Deputies are worth above threescore thousand Crowns. In the *Indies* the Laws are still more favourable to Traders, for tho' they are much more numerous than in *Persia,* they are nevertheless more set by. The Reason of this additional Respect, is, because in the *East,* Traders are Sacred Persons, who are never molested even in time of War; and are allowed a free Passage, they and their Effects, through the middle of Armies: 'Tis upon their account especially that the Roads are so safe all over *Asia,* and especially in *Persia.* The *Persians* call a Trader *Saudaguer, i. e.* Gain-Monger.

The Eastern Merchants affect Grandure in Trading, notwithstanding they send their Deputies into all Parts, and stay at Home themselves, as in the Center of their grand Concern; they make no Bargains themselves directly, there is no publick place of Exchange in their Towns; the Trade is carried on by Stock-jobbers, who are the subtilest, the cunningest, the slyest, the complaisantest, the patientest, and the most intriguing Men of the whole Society, having a valuable and insinuating Tongue beyond Expression: They are called *Delal,* which answers to Great Talkers, that Word being of a contrary Signification to *Lal, i. e.* Dumb. The *Mahometans* have a Proverb alluding to the Name of those Men, viz. That at the last Day, *Delal Lal,* the Stock-jobbers, or Talkers, will be Dumb; intimating that they will have nothing to say for themselves. 'Tis very curious to see them make Bargains: After they have Argued and Discoursed a while before the Seller, and commonly at his own House, they agree with their Fingers about the Price: They take hold of one another's right Hand under a Cloak or Handkerchief, and entertain one another in that manner; the strait Finger stands for Ten, the bent Finger for Five; the Finger end for One; the whole Hand for a Hundred; and the Fist for a Thousand. Thus they denote Pounds, Pence, and Farthings, with a Motion of their Fingers: While they bargain they put on such a grave and steady Countenance, that 'tis impossible to know in the least either what they think or say.

However, the *Mahometans* are not the greatest Traders in *Asia,* tho' they be dispers'd almost in every Part of it; and tho' their Religion bears sway in the larger part of it. Some of them are too Effeminate, and some too severe to apply themselves to Trade, especially foreign Trading. Wherefore in *Turky,* the *Christians* and *Jews* carry on the main foreign Trade: And in *Persia* the *Christians* and *Indian Gentiles.* As to the *Persians* they Trade with their own Countrymen, one Province with another, and most of them Trade with the *Indians.* The *Armenians* manage alone the whole European Trade; the Reason whereof is, because the *Mahometans* cannot strictly observe their Religion among the *Christians,* with relation to the outward Purity it requires of them; for Instance, Their Law forbids them to eat Flesh either Dress'd or Kill'd by a Man of a different Religion, and likewise to drink in the same Cup with such a one; it forbids to call upon God in a Place adorned with Figures; it even forbids in some Cases, the touching Persons of a contrary Opinion, which is a thing almost impossible to keep among the *Christians*. . . .

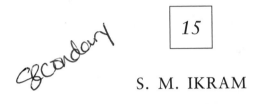

15

S. M. IKRAM

From *Muslim Civilization in India*

The Mughal Empire in India, the third of the great Muslim empires, was the largest, with a population between 100 and 150 million people and an area of 3.2 million square kilometers. Like the other Muslim empires, the Mughal Empire was founded by the descendants of Turkish and Mongol horsemen, and like the others it replaced earlier dynasties that also had come out of the grasslands of Central Asia. Its founder, Babur (r. 1527–1530), a descendant of Timur and Chinghiz Khan, conquered northern India. He and his son, Humayun (r. 1530–1556), espoused the Shia faith (as did Ismail Safavi and his descendants), but Akbar the Great (r. 1556–1605) consolidated Muslim rule of India by adopting the more accommodating Sunni faith of Islam, marrying a Hindu princess, abolishing discriminatory practices against Hindus, and appointing Hindus to government positions. Akbar's son, Jahangir (r. 1605–1627), and his grandson, Shah Jahan (r. 1628–1657), continued his policies of religious toleration and inclusion. These policies were reversed to a certain extent by Aurangzeb (r. 1658–1707).

S. M. Ikram is a scholar of Pakistan, the modern Muslim successor state to the Mughal Empire. In this selection from his survey of Muslim rule in India, Ikram discusses economic and social developments under the Mughals. This account, of course, is a secondary source, but Ikram makes use of primary sources in his study.

In what ways was the Mughal Empire similar to the other Muslim empires? In what ways was it different? In what ways were all three

S. M. Ikram, *Muslim Civilization in India*, ed. Ainslie T. Embree (New York: Columbia University Press, 1964), 223–33.

Muslim states like Ming China? In what ways were they different from a maritime state like Malacca?

Thinking Historically

This selection is about society and economy, but it contributes information about politics and culture as well.

One of the differences between the Mughal Empire and its sister Muslim empires is that the Mughals ruled a large "foreign" population with a different culture. To what extent did these Muslim and Hindu populations have different economies, politics, and societies? Is Mughal history two separate histories? Were its politics and economics separate?

It was the normal policy of the Timurid rulers,[1] both in their original Central Asian homelands and in India, to encourage trade. As in much else, Sher Shah Suri[2] during his brief reign (1538–1545) set a pattern that was followed by the later Mughals, especially Akbar, when he encouraged trade by linking together various parts of the country through an efficient system of roads and abolishing many inland tolls and duties. The Mughals maintained this general policy, but their rule was distinguished by the importance which foreign trade attained by the end of the sixteenth century. . . .

Trade and Industry

Both Akbar and Jahangir interested themselves in the foreign sea-borne trade, and Akbar himself took part in commercial activities for a time. The Mughals welcomed the foreign trader, provided ample protection and security for his transactions, and levied a very low custom duty (usually no more than 2.5 percent ad valorem). Furthermore, the expansion of local handicrafts and industry resulted in a reservoir of exportable goods. Indian exports consisted mainly of manufactured articles, with cotton cloth in great demand in Europe and elsewhere.

---

[1] Descendants of Timur (c. 1336–1405), in the West called Tamerlane (after Timur the Lame). The central Asian ruler of Samarkand, who also threatened India in 1398, was sacked by his troops. Babur and the Mughals were descendants of Timur and claimed Delhi as his descendant. [Ed.]

[2] An Afghan from Bengal, he usurped the Humayan throne and proved to be a forceful ruler. [Ed.]

Indigo, saltpeter, spices, opium, sugar, woolen and silk cloth of various kinds, yarn, asafoetida, salt, beads, borax, turmeric, lac, sealing wax, and drugs of various kinds were also exported. The principal imports were bullion, horses, and a certain quantity of luxury goods for the upper classes, like raw silk, coral, amber, precious stones, superior textiles (silk, velvet, brocade, broadcloth), perfumes, drugs, china goods, and European wines. By and large, however, in return for their goods Indian merchants insisted on payment in gold or silver. Naturally this was not popular in England and the rest of Europe, and writers on economic affairs in the seventeenth century frequently complained, as did Sir Thomas Roe, that "Europe bleedeth to enrich Asia." The demand for articles supplied by India was so great, however, and her requirements of European goods so limited, that Europe was obliged to trade on India's own terms until the eighteenth century, when special measures were taken in England and elsewhere to discourage the demand for Indian goods.

The manufacture of cotton goods had assumed such extensive proportions that in addition to satisfying her own needs India sent cloth to almost half the world: the east coast of Africa, Arabia, Egypt, Southeast Asia, as well as Europe. The textile industry, well established in Akbar's day, continued to flourish under his successors, and soon the operations of Dutch and English traders brought India into direct touch with Western markets. This resulted in great demand for Indian cotton goods from Europe, which naturally increased production at home. Even the silk industry — especially in Bengal — was in flourishing condition. [François] Bernier wrote: "There is in Bengal such a quantity of cotton and silk, that the kingdom may be called the common storehouse for these two kinds of merchandise, not of Hindoustan or the Empire of the Great Mogol only, but of all the neighbouring kingdoms, and even of Europe."

Apart from silk and cotton textiles, other industries were shawl and carpet weaving, woolen goods, pottery, leather goods, and articles made of wood. Owing to its proximity to sources of suitable timbers, Chittagong specialized in shipbuilding, and at one time supplied ships to distant Istanbul. The commercial side of the industry was in the hands of middlemen but the Mughal government, like the earlier sultans, made its own contribution. The emperor controlled a large number of royal workshops, busily turning out articles for his own use, for his household, for the court, and for the imperial army. Akbar took a special interest in the development of indigenous industry. He was directly responsible for expansion of silk weaving at Lahore, Agra, Fathpur-Sikri, and in Gujarat. He opened a large number of factories at important centers, importing master weavers from Persia, Kashmir, and Turkistan. Akbar frequently visited the workshops near the palace to watch the artisans at work, which encouraged the craftsmen and raised their status. It is said that he took such an interest in the industry that to foster demand he "ordered people of certain ranks to wear particular kinds of locally woven coverings . . . an order which resulted in the establishment of a large number of shawl manufactories in Lahore; and inducements were offered to foreign carpet-weavers to settle in Agra, Fathepur-Sikri, and Lahore, and manufacture carpets to compete with those imported from Persia." In course of time, the foreign traders established close contracts with important markets in India and new articles which were more in demand in Western Europe began to be produced in increasing quantities. Among the foreign inventions that excited Akbar's interest was an organ, "one of the wonders of creation," that had been brought from Europe.

Urban Life

All foreign travelers speak of the wealth and prosperity of Mughal cities and large towns. [Father Antonio] Monserrate stated that Lahore in 1581 was "not second to any city in Europe or Asia." Finch, who traveled in the early days of Jahangir, found both Agra and Lahore to be much larger than London, and his testimony is supported by others. Other cities like Surat ("A city of good quantity, with many fair merchants and houses therein"), Ahmadabad, Allahabad, Benares, and Patna similarly excited the admiration of visitors. The new port towns of Bombay, Calcutta, Madras, and Karachi developed under British rule, but they had their predecessors in Satgaon, Surat, Cambay, Lari Bunder, and other ports.

The efficient system of city government under the Mughals encouraged trade. The pivot of urban administration was the kotwal, the city governor. In addition to his executive and judicial powers, it was his duty to prevent and detect crime, to perform many of the functions now assigned to the municipal boards, to regulate prices, and in general, to be responsible for the peace and prosperity of the city. The efficient discharge of these duties depended on the personality of the individual city governor, but the Mughals tried to ensure high standards by making the kotwal personally responsible for the property and the security of the citizens. Akbar had decreed (probably following Sher Shah Suri's example of fixing the responsibility on village chiefs for highway robberies in their territory) that the kotwal was to either recover stolen goods or be held responsible for their loss. That this was not only a pious hope is borne out by the testimony of several foreign travelers who state that the kotwal was personally liable to make good the value of any stolen property which he was unable to recover. The kotawls often found pretexts to evade the ultimate responsibility, but in general they took elaborate measures to prevent thefts.

Most of this flourishing commerce was in the hands of the traditional Hindu merchant classes, whose business acumen was proverbial. Their caste guilds added to the skills in trade and commerce that they had learned through the centuries. Not only were their disputes settled by their *panchayats*,[3] but they would frequently impose pressure on the government by organized action. Foreign visitors record that the governors and kotwals were very sensitive to this, and in spite of hardships inseparable from a despotic system of administration, the business communities had their own means of obtaining redress. Bernier, writing during Aurangzeb's time, declared that the Hindus possessed "almost exclusively the trade and wealth of the country." If Muslims enjoyed advantages in higher administrative posts and in the army, Hindu merchants maintained the monopoly in trade and finance that they had had during the sultanate. A Dutch traveler in the early seventeenth century was struck by the fact that few Muslims engaged in handicraft industries, and that even when a Muslim merchant did have a large business, he employed Hindu bookkeepers and agents. Banking was almost exclusively in Hindu hands. In the years of the decline of the Mughals, a rich Hindu banker would finance his favorite rival claimant for the throne. The role of Jagat Seth of Murshidabad in the history of Bengal is well known. Even the "war of succession" out of which Aurangzeb emerged victorious was financed by a loan of five and a half lakhs of rupees from the Jain bankers of Ahmadabad. Here one sees a contrast with British rule, when the British monopolized not only the higher civil service posts but also controlled most of the major industries as well as the great banks and trading agencies.

Rural Conditions

Conditions in the rural areas during the Mughal period were much the same as at present, with one important difference — the Muslim rulers had scarcely disturbed the old organization of the villages. The *panchayats* continued to settle most disputes, with the state impinging very little on village life, except for the collection of land revenue, and even this was very often done on a village basis rather than through individuals, with the age-old arrangements being preserved. The incidence of land revenue was substantially higher under the Mughals and in Hindu

---

[3] Councils. [Ed.]

states like Vijayanagar than in British India, but the administration was more flexible, both in theory and in practice, in its assessment and collection. Apart from the remission of land revenue when crops failed, there was reduction in government demand even when bumper crops caused prices to fall. For example, between 1585 and 1590 very large sums had to be written off because a series of exceptionally good harvests had resulted in a surplus, and peasants could not sell their crops. The state also advanced loans to the cultivators and occasionally provided seed as well as implements for digging wells. Loans advanced to the cultivators for seeds, implements, bullocks, or digging of wells were called *taqavi* — an expression which has continued in modern land revenue administration.

Health and Medical Facilities

A feature noticed by many foreign travelers was the good health of the local inhabitants. Fryer, writing of the mortality among the English at Bombay and the adjacent parts, says that "the country people lived to a good old age, supposed to be the reward of their temperance." Bernier also speaks of "general habits of sobriety among the people," though this did not apply to a few cases among the upper classes or the royal family. The European travelers found "less vigour among the people than in the colder climates, but greater enjoyment of health." From their accounts, even the climate would appear to have been healthy. "Gout, stone complaints in the kidneys, catarrh . . . are nearly unknown; and persons who arrive in the country afflicted with any of these disorders soon experience a complete cure." The Mughal emphasis on physical fitness and encouragement of out-of-door manly games also raised the general standard of health. The ideal was that everyone was to be trained to be a soldier, a good rider, a keen *shikari,* and able to distinguish himself in games. Ovington found that the English at Surat were "much less vigorous and athletic in their bodies than Indians." It is possible that the drinking habits of the Europeans made them an easy prey to ill-health in the tropics.

Public hospitals had been provided in Muslim India, at least since the days of Firuz Tughluq (1351–1388), and though it would be ridiculous to compare them with the arrangements introduced by the British, the system seems to have been extended during the Mughal period. Jahangir states in his autobiography that on his accession to the throne he ordered the establishment, at government expense, of hospitals in large cities. . . .

REFLECTIONS

The land-based empires of Asia had vigorous systems of trade. Yet in none of these did the economy drive politics, as it did in Malacca. Rather, politics was driven by the emperor and imperial bureaucracy in China and by the military alliances of tribal confederacies in the Muslim empires.

In the Muslim empires, to counter the influence of tribal confederacies, the shahs relied on two special social groups: (1) slaves in central state armies, imperial offices, and as bodyguards, and (2) eunuchs in the harem and palace. Neither of these social groups shared the institutional conservatism of Chinese officialdom. Their value was loyalty and effectiveness rather than tradition and wisdom. In India, the Mughal emperor relied less on slave armies, because he was better able to counterbalance the competing tribal interests of a diverse population that included other central Asian peoples as well as dependent Hindu princes.

The Confucian culture of China demeaned the military. Chinese political centralization had long since curbed the ambitions of internal feudal princes. There were no sources of competing military power within China, only without. When the Mongols conquered China and established the Yuan dynasty (1271–1368), they could not govern with armies from Mongolia. Even though they diminished the role of the Chinese civil service, they had to appoint Chinese and Mongol officials to a vast bureaucracy that had operated for centuries according to its own laws.

As China absorbed its Mongol conquerors, so did India absorb the Mughals. Yet the Mongol Yuan dynasty was overthrown by the nativist Chinese Ming. Perhaps, with an aggressive revival of Hinduism during the Mughal reign of Aurangzeb and without incursions of new foreigners from Europe, India would have encountered a similar fate.

In any case, the political systems of China and the Muslim empires were rooted in the field and pasture; the ruling classes were landed aristocrats and tribal chieftains, not merchants. Although trade, markets, and economic activity were very important in all territorial empires and a number of both Chinese and Indian cities were the largest in the world, merchants did not constitute a separate social class in any of these empires. Chardin reminds us of the role of Europeans like himself and of Armenians in Persia. The Ottomans used Jews and Armenians to build long-distance trading networks. The Mughals used Hindu merchants and manufacturers, and some Indians (especially Gujaratis) traded in Persia and throughout the Indian Ocean. Economic activity was strong throughout Eurasia in the sixteenth and seventeenth century, but as a social class merchants were always subservient to the state. The lords of the land dominated the state.

Tiny Malacca carved out a different political structure as early as the fifteenth century. There were numerous merchant communities in a maritime state that depended on trade to survive, yet the political ruler, the sultan, was not a merchant. (That would come at a later stage in the history of capitalism.) Rather, Malacca owed its existence to the most powerful monarch on earth in the 1430s — the Ming emperor. And it was precisely the smaller, more marginal states like Malacca that were able to free themselves of the kings of the land, from trade as tribute, and from the politics of armies and officials, to create the modern business state. What do these readings suggest about the relationship between political power and economic prosperity?

The Scientific Revolution

HISTORICAL CONTEXT
Europe, America, India, China, and Japan, 1600–1800

Modern life is unthinkable apart from science. We surround ourselves with its products, from cars and computers to telephones and televisions; we are dependent on its institutions — its hospitals, universities and research laboratories; and we have internalized the methods and procedures of science in every aspect of our daily lives, from balancing checkbooks to counting calories. Even on social and humanitarian questions, the scientific method has become almost the exclusive model of knowledge in modern society.

We can trace the scientific focus of modern society to the "scientific revolution" of the seventeenth century. The seventeenth-century scientific revolution was a European phenomenon, with such notables as Copernicus in Poland, Galileo in Tuscany, and Newton in England. But it was also a global event, prompted initially by Europe's new knowledge of Asia, Africa, and the Americas, and ultimately spread as a universal method for understanding and manipulating the world.

What was the scientific revolution? How revolutionary was it? How similar, or different, was European science from that practiced elsewhere in the world? And how much did the European revolution affect scientific traditions elsewhere? These are some of the issues we will study in this chapter.

THINKING HISTORICALLY
Sifting Evidence: "Before" and "After"

This chapter's documents and essays concern intellectual or cultural history because they describe how people think. But it is obvious that scientific ideas, at least when put into practice, have an enormous impact on how people behave. Indeed, the idea of a scientific revolution implies not just a vast change of ideas but also transformation of the material world.

In order to evaluate the extent of the scientific revolution, in this chapter we will try to determine exactly what changed, by how much, and with what impact. Understanding change is a basic goal of historical study — some might say *the* basic goal of historical study. To understand change, then, we must be very precise about describing the "before" and "after."

In this chapter we will study both secondary articles in which a historian argues that a particular set of changes occurred and primary sources that we must critique to determine what is new and what is not. As we progress, we can use each source in conjunction with the others to answer larger questions about the scientific revolution.

$$\boxed{16}$$

FRANKLIN LE VAN BAUMER

The Scientific Revolution in the West

In this selection, an intellectual historian of Europe summarizes the scientific revolution. Without enumerating the achievements of European science in the seventeenth century, Baumer finds evidence of the "revolutionary" nature of the transformation by referring to the popularity of scientific societies and the powerful appeal of the new scientific mentality. How does he define the scientific revolution? How does he date it? Why does he believe that it was a revolution?

Thinking Historically

What intellectual or cultural changes did the scientific revolution bring about, according to Baumer? What ideas did Europeans have about nature before the scientific revolution? Baumer suggests that we can see the scientific revolution in new intellectual institutions, educational reforms, and new careers. What were these changes? Would you call them cultural or social changes?

Franklin Le Van Baumer, "The Scientific Revolution in the West," in *Main Currents of Western Thought*, ed. F. Le Van Baumer (New Haven: Yale University Press, 1978).

What were the causes of the scientific revolution? What political and economic events of the period before the seventeenth century helped to bring it about?

In his book *The Origins of Modern Science* Professor [Herbert] Butterfield of Cambridge writes that the "scientific revolution" of the sixteenth and seventeenth centuries "outshines everything since the rise of Christianity and reduces the Renaissance and Reformation to the rank of mere episodes, mere internal displacements, within the system of medieval Christendom." "It looms so large as the real origin both of the modern world and of the modern mentality that our customary periodisation of European history has become an anachronism and an encumbrance." This view can no longer be seriously questioned. The scientific achievements of the century and a half between the publication of Copernicus's *De Revolutionibus Orbium Celestium* (1543) and Newton's *Principia* (1687) marked the opening of a new period of intellectual and cultural life in the West, which I shall call the Age of Science. What chiefly distinguished this age from its predecessor was that science — meaning by science a body of knowledge, a method, an attitude of mind, a metaphysic (to be described below) — became the directive force of Western civilization, displacing theology and antique letters. Science made the world of the spirit, of Platonic Ideas, seem unreliable and dim by comparison with the material world. In the seventeenth century it drove revealed Christianity out of the physical universe into the region of history and private morals; to an ever growing number of people in the two succeeding centuries it made religion seem outmoded even there. Science invaded the schools, imposed literary canons, altered the world-picture of the philosophers, suggested new techniques to the social theorists. It changed profoundly man's attitude toward custom and tradition, enabling him to declare his independence of the past, to look down condescendingly upon the "ancients," and to envisage a rosy future. The Age of Science made the intoxicating discovery that melioration depends, not upon "change from within" (St. Paul's birth of the new man), but upon "change from without" (scientific and social mechanics).

1

Some people will perhaps object that there was no such thing as "scientific revolution" in the sixteenth and seventeenth centuries. They will say that history does not work that way, that the new science was not "revolutionary," but the cumulative effect of centuries of trial and error among scientists. But if by "scientific revolution" is meant the occasion when science became a real intellectual and cultural force in the West, this objection must surely evaporate. The evidence is rather overwhelming that sometime between 1543 and 1687, certainly by the late seventeenth century, science captured the interest of the intellectuals and upper classes. Francis Bacon's ringing of a bell to call the wits of Europe together to advance scientific learning did not go unheeded. Note the creation of new intellectual institutions to provide a home for science — the *Academia del Cimento* at Florence (1661), the Royal Society at London (1662), the *Académie des Sciences* at Paris (1666), the Berlin Academy (1700), to mention only the most important. These scientific academies signified the advent of science as an organized activity. Note the appearance of a literature of popular science, of which Fontenelle's *Plurality of Worlds* is only one example, and of popular lectures on scientific subjects. Note the movement for educational reform sponsored by Bacon and the Czech John Amos Comenius, who denounced the traditional education for its exclusive emphasis upon "words rather than things" (literature rather than nature itself). Evidently, by the end of the seventeenth century the prejudice against "mechanical" studies as belonging to practical rather than high mental life had all but disappeared. Bacon complained in 1605 that "matters mechanical" were esteemed "a kind of dishonour unto learning to descend to inquiry or meditation upon." But the Royal Society included in its roster a number of ecclesiastics and men of fashion. The second marquis of Worcester maintained a laboratory and published a book of inventions in 1663. Not a few men appear to have been "converted" from an ecclesiastical to a scientific career, and, as Butterfield notes, to have carried the gospel into the byways, with all the zest of the early Christian missionaries.

To account historically for the scientific revolution is no easy task. The problem becomes somewhat more manageable, however, if we exclude from the discussion the specific discoveries of the scientists. Only the internal history of science can explain how Harvey, for example, discovered the circulation of the blood, or Newton the universal law of gravitation.

But certain extrascientific factors were plainly instrumental in causing so many people to be simultaneously interested in "nature," and, moreover, to think about nature in the way they did. Professor [Alfred North] Whitehead reminds us that one of these factors was medieval Christianity itself and medieval scholasticism. Medieval Christianity sponsored the Greek, as opposed to the primitive, idea of a rationally ordered universe which made the orderly investigation of nature seem possible. Scholasticism trained western intellectuals in exact thinking. The Renaissance and the Protestant Reformation also prepared the ground for the scientific revolution — not by design, but as an indirect consequence of their thinking. . . . [H]umanism and Protestantism represented a movement toward the concrete. Erasmus preferred ethics to the metaphysical debates of the philosophers and theologians. The Protestants reduced the miraculous element in institutional Christianity and emphasized labor in a worldly calling. Furthermore, by attacking scholastic theology with which Aristotle was bound up, they made it easier for scientists to think about physics and astronomy in un-Aristotelian terms. As [philosopher] E. A. Burtt has noted of Copernicus, these men lived in a mental climate in which people generally were seeking new centers of reference. Copernicus, the architect of the heliocentric theory of the universe, was a contemporary of Luther and Archbishop Cranmer, who moved the religious center from Rome to Wittenberg and Canterbury. In the sixteenth century the economic center of gravity was similarly shifting from the Mediterranean to the English Channel and the Atlantic Ocean. The revival of ancient philosophies and ancient texts at the Renaissance also sharpened the scientific appetite. The Platonic and Phythagorean revival in fifteenth-century Italy undoubtedly did a good deal to accustom scientists to think of the universe in mathematical, quantitative terms. The translation of Galen and Archimedes worked the last rich vein of ancient science, and made it abundantly clear that the ancients had frequently disagreed on fundamentals, thus necessitating independent investigation. By their enthusiasm for natural beauty, the humanists helped to remove from nature the medieval stigma of sin, and thus to make possible the confident pronouncement of the scientific movement that God's Word could be read not only in the Bible but in the great book of nature.

But no one of these factors, nor all of them together, could have produced the scientific revolution. One is instantly reminded of Bacon's statement that "by the distant voyages and travels which have become frequent in our times, many things in nature have been laid open and discovered which may let in new light upon philosophy." The expansion of Europe, and increased travel in Europe itself, not only stimulated interest in nature but opened up to the West the vision of a "Kingdom of Man" upon earth. Much of Bacon's imagery was borrowed from the geographical discoveries: He aspired to be the Columbus of a new intellectual world, to sail through the Pillars of Hercules (symbol of the old knowledge) into the Atlantic Ocean in search of new and more useful knowledge. Bacon, however, failed to detect the coincidence of the scientific revolution with commercial prosperity and the rise of the middle class. Doubtless, the Marxist Professor Hessen greatly oversimplified when he wrote that "Newton was the typical representative of the rising bourgeoisie, and in his philosophy he embodies the characteristic features of his class." The theoretical scientists had mixed motives. Along with a concern for technology, they pursued truth for its own sake, and they sought God in his great creation. All the same, it is not stretching the imagination too far to see a rough correspondence between the mechanical universe of the seventeenth-century philosophers and the bourgeois desire for rational, predictable order. Science and business were a two-way street. If science affected business, so did business affect science — by its businesslike temper and its quantitative thinking, by its interest in "matter" and the rational control of matter.

2

The scientific revolution gave birth to a new conception of knowledge, a new methodology, and a new worldview substantially different from the old Aristotelian-Christian worldview. . . .

Knowledge now meant exact knowledge: what you know for certain, and not what may possibly or even probably be. Knowledge is what can be clearly apprehended by the mind, or measured by mathematics, or demonstrated by experiment. Galileo came close to saying this when he declared that without mathematics "it is impossible to comprehend a single word of (the great book of the universe);" likewise Descartes when he wrote that "we ought never to allow ourselves to be persuaded of the truth of anything unless on the evidence of our Reason." The distinction between "primary" and "secondary qualities" in seventeenth-century metaphysics carried the same implication. To Galileo, Descartes, and Robert Boyle those mathematical qualities that inhered in objects (size, weight, position, etc.) were "primary," i.e., matters of real knowledge; whereas all the other qualities that our senses tell us are in objects (color, odor, taste, etc.) were "secondary," less real because less amenable to measurement. The inference of all this is plain: Knowledge pertains to "natural philosophy" and possibly social theory, but not to theology or the older philosophy or poetry which involve opinion, belief, faith, but not knowledge. The Royal Society actually undertook to renovate the English language, by excluding from it metaphors and pulpit eloquence which conveyed no precise meaning. The "enthusiasm" of the religious man became suspect as did the "sixth sense" of the poet who could convey pleasure but not knowledge.

The odd thing about the scientific revolution is that for all its avowed distrust of hypotheses and systems, it created its own system of nature, or worldview. "I perceive," says the "Countess" in Fontenelle's popular dialogue of 1686, "Philosophy is now become very Mechanical." "I value (this universe) the more since I know it resembles a Watch, and the whole order of Nature the more plain and easy it is, to me it appears the more admirable." Descartes and other philosophers of science in the seventeenth century constructed a mechanical universe which resembled the machines — watches, pendulum clocks, steam engines — currently being built by scientists and artisans. However, it was not the observation of actual machines but the new astronomy and physics that made it possible to picture the universe in this way. The "Copernican revolution" destroyed Aristotle's "celestial world" of planets and stars which, because they were formed of a subtle substance having no weight, behaved differently from bodies on earth and in the "sublunary world." The new laws of motion formulated by a succession of physicists from Kepler to Newton explained the movement of bodies, both celestial and terrestrial, entirely on mechanical and mathematical principles. According to the law of inertia, the "natural" motion of bodies was in a straight line out into Euclidean space. The planets were pulled into their curvilinear orbits by gravitation which could operate at tremendous distances, and which varied inversely as the square of the distance.

Thus, the universe pictured by Fontenelle's Countess was very different from that of Dante in the thirteenth, or Richard Hooker in the sixteenth century. Gone was the Aristotelian-Christian universe of purposes, forms, and final causes. Gone were the spirits and intelligences which had been required to push the skies daily around the earth. The fundamental features of the new universe were numbers (mathematical quantities) and invariable laws. It was an economical universe in which nature did nothing in vain and performed its daily tasks without waste. In such a universe the scientist could delight and the bourgeois could live happily ever after — or at least up to the time of Darwin. The fact that nature appeared to have no spiritual purpose — Descartes said that it would continue to exist regardless of whether there were any human beings to think it — was more than compensated for by its dependability. Philosophy had indeed become very mechanical. Descartes kept God to start his machine going, and Newton did what he could to save the doctrine of providence. But for all practical purposes, God had become the First Cause, "very well skilled in mechanics and geometry." And the rage for mechanical explanation soon spread beyond the confines of physics to encompass the biological and social sciences. Thus did Descartes regard animals as a piece of clockwork, Robert Boyle the human body as a "matchless engine."

Under the circumstances, one would logically expect there to have been warfare between science and religion in the seventeenth century. But such was not the case. To be sure, some theologians expressed dismay at the downfall of Aristotelianism, and the Roman Church took steps to suppress Copernicanism when Giordano Bruno interpreted it to mean an infinite universe and a plurality of worlds. But the majority of the scientists and popularizers of science were sincerely religious men — not a few were actually ecclesiastics — who either saw no conflict or else went to some lengths to resolve it. Science itself was commonly regarded as a religious enterprise. . . .

In the final analysis, however, the new thing in seventeenth-century thought was the dethronement of theology from its proud position as the sun of the intellectual universe. Bacon and Descartes and Newton lived in an age that was finding it increasingly difficult to reconcile science and religion. To save the best features of both they effected a shaky compromise. For all practical purposes they eliminated religious purpose from nature — thus allowing science to get on with its work, while leaving religion in control of private belief and morals. By their insistence that religious truth itself must pass the tests of reason and reliable evidence, John Locke and the rationalists further reduced theology's prerogatives. Bacon was prepared to believe the word of God "though our reason be shocked at it." But not Locke: "'I believe because it is impossible,' might," he says, "in a good man, pass for a sally of zeal, but would prove a very ill rule for men to choose their opinions or religion by." Good Christian though Locke might be, his teaching had the effect of playing down the supernatural aspects of religion, of equating religion with simple ethics. . . .

17

GALILEO GALILEI

Letter to the Grand Duchess Christina

One reason for thinking of European scientific developments in the seventeenth century as a "revolution" lies in their condemnation by established authority, particularly religious authority. Both Protestants and Catholics condemned the sun-centered model of the universe proposed by Nicolas Copernicus (1473–1543) and modified by Tycho Brahe (1546–1601) and Johannes Kepler (1571–1630). Giordano Bruno, a religious philosopher and Copernican, was burned at the stake in 1600 by the Catholic Church. Galileo (1564–1642) was investigated in 1615 and 1616 for work that gave added weight to Copernicus's theory. His use of the telescope revealed more stars than

Galileo's Letter to the Grand Duchess Christina (1615), in *The Galileo Affair: A Documentary History,* ed. and trans. Maurice A. Finocchiaro (Berkeley and Los Angeles: University of California Press, 1989), 87–90, 114–18.

the fixed number seen by the naked eye or shown on the accepted model of the heavenly spheres of the ancient authority, Ptolemy. Galileo, by assuming that the earth revolved around the sun (and the moon around the earth), conceived orbits that were neater and closer to what had been observed.

This letter to the Grand Duchess Christina in 1615 shows Galileo already under siege. He had received a letter in 1613 from a supporter, Benedetto Castelli, who had been questioned by Christina (of Lorraine), the mother of the Grand Duke of Tuscany, Cosimo II de' Medici, about Galileo's views. Having left his twenty-year post at the University of Padua, Galileo was in 1613 philosopher and mathematician to the Duchy of Tuscany, and so he was in the delicate and precarious position of receiving notice of his employer's dissatisfaction with his views. This letter is his attempt to explain himself and to prevent the initiation of an inquisition. His efforts were unsuccessful. In 1633 Galileo was tried, condemned, forced to recant his views, and placed under house arrest. (The condemnation was retracted by the papacy in 1992.)

What seems to be Grand Duchess Christina's objections? How does Galileo try to answer them? How convincing would you find Galileo if you were the Grand Duchess?

Thinking Historically

What claims to new discoveries did Galileo make in this letter? In what respect did Galileo claim his work was not new? On balance, what did he perceive to be the differences between himself and his contemporaries?

Do you think that Galileo's argument in the concluding section of the letter (on Joshua) was radical for its time? Is his argument "modern" or scientific? Does this letter support Baumer's interpretation of the scientific revolution?

To the Most Serene Ladyship the Grand Duchess Dowager:

As Your Most Serene Highness knows very well, a few years ago I discovered in the heavens many particulars which had been invisible until our time. Because of their novelty, and because of some consequences deriving from them which contradict certain physical propositions[1] commonly accepted in philosophical schools, they roused against me no small number of such professors, as if I had placed these things

---

[1] In *The Starry Messenger* (Venice, 1610) Galileo had described his discovery, through telescopic observation, of lunar mountains, four satellites of Jupiter (which he named "Medicean planets"), the stellar composition of the Milky Way and of nebulas, and the existence of thousands of previously invisible fixed stars. Within a few years, Galileo added to these his observations of sunspots, the phases of Venus, and Saturn's rings.

in heaven with my hands in order to confound nature and the sciences. These people seemed to forget that a multitude of truths contribute to inquiry and to the growth and strength of disciplines rather than to their diminution or destruction, and at the same time they showed greater affection for their own opinions than for the true ones; thus they proceeded to deny and to try to nullify those novelties, about which the senses themselves could have rendered them certain, if they had wanted to look at those novelties carefully. To this end they produced various matters, and they published some writings full of useless discussions and sprinkled with quotations from the Holy Scripture, taken from passages which they do not properly understand and which they inappropriately adduce.[2] This was a very serious error, and they might not have fallen into it had they paid attention to St. Augustine's very useful advice concerning how to proceed with care in reaching definite decisions about matters which are obscure and difficult to understand by means of reason alone. For, speaking also about a particular physical conclusion pertaining to heavenly bodies, he writes this (*On the Literal Interpretation of Genesis,* book 2, at the end): "Now then, always practicing a pious and serious moderation, we ought not to believe anything lightly about an obscure subject, lest we reject (out of love for our error) something which later may be truly shown not to be in any way contrary to the holy books of either the Old or New Testament."

Then it developed that the passage of time disclosed to everyone the truths I had first pointed out, and, along with the truth of the matter, the difference in attitude between those who sincerely and without envy

---

[2] Galileo has been notified that Cardinal Bellarmine finds the Copernican theory heretical because the sun must go around the earth according to Psalm 19:

The heavens declare the glory of God;
. . . .
In them hath he set a tabernacle for the sun,
Which is as a bridegroom coming out of his chamber,
And rejoiceth as a strong man to run a race.
His going forth is from the end of the heaven,
And his circuit unto the ends of it:
And there is nothing hid from the heat thereof. (19:1, 4–6 King James Version)

The Grand Duchess mentioned to Castelli the passage in Joshua 10:12–13 (KJV):

Then spake Joshua to the Lord in the day when the Lord delivered the Amorites before the children of Israel, and he said in the sight of Israel, Sun, stand thou still upon Gibeon; and thou, Moon, in the valley of Ajalon. And the sun stood still, and the moon stayed, until the people had avenged themselves upon their enemies. Is not this written in the book of Jasher? So the sun stood still in the midst of heaven, and hastened not to go down about a whole day.

Thus, the Bible seemed to indicate that the sun revolved around the Earth. [Ed.]

did not accept these discoveries as true and those who added emotional agitation to disbelief. Thus, just as those who were most competent in astronomical and physical science were convinced by my first announcement, so gradually there has been a calming down of all the others whose denials and doubts were not sustained by anything other than the unexpected novelty and the lack of opportunity to see them and to experience them with the senses. However, there are those who are rendered ill-disposed, not so much toward the things as much as toward the author, by the love of their first error and by some interest which they imagine having but which escapes me. Unable to deny them any longer, these people became silent about them; but, embittered more than before by what has mellowed and quieted the others, they divert their thinking to other fictions and try to harm me in other ways. These would not really worry me any more than I was disturbed by the other oppositions, which I always laughed off, certain of the result that the business would have; I should not worry if I did not see that the new calumnies and persecutions are not limited to matters of greater or less theoretical understanding, which are relatively unimportant, but that they go further and try to damage me with stains which I do abhor and must abhor more than death. Nor can I be satisfied that these charges be known as false only by those who know me and them; their falsity must be known to every other person. These people are aware that in my astronomical and philosophical studies, on the question of the constitution of the world's parts, I hold that the sun is located at the center of the revolution of the heavenly orbs and does not change place, and that the earth rotates on itself and moves around it. Moreover, they hear how I confirm this view not only by refuting Ptolemy's and Aristotle's arguments, but also by producing many for the other side, especially some pertaining to physical effects whose causes perhaps cannot be determined in any other way, and other astronomical ones dependent on many features of the new celestial discoveries; these discoveries clearly confute the Ptolemaic system, and they agree admirably with this other position and confirm it. Now, these people are perhaps confounded by the known truth of the other propositions different from the ordinary which I hold, and so they may lack confidence to defend themselves as long as they remain in the philosophical field. Therefore, since they persist in their original self-appointed task of beating down me and my findings by every imaginable means, they have decided to try to shield the fallacies of their arguments with the cloak of simulated religiousness and with the authority of Holy Scripture, unintelligently using the latter for the confutation of arguments they neither understand nor have heard.

At first, they tried on their own to spread among common people the idea that such propositions are against Holy Scripture, and consequently damnable and heretical. Then they realized how by and large human nature is more inclined to join those ventures which result in the oppression of other people (even if unjustly) than those which result in their just improvement, and so it was not difficult for them to find someone who with unusual confidence did preach even from the pulpit that it is damnable and heretical; and this was done with little compassion and with little consideration of the injury not only to this doctrine and its followers, but also to mathematics and all mathematicians. Thus, having acquired more confidence, and with the vain hope that the seed which first took root in their insincere minds would grow into a tree and rise toward the sky, they are spreading among the people the rumor that it will shortly be declared heretical by the supreme authority. They also know that such a declaration not only would uproot these two conclusions, but also would render damnable all the other astronomical and physical observations and propositions which correspond and are necessarily connected with them; hence, they alleviate their task as much as they can by making it look, at least among common people, as if this opinion were new and especially mine, pretending not to know that Nicolaus Copernicus was its author or rather its reformer and confirmer. Now, Copernicus was not only a Catholic but also a clergyman and a canon, and he was so highly regarded that he was called to Rome from the remotest parts of Germany[3] when under Leo X the Lateran Council was discussing the reform of the ecclesiastical calendar; at that time this reform remained unfinished only because there was still no exact knowledge of the precise length of the year and the lunar month. Thus he was charged by the Bishop of Fossombrone,[4] who was then supervising this undertaking, to try by repeated studies and efforts to acquire more understanding and certainty about those celestial motions; and so he undertook this study, and, by truly Herculean labor and by his admirable mind, he made so much progress in this science and acquired such an exact knowledge of the periods of celestial motions that he earned the title of supreme astronomer; then in accordance with his doctrine not only was the calendar regularized,[5] but tables of all planetary motions were constructed. Having expounded this doctrine in six parts, he published it at the request of the Cardinal of Capua[6] and the Bishop of Kulm;[7] and since he had undertaken this task and these labors on orders from the Supreme Pontiff, he dedicated his book *On Heavenly Revolutions* to the successor of the latter, Paul III. Once printed this book was accepted by the Holy Church, and it was

[3] Actually Poland.

[4] Paul of Middelburg (1445–1533).

[5] Though the Copernican system did play a role in the reform of the calendar, the new Gregorian calendar was constructed on the basis of non-Copernican ideas.

[6] Cardinal Nicolaus von Schoenberg (1472–1537), archbishop of Capua.

[7] Tiedemann Giese (1480–1550), Polish friend of Copernicus.

read and studied all over the world without anyone ever having had the least scruple about its doctrine.[8] Finally, now that one is discovering how well founded upon clear observations and necessary demonstrations this doctrine is, some persons come along who, without having even seen the book, give its author the reward of so much work by trying to have him declared a heretic; this they do only in order to satisfy their special animosity, groundlessly conceived against someone else who has no greater connection with Copernicus than the endorsement of his doctrine.

Now, in matters of religion and reputation I have the greatest regard for how common people judge and view me; so, because of the false aspersions my enemies so unjustly try to cast upon me, I have thought it necessary to justify myself by discussing the details of what they produce to detest and abolish this opinion, in short, to declare it not just false but heretical. They always shield themselves with a simulated religious zeal, and they also try to involve Holy Scripture and to make it somehow subservient to their insincere objectives; against the intention of Scripture and the Holy Fathers (if I am not mistaken), they want to extend, not to say abuse, its authority, so that even for purely physical conclusions which are not matters of faith one must totally abandon the senses and demonstrative arguments in favor of any scriptural passage whose apparent words may contain a different indication. . . .

There remains one last thing for us to examine: to what extent it is true that the Joshua passage[9] can be taken without altering the literal meaning of the words and how it can be that, when the sun obeyed Joshua's order to stop, from this it followed that the day was prolonged by a large amount.

Given the heavenly motions in accordance with the Ptolemaic system, this is something which in no way can happen. For the sun's motion along the ecliptic takes place in the order of the signs of the zodiac, which is from west to east; this is contrary to the motion of the Prime Mobile from east to west, which is what causes day and night; therefore, it is clear that if the sun stops its own true motion, the day becomes shorter and not longer and that, on the contrary, the way to prolong it would be to speed up the sun's motion; thus, to make the sun stay for some time at the same place above the horizon, without going down toward the west, it would be necessary to accelerate its motion so as to equal the motion of the Prime Mobile, which would be to accelerate it to about three hundred and sixty times its usual motion. Hence if Joshua had wanted his words taken in their literal and most proper

---

[8] Of course, Galileo had no way of knowing that one Giovanni Maria Tolosani had had quite a few scruples about it.

[9] Joshua 10:12–13. [See footnote 2 (Ed.)]

meaning, he would have told the sun to accelerate its motion by an amount such that, when carried along by the Prime Mobile, it would not be made to set; but his words were being heard by people who perhaps had no other knowledge of heavenly motions except for the greatest and most common one from east to west; thus he adapted himself to their knowledge and spoke in accordance with their understanding because he did not want to teach them about the structure of the spheres but to make them understand the greatness of the miracle of the prolongation of the day.

Perhaps it was this consideration that first led Dionysius the Areopagite (in the Letter to Polycarpus) to say that in this miracle the Prime Mobile stopped and, as a consequence of its stopping, all other celestial spheres stopped. The same opinion is held by St. Augustine himself (in book 2 of *On the Miracles of the Holy Scripture*), and the Bishop of Avila supports it at length (in questions 22 and 24 of his commentary on chapter 10 of Joshua). Indeed one sees that Joshua himself intended to stop the whole system of celestial spheres, from his giving the order also to the moon, even though it has nothing to do with the prolongation of the day; in the injunction given to the moon one must include the orbs of the other planets, which are not mentioned here, as they are not in the rest of the Holy Scripture, since its intention has never been to teach us the astronomical sciences.

I think therefore, if I am not mistaken, that one can clearly see that, given the Ptolemaic system, it is necessary to interpret the words in a way different from their literal meaning. Guided by St. Agustine's very useful prescriptions, I should say that the best nonliteral interpretation is not necessarily this, if anyone can find another which is perhaps better and more suitable. So now I want to examine whether the same miracle could be understood in a way more in accordance with what we read in Joshua, if to the Copernican system we add another discovery which I recently made about the solar body. However, I continue to speak with the same reservations — to the effect that I am not so enamored with my own opinions as to want to place them ahead of others'; nor do I believe it is impossible to put forth interpretations which are better and more in accordance with the Holy Writ.

Let us first assume, in accordance with the opinion of the above-mentioned authors, that in the Joshua miracle the whole system of heavenly motions was stopped, so that the stopping of only one would not introduce unnecessarily universal confusion and great turmoil in the whole order of nature. Second, I think that although the solar body does not move from the same place, it turns on itself, completing an entire rotation in about one month, as I feel I have conclusively demonstrated in my *Sunspot Letters;* this motion is sensibly seen to be inclined southward in the upper part of the globe, and thus to tilt northward in the lower part, precisely in the same manner as the revolutions of all planetary orbs. Third, the sun may be regarded as a noble body, and it is the source of light illuminating not only the moon and the earth but also all the other planets, which are in themselves equally dark; having conclusively demonstrated this, I do not think it would be far from correct philosophizing to say that, insofar as it is the greatest minister of nature and, in a way, the heart and soul of the world, it transmits to the surrounding bodies not only light but also (by turning on itself) motion; thus, just as all motion of an animal's limbs would cease if the motion of its heart were to cease, in the same way if the sun's rotation stopped then all planetary revolutions would also stop. Now, concerning the admirable power and strength of the sun I could quote the supporting statements of many serious writers, but I want to restrict myself to just one passage from the book *The Divine Names* by the Blessed Dionysius the Areopagite. He writes this about the sun: "Light also gathers and attracts to itself all things that are seen, that move, that are illuminated, that are heated, and in a word that are surrounded by its splendor. Thus the sun is called Helios because it collects and gathers all things that are dispersed." And a little below that he again writes about the sun: "If in fact this sun, which we see and which (despite the multitude and dissimilarity of the essences and qualities of observed things) is nevertheless one, spreads its light equally and renews, nourishes, preserves, perfects, divides, joins, warms up, fertilizes, increases, changes, strengthens, produces, moves, and vitalizes all things; and if everything in this universe in accordance with its own power partakes of one and the same sun and contains within itself an equal anticipation of the causes of the many things which are shared; then certainly all the more reason, etc." Therefore, given that the sun is both the source of light and the origin of motion, and given that God wanted the whole world system to remain motionless for several hours as a result of Joshua's order, it was sufficient to stop the sun, and then its immobility stopped all the other turnings, so that the earth as well as the moon and the sun (and all the other planets) remained in the same arrangement; and during that whole time the night did not approach, and the day miraculously got longer. In this manner, by stopping the sun, and without changing or upsetting at all the way the other stars appear or their mutual arrangement, the day on the earth could have been lengthened in perfect accord with the literal meaning of the sacred text.

Furthermore, what deserves special appreciation, if I am not mistaken, is that with the Copernican system one can very clearly and very easily give a literal meaning to another detail which one reads about the same miracle; that is, that the sun stopped in the middle of heaven. Serious theologians have raised a difficulty about this passage: It seems very probable that, when Joshua asked for the prolongation of the day, the sun was close to setting and not at the meridian; for it was then about the time of the summer solstice, and consequently the days were very long, so that if the sun had been at the meridian then it does not seem likely that it would have been necessary to pray for a lengthening of the day in order to win a battle, since the still remaining time of seven hours or more could very well have been sufficient. Motivated by this argument, very serious theologians have held that the sun really was close to setting; this is also what the words "Sun, stand thou still"[10] seem to say, because if it had been at the meridian, then either there would have been no need to seek a miracle or it would have been sufficient to pray merely for some slowing down. This opinion is held by the Bishop of Gaeta,[11] and it is also accepted by Magalhaens, who confirms it by saying that on the same day, before the order to the sun, Joshua had done so many other things that it was impossible to complete them in half a day; thus they really resort to interpreting the words "in the midst of heaven"[12] somewhat implausibly, saying they mean the same as that the sun stopped while it was in our hemisphere, namely above the horizon. We can remove this and every other implausibility, if I am not mistaken, by placing the sun, as the Copernican system does and as it is most necessary to do, in the middle, namely at the center of the heavenly orbs and the planetary revolutions; for at any hour of the day, whether at noon or in the afternoon, the day would have been lengthened and all heavenly turnings stopped by the sun stopping in the middle of the heavens, namely at the center of the heavens, where it is located. . . .

[10] Joshua 10:12 (King James).

[11] Thomas de Vio (1468–1534), author of a commentary on St. Thomas Aquinas's *Summa Theologiae.*

[12] Joshua 10:13.

18

BONNIE S. ANDERSON
AND JUDITH P. ZINSSER

Women and Science

The Grand Duchess Christina slowed but did not block the ultimate acceptance of the Copernican sun-centered solar system. This selection from a history of European women shows how some women, especially the better educated, could participate in the scientific revolution of the seventeenth and eighteenth centuries. But Anderson and Zinsser also demonstrate how much of the scientific revolution endowed male prejudices with false scientific respectability. What factors seem to have enabled women to participate in the scientific revolution? In what ways was the scientific revolution a new bondage for women?

Thinking Historically

What do the authors mean when they say that for women "there was no scientific revolution"? In what ways were women's lives different after the scientific revolution? In what ways were they the same? Were the differences caused by the scientific revolution?

Women Scientists

In the same way that women responded to and participated in Humanism,[1] so they were drawn to the intellectual movement known as the Scientific Revolution. The excitement of the new discoveries of the seventeenth and eighteenth centuries, in particular, inspired a few gifted women scientists to formulate their own theories about the natural world, to perform their own experiments, and to publish their findings. In contrast to those educated strictly and formally according to Humanist precepts, these women had little formal training, and chose for themselves what they read and studied. Rather than encouraging them, their families at best left them to their excitement with the won-

---

[1] A faith in the capacities of humans that reached religious dimensions in the sixteenth century. [Ed.]

Bonnie S. Anderson and Judith P. Zinsser, *A History of Their Own: Women in Europe from Prehistory to the Present*, vol. II (New York: Harper & Row, 1988) 87–89, 96–99.

ders of the "Scientific Revolution"; at worst, parents criticized their daughters' absorption in such inappropriate, inelegant, and unfeminine endeavors.

All across Europe from the sixteenth to the eighteenth centuries these women found fascination in the natural sciences. They corresponded and studied with the male scientists of their day. They observed, and they formulated practical applications from their new knowledge of botany, horticulture, and chemistry. The Countess of Chinchon, wife of the Viceroy to Peru, brought quinine bark to Spain from Latin America because it had cured her malaria. Some noblewomen, like the German Anna of Saxony (1532–1582), found medical uses for the plants they studied. The most gifted of these early naturalists is remembered not as a scientist but as an artist. Maria Sibylla Merian (1647–1717) learned drawing and probably acquired her interest in plants and insects from her stepfather, a Flemish still-life artist. As a little girl she went with him into the fields to collect specimens. Though she married, bore two daughters, and ran a household, between 1679 and her death in 1717 she also managed to complete and have published six collections of engravings of European flowers and insects. These were more than artist's renderings. For example, her study of caterpillars was unique for the day. Unlike the still life done by her contemporaries, the drawings show the insect at every stage of development as observed from the specimens that she collected and nursed to maturity. She explained:

> From my youth I have been interested in insects, first I started with silkworms in my native Frankfurt-am-Main. After that . . . I started to collect all the caterpillars I could find to observe their changes.

Merian's enthusiasm, patience, and skill brought her to the attention of the director of the Amsterdam Botanical Gardens and other male collectors. When her daughter married and moved to the Dutch colony of Surinam, their support was important when she wanted to raise the money for a new scientific project. In 1699, at the age of fifty-two, Maria Sibylla Merian set off on what became a two-year expedition into the interior of South America. She collected, made notations and sketches. Only yellow fever finally forced her to return to Amsterdam in 1701. The resulting book of sixty engravings established her contemporary reputation as a naturalist.

Mathematics, astronomy, and studies of the universe also interested these self-taught women scientists. In 1566 in Paris Marie de Coste Blanche published *The Nature of the Sun and Earth*. Margaret Cavendish (1617–1673), the seventeenth-century Duchess of Newcastle, though haphazard in her approach to science, produced fourteen books on everything from natural history to atomic physics.

Even more exceptional in the eighteenth century was the French noblewoman and courtier, Emilie du Châtelet (1706–1749). She gained admission to the discussions of the foremost mathematicians and scientists of Paris, earned a reputation as a physicist and as an interpreter of the theories of Leibnitz and Newton. Emilie du Châtelet showed unusual intellectual abilities even as a child. By the age of ten she had read Cicero, studied mathematics and metaphysics. At twelve she could speak English, Italian, Spanish, and German and translated Greek and Latin texts like Aristotle and Virgil. Presentation at court and life as a courtier changed none of her scientific interests and hardly modified her studious habits. She seemed to need no sleep, read incredibly fast, and was said to appear in public with ink stains on her fingers from her notetaking and writing. When she took up the study of Descartes, her father complained to her uncle: "I argued with her in vain; she would not understand that no great lord will marry a woman who is seen reading every day." Her mother despaired of a proper future for such a daughter who "flaunts her mind, and frightens away the suitors her other excesses have not driven off." It was her lover and lifelong friend, the Duke de Richelieu, who encouraged her to continue and to formalize her studies by hiring professors in mathematics and physics from the Sorbonne to tutor her. In 1733 she stormed her way into the Café Gradot, the Parisian coffee-house where the scientists, mathematicians, and philosophers regularly met. Barred because she was a woman, she simply had a suit of men's clothes made for herself and reappeared, her long legs now in breeches and hose, to the delight of cheering colleagues and the consternation of the management.

From the early 1730s until the late 1740s her affair with the *philosophe* Voltaire made possible over ten years of study and writing. He paid for the renovation of her husband's country château in Champagne where they established a life filled with their work and time with each other. They had the windows draped so that shifts from day to night would not distract them. They collected a library of ten thousand volumes, more than the number at most universities. He had his duty; she hers.

Emilie du Châtelet usually rose at dawn, breakfasted on fish, bread, stew, and wine, then wrote letters, made the household arrangements for the day, and saw her children. Then she studied. She set up her experiments in the great hall of the château — pipes, rods, and wooden balls hung from the rafters as she set about duplicating the English physicist Newton's experiments. She and Voltaire broke the day with a meal together. Then more study and more writing. When she had trouble staying awake she put her hands in ice water until they were numb, then paced and beat them against her arms to restore the circulation.

Châtelet made her reputation as a scientist with her three-volume work on the German mathematician and philosopher Leibnitz, *The Institutions of Physics,* published in 1740. Contemporaries also knew of her work from her translation of Newton's *Principles of Mathematics,* her book on algebra, and her collaboration with Voltaire on his treatise about Newton.

From the fifteenth to the eighteenth centuries privileged women participated in the new intellectual movements. Like the men of their class, they became humanist scholars, naturalists, and scientists. Unfortunately, many of these women found themselves in conflict with their families and their society. A life devoted to scholarship conflicted with the roles that women, however learned, were still expected to fulfill.

Science Affirms Tradition

In the sixteenth and seventeenth centuries Europe's learned men questioned, altered, and dismissed some of the most hallowed precepts of Europe's inherited wisdom. The intellectual upheaval of the Scientific Revolution caused them to examine and describe anew the nature of the universe and its forces, the nature of the human body and its functions. Men used telescopes and rejected the traditional insistence on the smooth surface of the moon. Galileo, Leibnitz, and Newton studied and charted the movement of the planets, discovered gravity and the true relationship between the earth and the sun. Fallopio dissected the human body, Harvey discovered the circulation of the blood, and Leeuwenhoek found spermatozoa with his microscope.

For women, however, there was no Scientific Revolution. When men studied female anatomy, when they spoke of female physiology, of women's reproductive organs, of the female role in procreation, they ceased to be scientific. They suspended reason and did not accept the evidence of their senses. Tradition, prejudice, and imagination, not scientific observation, governed their conclusions about women. The writings of the classical authors like Aristotle and Galen continued to carry the same authority as they had when first written, long after they had been discarded in other areas. Men spoke in the name of the new "science" but mouthed words and phrases from the old misogyny. In the name of "science" they gave a supposed physiological basis to the traditional views of women's nature, function, and role. Science affirmed what men had always known, what custom, law, and religion had postulated and justified. With the authority of their "objective," "rational" inquiry they restated ancient premises and arrived at the same traditional conclusions: the innate superiority of the male and the justifiable subordination of the female.

In the face of such certainty, the challenges of women like Lucrezia Marinella and María de Zayas had little effect. As Marie de Gournay, the French essayist, had discovered at the beginning of the seventeenth century, those engaged in the scientific study of humanity viewed the female as if she were of a different species — less than human, at best; nature's mistake, fit only to "play the fool and serve [the male]."

The standard medical reference work, *Gynaecea,* reprinted throughout the last decades of the sixteenth century, included the old authorities like Aristotle and Galen, and thus the old premises about women's innate physical inferiority. A seventeenth-century examination for a doctor in Paris asked the rhetorical question "Is woman an imperfect work of nature?" All of the Aristotelian ideals about the different "humors" of the female and male survived in the popular press even after they had been rejected by the medical elite. The colder and moister humors of the female meant that women had a passive nature and thus took longer to develop in the womb. Once grown to maturity, they were better able to withstand the pain of childbirth.

Even without reference to the humors, medical and scientific texts supported the limited domestic role for women. Malebranche, a French seventeenth-century philosopher, noted that the delicate fibers of the woman's brain made her overly sensitive to all that came to it; thus she could not deal with ideas or form abstractions. Her body and mind were so relatively weak that she must stay within the protective confines of the home to be safe.

No amount of anatomical dissection dispelled old bits of misinformation or changed the old misconceptions about women's reproductive organs. Illustrations continued to show the uterus shaped like a flask with two horns, and guides for midwives gave the principal role in labor to the fetus. As in Greek and Roman medical texts these new "scientific" works assumed that women's bodies dictated their principal function, procreation. Yet even this role was devalued. All of the evidence of dissection and deductive reasoning reaffirmed the superiority of the male's role in reproduction. Men discovered the spermatazoon, but not the ovum. They believed that semen was the single active agent. Much as Aristotle had done almost two millennia earlier, seventeenth-century scientific study hypothesized that the female supplied the "matter," while the life and essence of the embryo came from the sperm alone.

These denigrating and erroneous conclusions were reaffirmed by the work of the seventeenth-century English scientist William Harvey. Having discovered the circulation of the blood, Harvey turned his considerable talents to the study of human reproduction and published his conclusions in 1651. He dissected female deer at all stages of their cycle, when pregnant and when not. He studied chickens and roosters. With all of this dissection and all of this observation he hypothesized an explanation for procreation and a rhapsody to male semen far more extreme than anything Aristotle had reasoned. The woman, like the hen with her unfertilized egg, supplies the matter, the man gives it form and life. The semen, he explained, had almost magical power to "elaborate, concoct"; it was "vivifying". . . . endowed with force and spirit and generative influence," coming as it did from "vessels so elaborate, and endowed with such vital energy." So powerful was this fluid that it did not even have to reach the woman's uterus or remain in the vagina. Rather he believed it gave off a "fecundating power," leaving the woman's body to play a passive, or secondary, role. Simple contact with this magical elixir of life worked like lightning, or — drawing on another set of his experiments — "in the same way as iron touched by the magnet is endowed with its powers and can attract other iron to it." The woman was but the receiver and the receptacle.

Anatomy and physiology confirmed the innate inferiority of woman and her limited reproductive function. They also proved as "scientific truth" all of the traditional negative images of the female nature. A sixteenth-century Italian anatomist accepted Galen's view and believed the ovaries to be internal testicles. He explained their strange placement so "as to keep her from perceiving and ascertaining her sufficient perfection," and to humble her "continual desire to dominate." An early-seventeenth-century French book on childbirth instructed the midwife to tie the umbilical cord far from the body to assure a long penis and a well-spoken young man for a male child and close to the body to give the female a straighter form and to ensure that she would talk less.

No one questioned the equally ancient and traditional connection between physiology and nature: the role of the uterus in determining a woman's behavior. The organ's potential influence confirmed the female's irrationality and her need to accept a subordinate role to the male. The sixteenth-century Italian anatomist Fallopio repeated Aristotle's idea that the womb lusted for the male in its desire to procreate. The French sixteenth-century doctor and writer Rabelais took Plato's view of the womb as insatiable, like an animal out of control when denied sexual intercourse, the cause of that singularly female ailment, "hysteria." Other sixteenth- and seventeenth-century writers on women and their health adopted all of the most misogynistic explanations of the traditional Greek and Roman authorities. No menstruation meant a diseased womb, an organ suffocating in a kind of female excrement. Only intercourse with a man could prevent or cure the condition. Left untreated the uterus would put pressure on other organs, cause convulsions, or drive the woman crazy. Thus, the male remained the key agent in the woman's life. She was innately inferior, potentially irrational, and lost to ill-health and madness without his timely intervention.

So much changed from the fifteenth to the eighteenth centuries in the ways in which women and men perceived their world, its institutions and attitudes. The Renaissance offered the exhilaration of a society in which the individual could be freed from traditional limitations.

In the spirit of Humanistic and scientific inquiry men questioned and reformulated assumptions about the mind's capabilities and the description of the natural universe. New methods of reasoning and discourse, of observation and experimentation, evolved and led to the reorientation of the natural universe and more accurate descriptions of the physical world, including man's own body. Yet when it came to questions and assumptions about women's function and role and to descriptions of her nature and her body, no new answers were formulated. Instead, inspired by the intellectual excitement of the times and the increasing confidence in their own perceptions of the spiritual and material world, men argued even more strongly from traditional premises, embellishing and revitalizing the ancient beliefs. Instead of breaking with tradition, descriptions of the female accumulated traditions: the classical, the religious, the literary, the customary, and the legal — all stated afresh in the secular language of the new age. Instead of being freed, women were ringed with yet more binding and seemingly incontrovertible versions of the traditional attitudes about their inferior nature, their proper function and role, and their subordinate relationship to men.

With the advent of printing, men were able to disseminate these negative conclusions about women as they never could before. From the sixteenth century on the printing presses brought the new tracts, pamphlets, treatises, broadsides, and engravings to increasing numbers of Europeans: pictures of the sperm as a tiny, fully formed infant; works by scholars and jurists explaining the female's "natural" physical and legal incapacity; romances and ballads telling of unchaste damsels and vengeful wives set to plague man.

Although these misogynistic attitudes about women flourished and spread, the defense of women had also begun. In her *Book of the City of Ladies* Christine de Pizan, the fifteenth-century writer, asks why no one had spoken on their behalf before, why the "accusations and slanders" had gone uncontradicted for so long? Her allegorical mentor, "Rectitude," replies, "Let me tell you that in the long run, everything comes to a head at the right time."

The world of the courts had widened the perimeters of women's expectations and given some women increased opportunities. However, for the vast majority of women, still not conscious of their disadvantaged and subordinate status, changes in material circumstances had a far greater impact. From the seventeenth to the twentieth centuries more women were able to live the life restricted in previous ages to the few. In Europe's salons and parlors they found increased comfort, greater security, and new ways to value their traditional roles and functions. For these women, "the right time" — the moment for questioning and rejecting the ancient premises of European society — lay in the future.

19

ZAHEER BABER

From *The Science of Empire: Scientific Knowledge, Civilization, and Colonial Rule in India*

The author of this secondary study points out that India had its own scientific tradition in the seventeenth century. In fact, India had a number of scientific traditions that dated back to the Middle Ages. Ayurvedic medicine — a body of pharmacological and surgical knowledge — was based on the idea of maintaining the proper balance of three humors (wind, bile, and phlegm) — an idea similar to the medieval European notion of the four humors (blood, phlegm, and two biles). There was also the indigenous Indian tradition of astrology. In addition, Indian scientific knowledge had made significant inroads in mathematics, botany, chemistry, and physics. By the seventeenth century, these Indian traditions had been combined with Muslim science and medicine from central Asia and the Middle East.

Which aspects of Indian science and medicine were most surprising to Europeans? How different was Indian science and medicine from that of Europe?

Thinking Historically

Is it possible that before the seventeenth century Indians were more "advanced" than Europeans in some fields of science and medicine? If so, in what fields? Was India more advanced than Europe in any areas of science or medicine after the seventeenth century? If so, in what areas? Could there have been a seventeenth-century scientific revolution in India?

Surgical Procedures in Medieval India

A number of early eighteenth-century accounts of English observers provide fascinating details about the practice of intricate medical procedures and surgical operations in India. According to Colonel Kyd, the founder of the Calcutta Botanic Gardens, "In Chirurgery (in which

Zaheer Baber, *The Science of Empire: Scientific Knowledge, Civilization, and Colonial Rule in India* (Albany: State University of New York Press, 1996), 79–85.

they are considered by us the least advanced) they often succeed in removing ulcers and cutaneous irruptions of the worst kind, which have baffled the skill of our surgeons, by the process of inducing inflammation and by means directly opposite to ours, and which they have probably long been in possession of." Similarly, Helenus Scott in his regular correspondence with Sir Joseph Banks provided an account of a surgical procedure to treat cataracts: "They practice with great success the operation of depressing the chrystalline lens when become opake and from time immemorial they cut for the stone at the same place which they now do in Europe. These are curious facts and I believe unknown before to us." Two years later, Dr. Scott, in another letter to Joseph Banks, referred to a "paper on putting on noses on those who have lost them" and promised to "send you by the later ships some of the Indian cement for uniting animal parts." On January 19, 1796, Scott sent Banks samples of a number of substances, including Indian steel with a note: "In this packet too you will find a piece of *Caute,* the cement for noses." Although these references to the substance and method for putting severed parts together have not been followed up in any detail, the ancient *Ayurvedic* text, the *Susruta-Samhita* does contain fragmentary references to roughly similar procedures.

Indigenous System of Inoculation against Smallpox

Perhaps the most interesting of the early accounts of medical practice are the detailed descriptions of the indigenous method of inoculation against smallpox in eighteenth-century India. Writing in 1737, one British observer noted that "the operation of inoculation called by the natives *tikah* has been known in the kingdom of Bengall as near as I can learn, about 150 years." The most complete account of the procedure was offered by Dr. J. Z. Holwell in a 1767 address to the College of Physicians in London. Holwell who practiced surgery in Calcutta and whose accounts of India attracted the attention of Voltaire, observed:

> Inoculation is performed in Indostan by a particular tribe of Bramins, who are delegated annually for this service from the different Colleges of Bindooband, Eleabas, Banaras, &c. over all the distant provinces; dividing themselves into small parties, of three or four each, they plan their travelling circuits in such wise as to arrive at the place of their respective destination some weeks before the usual return of the disease.

Holwell proceeded to describe the intricate details of the actual procedures adopted for inoculation:

Previous to the operation the Operator takes a piece of cloth in his hand, and with it gives a dry friction upon the part intended for inoculation, for the space of eight or ten minutes, then with a small instrument he wounds, by many slight touches, about the compass of a silver groat, just making the smallest appearance of blood, then opening a linen double rag takes from thence a small pledgit of cotton charged with the variolous matter, which he moistens with two or three drops of the Ganges water, and applies it to the wound, fixing it on with a slight bandage, and ordering it to remain on for six hours without being moved.

Holwell also described specific postinoculation procedures and regimens against which he was initially "prejudiced . . . but a few years experience gave me full conviction of the propriety of their method. . . . [T]his influenced my practice and I will venture to say, that every gentleman in the profession who did not adopt the same mode, have lost many a patient, which might otherwise have been saved."

From a scientific point of view, what is particularly significant is that, according to Holwell, the medical practitioners were aware of the causative principles underlying the disease of smallpox and the practice of inoculation. Based on extensive conversation with the practitioners, Holwell concluded:

They lay it down as a *principle* that the *immediate* cause of the small pox exists in the mortal part of every human and animal form; that the *mediate* (or second) *acting* cause, which stirs up the *first,* and throws it into a state of fermentation, is multitudes of *imperceptible animalculae* floating in the atmosphere; that these are the cause of all empidemical diseases, but more particularly of the small pox. . . . That when once this *peculiar* ferment, which produces the small pox, is raised in the blood, the *immediate cause* of the disease is totally expelled in the eruptions, or by other channels; and hence it is, that the blood is not susceptible of a second fermentation of the same kind.

Holwell also described a number of other procedures that were effective in curing full-blown smallpox, before concluding that "since this practice of the East has been followed without variation, and with uniform success from the remotest known times, it is but justice to conclude, it must have been originally founded on the basis of rational principles and experiments."

The practice of medicine and surgery was successful enough for the physicians to be accorded a fairly high status in medieval Indian society. In some regions the physicians were allowed to have hats or umbrellas carried over them — a practice that symbolized high social status and prestige. Thus, John Huyghen van Lichschoten, who lived in Goa for five years (1583–1588) observed:

There are in Goa many Heathen phisitions which observe their gravities with hats carried over them for the sunne, like the Portingales [Portugese], which no other heathens doe, but onely Ambassadors, or some rich Marchants. These Heathen phisitions doe not onely cure there owne nations and countrimen but the Portingales also, for the Viceroy himselfe, the Archbishop, and all the Monkes and Friers doe put more trust in them then in their own countrimen, whereby they get great [store of] money, and are much honoured and esteemed.

Apart from demonstrating the successful practice of medicine, the above account also establishes the fact that in certain regions physicians constituted a distinct occupational category or "profession" as early as the sixteenth century. Overall, it is evident that the practice of medicine flourished in medieval India, partly due to the patronage extended by some rulers. By the sixteenth century, the practice of medicine had also become established as a semi-independent occupation, and the practitioners were paid for their work.

Astronomy, Astrology, and Patronage:
The Science of the Heavens in Medieval India

. . . . The development of scientific thinking was especially evident in the field of astronomy. Due to extensive patronage extended by a number of Mughal rulers, medieval Indian society offered a conducive climate for the development of the indigenous as well as central and west Asian astronomical traditions.

A number of factors contributed to the patronage of astronomy by the Mughal rulers. Significant aspects of the lives of people were partly influenced by astrological considerations, which themselves depended on an accurate knowledge and understanding of the trajectories of planets and stars, and most of the medieval rulers and elites were well versed in and aware of the different astronomical traditions. For example, the first Mughal ruler, Babar, was cognizant of some of the practical uses of astronomical tables. In his discussion of the astronomical work of one of his ancestors, Mirza Ulugh Beg of Samarkand, Babar described a "fine building [which] is an observatory, that is, an instrument for writing Astronomical Tables. . . . [B]y its means the Mirza worked out the Kurkani Tables, now used all over the world." Another passage indicates that Babar was aware of other distinctive traditions of observational astronomy: "Not more than seven or eight observatories seem to have been constructed in the world. Mamum Khalifa made one with which the *Mamumi* Tables were written. Batalmus [Ptolemy] constructed another. Another was made, in Hindustan, in the time of Raja Vikramaditya Hindu in Ujjain and Dhar. . . . The Hindus of

Hindustan use the Tables of this Observatory." Astronomical observation and the calendars compiled as a result of such observations were useful in the sphere of religion as well as in the administration of the empire. For example, in the construction of mosques in south Asia, particular care had to be taken to ensure that they were built in such a way that people praying faced Mecca. In Babar's time, astronomical observation was being utilized to achieve accuracy in delineating the ritual specified directional orientation of the Muslim places of worship. In 1498 A.D. Babar recorded in his diary that "there is great discrepancy between the *qibla*[1] of this mosque and that of the College; that of the mosque seems to have been fixed by astronomical observation."

Babar's son and successor, Humayun (1530–1536), was also keenly interested in and patronized astronomy. In Jahangir's memoirs, a reference is made to a handwritten manuscript by Humayun that contained "an introduction to the science of astronomy, and other marvelous things, most of which he had studied and carried into practice." Abul Fazl records that shortly before his death, Humayun was planning to construct a large astronomical observatory and had even acquired a number of astronomical instruments. During the reign of his son, Akbar (1536–1605), patronage of astronomy and astrology continued. Abul Fazl in his *Akbar Nama* mentions "Maulana Chand, the astrologer, who possessed great acuteness and thorough dexterity in the science of the astrolabe, in the scrutinizing of astronomical tables, the construction of almanacs, and the interpretations of the stars." This reference from Abul Fazl's account of Akbar's reign explicitly establishes a symbiotic relationship between astrology and observational astronomy. Maulana Chand compiled a set of astronomical tables known as *Tahsilat-i-Akbar Shahi*, which was referred to by the astronomer-statesman, Raja Jai Singh, almost two hundred years later. Finally, astronomy was explicitly patronized during the reign of Akbar's son, Jahangir (1605–1627), who was an accomplished naturalist himself. His memoirs, the *Tuzuk-i-Jahangiri*, contain extensive accounts of the flora and fauna of medieval India. The following extract from Jahangir's memoirs illustrates his own keen interest in astronomical knowledge and provides evidence of the presence of astronomers in that period who were well versed in techniques of observation and measurement:

> On Saturday the 18th, the camp was at Ramgarh. For some nights before this there appeared, at three *gharis* before sunrise, in the atmosphere, a luminous vapour in the shape of a pillar. At each succeeding night it rose a *ghari* earlier. When it assumed its full form, it took the shape of a spear, thin at two ends, and thick in the middle.

---

[1] A niche in a mosque that points the direction to Mecca. [Ed.]

It was curved like a sickle, and had its back to the south, and its face to the north. It now showed itself a watch (*pahar*) before sunrise. Astronomers took its shape and size by the astrolabe, and ascertained that with differences of appearance it extended over twenty-four degrees. It moved in high heaven, but it had a movement of its own, differing from that of high heaven, for it was first in Scorpio and afterwards in Libra. Its declination (*harakat-i-arz*) was mainly southerly. . . . Sixteen nights after this phenomenon, a star showed itself in the same quarter. Its head was luminous, and its tail was two or three yards long, but the tail was not luminous. It has now appeared for eight nights; when it disappears, the fact will be noticed, as well as the results of it.

It is evident that due to a number of factors, astronomy attracted considerable patronage in medieval India. One of the factors that indirectly stimulated interest in astronomical observation was the widespread use of astrology for determining the auspicious as well as accurate timing for significant undertakings. Astronomy and astrology were not clearly demarcated from each other in the medieval or the ancient period, and the memoirs of the various Mughal rulers are replete with references that establish the significance accorded to the effect of the positions of the stars and constellations on human affairs. Thus Babar, while involved in a battle near Kabul in 1503, observed: "The reason I was so eager to engage was that on the day of the battle, the Eight stars were between the two armies; they would have been in the enemy's rear for thirteen or fourteen days if the fight had been deferred." Three years later, riding in the vicinity of Kabul, he recorded, "I had been in these parts several times before; drawing inferences from those times, I took the Pole-star on my right shoulder blade, and *with some anxiety,* moved on." In another march to Kabul in 1505, he noted: "I had never seen Suhail [Canopus]; when I came out of the pass, I saw a star, bright and low." Finally, while touring the newly conquered territory of Hindustan, or India, he defined the position of the city of Chanderi near Agra, by noting: "In Chanderi the altitude of the pole star is twenty-five degrees." These observations, recorded in Babar's memoirs, indicate both a concern with the possible influence of the position of stars on human action, as well as familiarity with observational and measurement techniques for accurately determining these positions.

The symbiotic relationship between astrology and astronomy and its significance in influencing some aspects of the administration of the Mughal empire continued under the rule of the later Mughals. Like Babar, Jahangir's memoirs are replete with observations like "the astrologers and astronomers chose the day of *Mubarak-shamba,* the 28th of the Divine month of Dai . . . as the proper time at which to enter the capital of Agra," and "as the auspicious hour for entering the city had been fixed for the 14th, I halted here, and at the selected auspicious hour proceeded to the fort." The concern with the influence of the position of stars is reflected in the determination of the exact timing of crucial celestial conjunctions, and each entry of Jahangir's memoirs is prefaced by observations like: "The transit of the sun into his house of Aries took place on Friday . . . after twelve and a half *gharis* or five sidereal hours," and "On Wednesday the 22nd *Zi-l-qada*, 1015 (March 10, 1607), when three and a half *gharis* of the day had passed, the sun rose to his House of Honour." These observations, recorded in the first decade of the seventeenth century, continued to be expressed in the late eighteenth century, when, according to a handwritten manuscript from 1780, "the return of the World Enlightening Sun into the sign of Aries . . . happens at 2 *Gurrys* and 3 *Puls* remaining of the latter part of the night." Considering the importance attached to the pursuit of astrology and astronomy, it is not surprising that its practitioners were patronized by the Mughal rulers. Thus, Jahangir explicitly refers to "Lachin Munajjim, astrologer [who was provided with] 1,000 personnel and 500 horses;" to another astrologer, "Jotik Ray [who was] weighed against money . . . [that] was given to him as a reward;" and to the provision of funds for "a brahman of the name of Rudar Bhattacharaj . . . who was engaged at Benares in teaching . . . [and] has studied well, both in the rational and traditional sciences, and is perfect in his own line."

A final reason for the patronage of astronomy was its practical use in the compilation and reform of different systems of calendars, which relied on, depending on the system adopted, solar or lunar observations. For example, in 1584, during the reign of Akbar, Fathullah Shiraz reinterpreted the astronomical data from the tables of the central Asian astronomer Ulugh Beg. As a result, a new and reformed solar Ilahi-era calendar was introduced and adopted as the official calendar of the Mughal empire for nearly seventy-five years. During Aurangzeb's reign in 1659, this solar calendar was replaced by the lunar Hejira calendar, which, in turn, was rejected after his death in 1708. Efforts at compiling a reformed solar calendar based on empirical observation of the trajectory of the sun led to the construction of the giant astronomical observatories by Jai Singh in early eighteenth-century India. Overall, regardless of the changing sociohistorical context, astrology and astronomy were patronized by successive rulers. In fact, the changing sociohistorical conditions were conducive to a partial synthesis of indigenous Indian, central, and west Asian astronomical traditions.

20

LYNDA NORENE SHAFFER

China, Technology, and Change

In this essay an important contemporary world historian asks us to compare the revolutionary consequences of scientific and technological changes that occurred in China and Europe before the seventeenth century. What is Shaffer's argument? In what ways was the European scientific revolution different from the changes in China she describes here?

Thinking Historically

What exactly was the impact of printing, the compass, and gunpowder in Europe? What was the "before" and "after" for each of these innovations? What, according to Shaffer, was the situation in China before and after each of these innovations? Which of these six causal explanations do you find most convincing? Were these innovations as revolutionary in China as they were in Europe?

Francis Bacon (1561–1626), an early advocate of the empirical method, upon which the scientific revolution was based, attributed Western Europe's early modern take-off to three things in particular: printing, the compass, and gunpowder. Bacon had no idea where these things had come from, but historians now know that all three were invented in China. Since, unlike Europe, China did not take off onto a path leading from the scientific to the Industrial Revolution, some historians are now asking why these inventions were so revolutionary in Western Europe and, apparently, so unrevolutionary in China.

In fact, the question has been posed by none other than Joseph Needham, the foremost English-language scholar of Chinese science and technology. It is only because of Needham's work that the Western academic community has become aware that until Europe's take-off, China was the unrivaled world leader in technological development. That is why it is so disturbing that Needham himself has posed this apparent puzzle. The English-speaking academic world relies upon him and repeats him; soon this question and the vision of China that it im-

Lynda Norene Shaffer, "China, Technology and Change," *World History Bulletin,* 4, no. 1 (Fall/Winter, 1986–87), 1–6.

plies will become dogma. Traditional China will take on supersociety qualities — able to contain the power of printing, to rein in the potential of the compass, even to muffle the blast of gunpowder.

The impact of these inventions on Western Europe is well known. Printing not only eliminated much of the opportunity for human copying errors, it also encouraged the production of more copies of old books and an increasing number of new books. As written material became both cheaper and more easily available, intellectual activity increased. Printing would eventually be held responsible, at least in part, for the spread of classical humanism and other ideas from the Renaissance. It is also said to have stimulated the Protestant Reformation, which urged a return to the Bible as the primary religious authority.

The introduction of gunpowder in Europe made castles and other medieval fortifications obsolete (since it could be used to blow holes in their walls) and thus helped to liberate Western Europe from feudal aristocratic power. As an aid to navigation the compass facilitated the Portuguese- and Spanish-sponsored voyages that led to Atlantic Europe's sole possession of the Western Hemisphere, as well as the Portuguese circumnavigation of Africa, which opened up the first all-sea route from Western Europe to the long-established ports of East Africa and Asia.

Needham's question can thus be understood to mean, Why didn't China use gunpowder to destroy feudal walls? Why didn't China use the compass to cross the Pacific and discover America, or to find an all-sea route to Western Europe? Why didn't China undergo a Renaissance or Reformation? The implication is that even though China possessed these technologies, it did not change much. Essentially Needham's question is asking, What was wrong with China?

Actually, there was nothing wrong with China. China was changed fundamentally by these inventions. But in order to see the changes, one must abandon the search for peculiarly European events in Chinese history, and look instead at China itself before and after these breakthroughs.

To begin, one should note that China possessed all three of these technologies by the latter part of the Tang dynasty (618–906) — between four and six hundred years before they appeared in Europe. And it was during just that time, from about 850, when the Tang dynasty began to falter, until 960, when the Song dynasty (960–1279) was established, that China underwent fundamental changes in all spheres. In fact, historians are now beginning to use the term *revolution* when referring to technological and commercial changes that culminated in the Song dynasty, in the same way that they refer to the changes in eighteenth- and nineteenth-century England as the Industrial Revolution. And the word might well be applied to other sorts of changes in China during this period.

For example, the Tang dynasty elite was aristocratic, but that of the

Song was not. No one has ever considered whether the invention of gunpowder contributed to the demise of China's aristocrats, which occurred between 750 and 960, shortly after its invention. Gunpowder may, indeed, have been a factor although it is unlikely that its importance lay in blowing up feudal walls. Tang China enjoyed such internal peace that its aristocratic lineages did not engage in castle-building of the sort typical in Europe. Thus, China did not have many feudal fortifications to blow up.

The only wall of significance in this respect was the Great Wall, which was designed to keep steppe nomads from invading China. In fact, gunpowder may have played a role in blowing holes in this wall, for the Chinese could not monopolize the terrible new weapon, and their nomadic enemies to the north soon learned to use it against them. The Song dynasty ultimately fell to the Mongols, the most formidable force ever to emerge from the Eurasian steppe. Gunpowder may have had a profound effect on China — exposing a united empire to foreign invasion and terrible devastation — but an effect quite opposite to the one it had on Western Europe.

On the other hand, the impact of printing on China was in some ways very similar to its later impact on Europe. For example, printing contributed to a rebirth of classical (that is, preceding the third century A.D.) Confucian learning, helping to revive a fundamentally humanistic outlook that had been pushed aside for several centuries.

After the fall of the Han dynasty (206 B.C.–A.D. 220), Confucianism had lost much of its credibility as a world view, and it eventually lost its central place in the scholarly world. It was replaced by Buddhism, which had come from India. Buddhists believed that much human pain and confusion resulted from the pursuit of illusory pleasures and dubious ambitions: Enlightenment and, ultimately, salvation would come from a progressive disengagement from the real world, which they also believed to be illusory. This point of view dominated Chinese intellectual life until the ninth century. Thus the academic and intellectual comeback of classical Confucianism was in essence a return to a more optimistic literature that affirmed the world as humans had made it.

The resurgence of Confucianism within the scholarly community was due to many factors, but printing was certainly one of the most important. Although it was invented by Buddhist monks in China, and at first benefited Buddhism, by the middle of the tenth century, printers were turning out innumerable copies of the classical Confucian corpus. This return of scholars to classical learning was part of a more general movement that shared not only its humanistic features with the later Western European Renaissance, but certain artistic trends as well.

Furthermore, the Protestant Reformation in Western Europe was in some ways reminiscent of the emergence and eventual triumph of Neo-Confucian philosophy. Although the roots of Neo-Confucianism can be found in the ninth century, the man who created what would become its most orthodox synthesis was Zhu Xi (Chu Hsi, 1130–1200). Neo-Confucianism was significantly different from classical Confucianism, for it had undergone an intellectual (and political) confrontation with Buddhism and had emerged profoundly changed. It is of the utmost importance to understand that not only was Neo-Confucianism new, it was also heresy, even during Zhu Xi's lifetime. It did not triumph until the thirteenth century, and it was not until 1313 (when Mongol conquerors ruled China) that Zhu Xi's commentaries on the classics became the single authoritative text against which all academic opinion was judged.

In the same way that Protestantism emerged out of a confrontation with the Roman Catholic establishment and asserted the individual Christian's autonomy, Neo-Confucianism emerged as a critique of Buddhist ideas that had taken hold in China, and it asserted an individual moral capacity totally unrelated to the ascetic practices and prayers of the Buddhist priesthood. In the twelfth century Neo-Confucianists lifted the work of Mencius (Meng Zi, 370–290 B.C.) out of obscurity and assigned it a place in the corpus second only to that of the *Analects of Confucius*. Many facets of Mencius appealed to the Neo-Confucianists, but one of the most important was his argument that humans by nature are fundamentally good. Within the context of the Song dynasty, this was an assertion that morally could be pursued through an engagement in human affairs, and that the Buddhist monk's withdrawal from life's mainstream did not bestow upon them any special virtue.

The importance of these philosophical developments notwithstanding, printing probably had its greatest impact on the Chinese political system. The origin of the civil service examination system in China can be traced back to the Han dynasty, but in the Song dynasty government-administered examinations became the most important route to political power in China. For almost a thousand years (except the early period of Mongol rule), China was governed by men who had come to power simply because they had done exceedingly well in examinations on the Neo-Confucian canon. At any one time thousands of students were studying for the exams, and thousands of inexpensive books were required. Without printing such a system would not have been possible.

The development of this alternative to aristocratic rule was one of the most radical changes in world history. Since the examinations were ultimately open to 98 percent of all males (actors were one of the few groups excluded), it was the most democratic system in the world prior to the development of representative democracy and popular suffrage in Western Europe in the eighteenth and nineteenth centuries. (There were some small-scale systems, such as the classical Greek city-states, which might be considered more democratic, but nothing comparable in size to Song China or even the modern nation-states of Europe.)

Finally we come to the compass. Suffice it to say that during the Song dynasty, China developed the world's largest and most technologically sophisticated merchant marine and navy. By the fifteenth century its ships were sailing from the north Pacific to the east coast of Africa. They could have made the arduous journey around the tip of Africa and on into Portuguese ports; however, they had no reason to do so. Although the Western European economy was prospering, it offered nothing that China could not acquire much closer to home at much less cost. In particular, wool, Western Europe's most important export, could easily be obtained along China's northern frontier.

Certainly, the Portuguese and the Spanish did not make their unprecedented voyages out of idle curiosity. They were trying to go to the Spice Islands, in what is now Indonesia, in order to acquire the most valuable commercial items of the time. In the fifteenth century these islands were the world's sole suppliers of the fine spices, such as cloves, nutmeg, and mace, as well as a source for the more generally available pepper. It was this spice market that lured Columbus westward from Spain and drew Vasco Da Gama around Africa and across the Indian Ocean.

After the invention of the compass, China also wanted to go to the Spice Islands and, in fact, did go, regularly — but Chinese ships did not have to go around the world to get there. The Atlantic nations of Western Europe, on the other hand, had to buy spices from Venice (which controlled the Mediterranean trade routes) or from other Italian city-states; or they had to find a new way to the Spice Islands. It was necessity that mothered those revolutionary routes that ultimately changed the world.

Gunpowder, printing, the compass — clearly these three inventions changed China as much as they changed Europe. And it should come as no surprise that changes wrought in China between the eighth and tenth centuries were different from changes wrought in Western Europe between the thirteenth and fifteenth centuries. It would, of course, be unfair and ahistorical to imply that something was wrong with Western Europe because the technologies appeared there later. It is equally unfair to ask why the Chinese did not accidentally bump into the Western Hemisphere while sailing east across the Pacific to find the wool markets of Spain.

$\boxed{21}$

SUGITA GEMPAKU

A Dutch Anatomy Lesson in Japan

Sugita Gempaku (1733–1817) was a Japanese physician who, as he tells us here, suddenly discovered the value of Western medical science when he chanced to witness a dissection shortly after he obtained a Dutch anatomy book.

What was it that Sugita Gempaku learned on that day in 1771? What were the differences between the treatments of anatomy in the Chinese *Book of Medicine* and the Dutch medical book? What accounts for these differences?

Thinking Historically

How did the Dutch book change the way the author practiced medicine? How did it change his knowledge of the human body? How did it change the relevance of his knowledge of the human body to the medicine he practiced?

Somehow, miraculously I obtained a book on anatomy written in [The Netherlands]. . . . It was a strange and even miraculous happening that I was able to obtain that book in that particular spring of 1771. Then at the night of the third day of the third month, I received a letter from a man by the name of Tokuno, who was in the service of the Town Commissioner. Tokuno stated in his letter that "A post-mortem examination of the body of a condemned criminal by a resident physician will be held tomorrow at Senjukotsugahara. You are welcome to witness it if you so desire."

The next day, when we arrived at the location . . . Ryotaku reached under his kimono to produce a Dutch book and showed it to us. "This is a Dutch book of anatomy called *Tabulae Anatomicae*. I bought this a few years ago when I went to Nagasaki, and kept it." As I examined it, it was the same book I had and was of the same edition. We held each other's hands and exclaimed: "What a coincidence!" Ryotaku continued by saying: "When I went to Nagasaki, I learned and heard," and opened this book. "These are called *long* in Dutch, they are lungs," he

Sugita Gempaku, "A Dutch Anatomy Lesson in Japan," in *Sources of Japanese History,* ed. David John Lu, vol. 1 (New York: McGraw-Hill, 1974), 253–55.

taught us. "This is *hart,* or the heart. When it says *maag* it is the stomach, and when it says *milt* it is the spleen." However, they did not look like the heart given in the Chinese medical books, and none of us were sure until we could actually see the dissection.

Thereafter we went together to the place which was especially set for us to observe the dissection. . . . That day, the old butcher pointed to this and that organ. After the heart, liver, gall bladder, and stomach were identified, he pointed to other parts for which there were no names. "I don't know their names. But I have dissected quite a few bodies from my youthful days. Inside of everyone's abdomen there were these parts and those parts." . . . The old butcher again said, "Every time I had a dissection, I pointed out to those physicians many of these parts, but not a single one of them questioned 'What was this?' or 'What was that?'" We compared the body as dissected against the charts both Ryotaku and I had, and could not find a single variance from the charts. The Chinese *Book of Medicine* says that the lungs are like the eight petals of the lotus flower, with three petals hanging in front, three in back, and two petals forming like two ears and that the liver has three petals to the left and four petals to the right. There were no such divisions, and the positions and shapes of intestines and gastric organs were all different from those taught by the old theories. The official physicians . . . had witnessed dissection seven or eight times. Whenever they witnessed the dissection, they found that the old theories contradicted reality. Each time they were perplexed and could not resolve their doubts. Every time they wrote down what they thought was strange. They wrote in their books, "The more we think of it, there must be fundamental differences in the bodies of Chinese and of the eastern barbarians." I could see why they wrote this way.

That day, after the dissection was over, we decided that we also should examine the shape of the skeletons left exposed on the execution ground. We collected the bones, and examined a number of them. Again, we were struck by the fact that they all differed from the old theories while conforming to the Dutch charts.

The three of us, Ryotaku, Junan, and I went home together. On the way home we spoke to each other and felt the same way. "How marvelous was our actual experience today. It is a shame that we were ignorant of these things until now. As physicians who serve their masters through medicine, we performed our duties in complete ignorance of the true form of the human body. How disgraceful it is. Somehow, through this experience, let us investigate further the truth about the human body. If we practice medicine with this knowledge behind us, we can make contributions for people under heaven and on this earth." Ryotaku spoke to us. "Indeed, I agree with you wholeheartedly." Then I spoke to my companion. "Somehow if we can translate anew this book called *Tabulae Anatomicae,* we can get a clear notion of the human body inside out. It will have great benefit in the treatment of our patients. Let us do our best to read it and understand it without the help of translators." . . .

The next day, we assembled at the house of Ryotaku and recalled the happenings of the previous day. When we faced that *Tabulae Anatomicae,* we felt as if we were setting sail on a great ocean in a ship without oars or a rudder. With the magnitude of the work before us, we were dumbfounded by our own ignorance. However, Ryotaku had been thinking of this for some time, and he had been in Nagasaki. He knew some Dutch through studying and hearing, and knew some sentence patterns and words. He was also ten years older than I, and we decided to make him head of our group and our teacher. At that time I did not know the twenty-five letters of the Dutch alphabet. I decided to study the language with firm determination, but I had to acquaint myself with letters and words gradually.

REFLECTIONS

It is important to emphasize the revolutionary impact of the European scientific revolution of the seventeenth century without slighting the scientific and technological achievements of other civilizations. The scientific developments in Europe sprang from foreign innovations, and in some fields Europe was not as advanced as other societies. Yet the scientific revolution's unique combination of observation and generalization, experimentation and mathematics, induction and deduction established a body of knowledge and a method for research that proved lasting and irreversible.

Why was it that China, so scientifically and technologically adept during the Sung dynasty, pictured hearts and lungs as flower petals in the late-Ming and early-Ch'ing seventeenth century? Was it that Chinese science lost momentum or changed direction? Or does such a question, as Lynda Shaffer warns, judge China unfairly by Western standards? Do the petal hearts reflect a different set of interests rather than a failure of Chinese science?

Chinese scientists excelled in acupuncture, massage, and herbal medicine, while European scientists excelled in surgery. It turned out that the inner workings of the human body were better revealed in surgical dissection than in muscle manipulation or in oral remedies. And, as Sugita Gempaku reminds us, the Europeans not only cut and removed, they also named what they found and tried to understand how it worked. Perhaps the major difference between science in Europe and that in India, China, and Japan in the seventeenth century was one of perspective: Europeans were beginning to imagine the human body as a machine and asking how it worked. In some respects, the metaphor of man as a machine proved more fruitful than organic metaphors of humans as plants or animals.

Probing questions also changed our understanding of the heavens. In Bertold Brecht's play *Galileo,* the great astronomer chides the cardinals of the church to look through a telescope so they can see the features of the moon and those revolving around Jupiter. Brecht opposes scientific observation with the church's reliance on biblical and Aristotelian authority, but this simple antithesis misses the mark. Galileo was a mathematician and an astronomer. Mathematics is not a matter of observation; it is quantifiable, an unbending authority. If mathematical calculations indicated that a star would appear at a particular spot in the heavens and it did not, Galileo might just as soon have questioned the observation as the math. From the seventeenth century on, scientists would check one or the other on the assumption that observation and mathematics could be brought together to understand the same event, that they would have to be in agreement, and that such agreement could lead to laws that could then be tested and proved or disproved.

It is this method of inquiry, not the discoveries, that was new. Astrology could lead to knowledge of astronomy, but they are not the same. The knowledge of the astrologer is metaphorical rather than scientific. The idea that a person born under Gemini, a stellar configuration that looks like twins, will be pulled in two directions is a psychological metaphor, not a matter of physics. It cannot be tested, validated, or built upon. On the other hand, physics and astronomy can. To the extent to which we combine astrology with astronomy, we lose the precision, quantifiability, and the reliability and certainty of science.

The scientific method is a systematic means of inquiry based on agreed-upon rules of hypothesis, experimentation, theory testing, law, and dissemination. Scientific inquiry is a social process in two important ways: First, any scientific discovery must be reproducible and recognized by other scientists to gain credence. Second, a community of scientists is needed to question, dismiss, or validate the work of its members.

Finally, we return to Baumer's emphasis on the societies of seventeenth-century science. The numerous organizations in Europe are testaments not only to a popular interest in science but to a continuing public conversation. Steven Shapin, a historian of science, has written of the importance of a class of "honorable gentlemen" with like interests who could trust each other's work and conclusions: "Truth flowed along the same personal channels as civil conversation. Knowledge was secured by trusting people with whom one was familiar, and familiarity could be used to gauge the truth of what they said."[1]

Ultimately, the difference between European science and that of India or China in the seventeenth century may have had more to do with society than with culture. The development of modern scientific methods relied on the numerous debates and discussions of a self-conscious class of gentlemen scientists in a Europe where news traveled quickly and ideas could be translated and tested with confidence across numerous borders. To what extent does science everywhere today demonstrate the hallmarks of the seventeenth-century scientific revolution? How does the spread of science make human behavior more uniform?

[1] Steven Shapin, *A Social History of Truth: Civility and Science in Seventeenth Century England* (Chicago: University of Chicago Press, 1994), 410.

5

Enlightenment
and Revolution

HISTORICAL CONTEXT
Europe and the Americas, 1650–1850

The modern world puts its faith in science, reason, and democracy. The seventeenth-century scientific revolution established reason as the key to understanding nature, and its application directed thought, organized society, and measured governments during the eighteenth-century Enlightenment. Most — though, as we shall see, not all — people believed that reason would eventually lead to freedom. Freedom of thought, religion, and association, and political liberties and representative governments were hailed as hallmarks of the Age of Enlightenment.

For some, enlightened society meant a more controlled rather than a more democratic society. Philosophers like Immanuel Kant and Jean-Jacques Rousseau wanted people to become free but thought most people were incapable of achieving such a state. Rulers who were called "enlightened despots" believed that the application of reason to society would make people happier, not necessarily freer.

Ultimately, however, the Enlightenment's faith in reason led to calls for political revolution as well as for schemes of order. In England in the seventeenth century, in America and France at the end of the eighteenth century, and in Latin America shortly thereafter, revolutionary governments were created according to rational principles of liberty and equality that dispatched monarchs and enshrined the rule of the people. In this chapter we will concentrate on the heritage of the Enlightenment, examining competing tendencies toward order and revolution, stability and liberty, equality and freedom. We will also compare the American and the French Revolutions, and these with the later revolutions in Latin America. Finally, in reflection, we will briefly compare these distinctly European and American developments with processes in other parts of the world.

THINKING HISTORICALLY
Close Reading and
Interpretation of Texts

At the core of the Enlightenment was a trust in reasoned discussion, a belief that people could understand each other, even if they were not in agreement. Such understanding demanded clear and concise communication in a world where the masses were often swayed by fiery sermons and flamboyant rhetoric. But the Enlightenment also put its faith in the written word and a literate public. Ideas were debated face to face in the salons and coffeehouses of Europe and in the meeting halls of America, but it was through letters, diaries, the new world of newspapers, and the burgeoning spread of printed books that the people of the Enlightenment learned what they and their neighbors thought.

It is appropriate then for us to read the selections in this chapter — all primary sources — in the spirit in which they were written. We will pay special attention to the words and language that the authors use and will attempt to understand exactly what they meant, even why they chose the words they did. Such explication is a twofold process; we must understand the words first and foremost; then we must strive to understand the words in their proper context, as they were intended by the author. To achieve our first goal, we will paraphrase, a difficult task because the eighteenth-century writing style differs greatly from our own: Sentences are longer and arguments are often complex. Vocabularies were broad during this period, and we may encounter words that are used in ways unknown to us. As to our latter goal, we must try to make the vocabulary and perspective of the authors our own. Grappling with what makes the least sense to us and trying to understand why it was said is the challenge.

22

DAVID HUME

On Miracles

The European Enlightenment of the eighteenth century was the expression of a new class of intellectuals, independent of the clergy but allied with the rising middle class. Their favorite words were *reason, nature,* and *progress.* They applied the systematic doubt of René Descartes (1596–1650) and the reasoning method of the scientific revolution to human affairs, including religion and politics. With caustic wit and good humor, they asked new questions and popularized new points of view that would eventually revolutionize Western politics and culture. While the French *philosophes* and Voltaire (1694–1778) may be the best known, the Scottish philosopher David Hume (1711–1776) may have been the most brilliant. What does Hume argue in this selection? Does he prove his point to your satisfaction? How does he use reason and nature to make his case? Is reason incompatible with religion?

Thinking Historically

The first step in understanding what Hume means in this essay must come from a careful reading — a sentence-by-sentence exploration. Try to paraphrase each sentence, putting it into your own words. For example, you might paraphrase the first sentence like this: "I've found a way to disprove superstition; this method should be useful as long as superstition exists, which may be forever." Notice the content of such words as *just* and *check.* What does Hume mean by these words and by *prodigies?*

The second sentence is a concise definition of the scientific method. How would you paraphrase it? The second and third sentences summarize the method Hume has discovered to counter superstition. What is the meaning of the third sentence?

In the rest of the essay, Hume offers four proofs, or reasons, why miracles do not exist. How would you paraphrase each of these? Do you find these more or less convincing than his more general opening and closing arguments? What does Hume mean by *miracles?*

The Philosophical Works of David Hume (Edinburgh: A. Black and W. Tait, 1826).

I flatter myself that I have discovered an argument . . . , which, if just, will, with the wise and learned, be an everlasting check to all kinds of superstitious delusion, and consequently will be useful as long as the world endures; for so long, I presume, will the accounts of miracles and prodigies be found in all history, sacred and profane. . . .

A wise man proportions his belief to the evidence. . . .

A miracle is a violation of the laws of nature; and as a firm and unalterable experience has established these laws, the proof against a miracle, from the very nature of the fact, is as entire as any argument from experience can possibly be imagined. . . . Nothing is esteemed a miracle, if it ever happens in the common course of nature. It is no miracle that a man, seemingly in good health, should die on a sudden; because such a kind of death, though more unusual than any other, has yet been frequently observed to happen. But it is a miracle that a dead man should come to life; because that has never been observed in any age or country. There must, therefore, be an uniform experience against every miraculous event, otherwise the event would not merit that appellation. And as an uniform experience amounts to a proof, there is here a direct and full *proof,* from the nature of the fact, against the existence of any miracle. . . .

(Further) there is not to be found, in all history, any miracle attested by a sufficient number of men, of such unquestioned good sense, education, and learning, as to secure us against all delusion in themselves; of such undoubted integrity, as to place them beyond all suspicion of any design to deceive others; of such credit and reputation in the eyes of mankind, as to have a great deal to lose in case of their being detected in any falsehood. . . .

Secondly, We may observe in human nature a principle which, if strictly examined, will be found to diminish extremely the assurance, which we might, from human testimony, have in any kind of prodigy. . . . The passion of *surprise* and *wonder,* arising from miracles, being an agreeable emotion, gives a sensible tendency towards the belief of those events from which it is derived. . . .

With what greediness are the miraculous accounts of travellers received, their descriptions of sea and land monsters, their relations of wonderful adventures, strange men, and uncouth manners? But if the spirit of religion join itself to the love of wonder, there is an end of common sense; and human testimony, in these circumstances, loses all pretensions to authority. A religionist may be an enthusiast, and imagine he sees what has no reality: He may know his narrative to be false, and yet persevere in it, with the best intentions in the world, for the sake of promoting so holy a cause: Or even where this delusion has not place, vanity, excited by so strong a temptation, operates on him more powerfully than on the rest of mankind in any other circumstances; and self-interest with equal force. . . .

The many instances of forged miracles and prophecies and supernatural events, which, in all ages, have either been detected by contrary evidence, or which detect themselves by their absurdity, prove sufficiently the strong propensity of mankind to the extraordinary and marvellous, and ought reasonably to beget a suspicion against all relations of this kind. . . .

Thirdly, It forms a strong presumption against all supernatural and miraculous relations, that they are observed chiefly to abound among ignorant and barbarous nations; or if a civilized people has ever given admission to any of them, that people will be found to have received them from ignorant and barbarous ancestors, who transmitted them with that inviolable sanction and authority which always attend received opinions. . . .

I may add, as a *fourth* reason, which diminishes the authority of prodigies, that there is no testimony for any, even those which have not been expressly detected, that is not opposed by any infinite number of witnesses; so that not only the miracle destroys the credit of testimony, but the testimony destroys itself. To make this the better understood, let us consider, that in matters of religion, whatever is different is contrary; and that it is impossible the religions of ancient Rome, of Turkey, of Siam, and of China, should all of them be established on any solid foundation. Every miracle, therefore, pretended to have been wrought in any of these religions (and all of them abound in miracles), as its direct scope is to establish the particular system to which it is attributed; so has it the same force, though more indirectly, to overthrow every other system. In destroying a rival system, it likewise destroys the credit of those miracles on which that system was established, so that all the prodigies of different religions are to be regarded as contrary facts, and the evidences of these prodigies, whether weak or strong, as opposite to each other. . . .

Upon the whole, then, it appears, that no testimony for any kind of miracle has ever amounted to a probability, much less to a proof; and that, even supposing it amounted to proof, it would be opposed by another proof, derived from the very nature of the fact which it would endeavour to establish. It is experience only which gives authority to human testimony; and it is the same experience which assures us of the laws of nature. When, therefore, these two kinds of experience are contrary, we have nothing to do but to subtract the one from the other, and embrace an opinion either on one side or the other, with that assurance which arises from the remainder. But according to the principle here explained, this subtraction with regard to all popular religions amounts to an entire annihilation; and therefore we may establish it as a maxim, that no human testimony can have such force as to prove a miracle, and make it a just foundation for any such system of religion.

23

IMMANUEL KANT

What Is Enlightenment?

Immanuel Kant (1724–1804), a university professor in the small town of Königsberg, East Prussia (now Kaliningrad, in Russia), is one of the most influential philosophers in European history. In this brief selection from his *Critique of Practical Reason*, he shows us how the Enlightenment's quest for scientific reason led to a demand, sometimes revolutionary, for political freedom. Do we, as Kant suggests, impose restrictions on our intellectual freedom? Do we need courage to use our own reason? What does he mean by "the freedom to make public use of one's reason"? Why is this so important?

Thinking Historically

Notice how Kant uses words like *tutelage, guardians,* and *age.* What does he mean by these words, and what image do they create when taken together? Without explicitly saying so, Kant makes childhood a metaphor for what? How does one get past childhood, according to Kant? Who are the guardians to whom Kant refers?

Compare Kant's faith in reason with that of the leaders of the scientific revolution. Does Kant believe that reason is politically revolutionary as well?

Notice how Kant distinguishes between the individual and the public. What is the point of this distinction? Does Kant believe that individuals can free themselves? Is it easier for the individual or for the public to achieve enlightenment?

How does Kant's view of the individual differ from Hume's? How does his view of the individual's courage to use reason differ from your own?

Enlightenment is man's release from his self-incurred tutelage. Tutelage is man's inability to make use of his understanding without direction from another. Self-incurred is this tutelage when its cause lies not in lack of reason but in lack of resolution and courage to use it without direction from another. *Sapere aude!* "Have courage to use your own reason!" — that is the motto of enlightenment.

Immanuel Kant, *Critique of Practical Reason,* 3rd ed., trans. Lewis White Beck (New York: Macmillan, 1993).

Laziness and cowardice are the reasons why so great a portion of mankind, after nature has long since discharged them from external direction, nevertheless remains under lifelong tutelage, and why it is so easy for others to set themselves up as their guardians. It is so easy not to be of age. If I have a book which understands for me, a pastor who has a conscience for me, a physician who decides my diet, and so forth, I need not trouble myself. I need not think, if I can only pay — others will readily undertake the irksome work for me.

That the step to competence is held to be very dangerous by the far greater portion of mankind (and by the entire fair sex) — quite apart from its being arduous — is seen to by those guardians who have so kindly assumed superintendence over them. After the guardians have first made their domestic cattle dumb and have made sure that these placid creatures will not dare take a single step without the harness of the cart to which they are confined, the guardians then show them the danger which threatens if they try to go alone. Actually, however, this danger is not so great, for by falling a few times they would finally learn to walk alone. But an example of this failure makes them timid and ordinarily frightens them away from all further trials.

For any single individual to work himself out of the life under tutelage which has become almost his nature is very difficult. He has come to be fond of this state, and he is for the present really incapable of making use of his reason, for no one has ever let him try it out. Statutes and formulas, those mechanical tools of the rational employment or rather mis-employment of his natural gifts, are the fetters of an everlasting tutelage. Whoever throws them off makes only an uncertain leap over the narrowest ditch because he is not accustomed to that kind of free motion. Therefore, there are only few who have succeeded by their own exercise of mind both in freeing themselves from incompetence and in achieving a steady pace.

But that the public should enlighten itself is more possible; indeed, if only freedom is granted, enlightenment is almost sure to follow. For there will always be some independent thinkers, even among the established guardians of the great masses, who, after throwing off the yoke of tutelage from their own shoulders, will disseminate the spirit of the rational appreciation of both their own worth and every man's vocation for thinking for himself. But be it noted that the public, which has first been brought under this yoke by their guardians, forces the guardians themselves to remain bound when it is incited to do so by some of the guardians who are themselves capable of some enlightenment — so harmful is it to implant prejudices, for they later take vengeance on their cultivators or on their descendants. Thus the public can only slowly attain enlightenment. Perhaps a fall of personal despotism or of avaricious or tyrannical oppression may be accomplished by revolution, but never a true reform in ways of thinking. Rather, new prejudices will serve as well as old ones to harness the great unthinking masses.

For this enlightenment, however, nothing is required but freedom, and indeed the most harmless among all the things to which this term can properly be applied. It is the freedom to make public use of one's reason at every point. But I hear on all sides, "Do not argue!" The officer says: "Do not argue but drill!" The tax-collector: "Do not argue but pay!" The cleric: "Do not argue but believe!" Everywhere freedom is restricted.

24

PETER THE GREAT

Westernizing Decrees

The application of the scientific method to human behavior was, as Hume's essay "On Miracles" reminds us, a dismissal of religious and spiritual approaches in favor of scientific and secular ones. Science was not necessarily seen as antireligious, at least in Protestant countries, but the eighteenth-century champions of a scientific social order were often more secular than religious.

Czar Peter the Great of Russia (1672–1725) was an early example of this new secularism. After a trip to Europe in 1699, he initiated a wide range of reforms intended to modernize Russia by imitating western Europe. He sought to make religion serve the interests of the secular state, much as he imagined Protestantism served the secular, national interests of northern European states. These reforms included abolishing the patriarchate (Russian papacy), putting the Orthodox church under lay control, and permitting members of the ruling family to marry foreign princesses who were not Orthodox. Increasingly in Peter the Great's Russia, one historian writes,[1] the often-used Russian word for soul (*dusha*) was used to indicate numbers of people to be

[1] James H. Billington, *The Icon and the Axe: An Interpretive History of Russian Culture* (New York: Vintage Books, 1966), 184.

A Source Book for Russian History: From Early Times to 1917, ed. George Vernadsky (New Haven: Yale University Press, 1972), 347, 365–66.

taxed or conscripted in the army. And while Peter allowed the building of the first Roman Catholic church in Russia, he approved of
Galileo's stand against Rome and organized the Orthodox church
along Protestant lines. His new capital, St. Petersburg, was intended to
draw in, from across the Baltic Sea, the western winds of change from
Scandinavia, Germany, and Holland. In a series of more than three
thousand decrees, Peter attempted to modernize Russia by westernizing everything from mathematics to mustaches.

This selection includes just a sampling of some of Peter's reforms.
Why do you suppose the czar passed decrees to change Russian clothing and shaving habits? In what way could such changes be considered scientific, rational, or enlightened? How would you characterize
a czar who forces people to be enlightened? European rulers who attempted to institute similar changes were called "enlightened
despots." This label may seem a contradiction in terms until we consider Kant's belief that individuals have been trained to be fond of
tutelage. The great French philosopher Jean-Jacques Rousseau expressed a similar notion when he said that humans must be "forced to
be free." Do you think people can be tutored or forced to be free? Do
you think science and reason can lead to despotism as easily as to freedom?

Thinking Historically

To read a document carefully means understanding what is said as
well as being sensitive to what is implied. What in these decrees suggests that they might have been resisted or opposed? Which elements
of Russian society would have been most likely to resist? Would these
laws undermine such social groups or just change their behavior?
Would the czar's reforms, if successful, have brought about a cultural
revolution, a social revolution, or a political revolution?

Decree on Western Dress (1701)

Western dress shall be worn by all the boyars, members of our councils and of our court . . . gentry of Moscow, secretaries . . . provincial
gentry, gosti, government officials, strel'tsy, members of the guilds purveying for our household, citizens of Moscow of all ranks, and residents of provincial cities . . . excepting the clergy and peasant tillers of
the soil.[2] The upper dress shall be of French or Saxon cut, and the

---

[2] "Boyars" were nobles; "gosti" were merchants; and "strel'tsy" were soldiers in the imperial guard.

lower dress . . . — (including) waistcoat, trousers, boots, shoes, and hats — shall be of the German type. They shall also ride German saddles. Likewise the womenfolk of all ranks, including the priests', deacons', and church attendants' wives, the wives of the dragoons, the soldiers, and the strel'tsy, and their children, shall wear Western dresses, hats, jackets, and underwear — undervests and petticoats — and shoes. From now on no one of the above-mentioned is to wear Russian dress or Circassian coats, sheepskin coats, or Russian peasant coats, trousers, boots, and shoes. It is also forbidden to ride Russian saddles, and the craftsmen shall not manufacture them or sell them at the marketplaces.

Decree on Shaving (1705)

A decree to be published in Moscow and in all the provincial cities: Henceforth, in accordance with this, His Majesty's decree, all court attendants . . . provincial service men, government officials of all ranks, military men, all the gosti, members of the wholesale merchants' guild, and members of the guilds purveying for our household must shave their beards and moustaches. But, if it happens that some of them do not wish to shave their beards and moustaches, let a yearly tax be collected from such persons; from court attendants . . . provincial service men, military men, and government officials of all ranks — 60 rubles per person; from the gosti and members of the wholesale merchants' guild of the first class — 100 rubles per person; from members of the wholesale merchants' guild of the middle and the lower class (and) . . . from (other) merchants and townsfolk — 60 rubles per person; . . . from townsfolk (of the lower rank), boyars' servants, stagecoachmen, waggoners, church attendants (with the exception of priests and deacons), and from Moscow residents of all ranks — 30 rubles per person. Special badges shall be issued to them from the Administrator of Land Affairs of Public Order . . . which they must wear. . . . As for the peasants, let a toll of two half-copecks per beard be collected at the town gates each time they enter or leave a town; and do not let the peasants pass the town gates, into or out of town, without paying this toll.

Decree on Compulsory Education of the Russian Nobility (1714)

Send to every administrative district some persons from mathematical schools to teach the children of the nobility — except those of freeholders and government clerks — mathematics and geometry; as a penalty for evasion establish a rule that no one will be allowed to marry unless he learns these subjects. Inform all prelates to issue no marriage certificates to those who are ordered to go to schools. . . .

The Great Sovereign has decreed; in all administrative districts children between the ages of ten and fifteen of the nobility, of government clerks, and of lesser officials, except those of freeholders, must be taught mathematics and some geometry. Toward that end, students should be sent from mathematical schools as teachers, several into each administrative district to prelates and to renowned monasteries to establish schools. During their instruction these teachers should be given food and financial remuneration . . . from district revenues set aside for that purpose by personal orders of His Imperial Majesty. No fees should be collected from students. When they have mastered the material, they should then be given certificates written in their own handwriting. When the students are released they ought to pay one ruble each for their training. Without these certificates they should not be allowed to marry nor receive marriage certificates.

An Instruction to Russian Students Abroad Studying Navigation (1714)

1. Learn how to draw plans and charts and how to use the compass and other naval indicators.
2. Learn how to navigate a vessel in battle as well as in a simple maneuver, and learn how to use all appropriate tools and instruments; namely, sails, ropes, and oars, and the like matters, on row boats and other vessels.
3. Discover as much as possible how to put ships to sea during a naval battle. Those who cannot succeed in this effort must diligently ascertain what action should be taken by the vessels that do and those that do not put to sea during such a situation (naval battle). Obtain from foreign naval officers written statements, bearing their signatures and seals, of how adequately you are prepared for naval duties.
4. If, upon his return, anyone wishes to receive from the Tsar greater favors for himself, he should learn, in addition to the above enumerated instructions, how to construct those vessels abroad in which he would like to demonstrate his skills.
5. Upon his return to Moscow, every foreign-trained Russian should bring with him at his own expense, for which he will later be reimbursed, at least two experienced masters of naval science. They the returnees will be assigned soldiers, one soldier per returnee, to teach them what they have learned abroad. And if they do not wish to accept soldiers, they may teach their acquaintances or their own people. The treasury will pay for transportation and maintenance of soldiers. And if anyone other

than soldiers learns the art of navigation the treasury will pay 100 rubles for the maintenance of every such individual.

$$\boxed{25}$$

The American Declaration of Independence

If anyone had taken a poll of American colonials in the thirteen lower colonies (and certainly the colony of Canada to the north) as late as 1775, independence would not have won a majority vote anywhere. Massachusetts might have come close, perhaps, but nowhere in the land was there a definitive urge to separate from the British empire. Still, tensions between the colonies and Britain were inevitable. Three thousand miles was a long way for news, views, appointees, and petitions to travel. While the colonists respected the king, George III, they found his ministers inadequately informed about events in their homeland. Royal governors were generally judged to be inept and punitive. And none of the colonies participated in the election of members of the British Parliament.

Of course, each side looked at the cost of colonial administration differently. The British believed that they had carried a large part of the costs of migration, administration of trade, and control of the sea, while the colonists found they had borne the costs and the humiliation resulting from the lack of political representation. Each effort at taxation — the Stamp Act of 1765, the Townshend Act of 1767, the Tea Act of 1773 — provoked violent responses from colonists, stiffened the resolve of both sides, and led to militant retribution by the parliament and the king. The Coercive Acts or, as the colonists called them, the "Intolerable Acts" (1774) intended to punish them — especially in Massachusetts after the Boston Tea Party — by closing the port of Boston, reducing colonial political authority, and imposing the quartering of British troops. In response, the first Continental Congress was called in the fall of 1774 and a second the following May. By the spring of 1775, events were rapidly pushing the colonies toward independence. In April, British troops engaged colonial forces at Lexington and Concord, instigating a land war that was to last until 1781.

A Documentary History of the United States, ed. Richard D. Heffner (New York: Penguin Books, 1991), 15–18.

In the midst of other urgent business, most notably raising an army, the Congress asked a committee that included Thomas Jefferson, Benjamin Franklin, and John Adams to compose a statement outlining the reasons for separation from Britain. Jefferson wrote the first draft, most of which became the final version approved by the committee and accepted by the Continental Congress on July 4, 1776.

The Declaration of Independence was preeminently a document of the Enlightenment. Its principal author, Thomas Jefferson, exemplified the Enlightenment intellectual. Conversant in European literature, law, and political thought, he made significant contributions to eighteenth-century knowledge in natural science and architecture. Likewise, Benjamin Franklin, a printer by profession, was a leading scientist, writer, and wit. Both men founded universities — the Universities of Virginia and Pennsylvania, respectively. Both were at home in France, where they served the new government of the United States as diplomats after the war. Other delegates to the Congress in Philadelphia were similarly accomplished.

It is no wonder, then, that the Declaration and the establishment of an independent United States of America should strike the world as the realization of the Enlightenment's basic tenets: That a new country could be created afresh by people with intelligence and foresight, according to principles of reason, and to realize human liberty seemed a fitting capstone to the eighteenth-century mind. Images of America as a virgin land ("In the beginning there was America," John Locke had declared) ignored the presence of native inhabitants. Declarations of freedom overlooked human slavery. But notions of the Enlightenment and the ideal of man, governing himself, rationally and for the common good, was a heady brew.

What were the goals of the authors of this document? In what ways is the Declaration of Independence similar to, and different from, other documents of the Enlightenment that you have read in this chapter? What common ideas could be shared by a revolutionary like Jefferson and an enlightened despot like Peter the Great? In what ways was the Declaration a call for democracy? In what ways was it not?

Thinking Historically

Before interpreting any document, we must read it carefully and put it into context — that is, determine the what, where, and why. Some of this information may be available in the text itself. For instance, who is the Declaration addressed to? What is the reason given for writing it?

We interpret or extract meaning from documents by asking questions that emerge from the reading. These questions may arise from passages we do not understand, from lack of clarity in the text, or from an incongruence between the text and our expectations. It may surprise some readers, for example, that the Declaration criticizes the king so sharply. To question this might lead us to explore the need for American colonists to defend their actions in terms of British legal tradition. For years, the American colonists blamed the king's ministers for their difficulties; in July 1776 they blamed the king — a traditional sign of revolutionary intent in England, which meant efforts toward independence were imminent. Yet while they cast blame upon the king, the colonists also sought the approval from the court of British opinion.

What about the disparity between the lofty sentiments of liberty and independence and the existence of slavery in the Americas? How is it possible, we ask ourselves, that Jefferson and some of the signers of the Declaration could own slaves while declaring it "self-evident that all men are created equal"? Did it not occur to them to think of slaves as men? Did they mean some abstract equality between "men" (or women) in Britain and America rather than between individuals?

You might also be struck by similarities or differences between the Declaration and other documents you have read in this chapter. How does the American Revolution differ from the changes envisioned by Peter the Great or Kant? Did Americans put more trust in common reason than Kant? How was their dismissal of tyrannical authority similar to, or different from, that of Kant or Hume?

In Congress, July 4, 1776, the Unanimous Declaration of the Thirteen United States of America

When in the course of human events, it becomes necessary for one people to dissolve the political bands which have connected them with another, and to assume among the powers of the earth, the separate and equal station to which the Laws of Nature and of Nature's God entitle them, a decent respect to the opinions of mankind requires that they should declare the causes which impel them to the separation.

We hold these truths to be self-evident, that all men are created equal, that they are endowed by their Creator with certain unalienable rights, that among these are life, liberty, and the pursuit of happiness. That to secure these rights, governments are instituted among men, deriving their just powers from the consent of the governed. That whenever any form of government becomes destructive of these ends, it is the right of the people to alter or to abolish it, and to institute new government, laying its foundation on such principles and organizing its powers in such form, as to them shall seem most likely to effect their safety and happiness. Prudence, indeed, will dictate that governments long established should not be changed for light and transient causes; and accordingly all experience hath shown, that mankind are more disposed to suffer, while evils are sufferable, than to right themselves by abolishing the forms to which they are accustomed. But when a long train of abuses and usurpations, pursuing invariably the same object evinces a design to reduce them under absolute despotism, it is their right, it is their duty, to throw off such government, and to provide new guards for their future security. Such has been the patient sufferance of these Colonies; and such is now the necessity which constrains them to alter their former systems of government. The history of the present King of Great Britain is a history of repeated injuries and usurpations, all having in direct object the establishment of an absolute tyranny over these States. To prove this, let facts be submitted to a candid world.

He has refused his assent to laws, the most wholesome and necessary for the public good.

He has forbidden his Governors to pass laws of immediate and pressing importance, unless suspended in their operation till his assent should be obtained; and when so suspended, he has utterly neglected to attend to them.

He has refused to pass other laws for the accommodation of large districts of people, unless those people would relinquish the right of representation in the Legislature, a right inestimable to them and formidable to tyrants only.

He has called together legislative bodies at places unusual, uncomfortable, and distant from the depository of their public records, for the sole purpose of fatiguing them into compliance with his measures.

He has dissolved representative houses repeatedly, for opposing with manly firmness his invasions on the rights of the people.

He has refused for a long time, after such dissolutions, to cause others to be elected; whereby the legislative powers, incapable of annihilation, have returned to the people at large for their exercise; the State remaining in the meantime exposed to all the dangers of invasion from without and convulsions within.

He has endeavoured to prevent the population of these states; for that purpose obstructing the laws of naturalization of foreigners; refusing to pass others to encourage their migration hither, and raising the conditions of new appropriations of lands.

He has obstructed the administration of justice, by refusing his assent to laws for establishing judiciary powers.

He has made judges dependent on his will alone, for the tenure of their offices, and the amount and payment of their salaries.

He has erected a multitude of new offices, and sent hither swarms of officers to harass our people, and eat out their substance.

He has kept among us, in times of peace, standing armies without the consent of our legislatures.

He has affected to render the military independent of and superior to the civil power.

He has combined with others to subject us to a jurisdiction foreign to our constitution, and unacknowledged by our laws; giving his assent to their acts of pretended legislation:

For quartering large bodies of armed troops among us:

For protecting them, by a mock trial, from punishment for any murders which they should commit on the inhabitants of these States:

For cutting off our trade with all parts of the world:

For imposing taxes on us without our consent:

For depriving us in many cases, of the benefits of trial by jury:

For transporting us beyond seas to be tried for pretended offences:

For abolishing the free system of English laws in a neighbouring Province, establishing therein an arbitrary government, and enlarging its boundaries so as to render it at once an example and fit instrument for introducing the same absolute rule into these Colonies:

For taking away our Charters, abolishing our most valuable laws, and altering fundamentally the forms of our governments:

For suspending our own Legislatures, and declaring themselves invested with power to legislate for us in all cases whatsoever.

He has abdicated government here, by declaring us out of his protection and waging war against us.

He has plundered our seas, ravaged our coasts, burnt our towns, and destroyed the lives of our people.

He is at this time transporting large armies of foreign mercenaries to complete the works of death, desolation, and tyranny, already begun with circumstances of cruelty and perfidy scarcely paralleled in the most barbarous ages, and totally unworthy the head of a civilized nation.

He has constrained our fellow citizens taken captive on the high seas to bear arms against their country, to become the executioners of their friends and brethren, or to fall themselves by their hands.

He has excited domestic insurrections amongst us, and has endeavoured to bring on the inhabitants of our frontiers, the merciless Indian savages, whose known rule of warfare, is an undistinguished destruction of all ages, sexes, and conditions.

In every state of these oppressions we have petitioned for redress in the most humble terms: our repeated petitions have been answered only by repeated injury. A prince whose character is thus marked by every act which may define a tyrant is unfit to be the ruler of a free people.

Nor have we been wanting in attention to our British brethren. We have warned them from time to time of attempts by their legislature to extend an unwarrantable jurisdiction over us. We have reminded them of the circumstances of our emigration and settlement here. We have appealed to their native justice and magnanimity, and we have conjured them by the ties of our common kindred to disavow these usurpations, which would inevitably interrupt our connections and correspondence. They too have been deaf to the voice of justice and of consanguinity. We must, therefore, acquiesce in the necessity, which denounces our separation, and hold them, as we hold the rest of mankind, enemies in war, in peace friends.

We, therefore, the Representatives of the United States of America, in General Congress assembled, appealing to the Supreme Judge of the world for the rectitude of our intentions, do, in the name, and by authority of the good people of these Colonies, solemnly publish and declare, That these United Colonies are, and of right ought to be Free and Independent States; that they are absolved from all allegiance to the British Crown, and that all political connection between them and the State of Great Britain, is and ought to be totally dissolved; and that as Free and Independent States, they have full power to levy war, conclude peace, contract alliances, establish commerce, and to do all other acts and things which Independent States may of right do. And for the support of this declaration, with a firm reliance on the protection of Divine Province, we mutually pledge to each other our lives, our fortunes, and our sacred honor.

26

The French Declaration of the Rights of Man and Citizen

The American Revolution began as a movement for independence and ended in the formation of a new government of the people — a republic without a king, without even a hereditary nobility like the British House of Lords. At that time, there were few historical republics to serve as models — ancient Greek and Italian Renaissance city-states and England under the revolutionary government of Oliver Cromwell (1599–1658) — and most did not last.

The founding of the Republic of the United States of America provided another model to emulate. Not suprisingly then, when the French movement to end political injustices turned to revolution in

A Documentary History of the French Revolution, ed. John Hall Stewart (London: Macmillan, 1979).

1789 and the revolutionaries convened at the National Assembly, the Marquis de Lafayette (1757–1834), hero of the American Revolution, proposed a Declaration of the Rights of Man and Citizen. Lafayette had the American Declaration in mind, and he had the assistance of Thomas Jefferson, present in Paris as the first United States ambassador to France, America's earliest ally.

While the resulting document appealed to a party of French revolutionaries who believed in natural and inalienable rights, the French were not able to start afresh as the Americans had done. The Americans established a republic because they had no king. In 1789 Louis XVI was still king of France: He could not be made to leave by a turn of phrase. Nor were men created equal in France in 1789. Those born into the nobility led lives different from those born into the Third Estate (the 99 percent of the population who were not nobility or clergy), and they had different legal rights as well. This disparity was precisely what the revolutionaries and the Declaration sought to change. Inevitably, though, such change would prove to be a more violent and revolutionary proposition than it had been in the American colonies. The American experience showed that it was rational and possible to create a society of citizens whose rights were protected by their own laws, but only French radicals believed that the American model could work in France.

In what ways did the Declaration of the Rights of Man and Citizen resemble the American Declaration of Independence? In what ways was it different? Which was more democratic?

Thinking Historically

As we have noted, the French Declaration is full of abstract, universal principles. But notice how such abstractions can claim our consent by their rationality without informing us as to how they will be implemented. What is meant by the first right, for instance? What does it mean to say that men are "born free"? Why is it necessary to distinguish between "born" and "remain"? What is meant by the phrase "general usefulness"? Do statements like these increase people's liberties, or are they intentionally vague so they can be interpreted at will?

The slogan of the French Revolution was "Liberty, Equality, Fraternity." Which of the rights in the French Declaration emphasize liberty, which equality? Can these two goals be opposed to each other? Was the French declaration more likely to create equality than the American Declaration of Independence?

The representatives of the French people, organized in National Assembly, considering that ignorance, forgetfulness, or contempt of the rights of man are the sole causes of public misfortunes and of the corruption of governments, have resolved to set forth in a solemn declaration the natural, inalienable, and sacred rights of man, in order that such declaration, continually before all members of the social body, may be a perpetual reminder of their rights and duties; in order that the acts of the legislative power and those of the executive power may constantly be compared with the aim of every political institution and may accordingly be more respected; in order that the demands of the citizens, founded henceforth upon simple and incontestable principles, may always be directed towards the maintenance of the Constitution and the welfare of all.

Accordingly, the National Assembly recognizes and proclaims, in the presence and under the auspices of the Supreme Being, the following rights of man and citizen.

1. Men are born and remain free and equal in rights; social distinctions may be based only upon general usefulness.

2. The aim of every political association is the preservation of the natural and inalienable rights of man; these rights are liberty, property, security, and resistance to oppression.

3. The source of all sovereignty resides essentially in the nation; no group, no individual may exercise authority not emanating expressly therefrom.

4. Liberty consists of the power to do whatever is not injurious to others; thus the enjoyment of the natural rights of every man has for its limits only those that assure other members of society the enjoyment of those same rights; such limits may be determined only by law.

5. The law has the right to forbid only actions which are injurious to society. Whatever is not forbidden by law may not be prevented, and no one may be constrained to do what it does not prescribe.

6. Law is the expression of the general will; all citizens have the right to concur personally, or through their representatives, in its formation; it must be the same for all, whether it protects or punishes. All citizens, being equal before it, are equally admissible to all public offices, positions, and employments, according to their capacity, and without other distinction than that of virtues and talents.

7. No man may be accused, arrested, or detained except in the cases determined by law, and according to the forms prescribed thereby. Whoever solicit, expedite, or execute arbitrary orders, or have them executed, must be punished; but every citizen summoned or apprehended in pursuance of the law must obey immediately; he renders himself culpable by resistance.

8. The law is to establish only penalties that are absolutely and obviously necessary; and no one may be punished except by virtue of a law established and promulgated prior to the offence and legally applied.

9. Since every man is presumed innocent until declared guilty, if arrest be deemed indispensable, all unnecessary severity for securing the person of the accused must be severely repressed by law.

10. No one is to be disquieted because of his opinions, even religious, provided their manifestation does not disturb the public order established by law.

11. Free communication of ideas and opinions is one of the most precious of the rights of man. Consequently, every citizen may speak, write, and print freely, subject to responsibility for the abuse of such liberty in the cases determined by law.

12. The guarantee of the rights of man and citizen necessitates a public force; therefore, is instituted for the advantage of all and not for the particular benefit of those to whom it is entrusted.

13. For the maintenance of the public force and for the expenses of administration a common tax is indispensable; it must be assessed equally on all citizens in proportion to their means.

14. Citizens have the right to ascertain, by themselves or through their representatives, the necessity of the public tax, to consent to it freely, to supervise its use, and to determine its quota, assessment, payment, and duration.

15. Society has the right to require of every public agent an accounting of his administration.

16. Every society in which the guarantee of rights is not assured or the separation of powers not determined has no constitution at all.

17. Since property is a sacred and inviolate right, no one may be deprived thereof unless a legally established public necessity obviously requires it, and upon condition of a just and previous indemnity.

27

The United States Bill of Rights

The Constitutional Convention that met in Philadelphia in 1787 comprised diverse interests: thirteen newly independent states representing North and South, merchants and planters, and urban and rural areas. Consequently, one of the serious matters of dispute at the convention

A Documentary History of the United States, ed. Richard D. Heffner (New York: Penguin Books, 1991), 34–36.

was how much sovereignty each state was prepared to relinquish to a federal government. Those who favored a vigorous executive and centralized government were known as the Federalists; those who feared a strong central government were known as Anti-Federalists.

Some were concerned about future limitations of individual liberties or state power by the federal government. One of the arguments the Anti-Federalists made against the proposed federal constitution was that it lacked a bill of rights, though this had hardly been an issue at the convention. George Madison of Virginia suggested such a bill late in the summer of 1787 when the delegates' work was almost done, so it was not included. As the Constitution was passed on to the states for ratification, Anti-Federalists drummed up support for a bill of rights. Two states, Rhode Island and North Carolina, refused to adopt the Constitution without one; other states passed the Constitution on the condition that a bill of rights would be forthcoming.

Most states had a bill of rights in their own constitutions; the absence of one in the federal constitution was a clear cause for concern. The Federalists, led by James Madison (1751–1836), the principal drafter of the Constitution, argued that a bill of rights was not necessary because the Constitution listed only powers that were delegated to the federal government — all other powers belonged to the states and individuals. Countering this, the Anti-Federalists noted that the Constitution named certain acts the federal government could *not* pass, making the failure to designate other restrictions on federal power troubling. Federalists believed that Anti-Federalists only wanted to weaken the federal government. With the mounting opposition of Anti-Federalists and an endorsement of a bill of rights by George Washington in his first inaugural address in April 1789, Madison agreed to work with the Congress to draft a bill of rights as the first ten amendments to the Constitution.

How do the protections of individual rights in the Bill of Rights differ from the principles enunciated in the Declaration of Independence or the French Declaration of the Rights of Man and Citizen? Do they do more than either of the earlier documents to protect individual rights and liberties? How so?

Thinking Historically

In reading historical texts, it is important to understand how words were used in their original context. Often the words are the same as or similar to our own, but the circumstances may be so foreign to us that we misinterpret their meaning. At other times, words in historical documents are used in the same way we would use them because in some sense past and present are not all that different.

In the debate between Federalists and Anti-Federalists, we might hear echoes of issues still alive in American politics. Yet our world in the twenty-first century is very different from that of the eighteenth century. Does this mean that the checks proposed by the Anti-Federalists are quaint anachronisms that no longer have meaning in the modern world? Or does the enormous power of the modern state make such protections even more necessary than they were two hundred years ago? Do we still need a well-trained militia? Must we still protect citizens from the quartering of troops? Is an eighteenth-century threshold of twenty dollars for a trial by jury appropriate today?

The Bill of Rights contains an odd combination of obvious fundamental principles and specific, time-bound prescriptions. Yet, the capacity of people to continually reinterpret language to find relevance and meaning causes some of the seemingly most dated rights (for example, the right to bear arms) to be vigorously defended even today.

Perhaps it is the notion of natural, innate rights that appeals to us today as strongly as it did in the eighteenth century. One historian writes, "The eighteenth century was a period (not, perhaps, unlike our own) in which the public's penchant for asserting its rights outran its ability to analyze them and to reach a consensus about their scope and meaning."[1]

The same historian points out that many English officials and commentators were struck by the unusual degree to which colonial Americans claimed *individual* rights. As early as 1704, James Logan, an agent of William Penn, ridiculed Pennsylvanians' obsession with the "Rattle of Rights and Privileges." English texts like the *Petition of Rights* in 1689 had claimed the rights of Parliament, but the notion that rights were held by individuals rather than by the community was perceived to be a distinctly American idea.

Is it still? Or is it again? The Bill of Rights was largely ignored from the time of its passage (1789–1791) until the twentieth century. The Fourteenth Amendment (1868), which made state matters a federal concern, was used increasingly in the twentieth century to defend the rights of minorities, women, even unions. The late twentieth century witnessed a civil rights movement and a proposal for an equal rights amendment, not to mention appeals for animal rights, plant rights, and even earth rights. And what of the vigorously argued issue of a "woman's right to choose" versus "the right to life"? We are also able to argue for human rights, minority rights, the right to die, and the rights of the dispossessed.

This legacy of the Enlightenment moves us still. Is it important that we struggle to define our rights more precisely? How does this com-

---

[1] James Hutson, "The Bill of Rights and the American Revolutionary Experience," in Michael J. Lacey and Knud Haakonssen, eds., *A Culture of Rights: The Bill of Rights in Philosophy, Politics, and Law 1791 and 1991* (New York: Cambridge University Press and the Woodrow Wilson Center for Scholarship, 1991), 63.

pare with the thinkers of the eighteenth century who declared their rights (that is, what they thought obvious, natural, and inalienable)? For many postmodern thinkers of the twentieth century, change has been so persistent that constancy has been all but eliminated. How ironic it is, then, that our age revived the notion of an individual's intrinsic, natural rights, when it seems that we can invent them as we go along. When we speak of rights today, do we mean what eighteenth-century thinkers did, or are we merely using the same word?

Amendment 1

Congress shall make no law respecting an establishment of religion, or prohibiting the free exercise thereof; or abridging the freedom of speech, or of the press; or the right of the people peaceably to assemble, and to petition the Government for a redress of grievances.

Amendment 2

A well-regulated Militia, being necessary to the security of a free State, the right of the people to keep and bear Arms, shall not be infringed.

Amendment 3

No Soldier shall, in time of peace, be quartered in any house without the consent of the Owner, nor in time of war, but in a manner to be prescribed by law.

Amendment 4

The right of the people to be secure in their persons, houses, papers, and effects, against unreasonable searches and seizures, shall not be violated, and no Warrants shall issue, but upon probable cause, supported by Oath or affirmation, and particularly describing the place to be searched, and the persons or things to be seized.

Amendment 5

No person shall be held to answer for a capital, or otherwise infamous crime, unless on a presentment or indictment of a Grand Jury, except in cases arising in the land or naval forces, or in the Militia, when an actual service in time of War or public danger; nor shall any person be subject for the same offence to be twice put in jeopardy of life or limb; nor shall be compelled in any criminal case to be a witness against himself, nor be deprived of life, liberty, or property, without due process of law; nor shall private property be taken for public use, without just compensation.

Amendment 6

In all criminal prosecutions, the accused shall enjoy the right to a speedy and public trial, by an impartial jury of the State and district wherein the crime shall have been committed, which district shall have been previously ascertained by law, and to be informed of the nature and cause of the accusation; to be confronted with the witness against him; to have compulsory process for obtaining witness in his favor, and to have the Assistance of Counsel for his defence.

Amendment 7

In Suits at common law, where the value in controversy shall exceed twenty dollars, the right of trial by jury shall be preserved, and no fact tried by a jury, shall be otherwise reexamined in any Court of the United States, than according to the rules of the common law.

Amendment 8

Excessive bail shall not be required, nor excessive fines imposed, nor cruel and unusual punishments inflicted.

Amendment 9

The enumeration in the Constitution, of certain rights, shall not be construed to deny or disparage others retained by the people.

Amendment 10

The powers not delegated to the United States by the Constitution, nor prohibited by it to the States, are reserved to the States respectively, or to the people.

28

SIMÓN BOLÍVAR

A Constitution for Venezuela

Simón Bolívar (1783–1830), called "the Liberator," successfully led the Latin American revolution for independence from Spain between 1810 and 1824. In 1819, he became president of Venezuela and of what is today Colombia, Ecuador, and Panama, and he gave the speech on the Constitution of Venezuela that follows.

What does he see as the difference between the independence of Spanish-American colonies and that of the American colonies? What does he mean when he says that Latin Americans have been denied "domestic tyranny"? Would you call Bolívar a "democrat"? Is he more or less democratic than the French or North American revolutionaries? What kind of society do you think would result from the constitution he envisions?

Thinking Historically

The language Bolívar uses to discuss the proposed Latin American constitution brings together a number of this chapter's threads. In what ways are Bolívar's language and ideas like those of the other Enlightenment thinkers you have read? Which of his ideas are like Kant's? Which are more like Jefferson's?

How does Bolívar characterize the revolutionary population of South America? How does this subjective characterization differ from that of North American revolutionaries? What do you think accounts for this difference?

In what ways did the revolutionaries of South America, North America, and France see their problems and needs differently? How did Bolívar propose to solve what he perceived to be the unique problems of South America? What do you think of his solution?

Let us review the past to discover the base upon which the Republic of Venezuela is founded.

America, in separating from the Spanish monarchy, found herself in a situation similar to that of the Roman Empire when its enormous

Selected Writings of Bolívar, comp. Vincent Lecuna, ed. Harold A. Bierck, Jr., 2 vols. (New York: Colonial Press, 1951), 175–91.

framework fell to pieces in the midst of the ancient world. Each Roman division then formed an independent nation in keeping with its location or interests; but this situation differed from America's in that those members proceeded to reestablish their former associations. We, on the contrary, do not even retain the vestiges of our original being. We are not Europeans; we are not Indians; we are but a mixed species of aborigines and Spaniards. Americans by birth and Europeans by law, we find ourselves engaged in a dual conflict: We are disputing with the natives for titles of ownership, and at the same time we are struggling to maintain ourselves in the country that gave us birth against the opposition of the invaders. Thus our position is most extraordinary and complicated. But there is more. As our role has always been strictly passive and political existence nil, we find that our quest for liberty is now even more difficult of accomplishment; for we, having been placed in a state lower than slavery, had been robbed not only of our freedom but also of the right to exercise an active domestic tyranny. Permit me to explain this paradox.

In absolute systems, the central power is unlimited. The will of the despot is the supreme law, arbitrarily enforced by subordinates who take part in the organized oppression in proportion to the authority that they wield. They are charged with civil, political, military, and religious functions; but, in the final analysis, the satraps of Persia are Persian, the pashas of the Grand Turk are Turks, and the sultans of Tartary are Tartars. China does not seek her mandarins in the homeland of Genghis Khan, her conqueror. America, on the contrary, received everything from Spain, who, in effect, deprived her of the experience that she would have gained from the exercise of an active tyranny by not allowing her to take part in her own domestic affairs and administration. This exclusion made it impossible for us to acquaint ourselves with the management of public affairs; nor did we enjoy that personal consideration, of such great value in major revolutions, that the brilliance of power inspires in the eyes of the multitude. In brief, Gentlemen, we were deliberately kept in ignorance and cut off from the world in all matters relating to the science of government.

Subject to the three-fold yoke of ignorance, tyranny, and vice, the American people have been unable to acquire knowledge, power, or [civic] virtue. The lessons we received and the models we studied, as pupils of such pernicious teachers, were most destructive. We have been ruled more by deceit than by force, and we have been degraded more by vice than by superstition. Slavery is the daughter of darkness: An ignorant people is a blind instrument of its own destruction. Ambition and intrigue abuse the credulity and experience of men lacking all political, economic, and civic knowledge; they adopt pure illusion as reality; they take license for liberty, treachery for patriotism, and vengeance for justice. This situation is similar to that of the robust blind man who, beguiled by his strength, strides forward with all the assurance of one who can see, but, upon hitting every variety of obstacle, finds himself unable to retrace his steps.

If a people, perverted by their training, succeed in achieving their liberty, they will soon lose it, for it would be of no avail to endeavor to explain to them that happiness consists in the practice of virtue; that the rule of law is more powerful than the rule of tyrants, because, as the laws are more inflexible, every one should submit to their beneficent austerity; that proper morals, and not force, are the bases of law; and that to practice justice is to practice liberty. Therefore, Legislators, your work is so much the more arduous, inasmuch as you have to reeducate men who have been corrupted by erroneous illusions and false incentives. Liberty, says Rousseau, is a succulent morsel, but one difficult to digest. Our weak fellow-citizens will have to strengthen their spirit greatly before they can digest the wholesome nutriment of freedom. Their limbs benumbed by chains, their sight dimmed by the darkness of dungeons, and their strength sapped by the pestilence of servitude, are they capable of marching toward the august temple of Liberty without faltering? Can they come near enough to bask in its brilliant rays and to breathe freely the pure air which reigns therein? . . . .

The more I admire the excellence of the federal Constitution of Venezuela, the more I am convinced of the impossibility of its application to our state. And to my way of thinking, it is a marvel that its prototype in North America endures so successfully and has not been overthrown at the first sign of adversity or danger. Although the people of North America are a singular model of political virtue and moral rectitude; although the nation was cradled in liberty, reared on freedom, and maintained by liberty alone; and — I must reveal everything — although those people, so lacking in many respects, are unique in the history of mankind, it is a marvel, I repeat, that so weak and complicated a government as the federal system has managed to govern them in the difficult and trying circumstances of their past. But, regardless of the effectiveness of this form of government with respect to North America, I must say that it has never for a moment entered my mind to compare the position and character of two states as dissimilar as the English-American and the Spanish-American. Would it not be most difficult to apply to Spain the English system of political, civil, and religious liberty? Hence, it would be even more difficult to adapt to Venezuela the laws of North America. Does not *L'Esprit des Lois* state that laws should be suited to the people for whom they are made; that it would be a major coincidence if those of one nation could be adapted to another; that laws must take into account the physical conditions of the country, climate, character of the land, location, size, and mode of living of the people; that they should be in keeping with the degree of liberty that the Constitution can sanction respecting the religion of the inhabitants, their inclinations, resources, number, commerce, habits, and customs? This is the code we must consult, not the code of Washington! . . .

Venezuela had, has, and should have a republican government. Its principles should be the sovereignty of the people, division of powers, civil liberty, proscription of slavery, and the abolition of monarchy and privileges. We need equality to recast, so to speak, into a unified nation, the classes of men, political opinions, and public customs.

Among the ancient and modern nations, Rome and Great Britain are the most outstanding. Both were born to govern and to be free and both were built not on ostentatious forms of freedom, but upon solid institutions. Thus I recommend to you, Representatives, the study of the British Constitution, for that body of laws appears destined to bring about the greatest possible good for the peoples that adopt it; but, however perfect it may be, I am by no means proposing that you imitate it slavishly. When I speak of the British government, I only refer to its republican features; and, indeed, can a political system be labelled a monarchy when it recognizes popular sovereignty, division and balance of powers, civil liberty, freedom of conscience and of press, and all that is politically sublime? Can there be more liberty in any other type of republic? Can more be asked of any society? I commend this Constitution to you as that most worthy of serving as model for those who aspire to the enjoyment of the rights of man and who seek all the political happiness which is compatible with the frailty of human nature.

Nothing in our fundamental laws would have to be altered were we to adopt a legislative power similar to that held by the British Parliament. Like the North Americans, we have divided national representation into two chambers; that of Representatives and the Senate. The first is very wisely constituted. It enjoys all its proper functions, and it requires no essential revision, because the Constitution, in creating it, gave it the form and powers which the people deemed necessary in order that they might be legally and properly represented. If the Senate were hereditary rather than elective, it would, in my opinion, be the basis, the tie, the very soul of our republic. In political storms this body would arrest the thunderbolts of the government and would repel any violent popular reaction. Devoted to the government because of a natural interest in its own preservation, a hereditary senate would always oppose any attempt on the part of the people to infringe upon the jurisdiction and authority of their magistrates. It must be confessed that most men are unaware of their best interests, and that they constantly endeavor to assail them in the hands of their custodians — the individual clashes with the mass, and the mass with authority. It is necessary, therefore, that in all governments there be a neutral body to protect the injured and disarm the offender. To be neutral, this body must not owe its origin to appointment by the government or to election by the people, if it is to enjoy a full measure of independence which neither fears nor expects anything from these two sources of authority. The hereditary senate, as a part of the people, shares its interests, its sentiments, and its spirit. For this reason it should not be presumed that a hereditary senate would ignore the interests of the people or forget its legislative duties. The senators in Rome and in the House of Lords in London have been the strongest pillars upon which the edifice of political and civil liberty has rested.

At the outset, these senators should be elected by Congress. The successors to this Senate must command the initial attention of the government, which should educate them in a *colegio* designed especially to train these guardians and future legislators of the nation. They ought to learn the arts, sciences, and letters that enrich the mind of a public figure. From childhood they should understand the career for which they have been destined by Providence, and from earliest youth they should prepare their minds for the dignity that awaits them.

The creation of a hereditary senate would in no way be a violation of political equality. I do not solicit the establishment of a nobility, for as a celebrated republican has said, that would simultaneously destroy equality and liberty. What I propose is an office for which the candidates must prepare themselves, an office that demands great knowledge and the ability to acquire such knowledge. All should not be left to chance and the outcome of elections. The people are more easily deceived than is Nature perfected by art; and, although these senators, it is true, would not be bred in an environment that is all virtue, it is equally true that they would be raised in an atmosphere of enlightened education. Furthermore, the liberators of Venezuela are entitled to occupy forever a high rank in the Republic that they have brought into existence. I believe that posterity would view with regret the effacement of the illustrious names of its first benefactors. I say, moreover, that it is a matter of public interest and national honor, of gratitude on Venezuela's part, to honor gloriously, until the end of time, a race of virtuous, prudent, and persevering men who, overcoming every obstacle, have founded the Republic at the price of the most heroic sacrifices. And if the people of Venezuela do not applaud the elevation of their benefactors, then they are unworthy to be free, and they will never be free.

A hereditary senate, I repeat, will be the fundamental basis of the legislative power, and therefore the foundation of the entire government. It will also serve as a counterweight to both government and people; and as a neutral power it will weaken the mutual attacks of these two eternally rival powers. In all conflicts the calm reasoning of a third party will serve as the means of reconciliation. Thus the Venezuelan senate will give strength to this delicate political structure, so sensitive to violent repercussions; it will be the mediator that will lull the storms and it will maintain harmony between the head and the other parts of the political body.

REFLECTIONS

The Enlightenment and its legacies — secular order and revolutionary republicanism — were European in origin but global in impact. In this chapter, we have touched on just a few of the crosscurrents of what some historians call an "Atlantic Revolution." A tide of revolutionary fervor swept through France, the United States, and Latin America, found sympathy in Russia in 1825, and echoed in the Muslim heartland, resulting in secular, modernizing regimes in Turkey and Egypt in the next century.

The Age of Revolution also marked the beginning of an age of mass migration, the earliest examples prompted by recruitment of soldiers for foreign wars. King George III of Britain shipped German Hessian troops across the Atlantic to suppress the American Revolution. The American revolutionaries moved quickly toward a Declaration of Independence in 1776 so that, as an independent nation, they could request military assistance from France, which they felt might be hesitant to meddle in British colonial affairs. Simón Bolívar owed a great deal of his success to Irish volunteers who saw the Liberator's struggle against Spain as comparable with their own against England.

The appeal of the Enlightenment, of rationally ordered society, and of democratic government continues. Elements of this eighteenth-century revolution — the rule of law; regular, popular elections of representatives; the separation of church and state, of government and politics, and of civil and military authority — are widely recognized ideals and emerging global realities. Like science, the principles of the Enlightenment are universal in their claims and often seem universal in their appeal. Nothing is simpler, more rational, or easier to follow than a call to reason, law, liberty, justice, or equality. And yet every society has evolved its own guidelines under different circumstances, often with lasting results. France had its king and still has a relatively centralized state. The United States began with slavery and still suffers from racism. South American states became free of Europe only to dominate Native Americans, and they continue to do so. One democratic society has a king, another a House of Lords, another a national church. Are these different adaptations of the Enlightenment ideal? Or are these examples of incomplete revolution, cases of special interests allowing their governments to fall short of principle?

The debate continues today as more societies seek to realize responsive, representative government and the rule of law while oftentimes respecting conflicting traditions. Muslim countries and Israel struggle with the competing demands of secular law and religion, citizenship and communalism. Former communist countries adopt market economies and struggle with traditions of collective support and the appeal of individual liberty.

Perhaps these are conflicts within the Enlightenment tradition itself. How is it possible to have both liberty and equality? How can we claim inalienable rights on the basis of a secular, scientific creed? How does a faith in human reason lead to revolution? And how can ideas of order or justice avoid the consequences of history and human nature?

6

Capitalism and the
Industrial Revolution

HISTORICAL CONTEXT
Europe and the World, 1750–1900

Two principal forces have shaped the modern world: capitalism and the industrial revolution. As influential as the transformations discussed in Chapter 5 (the rise of science and the democratic revolution), these two forces are sometimes considered to be one and the same, because the industrial revolution occurred first in capitalist countries such as England, Holland, and the United States. In fact, the rise of capitalism preceded the industrial revolution by centuries.

Capitalism denotes a particular economic organization of a society, whereas *industrial revolution* refers to a particular transformation of technology. Specifically, in capitalism market forces (supply and demand) set money prices that determine how goods are distributed. Markets for products and services are found in virtually all city societies, but throughout much of history these markets have played only minor roles in people's lives. Most economic behavior was regulated by family, religion, tradition, and political authority rather than by markets. Increasingly after 1500 in Europe, feudal dues were converted into money rents, periodic fairs became institutionalized, banks were established, modern book-keeping procedures were developed, and older systems of inherited economic status were loosened. After 1800, new populations of urban workers had to work for money to buy food and shelter; after 1850 even clothing had to be purchased in the new "department stores." By 1900, the market had become the operating metaphor of society: One sold oneself; everything had its price. Viewed positively, a capitalist society is one in which buyers and sellers, who together compose the market, make most decisions about the production and distribution of resources. Viewed less favorably, it is the capitalists — those who own the resources of the society — who make the

187

decisions about production and distribution. The democratic process of one person, one vote is supplanted by one dollar, one vote.

The industrial revolution made mass production possible with the use of power-driven machines. Mills driven by waterwheels existed in ancient times, but the construction of identical, replaceable machinery — the machine production of machines — revolutionized industry and enabled the coordination of production on a vast scale, occurring first in England's cotton textile mills at the end of the eighteenth century. The market for such textiles was capitalist, though the demand for many early mass-produced goods, such as muskets and uniforms, was government-driven.

The origins of capitalism are hotly debated among historians. Because the world's first cities, five thousand years ago, created markets, merchants, money, and private ownership of capital, some historians refer to an ancient capitalism. In this text, *capitalism* refers to those societies whose markets, merchants, money, and private ownership became central to the way society operated. As such, ancient Mesopotamia, Rome, and Sung dynasty China, which had extensive markets and paper money a thousand years ago, were not among the first capitalist societies. Smaller societies in which commercial interests and merchant classes took hold to direct political and economic matters were the capitalist forerunners. Malacca, Venice, Florence, Holland, and England, the mercantile states of the fifteenth to seventeenth centuries, exemplify *commercial capitalism* or mercantile capitalism. Thus, the shift to industrial capitalism was more than a change in scale; it was also a transition from a trade-based economy to a manufacturing-based economy, a difference that meant an enormous increase in productivity, profits, and prosperity.

THINKING HISTORICALLY
Distinguishing Causes of Change

Because industry and capitalism are so closely associated, it is difficult to distinguish the effects of one from the other. Still, such a distinction is necessary if we are to understand historical change.

Try to make an analytical distinction between capitalism and industrialization, even when the sources in this chapter do not. By determining what changes can be attributed to each, you will come to understand the changes that capitalism and industrialization might bring to other societies and the impact they may have had in other time periods.

Secondary

29

ARNOLD PACEY
Asia and the Industrial Revolution

Here a modern historian of technology demonstrates how Indian manufacturing techniques were assimilated by Europeans, particularly by the English successors of the Mughal Empire, providing a boost to the industrial revolution in Britain. In what ways was Indian technology considered superior prior to the industrial revolution? How did European products gain greater markets than those of India?

Thinking Historically

Notice how the author distinguishes between capitalism and the industrial revolution. Was India more industrially advanced than capitalistic? Did the British conquest of India benefit more from capitalism, industry, or something else?

Deindustrialization

During the eighteenth century, India participated in the European industrial revolution through the influence of its textile trade, and through the investments in shipping made by Indian bankers and merchants. Developments in textiles and shipbuilding constituted a significant industrial movement, but it would be wrong to suggest that India was on the verge of its own industrial revolution. There was no steam engine in India, no coal mines, and few machines. . . . [E]xpanding industries were mostly in coastal areas. Much of the interior was in economic decline, with irrigation works damaged and neglected as a result of the breakup of the Mughal Empire and the disruption of war. Though political weakness in the empire had been evident since 1707, and a Persian army heavily defeated Mughal forces at Delhi in 1739, it was the British who most fully took advantage of the collapse of the empire. Between 1757 and 1803, they took control of most of India except the Northwest. The result was that the East India Company now administered major sectors of the economy, and quickly reduced the role of the big Indian bankers by changes in taxes and methods of collecting them.

Meanwhile, India's markets in Europe were being eroded by competition from machine-spun yarns and printed calicoes made in Lancashire,

Arnold Pacey, *Technology in World Civilization* (Cambridge: MIT Press, 1990), 128–35.

189

and high customs duties were directed against Indian imports into Britain. Restrictions were also placed on the use of Indian-built ships for voyages to England. From 1812, there were extra duties on any imports they delivered, and that must be one factor in the decline in shipbuilding. A few Indian ships continued to make the voyage to Britain, however, and there was one in Liverpool Docks in 1839 when Herman Melville arrived from America. It was the *Irrawaddy* from Bombay and Melville commented: "Forty years ago, these merchantmen were nearly the largest in the world; and they still exceed the generality." They were "wholly built by the native shipwrights of India, who . . . surpassed the European artisans." Melville further commented on a point which an Indian historian confirms, that the coconut fibre rope used for rigging on most Indian ships was too elastic and needed constant attention. Thus the rigging on the *Irrawaddy* was being changed for hemp rope while it was in Liverpool. Sisal rope was an alternative in India, used with advantage on some ships based at Calcutta.

Attitudes to India changed markedly after the subcontinent had fallen into British hands. Before this, travellers found much to admire in technologies ranging from agriculture to metallurgy. After 1803, however, the arrogance of conquest was reinforced by the rapid development of British industry. This meant that Indian techniques which a few years earlier seemed remarkable could now be equalled at much lower cost by British factories. India was then made to appear rather primitive, and the idea grew that its proper role was to provide raw materials for western industry, including raw cotton and indigo dye, and to function as a market for British goods. This policy was reflected in 1813 by a relaxation of the East India Company's monopoly of trade so that other British companies could now bring in manufactured goods freely for sale in India. Thus the textile industry, iron production, and shipbuilding were all eroded by cheap imports from Britain, and by handicaps placed on Indian merchants.

By 1830, the situation had become so bad that even some of the British in India began to protest. One exclaimed, "We have destroyed the manufactures of India," pleading that there should be some protection for silk weaving, "the last of the expiring manufactures of India." Another observer was alarmed by a "commercial revolution" which produced "so much present suffering to numerous classes in India."

The question that remains is the speculative one of what might have happened if a strong Mughal government had survived. Fernand Braudel argues that although there was no lack of "capitalism" in India, the economy was not moving in the direction of home-grown industrialization. The historian of technology inevitably notes the lack of development of machines, even though there had been some increase in the use of water-wheels during the eighteenth century both in the iron industry and at gunpowder mills. However, it is impossible not to be struck by the achievements of the shipbuilding industry, which produced skilled carpenters and a model of large-scale organizations. It also trained up draughtsmen and people with mechanical interests. It is striking that one of the Wadia shipbuilders installed gas lighting in his home in 1834 and built a small foundry in which he made parts for steam engines. Given an independent and more prosperous India, it is difficult not to believe that a response to British industrialization might well have taken the form of a spread of skill and innovation from the shipyards into other industries.

As it was, such developments were delayed until the 1850s and later, when the first mechanized cotton mill opened. It is significant that some of the entrepreneurs who backed the development of this industry were from the same Parsi families as had built ships in Bombay and invested in overseas trade in the eighteenth century.

Guns and Rails: Asia, Britain, and America

Asian Stimulus

Britain's "conquest" of India cannot be attributed to superior armaments. Indian armies were also well equipped. More significant was the prior breakdown of Mughal government and the collaboration of many Indians. Some victories were also the result of good discipline and bold strategy, especially when Arthur Wellesley, the future Duke of Wellington, was in command. Wellesley's contribution also illustrates the distinctive western approach to the organizational aspect of technology. Indian armies might have had good armament, but because their guns were made in a great variety of different sizes, precise weapons drill was impossible and the supply of shot to the battlefield was unnecessarily complicated. By contrast, Wellesley's forces standardized on just three sizes of field gun, and the commander himself paid close attention to the design of gun carriages and to the bullocks which hauled them, so that his artillery could move as fast as his infantry, and without delays due to wheel breakages.

Significantly, the one major criticism regularly made of Indian artillery concerned the poor design of gun carriages. Many, particularly before 1760, were little better than four-wheeled trolleys. But the guns themselves were often of excellent design and workmanship. Whilst some were imported and others were made with the assistance of foreign craftworkers, there was many a brass cannon and mortar of Indian design, as well as heavy muskets for camel-mounted troops. Captured field guns were often taken over for use by the British, and after capturing ninety guns in one crucial battle, Wellesley wrote that seventy were "the finest brass ordnance I have ever seen." They were probably made in northern India, perhaps at the great Mughal arsenal at Agra.

Whilst Indians had been making guns from brass since the sixteenth century, Europeans could at first only produce this alloy in relatively small quantities because they had no technique for smelting zinc. By the eighteenth century, however, brass was being produced in large quantities in Europe, and brass cannon were being cast at Woolwich Arsenal near London. Several European countries were importing metallic zinc from China for this purpose. However, from 1743 there was a smelter near Bristol in England producing zinc, using coke[1] as fuel, and zinc smelters were also developed in Germany. At the end of the century, Britain's imports of zinc from the Far East were only about forty tons per year. Nevertheless, a British party which visited China in 1797 took particular note of zinc smelting methods. These were similar to the process used in India, which involved vaporizing the metal and then condensing it. There is a suspicion that the Bristol smelting works of 1743 was based on Indian practice, although the possibility of independent invention cannot be excluded.

A much clearer example of the transfer of technology from India occurred when British armies on the subcontinent encountered rockets, a type of weapon of which they had no previous experience. The basic technology had come from the Ottoman Turks or from Syria before 1500, although the Chinese had invented rockets even earlier. In the 1790s, some Indian armies included very large infantry units equipped with rockets. French mercenaries in Mysore had learned to make them, and the British Ordnance Office was enquiring for somebody with expertise on the subject. In response, William Congreve, whose father was head of the laboratory at Woolwich Arsenal, undertook to design a rocket on Indian lines. After a successful demonstration, about two hundred of his rockets were used by the British in an attack on Boulogne in 1806. Fired from over a kilometre away, they set fire to the town. After this success, rockets were adopted quite widely by European armies, though some commanders, notably the Duke of Wellington, frowned on such imprecise weapons, and they tended to drop out of use later in the century. What happened next, however, was typical of the whole British relationship with India. William Congreve set up a factory to manufacture the weapons in 1817, and part of its output was exported to India to equip rocket troops operating there under British command.

Yet another aspect of Asian technology in which eighteenth-century Europeans were interested was the design of farm implements. Reports on seed drills and ploughs were sent to the British Board of Agriculture from India in 1795. A century earlier the Dutch had found much of interest in ploughs and winnowing machines of a Chinese type which

[1] Fuel from soft coal. [Ed.]

they saw in Java. Then a Swedish party visiting Guangzhou (Canton) took a winnowing machine back home with them. Indeed, several of these machines were imported into different parts of Europe, and similar devices for cleaning threshed grain were soon being made there. The inventor of one of them, Jonas Norberg, admitted that he got "the initial idea" from three machines "brought here from China," but had to create a new type because the Chinese machines "do not suit our kinds of grain." Similarly, the Dutch saw that the Chinese plough did not suit their type of soil, but it stimulated them to produce new designs with curved metal mould-boards in contrast to the less efficient flat wooden boards used in Europe hitherto.

In most of these cases, and especially with zinc smelting, rockets, and winnowing machines, we have clear evidence of Europeans studying Asian technology in detail. With rockets and winnowers, though perhaps not with zinc, there was an element of imitation in the European inventions which followed. In other instances, however, the more usual course of technological dialogue between Europe and Asia was that European innovation was challenged by the quality or scale of Asian output, but took a different direction, as we have seen in many aspects of the textile industry. Sometimes, the dialogue was even more limited, and served mainly to give confidence in a technique that was already known. Such was the case with occasional references to China in the writings of engineers designing suspension bridges in Britain. The Chinese had a reputation for bridge construction, and before 1700 Peter the Great had asked for bridge-builders to be sent from China to work in Russia. Later, several books published in Europe described a variety of Chinese bridges, notably a long-span suspension bridge made with iron chains.

Among those who developed the suspension bridge in the West were James Finley in America, beginning in 1801, and Samuel Brown and Thomas Telford in Britain. About 1814, Brown devised a flat, wrought-iron chain link which Telford later used to form the main structural chains in his suspension bridges. But beyond borrowing this specific technique, what Telford needed was evidence that the suspension principle was applicable to the problem he was then tackling. Finley's two longest bridges had spanned seventy-four and ninety-three metres, over the Merrimac and Schuylkill Rivers in the eastern United States. Telford was aiming to span almost twice the larger distance with his 176-metre Menai Bridge. Experiments at a Shropshire ironworks gave confidence in the strength of the chains. But Telford may have looked for reassurance even further afield. One of his notebooks contains the reminder, "Examine Chinese bridges." It is clear from the wording which follows that he had seen a recent booklet advocating a "bridge of chains," partly based on a Chinese example, to cross the Firth of Forth in Scotland.

30

Primary

ADAM SMITH
From *The Wealth of Nations*

An Inquiry into the Nature and Causes of the Wealth of Nations might justly be called the bible of free-market capitalism. Written in 1776 in the context of the British (and European) debate over the proper role of government in the economy, Smith's work takes aim at *mercantilism,* or government supervision of the economy. Mercantilists believed that because there was a finite amount of wealth in the world, one country's gain would result in another country's loss. Therefore, the national economy required government assistance and direction to prosper. For example, after 1660 England imposed a series of acts on British colonies, requiring that they purchase British products and use British shipping — policies that were not well received in America.

Smith argues that free trade will produce greater wealth than mercantilist trade and that free markets allocate resources more efficiently than the government. At the time, Smith's ideas were not entirely new. His notion of *laissez-faire* (literally "let do") capitalism was advocated by the Physiocrat (economic) philosophers in France, although they believed wealth was only in land. Smith does not believe that capitalists are virtuous or that governments should absent themselves entirely from the economy. However, he does believe that the greed of capitalists generally negates itself and produces results that are advantageous to, but unimagined by, the individual. "It is not from the benevolence of the butcher, the brewer, or the baker, that we expect our dinner," Smith wrote, "but from their regard of their own interest. We address ourselves not to their humanity, but to their self-love, and never talk to them of our own necessities, but of their advantage."[1] Each person seeks to maximize his or her own gain, thereby creating an efficient market in which the cost of goods is instantly adjusted to exploit changes in supply and demand, while the market provides what is needed at the price people are willing to pay "as if by an invisible hand."

What would Smith say to a farmer or manufacturer who wanted to institute tariffs or quotas to limit the number of cheaper imports entering the country and to minimize competition? What would he say

[1] Book I, chapter 2.

Adam Smith, *The Wealth of Nations* (London: Everyman's Library, M. Dent & Sons, Ltd., 1910).

to a government official who wanted to protect an important domestic industry? What would he say to a worker who complained about low wages or boring work?

Thinking Historically

The Wealth of Nations was written in defense of free capitalism at a moment when the industrial revolution was just beginning. Some elements of Smith's writing suggest a preindustrial world, as in the quotation about the butcher, brewer, and baker mentioned earlier. Still, Smith was aware how new industrial methods were transforming age-old labor relations and manufacturing processes. In some respects, Smith recognized that capitalism could create wealth, not just redistribute it, because he appreciated the potential of industrial technology.

As you read this selection, note when Smith is discussing capitalism, the economic system, and the power of the new industrial technology. In his discussion of the division of labor, what relationship does Smith see between the development of a capitalistic market and the rise of industrial technology? According to Smith, what is the relationship between money and industry, and which is more important? What would Smith think about a "postindustrial" or "service" economy in which few workers actually make products? What would he think of a prosperous country that imported more than it exported?

Book I: Of the Causes of Improvement in the Productive Powers of Labour, and of the Order According to Which its Produce Is Naturally Distributed Among the Different Ranks of the People

Chapter 1: Of the Division of Labour

The greatest improvement in the productive powers of labour, and the greater part of the skill, dexterity, and judgment with which it is anywhere directed, or applied, seem to have been the effects of the division of labour.

The effects of the division of labour, in the general business of society, will be more easily understood by considering in what manner it operates in some particular manufactures. It is commonly supposed to be carried furthest in some very trifling ones; not perhaps that it really is carried further in them than in others of more importance: but in those trifling manufactures which are destined to supply the small wants of but a small number of people, the whole number of workmen must necessarily be small; and those employed in every different branch of the work can often be collected into the same workhouse, and placed at once under the view of the spectator. In those great manufactures, on the contrary, which are destined to supply the great wants of the great body of the people, every different branch of the work employs so great a number of workmen that it is impossible to collect them all into the same workhouse. We can seldom see more, at one time, than those employed in one single branch. Though in such manufactures, therefore, the work may really be divided into a much greater number of parts than in those of a more trifling nature, the division is not near so obvious, and has accordingly been much less observed.

To take an example, therefore, from a very trifling manufacture; but one in which the division of labour has been very often taken notice of, the trade of the pin-maker; a workman not educated to this business (which the division of labour has rendered a distinct trade), nor acquainted with the use of the machinery employed in it (to the invention of which the same division of labour has probably given occasion), could scarce, perhaps, with his utmost industry, make one pin in a day, and certainly could not make twenty. But in the way in which this business is now carried on, not only the whole work is a peculiar trade, but it is divided into a number of branches, of which the greater part are likewise peculiar trades. One man draws out the wire, another straights it, a third cuts it, a fourth points it, a fifth grinds it at the top for receiving the head; to make the head requires two or three distinct operations; to put it on is a peculiar business, to whiten the pins is another; it is even a trade by itself to put them into the paper; and the important business of making a pin is, in this manner, divided into about eighteen distinct operations, which, in some manufactories, are all performed by distinct hands, though in others the same man will sometimes perform two or three of them. I have seen a small manufactory of this kind where ten men only were employed, and where some of them consequently performed two or three distinct operations. But though they were very poor, and therefore but indifferently accommodated with the necessary machinery, they could, when they exerted themselves, make among them about twelve pounds of pins in a day. There are in a pound upwards of four thousand pins of a middling size. Those ten persons, therefore, could make among them upwards of forty-eight thousand pins in a day. Each person, therefore, making a tenth part of forty-eight thousand pins, might be considered as making four thousand eight hundred pins in a day. But if they had all wrought separately and independently, and without any of them having been educated to this peculiar business, they certainly could not each of them have made twenty, perhaps not one pin in a day; that is, certainly, not the two hundred and fortieth, perhaps not the four thousand eight hundredth part of what they are at present capable of performing, in consequence of a proper division and combination of their different operations.

In every other art and manufacture, the effects of the division of labour are similar to what they are in this very trifling one; though, in many of them, the labour can neither be so much subdivided, nor reduced to so great a simplicity of operation. . . .

Chapter 3: That the Division of Labour Is Limited by the Extent of the Market

As it is the power of exchanging that gives occasion to the division of labour, so the extent of this division must always be limited by the extent of that power, or, in other words, by the extent of the market. When the market is very small, no person can have any encouragement to dedicate himself entirely to one employment, for want of the power to exchange all that surplus part of the produce of his own labour, which is over and above his own consumption, for such parts of the produce of other men's labour as he has occasion for.

There are some sorts of industry, even of the lowest kind, which can be carried on nowhere but in a great town. A porter, for example, can find employment and subsistence in no other place. A village is by much too narrow a sphere for him. . . .

Chapter 5: Of the Real and Nominal Price of Commodities, or Their Price in Labour, and Their Price in Money

Every man is rich or poor according to the degree in which he can afford to enjoy the necessaries, conveniences, and amusements of human life. But after the division of labour has once thoroughly taken place, it is but a very small part of these with which a man's own labour can supply him. The far greater part of them he must derive from the labour of other people, and he must be rich or poor according to the quantity of that labour which he can command, or which he can afford to purchase. The value of any commodity, therefore, to the person who possesses it, and who means not to use or consume it himself, but to exchange it for other commodities, is equal to the quantity of labour which it enables him to purchase or command. Labour, therefore, is the real measure of the exchangeable value of all commodities. . . .

Chapter 7: Of the Natural and Market Price of Commodities

. . . When the quantity of any commodity which is brought to market falls short of the effectual demand, all those who are willing to pay the whole value of the rent, wages, and profit, which must be paid in order to bring it thither, cannot be supplied with the quantity which they want. Rather than want it altogether, some of them will be willing to give more. A competition will immediately begin among them, and the market price will rise more or less above the natural price, according as either the greatness of the deficiency, or the wealth and wanton luxury of the competitors, happen to animate more or less the eagerness of the competition. Among competitors of equal wealth and luxury the same deficiency will generally occasion a more or less eager competition, according as the acquisition of the commodity happens to be of more or less importance to them. Hence the exorbitant price of the necessaries of life during the blockade of a town or in a famine.

When the quantity brought to market exceeds the effectual demand, it cannot be all sold to those who are willing to pay the whole value of the rent, wages, and profit, which must be paid in order to bring it thither. Some part must be sold to those who are willing to pay less, and the low price which they give for it must reduce the price of the whole. The market price will sink more or less below the natural price, according as the greatness of the excess increases more or less the competition of the sellers, or according as it happens to be more or less important to them to get immediately rid of the commodity. The same excess in the importation of perishables will occasion a much greater competition than in that of durable commodities; in the importation of oranges, for example, than in that of old iron.

When the quantity brought to market is just sufficient to supply the effectual demand, and no more, the market price naturally comes to be either exactly, or as nearly as can be judged of, the same with the natural price. The whole quantity upon hand can be disposed of for this price, and cannot be disposed of for more. The competition of the different dealers obliges them all to accept of this price, but does not oblige them to accept of less.

The quantity of every commodity brought to market naturally suits itself to the effectual demand. It is the interest of all those who employ their land, labour, or stock, in bringing any commodity to market, that the quantity never should exceed the effectual demand; and it is the interest of all other people that it never should fall short of that demand.

Book II: On the Nature, Accumulation, and Employment of Stock

Chapter 3: Of the Accumulation of Capital, or of Productive and Unproductive Labour

There is one sort of labour which adds to the value of the subject upon which it is bestowed: There is another which has no such effect. The former, as it produces a value, may be called productive; the latter, unproductive labour. Thus the labour of a manufacturer adds, generally, to the value of the materials which he works upon, that of his own maintenance, and of his master's profit. The labour of a menial servant, on the contrary, adds to the value of nothing. Though the manufacturer has his wages advanced to him by his master, he, in reality, costs him no expence, the value of those wages being generally restored, together with a profit, in the improved value of the subject upon which his labour is bestowed. But the maintenance of a menial servant never is restored. A man grows rich by employing a multitude of manufacturers: He grows poor, by maintaining a multitude of menial servants. The labour of the latter, however, has its value, and deserves its reward as well as that of the former. But the labour of the manufacturer fixes and realizes itself in some particular subject or vendible commodity, which lasts for some time at least after that labour is past. . . .

The labour of some of the most respectable orders in the society is, like that of menial servants, unproductive of any value, and does not fix or realize itself in any permanent subject, or vendible commodity, which endures after that labour is past, and for which an equal quantity of labour could afterwards be procured. The sovereign, for example, with all the officers both of justice and war who serve under him, the whole army and navy, are unproductive labourers. They are the servants of the publick, and are maintained by a part of the annual produce of the industry of other people. Their service, how honourable, how useful, or how necessary soever, produces nothing for which an equal quantity of service can afterwards be procured. The protection, security, and defence of the commonwealth, the effect of their labour this year, will not purchase its protection, security, and defence, for the year to come. In the same class must be ranked, some both of the gravest and most important, and some of the most frivolous professions: churchmen, lawyers, physicians, men of letters of all kinds; players, buffoons, musicians, opera-singers, opera-dancers, and so forth. The labour of the meanest of these has a certain value, regulated by the very same principles which regulate that of every other sort of labour; and that of the noblest and most useful, produces nothing which could afterwards purchase or procure an equal quantity of labour. Like the declamation of the actor, the harangue of the orator, or the tune of the musician, the work of all of them perishes in the very instant of its production. . . .

Book IV: Of Systems of Political Economy

Chapter 1: Of the Principle of the Commercial or Mercantile System

I thought it necessary, though at the hazard of being tedious, to examine at full length this popular notion that wealth consists in money, or in gold and silver. Money in common language, as I have already observed, frequently signifies wealth, and this ambiguity of expression has rendered this popular notion so familiar to us that even they who are convinced of its absurdity are very apt to forget their own principles, and in the course of their reasonings to take it for granted as a certain and undeniable truth. Some of the best English writers upon commerce set out with observing that the wealth of a country consists, not in its gold and silver only, but in its lands, houses, and consumable goods of all different kinds. In the course of their reasonings, however, the lands, houses, and consumable goods seem to slip out of their memory, and the strain of their argument frequently supposes that all wealth consists in gold and silver, and that to multiply those metals is the great object of national industry and commerce. . . .

Chapter 2: Of Restraints upon the Importation from Foreign Countries of Such Goods as Can Be Produced at Home

. . . The produce of industry is what it adds to the subject or materials upon which it is employed. In proportion as the value of this produce is great or small, so will likewise be the profits of the employer. But it is only for the sake of profit that any man employs a capital in the support of industry; and he will always, therefore, endeavour to employ it in the support of that industry of which the produce is likely to be of the greatest value, or to exchange for the greatest quantity either of money or of other goods.

But the annual revenue of every society is always precisely equal to the exchangeable value of the whole annual produce of its industry, or rather is precisely the same thing with that exchangeable value. As every individual, therefore, endeavours as much as he can both to employ his capital in the support of domestic industry, and so to direct that industry that its produce may be of the greatest value; every individual necessarily labours to render the annual revenue of the society as great as he can. He generally, indeed, neither intends to promote the public interest, nor knows how much he is promoting it. By preferring the support of domestic to that of foreign industry, he intends only his own security; and by directing that industry in such a manner as its produce may be of the greatest value, he intends only his own gain, and he is in this, as in many other cases, led by an invisible hand to promote an end which was no part of his intention. Nor is it always the worse for the society that it was no part of it. By pursuing his own interest he frequently promotes that of the society more effectually than when he really intends to promote it. I have never known much good done by those who affected to trade for the public good. It is an affectation, indeed, not very common among merchants, and very few words need be employed in dissuading them from it.

What is the species of domestic industry which his capital can employ, and of which the produce is likely to be of the greatest value, every individual, it is evident, can, in his local situation, judge much better than any statesman or lawgiver can do for him. The statesman who should attempt to direct private people in what manner they ought to employ their capitals would not only load himself with a most unnecessary attention, but assume an authority which could safely be trusted, not only to no single person, but to no council or senate whatever, and which would nowhere be so dangerous as in the hands of a man who had folly and presumption enough to fancy himself fit to exercise it.

To give the monopoly of the home market to the produce of domestic industry, in any particular art or manufacture, is in some measure to direct private people in what manner they ought to employ their capitals, and must, in almost all cases, be either a useless or a hurtful regulation. If the produce of domestic can be brought there as cheap as that of foreign industry, the regulation is evidently useless. If it cannot, it must generally be hurtful. It is the maxim of every prudent master of a family never to attempt to make at home what it will cost him more to make than to buy. The tailor does not attempt to make his own shoes, but buys them of the shoemaker. The shoemaker does not attempt to make his own clothes, but employs a tailor. The farmer attempts to make neither the one nor the other, but employs those different artificers. All of them find it for their interest to employ their whole industry in a way in which they have some advantage over their neighbours, and to purchase with a part of its produce, or what is the same thing, with the price of a part of it, whatever else they have occasion for.

What is prudence in the conduct of every private family can scarce be folly in that of a great kingdom. If a foreign country can supply us with a commodity cheaper than we ourselves can make it, better buy it of them with some part of the produce of our own industry employed in a way in which we have some advantage. The general industry of the country, being always in proportion to the capital which employs it, will not thereby be diminished, no more than that of the above-mentioned artificers; but only left to find out the way in which it can be employed with the greatest advantage. It is certainly not employed to the greatest advantage when it is thus directed towards an object which it can buy cheaper than it can make. . . .

31

From *The Sadler Report of the House of Commons*

Although children were among the ideal workers in the factories of the industrial revolution, according to many factory owners, increasingly their exploitation became a concern of the British Parliament. One important parliamentary investigation, chaired by Michael Sadler, took volumes of testimony from child workers and older people who had worked as children in the mines and factories. The following is only a brief, representative sample of the testimony gathered in the Sadler Report. The report led to child-labor reform in the Factory Act of 1833.

What seem to be the causes of Crabtree's distress? How could they have been alleviated?

Thinking Historically

To what extent are the problems faced by Matthew Crabtree the inevitable results of machine production? To what extent are his problems caused by capitalism? How might the owner of this factory have addressed these issues?

If you asked the owner why he didn't pay more, shorten the workday, provide more time for meals, or provide medical assistance when it was needed, how do you think he would have responded? Do you think Matthew would have been in favor of reduced hours if it meant reduced wages?

Friday, 18 May 1832 — Michael Thomas Sadler, Esquire, in the Chair

Mr. Matthew Crabtree, *called in; and Examined.*
    What age are you? — Twenty-two.
    What is your occupation? — A blanket manufacturer.
    Have you ever been employed in a factory? — Yes.
    At what age did you first go to work in one? — Eight.
    How long did you continue in that occupation? — Four years.

From *The Sadler Report: Report from the Committee on the Bill to Regulate the Labour of Children in the Mills and Factories of the United Kingdom.* London: The House of Commons, 1832.

Will you state the hours of labour at the period when you first went to the factory, in ordinary times? — From 6 in the morning to 8 at night.

Fourteen hours? — Yes.

With what intervals for refreshment and rest? — An hour at noon.

Then you had no resting time allowed in which to take your breakfast, or what is in Yorkshire called your "drinking"? — No.

When trade was brisk what were your hours? — From 5 in the morning to 9 in the evening.

Sixteen hours? — Yes.

With what intervals at dinner? — An hour.

How far did you live from the mill? — About two miles.

Was there any time allowed for you to get your breakfast in the mill? — No.

Did you take it before you left your home? — Generally.

During those long hours of labour could you be punctual; how did you awake? — I seldom did awake spontaneously; I was most generally awoke or lifted out of bed, sometimes asleep, by my parents.

Were you always in time? — No.

What was the consequence if you had been too late? — I was most commonly beaten.

Severely? — Very severely, I thought.

In whose factory was this? — Messrs. Hague & Cook's, of Dewsbury.

Will you state the effect that those long hours had upon the state of your health and feelings? — I was, when working those long hours, commonly very much fatigued at night, when I left my work; so much so that I sometimes should have slept as I walked if I had not stumbled and started awake again; and so sick often that I could not eat, and what I did eat I vomited.

Did this labour destroy your appetite? — It did.

In what situation were you in that mill? — I was a piecener.

Will you state to this Committee whether piecening is a very laborious employment for children, or not? — It is a very laborious employment. Pieceners are continually running to and fro, and on their feet the whole day.

The duty of the piecener is to take the cardings from one part of the machinery, and to place them on another? — Yes.

So that the labour is not only continual, but it is unabated to the last? — It is unabated to the last.

Do you not think, from your own experience, that the speed of the machinery is so calculated as to demand the utmost exertions of a child supposing the hours were moderate? — It is as much as they could do at the best; they are always upon the stretch, and it is commonly very difficult to keep up with their work.

State the condition of the children toward the latter part of the day, who have thus to keep up with the machinery. — It is as much as they can do when they are not very much fatigued to keep up with their work, and toward the close of the day, when they come to be more fatigued, they cannot keep up with it very well, and the consequence is that they are beaten to spur them on.

Were you beaten under those circumstances? — Yes.

Frequently? — Very frequently.

And principally at the latter end of the day? — Yes.

And is it your belief that if you had not been so beaten, you should not have got through the work? — I should not if I had not been kept up to it by some means.

Does beating then principally occur at the latter end of the day, when the children are exceedingly fatigued? — It does at the latter end of the day, and in the morning sometimes, when they are very drowsy, and have not got rid of the fatigue of the day before.

What were you beaten with principally? — A strap.

Anything else? — Yes, a stick sometimes; and there is a kind of roller which runs on the top of the machine called a billy, perhaps two or three yards in length, and perhaps an inch and a half, or more in diameter; the circumference would be four or five inches; I cannot speak exactly.

Were you beaten with that instrument? — Yes.

Have you yourself been beaten, and have you seen other children struck severely with that roller? — I have been struck very severely with it myself, so much so as to knock me down, and I have seen other children have their heads broken with it.

You think that it is a general practice to beat the children with the roller? — It is.

You do not think then that you were worse treated than other children in the mill? — No, I was not, perhaps not so bad as some were.

In those mills is chastisement towards the latter part of the day going on perpetually? — Perpetually.

So that you can hardly be in a mill without hearing constant crying? — Never an hour, I believe.

Do you think that if the overlooker were naturally a humane person it would be still found necessary for him to beat the children, in order to keep up their attention and vigilance at the termination of those extraordinary days of labour? — Yes, the machine turns off a regular quantity of cardings, and of course they must keep as regularly to their work the whole of the day; they must keep with the machine, and therefore however humane the slubber may be, as he must keep up with the machine or be found fault with, he spurs the children to keep up also by various means but that which he commonly resorts to is to strap them when they become drowsy.

At the time when you were beaten for not keeping up with your work, were you anxious to have done it if you possibly could? — Yes; the dread of being beaten if we could not keep up with our work was a sufficient impulse to keep us to it if we could.

When you got home at night after this labour, did you feel much fatigued? — Very much so.

Had you any time to be with your parents, and to receive instruction from them? — No.

What did you do? — All that we did when we got home was to get the little bit of supper that was provided for us and go to bed immediately. If the supper had not been ready directly, we should have gone to sleep while it was preparing.

Did you not, as a child, feel it a very grievous hardship to be roused so soon in the morning? — I did.

Were the rest of the children similarly circumstanced? — Yes, all of them; but they were not all of them so far from their work as I was.

And if you had been too late you were under the apprehension of being cruelly beaten? — I generally was beaten when I happened to be too late; and when I got up in the morning the apprehension of that was so great, that I used to run, and cry all the way as I went to the mill.

That was the way by which your punctual attendance was secured? — Yes.

And you do not think it could have been secured by any other means? — No.

Then it is your impression from what you have seen, and from your own experience, that those long hours of labour have the effect of rendering young persons who are subject to them exceedingly unhappy? — Yes.

You have already said it had a considerable effect upon your health? — Yes.

Do you conceive that it diminished your growth? — I did not pay much attention to that; but I have been examined by some persons who said they thought I was rather stunted, and that I should have been taller if I had not worked at the mill.

What were your wages at that time? — Three shillings (per week).

And how much a day had you for overwork when you were worked so exceedingly long? — A halfpenny a day.

Did you frequently forfeit that if you were not always there to a moment? — Yes; I most frequently forfeited what was allowed for those long hours.

You took your food to the mill; was it in your mill, as is the case in cotton mills, much spoiled by being laid aside? — It was very frequently covered by flues from the wool; and in that case they had to be blown off with the mouth, and picked off with the fingers before it could be eaten.

So that not giving you a little leisure for eating your food, but obliging you to take it at the mill, spoiled your food when you did get it? — Yes, very commonly.

And that at the same time that this over-labour injured your appetite? — Yes.

Could you eat when you got home? — Not always.

What is the effect of this piecening upon the hands? — It makes them bleed; the skin is completely rubbed off, and in that case they bleed in perhaps a dozen parts.

The prominent parts of the hand? — Yes, all the prominent parts of the hand are rubbed down till they bleed; every day they are rubbed in that way.

All the time you continue at work? — All the time we are working. The hands never can be hardened in that work, for the grease keeps them soft in the first instance, and long and continual rubbing is always wearing them down, so that if they were hard they would be sure to bleed.

It is attended with much pain? — Very much.

Do they allow you to make use of the back of the hand? — No; the work cannot be so well done with the back of the hand, or I should have made use of that.

$$\boxed{32}$$

KARL MARX AND FRIEDRICH ENGELS

From *The Communist Manifesto*

The Communist Manifesto was written in 1848 in the midst of European upheaval, a time when capitalist industrialization had spread from England to France and Germany. Marx and Engels were Germans who studied and worked in France and England. In the *Manifesto,* they imagine a revolution that will transform all of Europe. What do they see as the inevitable causes of this revolution? How, according to their analysis, is the crisis of "modern" society different from previous crises? Were Marx and Engels correct?

Karl Marx and Friedrich Engels, *Manifesto of the Communist Party* (Arlington Heights, IL: Harlan Davidson, 1955). Reprinted in the Crofts Classics Series.

Thinking Historically

Notice how Marx and Engels describe the notions of capitalism and industrialization without using those words. The term *capitalism* developed later from Marx's classic *Das Kapital* (1859), but the term *bourgeoisie,* as Engels notes in this selection, stands for the capitalist class. For Marx and Engels, the industrial revolution (another, later phrase) is the product of a particular stage of capitalist development. Thus, if Marx and Engels were asked whether capitalism or industry was the principal force that created the modern world, what would their answer be?

The Communist Manifesto is widely known as the classic critique of capitalism, but a careful reading reveals a list of achievements of capitalist or "bourgeois civilization." What are these achievements? Did Marx and Engels consider them to be achievements? How could Marx and Engels both praise and criticize capitalism?

Bourgeois and Proletarians[1]

The history of all hitherto existing society is the history of class struggles.

Freeman and slave, patrician and plebeian, lord and serf, guildmaster and journeyman, in a word, oppressor and oppressed, stood in constant opposition to one another, carried on an uninterrupted, now hidden, now open fight, a fight that each time ended, either in a revolutionary reconstitution of society at large, or in the common ruin of the contending classes.

In the earlier epochs of history, we find almost everywhere a complicated arrangement of society into various orders, a manifold gradation of social rank. In ancient Rome we have patricians, knights, plebeians, slaves; in the Middle Ages, feudal lords, vassals, guildmasters, journeymen, apprentices, serfs; in almost all of these classes, again, subordinate gradations.

The modern bourgeois society that has sprouted from the ruins of feudal society, has not done away with class antagonisms. It has but established new classes, new conditions of oppression, new forms of struggle in place of the old ones.

---

[1] In French *bourgeois* means a town-dweller. *Proletarian* comes from the Latin, *proletarius,* which meant a person whose sole wealth was his offspring (*proles*). [Ed.]

[Note by Engels] By "bourgeoisie" is meant the class of modern capitalists, owners of the means of social production and employers of wage-labor; by "proletariat," the class of modern wage-laborers who, having no means of production of their own, are reduced to selling their labor power in order to live.

Our epoch, the epoch of the bourgeoisie, possesses, however, this distinctive feature: It has simplified the class antagonisms. Society as a whole is more and more splitting up into the two great hostile camps, into two great classes directly facing each other — bourgeoisie and proletariat.

From the serfs of the Middle Ages sprang the chartered burghers of the earliest towns. From these burgesses the first elements of the bourgeoisie were developed.

The discovery of America, the rounding of the Cape, opened up fresh ground for the rising bourgeoisie. The East-Indian and Chinese markets, the colonization of America, trade with the colonies, the increase in the means of exchange and in commodities generally, gave to commerce, to navigation, to industry, an impulse never before known, and thereby, to the revolutionary element in the tottering feudal society, a rapid development.

The feudal system of industry, in which industrial production was monopolized by closed guilds, now no longer sufficed for the growing wants of the new markets. The manufacturing system took its place. The guildmasters were pushed aside by the manufacturing middle class; division of labor between the different corporate guilds vanished in the face of division of labor in each single workshop.

Meantime the markets kept ever growing, the demand ever rising. Even manufacture[2] no longer sufficed. Thereupon, steam and machinery revolutionized industrial production. The place of manufacture was taken by the giant, modern industry, the place of the industrial middle class, by industrial millionaires — the leaders of whole industrial armies, the modern bourgeois.

Modern industry has established the world market, for which the discovery of America paved the way. This market has given an immense development to commerce, to navigation, to communication by land. This development has, in its turn, reacted on the extension of industry; and in proportion as industry, commerce, navigation, railways extended, in the same proportion the bourgeoisie developed, increased its capital, and pushed into the background every class handed down from the Middle Ages.

We see, therefore, how the modern bourgeoisie is itself the product of a long course of development, of a series of revolutions in the modes of production and of exchange.

Each step in the development of the bourgeoisie was accompanied by a corresponding political advance of that class. An oppressed class under the sway of the feudal nobility, it became an armed and self-governing association in the medieval commune; here independent

---

[2] By *manufacture* Marx meant the system of production which succeeded the guild system but which still relied mainly upon direct human labor for power. He distinguished it from modern industry which arose when machinery driven by water and steam was introduced. [Ed.]

urban republic (as in Italy and Germany), there taxable "third estate" of the monarchy (as in France); afterwards, in the period of manufacture proper, serving either the semifeudal or the absolute monarchy as a counterpoise against the nobility, and, in fact, cornerstone of the great monarchies in general — the bourgeoisie has at last, since the establishment of modern industry and of the world market, conquered for itself, in the modern representative state, exclusive political sway. The executive of the modern state is but a committee for managing the common affairs of the whole bourgeoisie.

The bourgeoisie has played a most revolutionary role in history.

The bourgeoisie, wherever it has got the upper hand, has put an end to all feudal, patriarchal, idyllic relations. It has pitilessly torn asunder the motley feudal ties that bound man to his "natural superiors," and has left no other bond between man and man than naked self-interest, than callous "cash payment." It has drowned the most heavenly ecstasies of religious fervor, of chivalrous enthusiasm, of philistine sentimentalism, in the icy water of egotistical calculation. It has resolved personal worth into exchange value, and in place of the numberless indefeasible chartered freedoms, has set up that single, unconscionable freedom — Free Trade. In one word, for exploitation, veiled by religious and political illusions, it has substituted naked, shameless, direct, brutal exploitation.

The bourgeoisie has stripped of its halo every occupation hitherto honored and looked up to with reverent awe. It has converted the physician, the lawyer, the priest, the poet, the man of science, into its paid wage-laborers.

The bourgeoisie has torn away from the family its sentimental veil, and has reduced the family relation to a mere money relation.

The bourgeoisie has disclosed how it came to pass that the brutal display of vigor in the Middle Ages, which reactionaries so much admire, found its fitting complement in the most slothful indolence. It has been the first to show what man's activity can bring about. It has accomplished wonders far surpassing Egyptian pyramids, Roman aqueducts, and Gothic cathedrals; it has conducted expeditions that put in the shade all former migrations of nations and crusades.

The bourgeoisie cannot exist without constantly revolutionizing the instruments of production, and thereby the relations of production, and with them the whole relations of society. Conservation of the old modes of production in unaltered form, was, on the contrary, the first condition of existence for all earlier industrial classes. Constant revolutionizing of production, uninterrupted disturbance of all social conditions, everlasting uncertainty and agitation distinguished the bourgeois epoch from all earlier ones. All fixed, fast-frozen relations, with their train of ancient and venerable prejudices and opinions, are swept away, all new-formed ones become antiquated before they can ossify. All that is solid melts into air, all that is holy is profaned, and man is at last compelled to face with sober senses his real conditions of life and his relations with his kind.

The need of a constantly expanding market for its products chases the bourgeoisie over the whole surface of the globe. It must nestle everywhere, settle everywhere, establish connections everywhere.

The bourgeoisie has through its exploitation of the world market given a cosmopolitan character to production and consumption in every country. To the great chagrin of reactionaries, it has drawn from under the feet of industry the national ground on which it stood. All old-established national industries have been destroyed or are daily being destroyed. They are dislodged by new industries, whose introduction becomes a life and death question for all civilized nations, by industries that no longer work up indigenous raw material, but raw material drawn from the remotest zones; industries whose products are consumed, not only at home, but in every quarter of the globe. In place of the old wants, satisfied by the production of the country, we find new wants, requiring for their satisfaction the products of distant lands and climes. In place of the old local and national seclusion and self-sufficiency, we have intercourse in every direction, universal interdependence of nations. And as in material, so also in intellectual production. The intellectual creations of individual nations become common property. National one-sidedness and narrow-mindedness become more and more impossible, and from the numerous national and local literatures there arises a world literature.

The bourgeoisie, by the rapid improvement of all instruments of production, by the immensely facilitated means of communication, draws all nations, even the most barbarian, into civilization. The cheap prices of its commodities are the heavy artillery with which it batters down all Chinese walls, with which it forces the barbarians' intensely obstinate hatred for foreigners to capitulate. It compels all nations, on pain of extinction, to adopt the bourgeois mode of production; it compels them to introduce what it calls civilization into their midst, i.e., to become bourgeois themselves. In a word, it creates a world after its own image.

The bourgeoisie has subjected the country to the rule of the towns. It has created enormous cities, has greatly increased the urban population as compared with the rural, and has thus rescued a considerable part of the population from the idiocy of rural life. Just as it has made the country dependent on the towns, so it has made barbarian and semi-barbarian countries dependent on the civilized ones, nations of peasants on nations of bourgeois, the East on the West.

More and more the bourgeoisie keeps doing away with the scattered state of the population, of the means of production, and of property. It has agglomerated population, centralized means of production, and has concentrated property in a few hands. The necessary consequence of this was political centralization. Independent, or but loosely connected provinces, with separate interests, laws, governments and systems of taxation, became lumped together into one nation, with one government, one code of laws, one national class interest, one frontier and one customs tariff.

The bourgeoisie, during its rule of scarce one hundred years, has created more massive and more colossal productive forces than have all preceding generations together. Subjection of nature's forces to man, machinery, application of chemistry to industry and agriculture, steam-navigation, railways, electric telegraphs, clearing of whole continents for cultivation, canalization of rivers, whole populations conjured out of the ground — what earlier century had even a presentiment that such productive forces slumbered in the lap of social labor?

We see then that the means of production and of exchange, which served as the foundation for the growth of the bourgeoisie, were generated in feudal society. At a certain stage in the development of these means of production and of exchange, the conditions under which feudal society produced and exchanged, the feudal organization of agriculture and manufacturing industry, in a word, the feudal relations of property became no longer compatible with the already developed productive forces; they became so many fetters. They had to be burst asunder; they were burst asunder.

Into their place stepped free competition, accompanied by a social and political constitution adapted to it, and by the economic and political sway of the bourgeois class.

A similar movement is going on before our own eyes. Modern bourgeois society with its relations of production, of exchange and of property, a society that has conjured up such gigantic means of production and exchange, is like the sorcerer who is no longer able to control the powers of the nether world whom he has called up by his spells. For many a decade past the history of industry and commerce is but the history of the revolt of modern productive forces against modern conditions of production, against the property relations that are the conditions for the existence of the bourgeoisie and of its rule. It is enough to mention the commercial crises that by their periodical return put the existence of the entire bourgeoisie society on trial, each time more threateningly. In these crises a great part not only of the existing products, but also of the previously created productive forces, are periodically destroyed. In these crises there breaks out an epidemic that, in all earlier epochs, would have seemed an absurdity — the epidemic of overproduction. Society suddenly finds itself put back into a state of momentary barbarism; it appears as if a famine, a universal war of devastation had cut off the supply of every means of subsistence; industry and commerce seem to be destroyed. And why? Because there is too much civilization, too much means of subsistence, too much industry, too much commerce. The productive forces at the disposal of society no longer tend to further the development of the conditions of bourgeois property; on the contrary, they have become too powerful for these conditions, by which they are fettered, and no sooner do they overcome these fetters than they bring disorder into the whole of bourgeois society, endanger the existence of bourgeois property. The conditions of bourgeois society are too narrow to comprise the wealth created by them. And how does the bourgeoisie get over these crises? On the one hand by enforced destruction of a mass of productive forces; on the other, by the conquest of new markets, and by the more thorough exploitation of the old ones. That is to say, by paving the way for more extensive and more destructive crises, and by diminishing the means whereby crises are prevented.

The weapons with which the bourgeoisie felled feudalism to the ground are now turned against the bourgeoisie itself.

But not only has the bourgeoisie forged the weapons that bring death to itself; it has also called into existence the men who are to wield those weapons — the modern working class — the proletarians.

33

PETER N. STEARNS

secondary

The Industrial Revolution Outside the West

Stearns, a modern historian, discusses the export of industrial machinery and techniques outside the West (Europe and North America) in the nineteenth century. Again and again, he finds that initial attempts at industrialization — in Russia, India, Egypt, and South America — led to increased production of export crops and resources but failed to stimulate true industrial revolutions. Consequently, as producers of raw materials, these countries became more deeply dependent on Western markets for their products, while at the same time importing

Peter N. Stearns, *The Industrial Revolution in World History* (Boulder, CO: Westview Press, 1993), 71–79.

from the West more valuable manufactured products like machinery. What common reasons can you find for these failures?

Thinking Historically

Did nineteenth-century efforts to ignite industrial revolutions outside the West fail because these societies neglected to develop capitalism, or did they fail because their local needs were subordinated to those of Western capitalists? Explain.

Before the 1870s no industrial revolution occurred outside Western society. The spread of industrialization within western Europe, while by no means automatic, followed from a host of shared economic, cultural, and political features. The quick ascension of the United States was somewhat more surprising — the area was not European and had been far less developed economically during the eighteenth century. Nevertheless, extensive commercial experience in the northern states and the close mercantile and cultural ties with Britain gave the new nation advantages for its rapid imitation of the British lead. Abundant natural resources and extensive investments from Europe kept the process going, joining the United States to the wider dynamic of industrialization in the nineteenth-century West.

Elsewhere, conditions did not permit an industrial revolution, an issue that must be explored in dealing with the international context for this first phase of the world's industrial experience. Yet the West's industrial revolution did have substantial impact. It led to a number of pilot projects whereby initial machinery and factories were established under Western guidance. More important, it led to new Western demands on the world's economies that instigated significant change without industrialization; indeed, these demands in several cases made industrialization more difficult.

Pilot Projects

Russia's contact with the West's industrial revolution before the 1870s offers an important case study that explains why many societies could not follow the lead of nations like France or the United States in imitating Britain. Yet Russia did introduce some new equipment for economic and military-political reasons, and these initiatives did generate change — they were not mere window dressing.

More than most societies not directly part of Western civilization, Russia had special advantages in reacting to the West's industrial lead and special motivation for paying attention to this lead. Russia had been part of Europe's diplomatic network since about 1700. It saw itself as one of Europe's great powers, a participant in international conferences and military alliances. The country also had close cultural ties with western Europe, sharing in artistic styles and scientific developments — though Russian leadership had stepped back from cultural alignment because of the shock of the French Revolution in 1789 and subsequent political disorders in the West. Russian aristocrats and intellectuals routinely visited western Europe. Finally, Russia had prior experience in imitating Western technology and manufacturing: importation of Western metallurgy and shipbuilding had formed a major part of Peter the Great's reform program in the early eighteenth century.

Contacts of this sort explain why Russia began to receive an industrial outreach from the West within a few decades of the advent of the industrial revolution. British textile machinery was imported beginning in 1843. Ernst Knoop, a German immigrant to Britain who had clerked in a Manchester cotton factory, set himself up as export agent to the Russians. He also sponsored British workers who installed the machinery in Russia and told any Russian entrepreneur brash enough to ask not simply for British models but for alterations or adaptations: "That is not your affair; in England they know better than you." Despite the snobbism, a number of Russian entrepreneurs set up small factories to produce cotton, aware that even in Russia's small urban market they could make a substantial profit by underselling traditional manufactured cloth. Other factories were established directly by Britons.

Europeans and Americans were particularly active in responding to calls by the tsar's government for assistance in establishing railway and steamship lines. The first steamship appeared in Russia in 1815, and by 1820 a regular service ran on the Volga River. The first public railroad, joining St. Petersburg to the imperial residence in the suburbs, opened in 1837. In 1851 the first major line connected St. Petersburg and Moscow, along a remarkably straight route desired by Tsar Nicholas I himself. American engineers were brought in, again by the government, to set up a railroad industry so that Russians could build their own locomotives and cars. George Whistler, the father of the painter James McNeill Whistler (and thus husband of Whistler's mother), played an important role in the effort. He and some American workers helped train Russians in the needed crafts, frequently complaining about their slovenly habits but appreciating their willingness to learn.

Russian imports of machinery increased rapidly; they were over thirty times as great in 1860 as they had been in 1825. While in 1851 the nation manufactured only about half as many machines as it imported, by 1860 the equation was reversed, and the number of machine-building factories had quintupled (from nineteen to ninety-nine). The new cotton industry surged forward with most production organized in factories using wage labor.

These were important changes. They revealed that some Russians were alert to the business advantages of Western methods and that some Westerners saw the great profits to be made by setting up shop in a huge but largely agricultural country. The role of the government was vital: The tsars used tax money to offer substantial premiums to Western entrepreneurs, who liked the adventure of dealing with the Russians but liked their superior profit margins even more.

But Russia did not then industrialize. Modern industrial operations did not sufficiently dent established economic practices. The nation remained overwhelmingly agricultural. High percentage increases in manufacturing proceeded from such a low base that they had little general impact. Several structural barriers impeded a genuine industrial revolution. Russia's cities had never boasted a manufacturing tradition; there were few artisans skilled even in preindustrial methods. Only by the 1860s and 1870s had cities grown enough for an artisan core to take shape — in printing, for example — and even then large numbers of foreigners (particularly Germans) had to be imported. Even more serious was the system of serfdom that kept most Russians bound to agricultural estates. While some free laborers could be found, most rural Russians could not legally leave their land, and their obligation to devote extensive work service to their lords' estates reduced their incentive even for agricultural production. Peter the Great had managed to adapt serfdom to a preindustrial metallurgical industry by allowing landlords to sell villages and the labor therein for expansion of ironworks. But this mongrel system was not suitable for change on a grander scale, which is precisely what the industrial revolution entailed.

Furthermore, the West's industrial revolution, while it provided tangible examples for Russia to imitate, also produced pressures to develop more traditional sectors in lieu of structural change. The West's growing cities and rising prosperity claimed rising levels of Russian timber, hemp, tallow, and, increasingly, grain. These were export goods that could be produced without new technology and without altering the existing labor system. Indeed, many landlords boosted the work-service obligations of the serfs in order to generate more grain production for sale to the West. The obvious temptation was to lock in an older economy — to respond to new opportunity by incremental changes within the traditional system and to maintain serfdom and the rural preponderance rather than to risk fundamental internal transformation.

The proof of Russia's lag showed in foreign trade. It rose but rather modestly, posting a threefold increase between 1800 and 1860. Exports of raw materials approximately paid for the imports of some machinery, factory-made goods from abroad, and a substantial volume of luxury products for the aristocracy. And the regions that participated most in the growing trade were not the tiny industrial enclaves (in St. Petersburg, Moscow, and the iron-rich Urals) but the wheat-growing areas of southern Russia where even industrial pilot projects had yet to surface. Russian manufacturing exported nothing at all to the West, though it did find a few customers in Turkey, central Asia, and China.

The proof of Russia's lag showed even more dramatically in Russia's new military disadvantage. Peter the Great's main goal had been to keep Russian military production near enough to Western levels to remain competitive, with the huge Russian population added into the equation. This strategy now failed, for the West's industrial revolution changed the rules of the game. A war in 1854 pitting Russia against Britain and France led to Russia's defeat in its own backyard. The British and French objected to new Russian territorial gains (won at the expense of Turkey's Ottoman Empire) that brought Russia greater access to the Black Sea. The battle-ground was the Crimea. Yet British and French steamships connected their armies more reliably with supplies and reinforcements from home than did Russia's ground transportation system with its few railroads and mere three thousand miles of first-class roads. And British and French industry could pour out more and higher-quality uniforms, guns, and munitions than traditional Russian manufacturing could hope to match. The Russians lost the Crimean War, surrendering their gains and swallowing their pride in 1856. Patchwork change had clearly proved insufficient to match the military, much less the economic, power the industrial revolution had generated in the West.

After a brief interlude, the Russians digested the implications of their defeat and launched a period of basic structural reforms. The linchpin was the abolition of serfdom in 1861. Peasants were not entirely freed, and rural discontent persisted, but many workers could now leave the land; the basis for a wage labor force was established. Other reforms focused on improving basic education and health, and while change in these areas was slow, it too set the basis for a genuine commitment to industrialization. A real industrial revolution lay in the future, however. By the 1870s Russia's contact with industrialization had deepened its economic gap vis-à-vis the West but had yielded a few interesting experiments with new methods and a growing realization of the need for further change.

Societies elsewhere in the world — those more removed from traditional ties to the West or more severely disadvantaged in the ties that did exist — saw even more tentative industrial pilot projects during the West's industrialization period. The Middle East and India tried some industrial imitation early on but largely failed — though not without generating some important economic change. Latin America also launched some revealingly limited technological change. Only eastern Asia and sub-Saharan Africa were largely untouched by any explicit industrial imitations until the late 1860s or beyond; they were too distant from European culture to venture a response so quickly.

Prior links with the West formed the key variable, as Russia's experience abundantly demonstrated. Societies that had some familiarity with Western merchants and some preindustrial awareness of the West's steady commercial gains mounted some early experiments in industrialization. Whether they benefited as a result compared with areas that did nothing before the late nineteenth century might be debated.

One industrial initiative in India developed around Calcutta, where British colonial rule had centered since the East India Company founded the city in 1690. A Hindu Brahman family, the Tagores, established close ties with many British administrators. Without becoming British, they sponsored a number of efforts to revivify India, including new colleges and research centers. Dwarkanath Tagore controlled tax collection in part of Bengal, and early in the nineteenth century he used part of his profit to found a bank. He also bought up a variety of commercial landholdings and traditional manufacturing operations. In 1834 he joined with British capitalists to establish a diversified company that boasted holdings in mines (including the first Indian coal mine), sugar refineries, and some new textile factories; the equipment was imported from Britain. Tagore's dominant idea was a British-Indian economic and cultural collaboration that would revitalize his country. He enjoyed a high reputation in Europe and for a short time made a success of his economic initiatives. Tagore died on a trip abroad, and his financial empire declined soon after.

This first taste of Indian industrialization was significant, but it brought few immediate results. The big news in India, even as Tagore launched his companies, was the rapid decline of traditional textiles under the bombardment of British factory competition; millions of Indian villagers were thrown out of work. Furthermore, relations between Britain and the Indian elite worsened after the mid-1830s as British officials sought a more active economic role and became more intolerant of Indian culture. One British official, admitting no knowledge of Indian scholarship, wrote that "all the historical information" and science available in Sanskrit was "less valuable than what may be found in the most paltry abridgements used at preparatory schools in England." With these attitudes, the kind of collaboration that might have aided Indian appropriation of British industry became impossible.

The next step in India's contact with the industrial revolution did not occur until the 1850s when the colonial government began to build a significant railroad network. The first passenger line opened in 1853. Some officials feared that Hindus might object to traveling on such smoke-filled monsters, but trains proved very popular and there ensued a period of rapid economic and social change. The principal result, however, was not industrial development but further extension of commercial agriculture (production of cotton and other goods for export) and intensification of British sales to India's interior. Coal mining did expand, but manufacturing continued to shrink. There was no hint of an industrial revolution in India.

Imitation in the Middle East was somewhat more elaborate, in part because most of this region, including parts of North Africa, retained independence from European colonialism. Muslims had long disdained Western culture and Christianity, and Muslim leaders, including the rulers of the great Ottoman Empire, had been very slow to recognize the West's growing dynamism after the fifteenth century. Some Western medicine was imported, but technology was ignored. Only in the eighteenth century did this attitude begin, haltingly, to change. The Ottoman government imported a printing press from Europe and began discussing Western-style technical training, primarily in relationship to the military.

In 1798 a French force briefly seized Egypt, providing a vivid symbol of Europe's growing technical superiority. Later an Ottoman governor, Muhammed Ali, seized Egypt from the imperial government and pursued an ambitious agenda of expansionism and modernization. Muhammed Ali sponsored many changes in Egyptian society in imitation of Western patterns, including a new tax system and new kinds of schooling. He also destroyed the traditional Egyptian elite. The government encouraged agricultural production by sponsoring major irrigation projects and began to import elements of the industrial revolution from the West in the 1830s. English machinery and technicians were brought in to build textile factories, sugar refineries, paper mills, and weapons shops. Muhammed Ali clearly contemplated a sweeping reform program in which industrialization would play a central role in making Egypt a powerhouse in the Middle East and an equal to the European powers. Many of his plans worked well, but the industrialization effort failed. Egyptian factories could not in the main compete with European imports, and the initial experiments either failed or stagnated. More durable changes involved the encouragement to the production of cash crops like sugar and cotton, which the government required in order to earn tax revenues to support its armies and its industrial imports. Growing concentration on cash crops also enriched a new group of Egyptian landlords and merchants. But the shift actually formalized Egypt's dependent position in the world economy, as European businesses and governments increasingly interfered with the internal economy. The Egyptian reaction to the West's industrial revolution, even more than the Russian response, was to generate massive economic redefinition without industrialization, a strategy that locked peasants into landlord control and made a manufacturing transformation at best a remote prospect.

Spurred by the West's example and by Muhammed Ali, the Ottoman government itself set up some factories after 1839, importing equipment from Europe to manufacture textiles, paper, and guns. Coal and iron mining were encouraged. The government established a postal system in 1834, a telegraph system in 1855, and steamships and the beginning of railway construction from 1866 onward. These changes increased the role of European traders and investors in the Ottoman economy and produced no overall industrial revolution. Again, the clearest result of improved transport and communication was a growing emphasis on the export of cash crops and minerals to pay for necessary manufactured imports from Europe. An industrial example had been set, and, as in Egypt, a growing though still tiny minority of Middle Easterners gained some factory experience, but no fundamental transformation occurred. . . .

Developments of preliminary industrial trappings — a few factories, a few railroads — nowhere outside Europe converted whole economies to an industrialization process until late in the nineteenth century, though they provided some relevant experience on which later (mainly after 1870) and more intensive efforts could build. A few workers became factory hands and experienced some of the same upheaval as their Western counterparts in terms of new routines and pressures on work pace. Many sought to limit their factory experience, leaving for other work or for the countryside after a short time; transience was a problem for much the same reasons as in the West: the clash with traditional work and leisure values. Some technical and business expertise also developed. Governments took the lead in most attempts to imitate the West, which was another portent for the future; with some exceptions, local merchant groups had neither the capital nor the motivation to undertake such ambitious and uncertain projects. By the 1850s a number of governments were clearly beginning to realize that some policy response to the industrial revolution was absolutely essential, lest Western influence become still more overwhelming. On balance, however, the principal results of very limited imitation tended to heighten the economic imbalance with western Europe, a disparity that made it easier to focus on nonindustrial exports. This too was a heritage for the future. . . .

34

IWASAKI YATARO

Mitsubishi Letter to Employees

Japan was the first country outside the West to undergo an industrial revolution. After 1854 when American Commodore Perry forced Japan to open its ports to the West, Japanese society underwent a wide range of changes. In 1868, the previously ceremonial emperor restored imperial power, moved the court to Edo (Tokyo), and undercut the power of aristocrats. This Meiji (Enlightened) Restoration government proceeded to mobilize the population to learn Western methods of industrial production and many other facets of Western culture and society. Many Japanese were educated in the United States and Europe, especially in Germany. Japanese industry was organized along the German model, with considerable government direction and power vested in leading families. Politics was not democratic, and the economy was not capitalist. In 1870, for example, the Meiji government launched a major railroad construction plan. It hoped to raise capital from private sources, but when none was offered, the government went ahead on its own. Gradually, with the help of foreign loans and Japanese capitalists, a mixed public and private economy developed.

One of the entrepreneurs who directed Japanese industrialization was Iwasaki Yataro, a clerk for a feudal lord, who used his ability and connections to create a steamship company that put the government Nippon line out of business and then went on to challenge the American and British lines. His company, Mitsubishi, was well on the way to becoming one of the great conglomerates of modern Japan.

In 1876, however, the British Peninsular and Oriental Steam Navigation Company challenged Mitsubishi's dominance in Japanese coastal trade. Mitsubishi responded by halving its coastal fares and cutting employee wages by one-third. In this letter to his employees, Iwasaki asks for their support.

Notice Iwasaki's appeal to national security and pride. Does the appeal strike you as genuine or contrived? Would it have been an unreasonable request to control Japanese coastal traffic, Japanese ports, and traffic from Japan to China? What would Adam Smith or Karl Marx have said about this request?

David John Lu, *Sources of Japanese History*, vol. 2 (New York: McGraw-Hill, 1974), 80–82.

Thinking Historically

Iwasaki Yataro was both a capitalist and an industrialist. While Japanese industrialization enjoyed greater state sponsorship than did British or American industrialization, entrepreneurs like Yataro played a crucial role. In this letter, does Iwasaki speak more as a capitalist or industrialist? Is there any disparity between these two roles, or are they woven together inextricably?

Comparing this document with the previous article by Stearns, what seems to have enabled Japan to succeed in industrializing when, at least in the nineteenth century, so many other countries could not?

Many people have expressed differing opinions concerning the principles to be followed and advantages to be obtained in engaging foreigners or Japanese in the task of coastal trade. Granted, we may permit a dissenting voice, which suggests that in principle both foreigners and Japanese must be permitted to engage in coastal trade, but once we look into the question of advantages, we know that coastal trade is too important a matter to be given over to the control of foreigners. If we allow the right of coastal navigation to fall into the hands of foreigners in peacetime, it means a loss of business and employment opportunities for our own people, and in wartime it means yielding the vital right of gathering information to foreigners. In fact, this is not too different from abandoning the rights of our country as an independent nation.

Looking back into the past, at the time when we abandoned the policy of seclusion and entered into an era of friendly intercourse and commerce with foreign nations, we should have been prepared for this very task. However, due to the fact that our people lack knowledge and wealth, we have yet to assemble a fleet sufficient to engage in coastal navigation. Furthermore, we have neither the necessary skills for navigation nor a plan for developing a maritime transportation industry. This condition has attracted foreign shipping companies to occupy our maritime transport lines. Yet our people show not a sense of surprise at it. Some people say that our treaties with foreign powers contain an express provision allowing foreign ships to proceed from Harbor A to Harbor B, and others claim that such a provision must not be regarded as granting foreign ships the right to coastal navigation inasmuch as it is intended not to impose unduly heavy taxes on them. I am not qualified to discuss its legal merit, but the issue remains an important one.

I now propose to do my utmost, and along with my 35 million compatriots, perform my duty as a citizen of this country. That is to recover the right of coastal trade in our hands and not to delegate that task to foreigners. Unless we propose to do so, it is useless for our government to revise the unequal treaties[1] or to change our entrenched customs. We need people who can respond, otherwise all the endeavors of the government will come to naught. This is the reason why the government protects our company, and I know that our responsibilities are even greater than the full weight of Mt. Fuji thrust upon our shoulders. There have been many who wish to hinder our progress in fulfilling our obligations. However, we have been able to eliminate one of our worst enemies, the Pacific Mail Company of the United States, from contention by applying appropriate means available to us. Now another rival has emerged. It is the Peninsula & Oriental Team Navigation Company of Great Britain, which is setting up a new line between Yokohama and Shanghai and is attempting to claim its rights over the ports of Nagasaki, Kobe, and Yokohama. The P & O Company is backed by its massive capital, its large fleet of ships, and by its experiences of operating in Oriental countries. In competing against this giant, what methods can we employ?

I have thought about this problem very carefully and have come to one conclusion. There is no other alternative but to eliminate unnecessary positions and unnecessary expenditures. This is a time-worn solution and no new wisdom is involved. Even though it is a familiar saying, it is much easier said than done, and this indeed has been the root cause of difficulties in the past and present times. Therefore, starting immediately, I propose that we engage in this task. By eliminating unnecessary personnel from the payroll, eliminating unnecessary expenditures, and engaging in hard and arduous tasks, we shall be able to solidify the foundation of our company. If there is a will, there is a way. Through our own efforts, we shall be able to repay the government for its protection and answer our nation for its confidence shown in us. Let us work together in discharging our obligations and let us not be ashamed of ourselves. Whether we succeed or fail, whether we can gain profit or sustain loss, we cannot anticipate at this time. Hopefully, all of you will join me in a singleness of heart to attain this cherished goal, forbearing and undaunted by setbacks, to restore to our own hands the right to our own coastal trade. If we succeed it will not only be an accomplishment for our company but also a glorious event for our Japanese Empire, which shall let its light shine to all four corners of the earth. We may succeed and we may fail, and it depends on your effort or lack of it. Do your utmost in this endeavor!

---

[1] *Unequal treaties* was a term the Chinese used to designate the treaties that were forced upon them by the opium wars; they were "unequal" in the sense that the superior power of the British forced the defeated Chinese to comply with British demands. Here the term refers to the commercial agreements that Japan was made to sign after Admiral Perry's arrival. [Ed.]

REFLECTIONS

Although this chapter focuses on the relative impact of capitalism and the industrial revolution, the differing fortunes of Europe and Asia are reviewed as well.

We began the chapter with an impressive summary of India's technological proficiency, particularly in fields that would become crucial to the European industrial revolution: textiles, shipbuilding, even cannon production. After our study of the industrial revolution in Europe, however, Peter Stearns explains that in nineteenth-century India, industrialization depended on the new money of the Tagore family and a joint British partnership that never occurred. Indian economic fortunes declined drastically as Britain spread its control over the subcontinent in the eighteenth and nineteenth centuries. Vast investments in railroads, ports, and communication facilities by the British only served, as Stearns reminds us, to expedite the flow of crops and raw materials to British ships. (We will learn the importance of two of those crops — tea and opium — in the next chapter.)

The story of Japanese development is also inconstant. The founder of Mitsubishi had to create coastal shipping from scratch on an island whose pirates, three hundred years earlier, had terrorized even China. Yet in a generation, between 1868 and 1900, Japan rose from a feudal backwater to the only industrialized country of Asia, able to defeat the armies of China and Russia.

So it would seem that industrialization does not evolve; rather, it is created: It is a reality easier to imitate than to invent. After the British industrial revolution, British artisans transported their skills to America, Holland, Belgium, France, and Germany. Czars, sultans, and shahs could replicate the process. And they did. But the failure to succeed also must be explained. For some, it was a matter of failing to define the Western system. To what extent was industrialization dependent on something else: capitalism, democracy, an independent class of capitalists, freedom from manipulation by Western capitalism? Was Japan's isolation from the West a fortuitous advantage?

And how about capitalism? If industrialization is easier to imitate than to invent, is directed industrialization inconsistent with a capitalist economy? The most successful industrializations between 1850 and 1950 were the Japanese and the Russian — both state-directed. Indeed, they became the models for countries of the Pacific rim in the second half of the twentieth century. Only in the last decade of the century (since 1989), with the decline of Russian and Japanese economies, did capitalist industrialization re-emerge as the global model, fairly late in the history of industrialization.

Free Trade and the Opium War

HISTORICAL CONTEXT
Britain and China, 1793–1844

The British war with China between 1840 and 1842 — the Opium War for the Chinese but a war for the principle of free trade for the British — offers a lens through which we can see the differences between Chinese and British ideas of trade and foreign relations during the era of capitalist industrialization. The war's roots reached back to before 1840, and the conflict did not end clearly in 1844. Nevertheless, an examination of the conflict from 1835 to 1842 provides a unique depth of focus at a critical moment for two of the leading powers in the world.

In this chapter, we compare the policies of Britain and China as their disagreements escalated to war. We also compare the various factors that led to the conflict: merchant capitalism and industrialization; profit and principle; personal and national interests. A relatively brief period like this gives us an opportunity to study in depth the motivation and decisions of individuals involved in the conflict. We also study the Opium War as a sort of archetype of Western imperialism in the nineteenth century, to understand one of the most significant dynamics of modern history — the age of European imperialism.

THINKING HISTORICALLY
Understanding "Both Sides" and Using Statistical Tables and Pictorial Images

A war offers an ideal vantage point from which to study how two sides can view the same conflict in entirely different terms. Often, two sides clash because their conflicts are irreconcilable and because their positions are mutually incomprehensible. As you read, try to view both sides of the Opium War. Ask yourself how it was possible for China and Britain to formulate such completely divergent positions regarding opium and trade in the decades before war broke out in 1840. To what extent was conflict a result of fundamentally different needs and interests? To what extent was conflict the result of imbalances in power?

As discussed in Chapter 6, the era of the triumph of capitalism and the industrial revolution in Britain is the backdrop of this war. To what extent did war occur as an inevitable consequence of the imbalance of the countries' military and technological capacities? To what extent did the war occur out of misunderstandings? Was the conflict bound to happen once Britain was transformed into a modern capitalist industrial state? Or was war inevitable at all?

Ask yourself how our sources — all primary documents in this chapter — reveal both sides of the conflict. What does it mean to understand *both* sides of a conflict? Notice the many debates and clashes that eventually escalated. Pay attention to the conflicts *within* China and Britain, as well as between Britain (and its allies including the United States) and China to enrich your understanding of why people and nations choose to go to war.

This chapter introduces statistical and visual sources, new elements of historical evidence that require a different kind of analysis. What and how does a statistical table add to our understanding of an issue? Is a picture worth a thousand words or something much more or less?

35   *primary*

CH'IEN LUNG

Letter to King George III

Lord Macartney, a cousin of King George III, sailed to China in 1793 with a retinue of eighty-four diplomats, scientists, artists, musicians, and Chinese-language specialists, and six hundred cases of scientific instruments, clocks, metalwork, knives, woolens, and other products. The expedition sought to expand trade between England and China, prompting the Chinese emperor, Ch'ien Lung (1726–1795), to write a letter to Macartney's king.

Harley Farnsworth MacNair, *Modern Chinese History, Selected Readings* (Shanghai: Commercial Press Ltd., 1923), 2–9.

Chinese trade had been a high priority of European merchants and kings for centuries. The European "discovery" and colonization of the Americas was, to a degree, a product of this quest — at least for the spices of what was presumed to be southern China. And for more than a thousand years, wealthy and powerful Europeans were among those throughout the world who prized Chinese silks and porcelains.

At the end of the eighteenth century, Britain was undergoing an industrial revolution, eagerly seeking markets for its increased production capacity. British trading interests extended far beyond the needs of the new industrialists, however. The British East India Company, a British trading monopoly that had been trading in India since the beginning of the seventeenth century, had to find markets for Indian cottons that British manufacturing had displaced from British markets. Indian cottons and agricultural products were thus shipped from India to China in exchange for Chinese silks (ceramics were now manufactured in Britain) and, increasingly, for Chinese tea.

As British workers were drawn from the country to factory towns and subjected to the discipline of the machine and meager wages, they were taught to drink more tea and less beer. Tea imports, negligible in the seventeenth century, climbed in Britain from four hundred thousand pounds in 1720 to twenty-three million pounds in 1800, at which time they constituted one-seventh of all the tea in China. Tea import taxes (like those the Americans refused to pay) covered one-tenth of British government expenses by 1800. Such enormous imports were not covered by a corresponding value of British or Indian exports. The East India Company, therefore, had to recoup the difference in gold and silver, a mercantilist's measure of ultimate wealth. Even those in Parliament who subscribed to Adam Smith's ideas on free trade worried because Britain was not given an opportunity to sell its manufactured goods in China.

What did Ch'ien Lung think of British manufactures? Does his response seem reasonable or mistaken? Why?

Thinking Historically

It is impossible to understand both sides of an issue by reading only one side's argument. But this document reveals a broader spectrum than most, because it summarizes the demands of Macartney in a fair, objective manner, provides the Chinese emperor's response point by point, and then indicates much of Ch'ien Lung's attitude and assumptions.

The specific points of disagreement have to be understood in the context of China and Britain's vastly different traditions concerning trade and foreign relations. For China, trade was a matter carried on by merchants, a class not highly esteemed. Other than limiting contact between Chinese and foreign merchants to specific areas, the emperor, like his predecessors, did not concern himself with these matters. As to foreign relations, the emperor received tribute missions from foreign princes as expressions of their subservience to the Celestial Kingdom presumed to shine from the center of the world.

What evidence do you see in Ch'ien Lung's letter that he viewed the Macartney mission as a traditional tribute mission? What evidence do you see that such was not Macartney's intention? What were the specific goals that Macartney sought to realize? How would you characterize the general (as opposed to specific) goals of Macartney's mission? Did either side understand the other?

You, O King, live beyond the confines of many seas, nevertheless, impelled by your humble desire to partake of the benefits of our civilisation, you have dispatched a mission respectfully bearing your memorial. Your Envoy has crossed the seas and paid his respects at my Court on the anniversary of my birthday. To show your devotion, you have also sent offerings of your country's produce.

I have perused your memorial: The earnest terms in which it is couched reveal a respectful humility on your part, which is highly praiseworthy. In consideration of the fact that your Ambassador and his deputy have come a long way with your memorial and tribute, I have shown them high favour and have allowed them to be introduced into my presence. To manifest my indulgence, I have entertained them at a banquet and made them numerous gifts. I have also caused presents to be forwarded to the Naval Commander and six hundred of his officers and men, although they did not come to Peking, so that they too may share in my all-embracing kindness.

As to your entreaty to send one of your nationals to be accredited to my Celestial Court and to be in control of your country's trade with China, this request is contrary to all usage of my dynasty and cannot possibly be entertained. It is true that Europeans, in the service of the dynasty, have been permitted to live at Peking, but they are compelled to adopt Chinese dress, they are strictly confined to their own precincts and are never permitted to return home. You are presumably familiar with our dynastic regulations. Your proposed Envoy to my Court could not be placed in a position similar to that of European officials in Peking who are forbidden to leave China, nor could he, on the other hand, be allowed liberty of movement and the privilege of corresponding with his own country; so that, you would gain nothing by his residence in our midst.

Moreover, Our Celestial dynasty possesses vast territories, and tribute missions from the dependencies are provided for by the Department for Tributary States, which ministers to their wants and exercises strict control over their movements. It would be quite impossible to leave them to their own devices. Supposing that your Envoy should come to our Court, his language and national dress differ from that of our people, and there would be no place in which to bestow him. It may be suggested that he might imitate the Europeans permanently resident in Peking and adopt the dress and customs of China, but, it has never been our dynasty's wish to force people to do things unseemly and inconvenient. Besides, supposing I sent an Ambassador to reside in your country, how could you possibly make for him the requisite arrangements? Europe consists of many other nations besides your own: If each and all demanded to be represented at our Court, how could we possibly consent? The thing is utterly impracticable. How can our dynasty alter its whole procedure and system of etiquette, established for more than a century, in order to meet your individual views? If it be said that your object is to exercise control over your country's trade, your nationals have had full liberty to trade at Canton for many a year, and have received the greatest consideration at our hands. Missions have been sent by Portugal and Italy, preferring similar requests. The Throne appreciated their sincerity and loaded them with favours, besides authorising measures to facilitate their trade with China. You are no doubt aware that, when my Canton merchant, Wu Chao-ping, was in debt to the foreign ships, I made the Viceroy advance the monies due, out of the provincial treasury, and ordered him to punish the culprit severely. Why then should foreign nations advance this utterly unreasonable request to be represented at my Court? Peking is nearly two thousand miles from Canton, and at such a distance what possible control could any British representative exercise?

If you assert that your reverence for Our Celestial dynasty fills you with a desire to acquire our civilisation, our ceremonies and code of laws differ so completely from your own that, even if your Envoy were able to acquire the rudiments of our civilisation, you could not possibly transplant our manners and customs to your alien soil. Therefore, however adept the Envoy might become, nothing would be gained thereby.

Swaying the wide world, I have but one aim in view, namely, to maintain a perfect governance and to fulfil the duties of the state: Strange and costly objects do not interest me. If I have commanded that the tribute offerings sent by you, O King, are to be accepted, this was solely consideration for the spirit which prompted you to dispatch them from afar. Our dynasty's majestic virtue has penetrated unto every country under Heaven, and Kings of all nations have offered their costly tribute by land and sea. As your Ambassador can see for himself, we possess all things. I set no value on objects strange or ingenious, and have no use for your country's manufactures. This then is my answer to your request to appoint a representative at my Court, a request contrary to our dynastic usage, which would only result in inconvenience to yourself. I have expounded my wishes in detail and have commanded your tribute Envoys to leave in peace on their homeward journey. It behooves you, O King, to respect my sentiments and to display even greater devotion and loyalty in future, so that, by perpetual submission to our Throne, you may secure peace and prosperity for your country hereafter. Besides making gifts (of which I enclose an inventory) to each member of your Mission, I confer upon you, O King, valuable presents in the number usually bestowed on such occasions, including silks and curios — a list of which is likewise enclosed. Do you reverently receive them and take note of goodwill towards you! A special mandate.

A further mandate to King George III dealt in detail with the British Ambassador's proposals and the Emperor's reasons for declining them:

You, O King, from afar have yearned after the blessings of our civilisation, and in your eagerness to come into touch with our converting influence have sent an Embassy across the sea bearing a memorial. I, already taken note of your respectful spirit of submission, have treated your mission with extreme favour and loaded it with gifts, besides issuing a mandate to you, O King, and honouring with the bestowal of valuable presents. Thus has my indulgence been manifested.

Yesterday your Ambassador petitioned my Ministers to memorialise me regarding your trade with China, but his proposal is not consistent with our dynastic usage and cannot be entertained. Hitherto, all European nations, including your own country's barbarian merchants, have carried on their trade with Our Celestial Empire at Canton. Such has been the procedure for many years, although Our Celestial Empire possesses all things in prolific abundance and lacks no product within its own borders. There was therefore no need to import the manufactures of outside barbarians in exchange for our own produce. But as the tea, silk, and porcelain which the Celestial Empire produces, are absolute necessities to European nations and to yourselves, we permitted, as a signal mark of favour, that foreign *hongs*[1] should be established at Canton, so that your wants might be supplied and your country thus participate in our beneficence. But your Ambassador has now put forward new requests which completely fail to recognise the Throne's principle to 'treat strangers from afar with indulgence,' and to exercise a pacifying control over barbarian tribes, the world over. Moreover, our dynasty, swaying the myriad races of the globe, extends the same benevolence towards all. Your England is not the only nation trading at Canton. If other nations, following your bad example, wrongfully importune my ear with further impossible requests, how will it be possible

---

[1] Companies.

for me to treat them with easy indulgence? Nevertheless, I do not forget the lonely remoteness of your island, cut off from the world by intervening wastes of sea, nor do I overlook your excusable ignorance of the usages of Our Celestial Empire. I have consequently commanded my Ministers to enlighten your Ambassador on the subject, and have ordered the departure of the mission. But I have doubts that, after your Envoy's return he may fail to acquaint you with my view in detail or that he may be lacking in lucidity, so that I shall now proceed to take your requests *seriatim* and to issue my mandate on each question separately. In this way you will, I trust, comprehend my meaning.

(1) Your Ambassador requests facilities for ships of your nation to call at Ningpo, Chusan, Tientsin and other places for purposes of trade. Until now trade with European nations has always been conducted at [Macao], where the foreign *hongs* are established to store and sell foreign merchandise. Your nation has obediently complied with this regulation for years past without raising any objection. In none of the other ports named have *hongs* been established, so that even if your vessels were to proceed thither, they would have no means of disposing of their cargoes. Furthermore, no interpreters are available, so you would have no means of explaining your wants, and nothing but general inconvenience would result. For the future, as in the past, I decree that your request is refused and that the trade shall be limited to [Macao].

(2) The request that your merchants may establish a repository in the capital of my Empire for the storing and sale of your produce, in accordance with the precedent granted to Russia, is even more impracticable than the last. My capital is the hub and centre about which all quarters of the globe revolve. Its ordinances are most august and its laws are strict in the extreme. The subjects of our dependencies have never been allowed to open places of business in Peking. Foreign trade has hitherto been conducted at [Macao], because it is conveniently near to the sea, and therefore an important gathering place for the ships of all nations sailing to and from. If warehouses were established in Peking, the remoteness of your country lying far to the north-west of my capital would render transport extremely difficult. Before Kiakhta was opened, the Russians were permitted to trade at Peking, but the accommodation furnished to them was only temporary. As soon as Kiakhta was available, they were compelled to withdraw from Peking, which has been closed to their trade these many years. Their frontier trade at Kiakhta, is on all fours with your trade at [Macao]. Possessing facilities at the latter place, you now ask for further privileges at Peking, although our dynasty observes the severest restrictions respecting the admission of foreigners within its boundaries, and has never permitted the subjects of dependencies to cross the Empire's barriers and mettle at will amongst the Chinese people. This request is also refused.

(3) Your request for a small island near Chusan, where merchants may reside and goods be warehoused, arises from your desire to develop trade. As there are neither foreign *hongs* nor interpreters in or near Chusan, where none of your ships have ever called, such an island would be utterly useless for your purposes. Every inch of the territory of our Empire is marked on the map and the strictest vigilance is exercised over it all: Even tiny islets and far-lying sandbanks are clearly defined as part of the provinces to which they belong. Consider, moreover, that England is not the only barbarian land which wishes to establish relations with our civilisation and trade with our Empire: Supposing that other nations were all to imitate your evil example and beseech me to present them each and all with a site for trading purposes, how could I possibly comply? This also is a flagrant infringement of the usage of my Empire and cannot possibly be entertained.

(4) The next request, for a small site in the vicinity of Canton city, where your barbarian merchants may lodge or, alternatively, that there be no longer any restrictions over their movements at [Macao], has arisen from the following causes. Hitherto, the barbarian merchants of Europe have had a definite locality assigned to them at [Macao] for residence and trade, and have been forbidden to encroach an inch beyond the limits assigned to that locality. Barbarian merchants having business with the *hongs* have never been allowed to enter the city of Canton; by these measures, disputes between Chinese and barbarians are prevented, and a firm barrier is raised between my subjects and those of other nations. The present request is quite contrary to precedent; furthermore, European nations have been trading with Canton for a number of years and, as they make large profits, the number of traders is constantly increasing. Now would it be possible to grant such a site to each country? The merchants of the foreign *hongs* are responsible to the local officials for the proceedings of barbarian merchants and they carry out periodical inspections. If these restrictions were withdrawn, friction would inevitably occur between the Chinese and your barbarian subjects, and the results would militate against the benevolent regard that I feel towards you. From every point of view, therefore, it is best that the regulations now in force should continue unchanged.

(5) Regarding your request for remission or reduction of duties on merchandise discharged by your British barbarian merchants at [Macao] and distributed throughout the interior, there is a regular tariff in force for barbarian merchants' goods, which applies equally to all European nations. It would be as wrong to increase the duty imposed on your nation's merchandise on the ground that the bulk of foreign trade is in your hands, as to make an exception in your case in the shape of specially reduced duties. In future, duties shall levied equitably without discrimination between your nation and any other, and, in

order to manifest my regard, your barbarian merchants shall continue to be shown every consideration at [Macao].

(6) As to your request that your ships shall pay the duties leviable by tariff, there are regular rules in force at the Canton house respecting the amounts payable, and since I have refused your request to be allowed to trade at other ports, this duty will naturally continue to be paid at Canton as heretofore.

(7) Regarding your nation's worship of the Lord of Heaven, it is the same religion as that of other European nations. Ever since the beginning of history, sage Emperors and wise rulers have bestowed on China a moral system and inculcated a code, which from time immemorial has been observed by the myriads of my subjects. There has been no hankering after heterodox doctrines. Even the European (missionary) officials in my capital are forbidden to hold intercourse with Chinese subjects; they are restricted within the limits of their appointed residences, and may not go about propagating their religion. The distinction between Chinese and barbarian is most strict, and your Ambassador's request that barbarians shall be given full liberty to disseminate religion is utterly unreasonable.

It may be, O King, that the above proposals have been wantonly made by your Ambassador on his own responsibility, or peradventure you yourself are ignorant of our dynastic regulations and had no intention of transgressing them when you expressed these wild ideas and hopes. I have ever shown the greatest condescension to the tribute missions of all States which sincerely yearn after the blessings of civilization, so as to manifest my kindly indulgence. I have even gone out of my way to grant any requests which were in any way consistent with Chinese usage. Above, all, upon you, who live in a remote and inaccessible region, far across the spaces of ocean, but who have shown your submissive loyalty by sending this tribune mission, I have heaped benefits far in excess of those accorded to other nations. But the demands presented by your Embassy are not only a contravention of dynastic tradition, but would be utterly unproductive of good result to yourself, besides being quite impracticable. I have accordingly stated the facts to you in detail, and it is your bounden duty reverently to appreciate my feelings and to obey these instructions henceforward for all time, so that you may enjoy the blessings of perpetual peace. If, after the receipt of this explicit decree, you lightly give ear to the representations of your subordinates and allow your barbarian merchants to proceed to Chêkiang and Tientsin, with the object of landing and trading there, the ordinances of my Celestial Empire are strict in the extreme, and the local officials, both civil and military, are bound reverently to obey the law of the land. Should your vessels touch the shore, your merchants will assuredly never be permitted to land or to reside there, but will be subject to instant expulsion. In that event your barbarian merchants will have had a long journey for nothing. Do not say that you were not warned in due time! Tremblingly obey and show no negligence! A special mandate!

36

Table 1. Opium Imported at Canton and Exported from India, 1816–1841

To avoid paying for tea and other Chinese imports in silver or gold, Britain sought an export that could be sold profitably to the Chinese. Even though Ch'ien Lung exaggerated China's self-sufficiency, finding a product that the Chinese needed in great quantities was not easy. Other countries had the same problem. The first American ship to sail to China in 1783 was loaded with ginseng, a root used in traditional Chinese medicine that grew in the eastern forests of the United States as well as in China. Britain could not grow ginseng, but it controlled India where the poppy grew and could be cultivated.

The opium sap from Chinese-grown poppies had been used in China for medicinal purposes for centuries. In the seventeenth century, the Chinese adopted the Southeast Asian practice of smoking opium with tobacco. In the beginning of the eighteenth century, the Chinese learned to increase the effect by smoking pure opium sap in a pipe. What had been in small doses a medicine was in large doses a debilitating poison. Opium dens sprang up — especially in Chinese cities — and produced a new class of degenerates: former officials and literati as well as the destitute, for whom the stupor of addiction was little worse than the terror of withdrawal or death.

In 1729 the Chinese enacted a law making the sale of opium illegal. Opium dealers were to be punished and conscripted for military service. Proprietors of opium dens would be executed. That year, the British East India Company produced two hundred chests of opium for sale in China. By 1767 the company was producing a thousand chests. In 1780, an imperial edict prohibited the consumption of opium and reiterated the prohibition of its sale. In 1800 the East India

Hsin-Pao Chang, *Commissioner Lin and the Opium War* (New York: Norton, 1970), 223. By arrangement with Harvard University Press, 1964.

Company contracted for the harvest of 4500 chests of opium for sale in China. The India-based company honored Chinese law by not selling the drug in China, but it sold even larger quantities to other British merchants. Company profits rose accordingly from 2.4 million rupees in 1800 to more than 8 million rupees in 1815.

Table 1 details the rise of the opium trade from the year after the Napoleonic War in 1816, to 1841, just before the war with China. (The table was compiled from figures available at the time.) What sort of increase does the table show? What else do you learn about the opium trade from this table?

Thinking Historically

Two methods can be used to measure the opium trade: imports and exports. The table lists imports to Canton from three East India Company sources of opium. Opium from Patna and Benares in the northeast was shipped through Bengal in the east. Opium grown in Malwa farther west (about halfway between Delhi and Bombay) was shipped from Bombay. These figures are totaled under the column "total." The second measure, of exports, appears in the two columns on the right.

Notice that the import and export figures do not always agree. There are various reasons for this. First, figures can be wrong. Second, not all exports went to Canton: Some went to British colonies in southeast Asia such as Malaya and Singapore and (in the later 1830s) other ports in China. Third, the imports in Canton included those from other countries as well as from Britain and India. Americans, for instance, carried opium from Turkey to Canton. Other European countries also traded in Canton. Nevertheless, the figures in the table indicate certain general trends. What are these trends? What can you say about the difference between the Bengal (Patna and Benares) and the Malwa imports to Canton? What does the table suggest about changes in the price of opium?

Table 1. Opium Imported at Canton and Exported from India, 1816–1841

| Years | IMPORTS TO CANTON | | | | | | EXPORTS FROM BENGAL AND BOMBAY | |
| | Bengal (Patna and Benares) | | Malwa | | Total | | | |
	Chests	Value $	Chests	Value $	Chests	Value $	Chests	Profits by EIC[1] (rupees)
1816–17	2,610	3,132,000	600	525,000	3,210	3,657,000	4,618	—
1817–18	2,530	3,200,450	1,150	703,800	3,680	3,904,250	3,692	—
1818–19	3,050	3,050,000	1,530	1,109,250	4,580	4,159,250	3,552	—
1819–20	2,970	3,667,950	1,630	1,915,250	4,600	5,583,200	4,006	—
1820–21	3,050	5,795,000	1,720	2,605,800	4,770	8,400,800	4,244	—
1821–22	2,910	6,038,250	1,718	2,276,350	4,628	8,314,600	5,576	—
1822–23	1,822	2,828,930	4,000	5,160,000	5,822	7,988,930	7,773	—
1823–24	2,910	4,656,000	4,172	3,859,100	7,082	8,515,100	8,895	—
1824–25	2,655	3,119,625	6,000	4,500,000	8,655	7,619,625	12,023	—
1825–26	3,442	3,141,755	6,179	4,466,450	9,621	7,608,205	9,373	—
1826–27	3,661	3,668,565	6,308	5,941,520	9,969	9,610,085	12,175	—
1827–28	5,114	5,105,073	4,361	5,251,760	9,475	10,356,833	11,154	—
1828–29	5,960	5,604,235	7,171	6,928,880	13,131	12,533,115	15,418	—
1829–30	7,143	6,149,577	6,857	5,907,580	14,000	12,057,157	16,877	—
1830–31	6,660	5,789,794	12,100	7,110,237	18,760	12,900,031	17,456	11,012,826
1831–32	5,672	5,484,340	7,831	5,447,355	13,503	10,931,695	22,138	13,269,945
1832–33	8,167	6,551,059	15,403	8,781,700	23,570	15,332,759	19,483	9,742,886
1833–34	8,672	6,545,845	11,114	7,510,695	19,786	14,056,540	23,902	11,110,385
1834–35	7,767	4,431,845	8,749	5,223,125	16,516	9,654,970	21,011	7,768,605
1835–36	11,992	8,838,000	14,208	8,550,622	26,200	17,388,622	30,202	14,920,068
1836–37	8,078	5,848,236	13,430	8,439,694	21,508	14,287,930	34,033	15,349,678
1837–38	6,165	3,903,129	13,875	6,980,028	20,040	10,883,157	34,373	15,864,440
1838–39	—	—	—	—	—	—	40,200	9,531,308
1839–40	—	—	—	—	—	—	20,619	3,377,775
1840–41	—	—	—	—	—	—	34,631	8,742,776

[1] British East India Company. [Ed.]

37

Table 2. British Imports and Exports at Port of Canton, April 1, 1835, to March 31, 1836

British merchants were permitted to trade only at the port of Canton. Like merchants from other countries, the British maintained warehouses along a strip of the port that was reserved for foreign trade. Opium was just one of the products that the British imported, and because its sale was outlawed, it was not unloaded at the port. Instead, the opium was transferred to Chinese ships in the waters off Lantin Island near Hong Kong and Canton, yet it was still considered to be, as demonstrated in this table, a British import to Canton. How important was opium compared with the other British imports listed here?

Thinking Historically

Had the British solved their problem of diminishing gold and silver reserves by 1835–36? How was the difference made up between total cost of imports and total cost of exports? What disadvantages would the Chinese have felt in the terms of this trade?

Table 2. British Imports and Exports at Port of Canton, April 1, 1835, to March 31, 1836

	IMPORTS (IN SPANISH DOLLARS)			
Item	Quantity	Average price	Per	Total value
Cotton	494,666	16.89	Picul	8,357,394
Sandalwood	3,982	19.98	"	79,584
Pepper	9,896	8.76	"	86,705
Rattans	16,414	3.15	"	51,843
Rice	372,929	2.08	"	776,492
Betel nut	29,948	3.00	"	89,845
Fish maws	4,458	29.10	"	129,740
Lead	19,385	6.22	"	120,632
Iron	28,011	3.78	"	105,930
Tin	32,510	17.17	"	558,437
Cotton yarn	12,336	39.95	"	492,867

Canton Register, 9–43:177 (Oct 25, 1836). Signed: "By order of the Superintendents of the trade of British Subjects in China, Edward Emslie, Secretary and Treasurer." [Ed.] Hsin-Pao Chang, *Commissioner Lin and the Opium War* (New York: Norton, 1970), 226–27.

Table 2. *(continued)*

IMPORTS (IN SPANISH DOLLARS)				
Item	Quantity	Average price	Per	Total value
Cotton piece goods, all sorts	164,699	4.70	Piece	775,466
Camlets	7,581	30.13	"	228,416
Long ells	21,805	13.53	"	295,026
Woollens, all sorts	—	—	—	963,224
Broadcloth	25,491	27.50	Piece	701,097
Tin plates	3,512	9.65	Box	33,921
Pearls and cornelians	—	—	—	184,723
Watches and clocks	—	—	—	60,193
Dollars	—	—	—	71,211
Sundries	—	—	—	359,629
Opium, Patna	9,692	744.82	Chest	7,218,800
Opium, Benares	2,300	704.00	"	1,619,200
Opium, Malwa	14,208	601.81	"	8,550,622
Opium, Turkey	911	566.00	Picul	515,626
				$32,426,623

EXPORTS (IN SPANISH DOLLARS)				
Black tea	312,481	31.79	Picul	9,936,835
Green tea	71,508	48.60	"	3,475,408
Raw silk, Nanking	7,920	412.91	"	3,270,291
Raw silk, Canton	1,948	253.50	"	493,824
Sugar candy	17,194	9.93	"	170,843
Soft sugar	33,933	5.42	"	184,177
Cassia lignea	14,699	9.87	"	145,113
Camphor	1,420	31.22	"	44,340
Alum	19,230	2.12	"	40,828
Aniseed star	2,923	11.25	"	32,911
Copper	4,277	16.95	"	72,503
Musk	1,106	49.18	Catty[1]	54,400
Vermilion	12,010	58.70	Box	705,000
Silk piece goods	—	—	—	314,021
Dollars	—	—	—	1,589,742
Sycee silver	—	—	—	2,384,606
Gold	21,251	23.24	Tael[2]	494,063
Sundries	—	—	—	443,994
				$23,852,899

[1] 100 catties = 1 picul (about 133⅓ pounds). [Ed.]
[2] 16 tael = 1 catty (about 20 ounces) = a British pound. [Ed.]

38

XU NAIJI AND YUAN YULIN

Memorials on the Legalization and Elimination of Opium

The rapid increase in opium addiction and the economic crisis brought on by the reverse in the balance of trade and the drain of Chinese silver stores led the Chinese court to consider legalizing the drug in order to control it. A *memorial,* or formal proposal, to that effect presented to the emperor on May 17, 1836, by Xu Naiji had an electrifying effect. What, according to Xu Naiji, would be the advantage of legalizing opium? What problems does he think it would solve?

By October 1836, it was widely believed among the Chinese officials and merchants in Hong Kong and the British trading community that opium would be legalized. Some believed that Xu Naiji's memorial was drawn up at the order of the emperor himself. At the same time, however, those opposed to legalization drafted memorials in response to Xu Naiji. One of these memorialists was Yuan Yulin. What are Yuan's objections to Xu's proposal to legalize opium? Which of the two arguments do you find more convincing and why?

Thinking Historically

While there were two sides to this debate, both Chinese memorialists agreed on the deleterious effects of opium. Legalization and elimination were alternative strategies to China's encounter with unscrupulous British merchants. The larger debate — between British demands that its merchants be given the freedom to expand their trade, whatever the products, and the Chinese attempt to control both the locations and items of trade — continued. Still, the larger debate might not have led to war had the smaller debate yielded a common ground.

What would the British find to their liking in Xu's proposal? What might trouble them? Would you expect a united British front on the issue of legalization, or might they have been as divided as the Chinese? Might legalization have prevented the war that came in 1839?

"Memorial from Heu-Naetse" in *Blue Book — Correspondence Relating to China, 1840,* 156–59; "Memorial from Yuan Yu-lin," in *A Critical Study of the First Anglo-Chinese War,* ed. P. C. Kuo (Shanghai: The Commercial Press Ltd., 1935), 211–13.

Xu Naiji: Legalization

Xu Naiji, Vice-President of the Sacrificial Court, presents the following memorial in regard to opium, to show that the more severe the interdicts against it are made, the more widely do the evils arising therefrom spread; and that it is right urgently to request, that a change be made in the arrangements respecting it; to which end he earnestly entreats His Sacred Majesty to cast a glance hereon and to issue secret orders for a faithful investigation of the subject.

I would humbly represent that opium was originally ranked among medicines; its qualities are stimulant; it also checks excessive secretions; and prevents the evil effects of noxious vapours. In the Materia Medica of Le Shechin, of the Ming dynasty, it is called Afooyung. When anyone is long habituated to inhaling it, it becomes necessary to resort to it at regular intervals, and the habit of using it, being inveterate, is destructive of time, injurious to property, and yet dear to one even as life. Of those who use it to great excess, the breath becomes feeble, the body wasted, the face sallow, the teeth black: The individuals themselves clearly see the evil effects of it, yet cannot refrain from it. It is, indeed, indispensably necessary to enact severe prohibitions in order to eradicate so vile a practice.

On inquiry, I find that there are three kinds of opium: One is called Company's, the outer covering of it is black, and hence it is also called "black earth"; it comes from Bengal; a second kind is called "whiteskin," and comes from Bombay; the third kind is called "redskin," and comes from Madras. These are places which belong to England.

In Keenlung's reign, as well as previously, opium was inserted in the tariff of Canton as a medicine, subject to a duty of three taels per hundred catties,[1] with an additional charge of two taels, four mace,[2] and five candareens,[3] under the name of charge per package. After this, it was prohibited. In the first year of Keaking, those found guilty of smoking opium were subject only to the punishment of the pillory and bamboo. Now they have, in the course of time, become liable to the severest penalties, transportation in various degrees, and death after the ordinary continuance in prison. Yet the smokers of the drug have increased in number, and the practice has spread almost throughout the whole empire. In Keenlung's and the previous reigns, when opium passed through the Custom-House and paid a duty, it was given into the hands of the Hong merchants in exchange for tea and other goods. But at the present time, the prohibitions of government being most strict against it, none dare openly to exchange goods for it; all secretly

[1] See footnote 2, page 237.
[2] A mace is equal to ¹⁄₁₀ of a tael.
[3] A candareen is a smaller Chinese measure of weight or money equal to ¹⁄₁₀₀ of a tael.

purchase it with money. In the reign of Keaking, there arrived, it may be, some hundred chests annually. The number has now increased to upwards of twenty thousand chests, containing each a hundred catties. The "black earth," which is the best, sells for about eight hundred dollars, foreign money, per chest; the "white-skin," which is next in quality, for about six hundred dollars; and the last, or "red-skin," for about four hundred dollars. The total quantity sold during the year amounts in value to ten and some odd millions of dollars; so that, in reckoning the dollar at seven mace, standard weight of silver, the annual waste of money somewhat exceeds ten millions of taels. Formerly, the barbarian merchants brought foreign money to China; which being paid in exchange for goods, was a source of pecuniary advantage to the people of all the sea-board provinces. But latterly, the barbarian merchants have clandestinely sold opium for money; which has rendered it unnecessary for them to import foreign silver. Thus foreign money has been going out of the country, while none comes into it.

It is proposed entirely to cut off the foreign trade, thus to remove the root, to dam up the source of the evil. The Celestial Dynasty would not, indeed, hesitate to relinquish the few millions of duties arising therefrom. But all the nations of the West have had a general market open to their ships for upwards of a thousand years; while the dealers in opium are the English alone; it would be wrong, for the sake of cutting off the English trade, to cut off that of all the other nations. Besides, the hundreds of thousands of people living on the sea-coast depend wholly on trade for their livelihood, and how are they to be disposed of? Moreover, the barbarian ships, being on the high seas, can repair to any island that may be selected as an entrepôt, and the native sea-going vessels can meet them there; it is then impossible to cut off the trade. Of late years, the foreign vessels have visited all the ports of Fuhkeen, Chekeang, Keangran, Shantung, even to Teentsin and Mantchouria, for the purpose of selling opium. And although at once expelled by the local authorities, yet it is reported that the quantity sold by them was not small. Thus it appears that, though the commerce of Canton should be cut off, yet it will not be possible to prevent the clandestine introduction of merchandise.

It will be found, on examination, that the smokers of opium are idle, lazy vagrants, having no useful purpose before them, and are unworthy of regard or even of contempt. And though there are smokers to be found who have overstepped the threshold of age, yet they do not attain to the long life of other men. But new births are daily increasing the population of the empire; and there is no cause to apprehend a diminution therein; while, on the other hand, we cannot adopt too great, or too early, precautions against the annual waste which is taking place in the resources, the very substance of China.

Since then, it will not answer to close our ports against (all trades), and since the laws issued against opium are quite inoperative, the only method left is to revert to the former system, to permit the barbarian merchants to import opium paying duty thereon as a medicine, and to require that, after having passed the Custom-House, it shall be delivered to the Hong merchants only in exchange for merchandise, and that no money be paid for it. The barbarians finding that the amount of dues to be paid on it, is less than what is now spent in bribes, will also gladly comply therein. Foreign money should be placed on the same footing with sycee silver, and the exportation of it should be equally prohibited. Offenders, when caught, should be punished by the entire destruction of the opium they may have, and the confiscation of the money that may be found with them. . . .

It becomes my duty, then, to request that it be enacted, that any officer, scholar, or soldier, found guilty of secretly smoking opium, shall be immediately dismissed from public employ, without being made liable to any other penalty. . . .

Lastly, that no regard be paid to the purchase and use of opium on the part of the people generally.

Does any suggest a doubt, that to remove the existing prohibitions will derogate from the dignity of the Government? I would ask, if he is ignorant that the pleasures of the table and of the nuptial couch may also be indulged in to the injury of health? Nor are the invigorating drugs *footsze* and *wootow* devoid of poisonous qualities: Yet it has never been heard that any one of these has been interdicted. Besides, the removal of the prohibitions refers only to the vulgar and common people, those who have no official duties to perform. So long as the officers of the Government, the scholars, and the military, are not included, I see no detriment to the dignity of the Government. And by allowing the proposed importation and exchange of the drug for other commodities, more than ten millions of money will annually be prevented from flowing out of the Central land. On which side then is the gain, — on which the loss? It is evident at a glance. . . . Perchance this may be found adequate to stop further oozing out of money, and to replenish the national resources. With inexpressible awe and trembling fear, I reverently present this memorial and await your Majesty's commands.

Yuan Yulin: Elimination

I, your minister, believe that the success or failure in government and the prosperity or decay of administration depend largely upon our capacity to distinguish between right and wrong, between what is safe and what is dangerous. . . . The prevailing evil of to-day is the excuse that things are hard to get done, and the foremost example of such hypocrisy is the proposal to legalize opium. . . .

In my humble opinion, the proposal for legalization has overlooked the distinction between right and wrong in three ways. Further, it fails to appreciate what is safe and what is dangerous in six respects. I beg leave to explain my views in detail.

Why has it overlooked the distinction between right and wrong? Namely:

The prohibition of opium is most solemnly recorded on the statute books. . . . The proposal to change the established law is thus a violation of an inherited institution and of the imperial edicts.

Uniformity is the most important element in the decrees of the Court. Now it has been proposed that the prohibition of opium-smoking would reach the officers of the Government, the scholars, and the military, but not the common people. But it is forgotten that the common people of to-day will be the officers, scholars, and the military of the future. Should they be allowed to smoke at first and then be prohibited from it in the future? Moreover, the officers, scholars, and the military of to-day may be degraded to the rank of the common people. In that ease, are they to be freed from the prohibition once imposed on them? Prohibition was proclaimed because opium is pernicious. It follows then that the ban should not be abolished until it ceases to be an evil. A partial prohibition or partial legalization is a confusion of rules by the government itself; consequently good faith in its observance can hardly be expected. When the law was all for prohibition, decrees had not been followed. How can the people respect the restrictions or punishments should the law be in confusion? The logical consequence will be the ruin of government and demoralization of our culture.

According to the old customs regulations, every 100 catties of opium are subject to a duty of 3 taels, and an additional duty of 2 taels, 4.5 mace. A chest of opium contains 100 catties, and the consumption in recent years amounted to more than 20,000 chests. If each chest pays a duty of 5 odd taels, the total would amount to no more than 120,000 or 130,000 taels. Even if the duties be raised to twofold, it would be only a little over 200,000 taels. Further doubled, the figure will stand at only 500,000 taels. . . . Hence, if our Government should seek its revenue from the duties on opium, it is to make an enormous sacrifice for a scanty profit.

As to the reasons why the proposed legalization fails to appreciate what is safe and what is dangerous:

The drain of silver, to be sure, arouses apprehension. But the point is whether inspection is faithfully enforced or not. Should the inspection be faithful, opium prohibition will be effective; so also will be the ban on the silver export. If it be not faithful, opium prohibition will come to naught, and so will the ban on silver export. It must not be supposed that inspection will be facilitated by relaxing opium prohibition or that it will be difficult if the prohibition is severe.

Further, I, your minister, believe that silver will continue to leave the country, no matter whether opium be prohibited or not. For the very object of the foreign barbarians in bringing opium into China is to fetch the silver in the interior of our country. The proposal now made to exchange goods by barter certainly runs counter to their desire. The logical consequence will be smuggling cloaked in an outward conformity to law, with the ultimate result of carrying away the silver as before. The prohibition on silver export is not unsevere to-day. Yet the annual drain in recent years amounts to the startling figure of 20,000,000 taels. If we cannot practice faithful inspection now, how can we expect to do so after the legalization of opium? . . .

It has been argued that since the imported opium costs an enormous sum of money, the cultivation of the poppy should be allowed in the interior of the country. . . . [But], the farm lands of our country are fixed in number. . . . The valuable acres yielding crops may easily be turned into a vast field of opium. This means to destroy agriculture and ruin the very foundation of the lives of the people.

If the habit of smoking secretly spreads over the country under the present prohibition, its legalization will mean greater disasters: fathers would no longer be able to teach their sons; husbands would no longer be able to admonish their wives; masters would no longer be able to restrain their servants; and teachers would no longer be able to train their pupils. The habitual smokers would continue it as a regular practice, while others would strive for imitation. The perpetration of evils will be fathomless. It would mean the end of the life of the people and the destruction of the soul of the nation.

As a result of the smoking of opium, the soldiers of Kwangtung were enfeebled. Your Majesty admonished them on that account during the late rebellion of the mountaineers in the said province. Now should the proposal be adhered to that soldiers, but not the people, be prohibited from smoking opium, then at the future recruitment of the army it would be found that old soldiers had already been spoiled by secret smoking, while fresh recruits would be habitual smokers! . . . The very trick of the cunning barbarians is to weaken our nation with poison. If they now actually succeed in fooling our people, it means the disintegration of our national defense and the opening up of the same to their penetration.

. . . The dishonest hong merchants had allied themselves with the lawless barbarians, employing fast crabs[1] and maintaining distilleries to smuggle opium. . . . Only by rigid enforcement of the law at the present time can its spread be prevented. Yet it is now suggested to allow their traffic! This is tantamount to confirming that their past conduct was

---

[1] A swift, transporting craft used for smuggling.

very politic: Henceforth they will be afraid of no punishment. It means help to traitorous citizens and coöperation with the foreign pirates [i.e., lawless foreigners]!

Further, what arouses our gravest apprehension is the perpetration of an evil which might completely go out of control. Once opium is legalized, the people will flock to it. When the evil becomes alarming and when we come to repent the wrong of legalization . . . we will readily find that the country is so heavily saddled with its bad results that recovery is well-nigh impossible. . . .

39

COMMISSIONER LIN

Letter to Queen Victoria

During the debate over legalization versus elimination in 1836, Lin Tse-hsu was a vigorous spokesman on behalf of eliminating opium smoking and its sale, the position eventually supported by the emperor. In recognition of his persuasive arguments and his success in confiscating opium as governor-general of Hupei and Hunan, the emperor appointed Lin as special commissioner to the port of Canton and charged him with putting an end to the importation of opium. Shortly after assuming his new duties in Canton in 1839 and armed with an imperial edict that made the importation, sale, or use of opium a capital offense, Lin demanded that all opium in Canton be confiscated and personally oversaw the destruction of more than twenty thousand chests. With the approval of the emperor, Lin also wrote the following letter to Queen Victoria of England. What seems to be the reason for this letter? What do you think of the argument Lin makes? Do you find it convincing?

Thinking Historically

Obviously, this letter was addressed to the Queen and the government of England. What assumptions does Lin make about the Queen, English policy, and opium? What would you expect the English re-

Modern Asia and Africa, ed. William H. McNeill and Mitsuko Iriye (New York: Oxford University Press, 1971).

sponse to be? Peter Parker, an American resident in Canton, read the letter at Lin's request and characterized it as "much nonsense and insult,"[1] adding that he did not think it would have the desired effect. What do you suppose Parker meant? If Lin had asked you about the letter, what advice would you have given him?

Lin, high imperial commissioner, a president of the Board of War, viceroy of the two Keäng provinces, &c., Tang, a president of the Board of War, viceroy of the two Kwang provinces, &c., and E, a vice-president of the Board of War, lieut.-governor of Kwangtung, &c., hereby conjointly address this public dispatch to the queen of England for the purpose of giving her clear and distinct information (on the state of affairs) &c.

It is only our high and mighty emperor, who alike supports and cherishes those of the Inner Land, and those from beyond the seas — who looks upon all mankind with equal benevolence — who, if a source of profit exists anywhere, diffuses it over the whole world — who, if the tree of evil takes root anywhere, plucks it up for the benefit of all nations — who, in a word, hath implanted in his breast that heart (by which beneficent nature herself) governs the heavens and the earth! You, the queen of your honorable nation, sit upon a throne occupied through successive generations by predecessors, all of whom have been styled respectful and obedient. Looking over the public documents accompanying the tribute sent (by your predecessors) on various occasions, we find the following — "All the people of my (i.e. the king of England's) country, arriving at the Central Land for purposes of trade, have to feel grateful to the great emperor for the most perfect justice, for the kindest treatment," and other words to that effect. Delighted did we feel that the kings of your honorable nation so clearly understood the great principles of propriety, and were so deeply grateful for the heavenly goodness (of our emperor): — therefore, it was that we of the heavenly dynasty nourished and cherished your people from afar, and bestowed upon them redoubled proofs of our urbanity and kindness. It is merely from these circumstances, that your country — deriving immense advantage from its commercial intercourse with us, which has endured now two hundred years — has become the rich and flourishing kingdom that it is said to be!

But, during the commercial intercourse which has existed so long, among the numerous foreign merchants resorting hither, are wheat and

---

[1] Hsin-Pao Chang, *Commissioner Lin and the Opium War* (New York: Norton, 1964), 137.

tares, good and bad; and of these latter are some, who, by means of introducing opium by stealth, have seduced our Chinese people, and caused every province of the land to overflow with that poison. These then know merely to advantage themselves, they care not about injuring others! This is a principle which heaven's Providence repugnates; and which mankind conjointly look upon with abhorrence! Moreover, the great emperor hearing of it, actually quivered with indignation, and especially dispatched me, the commissioner, to Canton, that in conjunction with the viceroy and lieut.-governor of the province, means might be taken for its suppression!

Every native of the Inner Land who sells opium, as also all who smoke it, are alike adjudged to death. Were we then to go back and take up the crimes of the foreigners, who, by selling it for many years have induced dreadful calamity and robbed us of enormous wealth, and punish them with equal severity, our laws could not but award to them absolute annihilation! But, considering that these said foreigners did yet repent of their crime, and with a sincere heart beg for mercy; that they took 20,283 chests of opium piled up in their store-ships, and through Elliot, the superintendent of the trade of your said country, petitioned that they might be delivered up to us, when the same were all utterly destroyed, of which we, the imperial commissioner and colleagues, made a duly prepared memorial to his majesty; — considering these circumstances, we have happily received a fresh proof of the extraordinary goodness of the great emperor, inasmuch as he who voluntarily comes forward, may yet be deemed a fit subject for mercy, and his crimes be graciously remitted him. But as for him who again knowingly violates the laws, difficult indeed will it be thus to go on repeatedly pardoning! He or they shall alike be doomed to the penalties of the new statute. We presume that you, the sovereign of your honorable nation, on pouring out your heart before the altar of eternal justice, cannot but command all foreigners with the deepest respect to reverence our laws! If we only lay clearly before your eyes, what is profitable and what is destructive, you will then know that the statutes of the heavenly dynasty cannot but be obeyed with fear and trembling!

We find that your country is distant from us about sixty or seventy thousand miles, that your foreign ships come hither striving the one with the other for our trade, and for the simple reason of their strong desire to reap a profit. Now, out of the wealth of our Inner Land, if we take a part to bestow upon foreigners from afar, it follows, that the immense wealth which the said foreigners amass, ought properly speaking to be portion of our own native Chinese people. By what principle of reason then, should these foreigners send in return a poisonous drug, which involves in destruction those very natives of China? Without meaning to say that the foreigners harbor such destructive intentions in their hearts, we yet positively assert that from their inordinate thirst after gain, they are perfectly careless about the injuries they inflict upon us! And such being the case, we should like to ask what has become of that conscience which heaven has implanted in the breasts of all men?

We have heard that in your own country opium is prohibited with the utmost strictness and severity: — this is a strong proof that you know full well how hurtful it is to mankind. Since then you do not permit it to injure your own country, you ought not to have the injurious drug transferred to another country, and above all others, how much less to the Inner Land! Of the products which China exports to your foreign countries, there is not one which is not beneficial to mankind in some shape or other. There are those which serve for food, those which are useful, and those which are calculated for resale; — but all are beneficial. Has China (we should like to ask) ever yet sent forth a noxious article from its soil? Not to speak of our tea and rhubarb, things which your foreign countries could not exist a single day without, if we of the Central Land were to grudge you what is beneficial, and not to compassionate your wants, then wherewithal could you foreigners manage to exist? And further, as regards your woolens, camlets, and longells, were it not that you get supplied with our native raw silk, you could not get these manufactured! If China were to grudge you those things which yield a profit, how could you foreigners scheme after any profit at all? Our other articles of food, such as sugar, ginger, cinnamon, &c., and our other articles for use, such as silk piece-goods, chinaware, &c., are also many necessaries of life to you; how can we reckon up their number! On the other hand, the things that come from your foreign countries are only calculated to make presents of, or serve for mere amusement. It is quite the same to us if we have them, or if we have them not. If these are of no material consequence to us of the Inner Land, what difficulty would there be in prohibiting and shutting our market against them? It is only that our heavenly dynasty most freely permits you to take off her tea, silk, and other commodities, and convey them for consumption everywhere, without the slightest stint or grudge, for no other reason, but that where a profit exists, we wish that it be diffused abroad for the benefit of all the earth!

Your honorable nation takes away the products of our Central Land, and not only do you thereby obtain food and support for yourselves, but moreover, by reselling these products to other countries you reap a threefold profit. Now if you would only not sell opium, this threefold profit would be secured to you: how can you possibly consent to forgo it for a drug that is hurtful to men, and an unbridled craving after gain that seems to know no bounds! Let us suppose that foreigners came from another country, and brought opium into England, and seduced the people of your country to smoke it, would not you, the sovereign of the said country, look upon such a procedure with anger, and in your just indignation endeavor to get rid of it? Now we have always heard that your highness possesses a most kind and benevolent heart, surely then you are incapable of doing or causing to be done unto another, that which you should not wish another to do unto you! We have at the same time heard that your ships which come to Canton do each and every of them carry a document by your highness' self, on which are written these words "you shall not be permitted to carry contraband goods"; this shows that the laws of your highness are in their origin both distinct and severe, and we can only suppose that because the ships coming here have been very numerous, due attention has not been given to search and examine; and for this reason it is that we now address you this public document, that you may clearly know how stern and severe are the laws of the central dynasty, and most certainly you will cause that they be not again rashly violated!

Moreover, we have heard that in London the metropolis where you dwell, as also in Scotland, Ireland, and other such places, no opium whatever is produced. It is only in sundry parts of your colonial kingdom of Hindostan, such as Bengal, Madras, Bombay, Patna, Malwa, Benares, Malacca, and other places where the very hills are covered with the opium plant, where tanks are made for the preparing of the drug; month by month, and year by year, the volume of the poison increases, its unclean stench ascends upwards, until heaven itself grows angry, and the very gods thereat get indignant! You, the queen of the said honorable nation, ought immediately to have the plant in those parts plucked up by the very root! Cause the land there to be hoed up afresh, sow in its stead the five grains, and if any man dare again to plant in these grounds a single poppy, visit his crime with the most severe punishment. By a truly benevolent system of government such as this, will you indeed reap advantage, and do away with a source of evil. Heaven must support you, and the gods will crown you with felicity! This will get for yourself the blessing of long life, and from this will proceed the security and stability of your descendants!

In reference to the foreign merchants who come to this our Central Land, the food that they eat, and the dwellings that they abide in, proceed entirely from the goodness of our heavenly dynasty: — the profits which they reap, and the fortunes which they amass, have their origin only in that portion of benefit which our heavenly dynasty kindly allots them: And as these pass but little of their time in your country, and the greater part of their time in ours, it is a generally received maxim of old and of modern times, that we should conjointly admonish, and clearly make known the punishment that awaits them.

Suppose the subject of another country were to come to England to trade, he would certainly be required to comply with the laws of England, then how much more does this apply to us of the celestial empire! Now it is a fixed statute of this empire, that any native Chinese who sells opium is punishable with death, and even he who merely smokes it, must no less die. Pause and reflect for a moment: If you foreigners did not bring the opium hither, where should our Chinese people get it to resell? It is you foreigners who involve our simple natives in the pit of death, and are they alone to be permitted to escape alive? If so much as one of those deprive one of our people of his life, he must forfeit his life in requital for that which he has taken: — how much more does this apply to him who by means of opium destroys his fellowmen? Does the havoc which he commits stop with a single life? Therefore it is that those foreigners who now import opium into the Central Land are condemned to be beheaded and strangled by the new statute, and this explains what we said at the beginning about plucking up the tree of evil, wherever it takes root, for the benefit of all nations.

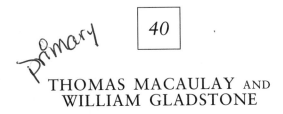

40

THOMAS MACAULAY AND WILLIAM GLADSTONE

The Parliamentary Debate

In January 1840, Lin found a ship captain who was willing to deliver his letter to the Queen (see selection 39). On his arrival in England in June, Captain Warner wrote to Lord Palmerston (1784–1865), the foreign minister since 1830, seeking to deliver Lin's letter, but was refused. Events were rapidly overtaking any efforts at peaceful settlement.

In addition to arresting Chinese opium smugglers, Commissioner Lin demanded the surrender of all British-controlled opium in China. To indicate his resolve, Lin blockaded the British warehouses in Canton and prevented the British from leaving until they complied. After a struggle of wills, Captain Elliot, representing the merchants and the government, agreed to accept the merchants' opium on behalf of the British government and turned it over to Commissioner Lin. Lin destroyed thousands of chests of the drug, and the British retired to Macao, from where they sent their ships to India for more supplies.

Hansard's Parliamentary Debates, Third Series, vol. 52, for April 7 and 8, 1840, 716–17, 718–19, 812–13, 816–18.

Thanks to the scarcity, opium could now be sold at much higher prices.

Meanwhile Captain Elliot, who personally opposed the opium trade, wrote to the British foreign secretary, Lord Palmerston, that the Chinese had committed an act of piracy for which they should be punished. Within a few months, in August 1839, another incident led to the first military engagement of what was to become the Opium War. A drunken British seaman wandering near anchorage had killed a Chinese subject in a fight. Commissioner Lin demanded that the responsible British sailor be turned over to Chinese authorities. Elliot refused, insisting that he did not know who the guilty sailor was. In retaliation for this and the renewed opium smuggling, Lin ordered the Chinese fleet to prevent British sailors from coming ashore — except at Canton, where they would be required to accept Chinese legal jurisdiction. On September 4, 1839, a British frigate, seeking supplies for those aboard, fired on the Chinese junks that barred access to Kowloon, the mainland peninsula opposite Hong Kong Island. In a second encounter near Canton two British ships sank four Chinese man-of-war junks. Only then did Lord Palmerston decide to send an armed fleet from India to China.

Palmerston had to work through the winter to prepare Parliament for war. William Jardine, one of the original opium traders and a partner of the leading firm, Jardine, Matheson, and Company, returned to England in 1839 and won a seat in Parliament, where he was able to amplify his complaints about Chinese injustices. Stories of an attack on a British sailor, China's demand that Britain turn over the killer of a Chinese subject, a suspension of British trading privileges, and the detainment of merchants in their warehouses in Canton inflamed public opinion.

Jardine privately informed Palmerston that the merchants, in surrendering their twenty thousand chests of opium to Elliot for delivery to Lin, fully expected to be compensated £2 million. Palmerston knew that British taxpayers would not take well to paying opium smugglers this enormous sum; pressing the Chinese to come up with the amount, by whatever means, seemed more feasible. On February 6, 1840, two weeks after meeting with Jardine, Palmerston wrote to the government of India, ordering them to prepare sixteen vessels of war with 540 guns, four armed steamers, and four thousand British, Irish, and Indian troops.

In the first months of 1840, members of Parliament rose intermittently to ask the government about rumors of military engagements in China. Finally, Palmerston allowed a debate on a subsidiary issue beginning on April 7, 1840. Among those who spoke for the government was the widely respected historian, poet, and veteran of India, Thomas Macaulay (1800–1859), the Secretary of State for War. The next day, William Gladstone (1809–1898) — champion of reform and free trade, who would become prime minister four times between 1868 and 1894 — spoke. At age thirty, he was already a conservative driven by moral conviction. He addressed opium — the issue that everyone else avoided.

How did Macaulay divert Parliament's attention from the issue of opium smuggling? What, according to Macaulay, were legitimate reasons to go to war?

Was Gladstone opposed to war and the opium trade? How did Gladstone counter the argument that the opium trade would be difficult to stop? How did he counter Macaulay's stirring call to defend the flag?

Thinking Historically

Macaulay and Gladstone gave different accounts of the events leading to the conflict. What were their different accounts? Do you find one more convincing than the other? Based on these accounts, what do you think actually happened?

Why was Gladstone more inclined to accept China's account of events than Macaulay? Can the differences between Macaulay and Gladstone be likened to the differences between China and Britain?

Macaulay Speech, April 7, 1840

Macaulay said that he had seen it asserted over and over again, that the Government was advocating the cause of the contraband trade, in order to force an opium war on the public; but he thought that it was impossible to be conceived that a thought so absurd and so atrocious should have ever entered the minds of the British Ministry. Their course was clear. They might doubt whether it were wise for the government of China to exclude from that country a drug which, if judiciously administered, was powerful in assuaging pain, and in promoting health, because it was occasionally used to excess by intemperate men — they might doubt whether it was wise policy on the part of that Government to attempt to stop the efflux of precious metals from the country in the due course of trade. They learned from history — and almost every country afforded proof, which was strengthened by existing circumstances in England, to which he had already alluded — that no machinery, however powerful, had been sufficient to keep out of any country those luxuries which the people enjoyed, or were able to purchase, or to prevent the efflux of precious metals, when it was demanded by the course of trade. What Great Britain could not effect with the finest marine, and the most trustworthy preventive service in the world, was not likely to be effected by the feeble efforts of the mandarins of China.

But, whatever their opinions on these points might be, the Governor of China alone, it must be remembered, was competent to decide; that government had a right to keep out opium, to keep in silver, and to enforce their prohibitory laws, by whatever means which they might possess, consistently with the principles of public morality, and of international law; and if, after having given fair notice of their intention, to seize all contraband goods introduced into their dominions; they seized our opium, we had no right to complain; but when the government, finding, that by just and lawful means, they could not carry out their prohibition, resorted to measures unjust and unlawful, confined our innocent countrymen, and insulted the Sovereign in the person of her representative, then he thought, the time had arrived when it was fit that we should interfere. Whether the proceedings of the Chinese were or were not founded on humanity, was not now to be decided. . . .

The Imperial Commissioner [Lin] began by confiscating property; his next demand was for innocent blood. A Chinese was slain; the most careful inquiry had been made, but was insufficient to discover the slayer, or even the nation to which he belonged; but it was caused to be notified that, guilty or not, some subject of the Queen's must be given up. Great Britain gave an unequivocal refusal to be a party to so barbarous a proceeding. The [British] people at Canton were seized; they were driven from Macao, suspected or not. Women with child, children at the breast, were treated with equal severity, were refused bread, or the means of subsistence; the innocent Lascars[1] were thrown into the sea; an English gentleman was barbarously mutilated, and England found itself at once assailed with a fury unknown to civilized countries. The place of this country among nations was not so mean or ill ascertained that we should trouble ourselves to resist every petty slight which we might receive. Conscious of her power, England could bear that her Sovereign could be called a barbarian, and her people described as savages, destitute of every useful art. When our Ambassadors were obliged to undergo a degrading prostration, in compliance with their regulations, conscious of our strength, we were more amused than irritated. But there was a limit to that forbearance. It would not have been worthy of us to take arms upon a small provocation, referring to rites and ceremonies merely; but every one in the scale of civilized nations should know that Englishmen were ever living under the protecting eye of their own country. [Macaulay] was much touched, and he thought that probably many others were so also, by one passage contained in the dispatch of Captain Elliot, in which he communicated his arrival at the factory at Canton. The moment at which he landed he

---

[1] East Indian sailors.

was surrounded by his countrymen in an agony of despair at their situation, but the first step which he took was to order the flag of Great Britain to be taken from the boat and to be planted in the balcony. This was an act which revived the drooping hopes of those who looked to him for protection. It was natural that they should look with confidence on the victorious flag which was hoisted over them, which reminded them that they belonged to a country unaccustomed to defeat, to submission, or to shame — it reminded them that they belonged to a country which had made the farthest ends of the earth ring with the fame of her exploits in redressing the wrongs of her children. . . .

Glastone Speech,
April 8, 1840

. . . [William Gladstone] thought that it was of importance to show that the Government of China, before it had resorted to violent measures to suppress the opium trade, had exhibited great moderation in the measures which it had adopted; and that by appeals to individuals and their agents, by serious warnings, by the constant confiscation of the opium found in the possession of natives, and in a word, by every means that could be devised, it had attempted to prove the sincerity of its endeavours to put an end to that illegal traffic. He thought that the noble Lord [Palmerston] ought to have co-operated, as far as he could, with the Government of China, when the sincerity of its endeavours was proved to him. The right hon. Gentleman opposite [Macaulay] asserted, that it was quite impossible for us to put down the opium trade in China ourselves. Admitting that to be the fact, still we might have shown a desire to co-operate with the Government of China; and if we had done so, we should, have put down the traffic to a great extent, though we might not have succeeded in abolishing it. We might have sent away the receiving ships — we might have refused them the protection of our flag. "But then," said the right hon. Gentleman opposite, "we should have created piracy, and should have converted the present illicit traffic into something much worse." Why, the trade in opium had already generated piracy not only on the river, but also all along the coast of China. But he was convinced in his own mind that if we had sent away the receiving ships, that measure would have produced other and very different measures on the part of the Chinese. The right hon. Gentleman opposite had also asked —

> "Shall we establish at our own expense a preventive service on the coast of China to put down the smuggling of opium into that country!"

Now to that question he would give an answer by asking another, and that was —

> "Did the right hon. Gentleman opposite know that the opium smuggled into China came exclusively from British ports — that was, from Bengal, and through Bombay!"

If that were the fact — and he defied the right hon. Gentleman to gainsay it — then we required no preventive service to put down this illegal traffic. We had only to stop the sailing of the opium vessels; and it was a matter of certainty, that if we had stopped the exportation of opium from Bengal, and broken up the depot at Lintin, and had checked the growth of it in Malwa, and had put a moral stigma upon it, we should have greatly crippled, if, indeed, we had not entirely extinguished, the trade in it. . . .

"You will be called upon," said Mr. Gladstone, addressing himself to the Ministers — "you will be called upon, even if you escape from condemnation on this motion, to show cause for your present intention of making war upon China. I do not mean to say that you ought not to send out an armament against China. Far from it. We have placed ourselves under your auspices in a position so unfavourable, that it is a matter of certainty that we cannot even demand terms of equity without a display of force. But we are going to exact reparation for insult, and compensation for confiscation which we allege ourselves to have suffered. If that be so, then I tell you that you are bound to show to us and to the world what the insult is for which we are to demand reparation. The right hon. Gentleman opposite has spoken to us of the cruel murder which he says the Chinese committed upon a boat's crew which they captured. Now, I beg leave to remind him that in one of his despatches Captain Elliot alleges that this was an act committed by pirates, and not by Chinese authorities. It is only in his last despatch that Captain Elliot says that his conviction now is that he was wrong in that allegation. Now, I must say, that all the conduct of the Chinese authorities militates against all this recent conviction of Captain Elliot. They had had not only the opportunity, but also the power, of putting to death other British subjects than the three Lascars whom they had captured, and if their object had been to inflict terror, the murder of the former would have answered their object better than the murder of the latter. Even in the case of the Lascars, the Chinese authorities had never been asked for explanation; and before explanation is asked, are we to be told that this outrage is a sufficient cause of war? But, says the right hon. Gentleman opposite, "The Chinese have poisoned their wells, and such a step would be certain to lead to retaliation and vengeance on the part of our sailors, who get their water from them." Now, as Captain Elliot declared to the Chinese authorities that he had no formal knowledge of what would be the orders of his own government when it heard of these transactions, and as he refused to give a formal injunction for the abandonment of the trade in opium, it appears to me that the Chinese were justified in saying, "We have no other alternative than to expel these smugglers from China," and they offered in consequence to Captain Elliot expulsion on the one hand, or legal traffic in the usual way on the other. Captain Elliot refused both. He would not let the shipping go up to Whampoa. Every objection that could be made was made by Captain Elliot to the renewal of the legal trade. The Chinese were anxious for the renewal of it; but "No," said Captain Elliot, "we will go to Lintin, we will establish ourselves there, we will maintain our right to procure provisions there, and at Lintin we will remain till more favourable circumstances arise." Now will the House consider what this language really amounted to? It was a claim on the part of the British merchants to go to the very focus of smuggling; and this afforded a suspicion — a seemingly well-founded suspicion — to the Chinese, that it was their intention that the opium trade should be resumed there. The Chinese had no armament ready wherewith to expel us from Lintin. They therefore said, "We will resort to another mode of bringing you to reason. We will expel you from our shores by refusing you provisions," and then of course they poisoned the wells. (*Cheers* from the Ministerial benches). I am ready to meet those cheers. I understand what they mean. I have not asserted — I do not mean to assert — that the Chinese actually poisoned their wells. All I mean to say is, that it was alleged that they had poisoned their wells. They gave you notice to abandon your contraband trade. When they found that you would not, they had a right to drive you from their coasts on account of your obstinacy in persisting in this infamous and atrocious traffic. You allowed your agent to aid and abet those who were concerned in carrying on that trade, and I do not know how it can be urged as a crime against the Chinese that they refused provisions to those who refused obedience to their laws whilst residing within their territories. I am not competent to judge how long this war may last, or how protracted may be its operations, but this I can say, that a war more unjust in its origin, a war more calculated in its progress to cover this country with permanent disgrace, I do not know, and I have not read of. The right hon. Gentleman opposite spoke last night in eloquent terms of the British flag waving in glory at Canton, and of the animating effects produced on the minds of our sailors by the knowledge, that in no country under heaven was it permitted to be insulted. We all know the animating effects which have been produced in the minds of British subjects on many critical occasions when that flag has been unfurled in the battlefield. But how comes it to pass that the sight of that flag always raises the spirit of Englishmen? It is because it has always been associated with the cause of justice, with opposition to oppression, with respect for national rights, with honourable commercial enterprize, but now, under the auspices of the noble Lord, that flag is hoisted to protect an infamous contraband traffic, and if it were never to be hoisted except as it is now hoisted on the coast of China, we should recoil from its sight with horror, and should never again feel our hearts thrill, as they now thrill with emotion, when it floats proudly and magnificently on the breeze.

41

Images of Chinese and British Soldiers and Naval Battle

The Chinese soldier in Figure 1 wears a tiger suit and cap designed to scare the enemy. Figure 2 is a Chinese portrayal of an English sailor as a fire devil. What do these images suggest about Chinese preparations and expectations for battle?

Figure 3 is a Western depiction of a naval battle between a British ship and Chinese junks. What advantage did the British ship enjoy over the junks? Figure 4 is a Chinese rendering of a British ship similar to the one depicted in Figure 3. What feature of the British ship most captured the attention of the Chinese artist? How does this vision of the ship relate to the Chinese image of the British soldier?

Thinking Historically

What, if anything, do pictorial images add to our understanding of this period? What, if anything, do they add to our understanding of Chinese and British perceptions of each other at the time of the Opium War?

The Opium War was one of the last wars fought before the development of photography. Would photographs of these people and events tell us more than the drawings? How so?

How would you describe the differences in the representative styles of Chinese and British artists at the time of the Opium War? What, if any, significance can you attribute to these differences?

A Chinese soldier wearing a "lucky" tiger cap and *The foreign devil himself*, Gamma Liasion Photo News Agency. *A sea battle during the Opium Wars*, National Maritime Museum, London. *A drawing of an English War steamer*, Mary Evans Picture Library.

Figure 1. A Chinese soldier wearing a "lucky" tiger cap.

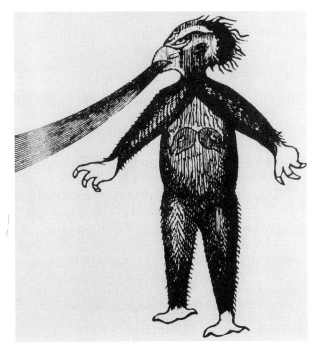

Figure 2. The foreign devil himself.

Figure 3. A sea battle during the Opium Wars.

Figure 4. A drawing of an English war steamer. The Chinese called these ships "fire devils."

42

Treaty of Nanking, 1842

The British threat to Nanking convinced China to sue for peace. The consequent Treaty of Nanking in 1842 brought an end to the Opium War. To what extent did the British succeed in achieving the goals they sought in the war? To what extent did they fulfill the aims of the Macartney mission?

Thinking Historically

This treaty has been labeled one of the "unequal treaties" by the Chinese. Why might it be characterized that way? What would have made it "equal"?

Victoria, by the Grace of God, Queen of the United Kingdom of Great Britain and Ireland, Defender of the Faith, etc., etc., etc. To all and Singular to whom these Presents shall come. Greetings! Whereas a Treaty between Us and Our Good Brother the Emperor of China, was concluded and signed, in the English and Chinese Languages, on board Our Ship the *Cornwallis,* at Nanking, on the Twenty-ninth day of August, in the Year of Our Lord One Thousand Eight Hundred and Forty-two, by the Plenipotentiaries of Us and of Our said Good Brother, duly and respectively authorized for that purpose; which Treaty is hereunto annexed in Original: —

Article I

There shall henceforward be Peace and Friendship between Her Majesty the Queen of the United Kingdom of Great Britain and Ireland, and His Majesty the Emperor of China, and between their respective Subjects, who shall enjoy full security and protection for their persons and property within the Dominions of the other.

Article II

His Majesty the Emperor of China agrees, that British Subjects, with their families and establishments, shall be allowed to reside, for the

Treaty of Nanking, in *Treaties, Conventions, etc., between China and Foreign States, Published at the Statistical Department of the Inspectorate General of Customs,* Vol. I, 1917, 351–56.

purpose of carrying on their Mercantile pursuits, without molestation or restraint at the Cities and Towns of Canton, Amoy, Foochow-fu, Ningpo, and Shanghai. . . .

Article III

It being obviously necessary and desirable, that British Subjects should have some Port whereat they may careen and refit their ships, when required, and keep Stores for that purpose, His Majesty the Emperor of China cedes to Her Majesty the Queen of Great Britain, etc., the Island of Hongkong. . . .

Article IV

The Emperor of China agrees to pay the sum of Six Millions of Dollars as the value of Opium which was delivered up at Canton in the month of March 1839, as a Ransom for the lives of Her Britannic Majesty's Superintendent and Subjects, who had been imprisoned and threatened with death by the Chinese High Officers. . . .

Article VI

The Government of Her Britannic Majesty having been obliged to send out an Expedition to demand and obtain redress for the violent and unjust Proceedings of the Chinese High Authorities towards Her Britannic Majesty's Officers and Subjects, the Emperor of China agrees to pay the sum of Twelve Millions of Dollars on account of the Expenses incurred. . . .

Article XII

On the assent of the Emperor of China to this Treaty being received and the discharge of the first instalment of money, Her Britannic Majesty's Forces will retire from Nanking and the Grand Canal, and will no longer molest or stop the Trade of China. The Military Post at Chinhai will also be withdrawn, but the Islands of Koolangsoo and that of Chusan will continue to be held by Her Majesty's Forces until the money payments, and the arrangements for opening the Ports to British Merchants be completed.

REFLECTIONS

The Treaty of Nanking said nothing about opium except for the provision that the Chinese would pay $6 million for the opium that Elliot had turned over to Lin in March of 1839. China continued the ban on the sale or importation of the drug while the British treaty established the principle of extraterritoriality, wherein citizens of foreign countries could be tried for offenses committed elsewhere by their own courts according to their own laws.

Of the new treaty ports opened on the Chinese coast, Shanghai proved to be the most successful by far. While other ports languished with a few foreign families, largely missionaries, Shanghai attracted a diverse population of merchants and missionaries from Europe and the United States. Forty-four ships entered the port in 1844; by 1855 the number had climbed to 437. By the mid-1850s Shanghai was exporting more than twenty million dollars' worth of silk per year and was receiving more than twenty thousand chests of opium per year. What does a comparison of these figures with those of Canton twenty years earlier (see Table 1 on page 235) suggest about changes in the China trade and the impact of the Opium War?

In Chapter 6 we explored the relative impact of capitalism and industrialization. In some ways, this chapter is a test case of that debate. We can chart the evolution of British policy between the Macartney expedition and the Opium War as industrialization takes hold. How did British policy change? What impact did industrialization have in the 1840s compared with the 1790s? In what ways did the industrial revolution change Britain's trade with China? In what ways did it change the terms of that trade?

It is interesting that opium exports to China increased after the Opium War. Industrial Britain could have substituted a wide range of manufactured products for opium to balance the importation of Chinese silks, porcelain, and tea, but capitalist Britain continued to receive enormous profits from the sale of opium.

To say that the Opium War was a product of mercantile capitalism is not to blame the merchants rather than politicians. Merchant capitalism was a state activity in the England of the British East India Company. Even with increasing insistence on free trade and an end to the company's monopoly over Indian trade in 1832, the boundaries between the interests of capital and the interests of the state were hard to draw.

Similarly, it makes little sense to debate whether the war was fought over trade or opium. Clearly, the war was fought to trade opium — for silk and tea and for whatever else would yield a profit. If the Opium War failed to end Chinese prohibition, it was largely because Chinese law could be bypassed in Shanghai and legally ignored in British-controlled Hong Kong. Nevertheless, the conflicts over trade and opium continued, leading to a second Opium War (1856–1860), at the conclusion of which the British secured more treaty ports, rights to interior trade, and the legalization of the opium trade throughout China.

While this chapter has shown us two sides to the Opium War, it also has replaced the simple notion of two clearly defined sides with a sense of the varying views and perspectives that come to bear on any issue. There were two sides to Macartney's demands, two sides to the Chinese debate over legalization, two sides to the Parliamentary debates. Indeed, we have viewed the two sides of import/export tables, images of ships, signatories to a treaty. One is led to conclude that there are at least two sides to every issue, and in any conflict many issues are involved. This is an important reminder to those who think there are only two sides to a story; indeed there are many more. We usually create two sides to an issue in an attempt to define and clarify it. We must recognize that these definitions are imperfect, yet they do not preclude our ability to render judgment; they only make that process more difficult.

8

Colonized and Colonizers

HISTORICAL CONTEXT
Europeans in Africa and Asia, 1850–1930

The British Opium War (1840–1842) was neither the beginning nor the end of European colonialism. In fact, the war occurred between two stages of European expansion. The first stage, beginning with Columbus, was a period in which Europeans — led by the Spanish and Portuguese — settled in the Western Hemisphere and created plantations with African labor. From 1492 to 1776, European settlement in Asia was limited to a few coastal port cities where merchants and missionaries operated. The second stage — the years between 1776, when Britain lost most of its American colonies, and 1880, when the European scramble for African territory began — has sometimes been called a period of *free-trade imperialism*. This term refers to the desire by European countries in general and by the British in particular to expand their zones of free-trade (as in the Opium War). It also refers to a widespread opposition to the expense of colonization, a conviction, especially among the British, who garnered all of the advantages of political empire without the costs of occupation and outright ownership.

The British used to say that their second global empire was created in the nineteenth century "in a fit of absentmindedness." But colonial policy in Britain and the rest of Europe was more planned and continuous than that schema might suggest. British control of India (including Burma) increased throughout the nineteenth century, as did British control of South Africa, Australia, the Pacific, and parts of the Americas. At the same time, France, having lost most of India to the British, began building an empire that included parts of North Africa, Southeast Asia, and the Pacific.

This new age of colonialism, beginning in the mid-nineteenth century, reached a fever pitch with the partition of Africa at the end of the century. The period spawned renewed settlement and massive population transfers, with most European migrants settling in the older colonies of the Americas (as well as in South Africa and Australia), where indigenous populations had been reduced. Even where settlement remained light, however, Europeans took political control of large areas of the Earth's surface.

In the first reading in this chapter, a historian offers a brief history of this second stage of European colonialism and describes what the renewed era of colonization meant, both for the colonizers and the colonized. Subsequent readings examine aspects of colonial society — in Dutch Java, British Burma, French Africa, and the Spanish Philippines.

THINKING HISTORICALLY
Using Literature in History

This chapter also explores whether literature can and should be used in the quest to better understand history. Beginning with some basic questions about the differences between literary and historical approaches, we examine a number of fictional accounts of colonialism, some written by the colonizers, others by the colonized or their descendants. How do these literary accounts add to, or detract from, a historical understanding of colonialism? The rich, evocative literature of the colonial period, both well informed and insightful, aids us in determining how we separate fact from fiction, construct historical knowledge, and appreciate the past in all its dimensions.

Secondary

| 43 |

JURGEN OSTERHAMMEL
From *Colonialism*

In this selection, modern historian Jurgen Osterhammel provides us with an overview of European colonialism. In the first part, "Colonial Epochs," the author discusses ways in which European colonialism changed from the late eighteenth to the early twentieth century. In the second section, "Colonial Societies," he discusses the special character of the colonial social order throughout this period.

Jurgen Osterhammel, *Colonialism*, trans. Shelly Frisch (Princeton: Markus Wiener, 1997), 32–34, 86–89.

How, according to Osterhammel, did colonialism change between 1760 and 1930? How were these changes reflected in the evolution of "colonial society"?

Thinking Historically

Unlike philosophy, which tends to deal with general principles, history studies specific details. Yet as this general overview of colonialism shows, history can include summaries of long-term change and generalizations about different parts of the world over entire centuries as well as specific names and dates. What sort of generalizations are made in this excerpt?

History, like fiction, is a form of storytelling. Fictional storytelling tends to be far more specific than history, usually documenting minutes or hours in the amount of space that it takes many historians to cover years and Osterhammel to cover centuries. Does this selection tell you a story in any sense, or is it too general to do that?

Colonial Epochs

. . . The most important colonial advance of the period [1760–1830] was the extension of the British position in *India*. The British East India Company (EIC) originally conducted trade from port cities. Later on, it becomes increasingly involved in Indian domestic politics, which were determined by the antagonisms of regional powers in the declining phase of the Mughal empire. Unlike the Spanish in Central America, the British in India at first pursued no plans to conquer and certainly no plans to proselytize. They were far from possessing military advantages over the Indian states until about the middle of the century. In Bengal, where British trade interests were increasingly concentrated, a mutually advantageous agreement was reached with the regional prince, the Nabob. Only when a collapse of this "collaboration" was brought about by a concatenation of causes did the idea of territorial rule originate. In 1755, Robert Clive, the future conqueror of Bengal, expressed a hitherto unthinkable idea: "We must indeed become the Nabobs ourselves." From then on the British pursued a strategy of subjugation within a polycentric Indian state system, interrupted repeatedly by phases of deadlock and consolidation. Until the end of the colonial period in 1947, hundreds of seemingly autonomous principalities continued to exist, but after 1818 the British could consider themselves the "paramount power" on the subcontinent.

The East India Company continued to play its double role as business enterprise and state organization. Under constant supervision of the government in London it accompanied the military expansion of its sphere of power with the gradual establishment of colonial structures, which, in rough schematic terms, passed through a characteristic sequences of steps: (1) securing an effective trade monopoly, (2) securing military dominance and disarmament of any subjugated indigenous powers, (3) achieving a tax collection system, (4) stabilizing government by comprehensive legal regulations and the establishment of a bureaucratic administration, and (5) intervening in the indigenous society for purposes of social and humanitarian reform. This fifth stage was reached in the early 1830s. Not only did the age of European rule over highly civilized Asian societies begin in India, but India also became the prototype of an exploitation colony without settlers, a model for British expansion in other parts of Asia and Africa.

The period between 1830 and 1880 was certainly not a calm interlude in the history of European expansion. Only the Caribbean, once so rich, became a "forgotten derelict corner of the world." In an age of "free trade imperialism," China, Japan, Siam (Thailand) and, to a greater extent than was previously the case, the Ottoman Empire as well as Egypt, now de facto independent from it, were forced to open their economies. Sovereignty limitations characteristic of "informal empires" were imposed on them. Latin America, which was *no longer* colonial, and West Africa, which was rid of the slave trade but *not yet* colonized, were integrated into the world economy more closely than ever. On Java, the major island of the Netherlands East Indies, direct colonial intervention in the utilization of land began after 1830; the outer Indonesian islands were gradually subjugated in the period to follow. Foreign encroachment on continental Southeast Asia began after about 1820. First the lowlands near the coast fell into foreign hands: in 1852–1853 Lower Burma, and in 1857 Cochin China. By 1870, the later colonial borders could be distinguished clearly. During the entire period, the Tsarist Empire advanced in the Caucasus and Central Asia with military force, and shortly thereafter in the Far East with somewhat more diplomatic means, thereby intensifying the so-called "Great Game," a sustained cold war between the two Asiatic Great Powers Russia and Great Britain.

Despite these continuities of European world conquest and of ties between classic European diplomacy and "high imperialism," there is something to be said for marking a new epoch around 1870–1880. Most of the reasons can be found in the broader imperialist environment of colonialism, that is, in the structural changes of the world economy and international system. In terms of *colonial* history, the chief development over the last two decades of the nineteenth century was the European occupation of Africa, a singularly condensed expropriation of an entire continent termed the "partition of Africa." On the eve of this process, only South Africa and Algeria had been regions of European colonization, South Africa since 1652 and Algeria since 1830. Elsewhere the Portuguese (Angola, Mozambique), French (Senegal), and British (Sierra Leone, Lagos) made their presence felt in a more limited way. After all, by 1870 over 270,000 white people were already living in Algeria and about 245,000 in South Africa (including the two Boer Republics). The further expansion of these early cores of colonization was also an impetus for the occupation of Africa in the last quarter of the century. The discovery of diamond deposits in 1867 and of gold in 1886 unleashed a development that changed South Africa into a capitalist center of growth and a magnet for international capital. At the same time, it strengthened white supremacy. In Algeria the same result was achieved simultaneously under almost purely agrarian conditions by extensive land transfers from the Arabs to a rapidly growing settlement population.

The actual "partition" of Africa in the years between the occupation of Tunis by the French in 1881 and of Egypt by the British in 1882 on the one hand and the Boer War of the years 1899–1902 on the other was initially a somewhat symbolic process. With treaties *amongst themselves,* the European Great Powers committed themselves to mutual recognition of colonies, protectorates, and spheres of influence. "Paper partition" was only slowly and incompletely transformed into effective occupation, "partition on the ground." However, the borders that were drawn endured with the later establishment of independent African national states. For Africans, the so-called partition of their continent often meant the brutal disruption of bonds and established ways of life. However, partition could also result in the exact opposite: "a ruthless act of political amalgamation, whereby something of the order of ten thousand units was reduced to a mere forty." Particularly in Islamic North Africa (Egypt, Morocco, Tunesia, and Algeria) as well as in parts of Asia (Vietnam, Korea, and Burma), colonialism encountered fairly complex proto-nation-states. Colonial rule in these countries was considered even less legitimate than elsewhere.

Colonial Societies

. . . Characteristic of the social and cultural history of modern colonialism, especially in Asia, was the increasing alienation between two societies that had shared the bond of a colonial relationship since the late eighteenth century. While the status scale in Iberian America was rapidly refined, thereby placing renewed emphasis on racial criteria, the dualization of the colonial social landscape intensified in Asia and Africa. Only in Portuguese Asia was there significant progress in societal interaction, especially where native clergy were concerned, owing to the enlightened politics of the crown under the Marquis de Pombal in the 1760s and 1770s. The sealing off of the European communities from the indigenous environment had many causes, which were manifested in varying combinations: (1) Although Portugal and the Netherlands in particular had officially encouraged marriage between European men and Asian women at first, and the other colonial powers had tolerated it tacitly, immigration of European women raised the sexual autarky of the colonial societies. (2) The transition from trade to rule and often to direct production with dependent workers transformed the "age of partnership" into an age of subordination. (3) Violent resistance by the natives, such as the Native American massacre of colonists in Virginia in 1622 and the Indian rebellion of 1857–1858, strengthened the resolve of white minorities to shield themselves for self-protection. (4) A European attitude of superiority over the rest of the world, stemming from the Christian Eurocentricism of early encounters, made it appear increasingly "unreasonable" to Europeans to maintain close egalitarian relationships with non-Europeans and to make cultural accommodations to them. (5) After the gradual abolition of slave trade and slavery, racist thought lived in the less blatant, but now "scientifically" legitimated forms. It bears pointing out, however, that racism is often not the *cause* of segregation, but the *effect*. Racism has often been used to justify segregation after the fact.

Ethnosocial distancing was an outgrowth of societal interaction and was not always based on discriminatory laws. A telling example was Batavia, the most populous and resplendent city in Asia that was governed by Europe. In the first half of the seventeenth century, a mixed society was formed based on house slavery and the expansion of "Creole" family and patronage networks with relatively high tolerance for interracial family relationships. This society resembled its counterpart in Mexico and was even more akin to Portuguese colonization in Asia (Goa). In the manner of living of its upper class, the mixed society of Batavia conformed almost as closely to its Javanese surroundings as it did to Holland. A distinct demarcation between the European and Asian spheres commenced with the British interregnum of 1811–1816. In the eyes of the British, the Batavian Dutch were appallingly infected by their contact with Asians. Cultural decontamination was decreed. The whites in the city and their mestizo relatives were told to develop an identity as civilized Europeans and clearly display it in their appearances before the Javanese public.

The English in India had always been somewhat more detached from the indigenous environment than the Dutch in Indonesia. After the 1780s, their isolation gradually intensified and became obvious with the decline in status of Eurasian Anglo-Indians, even though some influential Indian politicians in 1830 were still dreaming of a racially mixed India modelled on Mexico. The club became the center of British social life in India and the other Asian colonies during the Victorian era. In clubs, one could feel like a gentleman among other gentlemen while being served by a native staff. In Kuala Lumpur, very few non-Europeans were admitted before 1940; in Singapore no non-Europeans were allowed in at all. The large clubs of Calcutta remained closed to Indians until 1946. This type of color bar was especially disturbing because it excluded from social recognition the very people who had carried their self-Anglicizing the furthest and loyally supported British rule. Even Indian members of the Indian Civil Service were excluded.

In most regions of Africa, the colonial period began at a time when exclusionist thought and action were most pronounced. In Africa there was virtually no history of intercultural proximity and therefore no need for policies enforcing detachment. The Europeans saw themselves as foreign rulers separated from the African cultures by an abyss. This absolute aloofness extended even to Islam, which they certainly did not consider "primitive," but rather historically obsolete. Color bars in Africa varied in height; they were lowest in West Africa and highest in the settlement colonies of the far north and the deep south. A process of great symptomatic significance was the rejection of the highly educated West Africans who had worked with the early mission. They had envisioned the colonial takeover as an opportunity for a joint European-African effort to modernize and civilize Africa. Instead, they were now, as "white Negroes," despised by all. . . .

44

MULTATULI

From *Max Havelaar: Or the Coffee Auctions of the Dutch Trading Company*

Nineteenth-century colonial society, as Osterhammel notes in the previous selection, became a dual society in which Europeans increasingly separated themselves from non-Europeans whom they called "natives." But because that separation was uncommon in the early years of colonization — especially among Spanish, Portuguese, and to a lesser extent, Dutch colonialists — and because it was never univer-

Multatuli, *Max Havelaar: Or the Coffee Auctions of the Dutch Trading Company* (Amherst: University of Massachusetts Press, 1982), 100–02.

sal, there was always a class of people who remained apart from these two worlds. Thus, there arose in colonial societies another duality, "full" Europeans and "part" Europeans.

The latter duality is the subject of this selection, excerpted from the great Dutch novel *Max Havelaar* by Multatuli. Multatuli (Latin for "I suffered much") was the pen name of Eduard Douwes Dekker (1820–1887), who went to Java in 1838 to serve in the East Indian Civil Service. In 1856 he became a colonial official in Java, but within three months he resigned in protest against the treatment of the Javanese. His experiences and grievances are embodied in the character of Max Havelaar. How, according to Multatuli, were "liplaps" discriminated against? What groups of Dutch colonists were most discriminatory? Why?

Thinking Historically

Often called the *Uncle Tom's Cabin* of Dutch literature after its publication in 1859, *Max Havelaar* riveted Dutch attention on the abuses of colonialism in the Dutch East Indies much the way that Harriet Beecher Stowe's novel focused sentiment on slavery in the United States in the 1850s.

How does the author criticize Dutch colonialism and racism in this selection? Is criticism a proper role for history, or should history provide only the facts? What parts, if any, of this selection read like fiction rather than history? Does the fact that this account is fiction make it any less valuable to us as a lens through which to view the past?

European society in the Dutch East Indies is rather sharply divided into two parts: the real Europeans, and those who — although legally enjoying exactly the same rights — were not born in Europe, and have more or less "native" blood in their veins. In fairness to the conceptions of humanity in the East Indies I hasten to add here that however sharp the line which is drawn in social life between the two classes of individuals who, for the genuine natives, both equally bear the name of *Hollander*, this distinction has nothing of the barbarous character which prevails in the American status differentiation [between whites and slaves]. I cannot deny that, even so, there is still much in this mutual relationship which is unjust and repellent, and that the name *liplap* (half-caste) has often grated on my ear as proof of the distance which separates many a non-half-caste, a "white" person, from real civilization. It is true that only in exceptional cases is the half-caste admitted into European society, and that generally, if I may use a very slangy expression, he is not regarded as "one hundred per cent." But few people would present or defend such exclusion or disparagement as a *just principle*. Everyone is, of course, at liberty to choose his own environment and company, and one cannot blame the full European for preferring to mix with his own kind rather than with persons who — irrespective of their greater or lesser moral or intellectual value — do not share his impressions and ideas, or — and this, in a presumed difference in *civilization,* is perhaps very often the main thing — whose *prejudices have taken a different direction from his.*

A *liplap* — if I wanted to use the official, more polite term, I should have to say a "*so-called native child,*" but I beg leave to keep to an idiom which seems born of alliteration; *I* intend nothing impolite by it, and what does the word mean anyway? — a liplap may have many good qualities. The European may also have many good qualities. Both have many that are bad, and in this too they resemble each other. But the good and the bad qualities inherent in both are too divergent for commerce [relations] between them to be, as a rule, mutually satisfactory. Besides — and for this the Government is largely responsible — the liplap is often ill educated. We are not concerned here with what the European would be like if his mental development had been thus impeded from his youth; but it is certain that *in general* the liplap's poor schooling hinders his being placed on an equality with the European, even when some *individual* liplap may perhaps deserve to be ranked above some *individual* European, as regards culture or scientific or artistic attainments.

In this too there is nothing new. It was, for instance, the policy of William the Conqueror[1] to raise the most insignificant Norman above the most accomplished Saxon, and every Norman would appeal to the superiority of the Normans *in general,* in order to assert himself *in particular,* where he would have been the inferior *without* the influence of his countrymen as the dominant party.

Such a state of affairs naturally gives rise to a certain awkwardness in social intercourse, which nothing could remove except philosophical, broad-minded views and measures on the part of the Government.

It is obvious that the European, who is the gainer by such a relationship, feels perfectly comfortable in his artificial ascendancy. But it is often ludicrous to hear someone who acquired most of his culture and grammar in ZANDSTRAAT[2] in Rotterdam jeer at the liplap because, in speaking Dutch, he makes *glass* or *government* masculine, or *sun* or *moon* neuter.

A liplap may be well-bred, well-educated, even learned — there are such! But no sooner has the European who shammed sick in order to stay away from the ship on which he washed dishes, and who bases his claims to good manners on "ow are yer?" and "Beg pardon," become head of the commercial undertaking which made such "stupendous"

---

[1] The French Norman conqueror of England in 1066.
[2] Lower-class area.

profits out of indigo in 1800-and-something . . . nay, long before he becomes owner of the *toko,* the general store in which he sells hams and fowling-pieces — no sooner has this European noticed that the most well-bred liplap has difficulty in distinguishing between *b* and *g,* than he laughs at the stupidity of the man who does not know the difference between *bot* and *got.*

But, to take the grin off his face, our European would have to know that in Arabic and Malay those two consonants are expressed by one letter, that *Hieronymus* passes via *Geronimo* into *Jerôme,* that from *buano* we make *guano,* that our *hand* fits into a French *gant,* that *kous* in Dutch is *hose* in English, and that for *Guild Heaume* we say in Dutch *Huillem* or *Willem.* So much erudition is too much to ask from someone who made his fortune "in" indigo and got his education from success in throwing dice . . . or worse!

And such genuine Europeans surely cannot be expected to hobnob with liplaps!

I understand how *Willem* comes from *Guillaume,* and I must admit that, especially in the Moluccas, I have often met liplaps who amazed me by the extent of their knowledge and who gave me the idea that we Europeans, in spite of all the resources at our disposal, are often — and *absolutely,* not merely *relatively* — far behind these poor pariahs, who have to contend from the very cradle with artificial, studied, unjust subordination and with silly prejudice against their colour.

┌─────┐
│ *45* │
└─────┘

GEORGE ORWELL

From *Burmese Days*

This selection, from one of the great novels on colonialism, captures the life of the British colonial class in a remote "upcountry" town in Burma in the 1920s. The chapter is set in the European club. Flory, the principal character, is the only Englishman at all sympathetic to the Burmese. Though he has befriended the Indian physician, Dr. Veraswami, Flory is too weak to propose him as the first "native" member of the club. The other main characters are Westfield, District Superintendent of Police; Ellis, local company manager and the most

---

George Orwell, *Burmese Days* (1934; reprint, San Diego: Harcourt Brace, 1962), 17–27.

racist of the group; Lackersteen, local manager of a timber company who is usually drunk; Maxwell, a forest officer; and Macgregor, Deputy Commissioner and secretary of the club.

Why does the club loom so large in the lives of these Englishmen? If they complain so much, why are they in Burma? How do you account for the virulent racism of these men? Why does Ellis "correct" the butler's English? What does this story suggest about women in the colonial world?

Thinking Historically

As different as this selection is from Osterhammel's historical overview, both touch on the subjects of dual society, the European club, and colonial racism. How does this selection from Orwell support some of Osterhammel's generalizations? How does it deepen your understanding of these subjects?

The structure of a novel like this one bears certain similarities to history — a description of a place, proper names and biographies, descriptions of human interactions, an accounting of change, and a story. There are also structural differences in a novel — a lot of dialogue, greater attention to physical appearance and character, and a more prominent narrative. Do the fictional constructs in this selection detract from our historical understanding? Can such elements add to our understanding of what actually happened?

Of course, the problem with structural elements such as dialogue and story is that they are fiction. The author of a novel makes no pretense of telling the truth. Nevertheless, an author draws on what he or she knows to create a plausible scenario that is recognizable and consistent. Interestingly, Orwell knew Burma quite well. He was born in India in 1903. His father worked in the Opium Department of the Indian Civil Service. After attending school at Eton in England, Orwell returned to Burma, where he spent five years as a member of the Indian Imperial Police. Orwell, therefore, had a broad knowledge of Burma on which to base his story. Is there any way to determine what Orwell invented and what he merely described in this account?

Like Multatuli, Orwell also was politically engaged throughout his life. Would political ideas make him better or worse as a historian or novelist? How so?

. . . Flory's house was at the top of the maidan,[1] close to the edge of the jungle. From the gate the maidan sloped sharply down, scorched and khaki-coloured, with half a dozen dazzling white bungalows scat-

---

[1] Parade-ground. [Ed.]

tered round it. All quaked, shivered in the hot air. There was an English cemetery within a white wall half-way down the hill, and nearby a tiny tin-roofed church. Beyond that was the European Club, and when one looked at the Club — a dumpy one-storey wooden building — one looked at the real centre of the town. In any town in India the European Club is the spiritual citadel, the real seat of the British power, the Nirvana for which native officials and millionaires pine in vain. It was doubly so in this case, for it was the proud boast of Kyauktada Club that, almost alone of Clubs in Burma, it had never admitted an Oriental to membership. Beyond the Club, the Irrawaddy flowed huge and ochreous, glittering like diamonds in the patches that caught the sun; and beyond the river stretched great wastes of paddy fields, ending at the horizon in a range of blackish hills.

The native town, and the courts and the jail, were over to the right, mostly hidden in green groves of peepul trees. The spire of the pagoda rose from the trees like a slender spear tipped with gold. Kyauktada was a fairly typical Upper Burma town, that had not changed greatly between the days of Marco Polo and 1910, and might have slept in the Middle Ages for a century more if it had not proved a convenient spot for a railway terminus. In 1910 the Government made it the headquarters of a district and a seat of Progress — interpretable as a block of law courts, with their army of fat but ravenous pleaders, a hospital, a school, and one of those huge, durable jails which the English have built everywhere between Gibraltar and Hong Kong. The population was about four thousand, including a couple of hundred Indians, a few score Chinese and seven Europeans. There were also two Eurasians named Mr. Francis and Mr. Samuel, the sons of an American Baptist missionary and a Roman Catholic missionary respectively. The town contained no curiosities of any kind, except an Indian fakir who had lived for twenty years in a tree near the bazaar, drawing his food up in a basket every morning.

Flory yawned as he came out of the gate. He had been half drunk the night before, and the glare made him feel liverish. "Bloody, bloody hole!" he thought, looking down the hill. And, no one except the dog being near, he began to sing aloud, "Bloody, bloody, bloody, oh, how thou art bloody" to the tune of "Holy, holy, holy, oh how Thou art holy," as he walked down the hot red road, switching at the dried-up grasses with his stick. It was nearly nine o'clock and the sun was fiercer every minute. The heat throbbed down on one's head with a steady, rhythmic thumping, like blows from an enormous bolster. Flory stopped at the Club gate, wondering whether to go in or to go farther down the road and see Dr. Veraswami. Then he remembered that it was "English mail day" and the newspapers would have arrived. He went in, past the big tennis screen, which was overgrown by a creeper with starlike mauve flowers.

In the borders beside the path swathes of English flowers, phlox and larkspur, hollyhock and petunia, not yet slain by the sun, rioted in vast size and richness. The petunias were huge, like trees almost. There was no lawn, but instead a shrubbery of native trees and bushes — gold mohur trees like vast umbrellas of blood-red bloom, frangipanis with creamy, stalkless flowers, purple bougainvillea, scarlet hibiscus, and the pink, Chinese rose, bilious-green crotons, feathery fronds of tamarind. The clash of colours hurt one's eyes in the glare. A nearly naked *mali*,[2] watering-can in hand, was moving in the jungle of flowers like some large nectar-sucking bird.

On the Club steps a sandy-haired Englishman, with a prickly moustache, pale grey eyes too far apart, and abnormally thin calves to his legs, was standing with his hands in the pockets of his shorts. This was Mr. Westfield, the District Superintendent of Police. With a very bored air he was rocking himself backwards and forwards on his heels and pouting his upper lip so that his moustache tickled his nose. He greeted Flory with a slight sideways movement of his head. His way of speaking was clipped and soldierly, missing out every word that well could be missed out. Nearly everything he said was intended for a joke, but the tone of his voice was hollow and melancholy.

"Hullo, Flory me lad. Bloody awful morning, what?"

"We must expect it at this time of year, I suppose," Flory said. He had turned himself a little sideways, so that his birthmarked cheek was away from Westfield.

"Yes, dammit. Couple of months of this coming. Last year we didn't have a spot of rain till June. Look at that bloody sky, not a cloud in it. Like one of those damned great blue enamel saucepans. God! What'd you give to be in Piccadilly now, eh?"

"Have the English papers come?"

"Yes. Dear old *Punch, Pink'un,* and *Vie Parisienne.* Makes you homesick to read 'em, what? Let's come in and have a drink before the ice all goes. Old Lackersteen's been fairly bathing in it. Half pickled already."

They went in, Westfield remarking in his gloomy voice, "Lead on, Macduff." Inside, the Club was a teak-walled place smelling of earth-oil, and consisting of only four rooms, one of which contained a forlorn "library" of five hundred mildewed novels, and another an old and mangy billiard-table — this, however, seldom used, for during most of the year hordes of flying beetles came buzzing round the lamps and littered themselves over the cloth. There were also a card-room and a "lounge" which looked towards the river, over a wide veranda; but at this time of day all the verandas were curtained with green bamboo chicks. The lounge was an unhomelike room, with coco-nut matting on

2 Gardener. [Ed.]

the floor, and wicker chairs and tables which were littered with shiny illustrated papers. For ornament there were a number of "Bonzo" pictures, and the dusty skulls of sambhur. A punkah, lazily flapping, shook dust into the tepid air.

There were three men in the room. Under the punkah a florid, fine-looking, slightly bloated man of forty was sprawling across the table with his head in his hands, groaning in pain. This was Mr. Lackersteen, the local manager of a timber firm. He had been badly drunk the night before, and he was suffering for it. Ellis, local manager of yet another company, was standing before the notice board studying some notice with a look of bitter concentration. He was a tiny wiry-haired fellow with a pale, sharp-featured face and restless movements. Maxwell, the acting Divisional Forest Officer, was lying in one of the long chairs reading the *Field,* and invisible except for two large-boned legs and thick downy forearms.

"Look at this naughty old man," said Westfield, taking Mr. Lackersteen half affectionately by the shoulders and shaking him. "Example to the young, what? There, but for the grace of God and all that. Gives you an idea what you'll be like at forty."

Mr. Lackersteen gave a groan which sounded like "brandy."

"Poor old chap," said Westfield; "regular martyr to booze, eh? Look at it oozing out of his pores. Reminds me of the old colonel who used to sleep without a mosquito net. They asked his servant why and the servant said: 'At night, master too drunk to notice mosquitoes; in the morning, mosquitoes too drunk to notice master.' Look at him— boozed last night and then asking for more. Got a little niece coming to stay with him, too. Due tonight, isn't she, Lackersteen?"

"Oh, leave that drunken sot alone," said Ellis without turning round. He had a spiteful cockney voice. Mr. Lackersteen groaned again, "———the niece! Get me some brandy, for Christ's sake."

"Good education for the niece, eh? Seeing uncle under the table seven times a week. — Hey, butler! Bringing brandy for Lackersteen master!"

The butler, a dark, stout Dravidian with liquid, yellow-irised eyes like those of a dog, brought the brandy on a brass tray. Flory and Westfield ordered gin. Mr. Lackersteen swallowed a few spoonfuls of brandy and sat back in his chair, groaning in a more resigned way. He had a beefy, ingenuous face, with a toothbrush moustache. He was really a very simple-minded man, with no ambitions beyond having what he called "a good time." His wife governed him by the only possible method, namely, by never letting him out of her sight for more than an hour or two. Only once, a year after they were married, she had left him for a fortnight, and had returned unexpectedly a day before her time, to find Mr. Lackersteen, drunk, supported on either side by a naked Burmese girl, while a third up-ended a whisky bottle into his mouth. Since then she had watched him, as he used to complain, "like a cat over a bloody mousehole." However, he managed to enjoy quite a number of "good times," though they were usually rather hurried ones.

"My Christ, what a head I've got on me this morning," he said. "Call that butler again, Westfield. I've got to have another brandy before my missus gets here. She says she's going to cut my booze down to four pegs a day when our niece gets here. God rot them both!" he added gloomily.

"Stop playing the fool, all of you, and listen to this," said Ellis sourly. He had a queer wounding way of speaking, hardly ever opening his mouth without insulting somebody. He deliberately exaggerated his cockney accent, because of the sardonic tone it gave to his words. "Have you seen this notice of old Macgregor's? A little nosegay for everyone. Maxwell, wake up and listen!"

Maxwell lowered the *Field*. He was a fresh-coloured blond youth of not more than twenty-five or six — very young for the post he held. With his heavy limbs and thick white eyelashes he reminded one of a carthorse colt. Ellis nipped the notice from the board with a neat, spiteful little movement and began reading it aloud. It had been posted by Mr. Macgregor, who, besides being Deputy Commissioner, was secretary of the Club.

"Just listen to this. 'It has been suggested that as there are as yet no Oriental members of this club, and as it is now usual to admit officials of gazetted rank, whether native or European, to membership of most European Clubs, we should consider the question of following this practice in Kyauktada. The matter will be open for discussion at the next general meeting. On the one hand it may be pointed out' — oh, well, no need to wade through the rest of it. He can't even write out a notice without an attack of literary diarrhœa. Anyway, the point's this. He's asking us to break all our rules and take a dear little nigger-boy into this Club. *Dear* Dr. Veraswami, for instance. Dr. Very-slimy, I call him. That *would* be a treat, wouldn't it? Little pot-bellied niggers breathing garlic in your face over the bridge-table. Christ, to think of it! We've got to hang together and put our foot down on this at once. What do you say, Westfield? Flory?"

Westfield shrugged his thin shoulders philosophically. He had sat down at the table and lighted a black, stinking Burma cheroot.

"Got to put up with it, I suppose," he said. "B———s of natives are getting into all the Clubs nowadays. Even the Pegu Club, I'm told. Way this country's going, you know. We're about the last Club in Burma to hold out against 'em."

"We are; and what's more, we're damn well going to go on holding out. I'll die in the ditch before I'll see a nigger in here." Ellis had produced a stump of pencil. With the curious air of spite that some men can put into their tiniest action, he re-pinned the notice on the board and pencilled a tiny, neat "B. F." against Mr. Macgregor's signature — "There, that's what I think of his idea. I'll tell him so when he comes down. What do *you* say, Flory?"

Flory had not spoken all this time. Though by nature anything but a silent man, he seldom found much to say in Club conversations. He had sat down at the table and was reading G. K. Chesterton's article in the *London News,* at the same time caressing Flo's head with his left hand. Ellis, however, was one of those people who constantly nag others to echo their own opinions. He repeated his question, and Flory looked up, and their eyes met. The skin round Ellis's nose suddenly turned so pale that it was almost grey. In him it was a sign of anger. Without any prelude he burst into a stream of abuse that would have been startling, if the others had not been used to hearing something like it every morning.

"My God, I should have thought in a case like this, when it's a question of keeping those black, stinking swine out of the only place where we can enjoy ourselves, you'd have the decency to back me up. Even if that pot-bellied, greasy little sod of a nigger doctor *is* your best pal. *I* don't care if you choose to pal up with the scum of the bazaar. If it pleases you to go to Veraswami's house and drink whisky with all his nigger pals, that's your look-out. Do what you like outside the Club. But, by God, it's a different matter when you talk of bringing niggers in here. I suppose you'd like little Veraswami for a Club member, eh? Chipping into our conversation and pawing everyone with his sweaty hands and breathing his filthy garlic breath in our faces. By God, he'd go out with my boot behind him if ever I saw his black snout inside that door. Greasy, pot-bellied little———!" etc.

This went on for several minutes. It was curiously impressive, because it was so completely sincere. Ellis really did hate Orientals — hated them with a bitter, restless loathing as of something evil or unclean. Living and working, as the assistant of a timber firm must, in perpetual contact with the Burmese, he had never grown used to the sight of a black face. Any hint of friendly feeling towards an Oriental seemed to him a horrible perversity. He was an intelligent man and an able servant of his firm, but he was one of those Englishmen — common, unfortunately — who should never be allowed to set foot in the East.

Flory sat nursing Flo's head in his lap, unable to meet Ellis's eyes. At the best of times his birthmark made it difficult for him to look people straight in the face. And when he made ready to speak, he could feel his voice trembling — for it had a way of trembling when it should have been firm; his features, too, sometimes twitched uncontrollably.

"Steady on," he said at last, sullenly and rather feebly. "Steady on. There's no need to get so excited. *I* never suggested having any native members in here."

"Oh, didn't you? We all know bloody well you'd like to, though. Why else do you go to that oily little babu's house every morning, then? Sitting down at table with him as though he was a white man, and drinking out of glasses his filthy black lips have slobbered over — it makes me spew to think of it."

"Sit down, old chap, sit down," Westfield said. "Forget it. Have a drink on it. Not worth while quarrelling. Too hot."

"My God," said Ellis a little more calmly, taking a pace or two up and down, "my God, I don't understand you chaps. I simply don't. Here's that old fool Macgregor wanting to bring a nigger into this Club for no reason whatever, and you all sit down under it without a word. Good God, what are we supposed to be doing in this country? If we aren't going to rule, why the devil don't we clear out? Here we are, supposed to be governing a set of damn black swine who've been slaves since the beginning of history, and instead of ruling them in the only way they understand, we go and treat them as equals. And all you silly b——s take it for granted. There's Flory, makes his best pal of a black babu who calls himself a doctor because he's done two years at an Indian so-called university. And you, Westfield, proud as Punch of your knock-kneed, bribe-taking cowards of policemen. And there's Maxwell, spends his time running after Eurasian tarts. Yes, you do, Maxwell; I heard about your goings-on in Mandalay with some smelly little bitch called Molly Pereira. I supposed you'd have gone and married her if they hadn't transferred you up here? You all seem to *like* the dirty black brutes. Christ, I don't know what's come over us all. I really don't."

"Come on, have another drink," said Westfield. "Hey, butler! Spot of beer before the ice goes, eh? Beer, butler!"

The butler brought some bottles of Munich beer. Ellis presently sat down at the table with the others, and he nursed one of the cool bottles between his small hands. His forehead was sweating. He was sulky, but not in a rage any longer. At all times he was spiteful and perverse, but his violent fits of rage were soon over, and were never apologised for. Quarrels were a regular part of the routine of Club life. Mr. Lackersteen was feeling better and was studying the illustrations in *La Vie Parisienne*. It was after nine now, and the room, scented with the acrid smoke of Westfield's cheroot, was stifling hot. Everyone's shirt stuck to his back with the first sweat of the day. The invisible *chokra*[3] who pulled the punkah rope outside was falling asleep in the glare.

"Butler!" yelled Ellis, and as the butler appeared, "go and wake that bloody *chokra* up!"

"Yes, master."

---

[3] Person who pulls the punkah rope that moves a large panel to let in a breeze.

"And butler!"

"Yes, master?"

"How much ice have we got left?"

"'Bout twenty pounds, master. Will only last to-day, I think. I find it very difficult to keep ice cool now."

"Don't talk like that, damn you — 'I find it very difficult!' Have you swallowed a dictionary? 'Please, master, can't keeping ice cool' — that's how you ought to talk. We shall have to sack this fellow if he gets to talk English too well. I can't stick servants who talk English. D'you hear, butler?"

"Yes, master," said the butler, and retired.

"God! No ice till Monday," Westfield said. "You going back to the jungle, Flory?"

"Yes. I ought to be there now. I only came in because of the English mail."

"Go on tour myself, I think. Knock up a spot of Travelling Allowance. I can't stick my bloody office at this time of year. Sitting there under the damned punkah, signing one chit after another. Paper-chewing. God, how I wish the war was on again!"

"I'm going out the day after to-morrow," Ellis said. "Isn't that damned padre coming to hold his service this Sunday? I'll take care not to be in for that, anyway. Bloody knee-drill."

"Next Sunday," said Westfield. "Promised to be in for it myself. So's Macgregor. Bit hard on the poor devil of a padre, I must say. Only gets here once in six weeks. Might as well get up a congregation when he does come."

"Oh, hell! I'd snivel psalms to oblige the padre, but I can't stick the way these damned native Christians come shoving into our church. A pack of Madrassi servants and Karen school-teachers. And then those two yellow-bellies, Francis and Samuel — they call themselves Christians too. Last time the padre was here they had the nerve to come up and sit on the front pews with the white men. Someone ought to speak to the padre about that. What bloody fools we were ever to let those missionaries loose in this country! Teaching bazaar sweepers they're as good as we are. 'Please, sir, me Christian same like master.' Damned cheek." . . .

CHINUA ACHEBE

From *Things Fall Apart*

Missionaries, as the previous selection reminds us, were among the earliest European colonialists. The first missionaries went to the Americas with the Spanish conquistadors in the decades after Columbus. But long after the conquistadors were replaced by professional soldiers, administrators, policemen, mining engineers, company agents, and other representatives of a more bureaucratic and industrial age, the missionaries continued to seek out souls to save beyond the frontiers of colonial settlement.

In this selection from his novel, *Things Fall Apart*, Chinua Achebe imagines the arrival and impact of some of the first Anglican missionaries among the Ibo people of Nigeria — his own ancestors — after 1857. What, according to Achebe, were the principal obstacles faced by the missionaries? What elements in Christianity attracted some Africans? What elements repelled others? Judging from this selection, how would you characterize the overall impact of Christianity in Africa?

Thinking Historically

Unlike Multatuli and Orwell, Achebe is not describing historical events he witnessed, since he is writing about a period before he was born. And yet, he has a firsthand experience of Ibo culture. How does that experience make his fiction different from that of Multatuli and Orwell? What does Achebe's fiction add to a historical understanding of missionaries in Africa?

... The arrival of the missionaries had caused a considerable stir in the village of Mbanta. There were six of them and one was a white man. Every man and woman came out to see the white man. Stories about these strange men had grown since one of them had been killed in Abame and his iron horse tied to the sacred silk-cotton tree. And so everybody came to see the white man. It was the time of the year when everybody was at home. The harvest was over.

When they had all gathered, the white man began to speak to them. He spoke through an interpreter who was an Ibo man, though his di-

---

Chinua Achebe, *Things Fall Apart* (Oxford: Heinemann, 1958), 101–09.

alect was different and harsh to the ears of Mbanta. Many people laughed at his dialect and the way he used words strangely. Instead of saying "myself" he always said "my buttocks." But he was a man of commanding presence and the clansmen listened to him. He said he was one of them, as they could see from his colour and his language. The other four black men were also their brothers, although one of them did not speak Ibo. The white man was also their brother because they were all sons of God. And he told them about this new God, the Creator of all the world and all the men and women. He told them that they worshipped false gods, gods of wood and stone. A deep murmur went through the crowd when he said this. He told them that the true God lived on high and that all men when they died went before Him for judgment. Evil men and all the heathen who in their blindness bowed to wood and stone were thrown into a fire that burned like palm-oil. But good men who worshipped the true God lived for ever in His happy kingdom. "We have been sent by this great God to ask you to leave your wicked ways and false gods and turn to Him so that you may be saved when you die," he said.

"Your buttocks understand our language," said someone light-heartedly and the crowd laughed.

"What did he say?" the white man asked his interpreter. But before he could answer, another man asked a question: "Where is the white man's horse?" he asked. The Ibo evangelists consulted among themselves and decided that the man probably meant bicycle. They told the white man and he smiled benevolently.

"Tell them," he said, "that I shall bring many iron horses when we have settled down among them. Some of them will even ride the iron horse themselves." This was interpreted to them but very few of them heard. They were talking excitedly among themselves because the white man had said he was going to live among them. They had not thought about that.

At this point an old man said he had a question. "Which is this god of yours," he asked, "the goddess of the earth, the god of the sky, Amadiora of the thunderbolt, or what?"

The interpreter spoke to the white man and he immediately gave his answer. "All the gods you have named are not gods at all. They are gods of deceit who tell you to kill your fellows and destroy innocent children. There is only one true God and He has the earth, the sky, you and me, and all of us."

"If we leave our gods and follow your god," asked another man, "who will protect us from the anger of our neglected gods and ancestors?"

"Your gods are not alive and cannot do you any harm," replied the white man. "They are pieces of wood and stone."

When this was interpreted to the men of Mbanta they broke into derisive laughter. These men must be mad, they said to themselves.

How else could they say that Ani and Amadiora were harmless? And Idemili and Ogwugwu too? And some of them began to go away.

Then the missionaries burst into song. It was one of those gay and rollicking tunes of evangelism which had the power of plucking at silent and dusty chords in the heart of an Ibo man. The interpreter explained each verse to the audience, some of whom now stood enthralled. It was a story of brothers who lived in darkness and in fear, ignorant of the love of God. It told of one sheep out on the hills, away from the gates of God and from the tender shepherd's care.

After the singing the interpreter spoke about the Son of God whose name was Jesu Kristi. Okonkwo, who only stayed in the hope that it might come to chasing the men out of the village or whipping them, now said:

"You told us with your own mouth that there was only one god. Now you talk about his son. He must have a wife, then." The crowd agreed.

"I did not say He had a wife," said the interpreter, somewhat lamely.

"Your buttocks said he had a son," said the joker. "So he must have a wife and all of them must have buttocks."

The missionary ignored him and went on to talk about the Holy Trinity. At the end of it Okonkwo was fully convinced that the man was mad. He shrugged his shoulders and went away to tap his afternoon palm-wine.

But there was a young lad who had been captivated. His name was Nwoye, Okonkwo's first son. It was not the mad logic of the Trinity that captivated him. He did not understand it. It was the poetry of the new religion, something felt in the marrow. The hymn about brothers who sat in darkness and in fear seemed to answer a vague and persistent question that haunted his young soul — the question of the twins crying in the bush and the question of Ikemefuna who was killed. He felt a relief within as the hymn poured into his parched soul. The words of the hymn were like the drops of frozen rain melting on the dry plate of the panting earth. Nwoye's callow mind was greatly puzzled.

The missionaries spent their first four or five nights in the marketplace, and went into the village in the morning to preach the gospel. They asked who the king of the village was, but the villagers told them that there was no king. "We have men of high title and the chief priests and the elders," they said.

It was not very easy getting the men of high title and the elders together after the excitement of the first day. But the missionaries persevered, and in the end they were received by the rulers of Mbanta. They asked for a plot of land to build their church.

Every clan and village had its "evil forest." In it were buried all those who died of the really evil diseases, like leprosy and smallpox. It was also the dumping ground for the potent fetishes of great medicine-men when they died. An "evil forest" was, therefore, alive with sinister forces and powers of darkness. It was such a forest that the rulers of Mbanta gave to the missionaries. They did not really want them in their clan, and so they made them that offer which nobody in his right senses would accept.

"They want a piece of land to build their shrine," said Uchendu to his peers when they consulted among themselves. "We shall give them a piece of land." He paused, and there was a murmur of surprise and dis-agreement. "Let us give them a portion of the Evil Forest. They boast about victory over death. Let us give them a real battlefield in which to show their victory." They laughed and agreed, and sent for the mission-aries, whom they had asked to leave them for a while so that they might "whisper together." They offered them as much of the Evil For-est as they cared to take. And to their greatest amazement the mission-aries thanked them and burst into song.

"They do not understand," said some of the elders. "But they will understand when they go to their plot of land tomorrow morning." And they dispersed.

The next morning the crazy men actually began to clear a part of the forest and to build their house. The inhabitants of Mbanta ex-pected them all to be dead within four days. The first day passed and the second and third and fourth, and none of them died. Everyone was puzzled. And then it became known that the white man's fetish had unbelievable power. It was said that he wore glasses on his eyes so that he could see and talk to evil spirits. Not long after, he won his first three converts.

Although Nwoye had been attracted to the new faith from the very first day, he kept it secret. He dared not go too near the missionaries for fear of his father. But whenever they came to preach in the open market-place or the village playground, Nwoye was there. And he was already beginning to know some of the simple stories they told.

"We have now built a church," said Mr Kiaga, the interpreter, who was now in charge of the infant congregation. The white man had gone back to Umuofia, where he built his headquarters and from where he paid regular visits to Mr Kiaga's congregation at Mbanta.

"We have now built a church," said Mr Kiaga, "and we want you all to come in every seventh day to worship the true God."

On the following Sunday, Nwoye passed and re-passed the little red-earth and thatch building without summoning enough courage to enter. He heard the voice of singing and although it came from a hand-ful of men it was loud and confident. Their church stood on a circular clearing that looked like the open mouth of the Evil Forest. Was it waiting to snap its teeth together? After passing and re-passing by the church, Nwoye returned home.

It was well known among the people of Mbanta that their gods and ancestors were sometimes long-suffering and would deliberately allow a man to go on defying them. But even in such cases they set their limit at seven market weeks or twenty-eight days. Beyond that limit no man was suffered to go. And so excitement mounted in the village as the seventh week approached since the impudent missionaries built their church in the Evil Forest. The villagers were so certain about the doom that awaited these men that one or two converts thought it wise to suspend their allegiance to the new faith.

At last the day came by which all the missionaries should have died. But they were still alive, building a new red-earth and thatch house for their teacher, Mr Kiaga. That week they won a handful more converts. And for the first time they had a woman. Her name was Nneka, the wife of Amadi, who was a prosperous farmer. She was very heavy with child.

Nneka had had four previous pregnancies and childbirths. But each time she had borne twins, and they had been immediately thrown away. Her husband and his family were already becoming highly critical of such a woman and were not unduly perturbed when they found she had fled to join the Christians. It was a good riddance.

One morning Okonkwo's cousin, Amikwu, was passing by the church on his way from the neighbouring village, when he saw Nwoye among the Christians. He was greatly surprised, and when he got home he went straight to Okonkwo's hut and told him what he had seen. The women began to talk excitedly, but Okonkwo sat unmoved.

It was late afternoon before Nwoye returned. He went into the *obi* and saluted his father, but he did not answer. Nwoye turned round to walk into the inner compound when his father, suddenly overcome with fury, sprang to his feet and gripped him by the neck.

"Where have you been?" he stammered.

Nwoye struggled to free himself from the choking grip.

"Answer me," roared Okonkwo, "before I kill you!" He seized a heavy stick that lay on the dwarf wall and hit him two or three savage blows.

"Answer me!" he roared again. Nwoye stood looking at him and did not say a word. The women were screaming outside, afraid to go in.

"Leave that boy at once!" said a voice in the outer compound. It was Okonkwo's uncle Uchendu. "Are you mad?"

Okonkwo did not answer. But he left hold of Nwoye, who walked away and never returned.

He went back to the church and told Mr Kiaga that he had decided to go to Umuofia, where the white missionary had set up a school to teach young Christians to read and write.

Mr Kiaga's joy was very great. "Blessed is he who forsakes his father and his mother for my sake," he intoned. "Those that hear my words are my father and my mother."

Nwoye did not fully understand. But he was happy to leave his father. He would return later to his mother and his brothers and sisters and convert them to the new faith.

As Okonkwo sat in his hut that night, gazing into a log fire, he thought over the matter. A sudden fury rose within him and he felt a strong desire to take up his matchet, go to the church and wipe out the entire vile and miscreant gang. But on further thought he told himself that Nwoye was not worth fighting for. Why, he cried in his heart, should he, Okonkwo, of all people, be cursed with such a son? He saw clearly in it the finger of his personal god or *chi*. For how else could he explain his great misfortune and exile and now his despicable son's behaviour? Now that he had time to think of it, his son's crime stood out in its stark enormity. To abandon the gods of one's father and go about with a lot of effeminate men clucking like old hens was the very depth of abomination. Suppose when he died all his male children decided to follow Nwoye's steps and abandon their ancestors? Okonkwo felt a cold shudder run through him at the terrible prospect, like the prospect of annihilation. He saw himself and his father crowding round their ancestral shrine waiting in vain for worship and sacrifice and finding nothing but ashes of bygone days, and his children the while praying to the white man's god. If such a thing were ever to happen, he, Okonkwo, would wipe them off the face of the earth.

Okonkwo was popularly called the "Roaring Flame." As he looked into the log fire he recalled the name. He was a flaming fire. How then could he have begotten a son like Nwoye, degenerate and effeminate? Perhaps he was not his son. No! He could not be. His wife had played him false. He would teach her! But Nwoye resembled his grandfather, Unoka, who was Okonkwo's father. He pushed the thought out of his mind. He, Okonkwo, was called a flaming fire. How could he have begotten a woman for a son? At Nwoye's age Okonkwo had already become famous throughout Umuofia for his wrestling and his fearlessness.

He sighed heavily, and as if in sympathy the smouldering log also sighed. And immediately Okonkwo's eyes were opened and he saw the whole matter clearly. Living fire begets cold, impotent ash. He sighed again, deeply.

47

RUDYARD KIPLING

The White Man's Burden

This poem, written by Rudyard Kipling (1865–1936), is often presented as the epitome of colonialist sentiment, though some readers see in it a critical, satirical attitude toward colonialism. Do you find the poem to be for or against colonialism? Can it be both?

Thinking Historically

"The White Man's Burden" is a phrase normally associated with European colonialism in Africa. In fact, however, Kipling wrote the poem in response to the annexation of the Philippines by the United States. How does this historical context change the meaning of the poem for you? Does the meaning of a literary work depend on the motives of the writer, the historical context in which it is written, or both?

Take up the White Man's burden —
    Send forth the best ye breed —
Go, bind your sons to exile
    To serve your captives' need;
To wait, in heavy harness,
    On fluttered folk and wild —
Your new-caught sullen peoples,
    Half devil and half child.

Take up the White Man's burden —
    In patience to abide,
To veil the threat of terror
    And check the show of pride;
By open speech and simple,
    An hundred times made plain,
To seek another's profit
    And work another's gain.

Take up the White Man's burden —
    The savage wars of peace —

Rudyard Kipling, "The White Man's Burden," *McClure's Magazine* 12, no. 4 (February 1899): 290–91.

Fill full the mouth of Famine,
   And bid the sickness cease;
And when your goal is nearest
   (The end for others sought)
Watch sloth and heathen folly
   Bring all your hope to nought.

Take up the White Man's burden —
   No iron rule of kings,
But toil of serf and sweeper —
   The tale of common things.
The ports ye shall not enter,
   The roads ye shall not tread,
Go, make them with your living
   And mark them with your dead.

Take up the White Man's burden,
   And reap his own reward —
The blame of those ye better
   The hate of those ye guard —
The cry of hosts ye humour
   (Ah, slowly!) toward the light: —
"Why brought ye us from bondage,
   Our loved Egyptian night?"

Take up the White Man's burden —
   Ye dare not stoop to less —
Nor call too loud on Freedom
   To cloke your weariness.
By all ye will or whisper,
   By all ye leave or do,
The silent sullen peoples
   Shall weigh your God and you.

Take up the White Man's burden!
   Have done with childish days —
The lightly-proffered laurel,
   The easy ungrudged praise:
Comes now, to search your manhood
   Through all the thankless years,
Cold, edged with dear-bought wisdom,
   The judgment of your peers.

48

JOSE RIZAL

From *Noli Me Tangere*

Widely regarded as the great national Filipino novel, *Noli Me Tangere* (Latin for "touch me not") was published in 1887. It introduces the reader to a broad spectrum of life in colonial Manila just before the outbreak of the revolution against Spanish colonialism in 1896.

The selection begins with the opening scene of the novel: a party thrown by Don Santiago de los Santos. Notice the distinctions that are made between the Spanish and the Filipino "natives." Like other colonial worlds, the Philippines was a dual world, at least in the minds of those from Spain. But here we are reminded that not all natives are poor or powerless.

In the second part of the selection, the hero Ibarra, who has just left the dinner party given in his honor after a seven-year absence in Europe, learns how his father died. What does this reading suggest about the meaning of *Spaniard* and *native* in a colony approaching rebellion? How is it possible that a wealthy, well-connected Spaniard can be thought more subversive than a poor native?

Thinking Historically

Noli Me Tangere uniquely prefigured, reflected, and made history. When it was published in 1887, it was condemned as "heretical" and "subversive" by the Catholic Church and banned by the government, but it gave rise to a nationalist movement, and revolution in 1896 echoed the novel. For his prescience and presumed subversion, Rizal was arrested and executed in 1896.

Rizal's novel helped shape a Philippine national identity. When he formed the national organization called Filipino League in 1892, the Philippines (named after the Spanish King Philip) comprised thousands of islands of "Indios" in what was called "overseas Spain." Different indigenous peoples were identified by their particular island, region, dialect, or language. Rizal's novel helped to give people a sense of nationhood.

In one important respect, Rizal's fictional revolution was not the one that occurred. Instead of the national movement of middle-class intellectuals that Rizal envisioned, the revolution of 1896, led by Emilio Aguinaldo, galvanized the poor. And yet when Aguinaldo pro-

Jose Rizal, *Noli Me Tangere*, trans. Leon Ma Guerrero (New York: Norton, 1961), 1–8.

claimed the independence of the Philippines in 1898, creating the first republic in Asia, and became president in 1899, his support cut across all social classes and ethnic groups. How was this national unity a predictable consequence of the Manila that Rizal described in the novel? How does a work of fiction become a blueprint for history? To what extent do people use fictional characters or situations as models of behavior?

The United States did not accept Philippine independence. In its own imperial quest at the end of the century, the United States demanded the transfer of the Philippines from the defeated Spanish at the end of the Spanish-American War of 1898. U.S. troops captured President Aguinaldo in 1901 and brought an end to the ensuing guerrilla resistance the following year. How does Kipling's poem, "The White Man's Burden," apply to the U.S. seizure of the Philippines?

A Party

Don Santiago de los Santos was giving a dinner party one evening towards the end of October in the 1880's. Although, contrary to his usual practice, he had let it be known only on the afternoon of the same day, it was soon the topic of conversation in Binondo, where he lived, in other districts of Manila, and even in the Spanish walled city of Intramuros. Don Santiago was better known as Capitan Tiago — the rank was not military but political, and indicated that he had once been the native mayor of a town. In those days he had a reputation for lavishness. It was well known that his house, like his country, never closed its doors — except, of course, to trade and any idea that was new or daring.

So the news of his dinner party ran like an electric shock through the community of spongers, hangers-on, and gate-crashers whom God, in His infinite wisdom, had created and so fondly multiplied in Manila. Some of these set out to hunt polish for their boots; others, collar-buttons and cravats; but one and all gave the gravest thought to the manner in which they might greet their host with the assumed intimacy of long-standing friendship, or, if the occasion should arise, make a graceful apology for not having arrived earlier where presumably their presence was so eagerly awaited.

The dinner was being given in a house on Anloague Street which may still be recognised unless it has tumbled down in some earthquake. Certainly it will not have been pulled down by its owner; in the Philippines, that is usually left to God and Nature. In fact, one often thinks that they are under contract to the Government for just that purpose. The house was large enough, in a style common to those parts. It was situated in that section of the city which is crossed by a branch of the Pasig river, called by some the creek of Binondo, which, like all rivers of Manila at that time, combined the functions of public bath, sewer, laundry, fishery, waterway, and, should the Chinese water-pedlar find it convenient, even a source of drinking water. For a stretch of almost a kilometre this vital artery, with its bustling traffic and bewildering activity, hardly counted with one wooden bridge, and this one was under repair at one end for six months, and closed to traffic at the other end for the rest of the year. Indeed, in the hot season, carriage horses had been known to avail themselves of the situation and to jump into the water at this point, to the discomfiture of any day-dreamer in their vehicles who had dozed off while pondering the achievements of the century.

On the evening in question a visitor would have judged the house to be rather squat; its lines, not quite correct, although he would have hesitated to say whether this was due to the defective eyesight of its architect or to earthquake and typhoon. A wide staircase, green-banistered and partly carpeted, rose from the tiled court at the entrance. It led to the main floor along a double line of potted plants and flower vases set on stands of Chinese porcelain, remarkable for their fantastical colours and designs.

No porter or footman would have asked the visitor for his invitation card; he would have gone up freely, attracted by the strains of orchestra music and the suggestive tinkle of silver and china, and perhaps, if a foreigner, curious about the kind of dinner parties that were given in what was called the Pearl of the Orient.

Men are like turtles; they are classified and valued according to their shells. In this, and indeed in other respects, the inhabitants of the Philippines at that time were turtles, so that a description of Capitan Tiago's house is of some importance. At the head of the stairs the visitor would have found himself in a spacious entrance hall, serving for the occasion as a combination of music- and dining-room. The large table in the centre, richly and profusely decorated, would have been winking delectable promises to the uninvited guest at the same time that it threatened the timid and naïve young girl with two distressing hours in close company with strangers whose language and topics of conversation were apt to take the most extraordinary lines. In contrast with these earthly concerns would have been the paintings crowded on the walls, depicting such religious themes as *Purgatory, Hell, The Last Judgment, The Death of the Just Man,* and *The Death of the Sinner,* and, in the place of honour, set off by an elegant and splendid frame carved in the Renaissance style by the most renowned woodworker of the day, a strange canvas of formidable dimensions in which were to be seen two old crones, with the inscription: *Our Lady of Peace and Happy Voyage, Venerated in Antipolo, Visits in the Guise of a Beggar the Pious and Celebrated Capitana Inés, Who Lies Gravely Ill.* This composition made up for its lack of taste and artistry with a realism that some might have considered extreme; the blue and yellow tints of the patient's face suggested a corpse in an advanced state of decomposition, and the tumblers and other receptacles which were about her, the cortège of long illnesses, were reproduced so painstakingly as to make their contents almost identifiable. The sight of these paintings, so stimulating to the appetite, and so evocative of carefree ease, might have led the visitor to think that his cynical host had formed a very shrewd opinion of the character of his guests; and that indeed it was only to disguise his judgment that he had hung the room about with charming Chinese lanterns, empty bird-cages, silvered crystal balls in red, green, and blue, slightly withered air-plants, stuffed fishes, and other such decorations, the whole coming to a point in fanciful wooden arches, half Chinese, half European, which framed the side of the room overlooking the river, and gave a glimpse of a porch with trellises and kiosks dimly lighted by multi-coloured paper lanterns.

The dinner guests were gathered in the main reception room which had great mirrors and sparkling chandeliers. On a pinewood platform stood enthroned a magnificent grand piano, for which an exorbitant price had been paid, and which this night seemed more precious still because nobody was presumptuous enough to play on it. There was also a large portrait in oils of a good-looking man in a frock coat, stiff and straight, as well-balanced as the tasselled cane of office between his rigid ring-covered fingers, who seemed to be saying: "See what a lot of clothes I have on, and how dignified I look!"

The furniture was elegant; uncomfortable, perhaps, and not quite suited to the climate, but then the owner of the house would have been thinking of self-display rather than the health of his guests, and would have told them: "Shocking thing, this dysentery, I know, but after all you are now seated in armchairs come straight from Europe, and you can't always do that, can you?"

The salon was almost full, the men segregated from the women as in Catholic churches and in synagogues. The few ladies were mostly young girls, some Filipinas, Spaniards the others, hastily covering their mouths with their fans when they felt a yawn coming on, and scarcely saying a word. If someone ventured to start a conversation it died out in monosyllables, not unlike the night-noises of mice and lizards. Did the images of Our Lady in her various appellations, which hung from the walls in between the mirrors, oblige them to keep this curious silence and devout demeanour, or were women in the Philippines in those times simply an exception?

Only one took the trouble of making the lady guests welcome; she was a kindly-faced old woman, a cousin of Capitan Tiago, who spoke Spanish rather badly. Her hospitality and good manners did not extend beyond offering the Spanish ladies cigars and betel-nut chew on a tray, and giving her hand to be kissed by her compatriots, exactly like a friar. The poor old woman ended up by becoming thoroughly bored, and, hearing the crash of a broken plate, hurriedly seized the excuse to leave the room, muttering:

"*Jesús!* Just you wait, you wretches!"

She never came back.

The men, however, were already in higher spirits. In one corner a number of cadets were vivaciously whispering to one another, sharing scarcely muffled laughs as they glanced about the room, sometimes pointing openly to this or that person. On the other hand two foreigners, dressed in white, went striding up and down the salon, their hands clasped behind them, and without exchanging a single word, exactly like bored passengers pacing the deck of a ship. The centre of interest and liveliness seemed to be a group composed of two priests, two laymen, and an officer, who were at a small table with wine and English biscuits.

The officer was an ageing lieutenant, Guevara by name, tall, stern, with the air of a Duke of Alba left stranded in the lower ranks of the Constabulary roster. He said little, but what he said was heard to be sharp and brief. One of the friars was a young Dominican, Father Sibyla, handsome, well-groomed, and as bright as his gold-rimmed glasses. He had an air of premature gravity. Parish priest of Binondo, and formerly a professor at the Dominican College of San Juan de Letrán, he had the reputation of being a consummate casuist, so much so that in other times, when members of his Order still dared to match subtleties with laymen, the most skilful debater among the latter had never succeeded in trapping or confusing him; the agile distinctions of Father Sibyla had made his antagonist look like a fisherman trying to catch eels with a piece of string. The Dominican seemed to weigh his words and they were few.

By way of contrast, the other friar, a Franciscan, was a man of many words and even more numerous gestures. Although his hair was greying, his robust constitution seemed well preserved. His classic features, penetrating look, heavy jaws, and herculean build, gave him the appearance of a Roman patrician in disguise, and recalled one of those three monks in the German story who in the September equinox would cross a Tyrolean lake at midnight, and each time place in the hand of the terror-stricken boatman a silver coin, cold as ice. However, Father Dámaso was not so mysterious as that; he was a jovial man, and if the tone of his voice was rough, like that of a man who has never held his tongue and who thinks that what he says is dogma and beyond question, his frank and jolly laugh erased this disagreeable impression; one could even forgive him when he thrust out toward the company a naked pair of hairy legs that would have made a fortune at the freak-show of any suburban fair.

One of the civilians, Mr Laruja, was a small man with a black beard whose only notable feature was a nose so large that it seemed to belong to an entirely different person. The other was a fair-haired young man, apparently a newcomer to the country, who was just then engaged in an excited discussion with the Franciscan.

"You'll see," said the latter. "A few more months in this country, and you'll be agreeing with me; it's one thing to govern from Madrid, and quite another to make-do in the Philippines."

"But . . ."

"Take me, for example," Father Dámaso continued, raising his voice to keep the floor, "I've had twenty-three years of rice and bananas, and I can speak with authority on the matter. Don't come to me with theories and rhetoric; I know the natives. Listen, when I first arrived, I was assigned to a town, small it's true, but very hard-working in the fields. At that time I didn't know much Tagalog, but I was already hearing the women's Confessions; we understood one another, if you see what I mean. Well, sir, they came to like me so much that three years later, when I was transferred to a larger parish, left vacant by the death of a native priest, you should have seen all those women! They broke down and cried, they loaded me with presents, they saw me off with brass bands!"

"But that only goes to show . . ."

"Just a moment, one moment! Hold your horses! Now, my successor served a shorter time, and when he left, why, sir, he had an even greater escort, more tears were shed, more music played, and that in spite of the fact that he used to flog them more and had doubled the parish fees!"

"Permit me . . ."

"And that isn't all. Some time after, I served in the town of San Diego for twenty years; it's only a few months since I . . . left it." The recollection seemed to depress and anger him. "Well, twenty years! Nobody will deny that's time enough to know *any* town. There were six thousand souls in San Diego, and I couldn't have known each and every one of them better if I had given them birth and suck myself. I knew in which foot this little fellow limped, or where the shoe pinched that other little fellow, who was making love to that other dusky lady, and how many love affairs still another one had, and with whom, mind you, and who was the real father of this or that little urchin; all that sort of thing — after all, I was hearing the Confessions of each and every one of those rascals; they knew they had better be careful about fulfilling their religious duties, believe me. Santiago, our host, can tell you I'm speaking the honest truth; he has a lot of property there; in fact that is where we got to be friends. Well, sir, just to show you what the native is really like: When I left, there was scarcely a handful of old crones and lay members of our Order to see me off! That, after twenty years!"

"But I don't see the connection between this and the abolition of the tobacco monopoly," complained the new arrival when the Franciscan paused to refresh himself with a glass of sherry.

Father Dámaso was so taken aback that he almost dropped the glass. He glared at the young man for some time, and then exclaimed with unfeigned shock:

"What? How's that? But is it possible that you can't see what's clearer than daylight? Don't you see, my dear boy, that all this is tangible proof that the reforms proposed by the Ministers in Madrid are mad?"

It was the young man's turn to be puzzled. Beside him Lieutenant Guevara deepened his frown, while Mr Laruja moved his head ambiguously, uncertain whether to nod approval or shake disapproval of Father Dámaso. The Dominican, Father Sibyla, for his part, merely turned away from them.

"You believe . . ." the young Spaniard finally managed to blurt out, his face grave and inquiring.

"Believe it? Just as I believe in Holy Gospel! The native is so lazy!"

"Excuse me," said the new arrival, lowering his voice and drawing his chair closer. "What you have just said interests me very much indeed. Are the natives really *born* lazy? Or was that foreign traveller right who said that we Spaniards use this charge of laziness to excuse our own, as well as to explain the lack of progress and policy in our colonies? He was, of course, speaking of other colonies of ours, but I think the inhabitants there belong to the same race as these people."

"Rubbish! Pure envy! Mr Laruja here knows the country as well as I do; ask him, go on, ask him if the ignorance and laziness of these fellows can be matched."

"Quite right," Mr Laruja agreed promptly, "there is nobody lazier anywhere in the whole wide world than the native of these parts."

"None more vicious, or more ungrateful!"

"Or so ill-bred!"

The fair-haired young man looked uneasily around him.

"Gentlemen," he whispered, "I believe we are in the house of a native. Those young ladies . . ."

A Subversive Heretic

After leaving the dinner party Ibarra hesitated at the threshold of Capitan Tiago's house. The night air, already chilly at that time of year in Manila, seemed to clear his head. He bared his brow to the breeze, sighed, and went off toward the square of Binondo, looking searchingly about him.

Private carriages dashed past hansom cabs, their horses at a walk while waiting for a fare, and pedestrians of all nationalities. The streets looked exactly the same as when he had seen them last, with the same white-washed stucco-faced houses trimmed with blue. The lighted clock on the church tower, the Chinese corner-stores with their grimy curtains and iron railings, were all the same — even to the rail he himself had twisted out of shape one night as a prank.

"We go slow," he said to himself, turning down De la Sacristía Street.

Ice-cream pedlars were crying out their wares as of old, and the same kerosene lamps lighted the old fruit and vegetable stalls.

"Amazing," he thought, "why, that's the same Chinaman I saw there seven years ago, and that old woman . . . still there! It might've been last night, and I could have dreamed those seven years in Europe. And, good God, there's that cobblestone, just as I left it."

There it was indeed, dislodged from the sidewalk at the corner of San Jacinto and De la Sacristía.

He was thus pondering the phenomenon of an unchanging city in a country of uncertainties, when he felt the gentle touch of a hand on his shoulder. He turned and found himself face to face with Lieutenant Guevara, whose habitually hard frown had now softened almost into amiability.

"Watch your step, young fellow," he said. "Learn from your father."

"I beg your pardon, but you seem to have thought a lot of my father; could you tell me how and where he died?" asked Ibarra.

"What!" exclaimed the officer. "Don't you know?"

"I asked Don Santiago, but he put off telling me until tomorrow. Do you yourself happen to know?"

"Of course. Like everybody else. He died in prison."

The young man fell back a step, and stared astonished at the lieutenant.

"In prison? Who died in prison?"

"My dear sir, your father, of course." The officer seemed puzzled.

"My father in prison? What are you saying? Do you realise who my father was?" The young man was so distraught that he had seized the officer by the arm.

"I think I know," he replied. "Don Rafael Ibarra. You told me so yourself earlier this evening."

"Yes, Don Rafael Ibarra."

"But I thought you knew," Guevara protested pityingly, conscious of the turmoil in Ibarra's mind. "I supposed that . . . But come now, face it! In this country it's an honour to have gone to prison."

"You cannot be joking; I suppose I must believe you," said Ibarra in a strangled tone after a short silence. "Can you tell me why he was in prison?"

The old man reflected.

"Odd you should know so little about your family affairs."

"In his last letter, a year ago, my father asked me not to worry if I didn't hear from him; he said he expected to be very busy. He commended me to my studies, and sent his blessing."

"Then he must have written to you shortly before he died. It will be a year since he was buried in your home town."

"But why was my father imprisoned?"

"For a very honourable cause. But I'm due at the barracks. Come with me, take my arm, and I'll tell you as we go along."

This was the story he told.

"As you know yourself, your father was the richest man in your province, and, although he was loved and honoured by many, others hated or envied him. Unfortunately, those of us Spaniards who come to the Philippines aren't always what we should be. I mean not only your father's enemies, but one of your own grandparents, as you shall see. The continual changes in the administration, demoralisation in high places, favouritism, combined with the cheaper fares and shorter trip out here since the Suez Canal was opened, are to blame for everything; the worst elements of the Peninsula come here, and if a good man comes, he is soon corrupted by the present conditions of the country. It was among these Spaniards, including the friars, that your father had his enemies, and they were many.

"Some months after your departure your father began to have trouble with Father Dámaso; I don't really know why. The parish priest accused him of not going to Confession; but then, he hadn't gone to Confession before that, and it hadn't stopped them from being friends, as you yourself will remember. Anyway, Don Rafael was honest and just, more so than many who go to Confession, or hear Confessions, for that matter. He had his own strict code of ethics. When, for instance, we talked about his disagreements with Father Dámaso, he would ask me: "Mr Guevara, do you believe that God forgives a crime, say, a murder, merely upon Confession to a priest, a man who, after all, is bound to secrecy? And what do you say to a confession made in fear of hell, which is an act of mere attrition rather than contrition? Does one win forgiveness by being a coward and shamelessly playing it safe? I have a different idea of God. For myself I think that one wrong does not right another, and forgiveness cannot be won with useless tears or alms to the Church. I put it to you: If I had murdered the father of a family, if I had widowed some unhappy woman and turned happy children into destitute orphans, would I have satisfied divine justice by allowing myself to be hanged, or perhaps by confiding my secret to one sworn never to reveal it, by giving alms to priests who needed it least, by making a cash settlement of any penances imposed, or even by weeping night and day? What good would this have done the widow and the orphans? My conscience tells me that I should have taken in every possible way the place of my victim, dedicating myself, for the whole of my life, to the good of that family for whose misfortunes I was responsible, and even then, even then, who could make amends for the loss of a loving husband and father?" That was the way your father reasoned. He always acted in accordance with these exacting principles. One can truly say he never did anyone a conscious injury; on the contrary, he tried to atone with good deeds for certain injustices which, he said, had been committed by his grandparents. But to return to his troubles with the parish priest; things were beginning to look ugly; Father Dámaso was making allusions to your father from the very pulpit, and, considering that anything might be expected from a man like him, it was a miracle that he didn't name your father outright. I could see that sooner or later things were going to end badly.

"At that time there was a former artillery-man going the rounds in your province. He was so gross and stupid that he had been dismissed from the service, and, since he had to make a living and could not be allowed to do manual work, which would have hurt our prestige, someone gave him the job of collecting the tax on vehicles. This oaf had no schooling at all, and the natives soon found out. To them a Spaniard who didn't know how to read and write was a freak. So they all took to making fun of the poor wretch, who had to pay with humiliations for the taxes he collected. He knew he was the butt of their jokes, which further soured his already rough and evil temper. They would give him papers upside down; he would pretend to read them, and then would sign on the most likely blank space — and when I say sign, I mean he would make a series of clumsy squiggles. The natives paid their taxes, but they had their fun; he swallowed his pride, but collected. In this frame of mind he was in no mood to give anyone his due of respect, and he even had very harsh exchanges with your father.

"One day he was given an official paper in a shop, and he was turning it over and over trying to put it straight, when a schoolboy burst out laughing, pointing him out to his mates. Our man heard them laugh, and looking round him, he saw that people were trying hard to keep a straight face. He lost his temper and turned on the schoolboys. They ran away, mockingly reciting the alphabet as he chased them. He was blind with rage and, when he could not catch them up, he hurled his stick at them. It hit one of the boys on the head and knocked him down. The wretched tax-collector promptly ran up to him, and started kicking him; none of those who had been having such fun now dared to step in. Unfortunately, your father happened to be passing by. He was shocked and, seizing the tax-collector by the arm, was remonstrating

with him when the latter, still in a rage, started a wild swing. Your father did not give him time to finish it and, with the strength of a true
descendant of Basques . . . well, some say that he hit him, others, that
he did no more than give him a push. In any case the tax-collector staggered and fell a few feet away, hitting his head against a stone. Don
Rafael calmly lifted the hurt child in his arms and took him to the
town-hall. The tax-collector was throwing up blood; he never recovered consciousness and died a few minutes later. Naturally, the police
intervened, your father was imprisoned, and all his hidden enemies
showed their heads. All sorts of lies began to pour in; he was accused of
heresy and sedition. Heresy is always a very serious charge; more so in
this case, because the governor of the province at that time was a man
who made a great show of piety, even saying the Rosary in church in a
loud voice and with his servants for a chorus, perhaps so everyone
hearing him would start praying too. But subversion of the established
order is even worse than heresy, or the murder of *three* tax-collectors
capable of reading, writing, and making philosophical distinctions.
Your father was deserted by all; his papers and books were confiscated.
He was accused of subscribing to the *Overseas Mail* and other newspapers from Madrid, of having sent you to the German — and therefore
Protestant — part of Switzerland, of having in his possession a photograph and even letters from a native priest executed for complicity in
rebellion — and I don't know what else. Everything they could think of
was charged against him: even the fact that, being of Spanish blood, he
dressed like a native. Perhaps, if your father had been someone else, he
would have been released in a short time. One physician attributed the
tax-collector's death to apoplexy. But your father's great wealth, his
faith in justice, and his hatred of the illegal and the unjust, ruined him.
I did all I could; I hate begging favours, but I went to see the Governor
General himself, the predecessor of the present one, and submitted to
him that a man like your father, who took into his own house and fed
every Spaniard who was poor or homeless, and in whose veins there
ran good Spanish blood, could not be guilty of subversion. I offered to
stand surety for him. I swore to his innocence by my poverty and my
military honour. But all I got was a cold reception, an even colder dismissal, and the reputation of being a crank.

    "Your father asked me to take charge of his case. I first applied to a
young but already famous Filipino lawyer. He refused to undertake
your father's defence. "I would be ruined," he told me. "If I took the
case, that very fact could be made into a new charge against him, and
perhaps against myself." He suggested that I engage a Spanish lawyer,
and named one who was a fluent and forceful orator and enjoyed an
immense prestige. I did so, and renowned counsel accepted the defence,
which he carried out masterfully, brilliantly. But your father's enemies
were many, some of them hidden and unknown. There were plenty of

false witnesses, and their lies, which in other cases would have been exploded with a jibe from counsel, were now given credit for solidity and consistency. If counsel succeeded in discrediting them by showing their contradictions not only with each other, but even in themselves, new charges soon took the place of the old ones. He was accused of illegal and inequitable usurpation of many of his properties; indemnities and damages were demanded; he was said to have connections with bandits to buy protection for his fields and his herds. In short, the case became so complicated that after a year nobody could make head or tail of it. The governor left his post; his successor had a reputation for justice, but, alas, did not stay in office for more than a few months; and his successor, in turn, was too fond of fast horses.

"Your father's sufferings and disappointments, the rigours of prison, or perhaps grief at such ingratitude, broke his iron constitution, and he fell ill, of such an illness as only death can heal. He died in prison, with nobody by his side, just when everything was coming to an end, when he was about to be acquitted both of sedition and of murder. I arrived in time to see him die."

The old man fell silent. Ibarra had not said a word. They had reached the barracks gate. The officer paused and put out his hand.

"Ask Capitan Tiago for the details, my boy. And now, good-night. I must go in and see what's new."

Silently but with emotion, Ibarra gripped the withered old hand, and followed him with his eyes until he was lost from sight.

He turned slowly and hailed a passing carriage.

"Hotel Lala," he ordered, in an almost unintelligible voice.

"This chap must be just out of gaol," thought the coachman, whipping up his horses.

REFLECTIONS

All the novels excerpted in this chapter are well worth reading in their entirety, and many other excellent colonial novels can be chosen from this period as well as from the 1930s and 1940s. E. M. Forster's *A Passage to India* and Paul Scott's *The Raj Quartet* stand out as fictional introductions to British colonialism in India. (Both have also received excellent adaptations to film, the latter as the series for television called *The Jewel in the Crown*.) In addition to Chinua Achebe, Amos Tutuola and Wole Soyinka have written extensively on Nigeria; as well, Francis Bebey, Ferdinand Oyono, and Mongo Beti address French colonialism in Africa. On South Africa, the work of Alan Payton, Andre Brink, J. M. Coetzee, Peter Abrams, and James McClure, among many others, stands out.

The excerpts in this chapter call attention to such examples of colonialism as "liplaps." In English clubs, reading the entire novels from which those excerpts came, we might be drawn in to the story, involved to the extent of losing our objectivity. The advantage of becoming engrossed in a novel, of course, is that we feel part of the story and have a sense that we are learning something firsthand. Of course, we are reading a work of fiction, not gaining firsthand experience or reading an accurate historical account of events. A well-made film poses an even greater problem. Its visual and aural impact imparts a psychological reality that becomes part of our experience. If it is about a subject of which we know little, the film quickly becomes our "knowledge" of the subject, and this knowledge may be incomplete or inaccurate.

On the other hand, a well-written novel or film can whet our appetite and inspire us to learn more. Choose and read a novel about colonialism or some other historical subject. Then, read a biography of the author or research his or her background to determine how much the author knew about the subject. Next, read a historical account of the subject. How much attention does the historian give to the novelist's subject? How does the novel add depth to the historical account? How does the historical account place the novel in perspective? Finally how does the author's background place the novel in historical context?

9

Independence and Westernization

HISTORICAL CONTEXT
Japan, India, and China, 1880–1930

As the peoples of Asia and Africa adapted to Western colonialism or struggled to free themselves from it, they inevitably faced the issue of Westernization. To become Westernized was to accept and adopt the ways of the powerful colonial powers of the West: Western Europe and its more distant western offshoot, the United States. All colonized peoples were exposed to some degree of Western education, indoctrination, or control. As they sought their independence and worked to create their own national identities, they frequently revived older indigenous traditions, languages, and religions — ideas that had fallen into disuse or had been replaced by Western culture. This rebirth of traditional culture often meant a specific and determined rejection of Western ways.

This chapter explores a number of Asian responses to Westernization at the end of the nineteenth and the beginning of the twentieth century. The first reading gives a sense of how these societies came to grips with the West, culturally as well as politically. In every case, a people who sought its own national identity had to determine the degree of Westernization, if any, it desired to retain. Selections 50 and 51 explore this issue in Japan, the first Asian country to Westernize. Japan Westernized so successfully in fact, that in the minds of many Asians, and in other parts of the world, it was deemed a Western power. What was the range of attitudes toward the West in Japan, and how strong was the impact of Westernization on its people?

We next turn to India for comparison. While Japan adopted Western ways in its successful effort to escape Western colonization, India's submission to British colonization led to various forms of Westernization. However, the Westernization of India was not a single-minded process. There were both English colonial administrators who opposed it and Indians who favored it. India was more fully Westernized than Japan, but its opposition to Westernization was more thorough and intense (as we will see in Gandhi's criticism of Western technology in selection 53).

Finally, we compare China with India and Japan, as the degree of China's colonization fell somewhere between the other two. China also had an ancient cultural tradition and a long imperial political history. Borrowing from non-Chinese cultures seemed a far-fetched proposition. The attitude expressed by the emperor Ch'ien Lung in his letter to George III (selection 38) was held by many Chinese intellectuals long after the Opium War might have encouraged doubters in another society. And yet, rather suddenly, in the beginning of the twentieth century, Chinese intellectuals jettisoned age-old elements of Confucian and imperial traditions to embark on a new history, largely modeled on Western political ideas (first Franco-American and then Russian) and staffed and financed by overseas Chinese in Europe and the United States.

What accounted for the appeal of the West in these three different settings? Consider the label "the West." It can include the United States as well as Europe (Eastern Europe as well as Western Europe) and possibly even Japan. Did the intellectuals of Japan, China, and India mean the same thing by the West? Did the Westernizers seek to imitate different aspects of the West? And what motivated those who rejected the West? Did they have similar or different agendas?

THINKING HISTORICALLY
Appreciating Contradictions

The process of Westernization, like the experience of conquest and colonization that often preceded it, was wrought with conflict and led to frequent contradictions. Often, the struggle for national independence meant the borrowing of Western practices, words, even languages. In India, for instance, English was the only common language of all educated Indians. Therefore, it is not surprising that contradictory behavior and ambivalent relationships were endemic in the postcolonial world, just as they had been under colonialism. These contradictions usually manifested themselves in an individual's cultural identity. How do colonized persons adopt Western ways, embrace traditional culture, and not feel as though their identity has been divided between the two? Such individuals do not fit entirely into either world and so cannot help but be torn between who they were and who they have become. The somewhat anguished experiences of these colonized people are difficult to understand. We typically want to accept one view or another, to praise or to blame. But as we have learned, the history of peoples and nations is rarely that clear. In examining some of the fundamental contradictions in the history of Westernization, we might better understand how people were variously affected.

There is a tradition of historical thought, associated with the philosophies of G. W. F. Hegel and Karl Marx, which maintains that contradictions are the driving force of history. Contradictions are products of the historical process, results of social and cultural forces. Hegel and Marx would call this attention to how contradictions emerge, compete, and lead both to new levels of understanding and to new contradictions "thinking dialectically." We will content ourselves with identifying and appreciating contradictions in the following selections.

49

THEODORE VON LAUE

From *The World Revolution of Westernization*

Western colonialism, according to von Laue, a modern historian, brought about a "world revolution of Westernization," the victory of Western culture that accompanied Western political domination. What, according to von Laue, are these Western ideas that spread throughout the world during the nineteenth century? Did these ideas spread peacefully or were they forced on non-Western peoples? What groups of people were most attracted to Western ideas? Why did some non-Western people prefer Western culture to their own?

Does von Laue believe that this "world revolution" was a good thing? Does he believe it is over? What, according to von Laue, must still be done?

Thinking Historically

Von Laue is particularly interested in the plight of what he calls the "Westernized non-Western intelligentsia." Who are these people?

Theodore von Laue, *The World Revolution of Westernization* (New York: Oxford University Press, 1987), 27–34.

What is their problem? What does von Laue mean when he says that "as a result of their Westernization they became anti-Western nationalists"? How could Westernization make people anti-Western?

Throughout this selection, von Laue discusses paradoxical or ironic behavior. He writes of people learning lessons that were not formally taught and of psychological conflicts or love-hate attitudes. At one point he generalizes this phenomenon of seemingly contradictory behavior by quoting an eighteenth-century maxim that states, "To do just the opposite is also a form of imitation." Is von Laue describing some paradoxical aspect of human nature, or are these conflicts a particular product of colonialism?

While the world revolution of Westernization created a political world order radically above the horizons of all past human experience, it also unhinged, in the revolutionary manner sensed by Lord Lytton,[1] the depths of non-Western societies constituting the bulk of humanity. As he had said, "The application of the most refined principles of European government and some of the most artificial institutions of European society to a . . . vast population in whose history, habits, and traditions they have had no previous existence" was a risky enterprise, perhaps more than he had anticipated.

Examining the history of colonial expansion, one can discern a rough but generally applicable pattern for the revolutionary subversion of non-Western societies. Subversion began at the apex, with the defeat, humiliation, or even overthrow of traditional rulers. The key guarantee of law, order, and security from external interference was thus removed. With it went the continuity of tradition, whether of governance or of all other social institutions down to the subtle customs regulating the individual psyche. Thus ended not only political but also cultural self-determination. Henceforth, the initiatives shaping collective existence came from without, "mysterious formulas of a foreign and more or less uncongenial system" not only of administration but also of every aspect of life.

Once the authority of the ruler (who often was the semi-divine intermediary between Heaven and Earth) was subverted, the Western attack on the other props of society intensified. Missionaries, their security guaranteed by Western arms, discredited the local gods and their guardians, weakening the spiritual foundations of society. At the same time, colonial administrators interfered directly in indigenous affairs by suppressing hallowed practices repulsive to them, including human sac-

---

[1] British viceroy of India from 1876 to 1880.

rifice, slavery, and physical cruelty in its many forms. Meanwhile, Western businessmen and their local agents redirected the channels of trade and economic life, making local producers and consumers dependent on a world market beyond their comprehension and control. In a thousand ways the colonial administration and its allies, though not necessarily in agreement with each other, introduced a new set of rewards and punishments, of prestige and authority. The changeover was obvious even in the externals of dress. Africans became ashamed of their nudity, women covered their breasts; Chinese men cut off their queues and adopted Western clothes. The boldest even tried to become like Westerners "in taste, in opinion, in morals, and intellect."

The pathways of subversion here outlined indicate the general pattern and the directions which it followed over time. Its speed depended on Western policy and the resilience of local society. Things seemingly fell apart quickly in the case of the most vulnerable small-scale societies of Africa and much more slowly in India or China, if at all in Japan. Often the colonial administration itself, under the policy of "indirect rule," slowed the Western impact for fear of causing cultural chaos and making trouble for itself. In all cases, tradition (however subverted) persisted in a thousand forms, merely retreating from the external world into the subliminally conditioned responses of the human psyche, its last refuge. It is still lurking in the promptings of "soul" today.

And did things really fall apart? The world revolution of Westernization prevailed by the arts of both war and peace. Certain aspects of Western power possessed an intrinsic appeal which, even by indigenous judgment, enhanced life. New crops often brought ampler food; European rule often secured peace. Through their command of the seas and of worldwide trade Europeans and Americans opened access to survival and opportunity in foreign lands to countless millions of people in China and India. Or take even the persuasion of raw power: once convinced of the superiority of European weapons, who would not crave possession of them too? And more generally, being associated with European power also carried weight; it patently held the keys to the future. More directly perhaps, doing business with Westerners promised profit. If they played it right, compradors would get rich.

More subtly, certain categories of the local population eagerly took to foreign ways. Missionaries sheltered outcasts: slaves held for sacrifice, girls to be sold into prostitution or abandoned, or married women feeling abused and oppressed. The struggle for sexual equality is still raging in our midst, yet by comparison even Victorian England offered hope to women in Africa or East Asia. Regarding Japan, Fukuzawa[2] related the story of a highborn dowager lady who "had had some

2 See selection 50. [Ed.]

unhappy trials in earlier days." She was told of "the most remarkable of all the Western customs . . . the relations between men and women," where "men and women had equal rights, and monogamy was the strict rule in any class of people. . . ." It was, Fukuzawa reported, "as if her eyes were suddenly opened to something new. . . ." As a messenger of women's rights he certainly had Japanese women, "especially the ladies of the higher society," on his side. In China liberated women rushed to unbind their feet.

In addition, the Westerners introduced hospitals and medicines that relieved pain and saved lives, a fact not unappreciated. Besides, whose greed was not aroused by the plethora of Western goods, all fancier than local products: stronger liquor, gaudier textiles, faster transport? Simple minds soon preferred Western goods merely because they were Western. Given the comparative helplessness of local society, was it surprising that everything Western tended to be judged superior?

The Westerners with their sense of mission also introduced their education. It was perhaps not enough, according to anti-Western nationalist suspicious of European desires, to keep the natives down, yet it offered access to Western skills at some sacrifice on the part of teachers willing to forgo the easier life in their own culture. Privileged non-Westerners even attended schools and universities in the West. Thus, as part of the general pattern of Westernization, a new category of cultural half-breeds was created, the Westernized non-Western intelligentsia. It differed somewhat according to cultural origins, but shared a common predicament. Product of one culture, educated in another, it was caught in invidious comparison. As [philosopher] Thomas Hobbes observed "Man, whose Joy consisteth in comparing himselfe with other men, can relish nothing but what is eminent." Riveted to Western preeminence, this intelligentsia struggled for purpose, identity, and recognition in the treacherous no-man's-land in between — and most furiously in lands where skin color added to its disabilities. Talented and industrious, these intellectuals threw themselves heroically into the study of Western society and thought so alien to their own.

Along the way they soon acquired a taste for the dominant ideals of the West, foremost the liberal plea for equality, freedom, and self-determination and the socialists' cry of social justice for all exploited and oppressed peoples and classes. They were delighted by the bitter self-criticism they discovered among Westerners — Western society produced many doubters, especially among its fringes in central and eastern Europe. At the same time, non-Western intellectuals quickly perceived the pride that lurked behind Western humanitarianism. They might be treated as equals in London or Paris, but "east of Aden" on the Indian circuit or anywhere in the colonies, they were "natives" — natives hypersensitive to the hypocrisy behind the Western mission of exporting high ideals without the congenital ingredient of equality.

Thus they learned the lessons of power not formally taught by their masters. They needed power — state power — not only to carry the Western vision into practice on their own but also to make equality real.

Inevitably, the non-Western intellectuals turned their lessons to their own use. The ideals of freedom and self-determination justified giving free rein not only to the promptings of their own minds and souls, but also to protests over the humiliation of their countries and cultures. As a result of their Westernization they became anti-Western nationalists, outwardly curtailing, in themselves and their compatriots, the abject imitation of the West. Yet, as an 18th-century German wag had said, "To do just the opposite is also a form of imitation." Anti-Western self-assertion was a form of Westernization copying the cultural self-assertion of the West. Moreover, limiting western influence in fact undercut any chance of matching Western power (and the issue of power was never far from their minds). Thus anti-Western intellectuals were caught in a love-hate attitude toward the West, anti-Western purveyors of further Westernization.

Take Mohandas Gandhi,[3] perhaps the greatest among the Westernized non-Western intellectuals. Born into a prominent tradition-oriented Hindu family and of a lively, ambitious mind, he broke with Hindu taboo and studied English law in London, fashionably dressed and accepted in the best society, though by preference consorting with vegetarians and students of Eastern religion. After his return he confessed that "next to India, [he] would rather live in London than in any other place in the world." From 1892 to 1914, however, he lived in South Africa, using his legal training for defending the local Indian community against white discrimination. There he put together from Indian and Western sources a philosophy as well as a practice of non-violent resistance, strengthening the self-confidence and civil status of his clients. . . .

One of Gandhi's precursors, Narendranath Datta, better known as Swami Vivekananda,[4] had gone even further. At a lecture in Madras he exhorted his audience: "This is the great ideal before us, and everyone must be ready for it — the conquest of the whole world by India — nothing less than that. . . . Up India and conquer the world with your spirituality." Western globalized nationalism, obviously, was working its way around the world, escalating political ambition and cultural messianism to novel intensity. . . .

. . . [T]he run of Westernized non-Western intellectuals led awkward lives — "in a free state," as [Indian novelist] V. S. Naipaul has

---

[3] See selection 53. [Ed.]
[4] See selection 52. [Ed.]

put it — forever in search of roots, and certitude; inwardly split, part backward, part Western, camouflaging their imitation of the West by gestures of rejection; forever aspiring to build lofty halfway houses that bridged the disparate cultural universes, often in all-embracing designs, never admitting the fissures and cracks in their lives and opinions; and always covering up their unease with a compensating presumption of moral superiority based on the recognition that the promptings of heart and soul are superior to the dictates of reason. Knowing their own traditions and at least some of the essentials of the West, they sensed that they had a more elevated grasp of human reality; the future belonged to them rather than to the "decadent" West. Out of that existential misery of "heightened consciousness" (as [Russian novelist] Dostoyevsky called it) have come some of the most seminal contributions to the intellectual and political developments of the 20th century, including the anti-Western counterrevolutions.

. . . Let it be said first that the relations between the colonized and the colonizer are exceedingly subtle and complex, subject to keen controversy among all observers, all of them partisans, all of them now judging not by indigenous but by Westernized standards. Western ideals and practices have shaped and intensified the protests of Westernized non-Western intellectuals taking full advantage of the opportunities offered by Western society. Their protests, incidentally, were hardly ever turned against past inhumanities committed by their own kind (because traditionally they were not considered as such).

Next, having already surveyed the not inconsiderable side benefits of Western domination, let us ask: did the Westerners in their expansion behave toward the non-Westerners worse than they behaved toward themselves? While they never treated their colonial subjects as equals, they never killed as many people in all their colonial campaigns as they did in their own wars at home (the brutality of Europe's cultural evolution has been carefully rinsed out of all current historical accounts). And in their peaceful intercourse with non-Westerners we find the whole range of emotions common in Western society. It was darkness at heart on one extreme and saintliness on the other, and every mix in between, with the balance perhaps tending toward darkness. As one colonial officer in East Africa confided to his diary: "It is but a small percentage of white men whose characters do not in one way or another undergo a subtle process of deteriorization when they are compelled to live for any length of time among savage races and under conditions as exist in tropical climates." The colonial district commissioner, isolated among people whose ways sharply contradicted his own upbringing, often suffering from tropical sickness, and scared at heart, found himself perhaps in a worse dilemma than the Westernized non-Western intellectuals. Some of them, no doubt, were unscrupulous opportunists seeking escape from the trammels of civic conformity at home; they turned domineering sadists in the colonies. On the other hand, missionaries often sacrificed their lives, generally among uncomprehending local folk. It was perhaps a credit to the Westerners that the victims of imperialism found considerable sympathy in their own midst. The evils stood out while the good intentions were taken for granted.

Yet — to take a longer view — even compassionate Western observers generally overlook the fact that among all the gifts of the West the two most crucial boons were missing: cultural equality as the basis for political equality and reasonable harmony in the body politic. The world revolution of Westernization perpetuated inequality and ruinous cultural subversion while at the same time improving the material conditions of life. More people survived, forever subject to the agonies of inequality and disorientation resulting from enforced change originating beyond their ken. Collectively and individually, they straddled the border between West and non-West, on the one side enjoying the benefits of Western culture, on the other feeling exploited as victims of imperialism. Indigenous populations always remained backward and dependent, unable to match the resources and skills of a fast-advancing West.

What we should weigh, then, in any assessment of Western colonial expansion before World War I is perhaps not only the actions, good or evil, of the colonial powers, but also the long-run consequences thereafter. The victims of Western colonialism do not include only the casualties of colonial wars but also the far greater multitudes killed or brutalized in the civil commotions in the emerging modern nation-states. Whatever the mitigating circumstances, the anti-Western fury has its justifications indeed.

And yet, in the all-inclusive global perspective, is it morally justified? Was the outreach with all its outrages planned by the Westerners? Was it based on a deliberate design of conquest? Or was it the accidental result of stark imbalances in the resources of power for both war and peace which had come about through circumstances beyond human control? Why were the Westerners so powerful? Their stock answer has been: because of their ideals embedded in their religion, culture, and political institutions, adding up to their overwhelming material superiority. That answer, however, will not suffice for the overview appropriate to this age. In the enlarged contexts of global interaction human beings appear far more helpless than in their smaller settings, where they may claim a measure of control. As argued above, it was merely by historical and geographic accident that the Europeans were enabled to create the cultural hothouse that made them uniquely powerful in the world.

. . . As we now see the grand connections more clearly, we also understand that the burden of responsibility for bringing about cultural

equality falls more heavily on those who have been so privileged, so
spoiled, by circumstances beyond their control. They have furnished
the energies behind the world revolution of Westernization; they carry
the obligation to complete it according to their ideals of freedom,
equality, and human dignity and in a manner beneficial to all humanity. . . .

$$\boxed{50}$$

FUKUZAWA YUKICHI

Good-bye Asia

Fukuzawa Yukichi (1835–1901) was one of the most important
Japanese Westernizers during Japan's late-nineteenth-century rush to
catch up with the West. The son of a lower samurai (military) family,
Fukuzawa left home in 1854 to learn gunnery in the Dutch settlement
of Nagasaki. His pursuit of Western knowledge took him to a Dutch
school in Osaka, where he studied everything from the Dutch language to chemistry, physics, and anatomy, and to Yedo where he
studied English. Due to his privileged background and Western
schooling, he was naturally included in the first Japanese mission to
the United States in 1860 as well as in the first diplomatic mission to
Europe in 1862. When Fukuzawa returned to Japan, he found himself
to be the target of Japanese assassins who attacked foreigners and
Japanese suspected of being sympathizers with foreign ways.

Afraid to go out at night, Fukuzawa spent many years teaching in
his school and writing the books that would make him famous. The
best known of these was *Seiyo Jijo* (*Things Western*), which in 1866
introduced more than two hundred fifty thousand Japanese to the
daily life and typical institutions of Western society. For Fukuzawa,
the elements of Western success that Japan needed to imitate were scientific advancement and independence. According to Fukuzawa, the
main obstacle that prevented Japanese society from developing these

Fukuzawa Yukichi, "Datsu-a Ron" ("On Saying Good-bye to Asia"), in *Japan: A Documentary History*, vol. II, ed. David J. Lu (Armonk, NY: M. E. Sharpe, 1997), 351–53. From
Takeuchi Yoshimi, ed. *Azia Shugi (Asianism) Gendai Nihon Shisō Taikei (Great Compilation
of Modern Japanese Thought)*, vol. 8 (Tokyo: Chikuma Shobō, 1963), 38–40.

traits was a long heritage of Chinese Confucianism. Fukuzawa thought that Confucian emphasis on respect and order stifled educational independence.

In the years after the Meiji Restoration of 1868, in which feudalism was abolished and power was restored to the emperor, Fukuzawa became the most popular spokesman for the Westernizing policies of the new government. In this essay, "Good-bye Asia," written in 1885, Fukuzawa describes the spread of Western civilization in Japan. Does he believe that it is both inevitable and desirable? Why? What do you make of Fukuzawa's attitude toward Chinese and Korean civilizations? Do you think he is fair in the way he dismisses their potential?

Thinking Historically

Does this selection from Fukuzawa display any of the contradictions, ambivalence, or love-hate feelings that von Laue describes as common among Westernized non-Western intellectuals? Were such conflicts inevitable? How might someone like Fukuzawa avoid this conflict, ambivalence, or uncertainty? (A reading of *The Autobiography of Yukichi Fukuzawa* is recommended for deeper insight.)

Transportation has become so convenient these days that once the wind of Western civilization blows to the East, every blade of grass and every tree in the East follow what the Western wind brings. Ancient Westerners and present-day Westerners are from the same stock and are not much different from one another. The ancient ones moved slowly, but their contemporary counterparts move vivaciously at a fast pace. This is possible because present-day Westerners take advantage of the means of transportation available to them. For those of us who live in the Orient, unless we want to prevent the coming of Western civilization with a firm resolve, it is best that we cast our lot with them. If one observes carefully what is going on in today's world, one knows the futility of trying to prevent the onslaught of Western civilization. Why not float with them in the same ocean of civilization, sail the same waves, and enjoy the fruits and endeavors of civilization?

The movement of a civilization is like the spread of measles. Measles in Tokyo start in Nagasaki and come eastward with the spring thaw. We may hate the spread of this communicable disease, but is there any effective way of preventing it? I can prove that it is not possible. In a communicable disease, people receive only damages. In a civilization, damages may accompany benefits, but benefits always far outweigh them, and their force cannot be stopped. This being the case, there is no point in trying to prevent their spread. A wise man encourages the spread and allows our people to get used to its ways.

The opening to the modern civilization of the West began in the reign of Kaei (1848–58). Our people began to discover its utility and gradually and yet actively moved toward its acceptance. However, there was an old-fashioned and bloated government that stood in the way of progress. It was a problem impossible to solve. If the government were allowed to continue, the new civilization could not enter. The modern civilization and Japan's old conventions were mutually exclusive. If we were to discard our old conventions, that government also had to be abolished. We could have prevented the entry of this civilization, but it would have meant loss of our national independence. The struggles taking place in the world civilization were such that they would not allow an Eastern island nation to slumber in isolation. At that point, dedicated men (*shijin*) recognized the principle of "the country is more important than the government," relied on the dignity of the Imperial Household, and toppled the old government to establish a new one. With this, public and the private sectors alike, everyone in our country accepted the modern Western civilization. Not only were we able to cast aside Japan's old conventions, but we also succeeded in creating a new axle toward progress in Asia. Our basic assumptions could be summarized in two words: "Good-bye Asia (*Datsu-a*)."

Japan is located in the eastern extremities of Asia, but the spirit of her people have already moved away from the old conventions of Asia to the Western civilization. Unfortunately for Japan, there are two neighboring countries. One is called China and another Korea. These two peoples, like the Japanese people, have been nurtured by Asiatic political thoughts and mores. It may be that we are different races of people, or it may be due to the differences in our heredity or education; significant differences mark the three peoples. The Chinese and Koreans are more like each other and together they do not show as much similarity to the Japanese. These two peoples do not know how to progress either personally or as a nation. In this day and age with transportation becoming so convenient, they cannot be blind to the manifestations of Western civilization. But they say that what is seen or heard cannot influence the disposition of their minds. Their love affairs with ancient ways and old customs remain as strong as they were centuries ago. In this new and vibrant theater of civilization when we speak of education, they only refer back to Confucianism. As for school education, they can only cite [Chinese philosopher Mencius's] precepts of humanity, righteousness, decorum, and knowledge. While professing their abhorrence to ostentation, in reality they show their ignorance of truth and principles. As for their morality, one only has to observe their unspeakable acts of cruelty and shamelessness. Yet they remain arrogant and show no sign of self-examination.

In my view, these two countries cannot survive as independent nations with the onslaught of Western civilization to the East. Their concerned citizens might yet find a way to engage in a massive reform, on the scale of our Meiji Restoration, and they could change their governments and bring about a renewal of spirit among their peoples. If that could happen they would indeed be fortunate. However, it is more likely that would never happen, and within a few short years they will be wiped out from the world with their lands divided among the civilized nations. Why is this so? Simply at a time when the spread of civilization and enlightenment (*bummei kaika*) has a force akin to that of measles, China and Korea violate the natural law of its spread. They forcibly try to avoid it by shutting off air from their rooms. Without air, they suffocate to death. It is said that neighbors must extend helping hands to one another because their relations are inseparable. Today's China and Korea have not done a thing for Japan. From the perspectives of civilized Westerners, they may see what is happening in China and Korea and judge Japan accordingly, because of the three countries' geographical proximity. The governments of China and Korea still retain their autocratic manners and do not abide by the rule of law. Westerners may consider Japan likewise a lawless society. Natives of China and Korea are deep in their hocus pocus of nonscientific behavior. Western scholars may think that Japan still remains a country dedicated to the *yin* and *yang* and five elements.[1] Chinese are mean-spirited and shameless, and the chivalry of the Japanese people is lost to the Westerners. Koreans punish their convicts in an atrocious manner, and that is imputed to the Japanese as heartless people. There are many more examples I can cite. It is not different from the case of a righteous man living in a neighborhood of a town known for foolishness, lawlessness, atrocity, and heartlessness. His action is so rare that it is always buried under the ugliness of his neighbors' activities. When these incidents are multiplied, that can affect our normal conduct of diplomatic affairs. How unfortunate it is for Japan.

What must we do today? We do not have time to wait for the enlightenment of our neighbors so that we can work together toward the development of Asia. It is better for us to leave the ranks of Asian nations and cast our lot with civilized nations of the West. As for the way of dealing with China and Korea, no special treatment is necessary just because they happen to be our neighbors. We simply follow the manner of the Westerners in knowing how to treat them. Any person who cherishes a bad friend cannot escape his bad notoriety. We simply erase from our minds our bad friends in Asia.

1 *Yin* and *yang* is a traditional Chinese duality (hot/cold, active/passive, male/female) illustrated by a circle divided by an "s" to show unity within duality. The five elements suggest another traditional, prescientific idea that everything is made of five basic ingredients.

51

Images from Japan: Views of Westernization

This selection consists of three prints by Japanese artists. The first print, called *Beef Eater,* illustrates a character in Kanagaki Robun's *Aguranabe* (1871). The author, a popular newspaper humorist, parodies a new class of urban Westernized Japanese who carry watches and umbrellas and eat beef (banned by Buddhist law for centuries but added to the Japanese diet by Westerners).

The second piece, called *Monkey Show Dressing Room* (1879), by Honda Kinkachiro, shows monkeys dressing in a European style to "ape" the foreigners. Notice how much more Westernized the targets of this print are, just eight years after Figure 5 was created. What is this print's message? What is the artist's attitude toward Westernization?

The third piece, *The Exotic White Man,* shows a child born to a Western man and a Japanese woman. What is the artist's message? Does the artist favor such unions? What does the artist think of Westerners?

Thinking Historically

Prints, like cartoons, are a shorthand that must capture an easily recognizable trait. What, evidently, were the widely understood Japanese images of the West? Where do you think these stereotypes of the West came from? Do you see any signs in these prints of ambivalence on the part of the artist?

Beef Eater, from Kanagaki Robun, *Aguranabe* (1871) in G. B. Sansom, *The Western World and Japan* (Tokyo: Charles E. Tuttle Co., 1977). Honda Kinkachiro, *Monkey Show Dressing Room,* in Julia Meech-Pekarik, *The World of the Meiji Print* (New York: John Weatherhill, 1986). Japanese color print, late 19th c., Dutch private collection, in C. A. Burland, *The Exotic White Man* (New York: McGraw Hill, 1969), fig. 38.

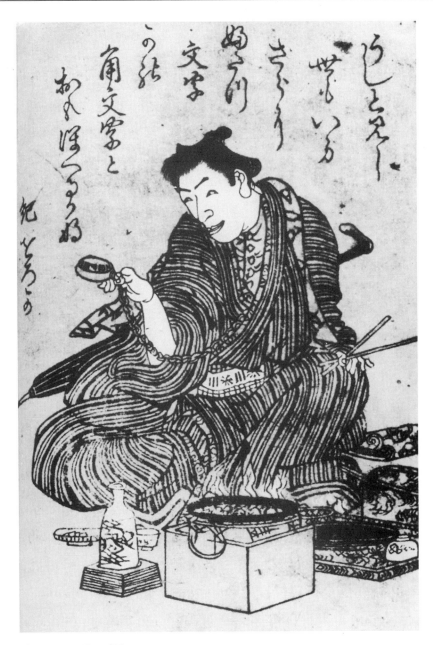

Figure 5. *Beef Eater.*

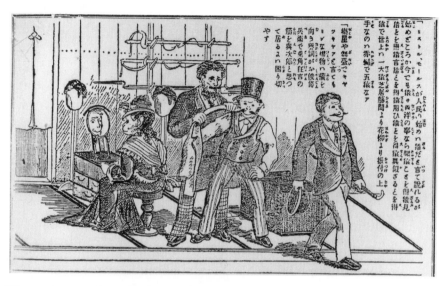

Figure 6. *Monkey Show Dressing Room.*

Figure 7. *The Exotic White Man.*

52

Primary

SWAMI VIVEKANANDA
Oh India, Forget Not

India's Westernization was less voluntary than Japan's. While Japan successfully limited European colonialism to a few seaports in the seventeenth century and was not forced to deal with the West again until after Admiral Perry's steam-age arrival in 1853, India became increasingly colonized by England throughout the eighteenth and nineteenth centuries. Because of India's long history as a British colony, aspects of Westernization there were deeper and more complex, the most obvious being use of the English language.

A colonial and foreign tongue, English had the advantage of uniting a country with dozens of regional languages (some of which were also imposed by foreign conquerors), while at the same time providing access to universities and a body of knowledge and literature as advanced as any in the world. English instruction — rather than ancient Sanskrit or Hindi or another Indian regional language — was championed by Britons who thought it would make Indians loyal and by Indians who thought it would unite them as a nation. The Indian use of English had its detractors, too: Britons who thought it dangerous or unseemly, and Britons and Indians who thought it patronizing and demeaning.

The debate over teaching English or Indian languages was part of a larger debate about the relative value of Western and Indian culture. Increasingly, toward the end of the nineteenth century as science took center stage in English culture, Indians found themselves torn between the claim of science and the appeal of traditional Indian religious knowledge.

Swami Vivekananda (1863–1902) was a Hindu religious leader who swayed Westerners as well as Indians with his eloquence. Reared in a middle-class family and intending to study law, he was transformed by the preaching of Sri Rāmakrishna (1836–1886), a poor peasant who had no formal training in either English or Sanskrit, the language of ancient Hinduism. Vivekananda traveled the world sharing his teacher's message that god was one, and all religions equal, a message of tolerance and brotherhood that pleased audiences from

From *The Complete Works of the Swami Vivekananda*, vol. 4, in *Sources of Indian Tradition*, vol. 2, ed. Stephen Hay (New York: Columbia University Press, 1986), 79–82.

Chicago (1893) to England. He returned to India to build institutions that would aid the poor, renew Hindu devotions, and give Indians pride in their heritage.

Written in Bengal in 1899, this selection is excerpted from one of his last essays. What kind of India does Vivekananda want Indians to create? Would you call his appeal anti-Western or pro-Indian? Do you see any drawbacks to his plan for India?

Thinking Historically

Notice how Vivekananda constructs his message dialectically out of opposing pairs. How does he transform a conflict between India and the West into a domestic conflict between Indians, and then into a personal, moral conflict for each of his readers? What is the effect of that persuasive rhetorical style? Does it encourage or discourage debate? Does it lead to new solutions or reinforce the old? Does Vivekananda want Indians to make decisions for themselves or to adopt a particular set of Hindu ideas?

It has been said before that India is slowly awakening through her friction with the outside nations, and, as the result of this little awakening is the appearance, to a certain extent, of free and independent thought in modern India. On one side is modern Western science, dazzling the eyes with the brilliance of myriad suns, and driving in the chariot of hard and fast facts collected by the application of tangible powers direct in their incision; on the other are the hopeful and strengthening traditions of her ancient forefathers, in the days when she was at the zenith of her glory — traditions that have been brought out of the pages of her history by the great sages of her own land and outside, that run for numberless years and centuries through her every vein with the quickening of life drawn from universal love, traditions that reveal unsurpassed valor, superhuman genius, and supreme spirituality, which are the envy of the gods — these inspire her with future hopes. On one side, rank materialism, plenitude of fortune, accumulation of gigantic power, and intense sense pursuits, have through foreign literature caused a tremendous stir; on the other, through the confounding din of all these discordant sounds, she hears, in low yet unmistakable accents, the heart-rending cries of her ancient gods, cutting her to the quick. There lie before her various strange luxuries introduced from the West — celestial drinks, costly well-served food, splendid apparel, magnificent palaces, new modes of conveyance — new manners, new fashions, dressed in which moves about the well-educated girl in shameless freedom; all these are arousing unfelt desires in her; again, the scene changes and in its place appear, with stern presence, Sītā,[1] Sāvitrī,[2] austere religious vows, fastings, the forest retreat, the matted locks and orange garb of the semi-naked Sannyasin, Samadhi, and the search after the Self. On one side, is the independence of Western societies based on self-interest; on the other, is the extreme self-sacrifice of the Aryan society. In this violent conflict, is it strange that Indian society should be tossed up and down? Of the West, the goal is — individual independence, the language — money-making education, the means — politics; of India, the goal is — Mukti [or *moksa*, release], the language — the Veda, the means — renunciation. For a time, modern India thinks, as it were: I am running this worldly life of mine in vain expectation of uncertain spiritual welfare hereafter, which has spread its fascination over me; and again, lo! spellbound she listens: "Here, in this world of death and change, O man, where is thy happiness?"

On one side, New India is saying: "We should have full freedom in the selection of husband and wife; because, the marriage in which are involved the happiness and misery of all our future life, we must have the right to determine, according to our own free will." On the other, Old India is dictating: "Marriage is not for sense enjoyment, but to perpetuate the race. This is the Indian conception of marriage. By the producing of children, you are contributing to, and are responsible for, the future good or evil of the society. Hence, society has the right to dictate whom you shall marry and whom you shall not. That form of marriage obtains in society, which is conducive most to its well-being; do you give up your desire of individual pleasure for the good of the many."

On one side New India is saying: "If we only adopt Western ideas, Western language, Western food, Western dress, and Western manners, we shall be as strong and powerful as the Western nations"; on the other, Old India is saying: "Fools! By imitation, other's ideas never become one's own — nothing, unless earned, is your own. Does the ass in the lion's skin become the lion?"

On one side, New India is saying: "What the Western nations do are surely good, otherwise how did they become so great?" On the other side, Old India is saying: "The flash of lightning is intensely bright, but only for a moment; look out, boys, it is dazzling your eyes. Beware!"

Have we not then to learn anything from the West? Must we not needs try and exert ourselves for better things? Are we perfect? Is our society entirely spotless, without any flaw? There are many things to learn, we must struggle for new and higher things till we die — struggle is the end of human life. Sri Rāmakrishna used to say: "As long as I

[1] Wife of Rama, the model of fidelity. [Ed.]
[2] High caste associated with clerical work. [Ed.]

live, so long I learn." That man or that society which has nothing to learn is already in the jaws of death. Yes, learn we must many things from the West, but there are fears as well.

A certain young man of little understanding used always to blame Hindu Shastras before Sri Rāmakrishna. One day he praised the *Bhagavad-Gītā,* on which Sri Rāmakrishna said: "Methinks some European pandit has praised the *Gītā,* and so he has also followed suit."

O India, this is your terrible danger. The spell of imitating the West is getting such a strong hold upon you, that what is good or what is bad is no longer decided by reason, judgment, discrimination, or reference to the Shastras. Whatever ideas, whatever manners the white men praise or like, are good; whatever things they dislike or censure are bad! Alas! What can be a more tangible proof of foolishness than this?

The Western ladies move freely everywhere — therefore, that is good; they choose for themselves their husbands — therefore, that is the highest step of advancement; the Westerners disapprove of our dress, decorations, food, and ways of living — therefore, they must be very bad; the Westerners condemn image-worship as sinful — surely then, image-worship is the greatest sin, there is no doubt of it!

The Westerners say that worshiping a single Deity is fruitful of the highest spiritual good — therefore, let us throw our Gods and Goddesses into the river Ganges! The Westerners hold caste distinctions to be obnoxious — therefore, let all the different castes be jumbled into one! The Westerners say that child-marriage is the root of all evils — therefore, that is also very bad, of a certainty it is!

We are not discussing here whether these customs deserve countenance or rejection; but if the mere disapproval of the Westerners be the measure of the abominableness of our manners and customs, then it is our duty to raise our emphatic protest against it. . . .

Oh India! With this mere echoing of others, with this base imitation of others, with this dependence on others, this slavish weakness, this vile detestable cruelty, wouldst thou, with these provisions only, scale the highest pinnacle of civilization and greatness? Wouldst thou attain, by means of thy disgraceful cowardice, that freedom deserved only by the brave and the heroic? Oh India! Forget not that the ideal of thy womanhood is Sītā, Sāvitrī, Damayanti; forget not that the God thou worshipest is the great Ascetic of ascetics, the all-renouncing Shankara, the Lord of Uma; forget not that thy marriage, thy wealth, thy life are not for sense-pleasure, are not for thy individual personal happiness; forget not that thou art born as a sacrifice to the *Mother's* altar; forget not that thy social order is but the reflex of the Infinite Universal Motherhood; forget not that the lower classes, the ignorant, the poor, the illiterate, the cobbler, the sweeper, are thy flesh and blood, thy brothers. Thou brave one, be bold, take courage, be proud that thou art an Indian, and proudly proclaim: "I am an Indian, every

Indian is my brother." Say: "The ignorant Indian, the poor and destitute Indian, the Brāhman Indian, the Pariah Indian, is my brother."
Thou too clad with but a rag round thy loins proudly proclaim at the
top of thy voice: "The Indian is my brother, the Indian is my life,
India's gods and goddesses are my God, India's society is the cradle of
my infancy, the pleasure-garden of my youth, the sacred heaven, the
Vārānasi, of my old age." Say, brother: "The soil of India is my highest
heaven, the good of India is my good," and repeat and pray day and
night: "O Thou Lord of Gauri, O Thou Mother of the Universe, vouch-
safe manliness unto me! O Thou Mother of Strength, take away my
weakness, take away my unmanliness, and — *Make me a Man!"*

53

MOHANDAS K. GANDHI
From *Hind Swaraj*

Swaraj means "self-rule" or "independence." At least, that is its literal meaning. This selection from Mohandas K. Gandhi's essay by
that title shows that the meaning may be more complex. Gandhi
began to develop his ideas of *Hind Swaraj,* or Indian Home Rule,
after he sailed from England to South Africa in 1908. An early version
of this essay, published then, was reissued in its present form in 1921,
two years after he returned to his birthplace, India, and again in 1938,
in the last years of struggle against British rule.

After Gandhi's introduction, the essay takes the form of questions
and answers. The questions are posed by a presumed "reader" of
Gandhi's paper. As "editor," Gandhi explains what he means. What
does he mean by "swaraj"? Is it more important to him that the English leave India, or that India not become like England? What does
Gandhi disapprove of in modern English civilization? What does he
mean by passive resistance or soul-force (Satyagraha)? Why does he
think it is preferable to violence, or body-force? What kind of India
would Gandhi have tried to create had he lived?

M. K. Gandhi, *Hind Swaraj* (Ahmedabad, India: Navajivan, 1938), 15–16, 26–27, 28, 30–31, 32–33, 58–60, 69–71, 82–85.

Thinking Historically

Notice the international background of this distinctly Indian independence movement, as Gandhi explains the circumstances of publication in the first section. Trained as a lawyer in England, Gandhi practiced law in South Africa. There he published a pamphlet in Gujarati, a regional Indian language, in a general Indian publication. Written in response to Indian anarchists that he met in London, the pamphlet was banned in India (its intended audience), so Gandhi translated it into English, which the English government of India allowed. The Indian independence movement — whether the anarachists' or Gandhi's — cannot be understood solely within the context of India; other languages, cultures, and peoples were intrinsic to its vitality. How is this "cross-cultural approach" in India different from the situation in Japan? Were the Japanese in a better position than the Indians to renounce the West and develop their own identity? Did they? Is Gandhi's renunciation of the West even more extreme?

Notice Gandhi's format for making his argument. Does the interview technique allow for an exchange of two points of view, or is it merely a guise for Gandhi to seem most persuasive?

Some have said that Gandhi's nonviolent and anti-Western plan for Indian independence was a distinctly Indian solution. If such is the case, how could a distinctly Indian solution come from someone who spent most of his adult life abroad? And how is it that a Western-trained lawyer like Gandhi should be the one to urge the creation of a non-Western, nonmodern India along the lines of Hindu holy men like Swami Vivekananda (who himself at one time had hoped to be a Western-trained lawyer)?

A Word of Explanation

It is certainly my good fortune that this booklet of mine is receiving wide attention. The original is in Gujarati. It has a chequered career. It was first published in the columns of the *Indian Opinion* of South Africa. It was written in 1908 during my return voyage from London to South Africa in answer to the Indian school of violence and its prototype in South Africa. I came in contact with every known Indian anarchist in London. Their bravery impressed me, but I felt that their zeal was misguided. I felt that violence was no remedy for India's ills, and that her civilization required the use of a different and higher weapon for self-protection. The Satyagraha of South Africa was still an infant hardly two years old. But it had developed sufficiently to permit me to write of it with some degree of confidence. What I wrote was so much appreciated that it was published as a booklet. It attracted some attention in India. The Bombay Government prohibited its circulation. I replied by publishing its translation. I thought it was due to my English friends that they should know its contents.

In my opinion it is a book which can be put into the hands of a child. It teaches the gospel of love in place of that of hate. It replaces violence with self-sacrifice. It pits soul force against brute force. It has gone through several editions and I commend it to those who would care to read it. I withdraw nothing except one word of it, and that in deference to a lady friend.

The booklet is a severe condemnation of "modern civilization." It was written in 1908. My conviction is deeper today than ever. I feel that if India will discard "modern civilization," she can only gain by doing so.

But I would warn the reader against thinking that I am today aiming at the Swaraj described therein. I know that India is not ripe for it. It may seem an impertinence to say so. But such is my conviction. I am individually working for the self-rule pictured therein. But today my corporate activity is undoubtedly devoted to the attainment of Parliamentary Swaraj in accordance with the wishes of the people of India. I am not aiming at destroying railways or hospitals, though I would certainly welcome their natural destruction. Neither railways nor hospitals are a test of a high and pure civilization. At best they are a necessary evil. Neither adds one inch to the moral stature of a nation. Nor am I aiming at a permanent destruction of law courts, much as I regard it as a "consummation devoutly to be wished." Still less am I trying to destroy all machinery and mills. It requires a higher simplicity and renunciation than the people are today prepared for.

The only part of the programme which is now being carried out is that of non-violence. But I regret to have to confess that even that is not being carried out in the spirit of the book. If it were, India would establish Swaraj in a day. If India adopted the doctrine of love as an active part of her religion and introduced it in her politics. Swaraj would descend upon India from heaven. But I am painfully aware that that event is far off as yet.

I offer these comments because I observe that much is being quoted from the booklet to discredit the present movement. I have even seen writings suggesting that I am playing a deep game, that I am using the present turmoil to foist my fads on India, and am making religious experiments at India's expense. I can only answer that Satyagraha is made of sterner stuff. There is nothing reserved and nothing secret in it. A portion of the whole theory of life described in *Hind Swaraj* is undoubtedly being carried into practice. There is no danger attendant upon the whole of it being practised. But it is not right to scare away people by reproducing from my writings passages that are irrelevant to the issue before the country.

Young India, January, 1921   M. K. Gandhi

What Is Swaraj?

READER: I have now learnt what the Congress has done to make India one nation, how the Partition has caused an awakening, and how discontent and unrest have spread through the land. I would now like to know your views on Swaraj. I fear that our interpretation is not the same as yours.

EDITOR: It is quite possible that we do not attach the same meaning to the term. You and I and all Indians are impatient to obtain Swaraj, but we are certainly not decided as to what it is. To drive the English out of India is a thought heard from many mouths, but it does not seem that many have properly considered why it should be so. I must ask you a question. Do you think that it is necessary to drive away the English, if we get all we want?

READER: I should ask of them only one thing, that is: "Please leave our country." If, after they have complied with this request, their withdrawal from India means that they are still in India, I should have no objection. Then we would understand that, in their language, the word "gone" is equivalent to "remained."

EDITOR: Well then, let us suppose that the English have retired. What will you do then?

READER: That question cannot be answered at this stage. The state after withdrawal will depend largely upon the manner of it. If, as you assume, they retire, it seems to me we shall still keep their constitution and shall carry on the Government. If they simply retire for the asking we should have an army, etc., ready at hand. We should, therefore, have no difficulty in carrying on the Government.

EDITOR: You may think so; I do not. But I will not discuss the matter just now. I have to answer your question, and that I can do well by asking you several questions. Why do you want to drive away the English?

READER: Because India has become impoverished by their Government. They take away our money from year to year. The most important posts are reserved for themselves. We are kept in a state of slavery. They behave insolently towards us and disregard our feelings.

EDITOR: If they do not take our money away, become gentle, and give us responsible posts, would you still consider their presence to be harmful?

READER: That question is useless. It is similar to the question whether there is any harm in associating with a tiger if he changes his nature. Such a question is sheer waste of time. When a tiger changes his nature, Englishmen will change theirs. This is not possible, and to believe it to be possible is contrary to human experience.

EDITOR: Supposing we get Self-Government similar to what the Canadians and the South Africans have, will it be good enough?

READER: That question also is useless. We may get it when we have the same powers; we shall then hoist our own flag. As is Japan, so must India be. We must own our navy, our army, and we must have our own splendour, and then will India's voice ring through the world.

EDITOR: You have drawn the picture well. In effect it means this: that we want English rule without the Englishman. You want the tiger's nature, but not the tiger; that is to say, you would make India English. And when it becomes English, it will be called not Hindustan but *Englistan*. This is not the Swaraj that I want.

Civilization

READER: Now you will have to explain what you mean by civilization.

EDITOR: Let us first consider what state of things is described by the word "civilization." Its true test lies in the fact that people living in it make bodily welfare the object of life. We will take some examples. The people of Europe today live in better-built houses than they did a hundred years ago. This is considered an emblem of civilization, and this is also a matter to promote bodily happiness. Formerly, they wore skins, and used spears as their weapons. Now, they wear long trousers, and, for embellishing their bodies, they wear a variety of clothing, and, instead of spears, they carry with them revolvers containing five or more chambers. If people of a certain country, who have hitherto not been in the habit of wearing much clothing, boots, etc., adopt European clothing, they are supposed to have become civilized out of savagery. Formerly, in Europe, people ploughed their lands mainly by manual labour. Now, one man can plough a vast tract by means of steam engines and can thus amass great wealth. This is called a sign of civilization. Formerly, only a few men wrote valuable books. Now, anybody writes and prints anything he likes and poisons people's minds. Formerly, men travelled in waggons. Now, they fly through the air in trains at the rate of four hundred and more miles per day. This is considered the height of civilization. It has been stated that, as men progress, they shall be able to travel in airship and reach any part of the world in a few hours. Men will not need the use of their hands and feet. They will press a button, and they will have their clothing at their side.

They will press another button, and they will have their newspaper. A third, and motor-car will be in waiting for them. They will have a variety of delicately dished up food. Everything will be done by machinery. Formerly, when people wanted to fight with one another, they measured between them their bodily strength; now it is possible to take away thousands of lives by one man working behind a gun from a hill. This is civilization. Formerly, men worked in the open air only as much as they liked. Now thousands of workmen meet together and for the sake of maintenance work in factories or mines. Their condition is worse than that of beasts. They are obliged to work, at the risk of their lives, at most dangerous occupations, for the sake of millionaires. Formerly, men were made slaves under physical compulsion. Now they are enslaved by temptation of money and of the luxuries that money can buy. There are now diseases of which people never dreamt before, and an army of doctors is engaged in finding out their cures, and so hospitals have increased. This is a test of civilization. Formerly, special messengers were required and much expense was incurred in order to send letters; today, anyone can abuse his fellow by means of a letter for one penny. True, at the same cost, one can send one's thanks also. Formerly, people had two or three meals consisting of home-made bread and vegetables; now, they require something to eat every two hours so that they have hardly leisure for anything else. What more need I say? All this you can ascertain from several authoritative books. These are all true tests of civilization. And if anyone speaks to the contrary, know that he is ignorant. This civilization takes note neither of morality nor of religion. Its votaries calmly state that their business is not to teach religion. Some even consider it to be a superstitious growth. Others put on the cloak of religion, and prate about morality. But, after twenty years' experience, I have come to the conclusion that immorality is often taught in the name of morality. Even a child can understand that in all I have described above there can be no inducement to morality. Civilization seeks to increase bodily comforts, and it fails miserably even in doing so. . . .

How Can India Become Free?

READER: I appreciate your views about civilization. I will have to think over them. I cannot take them in all at once. What, then, holding the views you do, would you suggest for freeing India?

EDITOR: I do not expect my views to be accepted all of a sudden. My duty is to place them before readers like yourself. Time can be trusted to do the rest. We have already examined the conditions for freeing India, but we have done so indirectly; we will now do so directly. It is a world-known maxim that the removal of the cause of a disease results in the removal of the disease itself. Similarly if the cause of India's slavery be removed, India can become free.

READER: If Indian civilization is, as you say, the best of all, how do you account for India's slavery?

EDITOR: This civilization is unquestionably the best, but it is to be observed that all civilizations have been on their trial. That civilization which is permanent outlives it. Because the sons of India were found wanting, its civilization has been placed in jeopardy. But its strength is to be seen in its ability to survive the shock. Moreover, the whole of India is not touched. Those alone who have been affected by Western civilization have become enslaved. We measure the universe by our own miserable foot-rule. When we are slaves, we think that the whole universe is enslaved. Because we are in an abject condition, we think that the whole of India is in that condition. As a matter of fact, it is not so, yet it is as well to impute our slavery to the whole of India. But if we bear in mind the above fact, we can see that if we become free, India is free. And in this thought you have a definition of Swaraj. It is Swaraj when we learn to rule ourselves. It is, therefore, in the palm of our hands. Do not consider this Swaraj to be like a dream. There is no idea of sitting still. The Swaraj that I wish to picture is such that, after we have once realized it, we shall endeavour to the end of our life-time to persuade others to do likewise. But such Swaraj has to be experienced, by each one for himself. One drowning man will never save another. Slaves ourselves, it would be a mere pretension to think of freeing others. Now you will have seen that it is not necessary for us to have as our goal the expulsion of the English. If the English become Indianized, we can accommodate them. If they wish to remain in India along with their civilization, there is no room for them. It lies with us to bring about such a state of things.

READER: It is impossible that Englishmen should ever become Indianized.

EDITOR: To say that is equivalent to saying that the English have no humanity in them. And it is really beside the point whether they become so or not. If we keep our own house in order, only those who are fit to live in it will remain. Others will leave of their own accord. Such things occur within the experience of all of us. . . .

Passive Resistance

READER: Is there any historical evidence as to the success of what you have called soul-force or truth-force? No instance seems to have happened of any nation having risen through soul-force. I still think that the evil-doers will not cease doing evil without physical punishment.

EDITOR: The [Hindu] poet Tulsidas [1532–1623] has said: "Of religion, pity, or love, is the root, as egotism of the body. Therefore, we should not abandon pity so long as we are alive." This appears to me to be a scientific truth. We have evidence of its working at every step. The universe would disappear without the existence of that force. . . .

The fact that there are so many men still alive in the world shows that it is based not on the force of arms but on the force of truth or love. Therefore, the greatest and most unimpeachable evidence of the success of this force is to be found in the fact that, in spite of the wars of the world, it still lives on.

Thousands, indeed tens of thousands, depend for their existence on a very active working of this force. Little quarrels of millions of families in their daily lives disappear before the exercise of this force. Hundreds of nations live in peace. History does not and cannot take note of this fact. History is really a record of every interruption of the even working of the force of love or of the soul. Two brothers quarrel; one of them repents and re-awakens the love that was lying dormant in him; the two again begin to live in peace; nobody takes note of this. But if the two brothers, through the intervention of solicitors or some other reason take up arms or go to law — which is another form of the exhibition of brute force, — their doings would be immediately noticed in the press, they would be the talk of their neighbours and would probably go down to history. And what is true of families and communities is true of nations. There is no reason to believe that there is one law for families and another for nations. History, then, is a record of an interruption of the course of nature. Soul-force, being natural, is not noted in history.

READER: According to what you say, it is plain that instances of this kind of passive resistance are not to be found in history. It is necessary to understand this passive resistance more fully. It will be better, therefore, if you enlarge upon it.

EDITOR: Passive resistance is a method of securing rights by personal suffering; it is the reverse of resistance by arms. When I refuse to do a thing that is repugnant to my conscience, I use soul-force. For instance, the Government of the day has passed a law which is applicable to me. I do not like it. If by using violence I force the Government to repeal the law, I am employing what may be termed body-force. If I do not obey the law and accept the penalty for its breach, I use soul-force. It involves sacrifice of self.

Everybody admits that sacrifice of self is infinitely superior to sacrifice of others. Moreover, if this kind of force is used in a cause that is unjust, only the person using it suffers. He does not make others suffer for his mistakes. Men have before now done many things which were subsequently found to have been wrong. No man can claim that he is absolutely in the right or that a particular thing is wrong because he thinks so, but it is wrong for him so long as that is his deliberate judgment. It is therefore meet that he should not do that which he knows to be wrong, and suffer the consequence whatever it may be. This is the key to the use of soul-force. . . .

54

JAWAHARLAL NEHRU

Gandhi

Mohandas K. Gandhi and Jawaharlal Nehru were the two most important leaders of India's national independence movement. Though they worked together and Nehru was Gandhi's choice as the first Indian prime minister, they expressed in their personalities and ideas two very different Indias. How would you describe these two Indias? Was it Gandhi's or Nehru's vision of the future that was realized? Who do you think was a better guide for India?

Thinking Historically

Think of Gandhi and Nehru as the two sides of the Indian struggle for independence. Did India benefit from having both of these sides represented? What would have happened if there had been only Gandhi's view or only Nehru's?

How was the debate in India about the influence of the West different from the debate in Japan?

I imagine that Gandhiji is not so vague about the objective as he sometimes appears to be. He is passionately desirous of going in a certain direction, but this is wholly at variance with modern ideas and conditions, and he has so far been unable to fit the two, or to chalk out all the intermediate steps leading to his goal. Hence the appearance of vagueness and avoidance of clarity. But his general inclination has been clear enough for a quarter of a century, ever since he started formulating his philosophy in South Africa. I do not know if those early writ-

J. Nehru, *Toward Freedom: The Autobiography of Jawaharlal Nehru* (New York: John Day Company, 1942).

ings still represent his views. I doubt if they do so in their entirety, but they do help us to understand the background of his thought.

"India's salvation consists," he wrote in 1909, "in unlearning what she has learned during the last fifty years. The railways, telegraphs, hospitals, lawyers, doctors, and suchlike have all to go; and the so-called upper classes have to learn consciously, religiously, and deliberately the simple peasant life, knowing it to be a life giving true happiness." And again: "Every time I get into a railway car or use a motor bus I know that I am doing violence to my sense of what is right"; "to attempt to reform the world by means of highly artificial and speedy locomotion is to attempt the impossible."

All this seems to me utterly wrong and harmful doctrine, and impossible of achievement. Behind it lies Gandhiji's love and praise of poverty and suffering and the ascetic life. For him progress and civilization consist not in the multiplication of wants, of higher standards of living, "but in the deliberate and voluntary restriction of wants, which promotes real happiness and contentment, and increases the capacity for service." If these premises are once accepted, it becomes easy to follow the rest of Gandhiji's thought and to have a better understanding of his activities. But most of us do not accept those premises, and yet we complain later on when we find that his activities are not to our liking.

Personally I dislike the praise of poverty and suffering. I do not think they are at all desirable, and they ought to be abolished. Nor do I appreciate the ascetic life as a social ideal, though it may suit individuals. I understand and appreciate simplicity, equality, self-control; but not the mortification of the flesh. Just as an athlete requires to train his body, I believe that the mind and habits have also to be trained and brought under control. It would be absurd to expect that a person who is given to too much self-indulgence can endure much suffering or show unusual self-control or behave like a hero when the crisis comes. To be in good moral condition requires at least as much training as to be in good physical condition. But that certainly does not mean asceticism or self-mortification.

Nor do I appreciate in the least the idealization of the "simple peasant life." I have almost a horror of it, and instead of submitting to it myself I want to drag out even the peasantry from it, not to urbanization, but to the spread of urban cultural facilities to rural areas. Far from his life's giving me true happiness, it would be almost as bad as imprisonment for me. What is there in "The Man with the Hoe" to idealize over? Crushed and exploited for innumerable generations, he is only little removed from the animals who keep him company.

> Who made him dead to rapture and despair,
> A thing that grieves not and that never hopes,
> Stolid and stunned, a brother to the ox?

This desire to get away from the mind of man to primitive conditions where mind does not count, seems to me quite incomprehensible. The very thing that is the glory and triumph of man is decried and discouraged, and a physical environment which will oppress the mind and prevent its growth is considered desirable. Present-day civilization is full of evils, but it is also full of good; and it has the capacity in it to rid itself of those evils. To destroy it root and branch is to remove that capacity from it and revert to a dull, sunless, and miserable existence. But even if that were desirable it is an impossible undertaking. We cannot stop the river of change or cut ourselves adrift from it, and psychologically we who have eaten of the apple of Eden cannot forget that taste and go back to primitiveness.

It is difficult to argue this, for the two standpoints are utterly different. Gandhiji is always thinking in terms of personal salvation and of sin, while most of us have society's welfare uppermost in our minds. I find it difficult to grasp the idea of sin, and perhaps it is because of this that I cannot appreciate Gandhiji's general outlook.

55

JIWEI CI

From *Dialectic of the Chinese Revolution*

Jiwei Ci, a modern philosopher and historian, argues that the Opium War (1840–1842) was a critical moment in the history of Chinese national consciousness. After the British defeat of China in 1842, the Chinese could no longer maintain their superiority in all things. Rather, they began to distinguish between cultural superiority (which they still claimed) and technological superiority (which they ceded to the West). Why, according to Jiwei Ci, was this distinction a recipe for disaster?

How was this Chinese distinction between culture and technology similar to the ways in which Vivekananda and Gandhi explained the

Jiwei Ci, *Dialectic of the Chinese Revolution: From Utopianism to Hedonism* (Stanford: Stanford University Press, 1994), 25–32, 34.

differences between India and the West? Would China and India have been more successful if they had, following the lead of a Fukuzawa or Nehru, adopted Western culture as well as Western technology?

Thinking Historically

Was it contradictory for Chinese thinkers to accept Western technology while retaining traditional culture, as Jiwei Ci maintains? Was it reasonable, or impossible, for China to borrow some aspects of the West while rejecting others? Is the lack of agreement between the "means" and the "ends" a sign of cultural crisis?

... It is arguable that China might have developed capitalism on its own initiative, in which case what would have happened would not be perceived as Westernization, with its implications of cultural defeat and loss of self-identity. Be that as it may, China's actual transformation occurred under, if it was not exactly set in motion by, the Western impact (a hackneyed but still accurate description). It made a world of difference, both to the actual process of change and to the perception of its nature, that what might (or might not) have happened voluntarily happened under coercion, that what might (or might not) have occurred through the dynamic of domestic factors occurred under the overwhelming influence of foreign powers. Without such influence, China might well have "modernized" in one or more of the ways that this problematic term implies, but the history of modern Chinese consciousness would have taken a vastly different course, and this in turn could not but have made an enormous difference to the course of modern Chinese history itself. But for this history of consciousness, China's Marxist detour on the road to capitalism, as well as the conscious peripheralization of a formerly self-centered civilization, would hardly have happened.

In this light, the Opium War marked, both materially and symbolically, the birth of "modern" China. It was a birth, however, that was to be recognized as such only when the effects of that violent encounter with the West, followed by more such encounters that ended in China's defeat, became clear and irreversible. One of the first such effects beyond the gradual territorial dismemberment of China by the Western powers was the division of a civilization the Chinese had hitherto viewed as *uniformly* excellent into the separate categories of value and technology, ends and means, culture and power. China could retain its sense of superiority only in the one but no longer in the other. Such a disjunction, with its traumatic acknowledgment of an alien culture as technologically superior and fitter for survival, had been totally absent from the Chinese way of viewing themselves and the world. And so had been the explicit formulation and rationale it was later to acquire in terms of *Zhongxue weiti, xixue weiyong* (Chinese learning as substance, Western learning as application), which proposed the opportunistic compromise of sticking to the Chinese way in what was supposedly important (*ti*) but adopting the Western way in what was necessary for self-preservation yet supposedly of merely practical significance (*yong*). Implicit in the willingness even to contemplate such a compromise was an awareness, a slow and reluctant awareness, of something that had never happened to China before.

China had seen alien rulers on its throne, the latest being the Manchus of the Qing dynasty (1644–1911), who ruled China at the time of the Opium War. But each time the victor ended up assimilating to, rather than assimilating, China. The Manchus, who themselves first conquered and then assimilated to China, could not be expected to know without one painful lesson after another that the entrance of the European powers had changed the rules of the game. "Unlike the Manchus, modern Europeans had no need to assimilate to China. And the Chinese, unable to take them in, were just as unable to throw them out so long as the technological gap endured." When the nature of this new situation finally began to sink in, however imperfectly, the fact that the West, which China regarded as culturally inferior, had repeatedly proved to be militarily and technologically superior took on a significance that earlier, superficially similar, events had never had. Where China had enjoyed a sense of uniform or integral superiority to the rest of the world, it now had to resort to what we may call the compartmentalization of superiority, with China still claiming superiority in cultural values but conceding superiority to the West in military might and technology.

It was, then, the function of the *ti-yong* formula to assign importance to the one realm and to deny it to the other. At a time when China had no choice but to adopt Western ways for the sake of self-preservation, the *ti-yong* rationale served conveniently, but only conceptually, to relegate those humiliating adoptions to the realm of cultural insignificance. The need for cultural change was thereby denied, and cultural pride seemingly preserved, in a desperate situation that imperiled nothing less than national survival. It had taken more than four decades following the Opium War, and no small amount of inventiveness, to arrive at a formula that allowed China to copy the West selectively with good conscience and at the same time ministered to China's cultural pride by finding a way of treating what China was copying as culturally irrelevant. . . .

For what had happened between China and the West was at bottom a confrontation between cultures. The West, driven by the dynamic of capitalism, could not but come and knock on the doors of China. China, following the dictates of its largely subsistence economy, with equal predictability tried to keep its doors shut. And in the ensuing contests of military strength, of which the Opium War was only the first, there was no way in which China could avoid defeat. For it can hardly be a matter for doubt which kind of culture, once it comes to fruition, has not only a greater need but also a greater capacity for conquest. There was thus a certain inevitability, first, about the confrontation between China and the West because of capitalism's *need* for conquest (in the interest of market expansion) and, second, about China's defeat because of capitalism's *capacity* for conquest. From the military point of view, the victory was one of rifles and gunboats over more primitive weapons. But behind the West's military victory was its more fundamental cultural triumph — the triumph of capitalism over feudalism. . . .

The triumph of the West was not, however, simply one of superior values. Who is to say that European civilization was superior to Chinese civilization, or vice versa, except in a de facto sense? The fact was that the West had won, and once the West had won, it was in a position to lay down, by maintaining a disparity in power, what was better. . . . [T]he defeated can attain parity with the victor only by becoming like the victor — first superficially, then more and more fundamentally. The defeated otherwise will stay in the shape that caused their defeat in the first place, until they swallow their defeat as if it were their desert, accede to the code of the victor, and change themselves in the victor's image. This is indeed what was to happen to China in due course, but not before the Chinese had realized that the West's victory was not merely one of military and technological superiority but one of the victor's cultural code as well.

Little did China know at the time that the Western technology capable of producing gunboats and rifles was itself the product, to use Marxian terms, of a different mode of production, with a unique level of productive forces and unique relations of production and, corresponding to the latter, unique social relations. Behind the rifles and gunboats was a whole history of social and economic development that the Chinese *ti-yong* reformers, armed with their magic *ti-yong* formula, ignored and tried to sidestep. What they wanted was only what they could see — rifles and gunboats — and they had only enough understanding of causality to know that the ability to produce rifles and gunboats required a certain level of productive forces. In their inability to extend the causal chain beyond mere technology, they could see no reason why it would not be possible to develop Western technology while holding fast to the traditional Chinese social relations and values. . . .

This desperate psychological balancing act was, as we have seen, an adjustment to a reality that had never before confronted imperial China. Only in a situation of irreconcilable conflict between culture and survival — things that for obvious reasons should always go together — would some such distinction between *ti* and *yong*, ends and means, be improvised in order both to secure survival and to preserve a culture that no longer guaranteed survival. This was an unmistakable sign of a culture in crisis, a culture in which it was no longer possible to pursue what was essential for survival as culturally important. Indeed, when culture and basic human needs are in harmony, as they should be, ends accord with means. And when ends accord with means, they do not appear to human consciousness as hierarchically differentiated realms of pure ends and mere means but simply as one continuous space for human willing and acting. Means become reified as a cultural or political category when they apparently serve but actually violate the highest values. Ends become reified as a cultural or political category when they are perceived not as immanent in human activity but as its superimposed rationale or end product. Thus the disjunction of human activity into ends and means, pure intention and mere activity, self-sufficient value and subservient instrumentality, is a symptom of a profound cultural crisis, not its solution. . . .

. . . And when they realized that this self-identity was no longer compatible with self-respect, indeed not even with self-preservation, they were quite prepared to give up their self-identity in order to regain their self-respect, and perhaps one day even their center mentality. By degrees, some of them even became prepared to refashion their cultural self-identity in the image of the West, whose cultural identity had given it power. As the vanquished finally accepted the code of the victor, the original code of the vanquished became the dumping ground to which a weak and sick people attributed and consigned their weakness and sickness and their debilitating memories so as to be strong and healthy again.

Thus, in the eyes of a new generation of Chinese, the technologically superior West came to be regarded as culturally superior; some even saw the West's technological and military superiority as but a symptom and effect of its cultural and political superiority. The separation of cultural realms into *ti* and *yong*, which had for a time helped sustain the nation's self-respect, had finally broken down, but when the two realms were once again joined to form one scale of evaluation, it was China — this time not just one realm of China but the whole of the Chinese tradition — that was found wanting. The cultural crisis had entered a new stage. . . .

56

SUN YAT-SEN

From *Memoirs of a Chinese Revolutionary*

The Chinese revolution of 1911 ended the Ch'ing dynasty and established a republic with Sun Yat-Sen as president. This is his account of the years leading up to the revolution. How is Sun Yat-Sen's Western experience different from Gandhi's? In what ways would you call Sun Yat-Sen a Westernizer? In what ways was he not?

Thinking Historically

Jiwei Ci argues that there could be no revolution in China as long as Chinese reformers sought to borrow from the West but retain Chinese culture. In what ways did Sun Yat-Sen abandon this strategy? What contradictions do you see in Sun Yat-Sen's nationalistic revolution? Why did Chinese nationalism require such a global seedbed?

My appeal for a revolution in China has been successful, and the destructive part of the Revolution, in the shape of the overthrow of the Manchu monarchy, has been achieved; but the constructive part has far from begun. Nevertheless, I do not lose hope in the successful completion of the Chinese Revolution; that is why I have devoted to it all my energies.

In the first year of the Republic, when European writers and scholars were writing thousands of articles about the Chinese Revolution, and approaching its facts more from the point of view of morality than of their meaning, I issued the first chapter of my *Notes on the Chinese Revolution* in which I set forth very briefly and concisely how, twenty years ago, the possibility of a successful revolution in China was a subject of great discussion.

Although I lived at the time in London, I could not name myself as one of the founders of the "Association for the Regeneration of China." This at the time involved the risk of persecution. Today I restore from memory the contents of that chapter of my reminiscences,

Sun Yat-Sen, *Memoirs of a Chinese Revolutionary* (London: Hutchinson & Co., Ltd., 1918), 184–224.

supplementing them with the facts of the last thirty years, which formerly I had to omit for conspirative reasons which will be understood.

From the moment that the idea of revolutionary struggle awoke within me up to the time of the foundation of the "Revolutionary League" (out of which the Kuomintang developed) I was a man who practiced revolution, and therefore all my revolutionary activities were not very complicated. I could count on my fingers the names of the persons who at that time recognized my ideas. From the time of the foundation of the "Revolutionary League," the work became much more complicated, and I cannot, of course, recount the names of all the emigrant patriots, still less of all the revolutionary heroes at home. I write my memoirs as materials for a future historian of the Koumintang.

From 1885, *i.e.*, from the time of our defeat in the war with France, I set before myself the object of the overthrow of the Ch'ing Dynasty and the establishment of a Chinese Republic on its ruins. At the very beginning I selected for my propaganda the college at which I was studying, regarding medical science as the kindly aunt who would bring me out onto the high road of politics.

Ten years passed like one day. In the Canton Medical School, I made friends with Chen-Shi-Liang, who had a very large circle of acquaintances amongst widely traveled people who knew China well. When I began talking of revolution, advocating its ideas, he gladly agreed with me, and declared that he would immediately enter a revolutionary party if I would agree to lead it. After staying a year in the school at Canton, I learned that an English Medical School with a wider program than that of the Canton School had been opened at Hong Kong. Thereupon, attracted also by the thought that there I should have a wider field for my revolutionary propaganda, I went to Hong Kong to continue my education. For four years I gave up all my time free from studies to the cause of revolutionary propaganda, traveling backward and forward between Hong Kong and Amoy. At that time I had scarcely any supporters, with the exception of three persons living in Hong Kong: Chen-Shao-Bo, Yu-Shao-Chi, and Yang-Ho-Lin, and one man at Shanghai, Lu-Ko-Tung. The others avoided me, as a rebel, as they would one stricken with plague.

Living together with my three friends Chen, Yu, and Yang, in Hong Kong, we were constantly discussing the revolution. Our thoughts were fixed on the problems of the Chinese Revolution. We studied chiefly the history of revolutions. When it happened that we came together and did not talk of revolution, we did not feel happy. Thus a few years went by, and we received from our friends the nickname of "the four great inseparable scoundrels." For me this was a period of revolutionary disputes and preparation. . . .

The First Revolt

Our committee was in Hong Kong and our branch at Yang-Chen. There worked at that time in the committee Ten-Yin-Nan, Yang-Tsui-Yun, Haun-Yun-Shan, Chen-Shao-Bo, and others, while in the branch at Yang-Chen there were Lu-Ko-Tung, Chen-Shi-Liang, and some instructors from America, and some generals. I often traveled between Canton and Hong Kong. Our tasks by that time were quite well defined. Preparations were in full blast. We had accumulated considerable strength, and we could by a single blow have effected a great deal. But just at this time the authorities discovered the arms we had smuggled in (five hundred revolvers), and one of our worthiest comrades, Lu-Ko-Tung, was executed. This was the first sacrifice made by us on the altar of the Chinese Revolution. At the same time there were arrested and executed Tse-Hsi and Chu-Gui. About seventy people were arrested, among them the Canton Admiral Tsin-Kui-Guan.

The day of September 9, 1895, I consider to be the day of my first revolutionary defeat. Three days after the defeat I was still in Canton, but ten days later I was forced to escape to Hong Kong by byroads, and thence left for Japan with comrades Chen-Shi-Liang and Chen-Shao-Bo, intending to land at Yokohama. I cut off my pigtail and put on European clothes, as the date of my return to China was indeterminate. Then I left for the Philippine islands. Chen-Shi-Liang returned to China to restore matters to the point reached before our defeat, while Chen-Shao-Bo remained in Japan to study the political situation. I was introduced at that time to the Japanese Sugawora, and later we made the acquaintance of Sonei and Miasaki, with whom we established connections. This was the beginning of friendly relations between the Chinese revolutionaries and the Japanese.

Having arrived in the Philippines, I began to gather comrades to strengthen our Association for the Regeneration of China, but even old comrades, owing to our defeat, did not conceal their despair, while some simply forswore our ideas. Owing to the absence of the necessary factors for the development of a revolutionary movement, the latter slowed down somewhat. There was no reason why I should stay long in the Philippines, and I decided to leave for America, in order to establish connections with the organization of Chinese emigrants there. . . .

Amongst the Chinese emigrants in America I found an even more sleepy atmosphere than in the Philippines. I crossed the continent from San Francisco to New York. On my way I stopped at various places for a few days — for ten days at the most — everywhere preaching that to save our mother country from threatening destruction we must overthrow the Ch'ing Dynasty, and that the duty of every Chinese citizen was to help to reconstruct China on a new democratic basis.

Although I spared no effort in this propaganda, the people to whom it was directed remained apathetic and little responsive to the ideas of the Chinese Revolution. . . .

Although my stay in America was of little importance for the further destinies of the Chinese Revolution, it nevertheless aroused fears and misgivings on the part of the Imperial government. Therefore on my arrival in London I almost fell into the clutches of the Imperial Embassy, but I was saved from peril by my teacher Kandeli. It was owing to him that I was saved from the great danger which threatened me.

After escaping from London, I went to Europe to study the methods of its political administration, and also to make the acquaintance of representatives of the opposition parties. In Europe I understood that, although the foremost European countries had achieved power and popular government, they could not accord complete happiness to their peoples. Therefore the leading European revolutionaries strive for a social revolution, and I conceived the idea of the simultaneous settlement, by means of the revolution, of the questions of national economy, national independence, and popular freedom. Hence arose my so-called *"san-min-chu,"* or the idea of democracy based on three principles.[1]

REFLECTIONS

The earliest phase of Westernization occurred in Russia under the direction of Czar Peter the Great (see Chapter 5, selection 24). Before and after Peter's efforts to import Western European institutions and values in order to "modernize" Russia, his country was riven by conflict between "Westernizers" and "Slavophiles," the latter determined to preserve an older Russian identity as ethnic Slavs in tradition, language, and religion. In some ways, the Russians were the first "non-Europeans" to struggle with the question of how much to borrow from the West. But due to Peter's reforms, the construction of a West-

---

[1] Sun Yat-Sen's three principles were nationalism, democracy, and "the people's livelihood." Nationalism was an appeal to the "Han Chinese" people to expel the northern Manchus whose Ch'ing dynasty had ruled China since 1644. Democracy meant getting rid of the monarchy and establishing a constitutional democracy. The constitution would establish "the five separate powers." These were the executive, judicial, and legislative powers that Sun found in British, French, and American constitutions with the addition of two more traditional Chinese powers: one to supervise an examination system to ensure well informed officials and the other to supervise officials and conduct impeachments. The "principle of the people's livelihood" meant the use of machinery and the abolition of taxes. Sun believed that the only tax necessary would be a 100 percent tax on increased market values of land. This "single tax," as the followers of the American socialist Henry George called it, would create a social revolution that would eliminate the economic inequalities of China.

ern capital at St. Petersburg, and the encouragement of Western education, military organization, and culture, Russia chose to align herself with Europe rather than with Asia. After the Russian Revolution of 1917, the Soviet Union became the "West of choice" for many Chinese revolutionaries. The Soviet Union (and Communist China) was Western in its commitment to German Marxism, economic modernization, social and economic equality, and its cosmopolitan opposition to religious or ethnic tribalism. Still, Slavophilism never completely disappeared.

With the end of communism, after 1989, anti-Western forces revived in Russia. When Russian capitalism floundered in the 1990s, the voices of religious orthodoxy, proponents of military might, and revivers of Slavic culture grew louder. In the new world of global markets, contradictions abounded. In 1999, Nikita Mikhakov, a Slavophile and internationally respected film director, built an international reputation and campaign chest to run for president of Russia, promising a return to the Russian values of the czars, one of whom, Alexander III, he played in his film, *Barber of Siberia*. This cinematic celebration of pre-Western Russia was filmed by a genius in Western marketing techniques, with 70 percent of the dialogue in English so that it might qualify for a "Best Picture" Oscar outside the foreign film category.

Our brief summary of Westernization in Asia recalls many stories like this. Why do so many nationalist leaders emerge from outside their native countries? Did Gandhi become more Indian in England or South Africa? Why did Sun Yat-Sen find the Chinese outside of China more revolutionary than those in China? Were the Chinese and Indians who lived overseas more free to express themselves, better able to contribute financially, or more optimistic about changing societies? We cannot overlook the international aspects of nationalist movements in the twentieth century. Westernizers and anti-Westernizers (Christian Sun Yat-Sen and Hindu Gandhi) seem to have been profoundly influenced by their foreign travel experiences. Is the history of Westernization, and of the opposition to Westernization, ultimately a global story? And are the global processes such that the story eventually becomes irrelevant?

At the end of the twentieth century, it is difficult to distinguish Westernization from globalization, as the forces that threaten the national economies or cultures of Asia, Africa, and Latin America tend to come from every direction. Perhaps future generations will see Westernization as only the initial stage of a larger process of economic and cultural integration which we now call globalization.

10

World War and
Its Consequences

The Europe that so many Asian intellectuals sought to imitate between 1880 and 1920 came very close to self-destructing between 1914 and 1918, and bringing many of the world's peoples from Asia, Africa, and the Americas down with it. The orgy of bloodletting, then known as the "Great War," put seventy million men in uniform, of whom ten million were killed and twenty million were wounded. Most of the soldiers were Europeans, though Russia contributed more soldiers than France or Germany, while Japan enlisted as many as the Austro-Hungarian empire that began the war. Other enlisted men came from the United States, Canada, Australia, New Zealand, South Africa, and the colonies: India, French West Africa, German East Africa, among others. Most casualties were suffered in Europe, especially along the German Western front — four hundred miles of trenches that spanned from Switzerland to the English Channel, across northeastern France. But battles were also fought along the borders of German and French (and German and English) colonies in Africa, and there were high Australian casualties on the coast of Gallipoli in Ottoman Turkey.

The readings in this chapter focus on the lives (and deaths) of the soldiers and the efforts of some of their political leaders. We examine the experiences of these soldiers and how the war changed the lives of those who survived its devastating toll. We compare the accounts of those who fought on either side of the great divide, for the Triple Entente (England, France, and Russia, and later the United States) and the Triple Alliance (Austria-Hungary, Germany, first Italy, and then the Ottoman Empire). We compare views across the generational divide that is part and parcel of all wars. Finally, we compare the view from the trenches with the view from distant capitals and government offices.

THINKING HISTORICALLY
Understanding Causes and Consequences

From 1914 to 1920, the greatest divide was the war itself. It marked the end of one era and the beginning of another. Few events have left the participants with such a profound sense of fundamental change. And so our study of the war is an appropriate place to ask two of the universal questions of major historical change: What caused it? and, What were the consequences?

The *causes* are those events or forces that came before; the *consequences* are the results, what the war itself prompted to occur. Thus, causes and consequences are part of the same continuum. Still, we must remember that not everything that happened before the war was a cause of the war. Similarly, not everything that happened afterward happened because of the war.

In this chapter we explore specific ideas about cause and consequence. Our goal is not to compile a definitive list of either but, rather, to explore some of the ways that historians and thoughtful readers can make sense of the past.

57   Q11
acdemic journal

ERNST ZU REVENTLOW

From *The Vampire of the Continent*

Count Ernst zu Reventlow (1869–1943), a German aristocrat, was a spokesman for German interests during the war. Like many of his contemporaries, he saw the German conflict with England as a clash of economic interests that had taken on global dimensions with the expansion of the British and German empires. In addition, the development of imperial alliances created a "balance of power" that caused

Ernst zu Reventlow, *The Vampire of the Continent* (New York: The Jackson Press, 1916), 132–57.

a rift across Europe, expanding even to European colonial possessions in Asia and Africa. The first block — the "triple alliance" — pledged Germany, Austria-Hungary, and Italy to defend each other from attack in 1882. In response, France and Russia signed a mutual assistance pact that same year. In 1904, after both pacts were renewed, England and France signed an "Entente Cordiale," creating a "triple entente" of England, France, and Russia. While such grand alliances were intended to prevent war, they were subject to the volatility of their weakest or least stable members. Thus, when Austrian Archduke Franz Ferdinand was assassinated on June 28, 1914, by a Bosnian Serb, Austria-Hungary — relying on German backing — gave Serbia a stiff ultimatum. With Russian backing, Serbia declined, and Austria declared war, dragging the rest of Europe into the conflict as a result of its treaty obligations.

That Germany and France should be enemies was hardly new. France had been defeated by Germany as recently as 1870. But there was nothing inevitable about the other alignments. English and French rivalries, as Reventlow notes, continued well beyond the Napoleonic Wars, especially in Egypt. English conflict with Russia in Central Asia periodically erupted into war in Afghanistan and the Crimea after 1850. At the same time, England and Germany shared many ties: The English royal family was German, their monarchs cousins, and much of the English and German upper and middle classes were educated in both countries. Yet, Reventlow writes as if England, rather than France, had become the main enemy of Germany by 1914. How do his charges support the view that England was Germany's most serious enemy?

Thinking Historically

Reventlow's argument can be read as an appeal to German interests in the war, as it was intended, but it can also be read as an explanation of the war's causes. In fact, we might be able to cull a number of causes from Reventlow's charge: English jealousy, German economic strength, economic conflict over world markets, the conflicting alliances. Which of these do you think Reventlow would call the most serious cause of the war? Why?

The prosperity of German industry, of German trade, of German shipping and the development of German capital began, about the middle of the nineties, to attract the attention of an ever-growing number of persons in Great Britain. Such attention on the part of the English is, as we know, invariably tainted by animosity. From all oversea countries arrived reports from British consuls and commercial agents, telling of German competition in the foreign markets. Everywhere was the German merchant to be found, who was unusually active, who spoke all languages, and who endeavored most skillfully to find out the wants and wishes of the native population, to which wants the manufactured goods were subsequently adapted.

The immense growth of German industry had been rendered possible by the protectionist policy inaugurated by Bismarck in 1879. The protection of those national forces which demanded to be developed, against foreign competition [and] especially against British industry, was an imperative necessity. Bismarck had not let himself be caught in the English net so carefully spread for continental birds, i.e., by the doctrine of the blessing of free trade for German industry. As soon as it was protected, German industry revealed a strength hitherto unsuspected; it could now thrive and the more it . . . [throve] the more could it expand; and thus was it ever more and more in a position to satisfy all requirements as to quality.

After a very short time, the English jeers about German industrial products, which were scoffed at as being "cheap and nasty," produced no effect. Then came England's great and irremediable mistake. In order to protect English buyers against worthless German products, the British Government decided that all manufactured goods imported into Great Britain, Ireland, and the colonies should be marked "Made in Germany." Thus did England, the champion of the magnificent ideal of Free Trade, decide. As is well known, the plan failed, and the German products, thanks to their good quality and their cheapness, obtained instead an unlooked-for success; for the English buyer got into the habit of asking for German instead of English goods. This failure, with the involuntary comedy and the still more involuntary English irony attached to it, produced its repercussion in the whole world and became a universal and well-deserved advertisement for German industry. . . .

It is by no means the superior capacity or the originality of the English people which . . . permitted them to obtain possession of the markets of the world. An exceptionally favorable geographical position; the ability to inflict in the most cunning and unscrupulous manner damage on other nations which were either exploited, if possible, by their best forces being drawn by England into her own service or which, if this was impossible, were paralyzed in such a way that they destroyed themselves: such have been the factors of the development of British wealth and power. The incurable madness of the Continental Powers, which perpetually tore each other to pieces and exhausted their resources for the greater glory of the British grocer, did the rest. But never did the superior productivity, the superior intelligence, and the honest work of the English have a share in the building up of England's monopoly. . . .

The Entente Cordiale [1904] . . . between France and England was an event of the highest importance in the history of the world for it marked the first great step taken on the road leading up to the war of 1914 which England so carefully organized and prepared and set in motion. The convention of 1904 put an end, once and for all, to all the colonial quarrels between England and France. . . . Bismarck had understood, by a skillful handling of African colonial problems, how to prevent a rapprochement between the two Western Powers; especially had he understood the art of keeping the Egyptian question, that chief bone of contention, alive. Fourteen years after Bismarck's departure, the last seeds of dissension sowed by this policy of his were dug up and destroyed. With the exception of a few unimportant reservations, France renounced all her claims to intervene in Egyptian matters. England promised, partly in public and partly in secret agreements, to assist her French friends in obtaining Morocco. . . . The most important point was the fact of the union of the two Western Powers. . . .

British statesmanship had not succeeded in reducing the German Empire to the position of England's humble servant. Consequently Germany was henceforth England's enemy. . . .

58

ERICH MARIA REMARQUE

From *All Quiet on the Western Front*

In this selection, the beginning of possibly the most famous war novel ever written, we are introduced to the main characters and to the daily routines of the German army on "the Western Front," the long line of trenches that stretched across northern France from Switzerland to the English Channel for most of the war between 1914 and 1918. What does this selection suggest about the types of people recruited to serve in the army? How does Remarque view friendship, authority, and discipline in the army? Do you imagine these German soldiers behaved very differently from French or English soldiers?

Erich Maria Remarque, *All Quiet on the Western Front,* trans. A. W. Wheen (New York: Fawcett Books, 1929), 1–18.

Thinking Historically

Remarque's novel is not intended as an explanation of the causes of war, but this excerpt offers an explanation of how young men were recruited to fight and gives us some idea of their mental state. How might you use material from this novel, assuming that it is factual, to propose at least one cause of World War I?

In this brief selection, the author also suggests something about the consequences of the war. What, according to Remarque, are the war's likely outcomes? The consequences described here are arrived at very early in the war. Is it likely that they will change significantly as the war continues?

We are at rest five miles behind the front. Yesterday we were relieved, and now our bellies are full of beef and haricot beans. We are satisfied and at peace. Each man has another mess-tin full for the evening; and, what is more, there is a double ration of sausage and bread. That puts a man in fine trim. We have not had such luck as this for a long time. The cook with his carroty head is begging us to eat; he beckons with his ladle to every one that passes, and spoons him out a great dollop. He does not see how he can empty his stew-pot in time for coffee. Tjaden and Müller have produced two washbasins and had them filled up to the brim as a reserve. In Tjaden this is voracity, in Müller it is foresight. Where Tjaden puts it all is a mystery, for he is and always will be as thin as a rake.

What's more important still is the issue of a double ration of smokes. Ten cigars, twenty cigarettes, and two quids of chew per man; now that is decent. I have exchanged my chewing tobacco with Katczinsky for his cigarettes, which means I have forty altogether. That's enough for a day.

It is true we have no right to this windfall. The Prussian is not so generous. We have only a miscalculation to thank for it.

Fourteen days ago we had to go up and relieve the front line. It was fairly quiet on our sector, so the quartermaster who remained in the rear had requisitioned the usual quantity of rations and provided for the full company of one hundred and fifty men. But on the last day an astonishing number of English heavies opened up on us with high-explosive, drumming ceaselessly on our position, so that we suffered severely and came back only eighty strong.

Last night we moved back and settled down to get a good sleep for once: Katczinsky is right when he says it would not be such a bad war if only one could get a little more sleep. In the line we have had next to none, and fourteen days is a long time at one stretch.

It was noon before the first of us crawled out of our quarters. Half an hour later every man had his mess-tin and we gathered at the cook-house, which smelt greasy and nourishing. At the head of the queue of course were the hungriest — little Albert Kropp, the clearest thinker among us and therefore only a lance-corporal; Müller, who still carries his school textbooks with him, dreams of examinations, and during a bombardment mutters propositions in physics; Leer, who wears a full beard and has a preference for the girls from officers' brothels. He swears that they are obliged by an army order to wear silk chemises and to bathe before entertaining guests of the rank of captain and upwards. And as the fourth, myself, Paul Bäumer. All four are nineteen years of age, and all four joined up from the same class as volunteers for the war.

Close behind us were our friends: Tjaden, a skinny locksmith of our own age, the biggest eater of the company. He sits down to eat as thin as a grasshopper and gets up as big as a bug in the family way; Haie Westhus, of the same age, a peat-digger, who can easily hold a ration-loaf in his hand and say: Guess what I've got in my fist; then Detering, a peasant, who thinks of nothing but his farm-yard and his wife; and finally Stanislaus Katczinsky, the leader of our group, shrewd, cunning, and hard-bitten, forty years of age, with a face of the soil, blue eyes, bent shoulders, and a remarkable nose for dirty weather, good food, and soft jobs.

Our gang formed the head of the queue before the cook-house. We were growing impatient, for the cook paid no attention to us.

Finally Katczinsky called to him: "Say, Heinrich, open up the soup-kitchen. Anyone can see the beans are done."

He shook his head sleepily: "You must all be there first." Tjaden grinned: "We are all here."

The sergeant-cook still took no notice. "That may do for you," he said. "But where are the others?"

"They won't be fed by you to-day. They're either in the dressing-station or pushing up daisies."

The cook was quite disconcerted as the facts dawned on him. He was staggered. "And I have cooked for one hundred and fifty men——"

Kropp poked him in the ribs. "Then for once we'll have enough. Come on, begin!"

Suddenly a vision came over Tjaden. His sharp, mousy features began to shine, his eyes grew small with cunning, his jaws twitched, and he whispered hoarsely: "Man! then you've got bread for one hundred and fifty men too, eh?"

The sergeant-cook nodded absent-minded, and bewildered.

Tjaden seized him by the tunic. "And sausage?"

Ginger nodded again.

Tjaden's chaps quivered. "Tobacco too?"

"Yes, everything."

Tjaden beamed: "What a bean-feast! That's all for us! Each man gets — wait a bit — yes, practically two issues."

Then Ginger stirred himself and said: "That won't do."

We got excited and began to crowd around.

"Why won't that do, you old carrot?" demanded Katczinsky.

"Eighty men can't have what is meant for a hundred and fifty."

"We'll soon show you," growled Müller.

"I don't care about the stew, but I can only issue rations for eighty men," persisted Ginger.

Katczinsky got angry. "You might be generous for once. You haven't drawn food for eighty men. You've drawn it for the Second Company. Good. Let's have it then. We are the Second Company."

We began to jostle the fellow. No one felt kindly toward him, for it was his fault that the food often came up to us in the line too late and cold. Under shellfire he wouldn't bring his kitchen up near enough, so that our soup-carriers had to go much farther than those of the other companies. Now Bulcke of the First Company is a much better fellow. He is as fat as a hamster in winter, but he trundles his pots when it comes to that right up to the very front-line.

We were in just the right mood, and there would certainly have been a dust-up if our company commander had not appeared. He informed himself of the dispute, and only remarked: "Yes, we did have heavy losses yesterday."

He glanced into the dixie. "The beans look good."

Ginger nodded. "Cooked with meat and fat."

The lieutenant looked at us. He knew what we were thinking. And he knew many other things too, because he came to the company as a non-com. and was promoted from the ranks. He lifted the lid from the dixie again and sniffed. Then passing on he said: "Bring me a plate full. Serve out all the rations. We can do with them."

Ginger looked sheepish as Tjaden danced round him.

"It doesn't cost you anything! Anyone would think the quartermaster's store belonged to him! And now get on with it, you old blubbersticker, and don't you miscount either."

"You be hanged!" spat out Ginger. When things get beyond him he throws up the sponge altogether; he just goes to pieces. And as if to show that all things were equal to him, of his own free will he issued in addition half a pound of synthetic honey to each man.

To-day is wonderfully good. The mail has come, and almost every man has a few letters and papers. We stroll over to the meadow behind the billets. Kropp has the round lid of a margarine tub under his arm.

On the right side of the meadow a large common latrine has been built, a roofed and durable construction. But that is for recruits who as yet have not learned how to make the most of whatever comes their way. We want something better. Scattered about everywhere there are separate, individual boxes for the same purpose. They are square, neat boxes with wooden sides all round, and have unimpeachably satisfactory seats. On the sides are hand grips enabling one to shift them about.

We move three together in a ring and sit down comfortably. And it will be two hours before we get up again.

I well remember how embarrassed we were as recruits in barracks when we had to use the general latrine. There were no doors and twenty men sat side by side as in a railway carriage, so that they could be reviewed all at one glance, for soldiers must always be under supervision.

Since then we have learned better than to be shy about such trifling immodesties. In time things far worse than that came easy to us.

Here in the open air though, the business is entirely a pleasure. I no longer understand why we should always have shied at these things before. They are, in fact, just as natural as eating and drinking. We might perhaps have paid no particular attention to them had they not figured so large in our experience, nor been such novelties to our minds — to the old hands they had long been a mere matter of course.

The soldier is on friendlier terms than other men with his stomach and intestines. Three-quarters of his vocabulary is derived from these regions, and they give an intimate flavour to expressions of his greatest joy as well as of his deepest indignation. It is impossible to express oneself in any other way so clearly and pithily. Our families and our teachers will be shocked when we go home, but here it is the universal language.

Enforced publicity has in our eyes restored the character of complete innocence to all these things. More than that, they are so much a matter of course that their comfortable performance is fully as much enjoyed as the playing of a safe top running flush. Not for nothing was the word "latrine-rumour" invented; these places are the regimental gossip-shop and common-rooms.

We feel ourselves for the time being better off than in any palatial white-tiled "convenience." *There* it can only be hygienic; *here* it is beautiful.

These are wonderfully care-free hours. Over us is the blue sky. On the horizon float the bright yellow, sunlit observation-balloons, and the many little white clouds of the anti-aircraft shells. Often they rise in a sheaf as they follow after an airman. We hear the muffled rumble of the front only as very distant thunder, bumblebees droning by quite drown it. Around us stretches the flowery meadow. The grasses sway their tall spears; the white butterflies flutter around and float on the soft warm wind of the late summer. We read letters and newspapers and smoke.

We take off our caps and lay them down beside us. The wind plays with our hair; it plays with our words and thoughts. The three boxes stand in the midst of the glowing, red field-poppies.

We set the lid of the margarine tub on our knees and so have a good table for a game of skat. Kropp has the cards with him. After every *misère ouverte* we have a round of nap. One could sit like this for ever.

The notes of an accordion float across from the billets. Often we lay aside the cards and look about us. One of us will say: "Well, boys. . . ." Or "It was a near thing that time. . . ." And for a moment we fall silent. There is in each of us a feeling of constraint. We are all sensible of it; it needs no words to communicate it. It might easily have happened that we should not be sitting here on our boxes to-day; it came damn near to that. And so everything is new and brave, red poppies and good food, cigarettes and summer breeze.

Kropp asks: "Anyone seen Kemmerich lately?"

"He's up at St. Joseph's," I tell him.

Müller explains that he has a flesh wound in his thigh; a good blighty.

We decide to go and see him this afternoon.

Kropp pulls out a letter. "Kantorek sends you all his best wishes."

We laugh. Müller throws his cigarette away and says: "I wish he was here."

Kantorek had been our schoolmaster, a stern little man in a grey tail-coat, with a face like a shrew mouse. He was about the same size as Corporal Himmelstoss, the "terror of Klosterberg." It is very queer that the unhappiness of the world is so often brought on by small men. They are so much more energetic and uncompromising than the big fellows. I have always taken good care to keep out of sections with small company commanders. They are mostly confounded little martinets.

During drill-time Kantorek gave us long lectures until the whole of our class went, under his shepherding, to the District Commandant and volunteered. I can see him now, as he used to glare at us through his spectacles and say in a moving voice: "Won't you join up, Comrades?"

These teachers always carry their feelings ready in their waistcoat pockets, and trot them out by the hour. But we didn't think of that then.

There was, indeed, one of us who hesitated and did not want to fall into line. That was Joseph Behm, a plump, homely fellow. But he did allow himself to be persuaded, otherwise he would have been ostracized. And perhaps more of us thought as he did, but no one could very well stand out, because at that time even one's parents were ready with the word "coward"; no one had the vaguest idea what we were in for. The wisest were just the poor and simple people. They knew the war to be a misfortune, whereas those who were better off, and should have been able to see more clearly what the consequences would be, were beside themselves with joy.

Katczinsky said that was a result of their upbringing. It made them stupid. And what Kat said, he had thought about.

Strange to say, Behm was one of the first to fall. He got hit in the eye during an attack, and we left him lying for dead. We couldn't bring him with us, because we had to come back helter-skelter. In the afternoon suddenly we heard him call, and saw him crawling about in No Man's Land. He had only been knocked unconscious. Because he could not see, and was mad with pain, he failed to keep under cover, and so was shot down before anyone could go and fetch him in.

Naturally we couldn't blame Kantorek for this. Where would the world be if one brought every man to book? There were thousands of Kantoreks, all of whom were convinced that they were acting for the best — in a way that cost them nothing.

And that is why they let us down so badly.

For us lads of eighteen they ought to have been mediators and guides to the world of maturity, the world of work, of duty, of culture, of progress — to the future. We often made fun of them and played jokes on them, but in our hearts we trusted them. The idea of authority, which they represented, was associated in our minds with a greater insight and a more humane wisdom. But the first death we saw shattered this belief. We had to recognize that our generation was more to be trusted than theirs. They surpassed us only in phrases and in cleverness. The first bombardment showed us our mistake, and under it the world as they had taught it to us broke in pieces.

While they continued to write and talk, we saw the wounded and dying. While they taught that duty to one's country is the greatest thing, we already knew that death-throes are stronger. But for all that we were no mutineers, no deserters, no cowards — they were very free with all these expressions. We loved our country as much as they; we went courageously into every action; but also we distinguished the false from true, we had suddenly learned to see. And we saw that there was nothing of their world left. We were all at once terribly alone; and alone we must see it through.

Before going over to see Kemmerich we pack up his things: He will need them on the way back.

In the dressing station there is great activity: It reeks as ever of carbolic, pus, and sweat. We are accustomed to a good deal in the billets, but this makes us feel faint. We ask for Kemmerich. He lies in a large room and receives us with feeble expressions of joy and helpless agitation. While he was unconscious someone had stolen his watch.

Müller shakes his head: "I always told you that nobody should carry as good a watch as that."

Müller is rather crude and tactless, otherwise he would hold his tongue, for anybody can see that Kemmerich will never come out of this place again. Whether he finds his watch or not will make no difference, at the most one will only be able to send it to his people.

"How goes it, Franz?" asks Kropp.

Kemmerich's head sinks.

"Not so bad . . . but I have such a damned pain in my foot."

We look at his bed covering. His leg lies under a wire basket. The bed covering arches over it. I kick Müller on the shin, for he is just about to tell Kemmerich what the orderlies told us outside: that Kemmerich has lost his foot. The leg is amputated. He looks ghastly, yellow and wan. In his face there are already the strained lines that we know so well, we have seen them now hundreds of times. They are not so much lines as marks. Under the skin the life no longer pulses, it has already pressed out the boundaries of the body. Death is working through from within. It already has command in the eyes. Here lies our comrade, Kemmerich, who a little while ago was roasting horse flesh with us and squatting in the shell-holes. He it is still and yet it is not he any longer. His features have become uncertain and faint, like a photographic plate from which two pictures have been taken. Even his voice sounds like ashes.

I think of the time when we went away. His mother, a good plump matron, brought him to the station. She wept continually, her face was bloated and swollen. Kemmerich felt embarrassed, for she was the least composed of all; she simply dissolved into fat and water. Then she caught sight of me and took hold of my arm again and again, and implored me to look after Franz out there. Indeed he did have a face like a child, and such frail bones that after four weeks' pack-carrying he already had flat feet. But how can a man look after anyone in the field!

"Now you will soon be going home," says Kropp. "You would have had to wait at least three or four months for your leave."

Kemmerich nods. I cannot bear to look at his hands, they are like wax. Under the nails is the dirt of the trenches, it shows through blue-black like poison. It strikes me that these nails will continue to grow like lean fantastic cellar-plants long after Kemmerich breathes no more. I see the picture before me. They twist themselves into corkscrews and grow and grow, and with them the hair on the decaying skull, just like grass in a good soil, just like grass, how can it be possible ———

Müller leans over. "We have brought your things, Franz."

Kemmerich signs with his hands. "Put them under the bed."

Müller does so. Kemmerich starts on again about the watch. How can one calm him without making him suspicious?

Müller reappears with a pair of airman's boots. They are fine English boots of soft, yellow leather which reach to the knees and lace up all the way — they are things to be coveted.

Müller is delighted at the sight of them. He matches their soles against his own clumsy boots and says: "Will you be taking them with you then, Franz?"

We all three have the same thought; even if he should get better, he would be able to use only one — they are no use to him. But as things are now it is a pity that they should stay here; the orderlies will of course grab them as soon as he is dead.

"Won't you leave them with us?" Müller repeats.

Kemmerich doesn't want to. They are his most prized possessions.

"Well, we could exchange," suggests Müller again. "Out here one can make some use of them." Still Kemmerich is not to be moved.

I tread on Müller's foot; reluctantly he puts the fine boots back again under the bed.

We talk a little more and then take our leave.

"Cheerio, Franz."

I promise him to come back in the morning. Müller talks of doing so, too. He is thinking of the lace-up boots and means to be on the spot.

Kemmerich groans. He is feverish. We get hold of an orderly outside and ask him to give Kemmerich a dose of morphia.

He refuses. "If we were to give morphia to everyone we would have to have tubs full ———"

"You only attend to officers properly," says Kropp viciously.

I hastily intervene and give him a cigarette. He takes it.

"Are you usually allowed to give it, then?" I ask him.

He is annoyed. "If you don't think so, then why do you ask?"

I press a few more cigarettes into his hand. "Do us the favour ———"

"Well, all right," he says.

Kropp goes in with him. He doesn't trust him and wants to see. We wait outside.

Müller returns to the subject of the boots. "They would fit me perfectly. In these boots I get blister after blister. Do you think he will last till tomorrow after drill?" If he passes out in the night, we know where the boots ———"

Kropp returns. "Do you think ———?" he asks.

"Done for," said Müller emphatically.

We go back to the huts. I think of the letter that I must write tomorrow to Kemmerich's mother. I am freezing. I could do with a tot of rum. Müller pulls up some grass and chews it. Suddenly little Kropp throws his cigarette away, stamps on it savagely, and looking around him with a broken and distracted face, stammers "Damned shit, the damned shit!"

We walk on for a long time. Kropp has calmed himself; we understand, he saw red; out there every man gets like that sometime.

"What has Kantorek written to you?" Müller asks him.

He laughs. "We are the Iron Youth."

We all three smile bitterly, Kropp rails: He is glad that he can speak.

Yes, that's the way they think, these hundred thousand Kantoreks! Iron Youth! Youth! We are none of us more than twenty years old. But young? Youth? That is long ago. We are old folk.

59

Government Posters: Enlistment and War Bonds

Posters were the communication medium of the First World War. In an age when governments had still not taught most people how to read but increasingly needed their consent or compliance, images spoke louder than words.

The American poster from 1917 and the German poster from 1915–1916 implored men to enlist in the army; the Italian poster from 1917 encouraged people to buy war bonds. What do you think accounts for the similar graphic style used in all three posters? How effective do you think the pointed finger of responsibility was? Some people have suggested that these images are the sign of a mass society where the individual can become anonymous but must be reached and motivated anyway. What do you think?

Thinking Historically

The rise of nationalism is often cited as one of the causes for the outbreak of the First World War. Do you see any hallmarks of separate national identity in these posters? Is the similarity of these posters an

James Montgomery Flagg, Recruiting poster for U.S. Army, 1917. Museum of Modern Art, New York. Achille Luciano Mauzan, Italian poster for national war loan, 1917. Museo Civico Luigi Bailo, Salce Collection, Treviso. German poster Anonymous, Recruiting poster for German Army, 1915–1916. Stuttgart Staatsgalerie. Max Gallo, *The Poster in History* (New York: American Heritage, McGraw-Hill, 1972), 132–33.

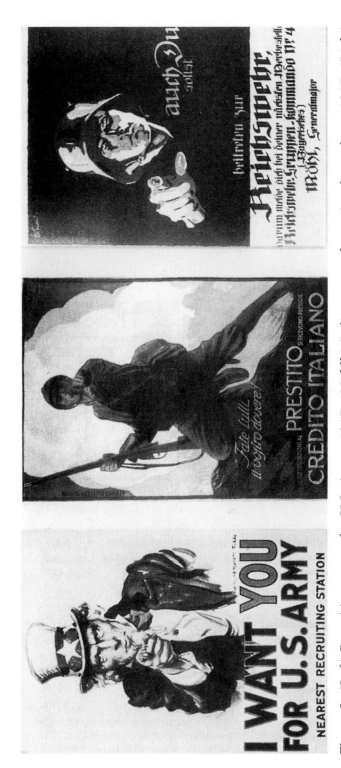

Figure 8. (*Left*) Recruiting poster for U.S. Army, 1917; (*Middle*) Italian poster for national war loan, 1917; (*Right*) Recruiting poster for German Army, 1915–16.

indication of the merging national identities of countries at war? Is it possible that one of the consequences of the war was such a convergence of identities, perhaps due to the similar experiences of each country in wartime?

60

S. V. BRITTEN, HUGO MULLER, BILL BLAND, AND KANDE KAMARA

Witness of Soldiers

These four soldiers came from different backgrounds and different parts of the world, but they all dug into the trenches on the Western Front in France. How were their experiences alike? How were they different? What do their experiences tell you about the daily lives of soldiers on the front?

Thinking Historically

While none of these accounts offers theories on the causes of the war, each provides evidence of the individual soldier's attitudes toward war and the enemy. If these individuals are representative of their country and social class, what do their comments suggest about the origins of the war?

The consequences of war for millions was death. Both Bland and Muller were killed in 1916 on the Western Front, Bland in June in the battle of the Somme River and Muller in October in the nearby Ancre Valley. We can only imagine the consequences for those they left behind. Judging from these accounts, however, what do you imagine were the consequences of the war for those who fought and survived? What impact might these veterans have had on their countries domestically and

Sergeant S. V. Britten, Diary of a Canadian, Sergeant S. V. Britten, The Royal Highlanders of Canada, Ack: 1915 diary, in *Voices and Images of the Great War* (Lyn Macdonald, 1988). Hugo Muller, German Army (1915 letter), in *German Students' War Letters* (Philip Witkopp, 1929). Captain Bill Bland, 22nd Battalion, The Manchester Regiment (7th Manchester Pais), Ack. reads: Bill Bland (1916 letter), Imperial War Museum. Kande Kamara, Oral Testimony recorded Sept. 22–24, 1976, from Joe Harris Lunn, "Kande Kamara Speaks: An Oral History of the West African Experience in France, 1914–1918," in *Africa and the First World War*, ed. Melvin E. Page (London: Macmillan, 1987), 44–45, 48.

internationally? Would their common experiences in war have prompted common consequences after the war, or would these people simply go back to their different lives?

Diary of a Canadian
[S. V. Britten]

Diary: 17 April 1915

Rose at 8.30, went down to Ypres with Capt. Morrisey & Rae, & spent day there, saw over the ruins of the Cathedral & Cloth Hall etc. Stopped all the afternoon, bought a handkerchief of Flemish Lace (& sending it to Vera as a souvenir), brought back a quantity of stuff for ourselves, including two bottles of wine. Witnessed an exciting battle between a British & a German biplane. The latter was brought down about 7 p.m. Terrific artillery fire started about 6 p.m., & lasted all night.

22 April

Left at 6.30 p.m. for reserve trenches and reached our reserve dugouts via St Julien. Just rat holes! One hell of accommodation! Got to the trenches as a fatigue party with stake & sandbags, and thought they were reserve trenches, they were so rotten. No trenches at all in parts, just isolated mounds. Found German's feet sticking up through the ground. The Gurkhas[1] had actually used human bodies instead of sandbags.

Right beside the stream where we were working were the bodies of two dead, since November last, one face downwards in full marching order, with his kit on his back. He died game! Stench something awful and dead all round. Water rats had made a home of their decomposed bodies. Visited the barbed wire with Rae — ordinary wire strung across. Quit about 1 a.m., came back to our dugouts and found them on fire. Had to march out to St Julien, & put up in a roofless house — not a roof left on anything in the whole place. Found our sack of food had been stolen and we were famished. Certainly a most unlucky day, for I lost my cherished pipe in the evening also. Bed at 4 a.m.

23 April

Up about noon and had no breakfast. Had a good view of the village of the dead, everything in a most heartbreaking state. We found a piano and had music. Furious shelling started about 4.30 p.m., and we took to the dugouts. Almost suffocated by the poisonous fumes! Got into marching order (without packs) & lined for action outside the village. Got to No. 7 station & found Captain Morrisey there, almost suffocated. Brought Lieutenant Molson out to St Jean, & we came to St Julien, getting a lift in

[1] Soldiers from Nepal.

an ambulance. Village a mess of dead horses, limbers, and men. Went on ration fatigue & tried to get up to the trenches but failed. Scouted the road, waited under heavy shell fire for about two hours, then moved off, & made a circumference up to the trenches via 48th communication trench. Getting there at almost daybreak.

23 April

Terrible day, no food or water, dead & dying all around.

Letter from a Former German Law Student
[Hugo Muller]

At Agny, near Arras,
17 October 1915

I am enclosing a French field-postcard, which I want you to put with my war-souvenirs. It came out of the letter-case of a dead French soldier. It has been extremely interesting to study the contents of the letter-cases of French killed and prisoners. The question frequently recurs, just as it does with us: "When will it all end?"

To my astonishment I practically never found any expression of hatred or abuse of Germany or German soldiers. On the other hand, many letters from relations revealed an absolute conviction of the justice of their cause, and sometimes also of confidence in victory. In every letter mother, fiancée, children, friends, whose photographs were often enclosed, spoke of a joyful return and a speedy meeting — and now they are all lying dead and hardly even buried between the trenches, while over them bullets and shells sing their gruesome dirge.

Letter from a Former
English University Lecturer
[Bill Bland]

18 February 1916
[France]

Darling, I can't bear you to be unhappy about me. Don't be grey and old, my darling. Think of the *cause,* the cause. It is England, England, England, always and all the time. The individual counts as nothing, the common cause everything. Have faith, my dear. If only you will have faith in the ultimate victory of the good, the true, and the beautiful, you will not be unhappy even if I never return to you. Dear, if one's number is up, one will go under. I am here, and I shall either survive or not survive. In the meantime, I have never been truly happier.

P.S. Hardship be damned! It's all one long blaze of glory.

Memories of a West African in France
[Kande Kamara]

... One of my younger brothers ... was shot in the thigh ... and he cried out ... "Brother, they've shot me." But I didn't look at him — I didn't help him — because during wartime, even if your friend is shot dead, you would continue facing the enemy to save your own life. Because [officers] were watching you, and if you were afraid to shoot the enemy ... your own people would shoot you down. ... I didn't say anything; I kept quiet. I wasn't looking at him, but tears were running down my face.

Soon the doctor came with the ambulance to look in the gutters [trenches]. And they found my brother there, and ... they picked him up, and my brother said, "I'm not going back in the vehicle." And he asked, "Why did I come here?" And they answered, "You came to fight." And he said, "I'm going to, just come tie my wound." And the doctor came and tied his leg and gave him some medicine. ... Then my brother said, "Let me go ... that's my brother down there, and wherever he dies, I will die there too." And that's when they said to him, "You have a really strong heart." ... And because he wasn't going to stop fighting, and he was already wounded, and he was going to stay with me, he was promoted to sergeant for his bravery.

At the beginning, the white people were always in the front line. ... But when we got to understand them ... and when they started trusting us ... that changed. ... At the very end we were all mixed, because by then everyone knew that mind and their heart and no one was afraid of color except for innocents.

[When] you see a black sergeant ... and a white corporal comes ... and he doesn't salute the black sergeant, and the black sergeant would arrest him ... [then you know you have] equality with the white man.

If we hadn't fought, if we — the black people — hadn't fought in western wars, and been taken overseas, and demonstrated some ability of human dignity, we wouldn't have been regarded today as anything.

61

WILFRED OWEN
Dulce et Decorum Est

Wilfred Owen enlisted in the British Army in 1915, was wounded in 1917, and was hospitalized, released, and sent back to the front, where he died November 4, 1918, one week before the end of the war. In this poem, he describes a poison gas attack. Like the machine gun and the airplane, gas was a common element of the new mechanized mass warfare. Owen describes how physically debilitating the effects of gas were. Why was gas such an effective and deadly weapon? How, according to Owen, had the nature of war changed?

Thinking Historically

The concluding phrase, which means "Sweet and proper it is to die for one's country," was a Latin declaration of patriotic duty that English students repeated as a lesson, not only in Latin classes but, more important, in their political education as subjects of the British empire. How does Owen portray this lesson as a cause of the war? What does he imagine to be the consequences of fighting a war with such patriotic slogans in mind?

Dulce et Decorum Est

Bent double, like old beggars under sacks,
Knock-kneed, coughing like hags, we cursed
   through sludge,
Till on the haunting flares we turned our backs
And towards our distant rest began the trudge.
Men marched asleep. Many had lost their boots
But limped on, blood-shod. All went lame; all
   blind;
Drunk with fatigue; deaf even to the hoots
Of tired, outstripped Five-Nines[1] that dropped
   behind.

Gas! GAS! Quick, boys! — An ecstasy of
   fumbling,

---

[1] German artillery shells.

Wilfred Owen, *Poems*, ed. Siegfried Sassoon (London: Chatto and Windus, 1920).

Fitting the clumsy helmets just in time;
But someone still was yelling out and stumbling,
And flound'ring like a man in fire or lime. . . .
Dim, through the misty panes and thick green
    light,
As under a green sea, I saw him drowning.

In all my dreams, before my helpless sight,
He plunges at me, guttering, choking,
    drowning.

If in some smothering dreams you too could
    pace
Behind the wagon that we flung him in,
And watch the white eyes writhing in his face,
His hanging face, like a devil's sick of sin;
If you could hear, at every jolt, the blood
Come gargling from the froth-corrupted lungs,
Obscene as cancer, bitter as the cud
Of vile, incurable sores on innocent tongues,
My friend, you would not tell with such high
    zest,
To children ardent for some desperate glory.
The old Lie: Dulce et decorum est
Pro patria mori.

62

ROSA LUXEMBURG

From *The Russian Revolution*

One of the great casualties of the First World War was the Russian empire, including the czar, his family, many of the members of their class, and its centuries-old autocratic system. The burden of war was simply too much for Russian society to bear. The disillusionment in the army and civilian society, along with the overwhelming costs of

Rosa Luxemburg, "The Russian Revolution," in *The Russian Revolution and Leninism or Marxism?* trans. Workers Age (Ann Arbor: University of Michigan Press, 1961), 69–72, 78–80.

war, forced Czar Nicholas II to abdicate in February of 1917 and to turn power over to a group of nobles and the Russian parliament. The government that emerged, under Alexander Kerensky, proved unable to satisfy the growing demands of peasants, veterans, and urban workers for "land, peace, and bread," a slogan that V. I. Lenin and the communists exploited, successfully seizing power from the moderate parliamentarians in October of that year.

As a Marxist, Lenin believed that he could establish a socialist society in Russia, but he argued that Russian conditions (e.g., economic underdevelopment; the devastation of war; the opposition of Europe, the United States, and Russian nobles to the revolution) made a democratic transition impossible. According to Lenin, a self-appointed government acting in the interests of the working class was the only way to a socialist Soviet Union. Lenin called this government "the dictatorship of the proletariat." And just as the government had to be protected from "counter-revolutionary" enemies who would take advantage of democratic procedures, so too did the governing party have to be administered tightly by a "vanguard" of professionals who would act secretly and ruthlessly to secure the interests of the proletariat. Thus, Lenin insisted, to secure socialism in a country at war with capitalism internally and externally, a highly motivated, tightly controlled Bolshevik party was needed to enforce the dictatorship of the proletariat.

Rosa Luxemburg (1870–1919) was born a Jew in Russian Poland, but at the age of nineteen fled to Switzerland, where she earned a doctorate in law and political science. At twenty-five she migrated to Germany where, as a journalist and theorist, she became an impassioned and influential voice in the German democratic socialist movement. She criticized its bureaucratic leadership and excoriated its submission to war hysteria. Her opposition to the war led to frequent imprisonment. While Luxemburg was imprisoned, Lenin seized power, and she composed her thoughts on the Russian Revolution in 1918.

As a cofounder of the German Spartacus League (which later became the German Communist Party), Luxemburg believed that the Bolshevik Revolution could mean the liberation of working people throughout Russia, then Germany and the rest of Europe. But after 1904 she disagreed with Lenin's ideas of centralized control and party discipline. What objections does she make to Lenin's revolution? What do you think of her arguments?

Ironically, the apparent success of Lenin's strategy in Russia led many in the German Spartacus League to agitate for a similar seizure of power in Germany at the end of the war. Rosa Luxemburg tried to dissuade them, believing it to be suicidal. Outvoted, she joined their uprising in Berlin in January 1919, and was subsequently arrested and murdered by the police.

Thinking Historically

Causes and consequences are often different sides of the same event. We might say that the First World War was a cause of the Russian Revolution or, conversely, that the Russian Revolution was a consequence of the First World War. Lenin argued that one of the consequences of the First World War was the particular sort of revolution he advocated, on the grounds that a democratic revolution was impossible under the circumstances. What do you think of that argument? Rosa Luxemburg disagreed that such draconian measures were necessary, and she argued that Lenin's revolutionary strategy would have its own consequences. What were the consequences she envisioned? Was she right?

[handwritten annotations: "Proletariat the lowest class" ; "Bourgeois — self-employed middle class"]

Lenin says: The bourgeois state is an instrument of oppression of the working class; the socialist state, of the bourgeoisie. To a certain extent, he says, it is only the capitalist state stood on its head. This simplified view misses the most essential thing: Bourgeois class rule has no need of the political training and education of the entire mass of the people, at least not beyond certain narrow limits. But for the proletarian dictatorship, that is the life element, the very air without which it is not able to exist. . . .

Freedom only for the supporters of the government, only for the members of one party — however numerous they may be — is no freedom at all. Freedom is always and exclusively freedom for the one who thinks differently. Not because of any fanatical concept of "justice" but because all that is instructive, wholesome, and purifying in political freedom depends on this essential characteristic, and its effectiveness vanishes when "freedom" becomes a special privilege.

The Bolsheviks themselves will not want, with hand on heart, to deny that, step by step, they have to feel out the ground, try out, experiment, test now one way now another, and that a good many of their measures do not represent priceless pearls of wisdom. Thus it must and will be with all of us when we get to the same point — even if the same difficult circumstances may not prevail everywhere.

The tacit assumption underlying the Lenin-Trotsky[1] theory of the dictatorship is this: that the socialist transformation is something for which a ready-made formula lies completed in the pocket of the revolutionary party, which needs only to be carried out energetically in practise. This is, unfortunately — or perhaps fortunately — not the case.

[1] Leon Trotsky (1899–1940) played a major role in the revolution in 1917, was appointed foreign minister in 1918, organized the Red Army in 1918–1920, and was exiled by Stalin in 1929. [Ed.]

Far from being a sum of ready-made prescriptions which have only to be applied, the practical realization of socialism as an economic, social, and juridical system is something which lies completely hidden in the mists of the future. What we possess in our program is nothing but a few main signposts which indicate the general direction in which to look for the necessary measures, and the indications are mainly negative in character at that. Thus we know more or less what we must eliminate at the outset in order to free the road for a socialist economy. But when it comes to the nature of the thousand concrete, practical measures, large and small, necessary to introduce socialist principles into economy, law, and all social relationships, there is no key in any socialist party program or textbook. That is not a shortcoming but rather the very thing that makes scientific socialism superior to the utopian varieties. The socialist system of society should only be, and can only be, an historical product, born out of the school of its own experiences, born in the course of its realization, as a result of the developments of living history, which — just like organic nature of which, in the last analysis, it forms a part — has the fine habit of always producing along with any real social need the means to its satisfaction, along with the task simultaneously the solution. However, if such is the case, then it is clear that socialism by its very nature cannot be decreed or introduced by *ukase*.[2] It has as its prerequisite a number of measures of force — against property, etc. The negative, the tearing down, can be decreed; the building up, the positive, cannot. New territory. A thousand problems. Only experience is capable of correcting and opening new ways. Only unobstructed, effervescing life falls into a thousand new forms and improvisations, brings to light creative force, itself corrects all mistaken attempts. The public life of countries with limited freedom is so poverty-stricken, so miserable, so rigid, so unfruitful, precisely because, through the exclusion of democracy, it cuts off the living sources of all spiritual riches and progress. (Proof: the year 1905 and the months from February to October 1917.)[3] There it was political in character; the same thing applies to economic and social life also. The whole mass of the people must take part in it. Otherwise, socialism will be decreed from behind a few official desks by a dozen intellectuals.

Public control is indispensably necessary. Otherwise the exchange of experiences remains only with the closed circle of the officials of the new regime. Corruption becomes inevitable. (Lenin's words, Bulletin No. 29) Socialism in life demands a complete spiritual transformation in the masses degraded by centuries of bourgeois class rule. Social instincts in place of egotistical ones, mass initiative in place of inertia, idealism which conquers all suffering, etc., etc. No one knows this

---

2 Order.
3 Periods of unsuccessful or limited revolution in Russia. [Ed.]

better, describes it more penetratingly; repeats it more stubbornly than Lenin. But he is completely mistaken in the means he employs. Decree, dictatorial force of the factory overseer, draconic penalties, rule by terror — all these things are but palliatives. The only way to a rebirth is the school of public life itself, the most unlimited, the broadest democracy, and public opinion. It is rule by terror which demoralizes.

When all this is eliminated, what really remains? In place of the representative bodies created by general, popular elections, Lenin and Trotsky have laid down the soviets as the only true representation of the laboring masses. But with the repression of political life in the land as a whole, life in the soviets must also become more and more crippled. Without general elections, without unrestricted freedom of press and assembly, without a free struggle of opinion, life dies out in every public institution, becomes a mere semblance of life, in which only the bureaucracy remains as the active element. Public life gradually falls asleep, a few dozen party leaders of inexhaustible energy and boundless experience direct and rule. Among them, in reality only a dozen outstanding heads do the leading and an elite of the working class is invited from time to time to meetings where they are to applaud the speeches of the leaders, and to approve proposed resolutions unanimously — at bottom, then, a clique affair — a dictatorship, to be sure, not the dictatorship of the proletariat, however, but only the dictatorship of a handful of politicians, that is a dictatorship in the bourgeois sense, in the sense of the rule of the Jacobins[4] (the postponement of the Soviet Congress from three-month periods to six-month period!) Yes, we can go even further: Such conditions must inevitably cause a brutalization of public life: attempted assassinations, shooting of hostages, etc. (Lenin's speech on discipline and corruption.)

. . . Everything that happens in Russia is comprehensible and represents an inevitable chain of causes and effects, the starting point and end term of which are: the failure of the German proletariat and the occupation of Russia by German imperialism. It would be demanding something superhuman from Lenin and his comrades if we should expect of them that under such circumstances they should conjure forth the finest democracy, the most exemplary dictatorship of the proletariat, and a flourishing socialist economy. By their determined revolutionary stand, their exemplary strength in action, and their unbreakable loyalty to international socialism, they have contributed whatever could possibly be contributed under such devilishly hard conditions. The danger begins only when they make a virtue of necessity and want to freeze into a complete theoretical system all the tactics forced upon them by these fatal circumstances, and want to recommend them to the

[4] Radicals in the French Revolution.

international proletariat as a model of socialist tactics. When they get in their own light in this way, and hide their genuine, unquestionable historical service under the bushel of false steps forced upon them by necessity, they render a poor service to international socialism for the sake of which they have fought and suffered; for they want to place in its storehouse as new discoveries all the distortions prescribed in Russia by necessity and compulsion — in the last analysis only by-products of the bankruptcy of international socialism in the present world war.

Let the German Government Socialists cry that the rule of the Bolsheviks in Russia is a distorted expression of the dictatorship of the proletariat. If it was or is such, that is only because it is a product of the behavior of the German proletariat, in itself a distorted expression of the socialist class struggle. All of us are subject to the laws of history, and it is only internationally that the socialist order of society can be realized. The Bolsheviks have shown that they are capable of everything that a genuine revolutionary party can contribute within the limits of the historical possibilities. They are not supposed to perform miracles. For a model and faultless proletarian revolution in an isolated land, exhausted by world war, strangled by imperialism, betrayed by the international proletariat, would be a miracle.

What is in order is to distinguish the essential from the non-essential, the kernel from the accidental excrescences in the policies of the Bolsheviks. In the present period, when we face decisive final struggles in all the world, the most important problem of socialism was and is the burning question of our time. It is not a matter of this or that secondary question of tactics, but of the capacity for action of the proletariat, the strength to act, the will to power of socialism as such. In this, Lenin and Trotsky and their friends were the *first,* those who went ahead as an example to the proletariat of the world; they are still the *only ones* up to now who can cry with [sixteenth-century reformer Urlich von] Hutten: "I have dared!"

This is the essential and *enduring* in Bolshevik policy. In *this* sense theirs is the immortal historical service of having marched at the head of the international proletariat with the conquest of political power and the practical placing of the problem of the realization of socialism, and of having advanced mightily the settlement of the score between capital and labor in the entire world. In Russia the problem could only be posed. It could not be solved in Russia. And in *this* sense, the future everywhere belongs to "Bolshevism."

63

WOODROW WILSON

Fourteen Points

Woodrow Wilson (1856–1924) was president of the United States during the First World War. He presented these "Fourteen Points" to Congress in January 1918 as a basis for a just peace treaty to end the war.

You may wish to compare these proposals with the actual peace settlement. Only points VII, VIII, X, and XIV were realized. Point IV was applied only to the defeated nations. The Versailles Treaty, which the defeated Germans were forced to sign on June 28, 1919, contained much harsher terms, including the famous "war guilt" clause (Article 231):

> The Allied and Associated Governments affirm and Germany accepts the responsibility of Germany and her allies for causing all the loss and damage to which the Allied and Associated Governments and their nationals have been subjected as a consequence of the war imposed upon them by the aggression of Germany and her allies.

Why do you think there was such a gap between Wilson's ideals and the actual treaty? How might Wilson have improved on these Fourteen Points? Could he reasonably expect all of them to be accepted?

Thinking Historically

What does the first paragraph suggest Wilson thought was one cause of the war? What does the beginning of the second paragraph suggest about the cause for U.S. entry into the war? What would have been the consequences of a peace fashioned along the lines Wilson envisioned in his Fourteen Points?

It will be our wish and purpose that the processes of peace, when they are begun, shall be absolutely open, and that they shall involve and permit henceforth no secret understandings of any kind. The day of con-

---

Woodrow Wilson, *War and Peace: Presidential Messages, Addresses, and Public Papers (1917–1924)*, vol. 1, ed. Ray Stannard Baker and William E. Dodd (New York: Harper Brothers, 1927).

quest and aggrandizement is gone by; so is also the day of secret covenants entered into in the interest of particular Governments and likely at some unlooked-for moment to upset the peace of the world. It is this happy fact, now clear to the view of every public man whose thoughts do not still linger in an age that is dead and gone, which makes it possible for every nation whose purposes are consistent with justice and the peace of the world to avow now or at any other time the objects it has in view.

We entered this war because violations of right had occurred which touched us to the quick and made the life of our own people impossible unless they were corrected and the world secured once for all against their recurrence. What we demand in this war, therefore, is nothing peculiar to ourselves. It is that the world be made fit and safe to live in; and particularly that it be made safe for every peace-loving nation which, like our own, wishes to live its own life, determine its own institutions, be assured of justice and fair dealing by the other peoples of the world as against force and selfish aggression. All the peoples of the world are in effect partners in this interest, and for our own part we see very clearly that unless justice be done to others it will not be done to us. The program of the world's peace, therefore, is our program; and that program, the only possible program, as we see it, is this:

I. Open covenants of peace, openly arrived at, after which there shall be no private international understandings of any kind but diplomacy shall proceed always frankly and in the public view.

II. Absolute freedom of navigation upon the seas, outside territorial waters, alike in peace and in war, except as the seas may be closed in whole or in part by international action. . . .

III. The removal, so far as possible, of all economic barriers and the establishment of an equality of trade conditions among all the nations consenting to the peace and associating themselves for its maintenance.

IV. Adequate guarantees given and taken that national armaments will be reduced to the lowest point consistent with domestic safety.

V. A free, open-minded, and absolutely impartial adjustment of all colonial claims, based upon a strict observance of the principle that in determining all such questions of sovereignty the interests of the populations concerned must have equal weight with the equitable claims of the government whose title is to be determined.

VI. The Evacuation of all Russian territory and such a settlement of all questions affecting Russia as will secure the best and freest cooperation of the other nations of the world in obtaining for her an unhampered and unembarrassed opportunity for the independent determination of her own political development and national policy and assure her of a sincere welcome into the society of free nations under institutions of her own choosing; and, more than a welcome, assistance also of every kind that she may need and may herself desire. The treatment accorded Russia by her sister nations in the months to come will be the acid test of their good will, of their comprehension of her needs as distinguished from their own interests, and of their intelligent and unselfish sympathy.

VII. Belgium, the whole world will agree, must be evacuated and restored, without any attempt to limit the sovereignty which she enjoys in common with all other free nations. No other single act will serve to restore confidence among the nations in the laws which they have themselves set and determined for the government of their relations with one another. Without this healing act the whole structure and validity of international law is forever impaired.

VIII. All French territory should be freed and the invaded portions restored, and the wrong done to France by Prussia in 1871 in the matter of Alsace-Lorraine, which has unsettled the peace of the world for nearly fifty years, should be righted, in order that peace may once more be made secure in the interest of all.

IX. A readjustment of the frontiers of Italy should be effected along clearly recognizable lines of nationality.

X. The peoples of Austria-Hungary, whose place among the nations we wish to see safeguarded and assured, should be accorded the freest opportunity of autonomous development.

XI. Rumania, Serbia, and Montenegro should be evacuated; occupied territories restored; Serbia accorded free and secure access to the sea; and the relations of the several Balkan states to one another determined by friendly counsel along historically established lines of allegiance and nationality; and international guarantees of the political and economic independence and territorial integrity of the several Balkan states should be entered into.

XII. The Turkish portions of the present Ottoman Empire should be assured a secure sovereignty, but the other nationalities which are now under Turkish rule should be assured an undoubted security of life and an absolutely unmolested opportunity of autonomous development, and the Dardanelles should be permanently opened as a free passage to the ships and commerce of all nations under international guarantees.

XIII. An independent Polish state should be erected which should include the territories inhabited by indisputably Polish populations, which should be assured a free and secure access to the sea, and whose political and economic independence and territorial integrity should be guaranteed by international covenant.

XIV. A general association of nations must be formed under specific covenants for the purpose of affording mutual guarantees of political independence and territorial integrity to great and small states alike.

In regard to these essential rectifications of wrong and assertions of right we feel ourselves to be intimate partners of all the governments and peoples associated together against the Imperialists. We cannot be separated in interest or divided in purpose. We stand together until the end.

For such arrangements and covenants we are willing to fight and to continue to fight until they are achieved; but only because we wish the right to prevail and desire a just and stable peace such as can be secured only by removing the chief provocations to war, which this program does remove. We have no jealousy of German greatness, and there is nothing in this program that impairs it. We grudge her no achievement or distinction of learning or of pacific enterprise such as have made her record very bright and very enviable. We do not wish to injure her or to block in any way her legitimate influence or power. We do not wish to fight her either with arms or with hostile arrangements of trade if she is willing to associate herself with us and the other peace-loving nations of the world in covenants of justice and law and fair dealing. We wish her only to accept a place of equality among the peoples of the world, — the new world in which we now live — instead of a place of mastery.

Neither do we presume to suggest to her any alteration or modification of her institutions. But it is necessary, we must frankly say, and necessary as a preliminary to any intelligent dealings with her on our part, that we should know whom her spokesmen speak for when they speak to us, whether for the Reichstag majority or for the military party and the men whose creed is imperial domination. We have spoken now, surely in terms too concrete to admit of any further doubt or question. An evident principle runs through the whole program I have outlined. It is the principle of justice to all peoples and nationalities, and their right to live on equal terms of liberty and safety with one another, whether they be strong or weak. Unless this principle be made its foundation no part of the structure of international justice can stand. The people of the United States could act upon no other principle; and to the vindication of this principle they are ready to devote their lives, their honor, and everything that they possess. The moral climax of this the culminating and final war for human liberty has come, and they are ready to put their own strength, their own highest purpose, their own integrity and devotion to the test.

The League of Nations Covenant

The League of Nations, in which President Woodrow Wilson could not persuade the United States Congress to approve U.S. membership, was the first attempt at world government. Like the United Nations that succeeded it, the league had as many flaws as hopes. This selection includes two articles from the Covenant of the League.

Article 22 concerns the mandates that the league established over the former colonies of the defeated powers (Germany, Austria, the Ottoman Empire) in the First World War. How consistent was this article with Wilson's Fourteen Points? What did this article promise the former colonies? How do you think these colonies would have responded?

Article 23 shows an array of concerns for the fledgling organization but little about how such ideals might have been implemented. Should these have been concerns of the League of Nations? Should they be concerns of the United Nations? How can such ideals be realized by international law or international organizations?

Thinking Historically

At the time of the covenant, the First World War was to be the war to end all wars, the war to make the world safe for democracy, the war to allow the self-determination of nations. Do any of these clauses of the League of Nations Covenant encourage such outcomes? Do any discourage them? What would be the likely consequences of the League's success in all of these areas?

Article 22

To those colonies and territories which as a consequence of the late war have ceased to be under the sovereignty of the States which formerly governed them and which are inhabited by peoples not yet able to stand by themselves under the strenuous conditions of the modern world, there should be applied the principle that the well-being and development of such peoples form a sacred trust of civilisation and that securities for the performance of this trust should be embodied in this Covenant.

The best method of giving practical effect to this principle is that the tutelage of such peoples should be entrusted to advanced nations who by reason of their resources, their experience, or their geographical position can best undertake this responsibility, and who are willing to accept it, and that this tutelage should be exercised by them as Mandatories on behalf of the League.

The character of the mandate must differ according to the stage of the development of the people, the geographical situation of the territory, its economic conditions, and other similar circumstances.

Certain communities formerly belonging to the Turkish Empire have reached a stage of development where their existence as independent nations can be provisionally recognised subject to the rendering of administrative advice and assistance by a Mandatory until such time as they are able to stand alone. The wishes of these communities must be a principal consideration in the selection of the Mandatory.

Other peoples, especially those of Central Africa, are at such a stage that the Mandatory must be responsible for the administration of the territory under conditions which will guarantee freedom of conscience and religion, subject only to the maintenance of public order and morals, the prohibition of abuses such as the slave trade, the arms traffic and the liquor traffic, and the prevention of the establishment of fortifications or military and naval bases and of military training of the natives for other than police purposes, and the defence of territory, and will also secure equal opportunities for the trade and commerce of other Members of the League.

There are territories, such as South-West Africa and certain of the South Pacific Islands, which, owing to the sparseness of their population, or their small size, or their remoteness from the centres of civilisation, or their geographical contiguity to the territory of the Mandatory, and other circumstances, can be best administered under the laws of the Mandatory as integral portions of its territory, subject to the safeguards above mentioned in the interests of the indigenous population.

In every case of mandate, the Mandatory shall render to the Council an annual report in reference to the territory committed to its charge.

The degree of authority, control, or administration to be exercised by the Mandatory shall, if not previously agreed upon by the Members of the League, be explicitly defined in each case by the council.

A permanent Commission shall be constituted to receive and examine the annual reports of the Mandatories and to advise the Council on all matters relating to the observance of the mandates.

Article 23

Subject to and in accordance with the provisions of international conventions existing or hereafter to be agreed upon, the Members of the League:

(*a*) will endeavour to secure and maintain fair and humane conditions of labour for men, women, and children, both in their own countries and in all countries to which their commercial and industrial relations extend, and for that purpose will establish and maintain the necessary international organisations;

(*b*) undertake to secure just treatment of the native inhabitants of territories under their control;

(*c*) will entrust the League with the general supervision over the execution of agreements with regard to the traffic in women and children, and the traffic in opium and other dangerous drugs;

(*d*) will entrust the League with the general supervision of the trade in arms and ammunition with the countries in which the control of this traffic is necessary in the common interest;

(*e*) will make provision to secure and maintain freedom of communications and of transit and equitable treatment for the commerce of all Members of the League. In this connection, the special necessities of the regions devastated during the war of 1914–1918 shall be borne in mind;

(*f*) will endeavour to take steps in matters of international concern for the prevention and control of disease.

65

Syrian Congress Memorandum

Article 22 of the League of Nations Covenant came as a shock to the peoples of the defeated Ottoman Empire who had fought with the English and French during the war and expected their independence. This selection is the Syrian statement of such expectations, sent as a memorandum to the King-Crane Commission, the body responsible for overseeing the transfer of Ottoman territory. What specifically was the Syrian Congress asking for? Who did they represent? Why did they ask the United States for aid? In what ways did European powers try to block Syrian independence?

Thinking Historically

Do you think this conflict could have been an expected consequence of the First World War? Do you think Wilson's Fourteen Points made the Syrian demands more likely? Do you think the European powers expected this response to the League Covenant?

The King-Crane Commission Report, in *Foreign Relations of the United States: Paris Peace Conference, 1919*, vol. 12, 780–81.

We the undersigned members of the General Syrian Congress, meeting in Damascus on Wednesday, July 2nd 1919, . . . provided with credentials and authorizations by the inhabitants of our various districts, Muslims, Christians, and Jews, have agreed upon the following statement of the desires of the people of the country who have elected us to present them to the American Section of the International Commission; the fifth article was passed by a very large majority; all the other articles were accepted unanimously.

1. We ask absolutely complete political independence for Syria within these boundaries. The Taurus System on the North; Rafah and a line running from Al Jauf to the south of the Syrian and the Hejazian line to Akaba on the south; the Euphrates and Khabur Rivers and a line extending east of Abu Kamal to the east of Al Jauf on the east; and the Mediterranean on the west.

2. We ask that the Government of this Syrian country should be a democratic civil constitutional Monarchy on broad decentralization principles, safeguarding the rights of minorities, and that the King be the Emir Feisal, who carried on a glorious struggle in the cause of our liberation and merited our full confidence and entire reliance.

3. Considering the fact that the Arabs inhabiting the Syrian area are not naturally less than other more advanced races and that they are by no means less developed than the Bulgarians, Serbians, Greeks, and Romanians at the beginning of their independence, we protest against Article 22 of the Covenant of the League of Nations, placing us among the nations in their middle stage of development which stand in need of a mandatory power.

4. In the event of the rejection by the Peace Conference of this just protest for certain considerations that we may not understand, we, relying on the declarations of President Wilson that his object in waging war was to put an end to the ambition of conquest and colonization, can only regard the mandate mentioned in the Covenant of the League of Nations as equivalent to the rendering of economical and technical assistance that does not prejudice our complete independence. And desiring that our country should not fall a prey to colonization and believing that the American Nation is furthest from any thought of colonization and has no political ambition in our country, we will seek the technical and economical assistance from the United States of America, provided that such assistance does not exceed 20 years.

5. In the event of America not finding herself in a position to accept our desire for assistance, we will seek this assistance from Great Britain, also provided that such assistance does not infringe the complete independence and unity of our country and that the duration of such assistance does not exceed that mentioned in the previous article.

6. We do not acknowledge any right claimed by the French Government in any part whatever of our Syrian country and refuse that she should assist us or have a hand in our country under any circumstances and in any place.

7. We oppose the pretensions of the Zionists to create a Jewish commonwealth in the southern part of Syria, known as Palestine, and oppose Zionist migration to any part of our country; for we do not acknowledge their title but consider them a grave peril to our people from the national, economical, and political points of view. Our Jewish compatriots shall enjoy our common rights and assume the common responsibilities.

8. We ask that there should be no separation of the southern part of Syria, known as Palestine, nor of the littoral western zone, which includes Lebanon, from the Syrian country. We desire that the unity of the country should be guaranteed against partition under whatever circumstances.

9. We ask complete independence for emancipated Mesopotamia and that there should be no economic barriers between the two countries.

10. The fundamental principles laid down by President Wilson in condemnation of secret treaties impel us to protest most emphatically against any treaty that stipulates the partition of our Syrian country and against any private engagement aiming at the establishment of Zionism in the southern part of Syria; therefore we ask the complete annulment of these conventions and agreements.

The noble principles enunciated by President Wilson strengthen our confidence that our desires emanating from the depths of our hearts, shall be the decisive factor in determining our future; and that President Wilson and the free American people will be our supporters for the realization of our hopes, thereby proving their sincerity and noble sympathy with the aspiration of the weaker nations in general and our Arab people in particular.

We also have the fullest confidence that the Peace Conference will realize that we would not have risen against the Turks, with whom we had participated in all civil, political, and representative privileges, but for their violation of our national rights, and so will grant us our desires in full in order that our political rights may not be less after the war than they were before, since we have shed so much blood in the cause of our liberty and independence.

We request to be allowed to send a delegation to represent us at the Peace Conference to defend our rights and secure the realization of our aspirations.

REFLECTIONS

By studying causes and consequences of world events, we learn how things change but more important we learn how to avoid repeating past mistakes. History is full of lessons that breed humility as well as confidence. In *The Origins of the First World War,*[1] historian James Joll points out how unprepared people were for the war as late as the summer of 1914. The lead article of the *London Times* on July 3, headlined "Efforts for Peace," declared ominously: "The public in England and Scotland do not realize how near the nation is to disaster." But those prophetic words concerned not the mounting European storm but rather the situation in Ireland. Even after the Austrian ultimatum to Serbia was issued on July 23 (almost a month after the assassination of the Archduke Franz Ferdinand on June 28), diplomats across Europe left for their summer holidays. By August, all of Europe was at war, though the expectation was that it would be over in a month.

We could make a good case for diplomatic blundering as an important cause of the First World War. It is safe to say that few statesmen had any inkling of the consequences of their actions in 1914. And yet, if we concentrate on the daily decisions of diplomats that summer, we may pay attention only to the tossing of lit matches by people sitting on powder kegs rather than on the origins of the powder kegs themselves.

In the years since 1914, there have been various accusations and explanations, each side blaming the other. German "war guilt" was established by force of arms and written into the Treaty of Versailles by the victors. But as English economist John Maynard Keynes argued in *The Economic Consequences of the Peace,* the saddling of moral guilt and heavy financial reparation payments for the war on Germany and Austria would have its own disastrous consequences: "The policy of reducing Germany to servitude for a generation," he wrote, "should be abhorrent and detestable, even if it were possible, even if it enriched ourselves, even if it did not sow the decay of the whole civilized life of Europe."[2] Writing in 1919, Keynes could not know how prophetic he was; he did not know that one of the consequences of declaring German acts the *cause* of the First World War would be an even more devastating Second World War.

President Wilson blamed secret diplomacy, the international system of alliances, and imperialism as the chief causes of the war. The idea that countries could be forced into war by secret treaties must have lost some of its cogency when the U.S. Congress refused to ratify Wilson's own negotiations, and neither alliances nor imperialism were regarded as un-American or likely to end in 1919. But Wilson's radical moral aversion to reviving Old World empires would have prevented, if successful, a new stage of imperialism in the League of Nations mandate system. One of the consequences of a Wilsonian peace might have been independent states in the Middle East and Africa a generation earlier.

1 James Joll, *The Origins of the First World War* (London: Longman, 1992), 200.
2 John Maynard Keynes, *The Economic Consequences of the Peace* (New York: Penguin, 1971), 225.

The principle of the "self-determination of nations" that Wilson espoused, however, was a double-edged sword. The fact that the war had
been "caused" by a Bosnian Serb nationalist assassin in 1914 might
have been a warning that national self-determination could become an
infinite regress in which smaller and smaller units sought to separate
themselves from foreign domination. On the issue of nationalism versus
internationalism, Wilson might have benefited from listening to Rosa
Luxemburg. When asked about antisemitism, this Jew from Russian
Poland answered:

> What do you want with this particular suffering of the Jews? The poor
> victims of the rubber plantations of Putumayo, the Negroes of Africa
> with whose bodies the Europeans play a game of catch are just as near
> to me. . . . I have no special corner of my heart reserved for the ghetto:
> I am at home wherever in the world there are clouds, birds, and human
> tears.[3]

Woodrow Wilson was a historian and president of Princeton University
before he became president of the United States. Rosa Luxemburg was
a professional revolutionary — perhaps the leading socialist theorist in
Europe. Both were trained to think historically. Which of the two better understood the causes and consequences of the First World War?
Which of the two had a better appreciation of the problems of nationalism that were to continue to haunt the twentieth century?

The rise of nationalist movements and international organizations
were only two consequences of the First World War. Historians have
attributed many other aspects of the twentieth century to the war. In an
engaging account of his own search for the evidence of war along the
Western Front, Stephen O'Shea writes:

> It is generally accepted that the Great War and its fifty-two months of
> senseless slaughter encouraged, or amplified, among other things: the
> loss of a belief in progress, a mistrust of technology, the loss of reli-
> gious faith, the loss of a belief in Western cultural superiority, the re-
> jection of class distinctions, the rejection of traditional sexual roles, the
> birth of the Modern [in art], the rejection of the past, the elevation of
> irony to a standard mode of apprehending the world, the unbuttoning
> of moral codes, and the conscious embrace of the irrational.[4]

What evidence can you find of any of these consequences in the participant accounts of this chapter?

---

[3] Jay Winter and Blaine Baggett, *The Great War* (New York: Penguin, 1996), 248, quoting Rosa Luxemburg.

[4] Stephen O'Shea, *Back to the Front: An Accidental Historian Walks the Trenches of
World War I* (New York: Avon Books, 1996), 9.

11

Fascism, World War II, and Genocide

HISTORICAL CONTEXT
Italy, Germany, Japan, China, and the Soviet Union, 1931–1945

It is easier to understand the causes of the Second World War than of the First World War. In 1914, we might have pointed to Serbia or Austria, Germany or England, even the bellicosity of Russia and France. But in 1939, it was Hitler's invasion of Poland that led to war with France (which was defeated along with most of Europe in 1940), England, and the nations of the British Commonwealth, followed by the Soviet Union after 1940 and the United States after 1941. As in 1914, Germany was allied with Austria (a remnant of the former empire annexed by Germany after 1937) and the new Axis alliance of Japan and Italy (until 1943).

World War II was even more of a global conflict than World War I. It began with the Japanese invasion of Manchuria in 1931, continuing with Japan's conquest of most of China in 1937 and of Southeast Asia and the Pacific in 1941. For Africans, the war began with the Italian invasion of Ethiopia in 1935. After 1940, North Africa became an increasingly important battleground. As in World War I, soldiers were drawn from all over the world, from Africa and India, the Caribbean and Middle East, but especially in the end, from the United States, Canada, Australia, and New Zealand.

The death toll from World War II may have approached one hundred million, soldiers and civilians combined. Russian deaths alone have been estimated to be between ten and forty million, an indication of the imprecision of such estimates. A common figure of fifty million deaths for all of Europe includes twenty million Russians. Asian casualties number around ten million in China alone. Civilian casualties in an age of lightning tank attacks, military occupation of cities, and aerial bombing were enormous. World War I blurred the distinction between soldiers and civilians; World War II ended it. Millions of civilians died in Eastern Europe — along the paths of invading armies — in the great cities of China, and in the bombed-out cities of Germany and Japan. The numbers of wounded, mentally or physically, cannot be counted. The destruction of property, the disruption of normal lives, the hunger, famine, disease, and deprivation continued long after the end of the war in 1945.

Death tolls offer a crude glimpse of war, and clearly World War II was one of the worst. This chapter focuses on a terrifying aspect of the conflict: the war within the war. Worse than the international struggles of armies, worse than the millions of collaborative casualties of civilians caught in harm's way was the mass murder of civilians, for which the war was no excuse. Hitler's attempt to rid the world of Jews was genocide. The systematic roundup and murder of gypsies, homosexuals, and psychiatric patients, among others, was part of his larger attempt at racial "cleansing" and "Aryan" domination for which the war was little more than a pretext. In addition, Hitler undertook the mass slaughter of all leaders and educated civilians in occupied Poland and Russia for the express purpose of turning those nations into docile armies of brute labor for German industry.

The Nazi racist agenda of genocide brought a particularly horrific dimension to war. The level of bestiality, of gross indifference to human life, of sadistic killing of defenseless civilians — among them women and children, the helpless, infirm, and aged — reached unimagined heights. Whether this was due to factors that distinguish the twentieth century from earlier eras (e.g., the anonymity of mass society, a global mix of populations, the rise of racist ideas, economic depression, the rise of fascist political parties and movements, the militarization of political life) we do not know. We do know that the Nazi experience was not singular. Imperial Japan, run by a militaristic fascist government in the 1930s, encouraged similar racist and inhumane behavior in its troops in Manchuria, China, and Southeast Asia. Both Germany and Japan gave scientists and common soldiers motive and approval for killing helpless wards in the most painful ways, without remorse or concern. Were such barbarities limited to these two countries? Certainly not. To a certain extent the encouragement of inhumanity was a product of dictatorship — the eclipse of individual will or power in fascist regimes and in Stalinist Russia as well.

THINKING HISTORICALLY
Understanding the Unforgivable

Occasionally when we learn of something horrendous, we simply say, "I don't believe it." Our disbelief harbors two feelings: first, our sense of outrage and anger, a rejection of what was done; second, our unwillingness to believe that such a thing could happen or did happen. Our choice of words expresses the difficulty we have making sense of the senseless.

We must try, however, to understand such catastrophes so that we can help to prevent similar horrors in the future. Understanding requires a level of empathy that is often difficult to arouse when we find someone's actions reprehensible. As you read these selections, you will be encouraged to understand, not to forgive.

┌─────┐
│ 66 │
└─────┘

JOACHIM C. FEST

The Rise of Hitler

World War II had its origins in World War I. The peace terms imposed by the victors demanded the removal of the kaiser, the demilitarization of Germany, the transfer of Germany's industrial heartland to France, and the payment of enormous sums in reparation for the war. In addition, the revolutionary establishment of a republic by the German socialist party was followed by the unsuccessful uprising by the far more radical Spartacus League, which had raised the specter of a Bolshevik coup that would later turn Germany into a communist state.

In this essay, historian Joachim Fest explores the response of German conservative, nationalist, and middle-class groups to these developments. The National Socialists (the Nazi party) was just one of many fascist groups in Germany. Initiated by Mussolini in Italy in 1922, fascism was a movement that spread throughout Europe. As defined by Mussolini, in fascism the state dominates everything else:

> For the Fascist the state is all-embracing; outside it no human or spiritual values exist, much less have worth. In this sense Fascism is totalitarian, and the Fascist State — a synthesis and a unity of all values — interprets, develops, and gives power to the whole life of the people.[1]

---

[1] *Enciclopedia Italiana*, vol. xiv, s.v. "fascism," signed by Mussolini but actually written by the philosopher Giovanni Gentile (1932), 847.

Joachim C. Fest, *Hitler*, trans. Clara and Richard Winston (New York: Harcourt Brace and Co., 1974), 89–91, 92–93, 99–102, 104–05.

Why did fascism appeal more to the middle-class than to the working class? Was Hitler typical of those who were attracted to fascism? Was Hitler out of touch with reality, or was he tuned in to the feelings of many?

Thinking Historically

Fest helps us understand some of the appeal of fascism by putting it into the context of Germany's defeat in World War I and the real or imagined threat of a Bolshevik revolution. Can you imagine empathizing with antirevolutionary fears if you lived then? Imagine how you might have responded to some of the other fascist appeals: fewer politicians, more police? The nobility of sacrificing for higher purposes; challenging the gray ordinariness of modern life; following instinct rather than reason; and war as authentic experience.

Are there mainstream Americans today who respond favorably to the idea of "revolt on behalf of order," who desire "authority, guidance, and order," or who are disgusted with liberalism?

At the end of the First World War the victory of the democratic idea seemed beyond question. Whatever its weaknesses might be, it rose above the turmoil of the times, the uprisings, the dislocations, and the continual quarrels among nations as the unifying principle of the new age. For the war had not only decided a claim to power. It had at the same time altered a conception of government. After the collapse of virtually all the governmental structures of Central and Eastern Europe, many new political entities had emerged out of turmoil and revolution. And these for the most part were organized on democratic principles. In 1914 there had been only three republics alongside of seventeen monarchies in Europe. Four years later there were as many republics as monarchies. The spirit of the age seemed to be pointing unequivocally toward various forms of popular rule.

Only Germany seemed to be opposing this mood of the times, after having been temporarily gripped and carried along by it. Those who would not acknowledge the reality created by the war organized into a fantastic swarm of *völkisch* (racist-nationalist) parties, clubs, and free corps. To these groups the revolution had been an act of treason; parliamentary democracy was something foreign and imposed from without, merely a synonym for "everything contrary to the German political will," or else an "institution for pillaging created by Allied capitalism."

Germany's former enemies regarded the multifarious symptoms of nationalistic protest as the response of an inveterately authoritarian people to democracy and civic responsibility. To be sure, the Germans were staggering beneath terrible political and psychological burdens:

There was the shock of defeat, the moral censure of the Versailles Treaty, the loss of territory and the demand for reparations, the impoverishment and spiritual undermining of much of the population. Nevertheless, the conviction remained that a great moral gap existed between the Germans and most of their neighbours. Full of resentment, refusing to learn a lesson, this incomprehensible country had withdrawn into its reactionary doctrines, made of them a special virtue, abjured Western rationality and humanity, and in general set itself against the universal trend of the age. For decades this picture of Germany dominated the discussion of the reasons for the rise of National Socialism.

But the image of democracy victorious was also deceptive. The moment in which democracy seemed to be achieving historic fulfillment simultaneously marked the beginning of its crisis. Only a few years later the idea of democracy was challenged in principle as it had never been before. Only a few years after it had celebrated its triumph it was overwhelmed or at least direly threatened by a new movement that had sprung to life in almost all European countries.

This movement recorded its most lasting successes in countries in which the war had aroused considerable discontent or made it conscious of existing discontent, and especially in countries in which the war had been followed by leftist revolutionary uprisings. In some places these movements were conservative, harking back to better times when men were more honorable, the valleys more peaceable, and money had more worth; in others these movements were revolutionary and vied with one another in their contempt for the existing order of things. Some attracted chiefly the petty bourgeois elements, others the peasants, others portions of the working class. Whatever their strange compound of classes, interests, and principles, all seemed to be drawing their dynamic force from the less conscious and more vital lower strata of society. National Socialism was merely one variant of this widespread European movement of protest and opposition aimed at overturning the general order of things.

National Socialism rose from provincial beginnings, from philistine clubs, as Hitler scornfully described them, which met in Munich bars over a few rounds of beer to talk over national and family troubles. No one would have dreamed that they could ever challenge, let alone outdo, the powerful, highly organized Marxist parties. But the following years proved that in these clubs of nationalistic beer drinkers, soon swelled by disillusioned homecoming soldiers and proletarianized members of the middle class, a tremendous force was waiting to be awakened, consolidated, and applied.

In Munich alone there existed, in 1919, nearly fifty more or less political associations, whose membership consisted chiefly of confused remnants of the prewar parties that had been broken up by war and revolution.

They had such names as New Fatherland, Council of Intellectual Work, Siegfried Ring, Universal League, Nova Vaconia, League of Socialist Women, Free Union of Socialist Pupils, and Ostara League. The German Workers' Party was one such group. What united them all and drew them together theoretically and in reality was nothing but an overwhelming feeling of anxiety.

First of all, and most immediate, there was the fear of revolution, that *grande peur* which after the French Revolution had haunted the European-bourgeoisie throughout the nineteenth century. The notion that revolutions were like forces of nature, elemental mechanisms operating without reference to the will of the actors in them, following their own logic and leading perforce to reigns of terror, destruction, killing, and chaos — that notion was seared into the public mind. That was the unforgettable experience, not [German philosopher Immanuel] Kant's belief that the French Revolution had also shown the potentiality for betterment inherent in human nature. For generations, particularly in Germany, this fear stood in the way of any practical revolutionary strivings and produced a mania for keeping things quiet, with the result that every revolutionary proclamation up to 1918 was countered by the standard appeal to law and order.

This old fear was revived by the pseudorevolutionary events in Germany and by the menace of the October Revolution in Russia. Diabolical traits were ascribed to the Reds. The refugees pouring into Munich described bloodthirsty barbarians on a rampage of killing. Such imagery had instant appeal to the nationalists. The following article from one of Munich's racist newspapers is a fair example of the fears of the period and the way these were expressed:

> Dreadful times in which Christian-hating, circumcised Asiatics everywhere are raising their bloodstained hands to strangle us in droves! The butcheries of Christians by the Jew Issachar Zederblum, alias Lenin, would have made even a Genghis Khan blush. In Hungary his pupil Cohn, alias Béla Kun, marched through the unhappy land with a band of Jewish terrorists schooled in murder and robbery, to set up, among brutal gallows, a mobile machine gallows and execute middle-class citizens and peasants on it. A splendidly equipped harem served him, in his stolen royal train, to rape and defile honorable Christian virgins by the dozen. His lieutenant Samuely has had sixty priests cruelly butchered in a single underground room. Their bellies are ripped open, their corpses mutilated, after they have been plundered to their blood-drenched skin. In the case of eight murdered priests it has been established that they were first crucified on the doors of their own churches! The very same atrocious scenes are . . . now reported from Munich. . . .

This threat dominated Hitler's speeches of the early years. In gar-ish colors he depicted the ravages of the "Red squads of butchers," the "murderous communists," the "bloody morass of Bolshevism." In Russia, he told his audiences, more than thirty million persons had been murdered, "partly on the scaffold, partly by machine guns and similar means, partly in veritable slaughterhouses, partly, millions upon millions, by hunger; and we all know that this wave of hunger is creeping on . . . and see that this scourge is approaching, that it is also coming upon Germany." The intelligentsia of the Soviet Union, he de-clared, had been exterminated by mass murder, the economy utterly smashed. Thousands of German prisoners-of-war had been drowned in the Neva or sold as slaves. Meanwhile, in Germany the enemy was boring away at the foundations of society "in unremitting, ever un-changing undermining work." The fate of Russia, he said again and again, would soon be ours! And years later, when he was already in power, he spoke again of "the horror of the Communist international hate dictatorship" that had preyed on his mind at the beginning of his career: "I tremble at the thought of what would become of our old, overcrowded continent if the chaos of the Bolshevik revolution were to be successful."

National Socialism owed a considerable part of its emotional ap-peal, its militancy, and its cohesion to this defensive attitude toward the threat of Marxist revolution. The aim of the National Socialist Party, Hitler repeatedly declared, "is very brief: Annihilation and extermina-tion of the Marxist world view." This was to be accomplished by an "incomparable, brilliantly orchestrated propaganda and information organization" side by side with a movement "of the most ruthless force and most brutal resolution, prepared to oppose all terrorism on the part of the Marxists with tenfold greater terrorism." At about the same time, for similar reasons, Mussolini was founding his Fasci di combatti-mento [battle group]. Henceforth, the new movements were to be iden-tified by the general name of "Fascism."

But the fear of revolution would not have been enough to endow the movement with that fierce energy, which for a time seemed to stem the universal trend toward democracy. After all, for many people revo-lution meant hope. A stronger and more elemental motivation had to be added. And in fact Marxism was feared as the precursor of a far more comprehensive assault upon all traditional ideas. It was viewed as the contemporary political aspect of a metaphysical upheaval, as a "dec-laration of war upon the European . . . idea of culture." Marxism itself was only the metaphor for something dreaded that escaped definition.

Anxiety was the permanent emotion of the time. It sprang from the intuition that the end of the war meant not only the end of familiar pre-war Europe with its grandeur and its urge to world domination, its monarchies, and gilt-edged securities, but also the end of an era. Along with the old forms of government, the accustomed framework of life was being destroyed. The unrest, the radicalism of the politicalized masses, the disorders of revolution were interpreted as the afterpains of the war and simultaneously as harbingers of a new, strange, and chaotic age. "That is why the foundations of life quake beneath our feet." . . .

This first phase of the postwar era was characterized both by fear of revolution and anticivilizational resentments; these together, curiously intertwined and reciprocally stimulating each other, produced a syndrome of extraordinary force. Into the brew went the hate and defense complexes of a society shaken to its foundations. German society had lost its imperial glory, its civil order, its national confidence, its prosperity, and its familiar authorities. The whole system had been turned topsy-turvy, and now many Germans blindly and bitterly wanted back what they thought had been unjustly taken from them. These general feelings of unhappiness were intensified and further radicalized by a variety of unsatisfied group interests. The class of white-collar workers, continuing to grow apace, proved especially susceptible to the grand gesture of total criticism. For the industrial revolution had just begun to affect office workers and was reducing the former "non-commissioned officers of capitalism" to the status of last victims of "modern slavery." It was all the worse for them because unlike the proletarians they had never developed a class pride of their own or imagined that the breakdown of the existing order was going to lead to their own apotheosis. Small businessmen were equally susceptible because of their fear of being crushed by corporations, department stores, and rationalized competition. Another unhappy group consisted of farmers who, slow to change and lacking capital, were fettered to backward modes of production. Another group were the academics and formerly solid bourgeois who felt themselves caught in the tremendous suction of proletarianization. Without outside support you found yourself "at once despised, declassed; to be unemployed is the same as being a communist," one victim stated in a questionnaire of the period. No statistics, no figures on rates of inflation, bankruptcies, and suicides can describe the feelings of those threatened by unemployment or poverty, or can express the anxieties of those others who still possessed some property and feared the consequences of so much accumulated discontent. Public institutions in their persistent weakness offered no bulwark against the seething collective emotions. It was all the worse because the widespread anxiety no longer, as in the time of Lagarde and Langbehn, was limited to cries of woe and impotent prophecies. The war had given arms to the fearful.

The vigilante groups and the free corps that were being organized in great numbers, partly on private initiative, partly with covert government support, chiefly to meet the threat of Communist revolution, formed centers of bewildered but determined resistance to the *status quo*. The members of these paramilitary groups were vaguely looking around for someone to lead them into a new system. At first there was another reservoir of militant energies alongside the parliamentary groups: the mass of homecoming soldiers. Many of these stayed in the barracks dragging out a pointless military life, baffled and unable to say good-bye to the warrior dreams of their recent youth. In the front-line trenches they had glimpsed the outlines of a new meaning to life; in the sluggishly resuming normality of the postwar period they tried in vain to find that meaning again. They had not fought and suffered for years for the sake of this weakened regime with its borrowed ideals which, as they saw it, could be pushed around by the most contemptible of their former enemies. And they also feared, after the exalting sense of life the war had given them, the ignobility of the commonplace bourgeois world.

It remained for Hitler to bring together these feelings and to appoint himself their spearhead. Indeed, Hitler regarded as a phenomenon seems like the synthetic product of all the anxiety, pessimism, nostalgia, and defensiveness we have discussed. For him, too, the war had been education and liberation. If there is a "Fascistic" type, it was embodied in him. More than any of his followers he expressed the underlying psychological, social, and ideological motives of the movement. He was never just its leader; he was also its exponent.

His early years had contributed their share to that experience of overwhelming anxiety which dominated his intellectual and emotional constitution. That lurking anxiety can be seen at the root of almost all his statements and reactions. It had everyday as well as cosmic dimensions. Many who knew him in his youth have described his pallid, "timorous" nature, which provided the fertile soil for his lush fantasies. His "constant fear" of contact with strangers was another aspect of that anxiety, as was his extreme distrust and his compulsion to wash frequently, which became more and more pronounced in later life. The same complex is apparent in his oft-expressed fear of venereal disease and his fear of contagion in general. He knew that "microbes are rushing at me." He was ridden by the Austrian Pan-German's fear of being overwhelmed by alien races, by fear of the "locust-like immigration of Russian and Polish Jews," by fear of "the niggerizing of the Germans," by fear of the Germans' "expulsion from Germany," and finally by fear that the Germans would be "exterminated." He had the *Völkische Boebachter* print an alleged French soldier's song whose refrain was: "Germans, we will possess your daughters!" Among his phobias were

American technology, the birth rate of the Slavs, big cities, "industrialization as unrestricted as it is harmful," the "economization of the nation," corporations, the "morass of metropolitan amusement culture," and modern art, which sought "to kill the soul of the people" by painting meadows blue and skies green. Wherever he looked he discovered the "signs of decay of a slowly ebbing world." Not an element of pessimistic anticivilizational criticism was missing from his imagination.

What linked Hitler with the leading Fascists of other countries was the resolve to halt this process of degeneration. What set him apart from them, however, was the manic single-mindedness with which he traced all the anxieties he had ever felt back to a single source. For at the heart of the towering structure of anxiety, black and hairy, stood the figure of the Jew: evil-smelling, smacking his lips, lusting after blonde girls, eternal contaminator of the blood, but "racially harder" than the Aryan, as Hitler uneasily declared as late as the summer of 1942. A prey to his psychosis, he saw Germany as the object of a worldwide conspiracy, pressed on all sides by Bolshevists, Freemasons, capitalists, Jesuits, all hand in glove with each other and directed in their nefarious projects by the "bloodthirsty and avaricious Jewish tyrant." *The* Jew had 75 per cent of world capital at his disposal. He dominated the stock exchanges and the Marxist parties, the Gold and Red Internationals. He was the "advocate of birth control and the idea of emigration." He undermined governments, bastardized races, glorified fratricide, fomented civil war, justified baseness, and poisoned nobility: "the wirepuller of the destinies of mankind." The whole world was in danger, Hitler cried imploringly; it had fallen "into the embrace of this octopus." He groped for images in which to make his horror tangible, saw "creeping venom," "belly-worms," and "adders devouring the nation's body." In formulating his anxiety he might equally hit on the maddest and most ludicrous phrases as on impressive or at least memorable ones. Thus he invented the "Jewification of our spiritual life," "the mammonization of our mating instinct," and "the resulting syphilization of our people." He could prophesy: "If, with the help of his Marxist creed, the Jew is victorious over the other peoples of the world, his crown will be the funeral wreath of humanity and the planet will, as it did millions of years ago, move through the ether devoid of men."

The appearance of Hitler signaled a union of those forces that in crisis conditions had great political potential. The Fascistic movements all centered on the charismatic appeal of a unique leader. The leader was to be the resolute voice of order controlling chaos. He would have looked further and thought deeper, would know the despairs but also the means of salvation. This looming giant had already been given established form in a prophetic literature that went back to German folklore. Like the mythology of many other nations unfortunate in their history, that of the Germans has its sleeping leaders dreaming away the centuries in the bowels of a mountain, but destined some day to return to rally their people and punish the guilty world. . . .

The same factors underlay the paramilitary aspects of the Fascistic movements, the uniforms, the rituals of saluting, reporting, standing at attention. The insigne of the movements all came down to a few basic motifs — various forms of crosses (such as the St. Olaf's cross of the Norwegian Nasjonal Samling and the red St. Andrew's cross of Portugal's National Syndicalists), also arrows, bundles of fasces, scythes. These symbols were constantly displayed on flags, badges, standards, or armbands. To some extent they were meant as defiance of the boring old bourgeois business of tailcoats and stiff collars. But primarily they seemed more in keeping with the brisk technological spirit of the age. Then, too, uniforms and military trappings could conceal social differences and bring some dash to the dullness and emotional barrenness of ordinary civilian life. . . .

The success of Fascism in contrast to many of its rivals was in large part due to its perceiving the essence of the crisis, of which it was itself the symptom. All the other parties affirmed the process of industrialization and emancipation, whereas the Fascists, evidently sharing the universal anxiety, tried to deal with it by translating it into violent action and histrionics. They also managed to leaven boring, prosaic everyday life by romantic rituals: torchlight processions, standards, death's heads, battle cries, and shouts of *Heil*, by the "new marriage of life with danger," and the idea of "glorious death." They presented men with modern tasks disguised in the costumery of the past. They deprecated material concerns and treated "politics as an area of self-denial and sacrifice of the individual for an idea." In taking this line they were addressing themselves to deeper needs than those who promised the masses higher wages. Ahead of all their rivals, the Fascists appeared to have recognized that the Marxist or liberal conception of man as guided only by reason and material interests was a monstrous abstraction.

Thus Fascism served the craving of the period for a general upheaval more effectively than its antagonists. It alone seemed to be articulating the feeling that everything had gone wrong, that the world had been led into an impasse. That Communism made fewer converts was not due solely to its stigma of being a class party and the agency of a foreign power. Rather, Communism suffered from a vague feeling that it represented part of the wrong turn the world had taken and part of the disease it pretended it could cure. Communism seemed not the negation of bourgeois materialism but merely its obverse, not the superseding of an unjust and inadequate system, but its mirror image turned upside down.

Hitler's unshakable confidence, which often seemed sheer madness, was based on the conviction that he was the only real revolutionary, that he had broken free of the existing system by reinstating the rights of human instincts. In alliance with these interests, he believed, he was invincible, for the instincts always won out in the end "against economic motivation, against the pressure of public opinion, even against reason." No doubt the appeal to instinct brought out a good deal of human baseness. No doubt what fascism wanted to restore was often a grotesque parody of the tradition they purported to honor, and the order they hailed was a hollow sham. But when Trotsky contemptuously dismissed the adherents of Fascistic movements as "human dust," he was only revealing the Left's characteristic ineptness in dealing with people's needs and impulses. That ineptness led to a multitude of clever errors of judgment by those who purported to understand the spirit of the age better than anyone else. . . .

67

HEINRICH HIMMLER

Speech to the SS

Heinrich Himmler (1900–1945) was one of the most powerful leaders of Nazi Germany. He was the head of the SS — the *Schutzstaffel*, the black-shirted elite army — which, among other responsibilities, ran the many concentration camps. Hitler gave Himmler the task of implementing the "final solution of the Jewish question": the policy of killing the Jewish population of Germany and the other countries the Nazis occupied. The horror that resulted is today often referred to by the biblical word *holocaust*.

The following reading consists of an excerpt from a speech Himmler gave to SS leaders on October 4, 1943. What seemed to be Himmler's concern in this speech? What kind of general support for the extermination of the Jews does this excerpt suggest existed?

Heinrich Himmler, "Secret Speech at Posen," *A Holocaust Reader,* ed. Lucy S. Dawidowicz (New York: Behrman House, 1976), 132–33.

Thinking Historically

Psychiatrists say that people use various strategies to cope when they must do something distasteful. We might summarize these strategies as denial, distancing, compartmentalizing, ennobling, rationalizing, and scapegoating. *Denial* pretends that something has not happened. *Distancing* removes the idea, memory, or reality from the mind, placing it at distance. *Compartmentalizing* separates one action, memory, or idea from others, allowing one to "put away" certain feelings. *Ennobling* makes the distasteful act a matter of pride rather than guilt, nobility rather than disgrace. *Rationalizing* creates "good" reasons for doing something, while *scapegoating* puts blame on someone else. These strategies overlap, and many of them might be used in the same situation.

What evidence do you see of these strategies in Himmler's speech? Judging from the speech, which of these strategies do you think his listeners used? To the extent that they rationalized their actions, what sorts of rationalizations or reasons do you think they offered?

I also want to make reference before you here, in complete frankness, to a really grave matter. Among ourselves, this once, it shall be uttered quite frankly; but in public we will never speak of it. Just as we did not hesitate on June 30, 1934, to do our duty as ordered, to stand up against the wall comrades who had transgressed,[1] and shoot them, so we have never talked about this and never will. It was the tact which I am glad to say is a matter of course to us that made us never discuss it among ourselves, never talk about it. Each of us shuddered, and yet each one knew that he would do it again if it were ordered and if it were necessary.

I am referring to the evacuation of the Jews, the annihilation of the Jewish people. This is one of those things that are easily said. "The Jewish people is going to be annihilated," says every party member. "Sure, it's in our program, elimination of the Jews, annihilation — we'll take care of it." And then they all come trudging, 80 million worthy Germans, and each one has his one decent Jew. Sure, the others are swine, but this one is an A-1 Jew. Of all those who talk this way, not one has seen it happen, not one has been through it. Most of you must know what it means to see a hundred corpses lie side by side, or five hundred, or a thousand. To have stuck this out — excepting cases of human weakness — to have kept our integrity, that is what has made us hard. In our history, this is an unwritten and never-to-be-written

---

[1] A reference to the "Night of the Long Knives," when Hitler ordered the SS to murder the leaders of the SA, a Nazi group he wished to suppress. [Ed.]

page of glory, for we know how difficult we would have made it for ourselves if today — amid the bombing raids, the hardships, and the deprivations of war — we still had the Jews in every city as secret saboteurs, agitators, and demagogues. If the Jews were still ensconced in the body of the German nation, we probably would have reached the 1916–17 stage by now.[2]

The wealth they had we have taken from them. I have issued a strict order, carried out by SS-Obergruppenfuhrer Pohl, that this wealth in its entirety is to be turned over to the Reich as a matter of course. We have taken none of it for ourselves. Individuals who transgress will be punished in accordance with an order I issued at the beginning, threatening that whoever takes so much as a mark of it for himself is a dead man. A number of SS men — not very many — have transgressed, and they will die, without mercy. We had the moral right, we had the duty toward our people, to kill this people which wanted to kill us. But we do not have the right to enrich ourselves with so much as a fur, a watch, a mark, or a cigarette, or anything else. Having exterminated a germ, we do not want, in the end, to be infected by the germ, and die of it. I will not stand by and let even a small rotten spot develop or take hold. Wherever it may form, we together will cauterize it. All in all, however, we can say that we have carried out this heaviest of our tasks in a spirit of love for our people. And our inward being, our soul, our character has not suffered injury from it.

68

JEAN-FRANÇOIS STEINER

From *Treblinka*

Treblinka, in Poland, was one of several Nazi death camps. (Auschwitz was the largest camp.) In these "death factories," the Nazis murdered millions of Jews as well as many thousands of gypsies, socialists, Soviet prisoners of war, and other people. In this selection, Steiner, who lost his father at Treblinka, reveals how "rational"

[2] Here Himmler is apparently referring to the stalemate on Germany's western front in World War I. [Ed.]

Jean-François Steiner, *Treblinka* (New York: Simon & Schuster, 1967), 153–54, 155–58, 159–60.

and "scientific" mass murder can be. How could this happen? Can it happen again?

Thinking Historically

Try to imagine what went through the mind of Lalka as he designed the extermination process at Treblinka. How did concerns for efficiency and humanity enter into his deliberations? Do you think he found his work distasteful? If so, which of the strategies mentioned in the previous selection did he adopt?

What would it have been like to be a sign-painter, guard, haircutter, "dentist," or body-carrier at Treblinka?

. . . Each poorly organized debarkation [of deportees from trains arriving at Treblinka] gave rise to unpleasant scenes — uncertainties and confusion for the deportees, who did not know where they were going and were sometimes seized with panic.

So, the first problem was to restore a minimum of hope. Lalka[1] had many faults, but he did not lack a certain creative imagination. After a few days of reflection he hit upon the idea of transforming the platform where the convoys [trains] arrived into a false station. He had the ground filled in to the level of the doors of the cars in order to give the appearance of a train platform and to make it easier to get off the trains. . . . On [a] wall Lalka had . . . doors and windows painted in gay and pleasing colors. The windows were decorated with cheerful curtains and framed by green blinds which were just as false as the rest. Each door was given a special name, stencilled at eye level: "Stationmaster," "Toilet," "Infirmary" (a red cross was painted on this door). Lalka carried his concern for detail so far as to have his men paint two doors leading to the waiting rooms, first and second class. The ticket window, which was barred with a horizontal sign reading, "Closed," was a little masterpiece with its ledge and false perspective and its grill, painted line for line. Next to the ticket window a large timetable announced the departure times of trains for Warsaw, Bialystok, Wolkowysk, etc. . . . Two doors were cut into the [wall]. The first led to the "hospital," bearing a wooden arrow on which "Wolkowysk" was painted. The second led to the place where the Jews were undressed; that arrow said "Bialystok." Lalka also had some flower beds designed, which gave the whole area a neat and cheery look.

. . . The windows were more real than real windows; from ten yards away you could not tell the difference. The arrows were conspicuous and reassuring. The flowers, which were real, made the whole

---

[1] Kurt Franz, whom the prisoners called Lalka, designed the highly efficient system of extermination at Treblinka. [Ed.]

scene resemble a pretty station in a little provincial town. Everything was perfect. . . .

Lalka also decided that better organization could save much time in the operations of undressing and recovery of the [deportees'] baggage. To do this you had only to rationalize the different operations, that is, to organize the undressing like an assembly line. But the rhythm of this assembly line was at the mercy of the sick, the old, and the wounded, who, since they were unable to keep the pace, threatened to bog down the operation and make it proceed even more slowly than before. . . . Individuals of both sexes over the age of ten, and children under ten, at a maximum rate of two children per adult, were judged fit to follow the complete circuit,[2] as long as they did not show serious wounds or marked disability. Victims who did not correspond to the norms were to be conducted to the "hospital" by members of the blue commando and turned over to the Ukrainians [guards] for special treatment. A bench was built all around the ditch of the "hospital" so that the victims would fall of their own weight after receiving the bullet in the back of the head. This bench was to be used only when Kurland[3] was swamped with work. On the platform, the door which these victims took was surmounted by the Wolkowysk arrow. In the Sibylline language of Treblinka, "Wolkowysk" meant the bullet in the back of the neck or the injection. "Bialystok" meant the gas chamber.

Beside the "Bialystok" door stood a tall Jew whose role was to shout endlessly, "Large bundles here, large bundles here!" He had been nicknamed "Groysse Pack." As soon as the victims had gone through, Groysse Pack and his men from the red commando carried the bundles at a run to the sorting square, where the sorting commandos immediately took possession of them. As soon as they had gone through the door came the order, "Women to the left, men to the right." This moment generally gave rise to painful scenes.

While the women were being led to the left-hand barracks to undress and go to the hairdresser, the men, who were lined up double file, slowly entered the production line. This production line included five stations. At each of these a group of "reds" shouted at the top of their lungs the name of the piece of clothing that it was in charge of receiving. At the first station the victim handed over his coat and hat. At the second, his jacket. (In exchange, he received a piece of string.) At the third he sat down, took off his shoes, and tied them together with the string he had just received.) Until then the shoes were not tied together in

---

[2] The "complete" circuit was getting off the train, walking along the platform through the door to the men's or women's barracks, undressing, and being led to the gas chamber "showers." [Ed.]

[3] Kurland was a Jew assigned to the "hospital," where he gave injections of poison to those who were too ill or crippled to make the complete circuit. [Ed.]

pairs, and since the yield was at least fifteen thousand pairs of shoes per day, they were all lost, since they could not be matched up again.) At the fourth station the victim left his trousers, and at the fifth his shirt and underwear.

After they had been stripped, the victims were conducted, as they came off the assembly line, to the right-hand barracks and penned in until the women had finished: ladies first. However, a small number chosen from among the most able-bodied, were singled out at the door to carry the clothing to the sorting square. They did this while running naked between two rows of Ukrainian guards. Without stopping once they threw their bundles onto the pile, turned around, and went back for another.

Meanwhile the women had been conducted to the barracks on the left. This barracks was divided into two parts: a dressing room and a beauty salon. "Put your clothes in a pile so you will be able to find them after the shower," they were ordered in the first room. The "beauty salon" was a room furnished with six benches, each of which could seat twenty women at a time. Behind each bench twenty prisoners of the red commando, wearing white tunics and armed with scissors, waited at attention until all the women were seated. Between haircutting sessions they sat down on the benches and, under the direction of a *kapo* [prisoner guard] who was transformed into a conductor, they had to sing old Yiddish melodies.

Lalka, who had insisted on taking personal responsibility for every detail, had perfected the technique of what he called the "Treblinka cut." With five well-placed slashes the whole head of hair was transferred to a sack placed beside each hairdresser for this purpose. It was simple and efficient. How many dramas did this "beauty salon" see? From the very beautiful young woman who wept when her hair was cut off, because she would be ugly, to the mother who grabbed a pair of scissors from one of the "hairdressers" and literally severed a Ukrainian's arm; from the sister who recognized one of the "hairdressers" as her brother to the young girl, Ruth Dorfman, who, suddenly understanding and fighting back her tears, asked whether it was difficult to die and admitted in a small brave voice that she was a little afraid and wished it were all over.

When they had been shorn the women left the "beauty salon" double file. Outside the door, they had to squat in a particular way also specified by Lalka, in order to be intimately searched. Up to this point, doubt had been carefully maintained. Of course, a discriminating eye might have observed that . . . the smell was the smell of rotting bodies. A thousand details proved that Treblinka was not a transient camp, and some realized this, but the majority had believed in the impossible for too long to begin to doubt at the last moment. The door of the barracks, which opened directly onto the "road to heaven," represented the turning point. Up to here the prisoners had been given a minimum of hope, from here on this policy was abandoned.

This was one of Lalka's great innovations. After what point was it no longer necessary to delude the victims? This detail had been the subject of rather heated controversy among the Technicians. At the Nuremberg trials, Rudolf Höss, Commandant of Auschwitz, criticized Treblinka where, according to him, the victims knew that they were going to be killed. Höss was an advocate of the towel distributed at the door to the gas chamber. He claimed that this system not only avoided disorder, but was more humane, and he was proud of it. But Höss did not invent this "towel technique"; it was in all the manuals, and it was utilized at Treblinka until Lalka's great reform.

Lalka's studies had led to what might be called the "principle of the cutoff." His reasoning was simple: Since sooner or later the victims must realize that they were going to be killed, to postpone this moment was only false humanity. The principle "the later the better" did not apply here. Lalka had been led to make an intensive study of this problem upon observing one day completely by chance, that winded victims died much more rapidly than the rest. The discovery had led him to make a clean sweep of accepted principles. Let us follow his industrialist's logic, keeping well in mind that his great preoccupation was the saving of time. A winded victim dies faster. Hence, a saving of time. The best way to wind a man is to make him run — another saving of time. Thus Lalka arrived at the conclusion that you must make the victims run. A new question had then arisen: At what point must you make the victims run and thus create panic (a further aid to breathlessness)? The question had answered itself: As soon as you have nothing more to make them do. Franz located the exact point, the point of no return: the door of the barracks.

The rest was merely a matter of working out the details. Along the "road to heaven" and in front of the gas chambers he stationed a cordon of guards armed with whips, whose function was to make the victims run, to make them rush into the gas chambers of their own accord in search of refuge. One can see that this system is more daring than the classic system, but one can also see the danger it represents. Suddenly abandoned to their despair, realizing that they no longer had anything to lose, the victims might attack the guards. Lalka was aware of this risk, but he maintained that everything depended on the pace. "It's close work," he said, "but if you maintain a very rapid pace and do not allow a single moment of hesitation, the method is absolutely without danger." There were still further elaborations later on, but from the first day, Lalka had only to pride himself on his innovation: It took no more than three quarters of an hour, by the clock, to put the victims through their last voyage, from the moment the doors of the cattle cars were unbolted to the moment the great trap doors of the gas chamber were opened to take out the bodies. Three quarters of an hour, door to door, compared to an hour and a quarter and sometimes even as much as two hours with the old system; it was a record. . . .

But let us return to the men. The timing was worked out so that by the time the last woman had emerged from the left-hand barracks, all the clothes had been transported to the sorting square. The men were immediately taken out of the right-hand barracks and driven after the women into the "road to heaven," which they reached by way of a special side path. By the time they arrived at the gas chambers the toughest, who had begun to run before the others to carry the bundles, were just as winded as the weakest. Everyone died in perfect unison for the greater satisfaction of that great Technician Kurt Franz, the Stakhanovite [model worker] of extermination.

Since a string of twenty cars arrived at the platform every half hour, the Lalka system made it possible to fully process twelve trains of twenty cars each — or four convoys, or twenty-four thousand persons — between seven o'clock in the morning and one-fifteen in the afternoon.

The rest of the day was devoted to the sorting of the clothing in Camp Number One and the disposal of the bodies in Camp Number Two.

Transported by two prisoners on litterlike affairs, the bodies, after they were removed from the gas chambers, were carefully stacked, to save room, in immense ditches in horizontal layers, which alternated with layers of sand. In this realm, too, Lalka introduced a number of improvements.

Until the great reform, the "dentists" had extracted gold teeth and bridges from the corpses by rummaging through the big piles that accumulated during the morning in front of the trap doors of the gas chambers. It was not very efficient, as Lalka realized. Thus he got the idea of stationing a line of dentists between the gas chambers and the ditches, a veritable gold filter. As they came abreast of the dentists, the carriers of the bodies, without setting down their litters, would pause long enough for the "dentists" to examine the mouths of the corpses and extract whatever needed extracting. For a trained "dentist" the operation never required more than a minute. He placed his booty in a basin which another "dentist" came to empty from time to time. After the take had been washed in the well, it was brought to the barracks where other "dentists" sorted, cleaned, and classified it.

Meanwhile, the carriers of the bodies resumed their race — all moving from one place to another was done on the double — to the ditch. Here Lalka had made another improvement: Previously the body carriers had gone down and stacked their bodies themselves. Lalka, that maniac for specialization, created a commando of body stackers which never left the bottom of the ditch. When they arrived, the carriers heaved their burdens with a practiced movement, the role of personal initiative being reduced to the minimum, and returned to the trap doors of the gas chambers by a lower route, as on a gymnastic platform, so as not to disturb the upward movement. When all the corpses had been removed from the gas chambers, which was generally between noon and one o'clock, the ramp commando in charge of removal of the bodies joined the carrier commando. The burial rites lasted all afternoon and continued even into the night. Lalka had made it a rule that nobody was to go to bed until the last corpse had been stacked in its place.

69

SUSAN ZUCCOTTI

A Village in Vichy France

When the Germans took Paris in the blitzkrieg, or lightning strike, of 1940, they imposed direct rule on northern France and a puppet government on the southern part of the country, led by World War I hero Marshall Philippe Pétain. Pétain governed from the old city of Vichy, about two hundred miles south of Paris. After 1941, the Germans began to impose their policy of anti-Semitism on the Vichy regime, as they had done in the north, insisting that Vichy capture and imprison Jews for shipment to concentration camps. Although much of southern France complied with the order, in a high plateau just a few hours south of Vichy, an area of independent French, many of them Protestants who had long resisted Catholic Paris, refused to do the Nazis' work. In this selection, a modern historian tells how the inhabitants of Le Chambon-sur-Lignon, risked their lives to save Jewish children in their schools and Jewish families in their homes. How did the people of Le Chambon save Jews? What gave them the courage to resist the orders of their government and the Nazis? How were they so successful?

Thinking Historically

To understand evil, we must first understand goodness. To condemn, we must first be able to praise. To understand how people could com-

Susan Zuccotti, *The Holocaust, the French and the Jews* (New York: Basic Books, 1993), 227–31.

mit horrendous acts, we must have some sense of their range of choice. Stories like that of Le Chambon-sur-Lignon aid us in that understanding. What supports did the people of this village have to disobey Nazi orders? Imagine yourself as a villager. What would you have done? Other pressures being equal, would you have gained strength from "doing the right thing"?

In interviews after the war, many of those — in France and throughout Europe — who had sheltered Jews at their own peril dismissed praise. In virtually every case, these protectors rejected the idea that they had done anything out of the ordinary. What did these people have that the Nazis had obviously taken away from so many others? How did the Nazis do it?

"Roughly fifty kilometers from Puy-en-Velay and about forty kilometers from Saint-Étienne, there is a little town, Le Chambon-sur-Lignon, the tiny capital of the plateau of the same name, an ancient Protestant village. There you can still find the caves where the Protestants gathered to practice their religion as well as to escape the king's dragoons." Thus begins Joseph Bass's postwar report on a remote village on a pine-studded plateau, about 960 meters above sea level, in the Massif Central west of Valence and the Rhône River. Léon Poliakov, who helped Bass hide Jews there, later described the department of Haute-Loire where Le Chambon is located as "one of the poorest and wildest regions of the Cévennes." Its Protestant inhabitants, he added, "distrust all authority, listening only to their conscience — or their pastors."

Long before Bass and Poliakov arrived there, hundreds of Jewish and non-Jewish refugees had already found their way to Le Chambon. Some had wandered into town as early as the winter of 1940–41. Most came independently at first, advised by friends or casual acquaintances of an isolated village of about one thousand people, reputedly sympathetic. Newcomers found shelter with village families or with the roughly two thousand peasants, most of them also Protestant, in the surrounding countryside. Others took rooms in one of more than a dozen hotels and boardinghouses in this popular summer resort area of pine forests, clear streams, and bracing air. Most were trying to escape internment, and most, needless to say, were not legally registered.

During the late spring and early summer of 1942, many foreign Jews and non-Jews released from internment camps to the care of charitable agencies also came to Le Chambon. Local institutions to care for them multiplied, openly and legally. Madeleine Barot and other young Protestant social workers of the CIMADE [a Protestant relief organization] established a family residence at the Hôtel Coteau Fleuri, outside of town. Quakers, with the help from Le Chambon's Pastor André

Trocmé, funded a boardinghouse for young children. Older students joined two farm-schools operated by the Secours suisse, or moved into residences of the École Cévenol, a private Protestant secondary school slightly north of the village. Still others were welcomed at the École des roches in the village itself.

In August 1942, French police rounding up recent Jewish immigrants in the unoccupied zone did not overlook Le Chambon. They arrived in the village with three empty buses, demanding that Pastor Trocmé provide a list of resident Jews. Trocmé not only claimed ignorance, somewhat truthfully, of names and addresses but promptly sent his Protestant Boy Scouts to even the most distant farms to warn Jews to hide. Other local residents had undoubtedly already seen the approach of the police up the valley, along a road visible for miles from the Plateau. Then and later, that visibility was one secret to security in Le Chambon. Police searched the region for two or three days and returned regularly for several weeks. They apparently netted only one victim, an Austrian who was later released because he was only half-Jewish.

Jews literally poured into Le Chambon after August 1942. By this point, their presence was totally unofficial. They came with the [Jewish resistance network] Service André — [its director Joseph] Bass later reported that the pastor never hesitated to help him — and with OSE [children's aid] and other clandestine networks. Some stayed in Le Chambon only long enough to find a guide to Switzerland, but many remained, hidden with families or in boardinghouses or schools. They kept coming until, as Poliakov observed, "in some hamlets, there was not a single farm which did not shelter a Jewish family." Roughly five thousand Jews are estimated to have been hidden among the three thousand native residents, all of whom knew about the refugees.

In his memoirs, Poliakov describes with touching detail his arrival at a local hotel with a group of Jewish children in 1943:

> Frightened, they hovered in a corner of the room. The first peasant couple enters: "We will take a little girl between eight and twelve years old," explains the woman. Little Myriam is called: "Will you go with this aunt and uncle?" Shy and frightened, Myriam does not answer. They muffle her up in blankets and carry her to the sleigh; she leaves for the farm where she will live a healthy and simple life with her temporary parents until the end of the war. . . . In a flash, all the children were similarly housed, under the benevolent eye of Pastor Trocmé.

Who was this pastor whose name appears in every account of Le Chambon-sur-Lignon during the war? Born in Saint-Quentin in Picardy in northern France in 1901, André Trocmé studied at the Union Theological Seminary in New York City, where he met his future wife, Italian-born Magda Grilli, in 1925. A pacifist and conscientious objector, Trocmé made no secret of his beliefs after his arrival in Le Chambon in 1934. Indeed, he and Pastor Édouard Theis, the director of the École Cévenol, were equally frank after 1940 about their dislike of the Vichy regime and the racial laws. Trocmé often spoke from the pulpit about the evils of racial persecution; Theis taught the same principles at the École Cévenol. On August 15, 1942, during a visit to the village by the Vichy youth minister, Georges Lamirand, and the departmental prefect and subprefect, several older students at the school presented the officials with a letter protesting the July 16 roundup [of Jews] in Paris and expressing local support of the Jews.

Trocmé, Theis, and Roger Darcissac, the director of the public school in Le Chambon, were arrested by French police in February 1943 and held for a month. At the end of the year, the two pastors went into hiding. During that period, Theis served as a guide for CIMADE, escorting refugees to Switzerland. Magda Trocmé continued her husband's work during his absence; one scholar has judged that she was at least as important as he in saving lives. Mildred Theis kept the École Cévenol open and continued to shelter refugees. The two women had many aides. Bass remembered pastors named Poivre, Leenhardt, Jeannet, Curtet, Betrix, Vienney, and Besson from surrounding hamlets, as well as the Trocmés' good friend Simone Mairesse. Municipal officials also cooperated, if only by looking the other way. And the people of the plateau, often influenced by their outspoken pastors but guided as well by their own sense of justice, continued to protect their Jewish guests until the Liberation. Of them, Bass wrote after the war, "The conduct of the Protestant pastors and men of action of the plateau of Le Chambon deserves to be told to Jews throughout the entire world."

In considering the rescue of Jews in Le Chambon, two questions arise: Why was the local population so sympathetic, and why was it so successful? To answer the first, Madeleine Barot stresses the special status of Protestants in France as a minority persecuted by Catholics. Protestants in Le Chambon still told tales of persecution around their hearths on cold winter nights and visited caves where their ancestors had hidden. The memory of persecution made them suspicious of authority, sympathetic to other minorities, and comfortable with clandestine life. In addition, many French Protestants were skeptical about the Vichy regime, in part because authoritarianism often bodes ill for minorities, but especially because, according to Barot, "Pétain dedicated France to the Virgin, and made it an intensely Catholic state." Finally, Christian anti-Semitism notwithstanding, Bible-reading Protestants of the type living around Le Chambon sometimes articulate a special affinity for the Jews, based on a shared reverence for the Old Testament and a common acceptance of God's special compact with his chosen people.

These various factors certainly did not apply to all French Protestants. Many, especially those of the assimilated and highly educated urban classes who were more removed from their historical and cultural roots, were favorably inclined toward the Vichy regime for the same economic and social reasons as their Catholic neighbors, and held the same variety of attitudes toward Jews. But Protestants around Le Chambon cherished their historic memory. That love, combined with the sturdy individualism and independence of mountain people and the leadership of a group of exceptional pastors, made Le Chambon an equally exceptional place.

But why were the rescuers of Le Chambon so successful? Admittedly, even they had their tragedies and their victims. In the spring of 1943, the Gestapo raided the École des roches, seizing many students along with their dedicated director, Daniel Trocmé, Pastor Trocmé's second cousin. Nearly all, including Daniel, died in deportation. But the Germans did not return and thus failed as miserably as the French police to find most of the Jews they knew were there. Why?

Geographic factors were important. The isolation of the area was made even more extreme by the closing of access roads in winter. Any movement on those same approach roads could be seen from the plateau. Thick forests were good for hiding. The Gestapo and the French Milice [volunteer fascist corps], busy elsewhere, were reluctant or perhaps afraid to enter a hostile area that, however dedicated by its pastor to nonviolence, was surrounded by armed Resistance fighters. Why stir up a sleeping hornets' nest? French police and gendarmes not only shared that reluctance but were also affected by local sympathies for refugees.

Two witnesses tell amusing stories. Madeleine Barot later declared of her own experience, "When the *gendarmes* in Tence [the nearest town] received an order for an arrest, they made a habit of dragging themselves along the road very visibly, of calling a halt at the café before tackling the steep ascent to the Coteau, announcing loudly that they were about to arrest some of those 'dirty Jews.'" Poliakov confirms the description, explaining that when the gendarmes received an arrest order, "they went to the [local] Hotel May and ordered a glass of wine: Comfortably seated at their table, they took their papers from their satchels and spelled out 'Goldberg . . . it's about someone named Jacques Goldberg.' Unnecessary to add that when they arrived at Goldberg's domicile half an hour later, the latter was long gone." Poliakov adds that when a more serious danger approached in the form of the Gestapo or the Milice, a telephone call of warning usually preceded them from the valley.

Barot's and Poliakov's accounts both allude to the most important factor in the rescue success rate in Le Chambon — the determination of local residents to protect their guests. The people of Le Chambon lived in a state of constant alertness, with a warning system prepared. Their solidarity also made it difficult for potential informers to act. To whom could they safely leak information? Municipal authorities sympathized with the majority, as did, it appeared, many of the police. Even local censors of mail were likely to prevent a denunciation. In such a situation, a careless informer might even put himself in danger. In addition, it was psychologically more difficult for a solitary anti-Semite or opportunist to express his bile in a region where he was bucking an obvious majority. He could not so easily convince himself that he was acting as a "good and loyal Frenchman." And in any part of France — where so many individual arrests of Jews by preoccupied and understaffed local Gestapo units were prompted by denunciations — the reluctance of informers was decisive.

$$\boxed{70}$$

IRIS CHANG

From *The Rape of Nanking*

Nazi genocide was not the only systematic murder of civilian populations during World War II. The military government of Japan, a German ally during the war, engaged in some of the same tactics of brutal and indiscriminate mass murder of civilians. In fact, atrocities in Japan preceded those in Germany.

While for Europeans World War II began with the German invasion of Poland on September 1, 1939, and for Americans with the Japanese attack at Pearl Harbor, Hawaii, on December 7, 1941, for the Chinese it began ten years earlier with the Japanese invasion of Manchuria in 1931. By 1937, Japanese troops occupied Peking and Shanghai as well as the old imperial capital of Nanking. It is estimated that more than twenty-five thousand civilians were killed by Japanese soldiers in the months after the fall of Nanking on December 13, 1937. But it was the appalling brutality of Japanese troops that foreign residents remembered, even those who could recall the brutality of the Chinese nationalist troops who captured the city in 1927. In the Introduction to *The Rape of Nanking,* Iris Chang writes:

Iris Chang, *The Rape of Nanking* (New York: Basic Books, 1997), 55–59.

The Rape of Nanking should be remembered not only for the number of people slaughtered but for the cruel manner in which many met their deaths. Chinese men were used for bayonet practice and in decapitation contests. An estimated 20,000 to 80,000 Chinese women were raped. Many soldiers went beyond rape to disembowel women, slice off their breasts, nail them alive to walls. Fathers were forced to rape their daughters, and sons their mothers, as other family members watched. Not only did live burials, castration, the carving of organs, and the roasting of people become routine, but more diabolical tortures were practiced, such as hanging people by their tongues on iron hooks or burying people to their waist and watching them get torn apart by German shepherds. So sickening was the spectacle that even the Nazis in the city were horrified, one declaring the massacre to be the work of "bestial machinery." (p. 6)

In the selection that follows, the author asks how Japanese soldiers were capable of such offenses. What is her answer?

Thinking Historically

What would have happened to these recruits if they had refused an order to kill a prisoner or noncombatant? Once they had killed one prisoner, why did they find it easier to kill another? Did they eventually enjoy it, feel pride, or think it insignificant? The last informant, Nagatomi, says he had been a "devil." Had he been possessed? By whom?

How then do we explain the raw brutality carried out day after day after day in the city of Nanking? Unlike their Nazi counterparts, who have mostly perished in prisons and before execution squads or, if alive, are spending their remaining days as fugitives from the law, many of the Japanese war criminals are still alive, living in peace and comfort, protected by the Japanese government. They are therefore some of the few people on this planet who, without concern for retaliation in a court of international law, can give authors and journalists a glimpse of their thoughts and feelings while committing World War II atrocities.

Here is what we learn. The Japanese soldier was not simply hardened for battle in China; he was hardened for the task of murdering Chinese combatants and noncombatants alike. Indeed, various games and exercises were set up by the Japanese military to numb its men to the human instinct against killing people who are not attacking.

For example, on their way to the capital, Japanese soldiers were made to participate in killing competitions, which were avidly covered by the Japanese media like sporting events. The most notorious one appeared in the December 7 issue of the *Japan Advertiser* under the headline "Sub-Lieutenants in Race to Fell 100 Chinese Running Close Contest."

> Sub-Lieutenant Mukai Toshiaki and Sub-Lieutenant Noda Takeshi, both of the Katagiri unit at Kuyung, in a friendly contest to see which of them will first fell 100 Chinese in individual sword combat before the Japanese forces completely occupy Nanking, are well in the final phase of their race, running almost neck to neck. On Sunday [December 5] . . . the "score," according to the Asahi, was: Sub-Lieutenant Mukai, 89, and Sub-Lieutenant Noda, 78.

A week later the paper reported that neither man could decide who had passed the 100 mark first, so they upped the goal to 150. "Mukai's blade was slightly damaged in the competition," the *Japan Advertiser* reported. "He explained that this was the result of cutting a Chinese in half, helmet and all. The contest was 'fun' he declared."

Such atrocities were not unique to the Nanking area. Rather, they were typical of the desensitization exercises practiced by the Japanese across China during the entire war. The following testimony by a Japanese private named Tajima is not unusual:

> One day Second Lieutenant Ono said to us, "You have never killed anyone yet, so today we shall have some killing practice. You must not consider the Chinese as a human being, but only as something of rather less value than a dog or cat. Be brave! Now, those who wish to volunteer for killing practice, step forward."
>
> No one moved. The lieutenant lost his temper.
>
> "You cowards!" he shouted. "Not one of you is fit to call himself a Japanese soldier. So no one will volunteer? Well then, I'll order you." And he began to call out names, "Otani — Furukawa — Ueno — Tajima!" (My God — me too!)
>
> I raised my bayoneted gun with trembling hands, and — directed by the lieutenant's almost hysterical cursing — I walked slowly towards the terror-stricken Chinese standing beside the pit — the grave he had helped to dig. In my heart, I begged his pardon, and — with my eyes shut and the lieutenant's curses in my ears — I plunged the bayonet into the petrified Chinese. When I opened my eyes again, he had slumped down into the pit. "Murderer! Criminal!" I called myself.

For new soldiers, horror was a natural impulse. One Japanese wartime memoir describes how a group of green Japanese recruits failed to conceal their shock when they witnessed seasoned soldiers torture a group of civilians to death. Their commander expected this reaction and wrote in his diary: "All new recruits are like this, but soon they will be doing the same things themselves."

But new officers also required desensitization. A veteran officer named Tominaga Shozo recalled vividly his own transformation from innocent youth to killing machine. Tominaga had been a fresh second lieutenant from a military academy when assigned to the 232nd Regiment of the 39th Division from Hiroshima. When he was introduced to the men under his command, Tominaga was stunned. "They had evil eyes," he remembered. "They weren't human eyes, but the eyes of leopards or tigers."

On the front Tominaga and other new candidate officers underwent intensive training to stiffen their endurance for war. In the program an instructor had pointed to a thin, emaciated Chinese in a detention center and told the officers: "These are the raw materials for your trial of courage." Day after day the instructor taught them how to cut off heads and bayonet living prisoners.

> On the final day, we were taken out to the site of our trial. Twenty-four prisoners were squatting there with their hands tied behind their backs. They were blindfolded. A big hole had been dug — ten meters long, two meters wide, and more than three meters deep. The regimental commander, the battalion commanders, and the company commanders all took the seats arranged for them. Second Lieutenant Tanaka bowed to the regimental commander and reported, "We shall now begin." He ordered a soldier on fatigue duty to haul one of the prisoners to the edge of the pit; the prisoner was kicked when he resisted. The soldiers finally dragged him over and forced him to his knees. Tanaka turned toward us and looked into each of our faces in turn. "Heads should be cut off like this," he said, unsheathing his army sword. He scooped water from a bucket with a dipper, then poured it over both sides of the blade. Swishing off the water, he raised his sword in a long arc. Standing behind the prisoner, Tanaka steadied himself, legs spread apart, and cut off the man's head with a shout, "Yo!" The head flew more than a meter away. Blood spurted up in two fountains from the body and sprayed into the hole.
>
> The scene was so appalling that I felt I couldn't breathe.

But gradually, Tominaga Shozo learned to kill. And as he grew more adept at it, he no longer felt that his men's eyes were evil. For him, atrocities became routine, almost banal. Looking back on his experience, he wrote: "We made them like this. Good sons, good daddies, good elder brothers at home were brought to the front to kill each other. Human beings turned into murdering demons. Everyone became a demon within three months."

Some Japanese soldiers admitted it was easy for them to kill because they had been taught that next to the emperor, all individual life — even their own — was valueless. Azuma Shiro, the Japanese soldier who witnessed a series of atrocities in Nanking, made an excellent point about his comrades' behavior in his letter to me. During his two years of military training in the 20th Infantry Regiment of Kyoto-fu Fukuchi-yama, he was taught that "loyalty is heavier than a mountain, and our life is lighter than a feather." He recalled that the highest honor a soldier could achieve during war was to come back dead: To die for the emperor was the greatest glory, to be caught alive by the enemy the greatest shame. "If my life was not important," Azuma wrote to me, "an enemy's life became inevitably much less important. . . . This philosophy led us to look down on the enemy and eventually to the mass murder and ill treatment of the captives."

In interview after interview, Japanese veterans from the Nanking massacre reported honestly that they experienced a complete lack of remorse or sense of wrongdoing, even when torturing helpless civilians. Nagatomi Hakudo spoke candidly about his emotions in the fallen capital:

> I remember being driven in a truck along a path that had been cleared through piles of thousands and thousands of slaughtered bodies. Wild dogs were gnawing at the dead flesh as we stopped and pulled a group of Chinese prisoners out of the back. Then the Japanese officer proposed a test of my courage. He unsheathed his sword, spat on it, and with a sudden mighty swing he brought it down on the neck of a Chinese boy cowering before us. The head was cut clean off and tumbled away on the group as the body slumped forward, blood spurting in two great gushing fountains from the neck. The officer suggested I take the head home as a souvenir. I remember smiling proudly as I took his sword and began killing people.

After almost sixty years of soul-searching, Nagatomi is a changed man. A doctor in Japan, he has built a shrine of remorse in his waiting room. Patients can watch videotapes of his trial in Nanking and a full confession of his crimes. The gentle and hospitable demeanor of the doctor belies the horror of his past, making it almost impossible for one to imagine that he had once been a ruthless murderer.

"Few know that soldiers impaled babies on bayonets and tossed them still alive into pots of boiling water," Nagatomi said. "They gang-raped women from the ages of twelve to eighty and then killed them when they could no longer satisfy sexual requirements. I beheaded people, starved them to death, burned them, and buried them alive, over two hundred in all. It is terrible that I could turn into an animal and do these things. There are really no words to explain what I was doing. I was truly a devil."

71

RALPH BLUMENTHAL

Japanese Germ-Warfare Atrocities

The Japanese concentration camps were not extermination camps, though many prisoners of the Japanese died in them and many survivors were brutalized. But, as did the Nazis, some Japanese doctors and scientists experimented on prisoners with deadly bacteria, chemical and biological agents, and surgical dismemberment without anesthesia and without any attempt to ease suffering or prevent death. Some of these experiments were concentrated under the command of Unit 731 of the Japanese army.

How did this come about? Who was responsible? Why have the Japanese been reticent in releasing information about these activities almost seventy years after they began? What interest did the United States have in keeping these activities secret?

Thinking Historically

Try to imagine the mental framework of Shiro Ishii, the founder of Unit 731 and of Toshimi Mizobuchi, a member of the unit. How do you think each of them viewed what they were doing? How would you characterize their responsibility for what occurred? How would you compare their responsibility with that of the soldiers at Nanking in the previous selection? How would you compare their responsibility to that of the soldiers at Treblinka?

More than fifty years after the Japanese Army attacked China with germ weapons and conducted gruesome experiments on thousands of human beings, Japan is resisting demands that it compensate the victims or make records of the atrocities public.

The Japanese Government has declined to cooperate with efforts by the Justice Department to put the names of several hundred surviving veterans of the germ warfare operations on a list of suspected war criminals barred from entering the United States, American officials say.

It has also rebuffed researchers seeking access to a vast archive of military documents in Tokyo that detail the World War II activities of

---

Ralph Blumenthal with Judith Miller, "Japan Rebuffs Requests for Information About Its Germ-Warfare Atrocities," *New York Times*, 4 March 1999, A12.

the Japanese Imperial Army, including its chief biological warfare arm, known as Unit 731.

The American authorities seized the archive after World War II but returned it to Japan in 1958 after only a small number of documents were copied.

Japan's approach stands in contrast to that of Germany, which has paid about $80 billion to war victims and their families. Private industries and banks in Germany and Switzerland plan to pay billions more.

Despite the refusal of the Japanese Government to release information, new details are emerging about the scope of the biological program. Research by scholars, campaigns by the Simon Wiesenthal Center of Los Angeles and the Global Alliance for Preserving the History of World War II in Asia, and a lawsuit in Japan by Chinese plaintiffs have unleashed a flood of new accounts that substantially expand the historical record.

The accounts have heightened tensions between Japan and its neighbors. They suggest that Japan's World War II germ attacks were even more widespread than first thought, stretching from Burma (now Myanmar), Thailand, Singapore, and the Dutch East Indies (now Indonesia) to Russia and Chinese cities and hamlets.

The Dead: The Numbers Remain in Dispute

The death toll from Japan's biological warfare remains in dispute. Some scholars assert that several hundred thousand people died, mostly in China. Others say the casualties were far lower. Scholars estimate that an additional ten thousand prisoners were killed in experiments, perhaps a dozen times the number who died at the hands of Dr. Josef Mengele and other Nazi scientists.

Eli M. Rosenbaum, director of the Office of Special Investigations in the Justice Department, said the dispute between Tokyo and Washington over suspected war criminals has been quietly building for three years.

The Justice Department's world-wide list of war crimes suspects now includes the names of about sixty thousand Germans and other Europeans, including Kurt Waldheim, the former United Nations Secretary General, President of Austria, and wartime intelligence officer in Hitler's army.

By contrast, Mr. Rosenbaum said the United States had dates of birth and other identifying data on fewer than one hundred suspected Japanese war criminals.

"For a friendly government to deny us access is astonishing, beyond the pale," Mr. Rosenbaum said. "Most outrageous of all is that the Japanese Government will not provide the dates of birth of war crimes suspects identified by O.S.I. so that they can be barred from the United States. They won't even tell us if they will ever assist us."

A Japanese Embassy spokesman in Washington, Tsuyoshi Yamamoto, said his Government would have no comment because the issue concerned "the specifics of Japanese cooperation with the United States, which are of a diplomatic nature."

Little was publicly known about Japan's germ operations until the 1980's, when scholars published their first accounts. More recently, veterans of Unit 731 have been speaking publicly in Japan about their misdeeds, seeking expiation.

According to participants, victims, and records, the unit mounted widespread germ attacks with anthrax, typhoid, and other pathogens. Among other experiments, its doctors infected prisoners with disease germs, removed organs and blood, and withheld water to collect data on how the human body copes with illness and deprivation. Many victims were then dissected alive.

Only one former member of the unit was ever turned away from entering the United States: Yushio Shinozuka, who arrived last summer to join a forum and publicly express anguish over having prepared victims for vivisection.

Rather than fading with time, diplomats and scholars say, sensitivities over the issue are becoming sharper as new generations re-examine wartime events, as they have with the Holocaust in Europe.

Complicating the issue is the complicity of American officials in shielding from prosecution top Japanese scientists who turned over their data to the United States, which was developing its own germ warfare program.

Among the questions that remain unresolved is whether doctors working with Unit 731 experimented on American prisoners of war.

"The cover-up continues," said Sheldon H. Harris, emeritus professor of history at California State University in Northridge and the author of *Factories of Death* (Routledge, 1994), an account of the Japanese germ warfare program and the American hunger for its secrets. . . .

Mr. Harris said in an interview that while he had unearthed American translations of three Japanese autopsy reports comprising nearly a thousand pages recounting wartime medical experiments on dead and living prisoners, seventeen other reports were missing, along with some eight thousand photographic slides documenting the experiments.

The Campaign: Germ Bombs in the 1930s

The origins of Unit 731 go back to 1930 and the Tokyo laboratory of an ultranationalist surgeon and microbiologist, Shiro Ishii, who was later made a general. Within two years, after Japanese troops overran

Manchuria in northeast China, General Ishii, using the cover of a sanitation unit, set up the first of several large biological warfare and human research centers in Ping Fan and other areas around Harbin, a heavily Russian city near the Soviet border.

Over the next decade, scholars and researchers say, the Japanese attacked hundreds of heavily populated communities and remote regions with germ bombs. Evidence of the attacks continues to emerge.

"There appears to have been a massive germ war campaign in Yunnan Province bordering Burma," said Daniel Barenblatt, a graduate psychologist and New York City researcher who has been assembling material for five years for a documentary with the film director David Irving, chairman of the undergraduate film and television department at New York University.

"They seem to have been killing ethnic minorities in a jungle campaign," Mr. Barenblatt said.

Many questions remain unanswered.

It is still not established, for example, whether American prisoners of war were among those experimented on. Some Americans have said they were sickened by contaminated feathers in their food, and Japanese accounts tell of jars containing body parts labeled American among other nationalities.

Frank James, 77, a survivor of the Bataan Death March, ended up in 1942 at a Japanese prison camp in Mukden, Manchuria, where, he said, he became a seventy-pound living skeleton. "They gave us shots, sprays in the face," he recounted in a telephone interview from his home in Redwood City, California, where he is confined with diabetes and lung disease.

He said one of his jobs at Mukden was to retrieve for dissection frozen corpses that he was certain were American. "They opened them up so they could look into the lining of the stomach," he recalled. "The light pink icicles in the stomach weren't thawed."

A new hourlong documentary . . . *Unit 731: Nightmare in Manchuria,* features interviews with other surviving American war prisoners who say they were victimized by Japanese experiments.

But records of their debriefings by American officials remain unavailable. Mr. Harris, the author, said he applied for the records under the Freedom of Information Act several years ago and was told by the Veterans Administration that they had been destroyed in a fire in St. Louis.

After the war, American interest in prosecuting members of Unit 731 for war crimes faded fast. While Germany was split in a four-power occupation, the United States had a largely free hand in rebuilding Japan and was forging close ties to the new Government.

In addition, Mr. Harris said, American scientists were "salivating" over the chance to obtain the forbidden secrets of Japan's human experiments. The American authorities granted General Ishii and his associates immunity from prosecution and in exchange received detailed information.

The Allies did prosecute 5,570 Japanese, none for biological warfare. Nine Japanese medical school professionals were convicted, and some executed, for vivisecting eight captured American fliers in 1945.

Toshimi Mizobuchi makes no secret of his years with Unit 731. A vigorous 76-year-old real estate manager living outside the Japanese city of Kobe, Mr. Mizobuchi is organizing this year's reunion for the several hundred surviving veterans of Unit 731. He says he did not take part in experiments on humans, though he knew of them and argues that they were justifiable.

In an interview at home near Kobe with Rabbi Abraham Cooper of the Simon Wiesenthal Center that was recorded and transcribed through an interpreter, Mr. Mizobuchi said he still regarded the victims of the experiments as "maruta," or logs.

"They were logs to me," said Mr. Mizobuchi, a training officer with the unit. "Logs were not considered to be human. They were either spies or conspirators." As such, he said, "they were already dead. So now they die a second time. We just executed a death sentence."

He said that there were about thirty veterans of the unit living near him and that a reunion was held almost every year, drawing forty or fifty. Mr. Mizobuchi said he had never visited the American mainland but had been to Hawaii twice for sightseeing.

"It's a stain on history," said Rabbi Cooper, associate dean of the Wiesenthal Center, founded in 1977 in the name of the Viennese concentration camp survivor and Nazi-hunter.

Rabbi Cooper said he had interviewed former germ war soldiers and others last month in Japan and planned to present Congress and the White House with evidence he had gathered. "This blanket amnesty can't stand," he said.

The Records: Japan Refuses Access to Files

Nearly sixty years later, Ada Pivo of Los Angeles is still looking for the truth about Unit 731's operations.

During the war, she said in an interview, she lived with her family in Harbin, where the unit made its headquarters. In 1940 her seventeen-year old sister, Leah, was one of two members of a Jewish youth group who contracted typhoid and died after an outing. Mrs. Pivo believes that her sister was infected by a bottle of lemonade spiked with bacteria by Japanese scientists.

It is known that food and drink and even children's sweets were sometimes laced with pathogens. But without access to records, it may never be possible to establish the link to a particular operation in Harbin.

Japan has long restricted access to military records, which were in the hands of the American authorities for nine years after the war.

The documents, first screened by the Central Intelligence Agency, include hundreds of thousands of pages of War Ministry records from 1868 to 1942, Navel Ministry records from 1868 to 1939, and operational records of many units throughout the war.

In 1948 the C.I.A. turned over the records to the National Archives, with no indication of what, if anything, had been removed. In 1957 the collection was ordered returned to Japan.

Concerned over the potential loss, a group of scholars including Edwin O. Reischauer of Harvard University and John Young of Georgetown University obtained a Ford Foundation grant to hurriedly microfilm what they could.

In February 1958, after about 5 percent of the records were copied, Mr. Young recalled in an interview, the documents were sent to Baltimore and loaded aboard a ship for Japan. "There was no way we could read them all," said Mr. Young, who deplored the loss.

In any case, Mr. Young, who assisted Allied war crimes investigators in China after the war, compiled a 144-page index to the pages that were microfilmed. A microfilm set was presented to the National Diet Library in Tokyo, an irony, Mr. Young said, considering that Japan has now closed off the collection. "I can tell you frankly, the militarists felt relieved," Mr. Young said. "As a historian I couldn't stand it."

72

NADEZHDA MANDELSTAM

From *Hope Against Hope*

During the 1930s and the period of World War II, Joseph Stalin (1879–1953) ruled the Soviet Union with an iron fist through secret police and terror. Nadezhda Mandelstam (1899–1980) was the wife of the great Russian poet Osip Mandelstam (1891–1938?). During the Stalin era, the poet was persecuted and twice arrested, and he

---

Nadezhda Mandelstam, *Hope Against Hope: A Memoir,* trans. Max Hayward (New York: Atheneum, 1970), 224–28.

eventually died in prison in Siberia. In her memoirs Mandelstam offers a heartrending, tough-minded, yet at times witty account of her life with her husband and of how innocent people suffered during Stalin's purges. Taking advantage of the relative "thaw" that followed Stalin's death in 1953, Mandelstam devoted the remainder of her life to trying to clear her husband's name and to have his work published in the Soviet Union. The first volume of the English translation of her memoirs is called *Hope Against Hope;* note that in Russian *nadezhda* means "hope." Why, according to the author, did the Stalinist terror last? What were its effects? How did it affect her own life? What does she mean by the "favor" of her husband's death certificate and the "good tidings" of his death? Why does she say, "The sooner he died, the better"?

Thinking Historically

While the Soviet Union was not a fascist state in the sense of being ruled by the military and large corporations, and its official ideology opposed such fascist values as violence, war, and a rejection of modern culture, Stalin controlled virtually every aspect of life through his network of spies, informers, and secret police. The effect was a climate of surveillance and an absence of privacy very much like the total control Mussolini, the founder of fascism, tried unsuccessfully to achieve in Italy.

How did this system of surveillance corrode individual judgment, identity, and will? How did it reduce people's humanity? How did it make people little more than obedient soldiers and spies?

When life becomes absolutely intolerable, you begin to think the horror will never end. In Kiev during the bombardment I understood that even the unbearable can come to an end, but I was not yet fully aware that it often does so only at death. As regards the Stalinist terror, we always knew that it might wax or wane, but that it might end — this we could never imagine. What reason was there for it to end? Everybody seemed intent on his daily round and went smilingly about the business of carrying out his instructions. It was essential to smile — if you didn't, it meant you were afraid or discontented. This nobody could afford to admit — if you were afraid, then you must have a bad conscience. Everybody who worked for the State — and in this country even the humblest stall-keeper is a bureaucrat — had to strut around wearing a cheerful expression, as though to say: "What's going on is no concern of mine, I have very important work to do, and I'm terribly busy. I am trying to do my best for the State, so do not get in my way.

My conscience is clear — if what's-his-name had been arrested, there must be good reason." The mask was taken off only at home, and then not always — even from your children you had to conceal how horror-struck you were; otherwise, God save you, they might let something slip in school. . . . Some people had adapted to the terror so well that they knew how to profit from it — there was nothing out of the ordinary about denouncing a neighbor to get his apartment or his job. But while wearing your smiling mask, it was important not to laugh — this could look suspicious to the neighbors and make them think you were indulging in sacrilegious mockery. We have lost the capacity to be spontaneously cheerful, and it will never come back to us. . . .

The principles and aims of mass terror have nothing in common with ordinary police work or with security. The only purpose of terror is intimidation. To plunge the whole country into a state of chronic fear, the number of victims must be raised to astronomical levels, and on every floor of every building there must always be several apartments from which the tenants have suddenly been taken away. The remaining inhabitants will be model citizens for the rest of their lives — this will be true for every street and every city through which the broom has swept. The only essential thing for those who rule by terror is not to overlook the new generations growing up without faith in their elders, and to keep on repeating the process in systematic fashion. Stalin ruled for a long time and saw to it that the waves of terror recurred from time to time, always on an even greater scale than before. But the champions of terror invariably leave one thing out of account — namely, that they can't kill everyone, and among their cowed, half-demented subjects there are always witnesses who survive to tell the tale. . . .

The only link with a person in prison was the window through which one handed parcels and money to be forwarded to him by the authorities. Once a month, after waiting three or four hours in line (the number of arrests was by now falling off, so this was not very long), I went up to the window and gave my name. The clerk behind the window thumbed through his list — I went on days when he dealt with the letter "M" — and asked me for my first name and initial. As soon as I replied, a hand stretched out of the window and I put my identity papers and some money into it. The hand then returned my papers with a receipt and I went away. Everybody envied me because I at least knew that my husband was alive and where he was. It happened only too often that the man behind the window barked: "No record. . . . Next!" All questions were useless — the official would simply shut his window in your face and one of the uniformed guards would come up to you. Order was immediately restored and the next in line moved up to the window. If anybody ever tried to linger, the guard found ready allies among the other people waiting.

The women who stood in line with me tried not to get drawn into conversation. They all, without exception, said that their husbands had been arrested by mistake and would soon be released. Their eyes were red from tears and lack of sleep, but I don't recall anyone ever crying while we stood in line. When they left their homes, they composed their features by some effort of the will and tried to look their best. Most of them came to hand in their parcels during working hours — they got off on some pretext or other — and on returning to their offices they had to be very careful not to show their feelings. Their faces had become masks.

After several months of standing in line at the window on the Sophia Embankment I was told one day that M. had been transferred to Butyrki. This was the prison in which people were held before being sent off in prison trains to the forced-labor camps. I rushed there to find out on what days they dealt with inquiries about people whose names began with the letter "M." In Butyrki I was only once able to hand over something for M.; the second time I tried, I was told that he had been sent to a camp for five years by decision of the Special Tribunal.[1]

This was confirmed to me in the Prosecutor's Office after I had stood in line there endlessly. There were special windows through which requests for information were handed, and I did the same as everybody else. Exactly a month after putting in a request, one was always informed that it had been turned down. This was the usual routine for a prisoner's wife — if she was lucky enough not to have been sent to a camp herself. In the smooth, impregnable wall against which we beat our heads they had cut these little windows through which we handed in parcels or requests for information. I was considered particularly lucky because I got a letter — the only one — from M. and thus learned where he was. I immediately sent a package to him there, but it was returned to me and I was told that the addressee was dead. A few months after this, M.'s brother Alexander Emilievich was given a document to certify his death. I know of no other prisoner's wife who ever received a certificate like this. I cannot imagine why such a favor was shown to me.

Nobody has said he actually saw M. dead. Nobody claims to have washed his body or put it in a grave. For those who went through the camps, life was like a delirium in which the sequence of time was lost and fact became mixed with fantasy. What these people have to say is no more reliable than similar accounts of any other calvary. Those few

---

[1] Established in 1934 to deal with "socially dangerous persons," the Special Tribunal was composed of high-ranking NKVD [the predecessor of the KGB] and militia officials and could impose sentences of exile or confinement to forced-labor camps.

who survived to bear witness, including such people as Dombrovski, had no chance to check their facts at the time, let alone to weigh hypotheses about them.

I can be certain of only one thing: that somewhere M.'s sufferings ended in death. Before his death, he must have lain dying on his bunk, like others around him. Perhaps he was waiting for a parcel — a parcel which never came in time and was sent back to me. For us its return was a sign that he had died. He, on the other hand, may have concluded from its non-arrival that something had happened to us: This because some well-fed official in military uniform, a trained killer, weary of searching through endless, constantly changing lists of prisoners for one unpronounceable name, had simply scrawled on the accompanying form the simplest thing that came into his head: "Addressee Dead" — and I, who had prayed for the merciful release of my husband, received these last, inevitable good tidings from a girl clerk in a Moscow post office.

And after his death — or even before it, perhaps — he lived on in camp legend as a demented old man of seventy who had once written poetry in the outside world and was therefore nicknamed "The Poet." And another old man — or was it the same one? — lived on in the transit camp at Vtoraya Rechka, waiting to be shipped to Kolyma,[2] and was thought by many people to be Osip Mandelstam — which, for all I know, he may have been.

That is all I have been able to find out about the last days, illness, and death of Mandelstam. Others know very much less about the death of their dear ones.

One Final Account

But there is still a little more to tell. The transport which took M. to Vladivostok left Moscow on September 9, 1938. Another person who was on it is a physicist called L. He does not wish to be identified because, as he says, "things are all right just now, but who knows what may happen later?" During the terror he worked in a Moscow technical college whose staff was completely decimated because one of its members was the son of a man hated by Stalin. L. was taken to join this transport from the Taganka prison. Others were brought from Butyrki, to which they had been transferred from the Ludianka[3] just before the transport was due to leave. As the train was traveling east, L. learned from another prisoner that M. was there, too. The other prisoner had learned this after he had fallen ill and been put in the sick bay, where he

---

[2] A notoriously brutal prison camp in Siberia. [Ed.]

[3] Another large prison in Moscow. [Ed.]

had met M. He reported to L. that M. just lay on his bunk all the time, his head covered with a blanket. He still had a little money and the guards sometimes bought bread rolls for him at stations. . . .

When he left the infirmary L. heard that M. had died. This must have been between December 1938 and April 1939 — in April L. was transferred to a work camp. He met no witnesses of M.'s death and knew about it only from hearsay. L.'s story seems to bear out what Kazarnovski had told me — namely, that M. died early. I also conclude from L.'s account that, since all typhus cases were taken to the infirmary, then M., who was found not to have it, must have died in quarantine. This means that he did not even die in his own bunk, covered by his own miserable convict's blanket.

There is nowhere I can make inquiries and nobody who will tell me anything. Who is likely to search through those grisly archives just for the sake of Mandelstam, when they won't even publish a volume of his work? Those who perished are lucky if they have been posthumously rehabilitated, or if, at any rate, their cases have been "discontinued for lack of evidence." . . .

All I can do, therefore, is to gather what meager evidence there is and speculate about the date of his death. As I constantly tell myself: The sooner he died, the better. There is nothing worse than a slow death. I hate to think that at the moment when my mind was set at rest on being told in the post office that he was dead, he may actually have been still alive and on his way to Kolyma. The date of death has not been established. And it is beyond my power to do anything more to establish it.

REFLECTIONS

The massacre of civilians in times of war and the forced expulsion and murder of people because of their race, religion, or ethnicity still go on today. At the end of the twentieth century, the expulsion of over a million ethnic Albanian Kosovars by the Serbian police and military remind many in the world of the events of the Nazi era.

Is the willingness to go to war to oppose genocide, ethnic cleansing, state-sponsored mass-murder, and the abrogation of human rights a sign of a new and welcome commitment in the world and in the United States? The United States entered World War II, "the good fight" against dictatorship, without knowledge of the holocaust and only after Japan attacked Pearl Harbor and Germany declared war on the United States. Oil, territory, or "national interest" more than principle has often motivated much of American foreign policy. Wars fought for principle are neither entirely new nor always salutary. In 1917 President Woodrow Wilson committed the United States to "a war to end all wars," but this noble if paradoxical goal was combined with a pledge to "make the world safe for democracy" and to ensure "the self-determination of nations." We have lived with some of the darker implications of those principles ever since. Spreading democracy has sometimes been viewed as a new form of Western imperialism, and the seemingly innocent goal of national self-determination bears some responsibility for unleashing the ethnic hatreds witnessed in the former Yugoslavia.

Short of war, the world community has adopted three other strategies to counter genocide and mass murder. The first is trial of war criminals. At the conclusion of World War II, war-crime trials of Nazis and Japanese were conducted. The terms *war crimes* and *war criminals* are unfortunate misnomers because they suggest a criminalization of military activities. In fact, the crimes recounted in this chapter were not crimes of the battlefield but, rather, massive crimes against civilian populations.

Developing and refining international laws respecting human rights is the second strategy. The "Declaration of Human Rights" passed by the United Nations, itself a shaper and guardian of international law, offers a recognized standard and continuing process for defining and preventing genocide, mass murder, and "crimes against humanity."

The third strategy, one in which all of us can participate, is the dissemination of information and concerted efforts toward understanding. To promote understanding, archives must be opened, and laws such as the "freedom of information act" must be used aggressively. We must develop sensitivity to the plight of victims, knowledge of the victimizers' motives, and understanding about the ways that the horrendous can happen.

In recent years "truth and reconciliation" commissions have been formed in South Africa and El Salvador to enable those countries to get beyond years of government-sponsored terrorism. In cases like these, when such governments have relinquished power but their personnel are either too powerful or too numerous to be brought to justice, the new democratic governments and their truth and reconciliation commissions have asked for a complete and remorseful accounting of past crimes. Some say these commissions have been able to accept truth instead of revenge; others find it to be truth instead of justice. But truth can be an amazing restorative, especially when it is linked with genuine contrition. The price of amnesty can hardly be less. Forgiveness may be much more. Which, if any, of the crimes recalled in this chapter would you be willing to forgive? What should be necessary for acquittal or amnesty? How do we prevent such things from occurring again and again?

12

New States and
New Struggles

HISTORICAL CONTEXT
Middle East, South Africa,
China, and Vietnam, 1945–1975

World War II, like World War I before it, left in its wake the means and the motives for the creation of new states and new struggles throughout the world. Perhaps most significantly, the end of war in 1945 signaled that it was time to bring an end to colonies, to victors and vanquished — an agenda only dimly recognized in 1919. Even if both wars had not been caused by colonialism, the participation of colonized peoples on battlefields, in hospitals and factories, at home and in Europe made the pretenses of a League of Nations "mandate" seem to those in Africa and Asia to be colonialism under a different name. Further, the utter devastation of Germany and Japan and the sheer exhaustion of England and France made the continuation of colonialism a dubious proposition.

But the new reality dawned slowly. The sudden availability of former colonies of Germany and Japan tempted France, whose pride, more so than England's, had been shattered by the war. Although England released the Indian subcontinent in 1947, France held on to its former colony in Vietnam in 1945 and retained it until defeated in 1954.

The new state of Israel, carved out of the colonial British Mandate over Palestine by the United Nations in 1947, was the result of the success of the Jewish Zionist movement that had long campaigned for a Jewish state in the ancient home of Judaism. Even before the Nazi Holocaust, European governments thought a Jewish state would provide a Western outpost in the Arab world, but the virtual genocide of European Jewry by the Nazis gave the project renewed support. Ignored were the claims of resident Palestinian Arabs displaced by Jewish refugees from Europe and North Africa.

Not all new states after 1945 were products of decolonization. The communist victory in China in 1949 came at the end of Japanese colonization in 1945 but also after four more years of the unpopular Nationalist regime of Chiang Kai-shek, supported by the United States. The new People's Republic of China, established by Mao Zedong (Tsetung) in 1949, extended communism from the world's largest political territory, the Soviet Union and much of Eastern Europe, to the world's most populated country.

Even before Mao Zedong defeated Chiang Kai-shek's Nationalist army, Vietnamese socialists, led by Ho Chi Minh, declared their independence from defeated Japan and from France, their former occupier. With U.S. support, the French attempted to regain their colony, and when that effort failed in 1954, the United States replaced France for reasons that pertained to the communist victory in China and the politics of the Cold War between the U.S. and the Soviet Union.

South Africa was almost the only African state that was not newly founded between 1945 and 1975, but the victory of the Nationalist Party in 1948 brought about revolutionary changes for the country. For more than forty years, during this age of decolonization, a minority of white Europeans found ways to keep the majority Africans strangers in their own land.

In this chapter we examine examples of post–World War II politics to understand the forces of nationalism and division. While none of the struggles that developed in these societies was as destructive as World Wars I and II, many proved intractable, and some continue even today.

THINKING HISTORICALLY
Diagnosing Rifts and
Noting the Uses of History

The new struggles of the post–World War II period had roots in the war. The expectation of the imminent end to colonialism released the forces of nationalism. Some of these forces were religious and communal, as in the partitions of India and Pakistan and of Palestine and Israel. In the context of the developing Cold War between the United States and the Soviet Union, national movements had to define their relationship to the superpowers: capitalism or communism, freedom and democracy or international socialist solidarity. In all cases, there were also local, indigenous roots of conflict and the sort of economic, political, cultural, and social conflict that can be found in virtually any society.

As you read these selections, look for the rifts in these societies. *Rifts* are divides or fault lines along which tensions mount and conflicts arise. Every society has rifts — sometimes they are recognized; other times they are glossed over and denied. This chapter is partly an exercise in scrutinizing sources (all selections in the chapter are primary sources) to determine what is *not* said but implied. Note the disputes that the speech or document attempts to solve or ignore and the consensus that is assumed. In some cases, most obviously the racial divide in South Africa during the 1950s and 1960s, the rift is obvious and highlighted in the source. In others, the divisions are harder to pinpoint. We look for divisions for two reasons. First, understanding rifts tells us a great deal about a society. Recognizing a rift may not tell us how fragile a society is, but it does reveal what the society holds most important and where frictions are likely to develop. We might also be able to compare societies that have similar rifts (ethnic, racial, religious, political, economic, or social). Second, because rifts are the dynamic forces in a society, they show us how things are changing.

As you read these selections, you will be asked to think about the ways in which a people uses its history. Most of these sources, like so many others we could include, use historical accounts — explanations or stories of the past — to support their arguments. How can a historical account support a particular idea of the present or a vision of the future? What, after all, is the value of history?

73

Arab Opposition to a State of Israel

After the defeat of the Ottoman Empire in World War I, the League of Nations gave Great Britain a mandate to administer the region known as Palestine. British rule was beset by, on one hand, pressure from the Zionist movement to establish a Jewish homeland in Palestine and, on the other, pressure from Palestinian Arabs and neighboring Arab states to resist the Zionist demands. In the meantime, Zionist-inspired Jewish immigration to Palestine — mainly from Europe — continued and then increased with the rise of anti-Semitism

The Israel-Arab Reader: A Documentary History of the Middle East Conflict, ed. Walter Laquer and Barry Rubin (New York: Viking Penguin, 1995), 80, 82, 85, 88.

after Hitler's coming to power in Germany in 1933. As World War II ended, the situation in Palestine worsened: Both Zionist and Arab pressures intensified, with both sides resorting sometimes to violence. The horrendous experience of the Jewish people in Europe under Hitler's murderous rule naturally added to the difficulty of resolving the problem.

In November 1945 the United States and Great Britain established a commission to investigate the issue. This reading contains a portion of the Arab presentation to the commission. Why did Arabs oppose a Jewish state? What claims to Palestine did they make? Would they have accepted a nonreligious state that included Jews and Arabs? Was any compromise possible at this point? Why did the Arabs oppose the partition of Palestine?

Thinking Historically

What seems to have been the main conflict in Palestine at the time this document was written? Would you call it religious, economic, political, or something else? In what ways was this conflict likely to get worse, according to the Arab authors?

1. The whole Arab people is unalterably opposed to the attempt to impose Jewish immigration and settlement upon it, and ultimately to establish a Jewish State in Palestine. Its opposition is based primarily upon right. The Arabs of Palestine are descendants of the indigenous inhabitants of the country, who have been in occupation of it since the beginning of history; they cannot agree that it is right to subject an indigenous population against its will to alien immigrants, whose claim is based upon a historical connection which ceased effectively many centuries ago. Moreover they form the majority of the population; as such they cannot submit to a policy of immigration which if pursued for long will turn them from a majority into a minority in an alien state; and they claim the democratic right of a majority to make its own decisions in matters of urgent national concern.

2. The entry of incessant waves of immigrants prevents normal economic and social development and causes constant dislocation of the country's life; in so far as it reacts upon prices and values and makes the whole economy dependent upon the constant inflow of capital from abroad it may even in certain circumstances lead to economic disaster. It is bound moreover to arouse continuous political unrest and prevent the establishment of that political stability on which the prosperity and health of the country depend. This unrest is likely to increase in frequency and violence as the Jews come nearer to being the majority and the Arabs a minority.

Even if economic and social equilibrium is reestablished, it will be to the detriment of the Arabs. The superior capital resources at the disposal of the Jews, their greater experience of modern economic technique, and the existence of a deliberate policy of expansion and domination have already gone far toward giving them the economic mastery of Palestine. The biggest concessionary companies are in their hands; they possess a large proportion of the total cultivable land, and an even larger one of the land in the highest category of fertility; and the land they possess is mostly inalienable to non-Jews. The continuance of land-purchase and immigration, taken together with the refusal of Jews to employ Arabs on their lands or in their enterprises and the great increase in the Arab population, will create a situation in which the Arab population is pushed to the margin of cultivation and a landless proletariat, rural and urban, comes into existence. This evil can be palliated but not cured by attempts at increasing the absorptive capacity or the industrial production of Palestine; the possibility of such improvements is limited, they would take a long time to carry out, and would scarcely do more than keep pace with the rapid growth of the Arab population; moreover in present circumstances they would be used primarily for the benefit of the Jews and thus might increase the disparity between the two communities.

Nor is the evil economic only. Zionism is essentially a political movement, aiming at the creation of a state: immigration, land-purchase, and economic expansion are only aspects of a general political strategy. If Zionism succeeds in its aim, the Arabs will become a minority in their own country; a minority which can hope for no more than a minor share in the government, for the state is to be a Jewish state, and which will find itself not only deprived of that international status which the other Arab countries possess but cut off from living contact with the Arab world of which it is an integral part. . . .

8. In the Arab view, any solution of the problem created by Zionist aspirations must satisfy certain conditions:

(i) It must recognize the right of the indigenous inhabitants of Palestine to continue in occupation of the country and to preserve its traditional character.

(ii) It must recognize that questions like immigration, which affect the whole nature and destiny of the country, should be decided in accordance with democratic principles by the will of the population.

(iii) It must accept the principle that the only way by which the will of the population can be expressed is through the establishment of responsible representative Government. (The Arabs find something inconsistent in the attitude of Zionists who demand the establishment of a free democratic commonwealth in Palestine and then hasten to add that this should not take place until the Jews are in a majority.)

(iv) This representative Government should be based upon the principle of absolute equality of all citizens irrespective of race and religion.

(v) The form of Government should be such as to make possible the development of a spirit of loyalty and cohesion among all elements of the community, which will override all sectional attachments. In other words it should be a Government which the whole community could regard as their own, which should be rooted in their consent and have a moral claim upon their obedience.

(vi) The settlement should recognize the fact that by geography and history Palestine is inescapably part of the Arab world; that the only alternative to its being part of the Arab world and accepting the implications of its position is complete isolation, which would be disastrous from every point of view; and that whether they like it or not the Jews in Palestine are dependent upon the goodwill of the Arabs.

(vii) The settlement should be such as to make possible a satisfactory definition within the framework of U.N.O. of the relations between Palestine and the Western Powers who possess interests in the country.

(viii) The settlement should take into account that Zionism is essentially a political movement aiming at the creation of a Jewish state and should therefore avoid making any concession which might encourage Zionists in the hope that this aim can be achieved in any circumstances. . . .

The idea of partition and the establishment of a Jewish state in a part of Palestine is inadmissible for the same reasons of principle as the idea of establishing a Jewish state in the whole country. If it is unjust to the Arabs to impose a Jewish state on the whole of Palestine, it is equally unjust to impose it in any part of the country. Moreover, as the Woodhead Commission showed, there are grave practical difficulties in the way of partition; commerce would be strangled, communications dislocated, and the public finances upset. It would also be impossible to devise frontiers which did not leave a large Arab minority in the Jewish state. This minority would not willingly accept its subjection to the Zionists, and it would not allow itself to be transferred to the Arab state. Moreover, partition would not satisfy the Zionists. It cannot be too often repeated that Zionism is a political movement aiming at the domination at least of the whole of Palestine; to give it a foothold in part of Palestine would be to encourage it to press for more and to provide it with a base for its activities. Because of this, because of the pressure of population, and in order to escape from its isolation it would inevitably be thrown into enmity with the surrounding Arab states and this enmity would disturb the stability of the whole Middle East.

74

Israel's Proclamation of Independence

The Anglo-American Commission failed to resolve the problem of competing Zionist and Arab claims to Palestine. In 1947 Britain informed the United Nations, which had replaced the League of Nations, that it could not continue indefinitely to administer Palestine. The United Nations then called for the partition of Palestine into Jewish and Arab states. On May 14, 1948, the Jews of Palestine proclaimed the independent State of Israel. The next day — when British authority officially ended — armies from the Arab nations invaded Israel. But the Arabs were defeated. At the end of the war, Israel controlled 77 percent of the former Palestine rather than the 57 percent the United Nations had allotted to a Jewish state. In the course of the war, 900,000 of the 1,300,000 Arabs who had been living in the Israeli part of Palestine became refugees.

What reasons does this document give for the establishment of Israel? What provision does the new state seem ready to make for Palestinian Arabs? Do these differ from the rights of Jews?

Thinking Historically

Can you see signs of any potential future conflicts in this document? Does this proclamation minimize or resolve any of the conflicts you read about in the previous selection? Does it magnify the conflicts mentioned in selection 73? If so, how?

Notice how the authors of this document use their view of history to support their position. How might the Palestinian-Arab view of history differ?

The Land of Israel was the birthplace of the Jewish people. Here their spiritual, religious, and national identity was formed. Here they achieved independence and created a culture of national and universal significance. Here they wrote and gave the Bible to the world.

Exiled from the Land of Israel the Jewish people remained faithful to it in all the countries of their dispersion, never ceasing to pray and hope for their return and the restoration of their national freedom.

Impelled by this historical association, Jews strove throughout the

The Israel-Arab Reader: A Documentary History of the Middle East Conflict, ed. Walter Laquer and Barry Rubin (New York: Viking Penguin, 1995), 107–09.

centuries to go back to the land of their fathers and regain their statehood. In recent decades they returned in their masses. They reclaimed the wilderness, revived their language, built cities and villages, and established a vigorous and ever-growing community, with its own economic and cultural life. They sought peace, yet were prepared to defend themselves. They brought the blessings of progress to all inhabitants of the country and looked forward to sovereign independence.

In the year 1897 the First Zionist Congress, inspired by Theodor Herzl's vision of the Jewish State, proclaimed the right of the Jewish people to national revival in their own country.

This right was acknowledged by the Balfour Declaration of November 2, 1917, and re-affirmed by the Mandate of the League of Nations, which gave explicit international recognition to the historic connection to the Jewish people with Palestine and their right to reconstitute their National Home.

The recent holocaust, which engulfed millions of Jews in Europe, proved anew the need to solve the problem of the homelessness and lack of independence of the Jewish people by means of the reestablishment of the Jewish State, which would open the gates to all Jews and endow the Jewish people with equality of status among the family of nations.

The survivors of the disastrous slaughter in Europe, and also Jews from other lands, have not desisted from their efforts to reach Eretz-Yisrael, in face of difficulties, obstacles, and perils; and have not ceased to urge their right to a life of dignity, freedom, and honest toil in their ancestral land.

In the second World War the Jewish people in Palestine made their full contribution to the struggle of the freedom-loving nations against the Nazi evil. The sacrifices of their soldiers and their war effort gained them the right to rank with the nations which founded the United Nations.

On November 29, 1947, the General Assembly of the United Nations adopted a Resolution requiring the establishment of a Jewish State in Palestine. The General Assembly called upon the inhabitants of the country to take all the necessary steps on their part to put the plan into effect. This recognition by the United Nations of the right of the Jewish people to establish their independent State is unassailable.

It is the natural right of the Jewish people to lead, as do all other nations, an independent existence in its sovereign State.

Accordingly we, the members of the National Council, representing the Jewish people in Palestine and the World Zionist Movement, are met together in solemn assembly today, the day of termination of the British Mandate for Palestine; and by virtue of the natural and historic right of the Jewish people and of the Resolution of the General Assembly of the United Nations.

We hereby proclaim the establishment of the Jewish State in Palestine, to be called Medinath Yisrael (The State of Israel).

The State of Israel will be open to the immigration of Jews from all countries of their dispersion; will promote the development of the country for the benefit of all its inhabitants; will be based on the principles of liberty, justice, and peace as conceived by the Prophets of Israel; will uphold the full social and political equality of all its citizens, without distinction of religion, race, or sex; will guarantee freedom of religion, conscience, education, and culture; will safeguard the Holy Places of all religions; and will loyally uphold the principles of the United Nations Charter.

The State of Israel will be ready to co-operate with the organs and representatives of the United Nations in the implementation of the Resolution of the Assembly of November 29, 1947, and will take steps to bring about the Economic Union over the whole of Palestine.

We appeal to the United Nations to assist the Jewish people in the building of its State and to admit Israel into the family of nations.

In the midst of wanton aggression [by Arab states], we yet call upon the Arab inhabitants of the State of Israel to preserve the ways of peace and play their part in the development of the State, on the basis of full and equal citizenship and due representation in all its bodies and institutions — provisional and permanent.

We extend our hand in peace, and neighbourliness to all the neighbouring states and their peoples, and invite them to cooperate with the independent Jewish nation for the common good of all. The State of Israel is prepared to make its contribution to the progress of the Middle East as a whole.

Our call goes out to the Jewish people all over the world to rally to our side in the task of immigration and development, and to stand by us in the great struggle for the fulfillment of the dream of generations for the redemption of Israel.

75

HENDRIK F. VERWOERD

On Apartheid

South Africa was settled by Europeans from Holland and England in the middle of the seventeenth century. From the beginning, Europeans had contact with the Khoikhoi indigenous people who were swiftly decimated by European diseases. As Europeans expanded inland from their original seacoast settlements, they farmed the interior with Khoikhoi labor and with slaves imported largely from Indonesia and Madagascar. By the end of the nineteenth century, European settlers engaged in frequent wars with the Xhosa and Zulu people (African Bantu speakers), who were ultimately subdued by machine guns. After the English defeated the Dutch in the Boer War at the turn of the century, the Republic of South Africa was declared in 1910. For most of the period before World War II, despite the English victory, moderate Dutch leaders ruled South Africa, restricting black African land ownership and civil rights. After the discovery of gold and diamonds in South Africa near the end of the nineteenth century, the need for workers from all races was great, and the friction between whites and blacks increased considerably.

During World War II, many white South Africans, some of whom had been educated in Germany, supported the Nazis. In 1948 a reconstituted Nationalist Party, backed by fascist and paramilitary movements, won a surprising electoral victory on the promise of a new, more segregationist policy called apartheid. In this selection, Hendrik F. Verwoerd explains the meaning of and rationale behind apartheid. Verwoerd, educated in Nazi Germany, was a key figure in the creation and execution of South African racial policy as the first "Native Minister" and later as prime minister (1958–1966).

The policy of apartheid was twofold: First, black "Bantu" speaking Africans (not the smaller and more absorbed populations of Khoikhoi and "people of mixed race"), who were needed for work but banned from "European cities," were declared to be no longer South African. Labeled instead "natives" of "independent homelands," this 70 percent of the population was moved to landlocked scrub, a paltry 13-percent share of former South African territory. Second, the needed black workers were allowed to commute weekly from these homelands to work in white South African mines and cities

A. N. Pelzer, ed., *Verwoerd Speaks: Speeches, 1948–1966* (Johannesburg: APB Publishers, 1966), 23–29.

if they carried appropriate passes and lived in designated dormitories while working. Of course, they were paid much less than their white counterparts who, it was thought, would then show greater appreciation for their privileges of race. Among the results of this policy were the effective elimination of what South African sociologists called "poor whiteism," the creation of a white middle class, clear color-coding of poverty, and increasing popularity for the Nationalist Party.

In the speech that follows, how does Verwoerd appeal to his white audience? How does he appeal to a black audience? Do you think he believed what he said? Did his audience?

In what ways does Verwoerd's policy toward black Africans resemble Israeli policy toward Palestinians or U.S. policy toward Native Americans? What are the differences?

Thinking Historically

Notice how Verwoerd argues that equality and intermingling will lead to conflict. What sort of conflict is he speaking about? Would you call it an economic conflict or an ethnic-racial conflict? How can ethnic-racial segregation minimize economic conflict? Is Verwoerd more interested in avoiding conflict or preserving privilege?

Next, I wish to accede to the wish which, I understand, has long been felt by members of this council, namely that a member of the Government should explain the main features of what is implied by the policy of Apartheid. . . .

As a premise, the question may be put: Must Bantu and European in future develop as intermixed communities, or as communities separated from one another in so far as this is practically possible? If the reply is "intermingled communities," then the following must be understood. There will be competition and conflict everywhere. So long as the points of contact are still comparatively few, as is the case now, friction and conflict will be few and less evident. The more this intermixing develops, however, the stronger the conflict will become. In such conflict, the Europeans will, at least for a long time, hold the stronger position, and the Bantu be the defeated party in every phase of the struggle. This must cause to rise in him an increasing sense of resentment and revenge. Neither for the European, nor for the Bantu, can this, namely increasing tension and conflict, be an ideal future, because the intermixed development involves disadvantage to both.

Perhaps, in such an eventuality, it is best frankly to face the situation which must arise in the political sphere. In the event of an intermixed development, the Bantu will undoubtedly desire a share in the government of the intermixed country. He will, in due course, not be satisfied with a limited share in the form of communal representation, but will desire full participation in the country's government on the basis of an equal franchise. For the sake of simplicity, I shall not enlarge here on the fact that, simultaneously with the development of this demand, he will desire the same in the social, economic, and other spheres of life, involving in due course, intermixed residence, intermixed labour, intermixed living, and, eventually, a miscegenated population — in spite of the well-known pride of both the Bantu and the European in their respective purity of descent. It follows logically, therefore, that, in an intermixed country, the Bantu must, in the political sphere, have as their object equal franchise with the European.

Now examine the same question from the European's point of view. A section of the Europeans, consisting of both Afrikaans- and English-speaking peoples, says equally clearly that, in regard to the above standpoint, the European must continue to dominate what will be the European part of South Africa. It should be noted that, notwithstanding false representations, these Europeans do not demand domination over the whole of South Africa, that is to say, over the Native territories according as the Bantu outgrow the need for their trusteeship. Because that section of the European population states its case very clearly, it must not be accepted, however, that the other section of the European population will support the above possible future demand of the Bantu. That section of the European population (English as well as Afrikaans) which is prepared to grant representation to the Bantu in the country's government does not wish to grant anything beyond communal representation, and that on a strictly limited basis. They do not yet realize that a balance of power may thereby be given to the non-European with which an attempt may later be made to secure full and equal franchise on the same voters' roll. The moment they realize that, or the moment when the attempt is made, this latter section of the European population will also throw in its weight with the first section in the interests of European supremacy in the European portion of the country. This appears clearly from its proposition that, in its belief on the basis of an inherent superiority, or greater knowledge, or whatever it may be, the European must remain master and leader. The section is, therefore, also a protagonist of separate residential areas, and of what it calls separation.

My point is this that, if mixed development is to be the policy of the future in South Africa, it will lead to the most terrific clash of interests imaginable. The endeavours and desires of the Bantu and the endeavours and objectives of *all* Europeans will be antagonistic. Such a clash can only bring unhappiness and misery to both. Both Bantu and European must, therefore, consider in good time how this misery can be averted from themselves and from their descendants. They must find a plan to provide the two population groups with opportunities for the full development of their respective powers and ambitions without coming into conflict.

The only possible way out is the second alternative, namely, that both adopt a development divorced from each other. That is all that the word apartheid means. Any word can be poisoned by attaching a false meaning to it. That has happened to this word. The Bantu have been made to believe that it means oppression, or even that the Native territories are to be taken away from them. In reality, however, exactly the opposite is intended with the policy of apartheid. To avoid the above-mentioned unpleasant and dangerous future for both sections of the population, the present Government adopts the attitude that it concedes and wishes to give to others precisely what it demands for itself. It believes in the supremacy (baasskap) of the European in his sphere but, then, it also believes equally in the supremacy (baasskap) of the Bantu in his own sphere. For the European child it wishes to create all the possible opportunities for its own development, prosperity, and national service in its own sphere; but for the Bantu it also wishes to create all the opportunities for the realization of ambitions and the rendering of service to *their* own people. There is thus no policy of oppression here, but one of creating a situation which has never existed for the Bantu; namely, that, taking into consideration their languages, traditions, history, and different national communities, they may pass through a development of their own. That opportunity arises for them as soon as such a division is brought into being between them and the Europeans that they need not be the imitators and henchmen of the latter. . . .

I trust that every Bantu will forget the misunderstandings of the past and choose not the road leading to conflict, but that which leads to peace and happiness for both the separate communities. Are the present leaders of the Bantu, under the influence of Communist agitators, going to seek a form of equality which they will not get? For in the long run they will come up against the whole of the European community, as well as the large section of their own compatriots who prefer the many advantages of self-government within a community of their own. I cannot believe that they will. Nobody can reject a form of independence, obtainable with everybody's co-operation, in favour of a futile striving after that which promises to be not freedom but downfall. . . .

76

NELSON MANDELA

Rivonia Trial Statement

On May 1, 1994, Nelson Mandela was elected president of South Africa in the first general election in which all South Africans, black and white, were permitted to vote. Mandela, the leader of the African National Congress (ANC), had spent twenty-seven years in jail when he was released by then-president F. W. de Klerk in 1990.

Mandela was born into a royal clan of the Thembu people in 1918 and, after his father's death, was prepared for the chieftainship by a cousin. He was educated at a British missionary school and Fort Harare University, experiences that broadened his identity as a South African so that he no longer "attached value to any kind of ethnicity." After earning a law degree, he joined the ANC, for which he rapidly became an important spokesman and organizer. As a political leader and attorney, Mandela worked peacefully and legally for the rights of black South Africans in the first decade of apartheid after 1948. But with mounting evidence of government oppression and, in 1961, the police killing of sixty-nine peaceful demonstrators in Sharpeville, Mandela led the ANC to adopt tactics of armed resistance, becoming the first commander of the new guerilla army. Eight months later he was arrested.

Mandela was already in prison when a raid by South African police on the Rivonia farm hideout of the ANC netted information implicating Mandela as organizer of the ANC's new military wing, Umkonto We Sizwe. At the trial he was given a life sentence. This selection is excerpted from the statement he made at his trial in 1964.

How was Mandela's vision for South Africa different from Verwoerd's? Was it inconsistent for Mandela to favor violence while claiming to be a democrat? Compare Mandela's nationalism with Gandhi's.

Thinking Historically

Notice how Mandela positioned himself as a modern force in the national struggle of South African blacks for full political participation. What, according to Mandela, were the tensions within the black community?

From Protest to Challenge: A Documentary History of African Politics in South Africa, 1882–1964, ed. Thomas Karis and Gwendolyn M. Carter, vol. III; Challenge and Violence, 1953–1964, ed. Thomas Karis and Gail M. Gerhart (Stanford: Hoover Institution Press, 1977), 771–77, 790–91, 795–96.

In the previous selection, Verwoerd defended racial and national division as a way of avoiding economic conflict. In this selection, Mandela defends the biracial policy of the ANC and the establishment of a democracy without racial or national distinctions. Does such a society run the risk of increasing economic and social conflict? How did Mandela hope to curtail such conflict?

How does Mandela's telling of the history of the ANC support his argument that violence against the state was nonracial and used only as a last resort?

I am the First Accused.

I hold a Bachelor's Degree in Arts and practised as an attorney in Johannesburg for a number of years in partnership with Oliver Tambo. I am a convicted prisoner serving five years for leaving the country without a permit and for inciting people to go on strike at the end of May, 1961.

At the outset, I want to say that the suggestion made by the State in its opening that the struggle in South Africa is under the influence of foreigners or communists is wholly incorrect. I have done whatever I did, both as an individual and as a leader of my people, because of my experience in South Africa and my own proudly-felt African background, and not because of what any outsider might have said.

In my youth in the Transkei I listened to the elders of my tribe telling stories of the old days. Amongst the tales they related to me were those of wars fought by our ancestors in defence of the fatherland. The names of Dingane and Bambata, Hintsa, and Makana, Squngthi and Dalasile, Moshoeshoe and Sekukhuni, were praised as the glory of the entire African nation. I hoped then that life might offer me the opportunity to serve my people and make my own humble contribution to their freedom struggle. This is what has motivated me in all that I have done in relation to the charges made against me in this case.

Having said this, I must deal immediately and at some length, with the question of violence. Some of the things so far told to the Court are true and some are untrue. I do not, however, deny that I planned sabotage. I did not plan it in a spirit of recklessness, nor because I have any love of violence. I planned it as the result of a calm and sober assessment of the political situation that had arisen after many years of tyranny, exploitation and oppression of my people by the Whites. . . .

But the violence which we chose to adopt was not terrorism. We who formed Umkonto were all members of the African National Congress, and had behind us the A.N.C. tradition of non-violence and negotiation as a means of solving political disputes. We believe that South Africa belonged to all the people who lived in it, and not to one group, be it Black or White. We did not want an inter-racial war, and tried to avoid it to the last minute. If the Court is in doubt about this, it will be seen that the whole history of our organization bears out what I have said, and what I will subsequently say, when I describe the tactics which Umkonto decided to adopt. I want, therefore, to say something about the African National Congress.

The African National Congress was formed in 1912 to defend the rights of the African people which had been seriously curtailed by the South Africa Act, and which were then being threatened by the Native Land Act. For thirty-seven years — that is until 1949 — it adhered strictly to a constitutional struggle. It put forward demands and resolutions; it sent delegations to the Government in the belief that African grievances could be settled through peaceful discussion and that Africans could advance gradually to full political rights. But White Governments remained unmoved, and the rights of Africans became less instead of becoming greater. In the words of my leader, Chief Luthuli, who became President of the A.N.C. in 1952, and who was later awarded the Nobel Peace Prize:

> who will deny that thirty years of my life have been spent knocking in vain, patiently, moderately, and modestly at a closed and barred door? What have been the fruits of moderation? The past thirty years have seen the greatest number of laws restricting our rights and progress, until today we have reached a stage where we have almost no rights at all.

Even after 1949, the A.N.C. remained determined to avoid violence. At this time, however, there was a change from the strictly constitutional means of protest which had been employed in the past. The change was embodied in a decision which was taken to protest against apartheid legislation by peaceful, but unlawful, demonstrations against certain laws. Pursuant to this policy the A.N.C. launched the Defiance Campaign, in which I was placed in charge of volunteers. This campaign was based on the principles of passive resistance. More than 8,500 people defied apartheid laws and went to gaol. Yet there was not a single instance of violence in the course of this campaign on the part of any defier. I, and nineteen colleagues were convicted for the role we played in organizing the campaign, but our sentences were suspended mainly because the Judge found that discipline and nonviolence had been stressed throughout. This was the time when the volunteer section of the A.N.C. was established, and the word "Amadelakufa" was first used: This was the time when the volunteers were asked to take a pledge to uphold certain principles. Evidence dealing with volunteers and their pledges has been introduced into this case, but completely out of context. The volunteers were not, and are not, the soldiers of a Black Army pledged to fight a civil war against the Whites. They were, and are, the dedicated workers who are prepared to lead campaigns initiated by the A.N.C. to distribute leaflets; to organize strikes, or do whatever the particular campaign required. They are called volunteers because they volunteer to face the penalties of imprisonment and whipping which are now prescribed by the legislature for such acts.

During the Defiance Campaign, the Public Safety Act and the Criminal Law Amendment Act were passed. These Statutes provided harsher penalties for offences committed by way of protests against laws. Despite this, the protests continued and the A.N.C. adhered to its policy of non-violence. In 1956, one hundred and fifty-six leading members of the Congress Alliance, including myself, were arrested on a charge of High Treason and charged under the Suppression of Communism Act. The non-violent policy of the A.N.C. was put into issue by the State, but when the Court gave judgment some five years later, it found that the A.N.C. did not have a policy of violence. We were acquitted on all counts, which included a count that the A.N.C. sought to set up a Communist State in place of the existing regime. The Government has always sought to label all its opponents as communists. This allegation has been repeated in the present case, but as I will show, the A.N.C. is not, and never has been, a communist organization.

In 1960, there was the shooting at Sharpeville, which resulted in the proclamation of a State of Emergency and the declaration of the A.N.C. as an unlawful organization. My colleagues and I, after careful consideration, decided that we would not obey this decree. The African people were not part of the Government and did not make the laws by which they were governed. We believed in the words of the Universal Declaration of Human Rights, that "the will of the people shall be the basis of the authority of the Government," and for us to accept the banning was equivalent to accepting the silencing of the Africans for all time. The A.N.C. refused to dissolve, but instead went underground. We believed it was our duty to preserve this organization which had been built up with almost fifty years of unremitting toil. I have no doubt that no self-respecting White political organization would disband itself if declared illegal by a Government in which it had no say. . . .

The lack of human dignity experienced by Africans is the direct result of the policy of White supremacy. White supremacy implies Black inferiority. Legislation designed to preserve White supremacy entrenches this notion. Menial tasks in South Africa are invariably performed by Africans. When anything has to be carried or cleaned the White man will look around for an African to do it for him, whether the African is employed by him or not. Because of this sort of attitude, Whites tend to regard Africans as a separate breed. They do not look upon them as people with families of their own; they do not realise that they have emotions — that they fall in love like White people do; that they want to be with their wives and children like White people want to be with theirs; that they want to earn enough money to support their families properly, to feed and clothe them and send them to school. And what "house-boy" or "garden-boy" or labourer can ever hope to do this?

Pass Laws, which to the Africans are among the most hated bits of legislation of South Africa, render any African liable to police surveillance at any time. I doubt whether there is a single African male in South Africa who has not at some stage had a brush with the police over his pass. Hundreds and thousands of Africans are thrown into gaol every year under pass laws. Even worse than this is the fact that pass laws keep husband and wife apart and lead to the breakdown of family life.

Poverty and the breakdown of family life have secondary effects. Children wander about the streets of the Townships because they have no schools to go to, or no money to enable them to go to school, or no parents at home to see that they go to school, because both parents (if there be two) have to work to keep the family alive. This leads to a breakdown in moral standards, to an alarming rise in illegitimacy, and to growing violence which erupts, not only politically, but everywhere. Life in the townships is dangerous. There is not a day that goes by without somebody being stabbed or assaulted. And violence is carried out of the townships in the White living areas. People are afraid to walk the streets after dark. Housebreakings and robberies are increasing, despite the fact that the death sentence can now be imposed for such offences. Death sentences cannot cure the festering sore.

Africans want to be paid a living wage. Africans want to perform work which they are capable of doing, and not work which the Government declares them to be capable of. Africans want to be allowed to live where they obtain work, and not be endorsed out of an area because they were not born there. Africans want to be allowed to own land in places where they work, and not to be obliged to live in rented houses which they can never call their own. Africans want to be part of the general population, and not confined to living in their own ghettos. African men want to have their wives and children to live with them where they work, and not be forced into an unnatural existence in men's hostels. African women want to be with their men folk and not be left permanently widowed in the reserves. Africans want to be allowed out after 11 o'clock at night and not to be confined to their rooms like little children. Africans want to be allowed to travel in their own country and to seek work where they want to and not where the Labour Bureau tells them to. Africans want a just share in the whole of South Africa; they want security and a stake in society.

Above all, we want equal political rights, because without them our disabilities will be permanent. I know this sounds revolutionary to the

Whites in this country, because the majority of voters will be Africans. This makes the White man fear democracy.

But this fear cannot be allowed to stand in the way of the only solution which will guarantee racial harmony and freedom for all. It is not true that the enfranchisement of all will result in racial domination. Political division, based on colour, is entirely artificial and, when it disappears, so will the domination of one colour group by another. The A.N.C. has spent half a century fighting against racialism. When it triumphs it will not change that policy.

This then is what the A.N.C. is fighting. Their struggle is a truly national one. It is a struggle of the African people, inspired by their own suffering and their own experience. It is a struggle for the right to live.

During my lifetime I have dedicated myself to this struggle of the African people. I have fought against White domination, and I have fought against Black domination. I have cherished the ideal of a democratic and free society in which all persons live together in harmony and with equal opportunities. It is an ideal which I hope to live for and to achieve. But if needs be, it is an ideal for which I am prepared to die.

77

MAO ZEDONG

On Letting a Hundred Flowers Blossom

When Mao Zedong (Tse-tung) and the Chinese Communist party came to power in 1949, they were faced with the ruins of Japanese occupation and World War II, the abject political failure of the Chinese Republic, decades of economic hardship, and the bitterness and pain of the recently concluded civil war. The Communists intended to return China to its former prosperity and stature in the world and to transform it into a modern state, doing away with the gross injustices that had plagued the vast masses of poor rural peasants and urban workers.

Mao Tse-tung, "On Letting a Hundred Flowers Blossom," from *Mao Tse-tung on Art and Literature* (Peking: Foreign Language Press, 1960).

In rural areas, "people's courts" were set up. Landlords were tried, subjected to self-criticism, and then forced to give up their property. Many were executed, with estimates varying from hundreds of thousands to tens of millions killed. While some of those classified as "rich peasants" lost their livelihoods, the vast majority of Chinese peasants (a group that numbered around 600 million, one-fifth of the world's population) benefited from the land redistribution that followed.

The Communists had less experience in the cities than in the country. In 1927 they had been routed from the cities by a Nationalist purge. Forced to regroup in western rural China, they developed new roots among the peasantry, as Mao revised the traditional Marxist-Leninist vision of socialist transformation based on the revolutionary potential of the urban proletariat. But the Communists brought the same zeal to the cities that they had to the countryside. They arrested thieves, burglars, smugglers, prostitutes, and beggars, had them "re-educated" to Marxist social responsibility, and employed them in useful work.

Intellectuals were long a privileged class in China, perhaps the most privileged class. Those who had not joined the communist movement in the country, choosing instead to remain in the city, were suspected of supporting the defeated Nationalists. Still, many intellectuals were won over by Communist success in ridding urban politics of corruption, reducing inflation and unemployment, increasing literacy, and championing justice for women and the poor.

By 1957, Mao felt confident enough of the support of the intellectual class that he called on them to help the cause by constructively criticizing the party. This was the point of his speech on art and literature, "On Letting a Hundred Flowers Blossom," that is excerpted here.

How did Mao distinguish between acceptable and unacceptable criticism? Does he seem to be more interested in finding fragrant flowers or poisonous weeds?

Thinking Historically

Mao discusses a cultural rift in the country — a disagreement about ideas. How does he see the difference between Marxist and non-Marxist intellectuals? To what extent does Mao see this cultural divide as one primarily of social class?

"Let a hundred flowers blossom," and "let a hundred schools of thought contend," "long-term coexistence and mutual supervision" — how did these slogans come to be put forward?

They were put forward in the light of the specific conditions existing in China, on the basis of the recognition that various kinds of contradictions still exist in a socialist society, and in to the country's urgent need to speed up its economic and cultural development.

The policy of letting a hundred flowers blossom and a hundred schools of thought contend is designed to promote the flourishing of the arts and the progress of science; it is designed to enable a socialist culture to thrive in our land. Different forms and styles in art can develop freely and different schools in science can contend freely. We think that it is harmful to the growth of art and science if administrative measures are used to impose one particular style of art or school of thought and to ban another. Questions of right and wrong in the arts and sciences should be settled through free discussion in artistic and scientific circles and in the course of practical work in the arts and sciences. They should not be settled in summary fashion. A period of trial is often needed to determine whether something is right or wrong. In the past, new and correct things often failed at the outset to win recognition from the majority of people and had to develop by twists and turns in struggle. Correct and good things have often at first been looked upon not as fragrant flowers but as poisonous weeds. Copernicus' theory of the solar system and Darwin's theory of evolution were once dismissed as erroneous and had to win through over bitter opposition. Chinese history offers many similar examples. In socialist society, conditions for the growth of new things are radically different from and far superior to those in the old society. Nevertheless, it still often happens that new, rising forces are held back and reasonable suggestions smothered.

The growth of new things can also be hindered, not because of deliberate suppression, but because of lack of discernment. That is why we should take a cautious attitude in regard to questions of right and wrong in the arts and sciences, encourage free discussion, and avoid hasty conclusions. We believe that this attitude will facilitate the growth of the arts and sciences.

Marxism has also developed through struggle. At the beginning, Marxism was subjected to all kinds of attack and regarded as a poisonous weed. It is still being attacked and regarded as a poisonous weed in many parts of the world. However, it enjoys a different position in the socialist countries. But even in these countries, there are non-Marxist as well as anti-Marxist ideologies. It is true that in China, socialist transformation, in so far as a change in the system of ownership is concerned, has in the main been completed, and the turbulent, large-scale, mass class struggles characteristic of the revolutionary periods have in the main concluded. But remnants of the overthrown landlord and comprador classes still exist, the bourgeoisie still exists, and the petty bourgeoisie has only just begun to remould itself. Class struggle is not yet over. The class struggle between the proletariat and the bourgeoisie, the class struggle between various political forces, and the class struggle in the ideological field between the proletariat and the bourgeoisie will still be long and devious and at times may even become very acute. The proletariat seeks to transform the world according to its own world outlook, so does the bourgeoisie. In this respect, the question whether socialism or capitalism will win is still not really settled. Marxists are still a minority of the entire population as well as of the intellectuals. Marxism therefore must still develop through struggle. Marxism can only develop through struggle — this is true not only in the past and present, it is necessarily true in the future also. What is correct always develops in the course of struggle with what is wrong. The true, the good, and the beautiful always exist in comparison with the false, the evil and the ugly, and grow in struggle with the latter. As mankind in general rejects an untruth and accepts a truth, a new truth will begin struggling with new erroneous ideas. Such struggles will never end. This is the law of development of truth and it is certainly also the law of development of Marxism.

It will take a considerable time to decide the issue in the ideological struggle between socialism and capitalism in our country. This is because the influence of the bourgeoisie and of the intellectuals who come from the old society will remain in our country as the ideology of a class for a long time to come. Failure to grasp this, or still worse, failure to understand it at all, can lead to the gravest mistakes — to ignoring the necessity of waging the struggle in the ideological field. Ideological struggle is not like other forms of struggle. Crude, coercive methods should not be used in this struggle, but only the method of painstaking reasoning. Today, socialism enjoys favourable conditions in the ideological struggle. The main power of the state is in the hands of the working people led by the proletariat. The Communist Party is strong and its prestige stands high. Although there are defects and mistakes in our work, every fair-minded person can see that we are loyal to the people, that we are both determined and able to build up our country together with the people, and that we have achieved great successes and will achieve still greater ones. The vast majority of the bourgeoisie and intellectuals who come from the old society are patriotic; they are willing to serve their flourishing socialist motherland, and they know that if they turn away from the socialist cause and the working people led by the Communist Party, they will have no one to rely on and no bright future to look forward to.

People may ask: Since Marxism is accepted by the majority of the people in our country as the guiding ideology, can it be criticized? Certainly it can. As a scientific truth, Marxism fears no criticism. If it did, and could be defeated in arguments, it would be worthless. In fact, aren't the idealists criticizing Marxism every day and in all sorts of ways? As for those who harbour bourgeois and petty-bourgeois ideas and do not wish to change, aren't they also criticizing Marxism in all sorts of ways? Marxists should not be afraid of criticism from any quarter. Quite the contrary, they need to steel and improve themselves and win new positions in the teeth of criticism and the storm and stress of struggle. Fighting against wrong ideas is like being vaccinated — a man develops greater immunity from disease after the vaccine takes effect. Plants raised in hot-houses are not likely to be robust. Carrying out the policy of "letting a hundred flowers blossom and a hundred schools of thought contend" will not weaken but strengthen the leading position of Marxism in the ideological field.

What should our policy be towards non-Marxist ideas? As far as unmistakable counter-revolutionaries and wreckers of the socialist cause are concerned, the matter is easy: We simply deprive them of their freedom of speech. But it is quite a different matter when we are faced with incorrect ideas among the people. Will it do to ban such ideas and give them no opportunity to express themselves? Certainly not. It is not only futile but very harmful to use crude and summary methods to deal with ideological questions among the people, with questions relating to the spiritual life of man. You may ban the expression of wrong ideas, but the ideas will still be there. On the other hand, correct ideas, if pampered in hot-houses without being exposed to the elements or immunized from disease, will not win out against wrong ones. That is why it is only by employing methods of discussion, criticism, and reasoning that we can really foster correct ideas, overcome wrong ideas, and really settle issues. . . .

On the surface, these two slogans — "let a hundred flowers blossom" and "let a hundred schools of thought contend" — have no class character: The proletariat can turn them to account, so can the bourgeoisie and other people. But different classes, strata, and social groups each have their own views on what are fragrant flowers and what are poisonous weeds. So what, from the point of view of the broad masses of the people, should be the criteria today for distinguishing between fragrant flowers and poisonous weeds?

In the political life of our country, how are our people to determine what is right and what is wrong in our words and actions? Basing ourselves on the principles of our Constitution, the will of the overwhelming majority of our people, and the political programmes jointly proclaimed on various occasions by our political parties and groups, we believe that, broadly speaking, words and actions can be judged right if they:

1. Help to unite the people of our various nationalities, and do not divide them;
2. Are beneficial, not harmful, to socialist transformation and socialist construction;

3. Help to consolidate, not undermine or weaken, the people's democratic dictatorship;
4. Help to consolidate, not undermine or weaken, democratic centralism;
5. Tend to strengthen, not to cast off or weaken, the leadership of the Communist Party;
6. Are beneficial, not harmful, to international socialist solidarity and the solidarity of the peace-loving peoples of the world.

Of these six criteria, the most important are the socialist path and the leadership of the Party. These criteria are put forward in order to foster, and not hinder, the free discussion of various questions among the people. Those who do not approve of these criteria can still put forward their own views and argue their case. When the majority of the people have clear-cut criteria to go by, criticism and self-criticism can be conducted along proper lines, and these criteria can be applied to people's words and actions to determine whether they are fragrant flowers or poisonous weeds. These are political criteria. Naturally, in judging the truthfulness of scientific theories or assessing the aesthetic value of works of art, other pertinent criteria are needed, but these six political criteria are also applicable to all activities in the arts or sciences. In a socialist country like ours, can there possibly be any useful scientific or artistic activity which runs counter to these political criteria?

All that is set out above stems from the specific historical conditions in our country. Since conditions vary in different socialist countries and with different Communist Parties, we do not think that other countries and Parties must or need to follow the Chinese way.

78

HAN SUYIN

The Cultural Revolution

The "Hundred Flowers" period was short. Mao, evidently overwhelmed by the outpouring and severity of criticism, turned on the intellectuals, labeling them as rightist and antisocialist. Many, perhaps a half million, were sent into the countryside to better understand peasant life and problems. The purge of professionals left Mao dependent

Han Suyin, *Phoenix Harvest*, bk. V of *China: Autobiography, History* (Vol. II of *My House Has Two Doors*) (Reading, Engl.: Triad/Granada of Jonathan Cape, 1980), 9–12, 16–20.

on party zealots for his next effort, the "Great Leap Forward." Impatient with Soviet-style economic development, Mao decided in 1957 to "will" China into modernity by turning the countryside into giant communes run by ordinary people rather than experts. Swayed by Mao's utopian vision, loyal party workers promised the realization of impossible goals and then fabricated harvest and production figures to match the promises. The result was three years of famine conditions between 1959 and 1962.

In 1963, at seventy years old, Mao found himself stung by his errors. In danger of losing control of the party to more practical, moderate, and younger officials, he decided to fight back. In 1966 he took advantage of mass meetings of young people called "Red Guards" to urge a new campaign against moderates in the party, government, and universities. Mao probably intended the "Great Proletarian Cultural Revolution" as a safeguard, to make sure that the Communist bureaucracy lived up to the goals of the revolution. While many would agree that the party was in need of a renewal of revolutionary ideals, Mao's Red Guards created instead a personality cult, chanting slogans of "Mao Tse-tung thought" from his ubiquitous "Little Red Book," and brought the country close to civil war.

Han Suyin lived in China before the war, published her memoirs and a number of novels on prewar China in the United States, then returned to China twice in 1966 as the cultural revolution took hold. She describes what she saw in this selection. The cultural revolution broke out in the spring of 1966. The author's visit in January offered glimpses of what was about to occur. Notice how people expected "another rectification movement" in art and literature. What was the attitude of Han Suyin's friend Hualan and Hualan's sister? What was the appeal of a cultural revolution for some of those whom the author met in January? What were the author's apprehensions? How were those apprehensions verified during her later visit that summer?

Thinking Historically

Notice how cultural conflicts became political and political conflicts became cultural. Which conflict — political or cultural — do you think was primary? Was Mao, for instance, overly sensitive about a historical play in Shanghai, or was historical theater the way in which his opponents expressed their criticism? If historical interpretation and cultural criticism were more political and more important in Chinese society than they would be in our own, what does that tell us about the difference between the two societies?

We have called the rift that divided China political and cultural, not national or racial. In that way, the struggles of postwar China were different from those of Israel and South Africa. But is there any evidence in the previous readings on Israel or South Africa that cultural differences were also part of what defined the opposing sides and led to conflict in those communities?

In January 1966 I went to Peking for ten days, because I had been invited to a seminar to be held on China at Chicago University. At least five such seminars were taking place in mid-western cities of the United States that year. I wanted to glean the latest thinking in Peking.

I filled a notebook with interviews on China's policies, on economics, and became thoroughly confused. I was not able to see Chou Enlai.[1] Little did I then know that the most intense confrontation was occurring at the top, between Mao Tsetung and Liu Shaochi. . . .

Mao in his interview with [journalist] Edgar Snow had been noncommittal. I had no opportunity to find out about the intense Party struggle that was going on; the pall of secrecy was clamped upon all hints. Hualan, not high enough in the cadre hierarchy to know, could only say that there would be another rectification movement "in art and literature and also in education." The Party establishment still envisaged the Cultural Revolution as merely another political campaign, of the style so customary in China.

Hualan's sister had returned from another stint in the rural areas, of "socialist education" and the "four cleans" in the countryside. The skin of her face was rough and her finger joints thickened with rheumatism. "My job was to try to break down feudal and capitalist ideas . . . I've had very little time to paint . . ." Many hundreds of thousands of cadres, intellectuals, and students had "gone down" in teams for this work. She was looking forward to teaching and painting again, "But at the moment we are having a great many political study classes on Mao Tsetung Thought." She added, "We are taking the army as a model." Hualan was full of enthusiasm. "It is very important: We are fighting revisionism in all its forms." The ballet, *The White-Haired Girl,* had been performed. It dated back to 1944 in Yenan, when it had been created (the music leaned heavily on Tchaikovsky). "Our workers–peasants–soldiers don't like Western ballet, they don't understand it. They want ballet, opera, with which they can identify, such as this one." A young man who was to

[1] Chou En-lai and Liu Shao-chi were leaders of the Communist party, along with Mao Zedong (Mao Tse-tung), from the 1920s. They were three of the five members of the "standing committee" that ran the politburo of the party when it took power in 1949; Mao was chairman. In the government structure, parallel to the party, Chou En-lai was premier and foreign minister. Liu Shao-chi, assumed to be Mao's successor, replaced Mao as head of state in 1959, after the disastrous "Great Leap Forward" of the previous year. But in the cultural revolution, Liu fell out of Mao's favor. Vilified and broken, Liu died in 1969. Both Chou and Mao died in 1976. [Ed.]

dance the role of the Prince in *Swan Lake* came from a poor peasant family; he had rejected the role; he felt he was "throwing away the face" of his family by dancing as a prince ... "Only after the dancers have been to the villages can they put real emotion into the scenes of our new ballets and operas," said Hualan.

There was hushed talk among the writers of the criticism of a theatre piece by the Vice-Mayor of Peking, Wu Han. In November 1965 a literary critic from Shanghai, Yao Wenyuan, already known for his acerbic condemnations of rightists in 1957, had written a long and scathing attack against Peking Vice-Mayor Wu Han's theatre play *Hai Jui is Dismissed from Office*. Hai Jui, an honest Ming dynasty (1368 to 1644) official, had upbraided the Emperor for not listening to the people. Now it was rumoured that his "historical play," first shown in 1960, was a plea for the rehabilitation of Minister of Defence Peng Tehuai, who in August 1959 had openly criticized the Leap.

At dinner with some friends, the distinguished chief editor of the People's Literature Printing Press, Yen Wenching, asked me what I thought of *Hai Jui*. I replied truthfully that I had not seen the play. Historical subjects, articles about personages who had died many centuries ago, were vehicles for expressing present-day situations, events, and people. This had always been done in China, and it continued to be done. But now not only Vice-Mayor Wu Han, but many other historians were being attacked and criticized as "promoting a bourgeois line in history."

A foreign resident in China told me that Teng To, chief editor of the monthly *Frontline* (the magazine of Peking's Party Committee), was undergoing criticism. He had written: "Everyone must have some leisure and only eight hours of work." "The idea of leisure time and the idea of revolution don't go together," said this man. Young workers in the factories had been infected by the habit of looking at the clock.

The January air was not only freezing but turgid with unvoiced apprehensions and abstruse theoretical argument. I interviewed three philosophers, who were to give me the latest "thinking." (I had not reckoned that the word "thinking" would involve me in the high spheres of theoretical abstraction.) The three talked of the necessity of a cultural revolution. Only a change of thinking in the people could propel advance: a transformation of ideas and habits and behaviour *before* a change in the material conditions of living could occur. But could mankind really overleap itself in thought, overleap the environment in which it dealt? Certainly, they replied. Had not men dreamt of flying machines before the aeroplane was invented? ...

In May 1966 I went back to China. She was entirely *other* that May. Again that unpleasant throat clamp as the raucous loudspeakers assaulted my eardrums for hours ... how was it possible to remain sane with the perpetual noise, the blaring and the shouting and the screaming and the singing? All the posters had changed. Now furious-fisted young people squashed diminutive snakes and bull-headed figures (imperialists and revisionists). A thousand portly, rosy-faced Maos everywhere. The customs officials remained calm and courteous, relaxed, impervious to the cacophony.

At the railway station no lunch was available; the waitresses were holding a political meeting. I saw them practising a dance in front of a large panel painted to represent Mao. Their hands lifted imaginary hearts from their breasts towards his smile. I listened to the loudspeakers but there were too many of them and the sound waves interfered with each other so that the result was a hopeless quack.

In Hongkong the Kuomintang newspapers had predicted a rupture between Mao Tsetung and Liu Shaochi. There had been rumours of an assassination plot against Mao. Here there was much talk of a "black line" which had for the past seventeen years infected, infested, deviated, twisted, distorted culture and education and the arts and literature in order to promote "restoration of capitalism." I groaned inwardly. "That's it. The intelligentsia is going to catch it once again." But I continued, of course, to smile and to hold myself tightly in control. And to hope my Family would not suffer too much — and that I would not break down.

In Kuangchow the well-cut suits of 1965 had disappeared. Every one of the cadres greeting me wore unpressed shirts and baggy pants and plastic sandals. There was no brilliantine upon the hair of the men, and the women cadres all had straight short hair. No more perms.

In Peking, however, the admirable Hsing Chiang continued to wear a crisp neat blouse and skirt; until one day in July when Kung Peng would say quietly to her, "Your clothes look a bit bourgeois." A friendly warning.

Nowhere in China, in the next few months, was there any hint that Liu Shaochi was the target of the upheaval. In fact I would see him twice. He remained visible, making speeches, receiving guests, and the Hsinhua news agency would report on the mass rallies he held for Vietnam in July. And yet, in 1970, Edgar Snow would be told by Mao that in January 1965 Mao had already decided that Liu Shaochi must go . . .

"We shall be going to Manchuria, as you asked," said Hsing Chiang. We would be back in June in Peking.

Manchuria. Limitless flat plains, length to abolish the horizon; space and a clean sky that ran its blueness in echoless silence. The kind of land that makes one want to be on horseback, the sound of hooves to pound the silence into music.

I saw factories, and communes, in Shenyang and Changchun and Fushun and Anshan and Harbin; the Anshan steel works; the Fushun opencast mines (where, in 1947, nineteen years previously, Pao my husband had died). So many notes, so many people telling me of their lives. And in every factory the *tatzepao,* the wall posters, pasted upon all the walls, swinging like banners, strung across from machine to machine, almost swamping every workshop. All of them uttered dire threats against "black liners" and "freaks and monsters."

On May 8th an editorial against the "black anti-Party line" had come out. "All those who oppose Mao Tsetung Thought must be toppled, no matter how high or how famous," shrieked the posters. "Down with seventeen years of black anti-Party line" blared the radios. Occasionally I discerned names . . . names of experts, engineers, factory managers, not prominent political figures; names of educators in the universities. But obviously the Party was still firmly in control, "directing and leading" the Cultural Revolution. And so the search for "freaks and monsters" and for "bull-headed devils and snake spirits" was among the middle ranks, the technical experts, and professors and engineers. Not a single top leader in the Party, at the time, was mentioned. The highest in rank were Party secretaries at city level and some university chancellors.

The higher Party cadres receive me and entertain me lavishly. I eat bear paws, an expensive delicacy. I am given a marvellous ginseng root worth thousands of *yuan,* which I shall give to Wanchun when I return to Peking.

After a few days of reading accusatory editorials and slogans and listening to the radio my brain goes into a stupor. I am numbed; even by imprecations. I smile and nod and because there is too much repetition I begin to speak like the people round me, and so my trip is a success as I am outstandingly docile. I read now with practised, jaded eye the posters above the machinery: "Sung Chiming is enforcing a revisionist line in the screws and bolts third workshop!"; "Wang Ahmeng has countered Mao Tsetung Thought for many years by saying: Too much political verbiage, not enough scientific work." I do not know Sung and Wang; I only hope that things won't be too hard for them.

At the Shenyang machine tool plant I meet a worker who is a specialist at cutting tools through sheer application of Mao Tsetung Thought to knife-cutting edges. In almost every factory I am told how much harm the Russians have done, and of the enormous amount of meat, rare metals, oranges, textiles, and shoes paid out for equipment.

At Anshan, the great steel works and China's pride, I am shown innovations attributed to Mao Tsetung Thought. In one workshop the Party man in charge introduces me to a pretty young woman worker who writes poetry. She has written decadent, bourgeois love poetry because in school her teacher was following the decadent revisionist black line and corrupting her with feudal poems. But since the intense political studies started in January she has remoulded herself and written some excellent proletarian poetry for workers–peasants–soldiers. The pretty worker begins to recite one of her old poems so that I may judge her wickedness. Then she recites a new one. "I would like to have some of your poems," I say, hoping she will also give me the old one she has recited. But alas, the Party cadre has seen through my bland cunning. "Not these, not these," he says as she riffles through her loose-leaf notebook. I get, at last, three rather tedious slogany scribbles. "These are the latest," says the Party cadre, beaming. He is kind, but I turn back to look at the girl and she too is watching me, and picking meditatively at her thumb. I now wonder what will happen to my dearest friend Yeh, who has printed in *Chinese Literature,* his English monthly, some of my translations of decadent feudal song-poems of the Sung dynasty (AD 960–1279).

In March, Lin Piao,[2] designated as Mao's "close comrade-in-arms," has issued a directive to "put politics in command." And production has gone up by so much and so much per cent everywhere, owing to the "heightening of revolutionary consciousness" among the workers. Production increase is no longer ascribed to the heroic, the fantastic, the real work of the marvellous, incredibly patient, and stoic people of China, but solely to the study of Mao Tsetung Thought . . . Cadres frown when I say that pump stations, canals, fertilizer factories, increase production . . . And that here in Manchuria electrification of communes started in 1948 with the Leap Forward . . .

In one commune I am shown earth mounds terraced for cultivation. This brigade has distinguished itself learning from China's model, Tachai, proclaimed by Mao in 1964 as *the* example for all China. Tachai is sited in the cratered, fissured, gullied loess region of Shansi province. There are not twenty square metres of uniform flat land in these canyons of silt. Tachai terraced its promontories and filled its gullies by hand labour. But here in Manchuria the plains are flat . . . whence, then, these earth mounds? Eleven years later I shall learn the hilarious and pitiful story: The mounds I saw were artificial; they had been raised up and fields laddered upon them to resemble Tachai. That is how "In all things learn from Tachai" had been interpreted by the literal-minded cadres.

But the official taking me around in 1966 tells me that these terraced fields are the product of the young educated middle school students sent out to labour in the countryside. "They built these fields with one hand while their other hand was occupied by the precious book of Chairman Mao," he says. I write it all down.

---

[2] Lin Piao was an old Communist ally of Mao, minister of defense, and head of the People's Liberation Army, and he was chosen Mao's successor in 1969 after the eclipse and death of Liu Shao-chi. Lin helped Mao politicize the army and militarize society in the Cultural Revolution (1966–1969) but died in a plane crash in 1971, as he was branded a traitor — perhaps because Mao sought to reassert the authority of the party over the army.

79

HO CHI MINH

The Vietnamese Declaration
of Independence

Colonized by France since 1858, Vietnam, like China, was occupied by Japan during World War II. With the defeat of Japanese forces, the Vietnamese declared their independence. This Declaration of Independence was written by Ho Chi Minh (1890–1969). Ho had been a student in France, where he became a poet, a socialist, and a Vietnamese nationalist. In 1919 while in Paris, he borrowed a suit and attended the Versailles peace conference, where he appealed to American president Woodrow Wilson to apply the principle of national self-determination to Vietnam, which had, after all, been an independent country for centuries before French occupation. When the victors merely dismantled the colonial empires of the defeated countries, Ho Chi Minh, like many other disappointed nationalists, found what he was looking for in Lenin's writings on nationalism and in the promise of support by the Congress of the Communist International in 1920. Ho Chi Minh became a founding member of both the French and the Indochinese Communist parties. For Ho Chi Minh, communism meant opposition to imperialism, to foreign control, and to "antipatriotic Vietnamese capitalists."

During the Japanese occupation in 1941, the broad-based nationalist organization, the Viet Minh, was formed and Ho was appointed its leader. On August 15, 1945, as news of the Japanese surrender reached Vietnam, the Viet Minh called for mass rallies. Thousands of peasants came to the cities of Saigon, Hanoi, and Hue to demonstrate against the emperor, Bao Dai, who had served as a Japanese puppet, as he had for the French and would again. On August 30, the emperor abdicated the throne.

On September 2, 1945, in front of half a million people in Hanoi, Ho Chi Minh read this Declaration of Independence. Notice the similarity between this document and the American Declaration of Independence. There was nothing inadvertent in the similarity. Ho had checked his translation of the opening phrases of the American Declaration with an American OSS (secret service) officer in Hanoi. After

Ho Chi Minh, Declaration of Independence of the Democratic Republic of Vietnam, in Nguyen Khac Vien and Hu Ngoc, *Vietnamese Literature* (Hanoi: Red River Foreign Languages Publishing House), 508–12.

Ho read the opening, he stopped, looked out over the crowd and asked, "Do you hear me distinctly, fellow countrymen?" They said they did, and Ho continued: "This immortal statement was made in the Declaration of Independence of the United States of America in 1776. In a broader sense, this means: All the people on earth are equal from birth, all the people have a right to live, to be happy and free."

In what other ways did the Vietnamese Declaration of Independence resemble that of the United States? Why do you think Ho Chi Minh wanted to take the U.S. Declaration as his model or make that connection? What were the grievances of the Vietnamese against the French?

Thinking Historically

A declaration of independence assumes a divide between the newly declared independent nation and the colonizing power, in this case France and Japan (but mainly France). Because declarations of independence are written at moments of unity against a foreigner, such documents rarely show internal rifts. Yet, we have noticed signs of internal differences in both the Israeli and American declarations of independence. What were they? Are there comparable signs of internal rifts in this document? If not, what might account for that? Was Vietnam more united in 1945 than Israel in 1947 or the United States in 1776?

"All men are created equal. They are endowed by their Creator with certain inalienable rights; among these are Life, Liberty, and the pursuit of Happiness."

This immortal statement was made in the Declaration of Independence of the United States of America in 1776. In a broader sense, this means: All the peoples on the earth are equal from birth, all the peoples have a right to live, to be happy and free.

The Declaration of the French Revolution made in 1791 on the Rights of Man and the Citizen also states: "All men are born free and with equal rights, and must always remain free and have equal rights."

Those are undeniable truths.

Nevertheless, for more than eighty years, the French imperialists, abusing the standard of Liberty, Equality, and Fraternity, have violated our Fatherland and oppressed our fellow-citizens. They have acted contrary to the ideals of humanity and justice.

In the field of politics, they have deprived our people of every democratic liberty.

They have enforced inhuman laws; they have set up three distinct political regimes in the North, the Center, and the South of Vietnam in order to wreck our national unity and prevent our people from being united.

They have built more prisons than schools. They have mercilessly slain our patriots; they have drowned our uprisings in rivers of blood.

They have fettered public opinion; they have practised obscurantism against our people.

To weaken our race they have forced us to use opium and alcohol.

In the field of economics, they have fleeced us to the backbone, impoverished our people, and devastated our land.

They have robbed us of our rice fields, our mines, our forests, and our raw materials. They have monopolized the issuing of bank-notes and the export trade.

They have invented numerous unjustifiable taxes and reduced our people, especially our peasantry, to a state of extreme poverty.

They have hampered the prospering of our national bourgeoisie; they have mercilessly exploited our workers.

In the autumn of 1940, when the Japanese Fascists violated Indochina's territory to establish new bases in their fight against the Allies, the French imperialists went down on their bended knees and handed over our country to them.

Thus, from that date, our people were subjected to the double yoke of the French and the Japanese. Their sufferings and miseries increased. The result was that towards the end of last year and the beginning of this year, from Quang Tri province to the North of Vietnam, more than two million of our fellow-citizens died from starvation. On March 9, the French troops were disarmed by the Japanese. The French colonialists either fled or surrendered, showing that not only were they incapable of "protecting" us, but that, in the span of five years, they had twice sold our country to the Japanese.

On several occasions before March 9, the Vietminh League urged the French to ally themselves with it against the Japanese. Instead of agreeing to this proposal, the French colonialists so intensified their terrorist activities against the Vietminh members that before fleeing they massacred a great number of our political prisoners detained at Yen Bay and Caobang.

Notwithstanding all this, our fellow-citizens have always manifested toward the French a tolerant and humane attitude. Even after the Japanese putsch of March 1945, the Vietminh League helped many Frenchmen to cross the frontier, rescued some of them from Japanese jails, and protected French lives and property.

From the autumn of 1940, our country had in fact ceased to be a French colony and had become a Japanese possession.

After the Japanese had surrendered to the Allies, our whole people rose to regain our national sovereignty and to found the Democratic Republic of Vietnam.

The truth is that we have wrested our independence from the Japanese and not from the French.

The French have fled, the Japanese have capitulated, Emperor Bao Dai has abdicated. Our people have broken the chains which for nearly a century have fettered them and have won independence for the Fatherland. Our people at the same time have overthrown the monarchic regime that has reigned supreme for dozens of centuries. In its place has been established the present Democratic Republic.

For these reasons, we, members of the Provisional Government, representing the whole Vietnamese people, declare that from now on we break off all relations of a colonial character with France; we repeal all the international obligation that France has so far subscribed to on behalf of Vietnam and we abolish all the special rights the French have unlawfully acquired in our Fatherland.

The whole Vietnamese people, animated by a common purpose, are determined to fight to the bitter end against any attempt by the French colonialists to reconquer their country.

We are convinced that the Allied nations which at Tehran and San Francisco have acknowledged the principles of self-determination and equality of nations, will not refuse to acknowledge the independence of Vietnam.

A people who have courageously opposed French domination for more than eight years, a people who have fought side by side with the Allies against the Fascists during these last years, such a people must be free and independent.

For these reasons, we, members of the Provisional Government of the Democratic Republic of Vietnam, solemnly declare to the world that Vietnam has the right to be a free and independent country — and in fact is so already. The entire Vietnamese people are determined to mobilize all their physical and mental strength, to sacrifice their lives and property in order to safeguard their independence and liberty.

80

ROBERT S. MCNAMARA

From *In Retrospect:*
The Tragedy and Lessons of Vietnam

The Democratic Republic of Vietnam, established in September 1945, did not remain intact beyond October. In deference to the French government's insistence on regaining its lost colonies, both Britain and the United States did everything possible to assist France but fight, an option avoided due to the popular yearning to bring American and British troops home. In October 1945, the United States detoured twelve merchant marine ships engaged in returning American troops, instructing them instead to transport French troops to Vietnam. Already on September 13, the British general in charge of disarming Japanese troops in Saigon interrupted his efforts in order to arm French prisoners of war. He lent the French the use of his own Indian Gurkha troops for a coup against the Viet Minh executive committee administration of Saigon. While waiting for the arrival of the French troops on American carriers, the British general armed the Japanese and instructed them to prevent the Vietnamese from retaking control of the city.

American policy toward Vietnam after 1945 was initially support of France, America's oldest ally (without whom, ironically, the United States' Declaration of Independence would have been short-lived). Ho Chi Minh pleaded for an independent Vietnam to President Truman as he had with Wilson, but both turned out to be more loyal to allies than to principles. After 1949 and the Communist victory in China, the American attitude toward Vietnam became part of a larger policy of containing the spread of communism. In some cases, as when Eisenhower offered the French the use of nuclear weapons as they faced their ultimate defeat in 1954, it became an American war.

John F. Kennedy came to the presidency in 1961, a vigorous anticommunist with a "brain trust" of advisers that rivaled its famous predecessor under Franklin D. Roosevelt. Among "the best and the brightest" that came from American business and academia to serve the country with Kennedy was Robert S. McNamara, the new secretary of defense. Over the course of the buildup of the Vietnam War, perhaps no one but the president — Kennedy and then Lyndon Johnson after him — had more to do with expanding and defending the

Robert S. McNamara, *In Retrospect: The Tragedy and Lessons of Vietnam* (New York: Vintage, 1995), 95–97, 101–02, 106–07.

U.S. military role than McNamara. To many, it became known as "McNamara's war."

In this selection from his memoir, "the book I planned never to write," says McNamara, he tries to explain how he "got it wrong," "terribly wrong." What do you think of McNamara's argument for an eventual Kennedy withdrawal (if Kennedy had not been assassinated November 22, 1963)? How, according to McNamara, did the United States become committed to the war in Vietnam in the beginning of the Johnson administration? What mistakes made by U.S. officials allowed this to happen?

Thinking Historically

The rifts in the United States during the 1960s are well known and are in good part attributable to the Vietnam War. The global reach of the United States peppered the period with global rifts as well. Pro-war and antiwar factions developed in Europe, Japan, Canada, Australia, New Zealand, among the U.S. allies asked to provide military or political support. Rifts between students and governments broke out throughout Europe as well as in the United States. Vietnamese relations with Russia and China were strained by fears that the United States would expand the war beyond Vietnam. Even the Chinese cultural revolution partially reflected Chinese fears of U.S. power in Asia. Rifts also divided Americans as "hawks" and "doves" and the Vietnamese as "communist" and "democrat," north and south, pro- and anti-American, although it was remarkable how often North Vietnamese leaders insisted that their quarrel was with the U.S. government, not the American people.

McNamara's memoir, published in 1995, reflects a different America, though the wounds of war have not completely healed some thirty years later. Readers who are struck by the author's sense of remorse and tragedy might want to ponder the other side of the question posed by Mao Zedong in the 1960s. Mao insisted that it was "better to be red than expert," better to have zeal than knowledge. In selection 78, we noted how this turned out to be a disastrous prescription for "the Great Leap Forward" and the cultural revolution. But even McNamara might warn us of the opposite problem — policy directed by brilliant experts who lack political sense. David Halberstam, whose book, *The Best and the Brightest,* defined the era and the problem, tells a story of how impressed Lyndon Johnson was with the Kennedy team of experts that he inherited on November 22, 1963. Johnson went reeling from his first meeting with McNamara and the others on November 24 to his mentor Sam Rayburn, the wily Texan, consummate legislator, and former Speaker of the House. Rayburn listened sympathetically to Johnson's praise, thought for a moment, and said:

"Well Lyndon, you may be right and they may be every bit as intelligent as you say, but I'd feel a whole lot better about them if just one of them had run for sheriff once."[1]

Would a team of sheriffs and other elected representatives have moderated the zeal of the experts who had all the answers (as the Congress showed less enthusiasm for the war than the presidential appointees and advisers)? If a democracy requires experts to get things done, does it also require politicians to determine what to do?

History was used by both proponents and opponents of the Vietnam War. McNamara mentions Kennedy's lesson (from Barbara Tuchman's history of the First World War, *The Guns of August*) of how easy it is to "blunder" into war. One of the arguments made in the 1960s was that appeasement (like that of British prime minister Chamberlain to Hitler's demand for part of Czechoslovakia at Munich in 1938) encouraged Hitler and made war more, rather than less, likely. Keeping in mind that no two wars are ever exactly alike, what lessons does McNamara's history offer us?

What would John F. Kennedy have done about Vietnam had he lived? I have been asked that question countless times over the last thirty years. Thus far, I have refused to answer for two reasons: Apart from what I have related, the president did not tell me what he planned to do in the future. Moreover, whatever his thoughts may have been before Diem's death,[2] they might have changed as the effect of that event on the political dynamics in South Vietnam became more apparent. Also, I saw no gain to our nation from speculation by me — or others — about how the dead president might have acted.

But today I feel differently. Having reviewed the record in detail, and with the advantage of hindsight, I think it highly probable that, had President Kennedy lived, he would have pulled us out of Vietnam. He would have concluded that the South Vietnamese were incapable of defending themselves, and that Saigon's grave political weaknesses made it unwise to try to offset the limitations of South Vietnamese forces by sending U.S. combat troops on a large scale. I think he would have come to that conclusion even if he reasoned, as I believe he would have, that South Vietnam and, ultimately, Southeast Asia would then be lost to Communism. He would have viewed that loss as more costly

---

[1] David Halberstam, *The Best and the Brightest* (New York: Random House, 1972), 53.

[2] Ngo Dinh Diem, U.S.-sponsored president of South Vietnam from 1954 until his assassination on November 2, 1963.

than we see it now. But he would have accepted that cost because he would have sensed that the conditions he had laid down — i.e., it was a South Vietnamese war, that it could only be won by them, and to win it they needed a sound political base — could not be met. Kennedy would have agreed that withdrawal would cause a fall of the "dominoes" but that staying in would ultimately lead to the same result, while exacting a terrible price in blood.

Early in his administration, President Kennedy asked his cabinet officials and members of the National Security Council to read Barbara Tuchman's book *The Guns of August.* He said it graphically portrayed how Europe's leaders had bungled into the debacle of World War I. And he emphasized: "I don't ever want to be in that position." Kennedy told us after we had done our reading, "We are not going to bungle into war." . . .

So I conclude that John Kennedy would have eventually gotten out of Vietnam rather than move more deeply in. I express this judgment now because, in light of it, I must explain how and why we — including Lyndon Johnson — who continued in policy-making roles after President Kennedy's death made the decisions leading to the eventual deployment to Vietnam of half a million U.S. combat troops. Why did we do what we did, and what lessons can be learned from our actions?

. . . Johnson was left with a national security team that, although it remained intact, was deeply split over Vietnam. Its senior members had failed to face up to the basic questions that had confronted first Eisenhower and then Kennedy: Would the loss of South Vietnam pose a threat to U.S. security serious enough to warrant extreme action to prevent it? If so, what kind of action should we take? Should it include the introduction of U.S. air and ground forces? Launching attacks against North Vietnam? Risking war with China? What would be the ultimate cost of such a program in economic, military, political, and human terms? Could it succeed? If the chances of success were low and the costs high, were there other courses — such as neutralization or withdrawal — that deserved careful study and debate?

Lyndon Johnson inherited these questions (although they were not presented clearly to him), and he inherited them without answers. They remained unanswered throughout his presidency, and for many years thereafter. In short, Johnson inherited a god-awful mess eminently more dangerous than the one Kennedy had inherited from Eisenhower. One evening not long after he took office, Johnson confessed to his aide Bill Moyers that he felt like a catfish that had "just grabbed a big juicy worm with a right sharp hook in the middle of it."

Contrary to popular myth, however, Lyndon Johnson was not oblivious to Vietnam when he became president. Although he had visited the country only once — in May 1961 — and had attended few meetings on the subject during Kennedy's tenure, he was keenly aware of the problem and his responsibility to deal with it. Among his first acts as president was to schedule the November 24 meeting with his Vietnam advisers.

Some say he called this meeting for domestic political reasons. With an election coming within a year, the story goes, he feared that if he did not appear involved and firm he would face strident attacks from hard-line, right-wing Republicans.

I disagree. Of course, domestic politics was always in the forefront of his mind, and, yes, he feared the domestic political consequences of appearing weak. He also feared the effect on our allies if the United States appeared unable or unwilling to meet our security obligations. But most of all Johnson was convinced that the Soviet Union and China were bent on achieving hegemony. He saw the takeover of South Vietnam as a step toward that objective — a break in our containment policy — and he was determined to prevent it. Johnson felt more certain than President Kennedy that the loss of South Vietnam had a higher cost than would the direct application of U.S. military force, and it was this view that shaped him and his policy decisions for the next five years. He failed to perceive the fundamentally political nature of the war. . . .

Shortly after my return to Washington, the president received a memorandum from Senate Majority Leader Mike Mansfield (D-Mont.), recommending that the United States try for a neutral Southeast Asia — neither dependent on U.S. military support nor subject to Chinese domination through some sort of truce or settlement. The president asked Dean, Mac, and me for our reactions.

All three of us felt Mansfield's path would lead to the loss of South Vietnam to Communist control with extremely serious consequences for the United States and the West. I stated the conventional wisdom among top U.S. civilian and military officials at the time:

> In Southeast Asia, Laos would almost certainly come under North Vietnamese domination, Cambodia might exhibit a façade of neutrality but would in fact accept Communist Chinese domination, Thailand would become very shaky, and Malaysia, already beset by Indonesia, the same; even Burma would see the developments as a clear sign that the whole of the area now had to accommodate completely to Communism (with serious consequences for the security of India as well).
>
> Basically, a truly "neutral" Southeast Asia is very unlikely to emerge from such a sequence of events, even if the U.S. itself tried to hold a firm position in Thailand, if Malaysia too tried to stand firm, and even if remote and uninvolved powers such as France backed the concept of "neutrality."

In the eyes of the rest of Asia and of key areas threatened by Communism in other areas as well, South Vietnam is both a test of U.S. firmness and specifically a test of U.S. capacity to deal with "wars of national liberation." Within Asia, there is evidence — for example, from Japan — that U.S. disengagement and the acceptance of Communist domination would have a serious effect on confidence. More broadly, there can be little doubt that any country threatened in the future by Communist subversion would have reason to doubt whether we would really see the thing through. This would apply even in such theoretically remote areas as Latin America.

I have quoted extensively from my memo for two reasons: to show how limited and shallow our analysis and discussion of the alternatives to our existing policy in Vietnam — i.e., neutralization or withdrawal — had been; and to illustrate that the consequences of Southeast Asia's loss to U.S. and Western security were now being presented to President Johnson with greater force and in more detail than on previous occasions.

This memo hardened the president's preexisting attitude. As the likely failure of our training strategy became more apparent in the months ahead, we tilted gradually — almost imperceptibly — toward approving the direct application of U.S. military force. We did so because of our increasing fear — and hindsight makes it clear it was an exaggerated fear — of what would happen if we did not. But we never carefully debated what U.S. force would ultimately be required, what our chances of success would be, or what the political, military, financial, and human costs would be if we provided it. Indeed, these basic questions went unexamined.

We were at the beginning of a slide down a tragic and slippery slope.

REFLECTIONS

In this chapter we looked at different parts of the world, mainly but not exclusively new states, involved in important struggles in the thirty years after World War II. These struggles represent many others that divided new and old nations, then and now. We distinguished between various types of struggles and their accompanying fault lines: national and religious in Palestine and Israel, racial and national in South Africa, cultural and political in China.

In Vietnam, we observed the international struggle — against France, Japan, and then the United States — but no internal rift, at least none in evidence, in the Vietnamese Declaration of Independence. There have, of course, been internal divisions in Vietnam as in any society. Much of the American propaganda war in the 1960s was based on the differences between "communist" and "democratic" Vietnam, symbolized as north and south. In Vietnam there were also traditional differences between Chinese Confucian cultural influences in the north and Indian Buddhist cultural influences in the south, between Catholics and Buddhists, between Vietnamese and Chinese inhabitants, and between landlords and peasants. Some of these divides were ancient; still others, like those between Vietnamese capitalists and urban workers, fairly recent. It is important to note how the Vietnam War represents a pivotal conflict in the development of the Cold War, and how it fundamentally shaped the world between 1945 and 1975.

Of course, the Vietnam War was not the only globalizing rift during the decades of the Cold War. To what extent were the rifts in Palestine and Israel or those of South Africa deepened by a Cold War in which the United States and the Soviet Union sought influence and advantage? Were the rifts in China deepened, or were new divides created in Vietnam as a result of the international conflict? McNamara finds one American policy error: the failure to recognize that Vietnam was engaged in a civil war, rather than a foreign invasion from the north. To what extent was that civil war aided and encouraged, if not created, by American promises, threats, and expenditures? What was the impact of America's Cold War support for the governing white minority party in South Africa?

We study rifts or divides, like we study contradictions, to understand change. In some cases, a rift, like a geological fault line, suggests how things are likely to continue to change. Have we seen such continuous tension without resolution in Israel and Palestine during these last fifty years?

Sometimes a rift causes a conflict that results in something new. Would the new South Africa or contemporary China rightly be considered such a development?

Often, one side of a conflict overwhelms and transforms the other into its own image. Of course, that is precisely what occurred as colonial powers struggled to impose their wills on their colonies. Is it happening again with the popularity of American ideas of democracy and free markets? How does this American influence affect the new states of South Africa, Vietnam, and China today?

13

Women's World

HISTORICAL CONTEXT
The World, 1950–2000

A surprising fact: Women make up about half the world's population and always have. Until recently, male historians focused only on the lives of men in their research, covering the lives of women by proxy. Today, historians both male and female try not to restrict their work to the activities or testimonies of men. Yet, because men dominated politics, war, and industry for many years, oftentimes important historical studies have ignored women. Historians now attempt to research and write more complete, balanced, historical accounts, addressing topics in which women have played important roles. Such topics include the history of the family, sexuality, privacy, popular culture, domesticity, and work, among others. In recent years, women's history and women's studies have become vibrant fields of specialization and discovery.

This chapter offers readings that, taken together, constitute a history of women during the latter half of the twentieth century. We will read women's accounts from various parts of the world, as they describe aspects of their lives and those of other women. We begin, however, with the Chinese Marriage Law of 1950 so we might consider the new legal baseline for one-fifth of the world's population. (This law was replicated in many other countries as well.) We then turn to the emerging women's movement in the United States, spearheaded by a far-reaching book, *The Feminine Mystique* (1963). Next, two African novelists — from Algeria and Nigeria — reflect on youth, adolescence, and family. Then two women from Latin America — an unemployed Brazilian and a revolutionary Guatemalan physician — talk about their lives. We conclude, moving from the personal to the political, with letters from Aung San Suu Kyi of Burma, recipient of the Nobel Peace Prize for her inspiring leadership in her country's struggle to return to democracy.

All of the women featured in this chapter are articulate, literate, self-conscious writers. Though atypical (most women in the world were illiterate), their eloquence allows us to reflect on the power of words for women, as well as for men.

THINKING HISTORICALLY
Constructing Theory

The notion of "constructing theory" may seem much more demanding than it is. It is little more than bringing together ideas that explain phenomena in history. Stated in words, a theory offers a possible answer to a question or an explanation of a problem. Theories are not necessarily true; they are guesses, called hypotheses, and have to be tested and supported with evidence. Theories might come to us from reading either primary or secondary sources, but ultimately a theory must make sense of the primary sources, the raw experience of history. (For that reason, this chapter contains only primary sources.) A theory organizes experience in a way that makes it more comprehensible. It seeks patterns or an explanation of patterns: causes, consequences, connections, relationships, reasons.

Ultimately, of course, a theory must be tested with new evidence. A good theory will interpret or incorporate new evidence without need for much change in theory. In this chapter, you are asked only to focus on constructing theory. Occasionally, you will be reminded of the limitations of the primary sources included here, but our emphasis will be on conceiving and expressing theories that give meaning to the material at hand.

$$\boxed{81}$$

The Marriage Law of the People's Republic of China

Chinese revolutionaries in the twentieth century frequently called for women's rights and equality. The "women question" was at the forefront of the Nationalist revolution of 1911 and, again, of the Communist revolution of 1949. Women who had been active in the revolution

---

The Marriage Law of the People's Republic of China (Peking: Foreign Languages Press, 1959).

of 1911 sought women's suffrage and an end to such patriarchal practices as foot-binding, the concubine system, child marriage, and prostitution. But the visions of Chinese revolutionaries often remained promises in word only.

The government of Chiang Kai-shek passed major resolutions in 1924 and 1926 to enact laws that would codify many of the aspirations of the women's movement: legal equality, right to own property, freely entered marriage, right to divorce, even equal pay for equal work. But in 1927, Chiang's Nationalist party broke its alliance with the communists and identified them with women's issues. In fact, many of the founders of the Communist party, including Mao Zedong, were proponents of family reform (free marriage and free love) before they were Marxists. Despite this, as they sought supporters and volunteers throughout China after 1927, especially in the more traditional and male-dominated countryside, they quickly dropped their calls for reform of the marriage and family laws.

When the Communists came to power in China in 1949, marriage reform again surfaced as a high-priority goal in constructing a new society. The 1950 Marriage Law, excerpted here, led to a widespread debate on the role of women in Chinese communist society. What practices did the Chinese Communists seek to curb with this law?

Thinking Historically

Construct a theory about how different groups of people in China might respond to this law. Among the groups you might consider are rich men, poor men, rich women, poor women, young and old, city and country people.

Chapter I. General Principles

Article 1. The arbitrary and compulsory feudal marriage system, which is based on the superiority of man over woman and which ignores the children's interests, shall be abolished.

The new democratic marriage system, which is based on free choice of partners, on monogamy, on equal rights for both sexes, and on protection of the lawful interests of women and children, shall be put into effect.
Article 2. Bigamy, concubinage, child betrothal, interference with the remarriage of widows, and the exaction of money or gifts in connection with marriage shall be prohibited. . . .

Chapter III. Rights and Duties of Husband and Wife

Article 7. Husband and wife are companions living together and shall enjoy equal status in the home.

Article 8. Husband and wife are in duty bound to love, respect, assist, and look after each other, to live in harmony, to engage in production, to care for the children, and to strive jointly for the welfare of the family and for the building up of a new society.

Article 9. Both husband and wife shall have the right to free choice of occupation and free participation in work or in social activities.

Article 10. Both husband and wife shall have equal right in the possession and management of family property.

82

BETTY FRIEDAN

From *The Feminine Mystique*

This book elicited an enormous response from women in the United States when it was published in 1963. What Friedan called "the problem that has no name" was immediately understood and widely discussed. What name would you give to the problem? What were its causes? Do women still feel it today?

Thinking Historically

In what ways were the needs of American women after World War II like those of Chinese women? In what ways were they different? Which do you find more striking, the similarities or the differences? What theories would explain why Chinese and American women had different problems in the 1950s and 1960s?

The problem lay buried, unspoken, for many years in the minds of American women. It was a strange stirring, a sense of dissatisfaction, a yearning that women suffered in the middle of the twentieth century in the United States. Each suburban wife struggled with it alone. As she made the beds, shopped for groceries, matched slipcover material, ate peanut butter sandwiches with her children, chauffeured Cub Scouts and Brownies, lay beside her husband at night — she was afraid to ask even of herself the silent question — "Is this all?"

Betty Friedan, *The Feminine Mystique* (New York: Dell, 1963), 11–12, 14, 15–16, 27.

For over fifteen years there was no word of this yearning in the millions of words written about women, for women, in all the columns, books, and articles by experts telling women their role was to seek fulfillment as wives and mothers. Over and over women heard in voices of tradition and of Freudian sophistication that they could desire no greater destiny than to glory in their own femininity. Experts told them how to catch a man and keep him, how to breastfeed children and handle their toilet training, how to cope with sibling rivalry and adolescent rebellion; how to buy a dishwasher, bake bread, cook gourmet snails, and build a swimming pool with their own hands; how to dress, look, and act more feminine and make marriage more exciting; how to keep their husbands from dying young and their sons from growing into delinquents. They were taught to pity the neurotic, unfeminine, unhappy women who wanted to be poets or physicists or presidents. They learned that truly feminine women do not want careers, higher education, political rights — the independence and the opportunities that the old-fashioned feminists fought for. Some women, in their forties and fifties, still remembered painfully giving up those dreams, but most of the younger women no longer even thought about them. A thousand expert voices applauded their femininity, their adjustment, their new maturity. All they had to do was devote their lives from earliest girlhood to finding a husband and bearing children. . . .

In the fifteen years after World War II, this mystique of feminine fulfillment became the cherished and self-perpetuating core of contemporary American culture. Millions of women lived their lives in the image of those pretty pictures of the American suburban housewife, kissing their husbands goodbye in front of the picture window, depositing their stationwagonsful of children at school, and smiling as they ran the new electric waxer over the spotless kitchen floor. They baked their own bread, sewed their own and their children's clothes, kept their new washing machines and dryers running all day. They changed the sheets on the beds twice a week instead of once, took the rug-hooking class in adult education, and pitied their poor frustrated mothers, who had dreamed of having a career. Their only dream was to be perfect wives and mothers; their highest ambition to have five children and a beautiful house, their only fight to get and keep their husbands. They had no thought for the unfeminine problems of the world outside the home; they wanted the men to make the major decisions. They gloried in their role as women, and wrote proudly on the census blank: "Occupation: housewife." . . .

If a woman had a problem in the 1950's and 1960's, she knew that something must be wrong with her marriage, or with herself. Other women were satisfied with their lives, she thought. What kind of a woman was she if she did not feel this mysterious fulfillment waxing the kitchen floor? She was so ashamed to admit her dissatisfaction that she never knew how many other women shared it. If she tried to tell her husband, he didn't understand what she was talking about. She did not really understand it herself. For over fifteen years women in America found it harder to talk about this problem than about sex. Even the psychoanalysts had no name for it. When a woman went to a psychiatrist for help, as many women did, she would say, "I'm so ashamed," or "I must be hopelessly neurotic." "I don't know what's wrong with women today," a suburban psychiatrist said uneasily. "I only know something is wrong because most of my patients happen to be women. And their problem isn't sexual." Most women with this problem did not go to see a psychoanalyst, however. "There's nothing wrong really," they kept telling themselves. "There isn't any problem."

But on an April morning in 1959, I heard a mother of four, having coffee with four other mothers in a suburban development fifteen miles from New York, say in a tone of quiet desperation, "the problem." And the others knew, without words, that she was not talking about a problem with her husband, or her children, or her home. Suddenly they realized they all shared the same problem, the problem that has no name. They began, hesitantly, to talk about it. Later, after they had picked up their children at nursery school and taken them home to nap, two of the women cried, in sheer relief, just to know they were not alone.

Gradually I came to realize that the problem that has no name was shared by countless women in America. As a magazine writer I often interviewed women about problems with their children, or their marriages, or their houses, or their communities. But after a while I began to recognize the telltale signs of this other problem. I saw the same signs in suburban ranch houses and split-levels on Long Island and in New Jersey and Westchester County; in colonial houses in a small Massachusetts town; on patios in Memphis; in suburban and city apartments; in living rooms in the Midwest. Sometimes I sensed the problem, not as a reporter, but as a suburban housewife, for during this time I was also bringing up my own three children in Rockland County, New York. I heard echoes of the problem in college dormitories and semi-private maternity wards, at PTA meetings and luncheons of the League of Women Voters, at suburban cocktail parties, in station wagons waiting for trains, and in snatches of conversation overheard at Schrafft's. The groping words I heard from other women, on quiet afternoons when children were at school or on quiet evenings when husbands worked late, I think I understood first as a woman long before I understood their larger social and psychological implications.

Just what was this problem that has no name? What were the words women used when they tried to express it? Sometimes a woman would say "I feel empty somehow . . . incomplete." Or she would say,

"I feel as if I don't exist." Sometimes she blotted out the feeling with a tranquilizer. Sometimes she thought the problem was with her husband, or her children, or that what she really needed was to redecorate her house, or move to a better neighborhood, or have an affair, or another baby. Sometimes, she went to a doctor with symptoms she could hardly describe: "A tired feeling . . . I get so angry with the children it scares me . . . I feel like crying without any reason." (A Cleveland doctor called it "the housewife's syndrome.") A number of women told me about great bleeding blisters that break out on their hands and arms. "I call it the housewife's blight," said a family doctor in Pennsylvania. "I see it so often lately in these young women with four, five and six children who bury themselves in their dishpans. But it isn't caused by detergent and it isn't cured by cortisone." . . .

If I am right, the problem that has no name stirring in the minds of so many American women today is not a matter of loss of femininity or too much education, or the demands of domesticity. It is far more important than anyone recognizes. It is the key to these other new and old problems which have been torturing women and their husbands and children, and puzzling their doctors and educators for years. It may well be the key to our future as a nation and a culture. We can no longer ignore that voice within women that says: "I want something more than my husband and my children and my home."

83

ASSIA DJEBAR

Growing Up in Algeria

Excerpted from a novel by an Algerian author, this selection is about growing up in Algeria just before the revolution for independence from France, which began in 1954. To the extent to which her account is autobiographical, what do you think it was like to grow up in Algeria as a young teenage girl around 1950? How typical do you think this girl's life and concerns were?

Assia Djebar, "Growing Up in Algeria," in *Fantasia: An Algerian Cavalcade*, trans. Dorothy S. Blair (Portsmouth, NH: Heinemann, 1993), 179–85.

The author discusses how her experiences in the French and Koranic religious school pulled her in different directions. What were they? Writing and reading were very important to her, but they both meant different things in Arabic Muslim culture and French culture. "Read!" or "Recite!" was the injunction of the Archangel Gabriel to the illiterate Muhammad, the Prophet, who on these instructions recited the words of God that became the Koran in the seventh century. In the Koranic schools, young people learn the Koran by reciting and memorizing it (just as Mohammed did). What was the meaning of reading in French for the author? What were the different meanings of writing for her? Do you think this exposure to both languages was making her more Arabic or French? Which identity was more real for her?

In what ways were the needs and interests of this teenage girl similar to, or different from, those of an American teenage girl in the same period? Do you think their lives have become more alike since then?

Thinking Historically

Construct a theory that answers one of the questions posed above. Keep in mind that a theory is not an answer — it is a guiding principle for an answer. So, for instance, if you choose to consider the question, "Which identity was more real for her?", an answer might be "Arabic," and a theory could be that "a person's mother tongue determines who she is." A theory is a general principle supported by evidence. (For example, you could interview bilingual people to find out if their first language played a greater role than their second in shaping their identities.) Keep in mind many different theories are possible in answer to each question.

At the age when I should be veiled already, I can still move about freely thanks to the French school: Every Monday the village bus takes me to the boarding school in the nearby town, and brings me back on Saturday to my parents' home.

I have a friend who is half Italian and who goes home every weekend to a fishing port on the coast; we go together to catch our respective buses and are tempted by all sorts of escapades ... With beating hearts we make our way into the centre of the town; to enter a smart cake-shop, wander along the edge of the park, stroll along the boulevard, which only runs alongside common barracks, seems the acme of freedom, after a week of boarding school! Excited by the proximity of forbidden pleasures, we eventually each catch our bus; the thrill lay in the risk of missing it!

As a young teenager I enjoy the exhilarating hours spent every Thursday in training on the sports field. I only have one worry: fear that my father might come to visit me! How can I tell him that it's compulsory for me to wear shorts, in other words, I have to show my legs? I keep this fear a secret, unable to confide in any of my schoolfriends; unlike me, they haven't got cousins who do not show their ankles or their arms, who do not even expose their faces. My panic is also compounded by an Arab woman's "shame." The French girls whirl around me; they do not suspect that my body is caught in invisible snares.

"Doesn't your daughter wear a veil yet?" asks one or other of the matrons, gazing questioningly at my mother with suspicious kohl-rimmed eyes, on the occasion of one of the summer weddings. I must be thirteen, or possibly fourteen.

"She reads!" my mother replies stiffly.

Everyone is swallowed up in the embarrassed silence that ensues. And in my own silence.

"She reads," that is to say in Arabic, "she studies." I think now that this command "to read" was not just casually included in the Quranic revelation made by the Angel Gabriel in the cave ... "She reads" is tantamount to saying that writing to be read, including that of the unbelievers, is always a source of revelation: in my case of the mobility of my body, and so of my future freedom.

When I am growing up — shortly before my native land throws off the colonial yoke — while the man still has the right to four legitimate wives, we girls, big and little, have at our command four languages to express desire before all that is left for us is sighs and moans: French for secret missives; Arabic for our stifled aspirations towards God-the-Father, the God of the religions of the Book; Lybico-Berber which takes us back to the pagan idols — mother-gods — of pre-Islamic Mecca. The fourth language, for all females, young or old, cloistered or half-emancipated, remains that of the body: the body which male neighbours' and cousins' eyes require to be deaf and blind, since they cannot completely incarcerate it; the body which, in trances, dances or vociferations, in fits of hope or despair, rebels, and unable to read or write, seeks some unknown shore as destination for its message of love.

In our towns, the first woman-reality is the voice, a dart which flies off into space, an arrow which slowly falls to earth; next comes writing with the scratching pointed quill forming amorous snares with its liana letters. By way of compensation, the need is felt to blot out women's bodies and they must be muffled up, tightly swathed, swaddled like infants or shrouded like corpses. Exposed, a woman's body would offend every eye, be an assault on the dimmest of desires, emphasize every separation. The voice, on the other hand, acts like a perfume, a draft of fresh water for the dry throat; and when it is savoured, it can be enjoyed by several simultaneously; a secret, polygamous pleasure . . .

When the hand writes, slow positioning of the arm, carefully bending forward or leaning to one side, crouching, swaying to and fro, as in an act of love. When reading, the eyes take their time, delight in caressing the curves, while the calligraphy suggests the rhythm of the scansion: as if the writing marked the beginning and the end of possession.

Writing: Everywhere, a wealth of burnished gold and in its vicinity there is no place for other imagery from either animal or vegetable kingdom; it looks in the mirror of its scrolls and curlicues and sees itself as woman, not the reflection of a voice. It emphasizes by its presence alone where to begin and where to retreat; it suggests, by the song that smoulders in its heart, the dance floor for rejoicing and hair-shirt for the ascetic; I speak of the Arabic script; to be separated from it is to be separated from a great love. This script, which I mastered only to write the sacred words, I see now spread out before me cloaked in innocence and whispering arabesques — and ever since, all other scripts (French, English, Greek) seem only to babble, are never cathartic; they may contain truth, indeed, but a blemished truth.

Just as the pentathlon runner of old needed the starter, so, as soon as I learned the foreign script, my body began to move as if by instinct.

As if the French language suddenly had eyes, and lent them me to see into liberty; as if the French language blinded the peeping-toms of my clan and, at this price, I could move freely, run headlong down every street, annex the outdoors for my cloistered companions, for the matriarchs of my family who endured a living death. As if . . . Derision! I know that every language is a dark depository for piled-up corpses, refuse, sewage, but faced with the language of the former conquerer, which offers me its ornaments, its jewels, its flowers, I find they are the flowers of death — chrysanthemums on tombs!

Its script is a public unveiling in front of sniggering onlookers . . . A queen walks down the street, white, anonymous, draped, but when the shroud of rough wool is torn away and drops sudddenly at her feet, which a moment ago were hidden, she becomes a beggar again, squatting in the dust, to be spat at, the target of cruel comments.

In my earliest childhood — from the age of five to ten — I attended the French school in the village, and every day after lessons there I went on to the Quranic school.

Classes were held in a back room lent by a grocer, one of the village notables. I can recall the place, and its dim light: Was it because the time for the lessons was just before dark, or because the lighting of the room was so parsimonious? . . .

The master's image has remained singularly clear: delicate features, pale complexion, a scholar's sunken cheeks; about forty families supported him. I was struck by the elegance of his bearing and his traditional attire: A spotless light muslin was wrapped around his headdress and floated behind his neck; his serge tunic was dazzling white. I never saw this man except sitting.

In comparison, the horde of misbehaving little urchins squatting on straw mats — sons of *fellaheen* [peasants] for the most part — seemed crude riffraff, from whom I kept my distance.

We were only four or five little girls. I suppose that our sex kept us apart, rather than my supercilious amazement at their behaviour. In spite of his aristocratic bearing, the *taleb* [teacher] did not hesitate to lift his cane and bring it down on the fingers of a recalcitrant or slow-witted lad. (I can still hear it whistle through the air.) We girls were spared this regular punishment.

I can remember the little impromptu parties my mother devised in our flat when I brought home (as later my brother was to do) the walnut table decorated with arabesques. This was the master's reward when we had learnt a long *sura* by heart. My mother and our village nanny, who was a second mother to us, then let out that semi-barbaric "you-you." That prolonged, irregular, spasmodic cooing, which in our building reserved for teachers' families — all European except for ours — must have appeared incongruous, a truly primitive cry. My mother considered the circumstances (the study of the Quran undertaken by her children) sufficiently important for her to let out this ancestral cry of jubilation in the middle of the village where she nevertheless felt herself an exile.

At every prize-giving ceremony at the French school, every prize I obtained strengthened my solidarity with my own family; but I felt there was more glory in this ostentatious clamour. The Quranic school, that dim cavern in which the haughty figure of the Sheikh was enthroned above the poor village children, this school became, thanks to the joy my mother demonstrated in this way, an island of bliss — Paradise regained.

Back in my native city, I learned that another Arab school was being opened, also funded by private contributions. One of my cousins attended it; she took me there. I was disappointed. The buildings, the timetable, the modern appearance of the masters, made it no different from a common-or-garden French school . . .

I understood later that in the village I had participated in the last of popular, secular teaching. In the city, thanks to the Nationalist movement of "Modernist Muslims," a new generation of Arab culture was being forged.

Since then these *medrasas* have sprung up everywhere. If I had attended one of them (if I'd grown up in the town where I was born)

I would have found it quite natural to swathe my head in a turban, to hide my hair, to cover my arms and calves, in a word to move about out of doors like a Muslim nun!

After the age of ten or eleven, shortly before puberty, I was no longer allowed to attend the Quranic school. At this age, boys are suddenly excluded from the women's Turkish bath — that emollient world of naked bodies stifling in a whirl of scalding steam . . . The same thing happened to my companions, the little village girls, one of whom I would like to describe here.

The daughter of the Kabyle baker must, like me, have attended the French school simultaneously with the Quranic school. But I can only recall her presence squatting at my side in front of the Sheikh: side by side, half smiling to each other, both already finding it uncomfortable to sit cross-legged! . . . My legs must have been too long, because of my height: It wasn't easy for me to hide them under my skirt.

For this reason alone I think that I would in any case have been weaned from Quranic instruction at this age: There is no doubt that it's easier to sit cross-legged when wearing a *seroual;* a young girl's body that is beginning to develop more easily conceals its form under the ample folds of the traditional costume. But my skirts, justified by my attendance at the French school, were ill adapted to such a posture.

When I was eleven I started secondary school and became a boarder. What happened to the baker's daughter? Certainly veiled, withdrawn overnight from school: betrayed by her figure. Her swelling breasts, her slender legs, in a word, the emergence of her woman's personality transformed her into an incarcerated body!

I remember how much this Quranic learning, as it is progressively acquired, is linked to the body.

The portion of the sacred verse, inscribed on both sides of the walnut tablet, had to be wiped off at least once a week, after we had shown that we could recite it off by heart. We scrubbed the piece of wood thoroughly, just like other people wash their clothes: The time it took to dry seemed to ensure the interval that the memory needed to digest what it had swallowed . . .

The learning was absorbed by the fingers, the arms, through the physical effort. The act of cleaning the tablet seemed like ingesting a portion of the Quranic text. The writing — itself a copy of writing which is considered immutable — could only continue to unfold before us if it relied, clause by clause, on this osmosis . . .

As the hand traces the liana-script, the mouth opens to repeat the words, obedient to their rhythm, partly to memorize, partly to relieve the muscular tension . . . The shrill voices of the drowsy children rise up in a monotonous, sing-song chorus.

Stumbling on, swaying from side to side, care taken to observe the tonic accents, to differentiate between long and short vowels, attentive to the rhythm of the chant; muscles of the larynx as well as the torso moving in harmony. Controlling the breath to allow the correct emission of the voice, and letting the understanding advance precariously along its tight-rope. Respecting the grammar by speaking it aloud, making it part of the chant.

This language which I learn demands the correct posture for the body, on which the memory rests for its support. The childish hand, spurred on — as in training for some sport — by willpower worthy of an adult, begins to write. "Read!" The fingers labouring on the tablet send back the signs to the body, which is simultaneously reader and servant. The lips having finished their muttering, the hand will once more do the washing, proceeding to wipe out what is written on the tablet: This is the moment of absolution, like touching the hem of death's garment. Again, it is the turn of writing, and the circle is completed.

And when I sit curled up like this to study my native language it is as though my body reproduces the architecture of my native city: the *medinas* with their tortuous alleyways closed off to the outside world, living their secret life. When I write and read the foreign language, my body travels far in subversive space, in spite of the neighbours and suspicious matrons; it would not need much for it to take wing and fly away!

As I approach a marriageable age, these two different apprenticeships, undertaken simultaneously, land me in a dichotomy of location. My father's preference will decide for me: light rather than darkness. I do not realize that an irrevocable choice is being made: the outdoors and the risk, instead of the prison of my peers. This stroke of luck brings me to the verge of breakdown.

I write and speak French outside: The words I use convey no flesh-and-blood reality. I learn the names of birds I've never seen, trees I shall take ten years or more to identify, lists of flowers and plants that I shall never smell until I travel north of the Mediterranean. In this respect, all vocabulary expresses what is missing in my life, exoticism without mystery, causing a kind of visual humiliation that it is not seemly to admit to . . . Settings and episodes in children's books are nothing but theoretical concepts; in the French family the mother comes to fetch her daughter or son from school; in the French street, the parents walk quite naturally side by side . . . So, the world of the school is expunged from the daily life of my native city, as it is from the life of my family. The latter is refused any referential rôle.

My conscious mind is here, huddled against my mother's knees, in the darkest corners of the flat which she never leaves. The ambit of the school is elsewhere: My search, my eyes are fixed on other regions. I do not realize, no-one around me realizes, that, in the conflict between these two worlds, lies an incipient vertigo.

$$84$$

SIMI BEDFORD

Growing Up in Nigeria

This selection is excerpted from a novel about a young girl growing up in Nigeria. What does this selection suggest to us about Nigeria, large wealthy families in the port city of Lagos, the history of slavery, Christianity, and life in modern Africa? How typical do you think this young girl is? In what ways is the life of this girl similar to that of the teenage girl in the previous selection?

Thinking Historically

What would be one problem with basing a theory about the life of young girls in Africa on this story? Did any ideas come to you after reading this piece that might be generalized into a theory? Can you think of a theory that would explain a difference in the lives of Simi Bedford and Assia Djebar (see selection 83)?

Both this selection and the previous one discuss language and religion. What are some of the similarities and differences in their approaches to these topics? Formulate a theory about the importance or meaning of language or religion for young women in Africa.

"Africans can talk oh!" Aunt Rose often said.

She was right, in our house we spoke four languages, and two of them were English, loudly from morning till night, so it was a mystery to us, the foster children and me, that Grandma and Grandpa never spoke to each other at all. It was a mystery too that I didn't wake up dead every morning, because unless I was cross with her, I slept with

Simi Bedford, "Growing Up in Nigeria," in *Yoruba Girl Dancing* (New York: Penguin, 1992), 1–10.

Grandma in her big brass bed. There were twelve pillows on it, six on either side, and if I hadn't slept practically standing up, spreadeagled against them with my head angled back over the top one for air, I would have suffocated for sure under the covers.

Grandma was asleep; I liked to look at her in the morning when she was sleeping, because then her eyes were tight shut. When they were open they were black and shiny like pebbles under water and knew what you were thinking. Her face was smooth and peaceful. I stroked her white hair, soft as duck down, back from her forehead and tugged at her plait but she didn't wake up; so I left her and ran next door to my nurse Patience and she dressed me. I was ready and waiting in my grandmother's sitting room for James when he arrived to escort me up to breakfast on the top floor. James was Grandpa's steward.

"Well madam, I see you ready," he said, knocking on Grandma's bedroom door, which was in the right-hand corner of the sitting room.

"Can we go now?" I was impatient to leave this morning, I had a choice piece of news.

"Yes yes, we dey go now," he replied, laughing down at me.

"Do I look pretty?"

"You are fine, fine," he said, as always.

Grandma's arm, plump and sepia coloured, appeared around the door with a white note folded in her hand and James plucked it from her fingers, sketched a small bow to the rest of her invisible behind the door, and ushered me out in front of him.

Grandpa was already in his armchair sorting through his post, which scattered onto the floor as, taking a running jump, I settled myself in his lap and lay back against his shirt front which appeared dazzlingly white in the darkened room. I had hoped for a glimpse of Grandma's note — Grandpa had taught me to read when I was three — but he raised his arms above my head and read the letter safely out of reach. Frustrated, I slipped from his knee to fetch the Bible, which I'd left on the table next to his desk the day before, I didn't expect to find it there though, because both table and desk were heaped with books. The walls of Grandpa's sitting room were painted cream but you couldn't see them either, they were lined with books filling the shelves from floor to ceiling. Books spilled out of the shelves ruckling up the rugs on the polished wooden floor, vying for space with mounds of newspapers and periodicals, old and new. I found the Bible on the floor at the same time as a shout of laughter from Grandpa signalled that he'd come to the end of Grandma's note and brought James's head enquiringly around the door of the next room, where he was busy preparing breakfast. Hopefully I turned around too, but the joke was not to be shared.

"Come here," Grandpa said and hugged me close so that my nose was filled with the scent of his cologne and coconut hair pomade. "Where did we finish yesterday?"

We were working our way day by day through the Old Testament, Grandpa had little truck with the New, that the meek should inherit the earth had no place in his philosophy.

"God killed all the firstborn," I said, opening the Bible with the green leather marker, "and the Pharaoh was just about to let all the Israelites go."

Frankly I thought the Pharaoh had brought his troubles on himself. Moses had told him in no uncertain terms that unless he was allowed to lead the Israelites out of Egypt, God would smite every firstborn in the land and Pharaoh had been given plenty of proof with the nine plagues already visited on him that God would keep his word. It was horrifying all the same, though, because, as I pointed out to Grandpa, that would have been me, I was the firstborn child in my family. Grandpa assured me he would not have allowed it to happen. I believed him, he would have made a deal and got the best of it.

"Begin now!" he said, gesturing towards the page.

Keeping my place by moving my forefinger carefully beneath each word, I began reading. But Grandpa was not in the mood; no sooner were the Israelites safely across the Red Sea and the pursuing Egyptians drowned in their chariots, than he called out to James that we were ready to eat.

I wasn't ready to let the Israelites go just yet though. I waited until James had finished wrapping me in a big white napkin in order to protect my dress and then I said, "Aunt Rose says that we used to be slaves, like the Israelites."

"Aunt Rose talks too much. What will you eat?"

"Did we, Grandpa?"

He spooned up his pawpaw and didn't answer; after a pause and another mouthful, he said testily, "Yes, in America, but that was a long time ago. The important thing for you to remember is that our family came back."

"To Lagos?"

"Not initially, they settled in Sierra Leone to begin with."

"Where Uncle Marcus and lots of the cousins live?"

"That's right. Are you not eating this morning?"

"Were you a slave, Grandpa?"

"Of course not! Do I look like a slave? However it is a fact that my grandfather was one. You know he was a very brave man: He fought, along with many other slaves, on the side of the British in their war against the Americans and in return for his help he was given his freedom. Afterwards the British brought all the freed slaves to Sierra Leone. They crossed the Atlantic Ocean in a big ship and it arrived just in time for my father, your great-grandfather, Elias Foster, to be born a free man in Africa again. When he became a grown man he came home: to Nigeria. He settled in Lagos and began trading in palm oil. He was very successful too."

"Like Moses!"

"Exactly."

"How did great-grandpa Elias know that this was his home?"

"Well he knew that according to our family tradition we came originally from the area around Abeokuta, so he made a journey up there and when he arrived he immediately recognised the tribal markings on the faces of the people, they were identical to the pattern handed down to his father by his grandfather in America. We are home for good now, I promise you."

"I don't think I'd like to go to America."

"But you would like to go to England some day, wouldn't you, to study?"

"Like Papa and Aunt Harriet? Some day maybe."

"Now! What are you going to eat?"

I looked at the bowl on the table, it was hard to choose from the mangoes, pawpaws, guavas, oranges, pineapple, grapefruit, and melon. I asked James, who'd been standing by, to cut me an avocado in half and sprinkle it with salt. We ate in silence and it wasn't until I was halfway through my second slice of pineapple — I loved pineapple — that I remembered my news for Grandpa. I felt sorry for Grandpa — he never knew anything, because he only ever left his eyrie to go to the Chamber of Commerce and to church on Sunday.

"Sisi Bola's getting married," I said, looking at him sideways.

"Don't speak with your mouth full. Who is she marrying?"

"Akin Ojo."

Grandpa raised his eyebrows, "She only recently left for England, are you sure?"

"Oh yes. She came back last week and Nimota says — you know my nurse Nimota? — she says that it must have been love at first look."

Grandpa roared with laughter. "Indeed."

"And Patience says — "

"Which one is Patience?"

"Grandpa you know my nurse Patience very well."

"Do I?"

"Yes! She says that the food in England have plenty magic, because Sisi Bola only stick out de back when she go, but she stick out the front too like a elephant when she come back."

My grandfather laughed again. "You are a disgraceful child! Eat up, eat up now."

"Don't you want to know when the wedding is?"

"I'm sure you will tell me."

"It's in three weeks' time. I'm to be a bridesmaid. Aunt Delma has asked Grandma."

Aunt Delma was Grandma's sister and Sisi Bola's mother.

Sisi Bola was to be married from our house and Aunt Rose said that Aunt Delma was exceedingly lucky to have a sister like Grandma who was not only generous but who was also wife to the richest man in Lagos. The wedding, she said, would be the wedding of the decade, we should mark her words. I repeated this to Yowande, the youngest of the foster children, who, although three years older than me, was my best friend in the house. She didn't know what wedding of the decade meant either, but she did know that Nimota, my second nanny, was planning to put a curse on Yetunde, her rival in love, so that she would be too sick to attend any of the celebrations. I must be careful not to say anything, she said, because if Grandma found out she would beat us all.

"I won't tell her," I said. Yowande looked sceptical. It wasn't fair, just because I was the youngest in the house. Even I knew how fanatical Grandma was about that kind of thing. She considered it a blasphemy against the Christian Religion. And anyway I never told tales now.

We all, the Fosters that is, lived a stone's throw from the Marina in the residential area off Broad Street: Broad Street, Aunt Rose said, was the commercial centre, whatever that meant, of Lagos, where, she said, men of substance like Grandpa had built their mansions in the European style. Nimota said that that simply meant Grandpa was a big man. Where she came from, up country, he would have been, she said, a Paramount Chief. It was a fact that Grandpa's warehouses, which we passed nearly every day on our constitutional along the Marina, stretched for half a mile around the bay, I'd been inside many times of course with Grandpa. Aunt Rose, who frequently accompanied Nimota and me, said that Grandpa's warehouses were filled with all the riches of the continent, but actually they contained quite ordinary everyday things, as Grandpa said. Palm oil, leather, timber, and stuff like that. You name it, Aunt Rose said, and Grandpa sold it. He had branches and factories throughout the country, even where Nimota came from, and that was very remote. Aunt Rose counted them up on her fingers, there were twenty-three in all, branches, that is, not fingers, Aunt Rose had the normal number, but you wouldn't think so, Nimota said, they were into everything. Our house was four storeys high and painted a bright strawberry pink with a cream pattern of whirls and fancy flourishes around the windows and doors. The Lagos sun which, Grandma said, can wreck such havoc with pink complexions, had been kind to this one and aged it gently, so that with time the colour had mellowed and become discreet. Long rows of windows each with its own wrought-iron balcony looked out across the front, and large double doors opened directly onto the street. At the back there was a large paved courtyard with a well in the centre. A huge avocado provided shade, as did the mango, pawpaw, guava, and banana trees; broad-leaved ferns masked the hot glitter of the paving stones.

During the day we liked to sit pleasantly and peacefully, on the benches under the trees; the light filtering down through the leaves was always green and forest cool. At night the courtyard was lit by the fires of the servants cooking their food in the outside kitchen and loud with the sound of crickets. The smoke from the fires kept the mosquitoes at bay.

We were a miniature village, thirty people lived in our house. Grandpa lived on the top floor and was attended by his own servants. He and Grandma had been effectively separated for fifteen years; he never came downstairs. Even so he ruled us all, his word was law and his power was absolute. Aunt Rose said that people were equally terrified of him outside the house, including the score of Europeans he employed. I heard her tell Patience that she herself was so in awe of him she had only dared to address him directly three or four times in the twenty years since she had been living under his roof. I thought that was pretty silly of Aunt Rose. I wasn't scared of Grandpa and he certainly wasn't frightening to look at. The neat whorls of his hair had turned to grey, but his moustache was marvellously black and glossy and so was his skin which had an almost metallic sheen. It seemed to me that he was always laughing and, unlike Grandma, who complained of the smell that clung to me when I came back down after breakfast upstairs, I liked his cigars. He was seldom without one, either clenched in his teeth or drifting smoke from between his long fingers. It was all right for me, Aunt Rose said, I was the favoured grandchild, the little princess.

My grandmother, Grandma Loretta, ruled the rest of the household from her sitting room, which served as another courtyard inside the house. All the other rooms on the first floor opened onto it. Stationed in her rocking chair in the corner by her bedroom door, no coming or going escaped her notice. I loved Grandma, she was fat and marvellously comfortable to sit on, her brown skin was soft to touch and she wore her hair plaited in a crown around her head. Any impression of cosiness however was dispelled by a second glance at her eyes, it was impossible to look into them and lie.

With the exception of my father Simon, all Grandpa and Grandma's children were still living at home. My father Simon was the eldest and my Aunt Harriet was next. In fact, however, they were not Grandma's children at all: They were Grandpa's two children by the Fante princess. So she was my real grandmother, but I never knew her, she was never seen in Lagos, and she died in Ghana which was her country long before I was born. Grandma brought up the two children as if they were her own. Aunt Harriet, who resembled her mother and kept a photograph of her locked in her drawer, was considered a great beauty. The photograph showed a magnificent woman with bare shoulders wrapped in a length of Kente cloth, which, so Aunt Harriet told me and I told Yowande, could only be worn by royalty. If the picture were in colour the cloth would be glowing red, green, and gold, like the stained-glass windows in Lagos cathedral. Her jet black hair was pulled up in a fan shape over a wooden frame and fastened with solid gold nuggets as befitted a Fante princess. Grandma said, and I heard her say it many times to Aunt Rose when they were sitting taking a glass of home-made ginger beer, that though Aunt Harriet, who was a barrister, was brilliant, she was too highly strung. Grandma was worried that Harriet might even be a little unstable. After all it was common knowledge that there was . . . well, instability, in the Fante princess's family. There was no denying Aunt Harriet was sensitive, because as Aunt Rose said, she had a habit of bursting into tears at the least little thing and rushing from the room.

Aunt Sylvia, Grandma's own elder daughter, was brilliant too, she was going to be a doctor. As Aunt Rose said, making sure that Grandma heard her, there was nothing unstable about that one. She was my father's favourite, he liked to hold her up as a perfect model of African womanhood. According to my father Aunt Sylvia was serious, clever, modest, and good. Nobody was perfect, Aunt Rose said. Aunt Grace, the youngest of my father's brothers and sisters, was my favourite, Yowande and I loved to play with her hair which was thick and shoulder length and watch her maid straightening it and curling it in the latest styles from England. Aunt Grace's eyebrows were two perfect arches, she was destined to be a film star. We knew it.

Grandma's only son Uncle George would normally have been at home too, but he had gone to England to fly aeroplanes and fight in the war. According to Patience he was a source of great pride, anger, and anxiety for my grandmother, not necessarily in that order. Opinion in the house was divided about Uncle George: We children thought he was a hero but Aunt Rose, and Patience too, believed he was downright foolhardy to get involved in dem white people war. They didn't say this to Grandma. Everyone had to be careful too on the subject of Uncle Henry. He was Grandpa's son by an outside wife and the spitting image of Grandpa. Yowande and I knew from listening to conversations around the house (we had our eyes to every keyhole and our ear to every door, Aunt Rose said, but she was no better, in Nimota's opinion) that Uncle Henry was one of the reasons Grandma never spoke to Grandpa, but no one explained why. Aunt Rose would only say that certain tenets of the Christian faith appealed to Grandpa more than others and one man one wife was not among them.

Aunt Rose had been living with my grandparents for twenty years, ever since she had arrived for a short holiday in her teens. Even the servants referred to her as poor Aunt Rose, not because she was a poor relation, which she was, but because she had never married, and even worse, Nimota said, she had no children. She was given to wearing dark coloured dresses with pale collars; thin and spindly, she hugged the corners of the house, delicate yet durable, like a cobweb.

Aunt Sylvia said that we made Aunt Rose's life intolerable. There were ten of us, nine foster children and me. The foster children were the sons and daughters of poor relations, like Aunt Rose; their parents sent them to live in Grandpa's house so that they could advance themselves. Yowande was the youngest, she was nine; Morenike was the eldest, she was fifteen and would be going home soon. In fact she would be leaving the CMS[1] just as I was beginning. Alaba who was my third nanny would miss her most, they were the same age. Aunt Rose said that when one of the foster children left, another appeared to take its place, miraculously, like shark's teeth. And then there was me: Everybody knew who I was. I was Remi Foster, the eldest of Simon Foster's three children, and Grandpa and Grandma's first grandchild. I lived with them because, as Grandpa said, Grandma would have been sad without a baby growing up in the house, and so would he. I was on permanent loan: It was the custom with the eldest grandchild and anyway, as Aunt Rose said, I was only a girl. She also said that no child required three nannies to trail after her all day long. I would be spoiled for life, we should mark her words. Well, the foster children certainly didn't spoil me, if I told tales they beat me up, and Grandma beat me too just to be sure. My life wasn't easy, like Aunt Rose thought. I couldn't tell her though, my lips were sealed.

85

CAROLINA MARIA DE JESUS

From *Child of the Dark: The Diary of Carolina Maria de Jesus*

This selection is from the diary of a common — and extraordinary — woman in Brazil in 1958. Carolina Maria de Jesus was born in 1913 in a small town in the interior of Brazil. Her mother, unmarried and unemployed, insisted that Carolina attend school, which she hated until the day she learned to read. She remembers reading out loud every sign

[1] School.

Carolina Maria de Jesus, *Child of the Dark: The Diary of Carolina Maria de Jesus,* trans. David St. Clair (New York: NAL Penguin, 1962), 32–34, 42–47.

and label she could find. It was the beginning of a lifetime fascination with words. But she was forced to leave school after the second grade.

When Carolina was sixteen, her mother moved to the suburbs of São Paulo. Carolina worked in a hospital, ran away to sing in a circus, and was employed in a long succession of jobs as cleaning woman and maid when, in 1947, she became pregnant. Her lover had abandoned her, and the family she worked for refused to let her into their house. Desperate, she moved into a *favela* (slum) in São Paulo, building her own shack with cardboard and cans taken from a Church construction site. In the next ten years she had two more children. In order to keep from thinking of her troubles, she wrote. Poems, plays, novels, "anything and everything, for when I was writing I was in a golden palace, with crystal windows and silver chandeliers." She also kept a diary that reveals the actual details of her daily life. It is a life still lived by many women in the favelas of Brazil.

What does the diary tell you about the lives of the poor in Brazil?

Thinking Historically

Of course, there are poor women in Africa and rich women in South America. And it need hardly be said that the poor outnumber the wealthy in Africa and Latin America as well as in China and the United States. Yet, it is difficult to imagine such desperate poverty as that described by Carolina Maria de Jesus. She is an articulate and thoughtful woman whose writing has helped her shape her own ideas. If you asked her what caused such poverty in her country, what might she say? Does she offer any theories about this? What is your theory for the existence of such poverty?

May 2, 1958 I'm not lazy. There are times when I try to keep up my diary. But then I think it's not worth it and figure I'm wasting my time.

I've made a promise to myself. I want to treat people that I know with more consideration. I want to have a pleasant smile for children and the employed.

I received a summons to appear at 8 P.M. at police station number 12. I spent the day looking for paper. At night my feet pained me so I couldn't walk. It started to rain. I went to the station and took José Carlos with me. The summons was for him. José Carlos is nine years old.

May 3 I went to the market at Carlos de Campos Street looking for any old thing. I got a lot of greens. But it didn't help much, for I've got no cooking fat. The children are upset because there's nothing to eat.

May 6 In the morning I went for water. I made João carry it. I was happy, then I received another summons. I was inspired yesterday and my verses were so pretty, I forgot to go to the station. It was 11:00

when I remembered the invitation from the illustrious lieutenant of the 12th precinct.

My advice to would-be politicians is that people do not tolerate hunger. It's necessary to know hunger to know how to describe it.

They are putting up a circus here at Araguaia Street. The Nilo Circus Theater.

May 9 I looked for paper but I didn't like it. Then I thought: I'll pretend that I'm dreaming.

May 10 I went to the police station and talked to the lieutenant. What a pleasant man! If I had known he was going to be so pleasant, I'd have gone on the first summons. The lieutenant was interested in my boys' education. He said the *favelas* have an unhealthy atmosphere where the people have more chance to go wrong than to become useful to state and country. I thought: If he knows this why doesn't he make a report and send it to the politicians? ... Now he tells me this, I a poor garbage collector. I can't even solve my own problems.

Brazil needs to be led by a person who has known hunger. Hunger is also a teacher.

Who has gone hungry learns to think of the future and of the children.

May 11 Today is Mother's Day. The sky is blue and white. It seems that even nature wants to pay homage to the mothers who feel unhappy because they can't realize the desires of their children.

The sun keeps climbing. Today it's not going to rain. Today is our day.

Dona Teresinha came to visit me. She gave me 15 cruzeiros and said it was for Vera to go to the circus. But I'm going to use the money to buy bread tomorrow because I only have four cruzeiros.

Yesterday I got half a pig's head at the slaughterhouse. We ate the meat and saved the bones. Today I put the bones on to boil and into the broth I put some potatoes. My children are always hungry. When they are starving they aren't so fussy about what they eat.

Night came. The stars are hidden. The shack is filled with mosquitoes. I lit a page from a newspaper and ran it over the walls. This is the way the *favela* dwellers kill mosquitoes.

May 13 At dawn it was raining. Today is a nice day for me, it's the anniversary of the Abolition. The day we celebrate the freeing of the slaves. In the jails the Negroes were the scapegoats. But now the whites are more educated and don't treat us any more with contempt. May God enlighten the whites so that the Negroes may have a happier life.

It continued to rain and I only have beans and salt. The rain is strong but even so I sent the boys to school. I'm writing until the rain goes away so I can go to Senhor Manuel and sell scrap. With that money I'm going to buy rice and sausage. The rain has stopped for a while. I'm going out.

I feel so sorry for my children. When they see the things to eat that I come home with they shout:

"*Viva Mama!*"

Their outbursts please me. I've lost the habit of smiling. Ten minutes later they want more food. I sent João to ask Dona Ida for a little pork fat. She didn't have any. I sent her a note:

"Dona Ida, I beg you to help me get a little pork fat, so I can make soup for the children. Today it's raining and I can't go looking for paper. Thank you, Carolina."

It rained and got colder. Winter had arrived and in winter people eat more. Vera asked for food, and I didn't have any. It was the same old show. I had two cruzeiros and wanted to buy a little flour to make a *virado*.[1] I went to ask Dona Alice for a little pork. She gave me pork and rice. It was 9 at night when we ate.

And that is the way on May 13, 1958 I fought against the real slavery — hunger!

May 15 On the nights they have a party they don't let anybody sleep. The neighbors in the brick houses near by have signed a petition to get rid of the *favelados*. But they won't get their way. The neighbors in the brick houses say:

"The politicians protect the *favelados*."

Who protects us are the public and the Order of St. Vincent Church. The politicians only show up here during election campaigns. Senhor Candido Sampaio, when he was city councilman in 1953, spent his Sundays here in the *favela*. He was so nice. He drank our coffee, drinking right out of our cups. He made us laugh with his jokes. He played with our children. He left a good impression here and when he was candidate for state deputy, he won. But the Chamber of Deputies didn't do one thing for the *favelados*. He doesn't visit us any more. . . .

May 22 Today I'm sad. I'm nervous. I don't know if I should start crying or start running until I fall unconscious. At dawn it was raining. I couldn't go out to get any money. I spent the day writing. I cooked the macaroni and I'll warm it up again for the children. I cooked the potatoes and they ate them. I have a few tin cans and a little scrap that I'm going to sell to Senhor Manuel. When João came home from school I sent him to sell the scrap. He got 13 cruzeiros. He bought a glass of mineral water: two cruzeiros. I was furious with him. Where had he seen a *favelado* with such highborn tastes?

The children eat a lot of bread. They like soft bread but when they don't have it, they eat hard bread.

Hard is the bread that we eat. Hard is the bed on which we sleep. Hard is the life of the *favelado*.

---

[1] A dish of black beans, manioc flour, pork, and eggs.

Oh, São Paulo! A queen that vainly shows her skyscrapers that are her crown of gold. All dressed up in velvet and silk but with cheap stockings underneath — the *favela*.

The money didn't stretch far enough to buy meat, so I cooked macaroni with a carrot. I didn't have any grease, it was horrible. Vera was the only one who complained yet asked for more.

"Mama, sell me to Dona Julita, because she has delicious food."

I know that there exist Brazilians here inside São Paulo who suffer more than I do. In June of '57 I felt sick and passed through the offices of the Social Service. I had carried a lot of scrap iron and got pains in my kidneys. So as not to see my children hungry I asked for help from the famous Social Service. It was there that I saw the tears slipping from the eyes of the poor. How painful it is to see the dramas that are played out there. The coldness in which they treat the poor. The only things they want to know about them is their name and address.

I went to the Governor's Palace.[2] The Palace sent me to an office at Brigadeiro Luis Antonio Avenue. They in turn sent me to the Social Service at the Santa Casa charity hospital. There I talked with Dona Maria Aparecida, who listened to me, said many things yet said nothing. I decided to go back to the Palace. I talked with Senhor Alcides. He is not Japanese yet is as yellow as rotten butter. I said to Senhor Alcides:

"I came here to ask for help because I'm ill. You sent me to Brigadeiro Luis Antonio Avenue, and I went. There they sent me to the Santa Casa. And I spent all the money I have on transportation."

"Take her!"

They wouldn't let me leave. A soldier put his bayonet at my chest. I looked the soldier in the eyes and saw that he had pity on me. I told him:

"I am poor. That's why I came here."

Dr. Osvaldo de Barros entered, a false philanthropist in São Paulo who is masquerading as St. Vincent de Paul. He said:

"Call a squad car!"

The policeman took me back to the *favela* and warned me that the next time I made a scene at the welfare agency I would be locked up.

Welfare agency! Welfare for whom? . . .

May 27 It seems that the slaughterhouse threw kerosene on their garbage dump so the *favelados* would not look for meat to eat. I didn't have any breakfast and walked around half dizzy. The daze of hunger is worse than that of alcohol. The daze of alcohol makes us sing, but the one of hunger makes us shake. I know how horrible it is to only have air in the stomach.

---

[2] Like most Brazilians, Carolina believes in going straight to the top to make her complaints.

I began to have a bitter taste in my mouth. I thought: Is there no end to the bitterness of life? I think that when I was born I was marked by fate to go hungry. I filled one sack of paper. When I entered Paulo Guimarães Street, a woman gave me some newspapers. They were clean and I went to the junk yard picking up everything that I found. Steel, tin, coal, everything serves the *favelado*. Leon weighed the paper and I got six cruzeiros.

I wanted to save the money to buy beans but I couldn't because my stomach was screaming and torturing me.

I decided to do something about it and bought a bread roll. What a surprising effect food has on our organisms. Before I ate, I saw the sky, the trees, and the birds all yellow, but after I ate, everything was normal to my eyes.

Food in the stomach is like fuel in machines. I was able to work better. My body stopped weighing me down. I started to walk faster. I had the feeling that I was gliding in space. I started to smile as if I was witnessing a beautiful play. And will there ever be a drama more beautiful than that of eating? I felt that I was eating for the first time in my life.

The Radio Patrol arrived. They came to take the two Negro boys who had broken into the power station. Four and six years old. It's easy to see that they are of the *favela*. *Favela* children are the most ragged children in the city. What they can find in the streets they eat. Banana peels, melon rind, and even pineapple husks. Anything that is too tough to chew, they grind. These boys had their pockets filled with aluminum coins, that new money in circulation.

May 28 It dawned raining. I only have three cruzeiros because I loaned Leila five so she could get her daughter in the hospital. I'm confused and don't know where to begin. I want to write, I want to work, I want to wash clothes. I'm cold and I don't have any shoes to wear. The children's shoes are worn out.

The worst thing in the *favela* is that there are children here. All the children of the *favela* know what a woman's body looks like. Because when the couples that are drunk fight, the woman, so as not to get a beating, runs naked into the street. When the fights start the *favelados* leave whatever they are doing to be present at the battle. So that when the woman goes running naked it's a real show for Joe Citizen. Afterward the comments begin among the children:

"Fernanda ran out nude when Armin was hitting her."

"Oh, I didn't see it. Damn!"

"What does a naked woman look like?"

And then the other, in order to tell him, puts his mouth near his ear. And the loud laughter echoes. Everything that is obscene or pornographic the *favelado* learns quickly.

There are some shacks where prostitutes play their love scenes right in front of the children.

The rich neighbors in the brick houses say we are protected by the politicians. They're wrong. The politicians only show up here in the Garbage Dump at election time. This year we had a visit from a candidate for deputy, Dr. Paulo de Campos Moura, who gave us beans and some wonderful blankets. He came at an opportune moment, before it got cold.

What I want to clear up about the people who live in the *favela* is the following: The only ones who really survive here are the *nordestinos.*[3] They work and don't squander. They buy a house or go back up north.

Here in the *favela* there are those who build shacks to live in and those who build them to rent. And the rents are from 500 to 700 cruzeiros. Those who make shacks to sell spend 4,000 cruzeiros and sell them for 11,000. Who made a lot of shacks to sell was Tiburcio.

May 29 It finally stopped raining. The clouds glided toward the horizon. Only the cold attacked us. Many people in the *favela* don't have warm clothing. When one has shoes he won't have a coat. I choke up watching the children walk in the mud. It seems that some new people have arrived in the *favela*. They are ragged with undernourished faces. They improvised a shack. It hurts me to see so much pain, reserved for the working class. I stared at my new companion in misfortune. She looked at the *favela* with its mud and sickly children. It was the saddest look I'd ever seen. Perhaps she has no more illusions. She had given her life over to misery.

There will be those who reading what I write will say — this is untrue. But misery is real.

What I revolt against is the greed of men who squeeze other men as if they were squeezing oranges.

---

[3] Forced by land-parching droughts and almost no industry, the poor of the north swarm into cities like São Paulo and Rio looking for work. Needing a place to live, they choose the *favelas* and end up worse off than they were before.

86

JENNIFER HARBURY

From *Bridge of Courage*

After graduating from Harvard Law School in 1978, Jennifer Harbury became engaged in human rights work that took her to Guatemala in 1985 and 1986. She returned to Guatemala in 1990 to record the oral history interviews that are the basis of the book from which this selection is excerpted. In Guatemala she met and married Commandante Everardo, who was later captured and disappeared. In 1995 her multiple hunger strikes forced the CIA to admit that her husband was dead, murdered by one of its paid agents.

U.S. policy in Guatemala switched from one of support to opposition in 1944 with the downfall of the dictator Jorge Chico and the election of a popular nationalist president, Jacobo Arbenz, who redistributed land to the poor, threatening the interests of U.S.–owned tropical fruit companies and U.S. investors. After securing his downfall in 1954, the United States trained the Guatemalan military and insured the continuance of conservative military regimes. In the 1980s these efforts were part of the U.S. campaign against neighboring Nicaragua and its support for the right-wing "death squads" of El Salvador. In 1999, an international Historical Clarification Commission issued a nine-volume report, "Guatemala: Memory of Silence," which held that the Guatemalan military, with the backing of the United States, engaged in a policy of genocide against the local population of Mayan Indians; 200,000 were tortured and murdered in a thirty-four-year war that ended in 1996.

This is the story of Anita, a physician who joined the Guatemalans and fought against this military regime. How did Anita become involved in the revolution against the government? Was her involvement unusual for an urban woman and for a physician?

Thinking Historically

How might Anita explain her various identities and activities? If you asked her if she had any theories about how a woman could become involved in all of these things, what might she say?

Compare Anita with Carolina from selection 85. How might you explain why Anita became a revolutionary and Carolina did not? Formulate a theory that generalizes and explains their differences.

Jennifer Harbury, "Anita," in *Bridge of Courage: Life Stories of the Guatemalan Companeros and Companeras* (Monroe, ME: Common Courage Press, 1995), 36–38, 103–06, 109–13.

Compare Anita with one of the African women you read about. What makes their experiences so different from Anita's? Formulate a theory that explains these differences.

... I joined the underground during my last year of medical school. I had just finished a rotation up in the jungle areas with the peasant co-operatives, and had learned a lot. What an eye opener that year was! It had been very difficult. My school supervisor hated women medical students and had sent me to the most remote regions in hopes that I would give up. Instead, though, I thrived, and came to love the villagers who took me in and cared for me. I loved their gentle ways, and their generosity, and I saw the unfairness and repression that they suffered. I never forgot it, even after I returned to the capital for my last year of study. And with my new awareness, I saw the things in the city that, perhaps, I hadn't wanted to see before.

I lived not far from a small union office, and on the way to the hospital each morning, I saw the fresh black ribbons on the union door, the new photographs, signaling yet another member dragged off to an ugly death in the middle of the night. And I saw the morgues. The tortures that had been inflicted on those poor people, the expressions on those dead faces, I will never forget. It is because of the morgues, I am positive, that so many of us medical students, and yes, even professors, joined up with the underground that year. Look, here is my graduation photo. See the two men handing me my diploma? They are both dead now; they were part of the city underground, but I didn't know it then. The two students next to me? They were with the guerrillas, too. I think they went to the mountains. None of us knew about each other, for security reasons. But I know now, and when I look at this photo, I feel doubly proud. Proud of the diploma and my completed studies, proud of all of us in the group, and proud of the courage represented in this image. It makes me happy to show it to you. I want these people remembered.

At first I worked in the city, with another medical student named Melissa. We had many small tasks: treating a wounded person brought in from the mountains, hiding medicines and passing them on, working in the clandestine clinics. It was all very dangerous. To be caught with medicines outside of the hospital meant death by torture. To be found treating a wounded combatant meant an immediate bullet. We both understood this, but we gave each other so much support, so much love. We were more than sisters. I still weep when I think of Melissa.

I don't know how she was found out, but she was. Things had grown so terrible in the city. Every day, our people were captured and tortured. And under that kind of torture, if people do not die quickly, they will talk. They cannot help it. So perhaps someone spoke of her, described her, gave away her next meeting point. Who knows — it doesn't matter. I found her in the morgue with so many others. She was naked and battered, her face bluish from strangulation, small razor cuts and cigarette burns up and down her arms and legs. Her autopsy report showed vaginal slashes, as if her captors, once finished with her themselves, had raped her with a broken bottle. Her eyes were gone, the sockets filled with mud. Looking down at her, I felt all my physician's arts were useless. It is so strange — it was not her injuries that hurt me the most. She was the same as all the others, there on the metal slabs that day. I had grown used to it. The pain was just from the loss of her, the loss for all of us left living.

That was the day I left for the mountains. I knew they would be coming for me soon. But that wasn't the real reason I left. I knew I could die just as quickly in the mountains. I could have fled the country to safety, but I chose not to. I had made a decision — I had decided to fight. I had decided that when those animals came looking for me, to kill me in that way, by God they were going to find me with a gun in my hands.

. . . I loved my work. I was the unit physician, but I was also responsible for physical fitness programs in the morning and for political education. The fitness program was often comical, especially when we got some macho young *compas* straight in from the city. I would always tell them to take it easy the first few days, to take things gradually and build up their bodies with time. But of course, they would always want to keep up with the women, even those of us who had been up there for months and months. After a heavy session of squats and abdominals, let alone the mountain climbing it takes just to get from tent to tent, it was not unusual to see some proud newcomer limping around sheepishly for a few days. But you must never laugh at a beginner. They learned for themselves, just as they learned that cooking and sewing and washing were no longer only women's work. All of us had a lot to learn, or unlearn, up there in the mountains.

It was the political work that I loved the best. We would all sit together in a big circle and talk about our heritage, the conquest, the problems of land distribution in our country, the racism. Most of our people were Maya from small villages, taught since birth that they were inferior. My goal, in teaching, was to convince them that they counted, that they had equal value, that they had much to say and much to give. My goal was to tell them that the new world, after our triumph, would be theirs. My reward was the expression on their faces. And you should hear the things they had to say, once they believed that they would be listened to with respect. So many ideas, so much wisdom these gentle people had stored up in their minds. Our country will be in good hands, some day. This much I know.

I would have stayed up in the mountains forever. I was happy enough with my work and my life, even though it was dangerous and often sad.

I was in love with another young *compa*, Mario. We fought side by side in combat, and we could talk about anything. He had little formal education, but he was very intelligent, and respected women as revolutionaries and as equals. He was very quiet and kindly, and completely dedicated. That is why we are not together now. When I was hurt later on, he could have stayed in the city with me while I recovered. But he chose to go back to combat. He knew how much he was needed in the mountains, and so that was the end of that. I respected his decision and I still do, but that doesn't mean it wasn't painful at the time. Most of the story I am going to tell you now is about painful memories, but I want to tell it anyway. I want you to write about it for us.

The day I was shot started out like any other day. I was on kitchen duty that morning, washing pots at the edge of the river. Some other *compas* were swimming nearby, getting cleaned up after hauling supplies from the bottom of the volcano, splashing water at me. What we didn't know was that one of our new people, a young *compa* named Marcelino, had slipped away during the night to head back towards his village. He had a serious alcoholism problem which he had not told us about, and in a moment of despair, he had decided he could not handle the situation, and had left all alone. We would have escorted him down, to safety, but he had been too ashamed to tell us of his problem. He did not get far before the army caught and tortured him, and it did not take long to make him talk. I am sorry for him, when I think of this. He only wanted to go home. Instead he met a bad death and almost took the rest of us with him.

I was bending over a large iron cauldron when the first hail of bullets hit us. It took me completely by surprise. I heard the explosion of gunfire, from so many, many guns and saw a river of blood pouring from my face. For a moment, I couldn't feel much and was able to crawl to safety behind some big rocks at the river's edge. Our *compas* had appeared instantly on the ledge above us, and fought back against the soldiers with so much strength that we were protected. It is thanks to them that I and the others in the river that day were neither killed nor captured. I lay behind the rocks for a long time while they fought. The bullet had taken off the right half of my jaw, and I was bleeding heavily, but all I could do was wrap up my face in the bandana I had been wearing and lie still. I knew the injury was very serious, and thought I would probably die, except that it hurt like hell. I had always been told that when you are truly close to death, there is no pain. So I lay there feeling cheated and mad — mad that not only was I going to die, but that this "no pain" stuff was just an old fairy tale. The worst part, though, was listening to the other wounded ones crying out for help. I was their doctor, but I couldn't even move a finger to help them. I could only lie there and listen, and wonder who was hurt, and how badly. This was the worst.

The battle went on for a long time, but I don't know how long. I fainted off and on, but I lived through it. I woke up to the sound of someone whispering my name nearby, and I tossed some pebbles to attract their attention. Then I saw the anxious faces of my friends leaning over me, gentle hands pulling me upright, checking my body for other injuries. People had seen me go down and thought I had been shot through the head, so they were really happy to find me not only alive but conscious, as well. They hauled me away from the river back to a hiding place where the rest of the *compas* were waiting. . . .

It took us ten days to get out of the mountains. . . .

On the tenth day . . . we staggered into a small village. It was a Mayan community, but you must not tell the name. Can you believe that the entire village came running to help us? There we were, ragged, bloody, armed and in uniform, and they still took us in and cared for us, even though the army was searching for us everywhere. I collapsed completely as we arrived. My legs had kept moving for as long as they had to, but once we reached safety, I had nothing left. A gray-haired, old *campesino* picked me up and carried me into a hut. His wife cleared off the bed for me, and they dressed me in clean clothes and washed my wounded face. Then — I will always remember this — she fixed me a good, strong soup that I could drink through the IV tubes. It was my first real food in so many days. I swear that this soup saved my life. Mario came to the hut, too, and stayed with me until I was taken away to the city.

Everyone was taken in and hidden. For most of our *compas,* hiding was easy. Dressed in civilian clothes, they became the Mayan *campesinos* they had been before the war. No one would know they had not been born there. They rested and helped work in the fields, while the villagers took care of the wounded and brought us food and news about the army activities nearby. The villagers also smuggled messages for us to the capital to help us reconnect with another platoon and to arrange medical care for us. The entire village could have been wiped out for this, but no one ever spoke of us, no one ever gave us away. A community commitment had been made to take care of us, and that commitment was honored by every single villager. Few words were spoken, and they never asked for thanks or payment. To me, it is people like these who are the true heroes of this war. Even though you must not tell the name of this village, you must tell what these people gave to us, what they risked for us.

I think we were there for close to a month while arrangements were made. Mario had made contact with his brother, Alejo, in the capital, and I was to stay with him in one of our safe houses while I received medical treatment. Alejo was the older one, and had brought Mario into the movement. The two brothers were incredibly close. I was happy to think that I would have a chance to know him, but when the car came to take me away, it was very difficult. I knew what Mario was going back to, and that we would probably never see each other again. And in fact we never did. Maybe this part I will not talk about. I arrived safely in the capital, which was no small achievement given my marked face and all the army roadblocks. Alejo took me in and cared for me as his own sister.

I wish this story had a happier ending, but it doesn't. It was early 1982, when the terror in the capital was at its height. The *compas* in our urban front fought bravely to the very end, but they came close to extermination. In the mountains, you stand a chance, but in the city there was just too much surveillance, too many terrified informants trying to get their own family members out of torture cells. We had a number of houses in the capital, but we watched them fall, one by one. Sometimes it was on television, the footage of tanks and bazookas destroying a quiet, middle-class home on a tree-lined street. Sometimes it was in the papers. There were many pictures of the dead, our *compas,* sometimes shot to death, often tortured. We all knew that our time was not far off. . . .

$$\boxed{87}$$

AUNG SAN SUU KYI

From *Letters from Burma*

The author of these letters heads the democratic political party that won election in Burma in 1980. In consequence, she was placed under house arrest by the brutal military junta (SLORC, for State Law and Order Restoration Council), which has continued to rule. Despite her receipt of the Nobel Prize in 1991 and continued devotional support from the Burmese people, the generals have refused to let this daughter of Aung San — Burma's national hero who was assassinated in 1947 just before Burma achieved independence — take office and sometimes even leave her house.

In these letters, written to a Japanese newspaper in 1996, Suu Kyi reveals an unusual combination of the personal and political, some might say the patriotic without the patriarchal. Is this a view of politics that a male politician would be unlikely to hold?

Aung San Suu Kyi, *Letters from Burma* (New York: Penguin, 1996), 19–21, 55–57.

Thinking Historically

Is there such a thing as women's politics? Do women vote differently than men? If so, what is that difference? Construct a theory that explains it.

Some people have pointed to the relatively large number of women presidents and prime ministers in South Asia in recent years. Women have been elected to govern India, Pakistan, Sri Lanka, as well as Burma. Can you formulate a theory that might explain this?

Many would say that particular women who have governed South Asia — Indira Gandhi of India, Benizar Bhutto of Pakistan, Sirimavo Bandaranaike of Sri Lanka — have not governed any differently than men. Perhaps politics has more to do with social background, interests, wealth, and class than it does with gender. Try to formulate a theory about women in politics that is based on the readings of this chapter.

The Peacock and the Dragon

The tenth day of the waning moon of the month of Tazaungdine marks National Day in Burma. It is the anniversary of the boycott against the 1920 Rangoon University Act which was seen by the Burmese as a move to restrict higher education to a privileged few. This boycott, which was initiated by university students, gained widespread support and could be said to have been the first step in the movement for an independent Burma. National Day is thus a symbol of the intimate and indissoluble link between political and intellectual freedom and of the vital role that students have played in the politics of Burma.

This year the seventy-fifth anniversary of National Day fell on 16 November. A committee headed by elder politicians and prominent men of letters was formed to plan the commemoration ceremony. It was decided that the celebrations should be on a modest scale in keeping with our financial resources and the economic situation of the country. The programme was very simple: some speeches, the presentation of prizes to those who had taken part in essay competitions organized by the National League for Democracy, and the playing of songs dating back to the days of the independence struggle. There was also a small exhibition of photographs, old books, and magazines.

An unseasonable rain had been falling for several days before the sixteenth but on the morning of National Day itself the weather turned out to be fine and dry. Many of the guests came clad in *pinni*, a hand-woven cotton cloth that ranges in colour from a flaxen beige through varying shades of apricot and orange to burnt umber. During the independence struggle *pinni* had acquired the same significance in Burma as *khaddi* in India, a symbol of patriotism and a practical sign of support for native goods.

Since 1988 it has also become the symbol of the movement for democracy. A *pinni* jacket worn with a white collarless shirt and a Kachin sarong (a tartan pattern in purple, black, and green) is the unofficial uniform for "democracy men." The dress for "democracy women" is a *pinni aingyi* (Burmese style blouse) with a traditional hand-woven sarong. During my campaign trip to the state of Kachin in 1989 I once drove through an area considered unsafe because it was within a zone where insurgents were known to be active. For mile upon mile men clad in *pinni* jackets on which the red badge of NLD [National League for Democracy] gleamed bravely stood as a "guard of honour" along the route, entirely unarmed. It was a proud and joyous sight.

The seventy-fifth anniversary of National Day brought a proud and joyous sight too. The guests were not all clad in *pinni* but there was about them a brightness that was pleasing to both the eye and the heart. The younger people were full of quiet enthusiasm and the older ones seemed rejuvenated. A well-known student politician of the 1930s who had become notorious in his mature years for the shapeless shirt, shabby denim trousers, scuffed shoes (gum boots during the monsoons), and battered hat in which he would tramp around town was suddenly transformed into a dapper gentleman in full Burmese national costume. All who knew him were stunned by the sudden picture of elegance he presented and our photographer hastened to record such an extraordinary vision.

The large bamboo and thatch pavilion that had been put up to receive the thousand guests was decorated with white banners on which were printed the green figure of a dancing peacock. As a backdrop to the stage there was a large dancing peacock, delicately executed on a white disc. This bird is the symbol of the students who first awoke the political consciousness of the people of Burma. It represents a national movement that culminated triumphantly with the independence of the country.

The orchestra had arrived a little late as there had been an attempt to try to "persuade" the musicians not to perform at our celebration. But their spirits were not dampened. They stayed on after the end of the official ceremony to play and sing nationalist songs from the old days. The most popular of these was *Nagani*, "Red Dragon." *Nagani* was the name of a book club founded by a group of young politicians in 1937 with the intention of making works on politics, economics, history, and literature accessible to the people of Burma. The name of the club became closely identified with patriotism and a song was written about the prosperity that would come to the country through the power of the Red Dragon.

Nagani was sung by a young man with a strong, beautiful voice and we all joined in the chorus while some of the guests went up on stage and performed Burmese dances. But beneath the light-hearted merriment ran a current of serious intent. The work of our national movement remains unfinished. We have still to achieve the prosperity promised by the dragon. It is not yet time for the triumphant dance of the peacock. . . .

A Baby in the Family

A couple of weeks ago some friends of mine became grandparents for the first time when their daughter gave birth to a little girl. The husband accepted his new status as grandfather with customary joviality, while the wife, too young-looking and pretty to get into the conventional idea of a cosily aged grandmother, found it a somewhat startling experience. The baby was the first grandchild for the "boy's side" as well, so she was truly a novel addition to the family circle, the subject of much adoring attention. I was told the paternal grandfather was especially pleased because the baby had been born in the Burmese month of *Pyatho* — an auspicious time for the birth of a girl child.

In societies where the birth of a girl is considered a disaster, the atmosphere of excitement and pride surrounding my friends' granddaughter would have caused astonishment. In Burma there is no prejudice against girl babies. In fact, there is a general belief that daughters are more dutiful and loving than sons and many Burmese parents welcome the birth of a daughter as an assurance that they will have somebody to take care of them in their old age.

My friends' granddaughter was only twelve days old when I went to admire her. She lay swaddled in pristine white on a comfortable pile of blankets and sheets spread on the wooden floor of my friends' bungalow, a small dome of mosquito netting arched prettily over her. It had been a long time since I had seen such a tiny baby and I was struck by its miniature perfection. I do not subscribe to the Wodehousian view that all babies look like poached eggs. Even if they do not have clearly defined features, babies have distinct expressions that mark them off as individuals from birth. And they certainly have individual cries, a fact I learned soon after the birth of my first son. It took me a few hours to realize that the yells of each tiny vociferous inmate of the maternity hospital had its own unique pitch, cadence, range, and grace-notes.

My friends' grandchild, however, did not provide me with a chance to familiarize myself with her particular milk call. Throughout my visit she remained as inanimate and still as a carved papoose on display in a museum, oblivious of the fuss and chatter around her. At one time her eyelids fluttered slightly and she showed signs of stirring but it was a false alarm. She remained resolutely asleep even when I picked her up and we all clustered around to have our photograph taken with the new star in our firmament.

Babies, I have read somewhere, are specially constructed to present an appealingly vulnerable appearance aimed at arousing tender, protective instincts: only then can tough adults be induced to act as willing slaves to demanding little beings utterly incapable of doing anything for themselves. It is claimed that there is something about the natural smell of a baby's skin that invites cuddles and kisses. Certainly I like both the shape and smell of babies, but I wonder whether their attraction does not lie in something more than merely physical attributes. Is it not the thought of a life stretching out like a shining clean slate on which might one day be written the most beautiful prose and poetry of existence that engenders such joy in the hearts of the parents and grandparents of a newly born child? The birth of a baby is an occasion for weaving hopeful dreams about the future.

However, in some families parents are not able to indulge in long dreams over their children. The infant mortality rate in Burma is 94 per 1000 live births, the fourth highest among the nations of the East Asia and Pacific Region. The mortality rate for those under the age of five too is the fourth highest in the region, 147 per 1000. And the maternal mortality rate is the third highest in the region at the official rate of 123 per 100 000 live births. (United Nations agencies surmise that the actual maternal mortality rate is in fact higher, 140 or more per 100 000.)

The reasons for these high mortality rates are malnutrition, lack of access to safe water and sanitation, lack of access to health services, and lack of caring capacity, which includes programmes for childhood development, primary education, and health education. In summary, there is a strong need in Burma for greater investment in health and education. Yet government expenditure in both sectors, as a proportion of the budget, has been falling steadily. Education accounted for 5.9 per cent of the budget in 1992–3, 5.2 per cent in 1993–4, and 5 per cent in 1994–5. Similarly, government spending on health care has dropped from 2.6 per cent in 1992–3, to 1.8 per cent in 1993–4, and 1.6 per cent in 1994–5.

Some of the best indicators of a country developing along the right lines are healthy mothers giving birth to healthy children who are assured of good care and a sound education that will enable them to face the challenges of a changing world. Our dreams for the future of the children of Burma have to be woven firmly around a commitment to better health care and better education.

REFLECTIONS

Can there be a history of women, even a history of women during the last half of the twentieth century? Or are the lives of women too diverse —

globally, economically, politically, culturally — to make a single, coherent story? Is the history of women during the last fifty years markedly different from the history of men or the history of humanity?

This chapter gives only a hint of the diversity of women's lives. We included China's hopeful marriage law at the beginning of the chapter but nothing about the failures to observe it, or about women who were forced out of work to make room for men, or about girls who were sold into virtual slavery, or about young women forced to work long hours in sweatshops. Nor did we include any discussion of glamorous models in Shanghai, rich capitalists and poor sex workers in Hong Kong, or ordinary mothers, wives, and workers for whom the law of 1950 *did* make a difference.

While Betty Friedan verbalized the feelings of many American women in 1963, how many women today, exhausted by working long hours that barely cover the costs of child care and commuting, would consider returning to a fifties world of motherhood and housework? How can two African novelists speak for poor, illiterate, rural women in areas devastated by civil wars or AIDS? How important are national differences? In what sense, if any, does an Algerian woman who is Muslim speak for a Muslim woman in Egypt or Iran or Pakistan, or for a Christian woman in Algeria? We have not even considered women from the Middle East, India, Russia, and Europe.

These questions are not meant to be an exercise in what literary critics call "deconstructing the text"; rather, they are intended to point out the enormous variety of women's experiences. Of course, the historian is forever seeking patterns and process, but finding even the general direction of change is not as simple as it might seem.

Have the lives of women improved over the course of the last hundred or the last fifty years? It is commonly thought that the twentieth century was extremely important in freeing women from the bonds of patriarchal limitations. Often, this process is divided into two stages, the first consisting of gaining the vote in the early decades of the century in Europe and America, and the second, the successes of the women's movement since 1960. This second wave broadened the feminist critique from concerns about elections to issues of equality in the workplace and patriarchy as a social and cultural force, ultimately resulting in a cohesive movement, improved public awareness, and specific legislation regarding women's rights. In this way, the movement of the sixties became public policy.

Yet, this history belongs only to women from Europe and North America. Is it accurate for women from Asia, Africa, and Latin America? To a certain extent, ideas about equal rights and the rights of women that were first instituted in Europe and North America have surfaced in less prosperous regions of the world, sometimes through the pressure of international organizations or the persuasion of Western-trained elites. Still, adoption of Western ways has not always benefited women. As nations in Asia and Africa became independent after World War II, male-dominated political bureaucracies often replaced more informal networks that had previously given greater prominence to women. In some cases, as in Algeria, women were given full equality with men during the national struggle, but as soon as independence was won they were forced out of the public realm, domiciled and veiled, becoming mute signs of male authority.

For most women today, the world has been shaped less by political struggles and more by the expanding global market. Poor women in Brazil, Indonesia, China, and the Philippines have seized the opportunity to escape the authority of fathers and village elders to work in modern factories that pay far more than they ever imagined, but barely enough to survive in distant cities after sending money home. The victory of market forces in former "command economies," like Russia, Poland, and Lithuania (countries where most doctors were women), has been accompanied by drastic declines in the employment of women and men, as well as declines in the percentage of professional women.

If there is not a single history of women that is different from a single history of humanity, there are millions, indeed billions, of histories of women, women's acts, women's worlds. The selections in this chapter hint at just a few of those histories. Perhaps the most useful service our brief discussions here can serve is to encourage you to explore women's stories further. In your studies, branch off in different directions: Study women in Algeria, maybe Muslim women or women in Africa, for example.

All of the women featured in this chapter are writers. Assia Djebar and Carolina Maria de Jesus give us especially poignant accounts of what their writing means to them. You might study the ways in which women use their writing as witness, mirror, and tools. After rereading the selections in this chapter and contemplating the role of writing, you might formulate a theory about women and words, or the link between writing and women's liberation. You might also notice that in many of these selections women refer to their bodies or their appearance. After carefully rereading the selections and giving the topic some quiet contemplation, you might ask yourself whether men and women write differently. You might ask yourself any number of questions and begin to formulate new theories that will help improve your level of understanding.

14

Globalization

HISTORICAL CONTEXT
The World, 1960–2000

Globalization is an ecological, political, cultural, and economic process whereby individuals, nations, and regions of the world become increasingly integrated and interdependent. We witness the process of globalization everywhere. Technologically, modes of communication are becoming more varied, instantaneous, and more continuous, and the time it takes to travel is becoming much less; all of these necessarily connect people and bring them closer. Economically, capital, labor, raw materials, and finished products are moved at increasing speeds and with more lasting impact by global, rather than national, markets. Culturally, the peoples of the world are watching the same films and television programs, speaking the same languages, wearing the same clothes, enjoying the same amusements, listening to the same music. National boundaries, cultures, allegiances, and languages have become quaint relics of the past.

Germany, among other countries, is openly embracing this trend. For example, a major German publishing house, Bertelsmann, with newspaper, magazine, and book holdings throughout the world, has decided to simplify communications by making English the official corporate language. Another German corporation, DaimlerChrysler, maker of Mercedes and new owner of Chrysler, recently considered moving its headquarters to New York City, which hails itself as "the capital of the world."

The process of globalization — the "shrinking" and integration of the world — is not a story that began in 1960. In some ways it dates back to 1492 and the integration of the eastern and western hemispheres, or to the nineteenth century, with the industrial network of railroads, steamships, and telegraph lines ushering in an age of great intercontinental migration. Nevertheless, this chapter focuses on globalization as it relates to the developments of the last forty years: commercial jet air travel, instant international phone connections, satellite

503

television, international corporations, the Internet, global markets, tourism, and entertainment.

The integration of the world has occurred at every level: ecological, political, cultural, and economic. We will briefly examine each of these levels in an effort to understand its impact on our lives today. In selection 88 we begin with the most fundamental level of global integration — the ecological and biological. While some ecological problems are local, their impact rarely is; population pressure, resource depletion, and species destruction all demand our attention and concern. In an age when seeds, germs, and animals have so few boundaries preventing their dispersal, we must heighten our awareness of their potential impact. The likelihood that the HIV (the virus that causes AIDS) virus originated in central Africa gives no protection to the children of HIV-positive drug users in Brazil, infected prostitutes in Thailand, or recipients of tainted blood in Russia. The continued enlargement of the hole in the earth's ozone layer over Antarctica does not have only local causes, consequences, or significance.

Selection 89 explores the disappearance of languages and cultures, every bit as alarming as the loss of biodiversity. We live in an age when a few international languages and cultures have put the displaced on the defensive, sometimes eliciting angry tribal responses. The conflict between the forces of tribalism (Jihad) and universalism in its coercive, consumerist form (McWorld) is explored in selection 90, while selection 91 examines a single case of cultural globalization, a Western exhibition of African art.

Selection 92 argues that globalization has led to new political alignments based on culture and religion — age-old distinctions that are in some ways more volatile than those of nation-states. Disputing this assessment, selection 93 insists that national and secular interests are reinforced by global integration. Finally, selection 94 explores the global impact of the expanding market economy and warns against the backlash that uncontrolled capitalism might cause.

THINKING HISTORICALLY
Understanding Process

All of the readings in this chapter propose large-scale theories of how things change. They provide overviews of recent global changes, citing dynamics that explain how the changes occurred, offering predictions as to where the changes may take us.

Read these selections to determine how the authors understand historical process. Historical process is large-scale change, interaction of significant forces. Some would characterize these forces as economic, technological, cultural, environmental, or political. Others might say that there can be no single or primary force of change. Yet, the authors featured in this chapter describe, from different tacks, a far-reaching transformative process operating in the world today.

In this chapter, we will evaluate theories of change and the problems that these changes pose. We will also critique how each author detects and diagnoses the most important changes, and how each understands the historical process by which our world is being transformed.

88

EDWARD O. WILSON

Conservation: The Next Hundred Years

A noted biologist, Edward O. Wilson has been writing on the problem of species depletion since the 1970s. What, according to Wilson, are the consequences of species losses? How much faster are species being lost today compared with the past? What does Wilson say should be done? What do you think of his recommendations?

Thinking Historically

Notice how Wilson describes the process by which species become extinct. In the first paragraph he writes of "accelerating technology guided by material acquisitiveness" and "vast numbers of seemingly innocent decisions." How do these phrases describe the process?

Wilson discusses population growth and deforestation. Does he see them as the problem or as causes of the problem? Will the process of correction require a major reversal of the process that originally caused the problem? If so, how does Wilson expect that to happen?

The tide of the earth's population is rising, the reservoir of the earth's living resources is falling. . . . There is only one solution: Man must recognize the necessity of cooperating with nature. He must temper his demands and use and conserve the natural living resources of this earth in a manner that alone can provide for the continuation of his civiliza-

---

Edward O. Wilson, "Conservation: The Next Hundred Years," in *Conservation for the Twenty-First Century*, ed. David Western and Mary Pearl (Oxford: Oxford University Press, 1989), 3–7.

tion. The final answer is to be found only through comprehension of the enduring processes of nature. The time for defiance is at an end.

Fairfield Osborn's closing declaration in *Our Plundered Planet* (1948) could have been written this morning. Its relevance after forty years serves as a reminder that accelerating technology guided by material acquisitiveness has brought no remedies, that a generation of new scientific research has only focused the problem into a sharper, more frightening image. The pace of population growth and environmental destruction has continued with no visible pause, having become a case study in the principle of unintended results wherein mass effects float up from vast numbers of seemingly innocent individual decisions.

What is needed is a fuller sense of what we possess, and stand to lose, by the innocent slippage. It can be said that every country has three forms of wealth: material, cultural, and biological. The first two are the basis of almost all our economic and political life. The third, composed of the fauna and flora and the uses put to natural diversity, is far more potent for long-term human welfare than generally appreciated, and it is declining irreversibly through the accelerating extinction of species and genetic strains. Furthermore, the problem is distinctively international in scope. By far the greatest variety of life occurs in the developing countries, especially in the tropics, and it is there also that population growth, environmental degradation, and species extinction have reached crisis levels.

The scope of the problem can be briefly summarized as follows: The rate of population growth has begun to slow on every continent except Africa, where it remains as rapid as ever. But even with a modest amount of global amelioration, most demographers still project a doubling of the standing population, from the present five billion to at least ten billion, before it finally levels off around the middle of the 2100s. Most of the growth is destined to be concentrated in just a few regions, principally the Indian subcontinent, the Middle East, Africa, and Latin America. So disproportionate is this distribution that the projected growth for North America, all of Europe, and the Soviet Union is less than the additions expected in either Bangladesh or Nigeria. The World Bank has estimated that Nigeria, now home to ninety-one million people, will add 527 million, more than the current population of the entire continent. Few believe that it can support this number and escape appalling misery.

Well over two billion people have already been added in the developing countries since 1932, more than the entire world population of that time. This spurt of growth is entirely unprecedented in the history of the world, and it has already led to a great deal of poverty and failed hopes. According to The World Bank, of the 2.5 billion people now living in the tropics, one billion live in a condition of absolute poverty. This means that the family head is unable to count on being able to provide food, shelter, and clothing for himself and his family from one day to the next. Furthermore, according to the World Health Organization, one of four persons in the tropics is malnourished. These are the people who are exerting the greatest pressure on the most species-rich habitats, with predictably devastating results. They are abetted by large-scale, poorly planned development projects initiated by governments and corporations. In light of these facts, the linkage between population growth, economic welfare, and the preservation of the earth's biological wealth becomes obvious. . . .

. . . The rate of tropical forest destruction is now reasonably well known, thanks to improvements in satellite scanning and increasingly accurate ground surveys. By the late 1970s, according to estimates from the Food and Agricultural Organization and United Nations Environmental Programme, 76,000 square kilometers, or nearly 1 percent of the total cover per annum, were being permanently cleared or converted into the shifting-cultivation cycle. The absolute amount is greater than the area of West Virginia or the entire country of Costa Rica. In effect, most of this land is being permanently cleared, that is, reduced to a state in which natural reforestation will be very difficult if not impossible to achieve. By the present time the reduction could easily be 100,000 square kilometers a year. . . .

The current reduction of diversity thus seems destined to approach that of the great natural catastrophes at the end of the Paleozoic and Mesozoic eras — in other words, the most extreme for 65 million years. In at least one important respect, the modern episode exceeds anything in the geological past. In the earlier mass extinctions, which some scientists believe were caused by large meteorite strikes, most of the plants survived even though animal diversity was severely reduced. Now, for the first time, due to deforestation, plant diversity is also declining sharply. The ultimate result is impossible to predict, but it is not something, I think, with which humanity will want to gamble.

What Is to Be Done?

A great many creative scholars and policymakers from previously unconnected disciplines have recently converged on the problems of international conservation. They foreshadow the collective enterprise likely to dominate the conservation movement during the twenty-first century. I will try to summarize the outlook very briefly in the form of seven trends or prospects, as follows.

1. A complete biotic survey. I am convinced that the needs of humanity in the context of the biodiversity crisis demand nothing less than a complete catalog of life on the earth. For how can we conserve and use our inherited biological wealth if we don't even know what it is? The beginning of wisdom, according to a Chinese maxim, is knowing things by their right names. Beyond that first step we will profit

from a vastly increased study of the distribution, biology, and evolutionary history of each species in turn. . . .

2. Ex situ conservation. The biotic survey should be accompanied by a more nearly comprehensive effort to build larger seed banks than now exist, as well as to expand populations of some of the most threatened species of plants and animals in zoos and botanical gardens. Central data centers, such as those now in existence for zoo animals, are needed to coordinate such activities and prevent entire loss of biotas and groups of organisms. . . .

3. Combining conservation and economic development. Conservation is inseparably linked to the future of economic development by a form of mutualistic symbiosis. Biodiversity will be impoverished without the shaping of land use in a form that preserves it, and economic development will be hindered and eventually reversed if it omits the kind of environmental policy that reserves and uses biodiversity. Applied scientists and land management experts agree with near unanimity that the crucial step is the improvement of land already in use, in order to take pressure off the natural habitats. . . .

4. Pressures from assistance and lending agencies. It is in the interest of each country in turn to use its natural resources so as to get a sustained yield rather than a short-term yield, even when the latter may be very high. The question for the pure utilitarian is whether to take a tidy one-time profit or a vastly larger profit over generations of time. There is only one moral choice. To cut down a virgin rain forest may produce a few million dollars during a ten-year period, but then it is gone forever, the age-old patrimony of the country having been diminished by the loss of many of its native species, the soil having been impoverished, and the hydrological cycle and water tables soon to be altered unfavorably. . . .

5. Restoration ecology. A major effort of the next century will almost certainly be in this relatively new subdiscipline. The trend will be animated by the heart-warming idea that it is possible not only to hold on to some natural areas, but also to start to enlarge them so as to secure the preservation of biodiversity for all time. We can heal the world, in other words, and in so doing make it a healthier, more stable place for our descendants. National parks and biosphere reserves can be expanded. Natural ecosystems can be reconstituted in forms that both restore the original biodiversity and add to productivity in agriculture and forestry. . . .

6. Engagement by the social sciences. One of the many weaknesses of the social sciences is their failure to make realistic assessments of the environment, including biodiversity. They have virtually nothing to say about how behavior and economic health are related to the living world in which the human mind evolved over millions of years. In this respect neoclassical economics is bankrupt. Its quantitative models of optimization and equilibrium have no realistic measure to place on the

value of the environment. Economists cannot factor in opportunity costs, the losses incurred when habitats are destroyed and species go extinct. They are unable to handle multiple margins outside a narrowly defined market economy. . . .

7. Aesthetic and moral reasoning. Environmental ethics, still a small and neglected branch of intellectual activity, deserves to become a major branch of the humanities during the next hundred years. In the end, when all the accounting is done, conservation will boil down to a decision of ethics based on empirical knowledge: How we value the natural world in which we evolved and now, increasingly, how we regard our status as individuals. We are fundamentally mammals and free spirits, not engines of economic and social progress, who reached our high level of rationality by the perpetual creation of new options. . . .

89

DAVID CRYSTAL

Vanishing Languages

As a speaker of Welsh, David Crystal has had firsthand experience with the declining use of a minority language as well as its adulteration by English, the majority language of Great Britain. He makes the case here for preserving the Welsh language he knows and loves and other languages that also are becoming extinct. If no one speaks these languages, why should he or anyone else care? In what ways is the loss of a language, or even many languages, a matter of concern for those who do not speak them?

Thinking Historically

What is the process, according to the author, that leads to the disappearance of languages? Is this process inevitable? Can it be stopped or controlled? What, if any, are the processes that can reverse the decline or disappearance of a language?

Notice the way in which Crystal calls for the help of international organizations to reverse the process of language loss. Does this involvement introduce a new force, one different from the cause of the problem?

David Crystal, "Vanishing Languages," in *Civilization* Vol. 4 (February/March 1997): 40–45.

There's a Welsh proverb I've known for as long as I can remember: *"Cenedl heb iaith, cenedl heb galon."* It means, "A nation without a language [is] a nation without a heart," and it's become more poignant over the years as more and more families who live around me in North Wales speak in English instead of Welsh across the dinner table.

Welsh, the direct descendant of the Celtic language that was spoken throughout most of Britain when the Anglo-Saxons invaded, has long been under threat from English. England's economic and technological dominance has made English the language of choice, causing a decline in the number of Welsh speakers. And although the decline has steadied in the past fifteen years, less than 20 percent of the population of Wales today can speak Welsh in addition to English.

The Welsh language is clearly in trouble. Someday, it may even join the rapidly growing list of extinct languages, which includes Gothic and Hittite, Manx and Cornish, Powhatan and Piscataway. If present trends continue, four of the world's languages will die [in the next two months]. Eighteen more will be gone [in a year]. A century from now, one-half of the world's six thousand or more languages may be extinct.

The decline is evident the world over. Consider the case of Sene: In 1978 there were fewer than ten elderly speakers remaining in the Morobe province of Papua New Guinea. Or Ngarla: In 1981 there were just two speakers of the Aboriginal language still alive in northwest Western Australia. And in 1982 there were ten surviving speakers of Achumawi out of a tribal population of eight hundred in northeastern California. Does it matter? When the last representatives of these peoples die, they take with them their oral history and culture, though their passing is rarely noticed. Sometimes, years later, we find hints of a culture's existence, in the form of inscriptions or fragments of text, but many of these — the Linear A inscriptions from ancient Crete, for example — remain undeciphered to this day. . . .

Taking a conservative estimate of six thousand languages worldwide, one fact becomes immediately clear: Languages reveal enormous differences in populations. At one extreme, there is English, spoken by more people globally than any other language in history, probably by a third of the world's population as a first, second, or foreign language. At the other extreme is Ngarla (and most of the other languages of the native peoples of Australia, Canada, and the United States), whose total population of speakers may amount to just one or two. And then there are closely related groups of languages like the Maric family in Queensland, Australia, which consists of twelve languages. When it was surveyed in 1981, only one of these, Bidyara, had as many as twenty speakers. Most had fewer than five. Five of them had only one speaker each.

The loss of languages may have accelerated recently, but it is hardly a new problem. In the nineteenth century, there were more than one thousand Indian languages in Brazil, many spoken in small, isolated villages in the rain forest; today there are a mere two hundred, most of which have never been written down or recorded. In North America, the three hundred or more indigenous languages spoken in the past have been halved. . . .

A dramatic illustration of how a language disappears took place in Venezuela in the 1960s. As part of the drive to tap the vast resources of the Amazonian rain forests, a group of Western explorers passed through a small village on the banks of the Coluene River. Unfortunately, they brought with them the influenza virus, and the villagers, who lacked any immunity, were immediately susceptible to the disease. Fewer than ten people survived. A human tragedy, it was a linguistic tragedy too, for this village contained the only speakers of the Trumai language. And with so few people left to pass it on, the language was doomed.

Other languages — such as Welsh and Scottish Gaelic — have been threatened when indigenous populations have moved or been split up. Brighter economic prospects tempt young members of the community away from their villages. And even if they choose to stay, it doesn't take much exposure to a dominant culture to motivate ambitious young people to replace their mother tongue with a language that gives them better access to education, jobs, and new technology.

A language's fortunes are tied to its culture's. Just as one language holds sway over others when its speakers gain power — politically, economically, or technologically — it diminishes, and may even die, when they lose that prominence. Latin, now used almost exclusively in its written form, had its day as a world language because of the power of Rome. English, once promoted by the British Empire, is thriving today chiefly because of the prominence of the U.S.A., but it was once an endangered language, threatened by the Norman invaders of Britain in the eleventh century, who brought with them a multitude of French words. In South America, Spanish and Portuguese, the languages of colonialists, have replaced many of the indigenous Indian tongues.

The death of languages is most noticeable in parts of the world where large numbers of languages are concentrated in a few small geographical regions. Travel to the tropical forests of the Morobe province in Papua New Guinea and you'll find five isolated villages in a mountain valley where fewer than one thousand people speak the Kapin language. They support themselves by agriculture and have little contact with outsiders. Other tiny communities, speaking completely different languages, live in neighboring valleys. Linguists estimate that in the country as a whole there is approximately one language for every two hundred people. Indeed, three countries, which together amount to less than 2 percent of the earth's land area, support seventeen hundred — or a quarter — of the world's living languages: Papua New Guinea has 862; Indonesia, 701; and Malaysia, 140. These countries' isolation and physical geography account in large part for the existence of such concentrations, and it is hardly surprising to find that, as remote areas of the globe have opened up for trade or tourism, there has been a dramatic increase in the rate of language death. Valuable reserves of gold, silver and timber in Papua New Guinea, for example, are bringing speculators to the islands — and with them their languages. . . .

Is it sensible to try to preserve a language (or culture) when its recent history suggests that it is heading for extinction? In the next few years, international organizations may have to decide, on chiefly economic grounds, which languages should be kept alive and which allowed to die.

The publication in the early 1900s of major surveys of the world's languages has brought some of these issues before the public. UNESCO's [United Nations Educational Scientific and Cultural Organization] Endangered Languages Project, the Foundation for Endangered Languages (established in the U.K. in 1995), and the Linguistic Society of America's Committee on Endangered Languages and Their Preservation are fostering research into the status of minority languages. Information is gradually becoming available on the Internet — such as through the World Wide Web site of the Summer Institute of Linguistics. And a clearinghouse for the world's endangered languages was established in 1995, by request of UNESCO, at the University of Tokyo.

But after the fact-finding, the really hard work consists of tape-recording and transcribing the endangered languages before they die. The fieldwork procedures are well established among a small number of dedicated linguists, who assess the urgency of the need, document what is already known about the languages, extend that knowledge as much as possible, and thus help preserve languages, if only in archive form.

The concept of a language as a "national treasure" still takes many people by surprise — and even English has no international conservation archive. It is hard to imagine the long hours and energy needed to document something as complex as a language — and it's often a race against time. Thirty years ago, when anthropologist J. V. Powell began working with the Quileute Indians in Washington state, seventy members of the tribe were fluent speakers. Around that time the tribal elders decided to try to revitalize the language, writing dictionaries and grammars, and imagining a day when their children would sit around chatting in Quileute. "But," says Powell, "their prayers haven't been answered. Now they've scaled back to a more modest goal: basic familiarity rather than fluency. Powell recognized that they will not save Quileute, but it will be preserved in recordings for future scholars — and will serve as a symbol of the tribe's group identity. That may seem like a small success, but it's a far better fate than the one facing most endangered languages.

90

BENJAMIN BARBER

From *Jihad vs. McWorld*

Barber uses the terms *Jihad* and *McWorld* to refer to what he sees as the two poles of the debate about modern global culture. *McWorld* is the force of Hollywood, fast-food outlets, jeans, and Americanization. *Jihad* (the Arab word for "crusade") is used to symbolize all of the nationalist, fundamentalist, ethnocentric, and tribal rejections of McWorld. Barber's argument is that these forces have largely shaped modern culture and that despite their opposition to each other, they both prevent the development of civic society and democracy: Jihad by terrorist opposition to discussion and debate, and McWorld by turning everyone into complacent, unthinking robots. What do you think of his argument? Is it persuasive? What sort of future does he predict?

Thinking Historically

Barber argues that Jihad originated in opposition to McWorld and that the two play off each other in a way that gives them both substance and support. Jihad thrives on the insensitivity, blandness, and oppression of McWorld; McWorld needs ethnic realities to give substance and soul to its theme parks and entertainments. Thus, according to Barber, they make each other stronger by struggling against each other. Their gains of these two extreme positions come at the expense of a genuine, polite, thoughtful, and civilized civic culture. Thus, Barber argues that the conflict between Jihad and McWorld is a dialectical process that transforms the world, but not for the better. Compare this idea of a dialectical process with the ideas of process in the two preceding selections. Which process do you think is more useful in explaining how things change?

History is not over. Nor are we arrived in the wondrous land of techné[1] promised by the futurologists. The collapse of state communism has not delivered people to a safe democratic haven, and the past,

---

[1] Technology.

Benjamin Barber, *Jihad vs. McWorld: How Globalism and Tribalism Are Reshaping the World* (New York: Ballantine, 1995), 3–8.

fratricide and civil discord perduring, still clouds the horizon just behind us. Those who look back see all of the horrors of the ancient slaughterbench reenacted in disintegral nations like Bosnia, Sri Lanka, Ossetia, and Rwanda and they declare that nothing has changed. Those who look forward prophesize commercial and technological interdependence — a virtual paradise made possible by spreading markets and global technology — and they proclaim that everything is or soon will be different. The rival observers seem to consult different almanacs drawn from the libraries of contrarian planets.

Yet anyone who reads the daily papers carefully, taking in the front page accounts of civil carnage as well as the business page stories on the mechanics of the information superhighway and the economics of communication mergers, anyone who turns deliberately to take in the whole 360-degree horizon, knows that our world and our lives are caught between what [Irish poet] William Butler Yeats called the two eternities of race and soul: that of race reflecting the tribal past, that of soul anticipating the cosmopolitan future. Our secular eternities are corrupted, however, race reduced to an insignia of resentment, and soul sized down to fit the demanding body by which it now measures its needs. Neither race nor soul offers us a future that is other than bleak, neither promises a polity that is remotely democratic.

The first scenario rooted in race holds out the grim prospect of a retribalization of large swaths of humankind by war and bloodshed: a threatened balkanization of nation-states in which culture is pitted against culture, people against people, tribe against tribe, a Jihad in the name of a hundred narrowly conceived faiths against every kind of interdependence, every kind of artificial social cooperation and mutuality: against technology, against pop culture, and against integrated markets; against modernity itself as well as the future in which modernity issues. The second paints that future in shimmering pastels, a busy portrait of onrushing economic, technological, and ecological forces that demand integration and uniformity and that mesmerize peoples everywhere with fast music, fast computers, and fast food — MTV, Macintosh, and McDonald's — pressing nations into one homogenous global theme park, one McWorld tied together by communications, information, entertainment, and commerce. Caught between Babel and Disneyland, the planet is falling precipitously apart and coming reluctantly together at the very same moment.

Some stunned observers notice only Babel, complaining about the thousand newly sundered "peoples" who prefer to address their neighbors with sniper rifles and mortars; others — zealots in Disneyland — seize on futurological platitudes and the promise of virtuality, exclaiming "It's a small world after all!" Both are right, but how can that be?

We are compelled to choose between what passes as "the twilight of sovereignty" and an entropic end of all history, or a return to the past's most fractious and demoralizing discord; to "the menace of global anarchy," to [John] Milton's capital of hell, Pandaemonium; to a world totally "out of control."

The apparent truth, which speaks to the paradox at the core of this book, is that the tendencies of both Jihad *and* McWorld are at work, both visible sometimes in the same country at the very same instant. Iranian zealots keep one ear tuned to the mullahs urging holy war and the other cocked to [Australian media mogul] Rupert Murdoch's Star television beaming in *Dynasty, Donahue,* and *The Simpsons* from hovering satellites. Chinese entrepreneurs vie for the attention of party cadres in Beijing and simultaneously pursue KFC franchises in cities like Nanjing, Hangzhou, and Xian where twenty-eight outlets serve over 100,000 customers a day. The Russian Orthodox church, even as it struggles to renew the ancient faith, has entered a joint venture with California businessmen to bottle and sell natural waters under the rubric Saint Springs Water Company. Serbian assassins wear Adidas sneakers and listen to Madonna on Walkman headphones as they take aim through their gunscopes at scurrying Sarajevo civilians looking to fill family watercans. Orthodox Hasids and brooding neo-Nazis have both turned to rock music to get their traditional messages out to the new generation, while fundamentalists plot virtual conspiracies on the Internet.

Now neither Jihad nor McWorld is in itself novel. History ending in the triumph of science and reason or some monstrous perversion thereof (Mary Shelley's Doctor Frankenstein) has been the leitmotiv of every philosopher and poet who has regretted the Age of Reason since the Enlightenment. Yeats lamented "the center will not hold, mere anarchy is loosed upon the world," and observers of Jihad today have little but historical detail to add. The Christian parable of the Fall and of the possibilities of redemption that it makes possible captures the eighteenth-century ambivalence — and our own — about past and future. I want, however, to do more than dress up the central paradox of human history in modern clothes. It is not Jihad and McWorld but the relationship between them that most interests me. For, squeezed between their opposing forces, the world has been sent spinning out of control. Can it be that what Jihad and McWorld have in common is anarchy: the absence of common will and that conscious and collective human control under the guidance of law we call democracy?

Progress moves in steps that sometimes lurch backwards; in history's twisting maze, Jihad not only revolts against but abets McWorld, while McWorld not only imperils but re-creates and reinforces Jihad. They produce their contraries and need one another. My object here then is not simply to offer sequential portraits of McWorld and Jihad, but while examining McWorld, to keep Jihad in my field of vision, and while dissecting Jihad, never to forget the context of McWorld. Call it a dialectic of McWorld: a study in the cunning of reason that does honor to the radical differences that distinguish Jihad and McWorld yet that acknowledges their powerful and paradoxical interdependence.

There is a crucial difference, however, between my modest attempt at dialectic and that of the masters of the nineteenth century. Still seduced by the Enlightenment's faith in progress, both [G. W. F.] Hegel and [Karl] Marx believed reason's cunning was on the side of progress. But it is harder to believe that the clash of Jihad and McWorld will issue in some overriding good. The outcome seems more likely to pervert than to nurture human liberty. The two may, in opposing each other, work to the same ends, work in apparent tension yet in covert harmony, but democracy is not their beneficiary. In East Berlin, tribal communism has yielded to capitalism. In Marx-Engelsplatz, the stolid, overbearing statues of Marx and [Friedrich] Engels face east, as if seeking distant solace from Moscow: but now, circling them along the streets that surround the park that is their prison are chain eateries like T.G.I. Friday's, international hotels like the Radisson, and a circle of neon billboards mocking them with brand names like Panasonic, Coke, and GoldStar. New gods, yes, but more liberty?

What then does it mean in concrete terms to view Jihad and Mc-World dialectically when the tendencies of the two sets of forces initially appear so intractably antithetical? After all, Jihad and McWorld operate with equal strength in opposite directions, the one driven by parochial hatreds, the other by universalizing markets, the one re-creating ancient subnational and ethnic borders from within, the other making national borders porous from without. Yet Jihad and McWorld have this in common: They both make war on the sovereign nation-state and thus undermine the nation-state's democratic institutions. Each eschews civil society and belittles democratic citizenship, neither seeks alternative democratic institutions. Their common thread is indifference to civil liberty. Jihad forges communities of blood rooted in exclusion and hatred, communities that slight democracy in favor of tyrannical paternalism or consensual tribalism. McWorld forges global markets rooted in consumption and profit, leaving to an untrustworthy, if not altogether fictitious, invisible hand issues of public interest and common good that once might have been nurtured by democratic citizenries and their watchful governments. Such governments, intimidated by market ideology, are actually pulling back at the very moment they ought to be aggressively intervening. What was once understood as protecting the public interest is now excoriated as heavy-handed regulatory browbeating. Justice yields to markets, even though, as [New York banker] Felix Rohatyn has bluntly confessed, "there is a brutal Darwinian logic to these markets. They are nervous and greedy. They look for stability and transparency, but what they reward is not always our preferred form of democracy." If the traditional conservators of freedom were democratic constitutions and Bills of Rights, "the new temples to liberty," [literary critic and philosopher] George Steiner suggests, "will be McDonald's and Kentucky Fried Chicken."

In being reduced to a choice between the market's universal church and a retribalizing politics of particularist identities, peoples around the globe are threatened with an atavistic return to medieval politics where local tribes and ambitious emperors together ruled the world entire, women and men united by the universal abstraction of Christianity even as they lived out isolated lives in warring fiefdoms defined by involuntary (ascriptive) forms of identity. This was a world in which princes and kings had little real power until they conceived the ideology of nationalism. Nationalism established government on a scale greater than the tribe yet less cosmopolitan than the universal church and in time gave birth to those intermediate, gradually more democratic institutions that would come to constitute the nation-state. Today, at the far end of this history, we seem intent on re-creating a world in which our only choices are the secular universalism of the cosmopolitan market and the everyday particularism of the fractious tribe.

In the tumult of the confrontation between global commerce and parochial ethnicity, the virtues of the democratic nation are lost and the instrumentalities by which it permitted peoples to transform themselves into nations and seize sovereign power in the name of liberty and the commonweal are put at risk. Neither Jihad nor McWorld aspires to resecure the civic virtues undermined by its denationalizing practices; neither global markets nor blood communities service public goods or pursue equality and justice. Impartial judiciaries and deliberate assemblies play no role in the roving killer bands that speak on behalf of newly liberated "peoples," and such democratic institutions have at best only marginal influence on the roving multinational corporations that speak on behalf of newly liberated markets. Jihad pursues a bloody politics of identity, McWorld a bloodless economics of profit. Belonging by default to McWorld, everyone is a consumer; seeking a repository for identity, everyone belongs to some tribe. But no one is a citizen. Without citizens, how can there be democracy?

91

KWAME ANTHONY APPIAH

African Art and Identity

In this selection, a modern African philosopher explores the meaning of an African identity, style, or work of art in an age of global cultural interaction. Note the rich ironies in the opening discussion of an American exhibition of African art. What does the author make of the roles of the Baule artist and David Rockefeller as curators or judges for the exhibit? What do Professor Appiah and [African-American author] James Baldwin seem to like about *Yoruba Man with a Bicycle*? What point is the author making about African identity?

Thinking Historically

What is the force of globalization that Appiah describes in this essay? To what extent is it Jihad or McWorld? Is there a different process at work here that brings these artists, curators, and critics together to make their judgments? Try to construct a theory that explains that process.

In 1987 the Center for African Art in New York organized a show entitled *Perspectives: Angles on African Art*. The curator, Susan Vogel, had worked with a number of "cocurators," whom I list in order of their appearance in the table of contents: Ekpo Eyo, quondam director of the Department of Antiquities of the National Museum of Nigeria; William Rubin, director of painting and sculpture at the Museum of Modern Art and organizer of its controversial Primitivism exhibit; Romare Bearden, African-American painter; Ivan Karp, curator of African ethnology at the Smithsonian; Nancy Graves, European-American painter, sculptor, and filmmaker; James Baldwin, who surely needs no qualifying glosses; David Rockefeller, art collector and friend of the mighty; Lela Kouakou, Baule artist and diviner, from Ivory Coast (this a delicious juxtaposition, richest and poorest, side by side); Iba N'Diaye, Senegalese sculptor; and Robert Farris Thompson, Yale professor and African and African-American art historian. Vogel describes the

Kwame Anthony Appiah, *In My Father's House: Africa in the Philosophy of Culture* (New York: Oxford University Press, 1992), 137–140, 147–148, 157. *Yoruba Man with a Bicycle* (Collection of the Newark Museum. Purchase 1977, Wallace M. Scudder Bequest Fund and the Members Fund).

Figure 9. *Yoruba Man with a Bicycle.*

process of selection in her introductory essay. The one woman and nine men were each offered a hundred-odd photographs of "African Art as varied in type and origin and as high in quality, as we could manage" and asked to select ten for the show. Or, I should say more exactly, that this is what was offered to eight of the men. For Vogel adds, "In the case of the Baule artist, a man familiar only with the art of his own people, only Baule objects were placed in the pool of photographs." At this point we are directed to a footnote to the essay, which reads:

Showing him the same assortment of photos the others saw would have been interesting, but confusing in terms of the reactions we sought here. Field aesthetic studies, my own and others, have shown that African informants will criticize sculptures from other ethnic groups in terms of their own traditional criteria, often assuming that such works are simply inept carvings of their own aesthetic tradition.

I shall return to this irresistible footnote in a moment. But let me pause to quote further, this time from the words of David Rockefeller, who would surely never "criticize sculptures from other ethnic groups in terms of [his] own traditional criteria," discussing what the catalog calls a "Fante female figure":

> I own somewhat similar things to this and I have always liked them. This is a rather more sophisticated version than the ones that I've seen, and I thought it was quite beautiful . . . the total composition has a very contemporary, very Western look to it. It's the kind of thing that goes very well with contemporary Western things. It would look good in a modern apartment or house.

We may suppose that David Rockefeller was delighted to discover that his final judgment was consistent with the intentions of the sculpture's creators. For a footnote to the earlier "Checklist" reveals that the Baltimore Museum of Art desires to "make public the fact that the authenticity of the Fante figure in its collection has been challenged." Indeed, work by Doran Ross suggests this object is almost certainly a modern piece introduced in my hometown of Kumasi by the workshop of a certain Francis Akwasi, which "specializes in carvings for the international market in the style of traditional sculpture. Many of its works are now in museums throughout the West, and were published as authentic by Cole and Ross" (yes, the same Doran Ross) in their classic catalog *The Arts of Ghana*.

But then it is hard to be *sure* what would please a man who gives as his reason for picking another piece (this time a Senufo helmet mask), "I have to say I picked this because I own it. It was given to me by President Houphouet Boigny of Ivory Coast." Or one who remarks, "concerning the market in African art":

> The best pieces are going for very high prices. Generally speaking, the less good pieces in terms of quality are not going up in price. And that's a fine reason for picking the good ones rather than the bad. They have a way of becoming more valuable.
>
> I like African art as objects I find would be appealing to use in a home or an office. . . . I don't think it goes with everything, necessarily — although the very best perhaps does. But I think it goes well with contemporary architecture.

There is something breathtakingly unpretentious in Mr. Rockefeller's easy movement between considerations of finance, of aesthetics, and of decor. In these responses we have surely a microcosm of the site of the African in contemporary — which is, then, surely to say, postmodern — America.

I have given so much of David Rockefeller not to emphasize the familiar fact that questions of what we call "aesthetic" value are crucially bound up with market value; not even to draw attention to the fact that this is known by those who play the art market. Rather, I want to keep clearly before us the fact that David Rockefeller is permitted to say *anything at all* about the arts of Africa because he is a *buyer* and because he is at the *center,* while Lela Kouakou, who merely makes art and who dwells at the margins, is a poor African whose words count only as parts of the commodification — both for those of us who constitute the museum public and for collectors, like Rockefeller — of Baule art. I want to remind you, in short, of how important it is that African art is a *commodity.*

But the cocurator whose choice will set us on our way is James Baldwin — the only cocurator who picked a piece that was not in the mold of the Africa of the exhibition Primitivism, a sculpture that will be my touchstone, a piece labeled by the museum *Yoruba Man with a Bicycle.* Here is some of what Baldwin said about it:

> This is something. This has got to be contemporary. He's really going to town. It's very jaunty, very authoritative. His errand might prove to be impossible. He is challenging something — or something has challenged him. He's grounded in immediate reality by the bicycle. . . . He's apparently a very proud and silent man. He's dressed sort of polyglot. Nothing looks like it fits him too well.

Baldwin's reading of this piece is, of course and inevitably, "in terms of [his] own . . . criteria," a reaction contextualized only by the knowledge that bicycles are new in Africa and that this piece, anyway, does not look anything like the works he recalls seeing from his earliest childhood at the Schomburg museum in Harlem. And his response torpedoes Vogel's argument for her notion that the only "authentically traditional" African — the only one whose responses, as she says, could have been found a century ago — must be refused a choice among Africa's art cultures because he, unlike the rest of the cocurators, who are Americans and the European-educated Africans, will use his "own . . . criteria." This Baule diviner, this authentically African villager, the message is, does not know what *we,* authentic postmodernists, now know: that the first and last mistake is to judge the Other on one's own terms. And so, in the name of this, the relativist insight, we impose our judgment that Lela Kouakou may not judge sculpture from beyond the Baule culture zone because he will — like all the other African "informants" we have met in the field — read them as if they meant to meet those Baule standards.

Worse than this, it is nonsense to explain Lela Kouakou's responses as deriving from an ignorance of other traditions — if indeed he is, as he is no doubt supposed to be, like most "traditional" artists today, if he is like, for example, Francis Akwasi of Kumasi. Kouakou may judge other artists by his own standards (what on earth else could he, could anyone, do, save make no judgment at all?), but to suppose that he is unaware that there are other standards within Africa (let alone without) is to ignore a piece of absolutely basic cultural knowledge, common to most precolonial as to most colonial and postcolonial cultures on the continent — the piece of cultural knowledge that explains why the people we now call "Baule" exist at all. To be Baule, for example, is, for a Baule, not to be a white person, not to be Senufo, not to be French. The ethnic groups — Lela Kouakou's Baule "tribe," for example — within which all African aesthetic life apparently occurs, are . . . the products of colonial and postcolonial articulations. And someone who knows enough to make himself up as a Baule for the twentieth century surely knows that there are other kinds of art.

But Baldwin's *Yoruba Man with a Bicycle* does more than give the lie to Vogel's strange footnote; it provides us with an image of an object that can serve as a point of entry to my theme: a piece of contemporary African art that will allow us to explore the articulation of the postcolonial and the postmodern. *Yoruba Man with a Bicycle* is described as follows in the catalog:

> Page 124
> Man with a Bicycle
> Yoruba, Nigeria 20th century
> Wood and paint H. 35¾ in.
> The Newark Museum
>
> The influence of the Western world is revealed in the clothes and bicycle of this neo-traditional Yoruba sculpture which probably represents a merchant en route to market.

And it is this word *neotraditional* — a word that is almost right — that provides, I think, the fundamental clue.

I do not know when the *Yoruba Man with a Bicycle* was made or by whom; African art has, until recently, been collected as the property of "ethnic" groups, not of individuals and workshops, so it is not unusual that not one of the pieces in the Perspectives show was identified in the "Checklist" by the name of an individual artist, even though many of them are twentieth-century (and no one will have been surprised, by contrast, that most of them *are* kindly labeled with the name of the people who own the largely private collections where they now live). As a result I cannot say if the piece is literally postcolonial, produced after Nigerian independence in 1960. But the piece belongs to a genre that has certainly been produced since then: the genre that is here called *neotraditional*. And, simply put, what is distinctive about this genre is that it is produced for the West.

I should qualify. Of course, many of the buyers of first instance live in Africa, many of them are juridically citizens of African states. But African bourgeois consumers of neotraditional art are educated in the Western style, and, if they want African art, they would often rather have a "genuinely" traditional piece — by which I mean a piece that they believe to be made precolonially, or at least in a style and by methods that were already established precolonially. And these buyers are a minority. Most of this art, which is *traditional* because it uses actually or supposedly precolonial techniques, but is *neo* — this, for what it is worth, is the explanation I promised earlier — because it has elements that are recognizably from the colonial or postcolonial in reference, has been made for Western tourists and other collectors. . . .

For all the while, in Africa's cultures, there are those who will not see themselves as Other. Despite the overwhelming reality of economic decline; despite unimaginable poverty; despite wars; despite malnutrition, disease, and political instability, African cultural productivity grows apace: Popular literatures, oral narrative and poetry, dance, drama, music, and visual art all thrive. The contemporary cultural production of many African societies — and the many traditions whose evidences so vigorously remain — is an antidote to the dark vision of the postcolonial novelist.

And I am grateful to James Baldwin for his introduction to the *Yoruba Man with a Bicycle* — a figure who is, as Baldwin so rightly saw, polyglot, speaking Yoruba and English, probably some Hausa and a little French for his trips to Cotonou or Cameroon; someone whose "clothes do not fit him too well." He and the other men and women among whom he mostly lives suggest to me that the place to look for hope is not just to the postcolonial novel — which has struggled to achieve the insights of a Ouologuem or Mudimbe [African novelists] — but to the all-consuming visions of this less-anxious creativity. It matters little who it was made *for;* what we should learn from is the imagination that produced it. The *Man with a Bicycle* is produced by someone who does not care that the bicycle is the white man's invention — it is not there to be Other to the Yoruba Self; it is there because someone cared for its solidity; it is there because it will take us further than our feet will take us; it is there because machines are now as African as novelists.

92

SAMUEL P. HUNTINGTON

The Clash of Civilizations?

In this influential essay, a political scientist proposes a model to understand the global rifts of the post–Cold War world. What does Huntington mean by a "civilization"? Is the clash of civilizations a new global development, according to Huntington? What is his strongest evidence?

Choose two or three examples of international conflicts from the daily newspaper. Do these examples fit Huntington's idea of a conflict between civilizations? If so, are there other conflicts in the world that do not?

Thinking Historically

Why, according to Huntington, are fault lines between civilizations more likely to cause conflict than other kinds of fault lines? What other kinds of global fault lines exist in the world? Do these also cause conflicts? How does the process of increased globalization figure into Huntington's model?

The Next Pattern of Conflict

World politics is entering a new phase, and intellectuals have not hesitated to proliferate visions of what it will be — the end of history, the return of traditional rivalries between nation states, and the decline of the nation state from the conflicting pulls of tribalism and globalism, among others. Each of these visions catches aspects of the emerging reality. Yet they all miss a crucial, indeed a central, aspect of what global politics is likely to be in the coming years.

It is my hypothesis that the fundamental source of conflict in this new world will not be primarily ideological or primarily economic. The great divisions among humankind and the dominating source of conflict will be cultural. Nation states will remain the most powerful actors in world affairs, but the principal conflicts of global politics will occur between nations and groups of different civilizations. The clash of civilizations will dominate global politics. The fault lines between civilizations will be the battle lines of the future.

Samuel P. Huntington, "The Clash of Civilizations?" in *The Clash of Civilizations? The Debate* (New York: Foreign Affairs, 1996), 1–5, 7–12.

Conflict between civilizations will be the latest phase in the evolution of conflict in the modern world. For a century and a half after the emergence of the modern international system with the Peace of Westphalia [1648], the conflicts of the Western world were largely among princes — emperors, absolute monarchs, and constitutional monarchs attempting to expand their bureaucracies, their armies, their mercantilist economic strength and, most important, the territory they ruled. In the process they created nation states, and beginning with the French Revolution the principal lines of conflict were between nations rather than princes. In 1793, as [historian] R. R. Palmer put it, "The wars of kings were over; the wars of peoples had begun." This nineteenth-century pattern lasted until the end of World War I. Then, as a result of the Russian Revolution and the reaction against it, the conflict of nations yielded to the conflict of ideologies, first among communism, fascism-Nazism and liberal democracy, and then between communism and liberal democracy. During the Cold War, this latter conflict became embodied in the struggle between the two superpowers, neither of which was a nation state in the classical European sense and each of which defined its identity in terms of its ideology.

These conflicts between princes, nation states, and ideologies were primarily conflicts within Western civilization, "Western civil wars," as [political scientist] William Lind has labeled them. This was as true of the Cold War as it was of the world wars and the earlier wars of the seventeenth, eighteenth, and nineteenth centuries. With the end of the Cold War, international politics moves out of its Western phase, and its centerpiece becomes the interaction between the West and non-Western civilizations and among non-Western civilizations. In the politics of civilizations, the peoples and governments of non-Western civilizations no longer remain the objects of history as targets of Western colonialism but join the West as movers and shapers of history.

The Nature of Civilizations

During the cold war the world was divided into the First, Second, and Third Worlds. Those divisions are no longer relevant. It is far more meaningful now to group countries not in terms of their political or economic systems or in terms of their level of economic development but rather in terms of their culture and civilization.

What do we mean when we talk of a civilization? A civilization is a cultural entity. Villages, regions, ethnic groups, nationalities, religious groups, all have distinct cultures at different levels of cultural heterogeneity. The culture of a village in southern Italy may be different from that of a village in northern Italy, but both will share in a common Italian culture that distinguishes them from German villages. European communities, in turn, will share cultural features that distinguish them from Arab or Chinese communities. Arabs, Chinese, and Westeners, however, are not part of any broader cultural entity. They constitute civilizations. A civilization is thus the highest cultural grouping of people and the broadest level of cultural identity people have short of that which distinguishes humans from other species. It is defined both by common objective elements, such as language, history, religion, customs, institutions, and by the subjective self-identification of people. People have levels of identity: A resident of Rome may define himself with varying degrees of intensity as a Roman, an Italian, a Catholic, a Christian, a European, a Westerner. The civilization to which he belongs is the broadest level of identification with which he intensely identifies. People can and do redefine their identities and, as a result, the composition and boundaries of civilizations change.

Civilizations may involve a large number of people, as with China ("a civilization pretending to be a state," as Lucian Pye put it), or a very small number of people, such as the Anglophone Caribbean. A civilization may include several nation states, as is the case with Western, Latin American, and Arab civilizations, or only one, as is the case with Japanese civilization. Civilizations obviously blend and overlap, and may include subcivilizations. Western civilization has two major variants, European and North American, and Islam has its Arab, Turkic, and Malay subdivisions. Civilizations are nonetheless meaningful entities, and while the lines between them are seldom sharp, they are real. Civilizations are dynamic; they rise and fall; they divide and merge. And, as any student of history knows, civilizations disappear and are buried in the sands of time.

Westerners tend to think of nation states as the principal actors in global affairs. They have been that, however, for only a few centuries. The broader reaches of human history have been the history of civilizations. In *A Study of History,* [historian] Arnold Toynbee identified twenty-one major civilizations; only six of them exist in the contemporary world.

Why Civilizations Will Clash

Civilization identity will be increasingly important in the future, and the world will be shaped in large measure by the interactions among seven or eight major civilizations. These include Western, Confucian, Japanese, Islamic, Hindu, Slavic-Orthodox, Latin American, and possibly African civilization. The most important conflicts of the future will occur along the cultural fault lines separating these civilizations from one another.

Why will this be the case?

First, differences among civilizations are not only real; they are basic. Civilizations are differentiated from each other by history, language, culture, tradition and, most important, religion. The people of different civilizations have different views on the relations between God and man, the individual and the group, the citizen and the state, parents and children, husband and wife, as well as differing views of the relative importance of rights and responsibilities, liberty and authority, equality and hierarchy. These differences are the product of centuries. They will not soon disappear. They are far more fundamental than differences among political ideologies and political regimes. Differences do not necessarily mean conflict, and conflict does not necessarily mean violence. Over the centuries, however, differences among civilizations have generated the most prolonged and the most violent conflicts.

Second, the world is becoming a smaller place. The interactions between peoples of different civilizations are increasing; these increasing interactions intensify civilization consciousness and awareness of differences between civilizations and commonalities within civilizations. North African immigration to France generates hostility among Frenchmen and at the same time increased receptivity to immigration by "good" European Catholic Poles. Americans react far more negatively to Japanese investment than to larger investments from Canada and European countries. Similarly, as [political scientist] Donald Horowitz has pointed out, "An Ibo may be . . . an Owerri Ibo or an Onitsha Ibo in what was the Eastern region of Nigeria. In Lagos, he is simply an Ibo. In London, he is a Nigerian. In New York, he is an African." The interactions among peoples of different civilizations enhance the civilization-consciousness of people that, in turn, invigorates differences and animosities stretching or thought to stretch back deep into history.

Third, the processes of economic modernization and social change throughout the world are separating people from longstanding local identities. They also weaken the nation state as a source of identity. In much of the world religion has moved in to fill this gap, often in the form of movements that are labeled "fundamentalist." Such movements are found in Western Christianity, Judaism, Buddhism, and Hinduism, as well as in Islam. In most countries and most religions the people active in fundamentalist movements are young, college-educated, middle-class technicians, professionals, and business persons. The "unsecularization of the world," [political scientist] George Weigel has remarked, "is one of the dominant social facts of life in the late twentieth century." The revival of religion, "la revanche de Dieu," as [French scholar of Islam] Gilles Kepel labeled it, provides a basis for identity and commitment that transcends national boundaries and unites civilizations.

Fourth, the growth of civilization-consciousness is enhanced by the dual role of the West. On the one hand, the West is at a peak of power.

At the same time, however, and perhaps as a result, a return to the roots phenomenon is occurring among non-Western civilizations. Increasingly one hears references to trends toward a turning inward and "Asianization" in Japan, the end of the Nehru legacy and the "Hinduization" of India, the failure of Western ideas of socialism and nationalism and hence "re-Islamization" of the Middle East, and now a debate over Westernization versus Russianization in Boris Yeltsin's country. A West at the peak of its power confronts non-Wests that increasingly have the desire, the will, and the resources to shape the world in non-Western ways.

In the past, the elites of non-Western societies were usually the people who were most involved with the West, had been educated at Oxford, the Sorbonne or Sandhurst, and had absorbed Western attitudes and values. At the same time, the populace in non-Western countries often remained deeply imbued with the indigenous culture. Now, however, these relationships are being reversed. A de-Westernization and indigenization of elites is occurring in many non-Western countries at the same time that Western, usually American, cultures, styles, and habits become more popular among the mass of the people.

Fifth, cultural characteristics and differences are less mutable and hence less easily compromised and resolved than political and economic ones. In the former Soviet Union, communists can become democrats, the rich can become poor and the poor rich, but Russians cannot become Estonians and Azeris cannot become Armenians. In class and ideological conflicts, the key question was "Which side are you on?" and people could and did choose sides and change sides. In conflicts between civilizations, the question is "What are you?" That is a given that cannot be changed. And as we know, from Bosnia to the Caucasus to the Sudan, the wrong answer to that question can mean a bullet in the head. Even more than ethnicity, religion discriminates sharply and exclusively among people. A person can be half-French and half-Arab and simultaneously even a citizen of two countries. It is more difficult to be half-Catholic and half-Muslim. . . .

As people define their identity in ethnic and religious terms, they are likely to see an "us" versus "them" relation existing between themselves and people of different ethnicity or religion. The end of ideologically defined states in Eastern Europe and the former Soviet Union permits traditional ethnic identities and animosities to come to the fore. Differences in culture and religion create differences over policy issues, ranging from human rights to immigration to trade and commerce to the environment. Geographical propinquity gives rise to conflicting territorial claims from Bosnia to Mindanao. Most important, the efforts of the West to promote its values of democracy and liberalism as universal values, to maintain its military predominance and to advance its economic interests engender countering responses from other civilizations. Decreasingly able to mobilize support and form coalitions on the basis of ideology, governments and groups will increasingly attempt to mobilize support by appealing to common religion and civilization identity.

The clash of civilizations thus occurs at two levels. At the micro-level, adjacent groups along the fault lines between civilizations struggle, often violently, over the control of territory and each other. At the macro-level, states from different civilizations compete for relative military and economic power, struggle over the control of international institutions and third parties, and competitively promote their particular political and religious values.

The Fault Lines Between Civilizations

The fault lines between civilizations are replacing the political and ideological boundaries of the Cold War as the flash points for crisis and bloodshed. The Cold War began when the Iron Curtain divided Europe politically and ideologically. The Cold War ended with the end of the Iron Curtain. As the ideological division of Europe has disappeared, the cultural division of Europe between Western Christianity, on the one hand, and Orthodox Christianity and Islam, on the other, has reemerged. The most significant dividing line in Europe, as [political scientist] William Wallace has suggested, may well be the eastern boundary of Western Christianity in the year 1500. This line runs along what are now the boundaries between Finland and Russia and between the Baltic states and Russia, cuts through Belarus and Ukraine separating the more Catholic western Ukraine from Orthodox eastern Ukraine, swings westward separating Transylvania from the rest of Romania, and then goes through Yugoslavia almost exactly along the line now separating Croatia and Slovenia from the rest of Yugoslavia. In the Balkans this line, of course, coincides with the historic boundary between the Hapsburg and Ottoman empires. The peoples to the north and west of this line are Protestant or Catholic; they shared the common experiences of European history — feudalism, the Renaissance, the Reformation, the Enlightenment, the French Revolution, the Industrial Revolution; they are generally economically better off than the peoples to the east; and they may now look forward to increasing involvement in a common European economy and to the consolidation of democratic political systems. The peoples to the east and south of this line are Orthodox or Muslim; they historically belonged to the Ottoman or Tsarist empires and were only lightly touched by the shaping events in the rest of Europe; they are generally less advanced economically; they seem much less likely to develop stable democratic political systems. The Velvet Curtain of culture has replaced the Iron Curtain of

Western Christianity circa 1500 / Orthodox Christianity and Islam

RUSSIA

FINLAND

SWEDEN

ESTONIA

LATVIA

LITHUANIA

BELARUS

POLAND

CZECH REP.

SLOVAKIA

UKRAINE

SLOVENIA

HUNG.

MOLD.

CROATIA

ROMANIA

BOSNIA

SERBIA

Black Sea

MONTE-NEGRO

BULGARIA

MACEDONIA

ALB.

ITALY

GREECE

N

TURKEY

0 ──── 200
MILES

Source: W. Wallace, THE TRANSFORMATION OF WESTERN EUROPE. London: Pinter, 1990. Map by Ib Ohlsson for FOREIGN AFFAIRS.

Figure 10. Civilization Divide, circa 1500.

ideology as the most significant dividing line in Europe. As the events in Yugoslavia show, it is not only a line of difference; it is also at times a line of bloody conflict.

Conflict along the fault line between Western and Islamic civilizations has been going on for thirteen hundred years. After the founding of Islam, the Arab and Moorish surge west and north only ended at Tours in 732. From the eleventh to the thirteenth century the Crusaders attempted with temporary success to bring Christianity and Christian rule to the Holy Land. From the fourteenth to the seventeenth century, the Ottoman Turks reversed the balance, extended their sway over the Middle East and the Balkans, captured Constantinople, and twice laid siege to Vienna. In the nineteenth and early twentieth centuries as Ottoman power declined Britain, France, and Italy established Western control over most of North Africa and the Middle East.

After World War II, the West, in turn, began to retreat; the colonial empires disappeared; first Arab nationalism and then Islamic fundamentalism manifested themselves; the West became heavily dependent on the Persian Gulf countries for its energy; the oil-rich Muslim countries became money-rich and, when they wished to, weapons-rich. Several wars occurred between Arabs and Israel (created by the West). France fought a bloody and ruthless war in Algeria for most of the 1950s; British and French forces invaded Egypt in 1956; American forces went into Lebanon in 1958; subsequently American forces returned to Lebanon, attacked Libya, and engaged in various military encounters with Iran; Arab and Islamic terrorists, supported by at least three Middle Eastern governments, employed the weapon of the weak and bombed Western planes and installations and seized Western hostages. This warfare between Arabs and the West culminated in 1990, when the United States sent a massive army to the Persian Gulf to defend some Arab countries against aggression by another. In its aftermath NATO planning is increasingly directed to potential threats and instability along its "southern tier."

This centuries-old military interaction between the West and Islam is unlikely to decline. It could become more virulent. The Gulf War left some Arabs feeling proud that Saddam Hussein had attacked Israel and stood up to the West. It also left many feeling humiliated and resentful of the West's military presence in the Persian Gulf, the West's overwhelming military dominance, and their apparent inability to shape their own destiny. Many Arab countries, in addition to the oil exporters, are reaching levels of economic and social development where autocratic forms of government become inappropriate and efforts to introduce democracy become stronger. Some openings in Arab political systems have already occurred. The principal beneficiaries of these openings have been Islamist movements. In the Arab world, in short, Western democracy strengthens anti-Western political forces. This may be a passing phenomenon, but it surely complicates relations between Islamic countries and the West.

Those relations are also complicated by demography. The spectacular population growth in Arab countries, particularly in North Africa, has led to increased migration to Western Europe. The movement within Western Europe toward minimizing internal boundaries has sharpened political sensitivities with respect to this development. In Italy, France, and Germany, racism is increasingly open, and political reactions and violence against Arab and Turkish migrants have become more intense and more widespread since 1990.

On both sides the interaction between Islam and the West is seen as a clash of civilizations. The West's "next confrontation," observes M. J. Akbar, an Indian Muslim author, "is definitely going to come from the Muslim world. It is in the sweep of the Islamic nations from the Maghreb to Pakistan that the struggle for a new world order will begin." [Historian of Islam] Bernard Lewis comes to a similar conclusion:

> We are facing a mood and a movement far transcending the level of issues and policies and the governments that pursue them. This is no less than a clash of civilizations — the perhaps irrational but surely historic reaction of an ancient rival against our Judeo-Christian heritage, our secular present, and the worldwide expansion of both.

Historically, the other great antagonistic interaction of Arab Islamic civilization has been with the pagan, animist, and now increasingly

Christian black peoples to the south. In the past, this antagonism was epitomized in the image of Arab slave dealers and black slaves. It has been reflected in the on-going civil war in the Sudan between Arabs and blacks, the fighting in Chad between Libyan-supported insurgents and the government, the tensions between Orthodox Christians and Muslims in the Horn of Africa, and the political conflicts, recurring riots, and communal violence between Muslims and Christians in Nigeria. The modernization of Africa and the spread of Christianity are likely to enhance the probability of violence along this fault line. Symptomatic of the intensification of this conflict was Pope John Paul II's speech in Khartoum in February 1993 attacking the actions of the Sudan's Islamist government against the Christian minority there.

On the northern border of Islam, conflict has increasingly erupted between Orthodox and Muslim peoples, including the carnage of Bosnia and Sarajevo, the simmering violence between Serb and Albanian [as in Kosovo], the tenuous relations between Bulgarians and their Turkish minority, the violence between Ossetians and Ingush, the unremitting slaughter of each other by Armenians and Azeris, the tense relations between Russians and Muslims in Central Asia, and the deployment of Russian troops to protect Russian interests in the Caucasus and Central Asia. Religion reinforces the revival of ethnic identities and restimulates Russian fears about the security of their southern borders. This concern is well captured by [Intelligence Officer] Archie Roosevelt:

> Much of Russian history concerns the struggle between the Slavs and the Turkic peoples on their borders, which dates back to the foundation of the Russian state more than a thousand years ago. In the Slavs' millennium-long confrontation with their eastern neighbors lies the key to an understanding not only of Russian history, but Russian character. To understand Russian realities today one has to have a concept of the great Turkic ethnic group that has preoccupied Russians through the centuries.

The conflict of civilizations is deeply rooted elsewhere in Asia. The historic clash between Muslim and Hindu in the subcontinent manifests itself now not only in the rivalry between Pakistan and India but also in intensifying religious strife within India between increasingly militant Hindu groups and India's substantial Muslim minority. The destruction of the Ayodhya mosque in December 1992 brought to the fore the issue of whether India will remain a secular democratic state or become a Hindu one. In East Asia, China has outstanding territorial disputes with most of its neighbors. It has pursued a ruthless policy toward the Buddhist people of Tibet, and it is pursuing an increasingly ruthless policy toward its Turkic-Muslim minority. With the Cold War over, the underlying differences between China and the United States have reasserted themselves in areas such as human rights, trade, and weapons proliferation. These differences are unlikely to moderate. A "new cold war," [former premier of China] Deng Xaioping reportedly asserted in 1991, is under way between China and America.

The same phrase has been applied to the increasingly difficult relations between Japan and the United States. Here cultural difference exacerbates economic conflict. People on each side allege racism on the other, but at least on the American side the antipathies are not racial but cultural. The basic values, attitudes, behavioral patterns of the two societies could hardly be more different. The economic issues between the United States and Europe are no less serious than those between the United States and Japan, but they do not have the same political salience and emotional intensity because the differences between American culture and European culture are so much less than those between American civilization and Japanese civilization.

The interactions between civilizations vary greatly in the extent to which they are likely to be characterized by violence. Economic competition clearly predominates between the American and European sub-civilizations of the West and between both of them and Japan. On the Eurasian continent, however, the proliferation of ethnic conflict, epitomized at the extreme in "ethnic cleansing," has not been totally random. It has been most frequent and most violent between groups belonging to different civilizations. In Eurasia the great historic fault lines between civilizations are once more aflame. This is particularly true along the boundaries of the crescent-shaped Islamic bloc of nations from the bulge of Africa to central Asia. Violence also occurs between Muslims, on the one hand, and Orthodox Serbs in the Balkans, Jews in Israel, Hindus in India, Buddhists in Burma, and Catholics in the Philippines. Islam has bloody borders.

93

FOUAD AJAMI

The Summoning

The author of this selection specializes in Middle East studies. His criticism of Huntington is theoretical and directed to specific cases (mainly in the Middle East). What is his theoretical criticism? What are his arguments about specific countries in the Middle East? Which of these arguments do you find most persuasive? What do you think of Huntington's argument after reading Ajami's piece?

Thinking Historically

How are the first sentences of Ajami's essay — about civilizations rising and dusting themselves off after the Cold War — a criticism of Huntington's idea of process? What, according to Ajami, is the problem with Huntington's idea of civilizations as dynamic entities that change the world? What dynamic forces does Ajami think are more important or powerful than civilizations?

In a curious essay, "The Clash of Civilizations," Huntington has found his civilizations whole and intact, watertight under an eternal sky. Buried alive, as it were, during the years of the Cold War, these civilizations (Islamic, Slavic-Orthodox, Western, Confucian, Japanese, Hindu, etc.) rose as soon as the stone was rolled off, dusted themselves off, and proceeded to claim the loyalty of their adherents. For this student of history and culture, civilizations have always seemed messy creatures. Furrows run across whole civilizations, across individuals themselves — that was modernity's verdict. But Huntington looks past all that. The crooked and meandering alleyways of the world are straightened out. With a sharp pencil and a steady hand Huntington marks out where one civilization ends and the wilderness of "the other" begins.

More surprising still is Huntington's attitude toward states, and their place in his scheme of things. From one of the most influential and brilliant students of the state and its national interest there now comes an essay that misses the slyness of states, the unsentimental and cold-blooded nature of so much of what they do as they pick their way through chaos. Despite the obligatory passage that states will remain

---

Fouad Ajami, "The Summoning," in Samuel Huntington, *The Clash of Civilizations? The Debate* (New York: Foreign Affairs, 1996), 26–32.

"the most powerful actors in world affairs," states are written off, their place given over to clashing civilizations. In Huntington's words, "The next world war, if there is one, will be a war between civilizations."

The Power of Modernity

Huntington's meditation is occasioned by his concern about the state of the West, its power and the terms of its engagement with "the rest."[1] "He who gives, dominates," the great historian Fernand Braudel observed of the traffic of civilizations. In making itself over the centuries, the West helped make the others as well. We have come to the end of this trail, Huntington is sure. He is impressed by the "de-Westernization" of societies, their "indigenization" and apparent willingness to go their own way. In his view of things such phenomena as the "Hinduization" of India and Islamic fundamentalism are ascendant. To these detours into "tradition" Huntington has assigned great force and power.

But Huntington is wrong. He has underestimated the tenacity of modernity and secularism in places that acquired these ways against great odds, always perilously close to the abyss, the darkness never far. India will not become a Hindu state. The inheritance of Indian secularism will hold. The vast middle class will defend it, keep the order intact to maintain India's — and its own — place in the modern world of nations. There exists in that anarchic polity an instinctive dread of playing with fires that might consume it. Hindu chauvinism may coarsen the public life of the country, but the state and the middle class that sustains it know that a detour into religious fanaticism is a fling with ruin. A resourceful middle class partakes of global culture and norms. A century has passed since the Indian bourgeoisie, through its political vehicle the Indian National Congress, set out to claim for itself and India a place among nations. Out of that long struggle to overturn British rule and the parallel struggle against "communalism," the advocates of the national idea built a large and durable state. They will not cede all this for a political kingdom of Hindu purity.

We have been hearing from the traditionalists, but we should not exaggerate their power, for traditions are often more insistent and loud when they rupture, when people no longer really believe and when age-old customs lose their ability to keep men and women at home. The phenomenon we have dubbed as Islamic fundamentalism is less a sign of resurgence than of panic and bewilderment and guilt that the border

---

1 The West itself is unexamined in Huntington's essay. No fissures run through it. No multiculturalists are heard from. It is orderly within its ramparts. What doubts Huntington has about the will within the walls, he has kept within himself. He has assumed that his call to unity will be answered, for outside flutter the banners of the Saracens and the Confucians.

with "the other" has been crossed. Those young urban poor, half-educated in the cities of the Arab world, and their Sorbonne-educated lay preachers, can they be evidence of a genuine return to tradition? They crash Europe's and America's gates in search of liberty and work, and they rail against the sins of the West. It is easy to understand Huntington's frustration with this kind of complexity, with the strange mixture of attraction and repulsion that the West breeds, and his need to simplify matters, to mark out the borders of civilizations.

Tradition-mongering is no proof, though, that these civilizations outside the West are intact, or that their thrashing about is an indication of their vitality, or that they present a conventional threat of arms. Even so thorough and far-reaching an attack against Western hegemony as Iran's theocratic revolution could yet fail to wean that society from the culture of the West. That country's cruel revolution was born of the realization of the "armed Imam" that his people were being seduced by America's ways. The gates had been thrown wide open in the 1970s, and the high walls Ayatollah Khomeini built around his polity were a response to that cultural seduction. Swamped Iran was "rescued" by men claiming authenticity as their banner. One extreme led to another.

"We prayed for the rain of mercy and received floods," was the way Mehdi Bazargan, the decent modernist who was Khomeini's first prime minister, put it. But the millennium has been brought down to earth, and the dream of a pan-Islamic revolt in Iran's image has vanished into the wind. The terror and the shabbiness have caught up with the utopia. Sudan could emulate the Iranian "revolutionary example." But this will only mean the further pauperization and ruin of a desperate land. There is no rehabilitation of the Iranian example.

A battle rages in Algeria, a society of the Mediterranean, close to Europe — a wine-producing country for that matter — and in Egypt between the secular powers that be and an Islamic alternative. But we should not rush to print with obituaries of these states. In Algeria the nomenklatura of the National Liberation Front failed and triggered a revolt of the young, the underclass, and the excluded. The revolt raised an Islamic banner. Caught between a regime they despised and a reign of virtue they feared, the professionals and the women and the modernists of the middle class threw their support to the forces of "order." They hailed the army's crackdown on the Islamicists; they allowed the interruption of a democratic process sure to bring the Islamicists to power; they accepted the "liberties" protected by the repression, the devil you know rather than the one you don't.

The Algerian themes repeat in the Egyptian case, although Egypt's dilemma over its Islamicist opposition is not as acute. The Islamicists continue to hound the state, but they cannot bring it down. There is no likelihood that the Egyptian state — now riddled with enough complacency and corruption to try the celebrated patience and good humor of the Egyptians — will go under. This is an old and skeptical country. It knows better than to trust its fate to enforcers of radical religious dogma. These are not deep and secure structures of order that the national middle classes have put in place. But they will not be blown away overnight.

Nor will Turkey lose its way, turn its back on Europe, and chase after some imperial temptation in the scorched domains of Central Asia. Huntington sells that country's modernity and secularism short when he writes that the Turks — rejecting Mecca and rejected by Brussels — are likely to head to Tashkent in search of a Pan-Turkic role. There is no journey to that imperial past. Ataturk severed that link with fury, pointed his country westward, embraced the civilization of Europe, and did it without qualms or second thoughts. It is on Frankfurt and Bonn — and Washington — not on Baku and Tashkent that the attention of the Turks is fixed. The inheritors of Ataturk's legacy are too shrewd to go chasing after imperial glory, gathering about them the scattered domains of the Turkish peoples. After their European possessions were lost, the Turks clung to Thrace and to all that this link to Europe represents.

Huntington would have nations battle for civilizational ties and fidelities when they would rather scramble for their market shares, learn how to compete in a merciless world economy, provide jobs, move out of poverty. For their part, the "management gurus" and those who believe that the interests have vanquished the passions in today's world tell us that men want Sony, nor soil. There is a good deal of truth in what they say, a terrible exhaustion with utopias, a reluctance to set out on expeditions of principle or belief. It is hard to think of Russia, ravaged as it is by inflation, taking up the grand cause of a "second Byzantium," the bearer of the orthodox-Slavic torch.

And where is the Confucian world Huntington speaks of? In the busy and booming lands of the Pacific Rim, so much of politics and ideology has been sublimated into finance that the nations of East Asia have turned into veritable workshops. The civilization of Cathay is dead; the Indonesian archipelago is deaf to the call of the religious radicals in Tehran as it tries to catch up with Malaysia and Singapore. A different wind blows in the lands of the Pacific. In that world economics, not politics, is in command. The world is far less antiseptic than Lee Kuan Yew, the sage of Singapore, would want it to be. A nemesis could lie in wait for all the prosperity that the 1980s brought to the Pacific. But the lands of the Pacific Rim — protected, to be sure, by an American security umbrella — are not ready for a great falling out among the nations. And were troubles to visit that world they would erupt within its boundaries, not across civilizational lines.

The things and ways that the West took to "the rest" ... have become the ways of the world. The secular idea, the state system and the balance of power, pop culture jumping tariff walls and barriers, the state as an instrument of welfare, all these have been internalized in the remotest places. We have stirred up the very storms into which we now ride.

The Weakness of Tradition

Nations "cheat": They juggle identities and interests. Their ways meander. One would think that the traffic of arms from North Korea and China to Libya and Iran and Syria shows this — that states will consort with any civilization, however alien, as long as the price is right and the goods are ready. Huntington turns this routine act of selfishness into a sinister "Confucian-Islamic connection." There are better explanations: the commerce of renegades, plain piracy, an "underground economy" that picks up the slack left by the great arms suppliers (the United States, Russia, Britain, and France).

Contrast the way Huntington sees things with [historian Fernand] Braudel's depiction of the traffic between Christendom and Islam across the Mediterranean in the sixteenth century — and this was in a religious age, after the fall of Constantinople to the Turks and of Granada to the Spanish: "Men passed to and fro, indifferent to frontiers, states and creeds. They were more aware of the necessities for shipping and trade, the hazards of war and piracy, the opportunities for complicity or betrayal provided by circumstances."

Those kinds of "complicities" and ambiguities are missing in Huntington's analysis. Civilizations are crammed into the nooks and crannies — and checkpoints — of the Balkans. Huntington goes where only the brave would venture, into that belt of mixed populations stretching from the Adriatic to the Baltic. Countless nationalisms make their home there, all aggrieved, all possessed of memories of a fabled past and equally ready for the demagogues vowing to straighten a messy map. In the thicket of these pan-movements he finds the line that marked "the eastern boundary of Western Christianity in the year 1500." The scramble for turf between Croatian nationalism and its Serbian counterpart, their "joint venture" in carving up Bosnia, are made into a fight of the inheritors of Rome, Byzantium, and Islam.

But why should we fall for this kind of determinism? "An outsider who travels the highway between Zagreb and Belgrade is struck not by the decisive historical fault line which falls across the lush Slavonian plain but by the opposite. Serbs and Croats speak the same language, give or take a few hundred words, have shared the same village way of life for centuries." The cruel genius of [president of Yugoslavia] Slobodan Milosevic[2] and [former Croatian dictator] Franjo Tudjman, men on horseback familiar in lands and situations of distress, was to make their bids for power into grand civilizational undertakings — the ramparts of their Enlightenment defended against Islam or, in Tudjman's case, against the heirs of the Slavic-Orthodox faith. Differences had to be magnified. Once [former president of Yugoslavia Josip Broz] Tito, an equal opportunity oppressor, had passed from the scene, the balancing act among the nationalities was bound to come apart. Serbia had had a measure of hegemony in the old system. But of the world that loomed over the horizon — privatization and economic reform — the Serbs were less confident. The citizens of Sarajevo and the Croats and the Slovenes had a head start on the rural Serbs. And so the Serbs hacked at the new order of things with desperate abandon.

Some Muslim volunteers came to Bosnia, driven by faith and zeal. Huntington sees in these few stragglers the sweeping power of "civilizational rallying," proof of the hold of what he calls the "kin-country syndrome." This is delusion. No Muslim cavalry was ever going to ride to the rescue. The Iranians may have railed about holy warfare, but the Chetniks went on with their work. The work of order and mercy would have had to be done by the United States if the cruel utopia of the Serbs was to be contested.

It should have taken no powers of prophecy to foretell where the fight in the Balkans would end. The abandonment of Bosnia was of a piece with the ways of the world. No one wanted to die for Srebrenica. The Europeans averted their gaze, as has been their habit. The Americans hesitated for a moment as the urge to stay out of the Balkans did battle with the scenes of horror. Then "prudence" won out. Milosevic and Tudjman may need civilizational legends, but there is no need to invest their projects of conquest with this kind of meaning. . . .

---

2 Serbian dictator whose militant Serbian nationalism led to the disintegration of Yugoslavia in the 1990s. Indicted as a war criminal in 1999, for expulsion and deaths of Albanian Kosovars.

94

GEORGE SOROS

From *The Crisis of Global Capitalism*

The author of this selection is a leading investor and philanthropist known for "breaking the Bank of England" in 1992, successfully betting against the British pound, lending major financing to the Russian economy, and becoming the scapegoat of the prime minister of Malaysia during that country's financial crisis in 1998.

What does Soros see as the crisis facing global capitalism? Why is "market fundamentalism" a threat to capitalism? What does Soros think must be done to ensure that capitalism will continue to operate in the future?

Thinking Historically

What is the dynamic process by which, according to Soros, the capital markets tend to boom and bust and create instability in global society? By what process is global capitalism at odds with global democracy and what Soros calls an "open society"? What process does Soros want to set in motion in order to prevent global markets from undermining global society?

. . . We live in a global economy, but the political organization of our global society is woefully inadequate. We are bereft of the capacity to preserve peace and to counteract the excesses of the financial markets. Without these controls, the global economy is liable to break down.

The global economy is characterized not only by free trade in goods and services but even more by the free movement of capital. Interest rates, exchange rates, and stock prices in various countries are intimately interrelated, and global financial markets exert tremendous influence on economic conditions. Given the decisive role that international financial capital plays in the fortunes of individual countries, it is not inappropriate to speak of a global capitalist system.

Financial capital enjoys a privileged position. Capital is more mobile than the other factors of production and financial capital is even more mobile than direct investment. Financial capital moves wherever

---

George Soros, *The Crisis of Global Capitalism* (New York: Public Affairs, 1998), xix–xxi, xxv–xxx.

it is best rewarded; as it is the harbinger of prosperity, individual countries compete to attract it. Due to these advantages, capital is increasingly accumulated in financial institutions and publicly traded multinational corporations; the process is intermediated by financial markets.

The development of a global economy has not been matched by the development of a global society. The basic unit for political and social life remains the nation-state. International law and international institutions, insofar as they exist, are not strong enough to prevent war or the large-scale abuse of human rights in individual countries. Ecological threats are not adequately dealt with. Global financial markets are largely beyond the control of national or international authorities.

I argue that the current state of affairs is unsound and unsustainable. Financial markets are inherently unstable and there are social needs that cannot be met by giving market forces free rein. Unfortunately these defects are not recognized. Instead there is a widespread belief that markets are self-correcting and a global economy can flourish without any need for a global society. It is claimed that the common interest is best served by allowing everyone to look out for his or her own interests and that attempts to protect the common interest by collective decision making distort the market mechanism. This idea was called laissez faire in the nineteenth century but it may not be such a good name today because it is a French word and most of the people who believe in the magic of the marketplace do not speak French. I have found a better name for it: market fundamentalism.

It is market fundamentalism that has rendered the global capitalist system unsound and unsustainable. This is a relatively recent state of affairs. At the end of the Second World War, the international movement of capital was restricted and the Bretton Woods institutions[1] were set up to facilitate trade in the absence of capital movements. Restrictions were removed only gradually and it was only when [conservative prime minister of the United Kingdom] Margaret Thatcher and [conservative Republican president of the United States] Ronald Reagan came to power around 1980 that market fundamentalism became the dominant ideology. It is market fundamentalism that has put financial capital into the driver's seat.

This is, of course, not the first time that we have had a global capitalist system. Its main features were first identified in rather prophetic fashion by Karl Marx and Friedrich Engels in the *Communist Manifesto,* published in 1848. The system that prevailed in the second half of the nineteenth century was in some ways more stable than the contemporary version. First, there were imperial powers, Great Britain foremost among them, that derived large enough benefits from being at

[1] International Monetary Fund (IMF) and International Bank For Reconstruction and Development.

the center of the system to find it worthwhile to preserve it. Second, there was a single international currency in the form of gold; today there are three major currencies — the dollar; the German mark, [and now] the euro; and the yen — which are rubbing against each other like tectonic plates, often creating earthquakes, crashing minor currencies in the process. Third, and most important, there were certain shared beliefs and ethical standards, which were not necessarily practiced but were nevertheless quite universally accepted as desirable. These values combined a faith in reason and a respect for science with the Judeo-Christian ethical tradition and on the whole provided a more reliable guide to what is right and what is wrong than the values that prevail today. . . .

The nineteenth-century incarnation of the global capitalist system, in spite of its relative stability, was destroyed by the First World War. After the end of the war, there was a feeble attempt to reconstruct it, which came to a bad end in the crash of 1929 and the subsequent Great Depression. How much more likely is it, then, that the current version of global capitalism will also come to a bad end, given that the elements of stability that were present in the nineteenth century are now missing? . . .

I believe that the failures of the market mechanism pale into insignificance compared to the failure of what I call the nonmarket sector of society. When I speak of the nonmarket sector, I mean the collective interests of society, the social values that do not find expression in markets. There are people who question whether such collective interests exist at all. Society, they maintain, consists of individuals, and their interests are best expressed by their decisions as market participants. For instance, if they feel philanthropic they can express it by giving money away. In this way, everything can be reduced to monetary values.

It hardly needs saying that this view is false. There are things we can decide individually; there are other things that can only be dealt with collectively. As a market participant, I try to maximize my profits. As a citizen, I am concerned about social values: peace, justice, freedom, or whatever. I cannot give expression to those values as a market participant. Let us suppose that the rules that govern financial markets ought to be changed. I cannot change them unilaterally. If I impose the rules on myself but not on others, it would effect my own performance in the market but it would have no effect on what happens in the markets because no single participant is supposed to be able to influence the outcome.

We must make a distinction between making the rules and playing by those rules. Rule making involves collective decisions, or politics. Playing by the rules involves individual decisions, or market behavior. Unfortunately the distinction is rarely observed. People seem largely to vote their pocketbooks and they lobby for legislation that serves their personal interests. What is worse, elected representatives also frequently put their personal interests ahead of the common interest. Instead of standing for certain intrinsic values, political leaders want to be elected at all costs — and under the prevailing ideology of market fundamentalism, or untrammeled individualism, this is regarded as a natural, rational, and even perhaps desirable way for politicians to behave. This attitude toward politics undermines the postulate on which the principle of representative democracy was built. The contradiction between politicians' personal and public interests was, of course, always present, but it has been greatly aggravated by prevailing attitudes that put success as measured by money ahead of intrinsic values such as honesty. Thus the ascendancy of the profit motive and the decline in the effectiveness of the collective decision-making process have reinforced each other in a reflexive fashion. The promotion of self-interest to a moral principle has corrupted politics and the failure of politics has become the strongest argument in favor of giving markets an ever freer reign.

The functions that cannot and should not be governed purely by market forces include many of the most important things in human life, ranging from moral values to family relationships to aesthetic and intellectual achievements. Yet market fundamentalism is constantly attempting to extend its sway into these regions, in a form of ideological imperialism. According to market fundamentalism, all social activities and human interactions should be looked at as transactional, contract-based relationships and valued in terms of a single common denominator, money. Activities should be regulated, as far as possible, by nothing more intrusive than the invisible hand of profit-maximizing competition. The incursions of market ideology into fields far outside business and economics are having destructive and demoralizing social effects. But market fundamentalism has become so powerful that any political forces that dare to resist it are branded as sentimental, illogical, and naive.

Yet the truth is that market fundamentalism is itself naive and illogical. Even if we put aside the bigger moral and ethical questions and concentrate solely on the economic arena, the ideology of market fundamentalism is profoundly and irredeemably flawed. To put the matter simply, market forces, if they are given complete authority even in the purely economic and financial arenas, produce chaos and could ultimately lead to the downfall of the global capitalist system. . . .

There is a widespread presumption that democracy and capitalism go hand in hand. In fact the relationship is much more complicated. Capitalism needs democracy as a counterweight because the capitalist system by itself shows no tendency toward equilibrium. The owners of capital seek to maximize their profits. Left to their own devices, they would continue to accumulate capital until the situation became unbalanced. Marx and Engels gave a very good analysis of the capitalist system 150 years ago, better in some ways, I must say, than the equilibrium theory of classical economics. The remedy they prescribed — Communism — was worse than the disease. But the main reason why their dire predictions did not come true was because of countervailing political interventions in democratic countries.

Unfortunately we are once again in danger of drawing the wrong conclusions from the lessons of history. This time the danger comes not from Communism but from market fundamentalism. Communism abolished the market mechanism and imposed collective control over all economic activities. Market fundamentalism seeks to abolish collective decision making and to impose the supremacy of market values over all political and social values. Both extremes are wrong. What we need is a correct balance between politics and markets, between rule making and playing by the rules.

But even if we recognized this need, how could we achieve it? The world has entered a period of profound imbalance in which no individual state can resist the power of global financial markets and there are practically no institutions for rule making on an international scale. Collective decision-making mechanisms for the global economy simply do not exist. These conditions are widely acclaimed as the triumph of market discipline, but if financial markets are inherently unstable, imposing market discipline means imposing instability — and how much instability can society tolerate?

Yet the situation is far from hopeless. We must learn to distinguish between individual decision making as expressed in market behavior and collective decision making as expressed in social behavior in general and politics in particular. In both cases, we are guided by self-interest; but in collective decision making we must put the common interest ahead of our individual self-interest *even if others fail to do so.* That is the only way the common interest can prevail.

Today the global capitalist system still stands near the height of its powers. It is certainly endangered by the present global crisis, but its ideological supremacy knows no bounds. The Asian crisis has swept away the autocratic regimes that combined personal profits with Confucian ethics and replaced them with more democratic, reform-minded governments. But the crisis has also undermined the ability of the international financial authorities to prevent and resolve financial crises. How long before the crisis starts sweeping away reform-minded governments? I am afraid that the political developments triggered by the financial crisis may eventually sweep away the global capitalist system itself. It has happened before.

I want to make it clear that I do not want to abolish capitalism. In spite of its shortcomings, it is better than the alternatives. Instead, I want to prevent the global capitalist system from destroying itself. . . .

To stabilize and regulate a truly global economy, we need some global system of political decision making. In short, we need a global society to support our global economy. A global society does not mean a global state. To abolish the existence of states is neither feasible nor desirable; but insofar as there are collective interests that transcend state boundaries, the sovereignty of states must be subordinated to international law and international institutions. Interestingly, the greatest opposition to this idea is coming from the United States, which, as the sole remaining superpower, is unwilling to subordinate itself to any international authority. The United States faces a crisis of identity: Does it want to be a solitary superpower or the leader of the free world? The two roles could be blurred as long as the free world was confronting an "evil empire," but the choice now presents itself in much starker terms. Unfortunately we have not even started to consider it. The popular inclination in the United States is to go it alone, but that would deprive the world of the leadership it so badly needs. Isolationism could be justified only if the market fundamentalists were right and the global economy could sustain itself without a global society.

The alternative is for the United States to forge an alliance with like-minded nations to establish the laws and institutions that are necessary to the preservation of peace, freedom, prosperity, and stability. What these laws and institutions are cannot be decided once and for all; what we need is to set in motion a cooperative, iterative process that defines the open society ideal — a process in which we openly admit the imperfections of the global capitalist system and try to learn from our mistakes. It cannot happen without the United States. But conversely, there has never been a time when a strong lead from the United States and other like-minded countries could achieve such powerful and benign results. With the right sense of leadership and with clarity of purpose, the United States and its allies could begin to create a global open society that could help to stabilize the global economic system and to extend and uphold universal human values. The opportunity is waiting to be grasped.

REFLECTIONS

What are the processes that are changing our world? The readings in this chapter propose a number of theories, some perhaps more persuasive than others. In the first selection Wilson emphasizes the consequences of population growth, a factor that strains the resources of the earth while increasing human impact on nature. Wilson also mentions that future population growth will occur in the poor rather than the wealthy areas of the world, as the latter have reduced their growth rates close to a replacement level. (For example, we now know that the populations of some countries in Europe are actually diminishing.) So the dynamic of population growth does not appear to be one of eternal increase; there is a late stage on the road to development where equilibrium returns. That the increase is continuing in those countries that have the least capacity for absorption — and also the greatest biodiversity — is tragic, perhaps repeating what happened centuries ago in Europe and North America.

There are two schools of thought regarding process: The first recognizes something — like population growth — as continually expanding, with the expansion necessarily affecting everything else; the second recognizes some sort of struggle, conflict, or rift in the world, a change resulting from the pressure of one side on the other. David Crystal's notion of majority languages making minority languages unnecessary, obsolete, or extinct belongs to the latter category — conflict — in this case the periodic conflict between cultures, nations, and language communities.

Benjamin Barber also finds conflict to be a prime mover in history, but for him it is not the occasional conquest of one group over another that prompts change. Rather, Barber believes modern society is marked by a special conflict between nationalist-tribal forces and international-market forces. The dynamic of the historical process for Barber is a dialectical interaction in which each force gains strength for the conflict, reducing the middle ground of civil society and responsible politics in the process. Anthony Appiah shows how international cultural and financial forces can overcome local visions, not for being "tribal" but for embracing global, cosmopolitan currents and challenging the stereotypes of those global forces.

The debate over the Huntington thesis raises different, less dialectical visions of conflict. Huntington sees "fault lines," tectonic plates moving in opposite directions, sometimes tearing apart nations and communities, sometimes burying one in the debris of an earthquake. Fouad Ajami found such fault lines less obvious, permanent, or predictable, and wondered how they emerged in pristine sixteenth-century condition the moment they were uncovered by the end of the Cold War. Instead, Ajami insists that nation states were still the main source of conflict in the world and that they are sly, unsentimental, and unpredictable.

Ajami argues that there are other more important forces than traditional cultural identity that shape the modern world: secularism, Westernization, modernity itself, and market share. Thus Ajami sees the goal of the secular, Westernized middle classes of Islam and other "civilizations" as being in agreement on fundmental issues.

George Soros reminds us of the power of the market to create its own world, even as it ignores the common needs of society. Perhaps the market, by legitimating and institutionalizing greed and egoism, unleashes the greatest forces of change and the most severe threat to stability, society, and common needs.

Which of the forces discussed in this chapter do you find most powerful? Are there other forces, not included here, that are also transforming the world in which you live? How do we counter the forces that change us in ways we find unacceptable? How do we retard or reverse such powerful processes of change? Some of these authors (Wilson is an example) suggest that knowledge, good feeling, and good will can reverse a destructive process. Others (Crystal and Soros, especially) believe that a correction must come by establishing a new international force in order to control nations and markets successfully. What do you think?

Understanding the process of change is the most useful "habit of mind" we gain from studying the past. Although the facts are many and the details overwhelming, process only appears through the study of the specific. And we must continually check our theories of change with the facts, and revise them to conform to new information.

More important, understanding change does not necessarily mean that we must submit to it. Of the processes of globalization discussed in this chapter — population growth, species and language loss, cultural conflict, secularization, commercialization, and market expansion — some may seem "inevitable," some merely strong, some even reversible. Intelligent action requires an appreciation of the possible as well as the identification of the improbable.

History is not an exact science. Fortunately human beings are creators, as well as subjects, of change. Even winds that cannot be changed can be deflected and harnessed. Which way is the world moving? What are we becoming? What can we do? What kind of world can we create? These are questions that can only be answered by studying the past as process. Worlds of history converge upon us, but only one world will emerge from our wishes, our wisdom, and our will.

Ghislain de Busbecq, "The Ottoman Empire under Suleiman" from *The Turkish Letters of Ogier Ghislain de Busbecq, Imperial Ambassador at Constantinople, 1534–1562,* translated by Edward S. Foster. Copyright © 1927. Reprinted with the permission of Oxford University Press, Ltd.

Carolina Maria de Jesus, excerpts from *Child of the Dark: The Diary of Carolina Maria de Jesus,* translated by David St. Clair. Translation copyright © 1962 by E. P. Dutton & Co., Inc., New York and Souvenir Press Ltd., London. Reprinted with the permission of the publisher, Dutton, an imprint of the New American Library, a division of Penguin Putnam, Inc.

Bernal Díaz, excerpt from *The Conquest of New Spain,* translated by J. M. Cohen. Copyright © 1963 by J. M. Cohen. Reprinted with the permission of Penguin Books, Ltd.

Assia Djebar, "Growing Up in Algeria" from *Fantasia: An Algerian Cavalcade, translated by Dorothy S. Blair.* Copyright © 1993. Reprinted with the permission of Quartet Books Limited.

Olaudah Equiano, excerpt from "Olaudah Equiano of the Niger Ibo," edited by G.I. Jones, in Philip D. Curtin (ed.), *Africa Remembered.* Copyright © 1967 (reissued 1997). Reprinted with the permission of Waveland Press.

Joachim C. Fest, "The Rise of Hitler" from *Hitler,* translated by Clara and Richard Winston. Copyright © 1974 by Harcourt, Inc. English translation copyright © 1974 by Harcourt, Inc. Reprinted with the permission of the publishers.

"The French Declaration of the Rights of Man and Citizen" from John Hall Stewart (ed.), *A Documentary History of the French Revolution.* Copyright 1951 by Macmillan Publishing Company, renewed © 1979 by John Hall Stewart. Reprinted with the permission of Prentice-Hall, Inc., Upper Saddle River, NJ.

Betty Friedan, excerpts from "The Problem That Has No Name" from *The Feminine Mystique.* Copyright © 1963 by Betty Friedan. Reprinted with the permission of W. W. Norton & Company, Inc.

Fukuzawa Yukichi, "Datsu-a Ron (On Saying Goodbye to Asia)" from David John Lu (ed.), *Japan, A Documentary History,* Volume II (Armonk, New York: M.E. Sharpe, 1997), 351–53. Reprinted with the permission of M.E. Sharpe, Inc., Armonk, NY 10504.

Galileo Galilei, "Letter to the Grand Duchess Christina" from Maurice A. Finocchiaro (ed. and trans.), *The Galileo Affair: A Documentary History.* Copyright © 1989 by The Regents of the University of California. Reprinted with the permission of the University of California Press.

Mohandas K. Gandhi, excerpt from *Hind Swaraj or Indian Home Rule.* Copyright © 1938 by The Navajivan Trust. Reprinted with the permission of The Navajivan Trust.

Sugita Gempaku, "A Dutch Anatomy Lesson in Japan" from David John Lu (ed.), *Sources of Japanese History, Volume I.* (New York: McGraw-Hill, 1974).

Han Suyin, excerpt from "The Lowering Sky—The Cultural Revolution: 1966" from *Phoenix Harvest.* Copyright © 1980. Reprinted with the permission of Jonathan Cape Ltd.

Jennifer Harbury, excerpts from *Bridge of Courage: Life Stories of the Guatemalan Companeros and Companeras.* Reprinted with the permission of Common Courage Press, Monroe, Maine.

Heinrich Himmler, "Secret Speech at Posen" from Lucy Dawidowicz (ed.), *A Holocaust Reader.* Copyright © 1976 by Lucy Dawidowicz. Reprinted with the permission of Behrman House, 235 Watchung Avenue, West Orange, New Jersey, 07052.

Sarnia Hayes Hoyt, excerpt from *Old Malacca.* Copyright © 1993. Reprinted with the permission of Oxford University Press, Ltd.

Samuel P. Huntington, "The Clash of Civilizations?" from *The Clash of Civilizations? The Debate.* Copyright © 1996 by the Council on Foreign Relations, Inc. Reprinted with the permission of *Foreign Affairs.*

S. M. Ikram, excerpt from Ainslie T. Embree (ed.), *Muslim Civilization in India.* Copyright © 1964 by Columbia University Press. Reprinted with the permission of the publishers via the Copyright Clearance Center, Inc.

Jiwei Ci, excerpt from *Dialectic of the Chinese Revolution: From Utopianism to Hedonism.* Copyright © 1994 by the Board of Trustees of the Leland Stanford Junior University. Reprinted with the permission of Stanford University Press.

Immanuel Kant, "What Is Enlightenment?" from *Critique of Practical Reason,* Third Edition, translated by Lewis White Beck. Copyright © 1993. Reprinted with the permission of Prentice-Hall, Inc., Upper Saddle River, NJ.

Nicholas D. Kristof, "1492: The Prequel" from *The New York Times Magazine* (June 6, 1999). Copyright © 1999 by The New York Times. Reprinted by permission.

Franklin Le Van Baumer, "The Scientific Revolution in the West" from F. Le Van Baumer (ed.), *Main Currents of Western Thought, Fourth Edition.* Copyright © 1978 by Yale University. Reprinted with the permission of Yale University Press.

Nelson Mandela, "Rivonia Trial Statement." Reprinted with the permission of Maribuye Books, University of Western Cape.

Nadezhda Mandelstam, excerpt from *Hope Against Hope: A Memoir,* translated by Max Hayward. Copyright © 1970 by Atheneum Publishers. Reprinted with the permission of Scribner, a division of Simon & Schuster, Inc.

Karl Marx and Friedrich Engels, "The Communist Manifesto" from *Manifesto of the Communist Party.* Copyright © 1955. Reprinted with the permission of Harlan Davidson, Inc.

Nzinga Mbemba, "Affonso of Congo: Evils of the Trade" from Basil Davidson, ed., *The African Past: Chronicles from Antiquity to Modern Times* (Boston: Little, Brown and Company, 1964). Copyright © 1964 by Basil Davidson. Reprinted with the permission of Curtis Brown, Ltd.

Robert S. McNamara, excerpt from "A Time of Transition" from *In Retrospect: The Tragedy and Lessons of Vietnam.* Copyright © 1995 by Robert S. McNamara. Reprinted with the permission of Times Books, a division of Random House, Inc.

Hugo Muller, letter to his family (October 17, 1915) from *German Students' War Letters.* Copyright 1929. Reprinted with the permission of Methuen.

Multatuli (Eduard Douwes Dekker), excerpt from *Max Havelaar: Or the Coffee Auctions of the Dutch Trading Company.* Copyright © 1982 by The University of Massachusetts Press. Reprinted with the permission of the publishers.

Jawaharlal Nehru, "Gandhi" from *Toward Freedom: The Autobiography of Jawaharlal Nehru* (New York: John Day Co., 1942). Reprinted by permission of the Jawaharlal Nehru Memorial Fund.

George Orwell, excerpt from *Burmese Days.* Copyright © 1934 by George Orwell, renewed © 1961 by Sonia Brownell Orwell. Reprinted with the permission of Harcourt, Inc. and Bill Hamilton as the Literary Executor of the Estate of Sonia Brownell Orwell, and Martin Secker and Warburg Ltd.

Jurgen Osterhammel, excerpt from *Colonialism,* translated by Shelly Frisch. Copyright © 1997 by Shelly L. Frisch. Reprinted with the permission of Markus Wiener Publishers.

Arnold Pacey, "Asia and the Industrial Revolution" from *Technology in World Civilization.* Copyright © 1990. Reprinted with the permission of MIT Press.

Erich Maria Remarque, excerpt from *All Quiet on the Western Front,* translated by A.W. Wheen. Copyright © 1928 by Ullstein A.G., renewed © 1956 by Erich Maria Remarque. Copyright © 1929, 1930 by Little, Brown and Company, renewed © 1957, 1958 by Erich Maria Remarque. Reprinted with the permission of the Estate of Paulette Goddard Remarque, c/o Pryor, Cashman, Sherman & Flynn, New York, NY. All rights reserved.

Jose Rizal, excerpt from *Noli Me Tangere,* translated by Leon Ma Guerrero. Copyright © 1961. Reprinted with the permission of Indiana University Press.

Russian Law Code, "Westernizing by Peter the Great, 1701–1714" from George Vernadsky (ed.), *A Source Book for Russian History: From Early Times to 1917.* Copyright © 1972 by Yale University. Reprinted with the permission of Yale University Press.

Kirkpatrick Sale, excerpts from "1492–93" (Chapter Five) from *The Conquest of Paradise.* Copyright © 1991 by Kirkpatrick Sale. Reprinted with the permission of Alfred A. Knopf, Inc.

Lynda Norene Shaffer, "China, Technology and Change" from *World History Bulletin* (Fall/Winter 1986–87) 4, no. 1. Reprinted with the permission of the author.

George Soros, excerpt from *The Crisis of Global Capitalism: Open Society Endangered.* Copyright © 1998. Reprinted with the permission of Public Affairs, Inc., a member of Perseus Books, L.L.C.

Jonathan Spence, "The Late Ming Empire" from *The Search for Modern China.* Copyright © 1990 by Jonathan D. Spence. Reprinted with the permission of W. W. Norton & Company, Inc. Includes Tang Xianzu, excerpts from *The Peony Pavilion,* translated by Cyril Birch. Copyright © 1980 by Indiana University Press. Reprinted with the permission of the publishers.

Peter N. Stearns, "The Industrial Revolution Outside the West" from *The Industrial Revolution in World History.* Copyright © 1993 by Westview Press, Inc. Reprinted with the permission of Westview Press, a subsidiary of Perseus Books Group L.L.C.

Jean-François Steiner, excerpt from *Treblinka.* English translation copyright © 1967 by Simon & Schuster. Reprinted with the permission of Simon & Schuster, Inc.

Table 1: "Opium Imports" from Hsin-Pao Chang, *Commissioner Lin and the Opium War.* Copyright © 1964 by the President and Fellows of Harvard College. Reprinted with the permission of Harvard University Press.

Hendrik F. Verwoerd, "On Apartheid" from A.N. Pelzer (ed.), *Verwoerd Speaks: Speeches, 1948–1966.* Copyright © 1966. Reprinted by permission.

Swami Vivekananda, "Oh India, Forget Not" from *The Complete Works of the Swami Vivekananda,* Reprinted by permission of Advaita Ashrama, 4:408–14.

Theodore von Laue, excerpt from *The World Revolution of Westernization.* Copyright © 1987 by Oxford University Press, Inc. Reprinted with the permission of the publishers.

Edward O. Wilson, excerpts from "Conservation: The Next Hundred Years" from David Western and Mary Pearl (eds.).

Susan Zuccotti, excerpt from "A Village in Vichy, France" from *The Holocaust, the French and the Jews*. Copyright © 1993 by Basic Books, Inc. Reprinted with the permission of Basic Books, a member of Perseus Books.

ILLUSTRATIONS

Figure 1. Gamma Liasion Photo News Agency.
Figure 2. Gamma Liasion Photo News Agency.
Figure 3. National Maritime Museum.
Figure 4. Mary Evans Picture Library.
Figure 6. Courtesy of The Metropolitan Museum of Art.
Figure 7. Werner Forman/Art Resource, NY.
Figure 8a. The Museum of Modern Art, New York. Acquired by exchange. Photograph © 2000 by The Museum of Modern Art, New York.
Figure 8b. Courtesy Museo Civico Luigi Bailo and Soprintendenza ai Beni Artistici e Storici del Veneto.
Figure 8c. Courtesy of Graphische Sammlung der Stuttgart Staatsgalerie.
Figure 9. The Newark Museum/Art Resource, NY.
Figure 10. Map by Ib Ohlsson. Courtesy of Foreign Affairs.